16th Nordic Conference of Computational Linguistics (NODALIDA 2007)

Tartu, Estonia
25 – 26 May 2007

Editors:

Joakim Nivre
Heiki-Jaan Kaalep

Kadri Muischnek
Mare Koit

ISBN: 978-1-5108-3519-1

PROCEEDINGS of the 16th Nordic Conference of Computational Linguistics

NODALIDA-2007

Editors: Joakim Nivre, Heiki-Jaan Kaalep, Kadri Muischnek and Mare Koit

University of Tartu
Tartu 2007

Contents

Preface

Language technology research in Northern Europe is thriving. One clear sign of this is the fact that the NODALIDA conference (also known as the Nordic Conference of Computational Linguistics) has grown to the point where it is no longer manageable to let the local organization committee do all the work in putting together the program. Hence, the need for a separate program committee.

When trusted with the responsibility of chairing the program committee, the program chair made an informal survey of expectations in the community through an e-mail questionnaire sent out on the NODALI list. (Thanks to everyone who responded.) Four things emerged clearly from this survey: People wanted a high-quality technical track with review of full papers. However, people also wanted an opportunity for students to present their work, and an opportunity to get feedback on work in progress in the form of posters. Last but not least, people wanted workshops. Hence, we give you regular paper sessions, student paper sessions, a poster session, and a full day of workshops. As a bonus, we also give you two distinguished keynote speakers, Diana McCarthy and Walter Daelemans, the first business meeting of the newly established Northern European Association for Language Technology (NEALT), and a tutorial on the Estonian language, hoping to establish a new NODALIDA tradition of local language tutorials. (Thanks to Koenraad de Smedt for this great idea.)

When issuing the call for workshops, regular papers, student papers, and posters, we were unsure whether there would be enough work going on in Northern Europe and the rest of the world to fill all the categories. The community response surpassed all our expectations. We received 41 regular paper submissions, 24 student paper submissions, 32 poster submissions, and 7 workshop proposals, for a total of 104 submissions, an all time record for NODALIDA. (Thanks to everyone who submitted their work.) Moreover, a fair share of these submissions came from countries outside our region, clearly showing that NODALIDA, while remaining a conference with a strong regional character, is also being recognized in the rest of the world. In the final program, there are 26 regular papers, 12 student papers, 26 posters, and 4 workshops. We want to thank the program committee and all our 69 reviewers for their hard work in putting together the program.

Finally, NODALIDA 2007 is special not only for being the biggest ever in terms of submissions, but also for being the first NODALIDA held in Estonia, in the beautiful city of Tartu, at one of the oldest universities in the region, founded

in 1632. We want to thank the local organization committee for all their hard work
to welcome the NODALIDA participants in Tartu.

We wish you all an enjoyable NODALIDA 2007!

Joakim Nivre
Program Chair
NODALIDA 2007

Mare Koit and Tiit Roosmaa
Local Co-Chairs
NODALIDA 2007

Committees

Program Committee

Joakim Nivre (chair), Växjö University and Uppsala University
Helena Ahonen-Myka, University of Helsinki
Daniel Hardt, Copenhagen Business School
Kristiina Jokinen, University of Helsinki and University of Tartu
Pierre Nugues, Lund University
Stephan Oepen, University of Oslo, NTNU Trondheim and Stanford University
Patrizia Paggio, University of Copenhagen
Torbjørn Svendsen, NTNU Trondheim

Local Organization Committee

Mare Koit (co-chair), University of Tartu
Tiit Roosmaa (co-chair), University of Tartu
Urve Talvik, University of Tartu
Heli Uibo, University of Tartu
Kadri Vider, University of Tartu

Reviewers

Lars Ahrenberg
Ingunn Amdal
Beáta Bandmann Megyesi
Francis Bond
Janne Bondi Johannessen
Lars Borin
Matthias Buch-Kromann
Rolf Carlson
Mathias Creutz
Antoine Doucet
Laila Dybkjær
Helge Dyvik
Eva Ejerhed
Björn Gambäck
Barbara Gawronska
Jerneja Zganec Gros
Nina Grønnum
Petter Haugereid
Peter Juel Henrichsen
Merle Horne
Hannes Högni Vilhjálmsson
Richard Johansson
Magne H. Johnsen
Arne Jönsson
Viggo Kann
Jussi Karlgren
Sabine Kirchmeier-Andersen
Ola Knutsson
Mare Koit
Jacques Koreman
Kimmo Koskenniemi
Mikko Kurimo
Leena Kuure
Knut Kvale
Juha-Pertti Laaksonen

Torbjörn Lager
Birger Larsen
Krister Lindén
Jan Tore Lønning
Ramón López-Cózar Delgado
Bodil Nistrup Madsen
Bente Maegaard
Jean-Claude Martin
Bilyana Martinovski
Michael McTear
Tor Andre Myrvoll
Costanza Navarretta
Anders Nøklestad
Torbjørn Nordgård
Bjarne Ørsnes
Maria Teresa Pazienza
Bolette Pedersen
Jussi Piitulainen
Ari Pirkola
Aarne Ranta
Victoria Rosén
Eiríkur Rögnvaldsson
Rune Sætre
Anders Søgaard
Markku Turunen
Wim van Dommelen
Martin Volk
Jürgen Wedekind
Stefan Werner
Mats Wirén
Roman Yangarber
Zhang Yi
Anssi Yli-Jyrä
Fabio Massimo Zanzotto

Conference program
NODALIDA-2007 Main Conference

Friday, May 25, 2007

9.00–10.30   **Opening Session**
9.00– 9.30   Opening
9.30–10.30   Invited Talk
             Evaluating Automatic Approaches for Word Meaning Discovery and Disam-
             biguation using Lexical Substitution
             Diana F. McCarthy, University of Sussex
10.30–11.00 **Coffee Break**
11.00–12.30 **Parallel Paper Sessions**

	Parsing	**Multilingual Resources and Translation**	**Speech Technology**
11.00– 11.30	*IceParser: An Incremental Finite-State Parser for Icelandic* Hrafn Loftsson and Eiríkur Rögnvaldsson	*Using Danish as a CG Interlingua: A Wide-Coverage Norwegian-English Machine Translation System* Eckhard Bick and Lars Nygaard	*Automatic Compound Word Reconstruction for Speech Recognition of Compounding Languages* Tanel Alumäe
11.30– 12.00	*Combining Contexts in Lexicon Learning for Semantic Parsing* Richard Socher, Chris Biemann and Rainer Osswald	*Identifying Cross Language Term Equivalents Using Statistical Machine Translation and Distributional Association Measures* Hans Hjelm	*Multivariate Cepstral Feature Compensation on Band-limited Data for Robust Speech Recognition* Nicolas Morales, John H. L. Hansen, Doroteo T. Toledano and Javier Garrido
12.00– 12.30	*Polynomial Charts for Totally Unordered Languages* Anders Søgaard	*The Swedish-Turkish Parallel Corpus and Tools for its Creation* Beata B. Megyesi and Bengt Dahlqvist	*Development of Text-To-Speech System for Latvian* Kārlis Goba and Andrejs Vasiļjevs

12.30–14.00 **Lunch**

xiii

14.00–15.30 **Parallel Paper Sessions**

	Treebanks	**Information Extraction and Summarization**	**Phonetics and Speech**
14.00–14.30	*Theoretically Motivated Treebank Coverage* Victoria Rosén and Koenraad De Smedt	*Time Extraction from Real-time Generated Football Reports* Markus Borg	*Utterance-initial Duration of Finnish Non-plosive Consonants* Tuomo Saarni, Jussi Hakokari, Olli Aaltonen, Jouni Isoaho and Tapio Salakoski
14.30–15.00	*Extended Constituent-to-Dependency Conversion for English* Richard Johansson and Pierre Nugues	*The Extraction of Trajectories from Real Texts Based on Linear Classification* Hanjing Li, Tiejun Zhao, Sheng Li, Jiyuan Zhao	*An Advanced Speech Corpus for Norwegian* Janne Bondi Johannessen, Kristin Hagen, Joel James Priestley and Lars Nygaard
15.00–15.30	*Clausal Coordinate Ellipsis in German: The TIGER Treebank as a Source of Evidence* Karin Harbusch and Gerard Kempen	*Widening the HolSum Search Scope* Martin Hassel and Jonas Sjöbergh	*Spoken Document Retrieval in a Highly Inflectional Language* Inger Ekman and Kalervo Järvelin

15.30–16.00 **Coffee Break**

16.00–17.00 **Poster Session 1**

LinES: An English-Swedish Parallel Treebank
Lars Ahrenberg

Posterior Probability Based Confidence Measures Applied to a Children's Speech Reading Tracking System
Daniel Bolanos and Wayne H. Ward

Estonian-English Statistical Machine Translation: the First Results
Mark Fishel, Heiki-Jaan Kaalep and Kadri Muischnek

A Hybrid Constituency-Dependency Parser for Swedish
Johan Hall, Joakim Nivre and Jens Nilsson

Íslenskur Orðasjóður – Building a Large Icelandic Corpus
Erla Hallsteinsdóttir, Thomas Eckart, Chris Biemann, Uwe Quasthoff and
Matthias Richter

A Survey and Classification of Methods for (Mostly) Unsupervised Learning

Role of Different Spectral Attributes in Vowel Categorization: the Case of Udmurt
Janne Savela, Stina Ojala, Olli Aaltonen and Tapio Salakoski

Recreating Humorous Split Compound Errors in Swedish by Using Grammaticality
Jonas Sjöbergh and Kenji Araki

A Re-examination of Question Classification
Håkan Sundblad

Interpretation of Yes/No Questions as Metaphor Recognition
Tarmo Truu, Haldur Õim and Mare Koit

Rule-based Logical Forms Extraction
Cenny Wenner

19.00– Conference Dinner

Saturday, May 26, 2007

9.00–10.00 **Plenary Session**
Invited Talk
Text Analysis and Machine Learning for Stylometrics and Stylogenetics
Walter Daelemans, University of Antwerp

10.00–10.30 **Coffee Break**

10.30–12.30 **Parallel Student Sessions**

	Spoken Language Processing	**Multilingual Resources and Translation**	**Natural Language Processing**
10.30–11.00	*Clause Boundary Detection in Transcribed Spoken Language* Fredrik Jørgensen	*Memory-Based Learning of Word Translation* Maria Holmqvist	*Unmediated Data-Oriented Generation* Dave Cochran
11.00–11.30	*The Effects of Disfluency Detection in Parsing Spoken Language* Fredrik Jørgensen	*Using Parallel Corpora to Create a Greek-English Dictionary with UPLUG* Konstantinos Charitakis	*Linguistically Fuelled Text Similarity* Björn Andrist and Martin Hassel

11.30–12.00	*Tagging a Norwegian Speech Corpus* Anders Nøklestad and Åshild Søfteland	*Using a Wizard of Oz as a Baseline to Determine Which System Architecture Is the Best for a Spoken Language Translation System* Marianne Starlander	*Decomposing Swedish Compounds Using Memory-Based Learning* Karin Friberg
12.00–12.30	*Initial Experiments with Estonian Speech Recognition* Anton Ragni	*Grammar Sharing Techniques for Rule-based Multilingual NLP Systems* Marianne Santaholma	*A Method for Resolution of Temporal Expressions in Estonian Natural Language Dialogue Systems* Margus Treumuth

12.30–14.00   **Lunch**
14.00–15.30   **Parallel Paper Sessions**

	Parsing and Translation	**Machine Learning**	**Dialogue**
14.00–14.30	*Dependency-Based Hybrid Model of Syntactic Analysis for the Languages with a Rather Free Word Order* Guntis Bārzdiņs, Normunds Grūzītis, Gunta Nešpore and Baiba Saulīte	*Comparison of the Self-Organizing Map and Multidimensional Scaling in Analysis of Estonian Emotion Concepts* Toomas Kirt and Ene Vainik	*Interview and Delivery: Dialogue Strategies for Conversational Recommender Systems* Pontus Wärnestål, Lars Degerstedt and Arne Jönsson
14.30–15.00	*Comparing French PP-attachment to English, German and Swedish* Martin Volk and Frida Tidström	*Evaluating Stages of Development in Second Language French: A Machine-Learning Approach* Jonas Granfeldt and Pierre Nugues	*Achieving Goals in Collaboration: Analysis of Estonian Institutional Calls* Olga Gerassimenko, Mare Koit, Andriela Rääbis and Krista Strandson

15.00–15.30	*Comprehension Assistant for Languages of Baltic States* Inguna Skadiņa, Andrejs Vasiļjevs, Daiga Deksne, Raivis Skadiņš and Linda Goldberga	*Inducing Baseform Models from a Swedish Vocabulary Pool* Eva Forsbom	

15.30–16.00   **Coffee Break**
16.00–17.30   **Closing Session**
16.00–17.00   Business Meeting of the Northern European Association for Language Technology (NEALT)
17.00–17.30   Closing

I Invited Talks

Evaluating Automatic Approaches
for Word Meaning Discovery and Disambiguation
using Lexical Substitution

Diana F. McCarthy
University of Sussex

Abstract

There has been a surge of interest in Computational Linguistics in word sense disambiguation (WSD). A major catalyst has been the SENSEVAL evaluation exercises which have provided standard datasets for the field over the past decade. Whilst researchers believe that WSD will ultimately prove useful for applications which need some degree of semantic interpretation, the jury is still out on this point. One significant problem is that there is no clear choice of inventory for any given task, other than the use of a parallel corpus for a specific language pair for a machine translation application. Most of the datasets produced, certainly in English, have used WordNet. Whilst WordNet is a wonderful resource it would be beneficial if systems using other inventories could enter the WSD arena without the need for mappings between the inventories which may mask results. As well as the work in disambiguation, there is a growing interest in automatic acquisition of inventories of word meaning. It would be useful to investigate the merits of predefined inventories themselves, aside from their use for disambiguation, and compare automatic methods of acquring inventories. In this talk I will discuss these issues and some results in the context of the English Lexical Substitution Task, organised by myself and Roberto Navigli (University of Rome, "La Sapienza") earlier this year under the auspices of SEMEVAL.

Text Analysis and Machine Learning
for Stylometrics and Stylogenetics

Walter Daelemans
University of Antwerp

Abstract

Automatic Text Categorization, learning to assign documents to specific categories (e.g. in topic assignment or spam filtering), has been an influential application in Natural Language Processing. These systems consist of two components: a first one that constructs representations of documents (mostly bags of words represented as binary or numeric vectors), and a second one that uses standard machine learning techniques to learn mappings between such document vectors and their topics. Recently, this general approach has been put to use for other, more linguistically interesting "stylometric" applications, such as assigning authorship to documents or determining the gender of the author of a document. Such applications need linguistically more sophisticated document representations and provide insight into which linguistic properties of documents are relevant for predicting the (gender of) the author. In my presentation, I will give a brief overview of results in this approach and describe a number of applications of the methodology we are currently investigating in the CNTS research group. For creating linguistically more interesting document representations, we use a memory-based shallow parser that analyzes documents at the levels of morphology, part of speech, phrases, and grammatical relations. More specifically I will describe results on authorship attribution in the context of journalists writing about the same topic (politics). A more challenging task is personality assignment on the basis of text. We constructed a corpus consisting of 145 documents describing the contents of the same documentary, written by 145 different students who also took a personality test. We show which linguistic features correlate with different dimensions of personality and the predictability of personality from these features. Finally, I will describe work on what we dubbed "stylogenetics", stylistic analysis of literary works based on the same general architecture, but using clustering as a machine learning technique rather than supervised learning.

II Regular Papers

Automatic Compound Word Reconstruction for Speech Recognition of Compounding Languages

Tanel Alumäe
Laboratory of Phonetics and Speech Technology
Institute of Cybernetics at Tallinn University of Technology
Estonia
`tanel.alumae@phon.ioc.ee`

Abstract

This paper compares two approaches to lexical compound word reconstruction from a speech recognizer output where compound words are decomposed. The first method has been proposed earlier and uses a dedicated language model that models compound tails in the context of the preceding words and compound heads only in the context of the tail. A novel approach models imaginable compound particle connectors as hidden events and predicts such events using a simple N-gram language model. Experiments on two Estonian speech recognition tasks show that the second approach performs consistently better and achieves high accuracy.

1 Introduction

In many languages, compound words can be formed by concatenating two or more word-like particles. In Estonian (but also in other languages, such as German), compound words occur abundantly and can even be built spontaneously. In a corpus of written Estonian consisting of roughly 70 million words, the number of different word types (including inflected words forms) is around 1.7 million and among those, around 1.1 million (68%) are compound words.

In large vocabulary continuous speech recognition (LVCSR) systems, an N-gram statistical language model is used to estimate prior word probabilities in various contexts. The language model vocabulary specifies which words are known to the system and therefore can be recognized. However,

the large amount and spontaneous nature of compound words makes it difficult to design a language model that has a good coverage of the language. In addition, when vocabulary is increased, it becomes more difficult to robustly estimate language model probabilities for all words in different contexts. In order to decrease the lexical variety and the resulting out-of-vocabulary (OOV) rate, compound words can be split into separate particles and modeled as separate language modeling units. As a result however, the output of the recognizer consists of a stream of non-compound units that must later be reassembled into compound words where necessary.

In this paper, we compare the accuracy of two different methods for compound word reconstruction from recognizer output. The first model was proposed by Spies (1995) and is based on the assumption that a compound word can be decomposed into its first part(s) and the tail part. The predictive effect of the preceding context is only applied to the tail of the compound word. The head part, on the other hand, is assumed to be independent of the preceding context and its probability is calculated given only the tail. The second approach treats imaginable connectors between compound word particles as hidden events in the language model. Such a language model is typically used for sentence segmentation of conversational speech based on recognized words (Stolcke and Shriberg, 1996), but can be generalized for detecting other hidden events between recognized units. The latter approach is in essence similar to the method used in the morph-based speech recognition system described in (Siivola et al., 2003), except that they model word boundaries, not compound word connectors as seperate units, and do it already in the decoder.

Joakim Nivre, Heiki-Jaan Kaalep, Kadri Muischnek and Mare Koit (Eds.)
NODALIDA 2007 Conference Proceedings, pp. 5–12

The paper is organized as follows. In section 2 we describe the approach to statistical large vocabulary language modeling for Estonian. Section 3 describes the two approaches for compound word reconstruction in more detail. Results of a variety of experiments are reported in section 4. Some interesting error patterns are identified and analyzed. We end with a conclusion and some suggestions for future work.

2   Language modelling for Estonian

Estonian is an agglutinative and highly inflective language. One or many suffixes can be appended to verb and noun stems, depending on their syntactic and semantic role in the sentence.

Estonian is also a so-called compounding language, i.e. compound words can be formed from shorter particles to express complex concepts as single words. For example, the words *rahva* 'folk' and *muusika* 'music' can be combined to form a word *rahvamuusika* 'folk music' and this in turn can be combined with the word *ansambel* to form *rahvamuusikaansambel* 'folk music group'.

As a result, the lexical variety of Estonian is very high and it is not possible to achieve a good vocabulary coverage when using words as basic units for language modelling. Figure 1 compares the out-of-vocabulary (OOV) rates of three different vocabularies: words, words after decompounding, and after full morphological decomposition. The vocabularies are selected from a corpus described in section 4.1 and the OOV-rates are measured against a set of sentence transcripts used for speech recognition. The OOV-rate was measured using varying vocabulary sizes.

It is clear from the experiments that neither words nor decompounded words are suitable for language modelling using a conventionally sized vocabulary. The OOV-rate of the word-based vocabularies is much over what can be tolerated even when using a very large 800K size vocabulary. It can be seen that after splitting the compound words, the OOV-rate is roughly halved. Still, even when using a large 100K vocabulary, the OOV-rate is about 6% – too much to be used in large vocabulary speech recognition. However, the OOV-rates of morphemes is much lower and can be compared with the OOV-

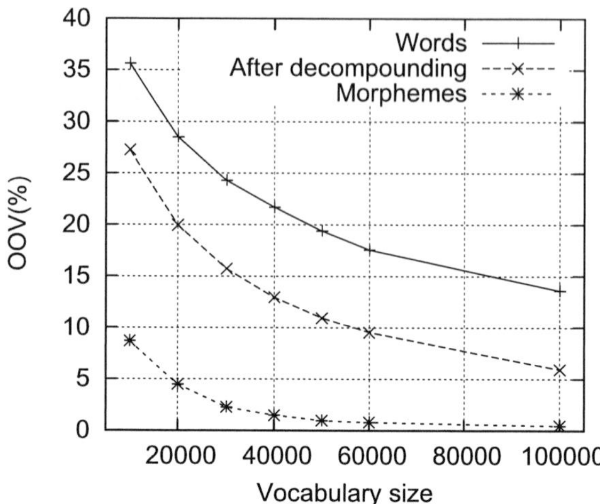

Figure 1: Out-of-vocabulary rate of different vocabularies.

rates of English word-based vocabularies of similar sizes. The OOV-rate of the morpheme-based vocabulary reaches the 2% threshold already when using a 40K vocabulary.

When using morphemes as basic units for language modelling, the output of the decoder is a sequence of morphemes. The set of different suffix morphemes is rather small and thus the suffixes can be tagged in the vocabulary so that they can be concatenated to the previous stem after decoding. However, this approach can not be applied for reconstructing compound words as the set of stems and morphemes that take part in forming compound words is very large and sparse. The rest of the paper describes and compares two methods that attempt to reconstruct compound words from the sequence of morphemes.

3   Methods

This section describes two independent approaches to compound word reconstruction. Both of those methods enable us to compute a posterior probability of a compound word once its subsequent composing words have been recognized.

3.1   Compound word language model

The compound word language model proposed by Spies (1995) is based on the observation that the grammatically determining part of a compound word in many languages is the last particle. This is true for both German, for which the model was originally developed, as well as for Estonian. The head words of a compound may be considered as semantic modifiers of the last particle.

This observation suggests that when calculating language model scores for compound words, the predictive effect of the preceding context should be applied only to the tail part of the compound, while the probabilities of head words are computed given the tail. Let h_1 denote the first head of a compound, $h_2...h_n$ the (optional) remaining heads, t the tail of part of the compound and w_1w_2 the two preceding context words. Then, the total probability of a compound word $h_1..h_nt$ given the two preceding words w_1w_2 can be calculated as

$$P(h_1..h_nt|w_1w_2) = \\ P_h(h_1) \prod_{i=2}^{n} P_h(h_i|h_{i-1}) \frac{P_{bw}(h_n|t)P_{tail}(t|w_1w_2)}{P(h_n)}$$

Here, $P_h(h_i|h_{i-1})$ is the within-head bigram probability, i.e., the probability that the compound head h_i occurs after the compound head h_{i-1}. $P_{bw}(h_n|t)$ is the backward bigram probability of compound head h_n followed by tail t, i.e., the probability of the last head given the tail. $P_{tail}(t|w_1w_2)$ is the distant trigram probability of the compound tail, i.e. the probability of a compound ending with the tail t given the last two context words. The given equation consists of two parts: the first part amounts to a simple bigram probability of the compound head sequence, independent of the observed context, while the last fraction expresses the distant trigram probability of the tail, multiplied by the gain in probability of the last head due to the observed tail. See the original proposal of this model (Spies, 1995) for more details about the derivation of this equation.

Given a sequence of recognized units (that are either true words or compound particles), the most probable reconstruction is found as follows:

1. Any unit can be regarded as a non-compound part. Unit probability is then calculated using the trigram distribution.
2. In case the unit has occurred as a compound head in the training corpus, a new compound branch is created. The compound branch continues as follows:

(a) If the next word is again a head candidate, a new compound branch is created, and the processing in the new branch is continued as in step 2.
(b) If the next word is a compound tail candidate, a new possible compound word has been found. The compound word probability is calculated according to the compound word model equation. Processing in this branch continues as in step 1.
(c) If the next word is neither a head nor a tail candidate, the current branch is discarded.
3. The most probable reconstruction of a sentence is the one that corresponds to the path with the highest product score.

3.2 Hidden event language model

The hidden event language model (Stolcke and Shriberg, 1996) describes the joint distribution of words and events, $P_{LM}(W, E)$. In our case, words correspond to the recognized units and events to the imaginable interword compound particle connectors. Let W denote the recognized tokens $w_1, w_2, ..., w_n$ and E denote the sequence of interword events $e_1, e_2, ..., e_n$. The hidden event language model describes the joint distribution of words and events, $P(W, E) = P(w_1, e_1, w_2, e_2, ..., w_n, e_n)$.

For training such a hidden event language model, a training corpus is used such that the compound words are decomposed into separate units, and the compound connector event is represented by an additional nonword token (<CC>), for example:

```
gruusia rahva <CC> muusika <CC>
ansambel andis meelde <CC> jääva
kontserdi
```

'Georgian folk music group gave a memorable concert'.

The language model used for recognition is trained on the corpus where the compound connector tags are removed. The vocabulary of the compound reconstruction language model is the same as that of the main language model, with an additional token "<CC>". We do not explicitly model the "non-CC" event in order to make more effective use of the contextual information. During compound reconstruction, the Viterbi algorithm is used to find the most likely sequence of words and hidden tokens for the given input sequence. The word/event pairs correspond to states and the words to observations, and the transition probabilities are given by the the hidden event N-gram model.

4 Experiments

4.1 Training data

We tested the concepts and algorithms described here using two different Estonian speech databases, BABEL and SpeechDat.

The Estonian subset of the BABEL multilanguage database (Eek and Meister, 1999) contains speech recordings made in an anechoic chamber, directly digitized using 16-bits and a sampling rate of 20 kHz. The textual content of the database consists of numbers, artificial CVC-constructs, 5-sentence mini-passages and isolated filler sentences. The isolated sentences were designed by phoneticians to be especially rich in phonologically interesting variations. The sentences are also designed to reflect the syntactic and semantic complexity and variability of the language. For training acoustic models, the mini-passage and isolated sentence recordings of 60 speakers were used, totalling in about 6 hours of audio data. For evaluation, 138 isolated sentence utterances by six different speakers were used.

The SpeechDat-like speech database project (Meister et al., 2002) was aimed to collect telephone speech from a large number of speakers for speech and speaker recognition purposes. The main technical characteristics of the database are as follows: sampling rate 8 kHz, 8-bit mono A-law encoding, calls from fixed and cellular phones as the signal source, calls from both home and office environments. Each recording session consists of a fixed set of utterance types, such as isolated and connected digits, numbers, money amounts, spelled words, time and date phrases, yes/no answers, proper names, application words and phrases, phonetically rich words and sentences. The database contains about 241.1 hours of audio data from 1332 different speakers. For recognition experiments, the database was divided into training, development and test set. The development and test sets were chosen by randomly assigning 40 different speakers to each of the sets. To avoid using the same speaker's data for both training and evaluation, those 80 speakers were chosen out of those contributors who only made one call session. Only the prompted sentence utterances were used in evaluations, thus both the development and test set contained 320 utterances.

For training language models, we used a the following subset of the Mixed Corpus of Estonian (Kaalep and Muischnek, 2005), compiled by the Working Group of Computational Linguistics at the University of Tartu: daily newspaper "Postimees" (33 million words), weekly newspaper "Eesti Ekspress" (7.5 million words), Estonian original prose from 1995 onwards (4.2 million words), academic journal "Akadeemia" (7 million words), transcripts of Estonian Parliament (13 million words), weekly magazine "Kroonika" (0.6 million words).

4.2 LVCSR system

The CMU Sphinx (Placeway et al., 1997) speech recognition system was used used for speech recognition experiments. The latest version of Sphinx-Train was used for training and Sphinx 3.6.3 was used for decoding test utterances. For acoustic features, MFCC coefficients were used, extracted from a window of 0.0256 seconds with a frame rate of 100 frames/second. All acoustic units are modeled by continuous left-to-right HMMs with three emitting states and no skip transitions. The output vectors are 39-dimensional and are composed of 13 cepstral coefficients, delta and double delta coefficients. Data-driven decision trees were used for creating tied-state triphone models. Each state is modeled by 8 Gaussian mixture components. The BABEL-based acoustic models use a sample rate of 16 kHz, the number of senones is fixed to 3000. The SpeechDat-based models use a sample rate of 8000 Hz, a frequency band of 130 Hz - 3400 Hz, and the number of senones was fixed to 6000. Models were created for 25 phonemes, silence, and five filler/noise types (the latter only for the SpeechDat-based system). Long phonemes as well as diphthongs are modelled by sequences of two corresponding phone units. The only exception in the handling of short and long phonemes lies in the modelling of plosives since the realization of long plosives is clearly different from concatenation of two short plosives. Therefore, we model short and long plosives using separate units. Pairs of palatalised and unpalatalised phonemes are merged into one acoustic unit.

The SRILM toolkit (Stolcke, 2002) was used for selecting language model vocabulary and compiling the language model. The language model was created by first processing the text corpora using the Estonian morphological analyzer and disambiguator (Kaalep and Vaino, 2001). Using the information from morphological analysis, it is possible to split compounds words into particles and separate morphological suffixes from preceding stems. Language model vocabulary was created by selecting the most likely 60 000 units from the mixture of the corpora, using sentences in the SpeechDat training set as heldout text for optimization. The resulting vocabulary has a OOV-rate of 2.05% against the sentences in the BABEL test set and 2.20% against the sentences in the SpeechDat test set. Using the vocabulary of 60 000 particles, a trigram language model was estimated for each training corpus subset. The cutoff value was 1 for both bigrams and trigrams, i.e. singleton n-grams were included in the models. A modified version of Kneser-Ney smoothing as implemented in SRILM was applied. Finally, a single LM was built by merging the six models, using interpolation coefficients optimized on the sentences in the SpeechDat training set.

Since Estonian is almost a phonetic language, a simple rule-based grapheme-to-phoneme algorithm described in (Alumäe, 2006) could be used for generating pronunciations for both training data as well as for the words in the language model used for decoding. The pronunciation of foreign proper names deviates obviously from rule-based pronunciation but since our test set did not contain many proper names, we limited the amount of proper names in the vocabulary to most frequent 500, which were mostly of Estonian origin. No manual correction of the pronunciation lexicon was done.

4.3 Training models for compound word reconstruction

The models for compound word reconstructions were estimated using the morphologically analyzed corpora, that is, words were split into morphemes and compound word connector symbols marked places where compound words are formed.

The compound word language model consists of three sub-models: the distant trigram model, inner-compound head bigram model and head-given-tail bigram model. All given models were trained over the union of the text corpora as follows: for training the distant trigram model, all head compound particles were removed from the texts and a trigram language model was estimated; for training the inner-compound head bigram, all compound head sequences were extracted from the corpus, and a bigram language model was estimated; for training the head-given-tail bigram model, all compounds were extracted from the corpus, all but the last head and tail were removed from the compound words, the remaining word pairs were reversed and a bigram language model was estimated. In all cases, modified Kneser-Ney smoothing using a cutoff value of 2 was applied.

For training the hidden event language model, we took the same vocabulary as was used for training the main language model, added the compound connector symbol to it, and estimated a trigram model over the union of the subcorpora, using a cutoff value of 2 and Kneser-Ney smoothing.

4.4 Evaluation metrics

We tested both compound word models on two kinds of test data:

- reference transcripts, split into morphemes. This corresponds to perfect recognizer output;
- actual recognizer output, consisting of recognized morphemes.

To evaluate the accuracy of reconstructing compound words in reference transcripts, the reconstructed sentences were simply compared with original sentences. However, it is not obvious what to use as reference when evaluating reconstruction of recognizer output. We chose to use dynamic programming for inserting compound word connectors in the recognizer output by aligning the recognized units with reference units and inserting compound word connectors according to their location in reference transcripts. This approach however sometimes inserts compound word connectors in places where they are linguistically not legitimate. For example, consider a reference sentence

```
.. pälvis suure tähele <CC> panu
```

and the recognized token stream

```
... pälvis suure tähele PANNA
```

Test set	Model	Inserted tags	Precision	Recall	F measure	WER
BABEL	Compound word LM	154	0.64	0.83	0.72	8.2
	Hidden event LM	122	0.82	0.85	0.83	4.4
Speechdat	Compound word LM	395	0.84	0.89	0.86	6.5
	Hidden event LM	352	0.89	0.94	0.91	4.2

Table 1: Compound word connector tagging accuracies and the resulting would-be word error rate resulting from incorrect tagging, given perfect morpheme output by the decoder.

According to the alignment, the token *tähele* and the misrecognized token *panna* should be recomposed, although in reality, those two words often occur together and are never written as a compound word (as opposed to *tähele* and *panu* which are always written as a compound word).

For measuring compound reconstruction accuracy, we calculated compound connector insertion precision and recall. Precision is defined as a measure of the proportion of tags that the automatic procedure inserted correctly:

$$P = \frac{t_p}{t_p + f_p}$$

where t_p is the number of correctly inserted tags (true positives) and f_p the number of incorrectly inserted tags (false positives). Recall is defined as the proportion of actual compound word connector tags that the system found:

$$R = \frac{t_p}{t_p + f_n}$$

where f_n is the number of tags that the system failed to insert (false negatives).

Precision and recall can be combined into a single measure of overall performance by using the F measure which is defined as follows:

$$F = \frac{1}{\alpha \frac{1}{P} + (1 - \alpha) \frac{1}{R}} \overset{[\alpha=0.5]}{=} \frac{2PR}{P + R}$$

where α is a factor which determines the relative importance of precision versus recall.

Another measure we used was the word error rate, calculated after compound word reconstruction, after alignment with the original reference transcripts. Word error rate is calculated as usual:

$$WER = \frac{S + D + I}{N}$$

where S is the number of substitution errors, D the number of deletion errors, I the number of insertion errors and N the number of words in the reference.

4.5 Results

As the first test, the method was tested on the reference transcripts from the BABEL and SpeechDat speech databases. The input consists of morphemes where compound word connectors are deleted. Results are shown in table 1.

As can be seen, the hidden event language model does better than the compound word language model. The latter seems to have a big problem with overgenerating compound words which lowers the precision figures.

The second test analyzed compound word reconstruction, given the recognized hypotheses from the decoder. Results are listed in table 2. The table also gives the "oracle" WER for each test set, that is, the WER given the perfect compound word reconstruction based on alignment with reference sentences.

The precision and recall of the models is much lower than when using reference sentences as input. This is expected, as often one particle of a compound word is misrecognized which "confuses" the models and gives them no reason to suggest a compound word.

For both test sets, the hidden event language model performed better in terms of both precision/recall as well as the final WER. The relative improvement in WER of the hidden event language model over the compound word language model was 5.0% for the BABEL test set and 4.7% for the SpeechDat test set.

4.6 Analysis

Table 3 lists some sentences from the SpeechDat test set that contain mistakenly compounded or uncom-

Test set	Model	Inserted tags	Precision	Recall	F measure	WER	Oracle WER
BABEL	Compound word LM	160	0.54	0.73	0.62	31.7	28.9
	Hidden event LM	123	0.67	0.70	0.68	30.2	
Speechdat	Compound word LM	378	0.66	0.67	0.66	44.2	40.0
	Hidden event LM	338	0.74	0.67	0.70	42.2	

Table 2: Compound word connector tagging accuracies and the resulting word error rate compared to the "oracle" word error rate, given the actual recognized hypotheses from the decoder.

pounded words, using the hidden event LM. The errors are written in upper case and the correct words are written in the right column. Quick investigation reveals at least three common patterns where compound recomposition errors occur:

1. a compound word is not recognized when both of the compound word particles are very infrequent: the result is that there is not enough occurrences of the pair, nor occurrences where the head word is a head in a compound, neither where the tail word is a tail in a compound; as a result, the statistical model has no reason to insert a compound connector between them (e.g. *piirde-tross*, *traks-tunkedes*, *ainu-autorsusest*, *broiler-küülik*)

2. two words are mistakenly recognized as a compound word when the first word is often a head word in compound words, and/or the second word is often a tail word in compound words, although their pair may actually never occur as a compound, and it also does not occur as an uncompounded pair often enough (e.g. *suur laud / suur-laud, kuue meetri / kuue-meetri*)

3. in some cases, words are mistakenly recomposed into a compound word when the fact that the words should be written separately comes from the surrounding context (e.g. *laulu looja / laulu-looja, kunsti tekke põhjuseks / tekke-põhjuseks, eri värvi osadest / värvi-osadest*). Those errors are probably the hardest to handle since the correct behavior would often require understanding of the discourse. Often, it is arguable whether the words should be written as a compound or not (e.g. *tekke-põhjuseks, taime-seemnetes*.

Manual analysis of the compounding errors of the SpeechDat reference texts shows that the majority of errors (around 60%) were of type 1. About 30% of the errors could be classified as context errors (type 3) and the rest (around 10%) were of type 2.

5 Conclusion

We tested two separate methods for reconstructing compound words from a stream of recognized morphemes, using only linguistic information. The first method, using a special compound word language model, relies on the assumption that the head part of a compound word is independent of the preceding context and its probability is calculated given only the tail. Probability of the tail, on the other hand, is calculated given the preceding context words. As an alternative approach, we proposed to use a trigram language model for locations of hidden compound word connector symbols between compound particles. Experiments with two test sets showed that the method based on hidden event language model performs consistently better than the compound word language model based approach.

The proposed compound word reconstruction technique could be improved. The analysis of reconstruction errors revealed two kinds of problems caused by data sparseness issues. Some of such issues could probably be eliminated by using a class-based language model. An added area for further study is to combine acoustic and prosodic cues, such as pause length, phone duration and pitch around the boundary between possible compound particles, with the linguistic model, as has been done for automatic sentence segmentation (Stolcke et al., 1998).

Acknowledgments

This research was partly funded by the Estonian Information Technology Foundation as part of the Tiigriülikool program and by the Estonian Associ-

Recognized	Actual
ühevärviline kostüüm pikendab teie figuuri samas kui eri VÄRVIOSADEST lühendab	.. VÄRVI OSADEST ..
üles pannakse uued liiklusmärgid PIIRDE TROSS tõmmatakse pingule	.. PIIRDETROSS ..
üheks kunsti TEKKEPÕHJUSEKS peetakse inimese tarvet ilu ja loomisrõõmu järele	.. TEKKE PÕHJUSEKS ..
väikeses ja pimedas kambris oli näha vaid voodi ja SUURLAUD	.. SUUR LAUD ..
väga soodsalt mõjuvad organismile tsitrused küüslauk ja TAIME SEEMNETES leiduvad ained	.. TAIMESEEMNETES ..
viis miljonit aastat tagasi VÄLJA SURNUD hiire fossiil oli üllatavalt hästi säilinud	.. VÄLJASURNUD ..
vaikne ja ennast ise kütusega varustav liikur on KUUEMEETRI pikkune silindriline puur	.. KUUE MEETRI ..
vaguniuksel istub taburetil õlistes TRAKS TUNKEDES naine	.. TRAKSTUNKEDES ..
vaesed MAA INIMESED said aru et see oli pogromm nende vastu	.. MAAINIMESED ..
LAULULOOJA oli huvitatud AINU AUTORSUSEST	LAULU LOOJA .. AINU-AUTORSUSEST
kuigi broileriks nimetatakse noort kana saab maitsva prae ka BROILER KÜÜLIKUST	.. BROILERKÜÜLIKUST

Table 3: Some sample compound word reconstruction errors from the SpeechDat test set.

ation of Information Technology and Telecommunications.

References

Tanel Alumäe. 2006. *Methods for Estonian large vocabulary speech recognition*. Ph.D. thesis, Tallinn University of Technology.

Arvo Eek and Einar Meister. 1999. Estonian speech in the BABEL multi-language database: Phonetic-phonological problems revealed in the text corpus. In *Proceedings of LP'98. Vol II.*, pages 529–546.

Heiki-Jaan Kaalep and Kadri Muischnek. 2005. The corpora of Estonian at the University of Tartu: the current situation. In *The Second Baltic Conference on Human Language Technologies : Proceedings*, pages 267–272, Tallinn, Estonia.

Heiki-Jaan Kaalep and Tarmo Vaino. 2001. Complete morphological analysis in the linguist's toolbox. In *Congressus Nonus Internationalis Fenno-Ugristarum Pars V*, pages 9–16, Tartu, Estonia.

Einar Meister, Jürgen Lasn, and Lya Meister. 2002. Estonian SpeechDat: a project in progress. In *Fonetiikan Päivät 2002 — The Phonetics Symposium 2002*, pages 21–26.

P. Placeway, S. Chen, M. Eskenazi, U. Jain, V. Parikh, B. Raj, M. Ravishankar, R. Rosenfeld, K. Seymore, M. Siegler, R. Stern, and E. Thayer. 1997. Hub-4 Sphinx-3 system. In *Proceedings of the DARPA Speech Recognition Workshop*, pages 95–100.

Vesa Siivola, Teemu Hirsimäki, Mathias Creutz, and Mikko Kurimo. 2003. Unlimited vocabulary speech recognition based on morphs discovered in an unsupervised manner. In *Proceedings of Eurospeech*, Geneva, Switzerland.

M. Spies. 1995. A language model for compound words. In *Proceedings of Eurospeech*, pages 1767–1779.

A. Stolcke and E. Shriberg. 1996. Automatic linguistic segmentation of conversational speech. In *Proceedings of ICSLP*, volume 2, pages 1005–1008, Philadelphia, PA, USA.

A. Stolcke, E. Shriberg, R. Bates, M. Ostendorf, D. Hakkani, M. Plauche, G. Tur, and Y. Lu. 1998. Automatic detection of sentence boundaries and disfluencies based on recognized words. In *Proceedings of ICSLP*, volume 5, pages 2247–2250, Sydney, Australia.

Andreas Stolcke. 2002. SRILM – an extensible language modeling toolkit. In *Proceedings of ICSLP*, volume 2, pages 901–904, Denver, USA.

Dependency-Based Hybrid Model of Syntactic Analysis
for the Languages with a Rather Free Word Order

Guntis Bārzdiņš, Normunds Grūzītis, Gunta Nešpore and Baiba Saulīte
Institute of Mathematics and Computer Science
University of Latvia
Raiņa bulv. 29, Rīga, LV-1459, Latvia
`guntis@latnet.lv, {normundsg,gunta,baiba}@ailab.lv`

Abstract

Although phrase structure grammars have turned out to be a more popular approach for analysis and representation of the natural language syntactic structures, dependency grammars are often considered as being more appropriate for free word order languages. While building a parser for Latvian, a language with a rather free word order, we found (similarly to TIGER project for German and Talbanken05 for Swedish) that none of these models alone is adequate. Instead, we are proposing an original hybrid formalism that is strongly built on top of the dependency model borrowing the concept of a constituent from the phrase structure approach for representing analytical (multi-word) forms. The proposed model has been implemented in an experimental parser and is being successfully applied for description of a wide coverage grammar for Latvian.

1   Introduction

The reported research is part of an interdisciplinary project[*] that aims to develop semantic resources and methodologies for automatic meaning extraction from Latvian texts. This ultimate goal requires the lower levels of the language analysis, namely, morphology, syntax and lexical semantics, to be properly understood and implemented in the first place. The advantage of our semantic framework is that we are not concerned with the full disambiguation at the level of parsing, as the final disambiguation can be, hopefully, postponed to the semantic processing layers involving frame semantics (like FrameNet) and ontologies (like SUMO) and reasoning techniques. Our experiences of building such syntax parser for Latvian via original hybrid model techniques are described in this paper.

Morphological analysis nowadays is a solved problem for virtually any language group. However, a deep and comprehensive analysis and representation of the syntactic structure of an arbitrary sentence, is still a challenge, illustrated by the wide variety of formalisms attempted in non-English treebanks, such as TIGER for German (Brants et. al., 2002) or Talbanken05 for Swedish (Nivre et. al., 2006). To name a few, difficulties are typically caused by discontinuous constituents, coordinate structures and analytical forms (like the ambiguous prepositional phrases (Volk, 2006)).

Latvian belongs to the Baltic language group — it is a highly inflective synthetic language with a rather free word order. We are using the term *rather* due to the fact that there is virtually no language with an absolutely free word order and vice versa (Saussure, 1966). We are claiming that Latvian has one of the most liberal word orderings. In terms of the grammar structure Latvian is closely related to Lithuanian and also to Slavonic languages (int. al. many Central European languages). Therefore the model we have developed and tested for Latvian might be of interest also for other languages.

---

[*] SemTi-Kamols project at the Institute of Mathematics and Computer Science (UL). Anno 2005. www.semti-kamols.lv

Joakim Nivre, Heiki-Jaan Kaalep, Kadri Muischnek and Mare Koit (Eds.)
NODALIDA 2007 Conference Proceedings, pp. 13–20

There are two mainstream approaches that are typically considered when developing a syntactically annotated corpus and a forthcoming parser — phrase structure (constituency) model or dependency model (Nivre, 2002). Although constituency and dependency grammars are at least weakly equivalent (Gaifman, 1965), i.e. mutually transformable, they suggest significantly different views and methodologies with their own respective advantages and disadvantages.

Parsers for languages with a rather strict word order typically follow a top-down approach: sentences are split into phrases or constituents, which are then split into more fine-grained constituents. Conventionally, formalization of constituents is done by means of a *phrase structure* (*constituency*, *generative*) *grammar* (Chomsky, 1957; Marcus et. al., 1993).

Languages with a rather free word order can be more naturally (with considerably smaller number of rules) described following the bottom-up approach: from the surface to the model by drawing subordination links that are connecting individual words. Conventionally, these links are formalized via a *dependency grammar* (Tesnière, 1959; Mel'čuk, 1988; Hajičová et. al., 2001).

However, in practice the argument of the word order has not been a very strong one. Phrase structure rather than dependency structure treebanks have turned out to be a more popular approach also for synthetic free word order languages, although additions like functional annotations there are often added (Nivre, 2002) or efforts are made to create both types of syntactically annotated corpora, e.g. (Nivre et. al., 2006). One of the phrase structure popularity reasons might be the compatibility in methods, algorithms and tools with the English-speaking community.

The choice of an annotation scheme in fact is not limited just to the one or the other candidate. Various hybrid models have been proposed also before, like the different versions of head-driven phrase structure grammars (HPSG) (Pollard and Sag, 1994) or the TIGER annotation scheme (Brants and Hansen, 2002) and its predecessor (Skut et. al., 1997). The latter one seems to be the most advanced approach towards a real hybrid model for syntactic analysis: a sentence there is represented as a graph whose nodes are constituents and edges — syntactic functions. This allows TIGER to adequately represent such phenomena as discontinuous constituents, which are typical for the free word order languages. However, to support languages with even more liberal word order than in the case of German, the TIGER model can be further empowered with more explicit dependency grammar elements as will be described in the sections 2 and 3, where we present our original hybrid approach. An initial evaluation of the approach is given in the section 4.

2 Our Hybrid Parsing Method

Our hybrid parsing method is strongly based on the pure dependency parsing mechanism described by Covington (2001; 2003). Meanwhile it is fundamentally extended with a constituency mechanism to handle analytical multi-word forms consisting of fixed order mandatory words. This enables us to elegantly overcome the limitation of the pure dependency grammars, where all dependants are optional and totally free-order. In our approach a head and a dependant don't have to be single orthographic words anymore.

The merging of the two approaches though is not straightforward — to do so we had to introduce a concept of "x-word", which in a sense is the core idea of our method. As will be seen in the further explanation, x-words are devices that cancel off substrings in parsing and they act as glue between the two worlds due to their dual nature:

- x-words can be viewed as non-terminal symbols in the phrase structure grammar, and as such during the parsing process substitute all entities forming respective constituents;

- the dependency parser treats x-words as regular words, i.e., an x-word can act as a head for depending words and/or as a dependent of another head word.

The concept of x-word, in fact, is analogous to the "nucleus" — the primitive element of syntactic description introduced by (Tesnière, 1959) and discussed in-depth and exploited in (Järvinen and Tapanainen, 1998).

It also bears some similarity to the "classical" HPSG approach (Pollard and Sag, 1994), where features of a phrase are handed over via the head of the phrase (i.e. a constituent as whole is represented only by the features of its head). The main difference of our model is that x-word is a new artificial word with artificial morphological properties inherited in the controlled way from all constituents that are forming the x-word.

In our approach all complex text structures with fixed word order, like prepositional phrases and analytical forms (perfect tenses) of a predicate, can be seen as (substituted by) x-words (see Figure 1). Section 3 provides a more detailed description of the intended x-word usage.

By iteratively substituting all analytical word forms in the text with the corresponding x-words, we are ending up with a simple sentence structure, which can be described and parsed by simple word-to-word (including x-word) dependencies. The only requirement thus is an agreement on the specified morphological features (as in Figure 1). Agreement is established via Prolog-style feature unification (Covington, 2003).

```
([_,[v,aux,Tense,Nr,_]],
 [_,[v,aux,past,Nr,_]],
 [_,[v,m,0,0,Trans]])→

[x-verb,[v,m,Tense,Nr,Trans,perf]]
```

Figure 1. A simplified example of an x-word declaration: substitution of an analytical form of a verb (like *ir bijis jādod* 'have had to give'). Constants are in lower case. Capitalized are variables that have to agree on values or are to be inherited.

For languages with a rather free word order constituents of analytic forms are required to appear in a fixed order, however, dependants of such constituents in general appear in a free order according to the rules of the dependency grammar and thus can interleave in between. The consequence is that x-words are defined only by their mandatory constituents while the optional ones (if any) are attached implicitly via the pure dependency grammar.

An illustration of a hybrid parse tree generated according to the described x-word based hybrid model is shown in Figure 3.

Despite its conceptual simplicity, the proposed method is very powerful and can be used to parse different phenomena (see section 3) in languages both with rather free or strict word order.

2.1 Implementation

In general, parsing of dependencies can be based on two simple tables (Covington, 1990):

- a list of word forms and their morphological descriptions (let us name it A-table);

- a list of possible head-dependent dependency pairs, declaring which word forms may be linked by which syntactical roles (let us name it B-table).

The parsing is reduced to the search problem for the parse tree satisfying these given constraints.

In our implementation an automatic acquisition of the table A is done on-the-fly by exploiting a morphological analyzer over the words of input sentence (see Figure 2 for an illustration of the resulting A-table).

Additionally to this infrastructure inherited from Covington (1990; 2003), we have introduced one more table (X-table), which is a list of complex, fixed word order patterns along with their x-word substitutions (as sketched in Figure 2). An x-word is composed via production rules analogous to those of the constituency grammar (only it is written in a bottom-up direction). The difference is that only the mandatory constituents of an x-word are explicitly declared, while their optional dependents are described by the regular dependency rules (B-table). X-words can be nested in other x-words as well — either directly like in a constituency grammar, or indirectly via dependency rules of B-table.

From the point of view of the B-table, simple word or x-word heads/dependants are treated equally.

A-Table	
Word	Morphological Features
vasarā	`[n,f,sg,loc]`
var	`[v,aux,present,pl,trans]`
peldēties	`[v,m,inf,0,intrans]`

X-Table		
x-Word	Morphology	Constituents
`x-coord`	. . .	. . .
`x-prep`	. . .	. . .
`x-verb`	. . .	. . .

B-Table		
Function	Head	Dependant
`modifier`	`[_,{v,m}]`	`[_,{n,loc}]`
`subject`	`[x-verb,{v,m,Nr}]`	`[_,{n,Nr,nom}]`
`attribute`	`[_,{n}]`	`[_,{n,gen}]`

Figure 2. Simplified illustration of the tables A, X and B. Notation {..} — unordered conditions.

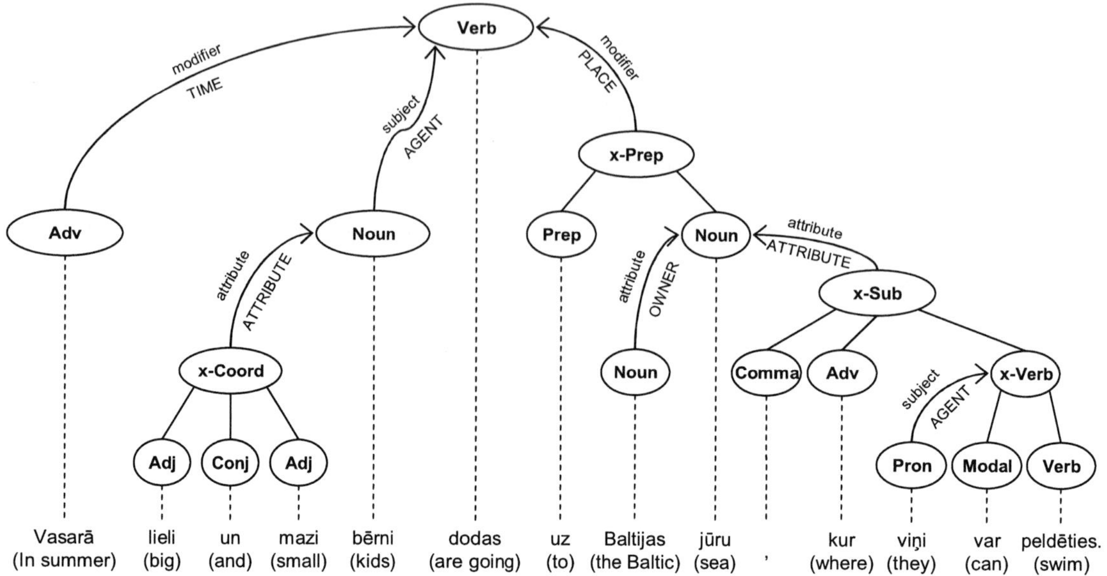

Figure 3. A shallow parse tree conforming to the hybrid model. Directed arcs stand for dependencies (optional), undirected — for constituents (mandatory). Nodes are words, either simple or complex (x-words).

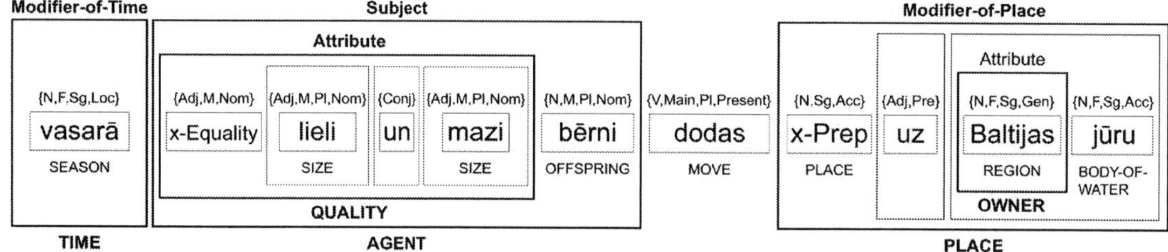

Figure 4. A chunk of the sentence presented in the Figure 3. Tree representation is encoded in the notation of the nested boxes.

Although an x-word as such in its adjacency is seen as syntactic primitive, its internal structure is parsed further as an independent subtree exploiting the fixed patterns and dependency connections defined in the X- and B-table respectively. Note that both explicit and implicit constituents interleave (e.g., 'UZ Baltijas JŪRU' in Figure 3).

To reduce parsing ambiguity, we have introduced one additional constraint in our parsing engine: each head is allowed to have only one dependant with the same syntactic role (function column in the B-table). For instance, this avoids more than one (uncoordinated) subject per predicate, which seems to be a natural constraint.

The proposal can be summarized as follows: we have added the mechanism of x-words to a combination of (Covington, 2003) + (Brants and Hansen, 2002). By introducing the x-words we have made the hybrid approach already proposed by the TIGER schema more straightforward and more powerful.

2.2 Visualization

Along with an original method of parsing, we have also introduced a space-saving graphical notation — nested boxes — in addition to the classical tree representation. In our notation each box corresponds to a single word (simple or complex x-word) and has both syntactic and semantic annotations. A list of morphological features and syntactic role is given at the top of a word/box; a label of an ontological concept and semantic role is given at the bottom (see Figure 4, illustrating the box-representation of the parse tree shown in Figure 3).

3 Methodology

In this section we will show how different well-known phenomena of syntactical analysis are handled by our hybrid parser.

3.1 Free Word Order

Considering analysis of a free word order, subordination relations are declared between parts of a simple sentence, assuming that each part basically is represented by a single word (see Figure 5). As a result, dependency grammar is defined by a set of head-dependent pairs, where only the agreement of morphological forms between both parts is significant, but not the order in which they appear in a sentence, since it doesn't have impact on the syntactic model.

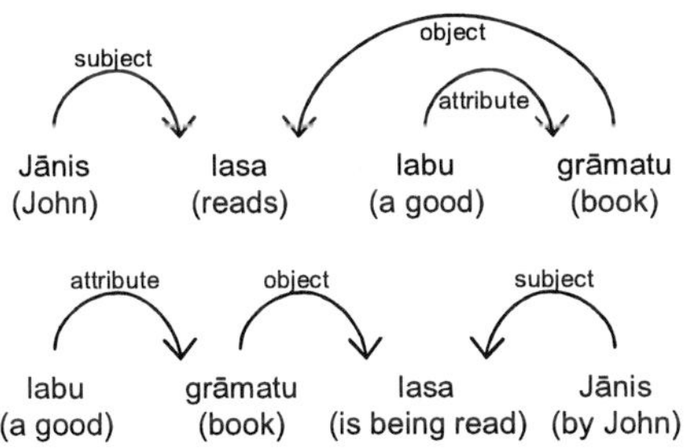

Figure 5. Dependency tree (arcs) remains the same for different readings of a sentence.

Out of the six possible subject-predicate-object orderings all the six are allowed in Latvian. Position of an adverb also is not constrained. Only attributes traditionally go before their heads.

3.2 Agreement

In Latvian as an inflective language agreement is very important phenomenon. It happens in both nominal (e.g. *lielā mājā* 'in a big house'), and verbal forms.

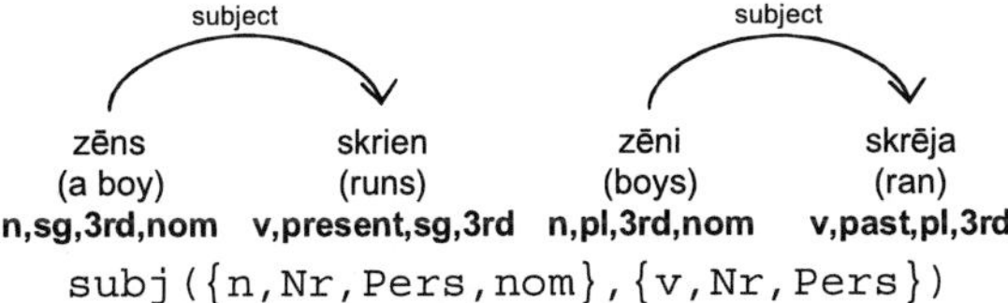


```
subj({n,Nr,Pers,nom},{v,Nr,Pers})
```

Figure 6. A single unification-based dependency rule will correctly accept all the subject(noun)-predicate pairs.

The head and the dependant of each dependency pair can be easily turned into constrained patterns (see Figure 6 for a simplified example), stating conditions on rich morphological features and inflectional agreement between both parts.

3.3 Constraints on the Left/Right Position

Apart form the internal structure of complex words, positional restrictions can be imposed on words per se. Although we are dealing with a language with a free word order in some cases the order of constituents is quite important. For example, in the already mentioned construction `attr([adj|_],[n|_])`, the constituents normally can not change their order.

The parser can be guided by an additional parameter of a dependency rule, indicating whether a head goes first or last against its dependant: `attr([adj|_],[n|_],right)`.

The fixed order of the words does not prevent them from being involved in other dependencies — they do not necessarily have to be placed together. For instance, the parser also accepts constructions like *liels koka galds* 'big wooden table'.

3.4 Analytical Forms of a Predicate

Rather free word order means that there exist rather strict constructions as well, i.e. analytical forms. The main part of a sentence that often is made up by few words in the same function is the predicate. We have described the following patterns of an analytical predicate in the X-table: perfect tenses, moods, passive voice, semantic modifiers (e.g. modal verbs), nominal and adverbial predicates.

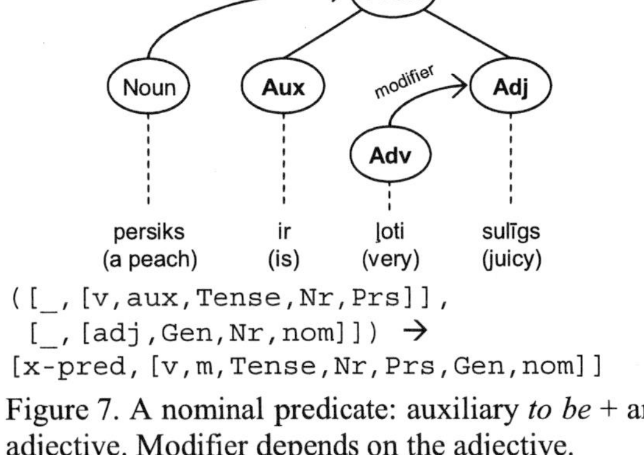


```
([_,[v,aux,Tense,Nr,Prs]],
 [_,[adj,Gen,Nr,nom]]) →
[x-pred,[v,m,Tense,Nr,Prs,Gen,nom]]
```

Figure 7. A nominal predicate: auxiliary *to be* + an adjective. Modifier depends on the adjective.

Between the constituents of an analytical predicate other (dependant) parts of sentence may appear that is acceptable by the parser. In case of Latvian they are typically modifiers and attributes, which are related either to the predicate as whole or to a particular constituent (e.g., Figure 7). Note that such cases are also related to the phenomenon of discontinuous constituents (see section 3.7).

3.5 Prepositional Phrases

Prepositional phrases are regarded as x-words consisting of a preposition (or rarely — postposition) and a nomen in an appropriate (fixed) form. The nomen may be further involved as a root for a rich sub tree of dependants — all the structure will be regarded as a single x-word like in Figure 8.

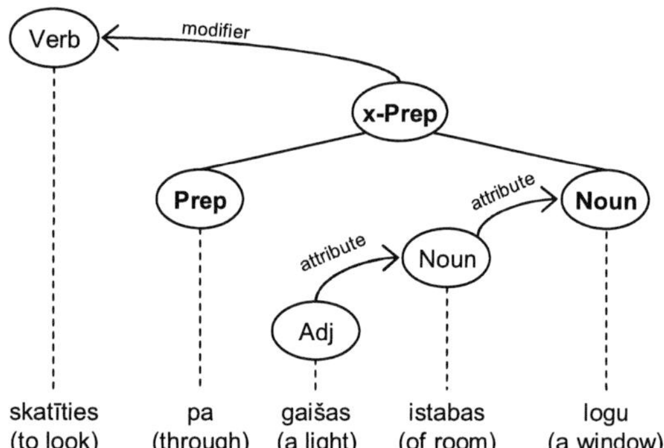

Figure 8. An x-word-driven prepositional phrase (*to look through a window of a light room*).

3.6 Coordinate Structures

Another well known issue concerns coordinate structures. The notion of an x-word can be clearly used to describe coordinated parts of a sentence as well (as illustrated in Figure 9).

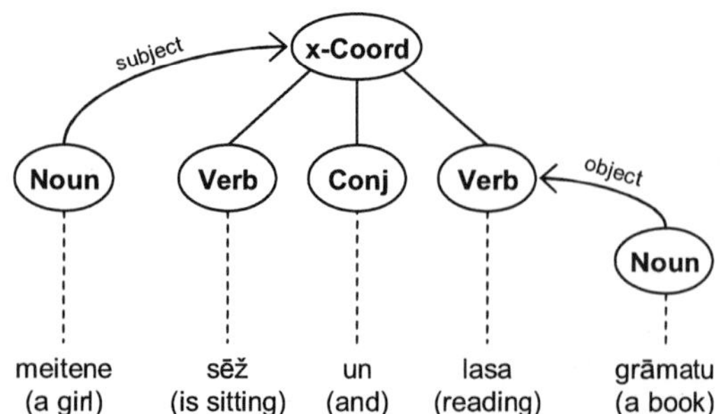

Figure 9. A typical pattern of a coordination structure that is parsed using the x-word mechanism. In this case the coordination results in a predicate.

Coordinated parts of sentence can be regarded as a single x-word, because syntactically they take the same position. Morphological features are in agreement, thus can be inherited with no loss of information.

3.7 Discontinuous Constituents

The widely discussed phenomenon of discontinuous constituents is one of the main issues if dealing with a phrase structure grammar. Dependency grammars on the contrary are not affected much by this problem — non-projective parse trees are very infrequent phenomena, since dependency grammars are not based on constituents and the root element of each parse tree is a verb (predicate) to which all the other syntactic primitives are connected, either directly or recursively via its dependants. Moreover, we are basically interested in texts where neutral word order prevails, i.e., in a written text but not in a speech. We also exclude from the scope of written texts some specific usages of a language, e.g. poetry.

In our approach discontinuous x-words are implicitly covered by the natural interleaving of dependants within the x-words (see sections 2.1 and 3.4). However, there is a limitation — dependants that linearly stand inside of an x-word are not allowed to be connected to the x-word as whole but to a particular constituent of it — which, in fact, is a semantically motivated restriction (at least for Latvian).

3.8 Subordinate and Coordinate Clauses

It is obvious that subordinate and coordinate clauses are based on a simple sentence structure. Therefore in our model subordinate clauses are seen as x-words as well — they link to the principal clause as a single part of a sentence (both syntactically and semantically), and typically they are dependants of a single word (simple or complex one). An example has been already shown in Figure 3. Thereby, an artificial part-of-speech must be introduced for a subordinate clause.

Clauses being in coordination relationship could be joined under an artificial node *sentence*, similarly as it is illustrated with coordinate structures in section 3.6. However, from the point of view of semantic structure each coordinated clause is treated as a separate sentence. Such an x-word would only introduce unnecessary ambiguity together with grammar patterns for coordinated verbs: by application of dependency rules the co-ordinated parts of sentence can be expanded up to coordinated clauses.

4   Evaluation

It should be noted that we are not considering any performance and algorithmic complexity aspects in the scope of this paper. Moreover, we would like to avoid any premature discussion on optimization or disambiguation to keep the model descriptive and clean until the stage of the semantic analysis.

The described hybrid parsing method has been implemented in a running parser of Latvian. Performance of the naïve and straightforward implementation is in the range of few seconds per sentence and is acceptable for verification purposes of the grammar.

The grammar is already able to recognize most types of frequent syntactic structures. If an arbitrary sentence can not be parsed successfully, it is mainly because of "routine" work needed to add the missing table entries to the system. However, it is feasible that a significant amount of work is still pending to accomplish a near-complete coverage.

Currently we have formalized ~450 patterns of x-words (X-table) and ~200 dependency rules (B-table). A-table, as it was mentioned earlier, for each sentence is built on-the-fly by exploiting a morphological analyzer of Latvian. Although the number of patterns/rules is still small, part of them have been detected as overlapping, or are too general. This results in high number of ambiguities for the respective sentences. Due to this, in parallel we are developing an automated consistency checker to detect the possible inconsistencies or overlapping in the hand-crafted rules.

On the other hand, free word order structures by default are more ambiguous than the corresponding analytical constructions. Therefore, we produce all the possible parse trees for each sentence and consider the result correct and sufficient for the further semantic parsing stage, if all these trees are syntactically correct and the semantically correct tree is among them. We agree with (Tesnière, 1959) that the syntactic structure follows from the semantic structure. Therefore we regard disambiguation as a separate problem and in the current stage of analysis we only do care that there are syntactically valid trees produced.

Some constructions are not implemented in the parser yet (e.g. semi-predicative components and participial phrases), but we believe that there are no principal problems in dealing with these constructions.

A screenshot of a running application is given in Figure 11. Although the model and the parser were made taking into account the Latvian language only, the parser that is based on the three clear-cut tables has turned out to be language independent.

One might ask why we haven't tried to extract the grammar from a treebank. It has been shown that if there is a sufficiently large treebank available (at least about 20 000 manually annotated sentences), it is possible to learn the grammar at a certain extent from the treebank (Charniak, 1996). Unfortunately there is no large scale Latvian treebank available. Actually, there is no publicly accessible treebank at all. Moreover, the corpus has to be annotated with a grammar of interest. Instead we are planning to develop an experimental treebank on the basis of the approach and the parser presented.

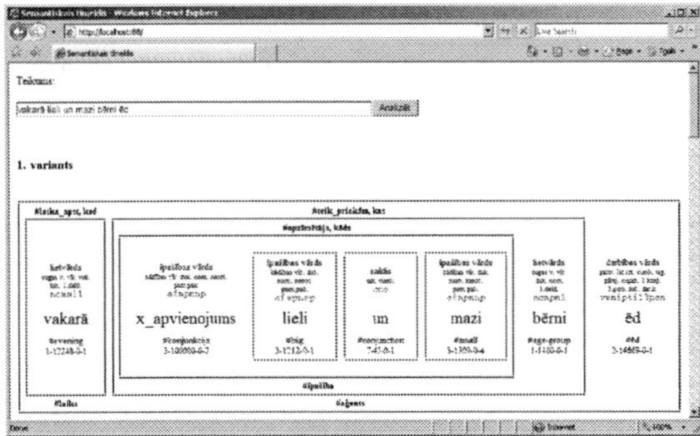

Figure 11. A screenshot of the user-interface of the experimental Latvian syntax parser. It is implemented in SWI-Prolog with a web-browser front-end.

5   Conclusion

We have experimentally verified that the proposed hybrid model, which is strongly based on the dependency grammar approach, can be used to describe languages both with rather free or strict word order. Even if the computational performance and simplicity is better for phrase-structure grammars, the construction of a wide coverage grammar might be more convenient via a layer of the proposed hybrid approach. Straightforward compatibility between the syntactic and semantic structures in case of the dependency grammar is also of a great importance.

In order to adapt the parser for other languages "only" the three tables (A, X and B) have to be produced describing morphology and syntax of the particular language.

Acknowledgements

Project is funded by the National Research Program in Information Technologies and is partially supported by European Social Fund. Also we thank our colleagues and reviewers of this paper for their valuable comments and references.

References

Sabine Brants and Silvia Hansen. 2002. *Developments in the TIGER Annotation Scheme and their Realization in the Corpus*. In Proceedings of the Third Conference on Language Resources and Evaluation (LREC 2002), pp. 1643–1649

Sabine Brants, Stefanie Dipper, Silvia Hansen, Wolfgang Lezius and George Smith. 2002. *The TIGER Treebank*. In Proceedings of the Workshop on Treebanks and Linguistic Theories

Eugene Charniak. 1996. *Tree-Bank Grammars*. In AAAI/IAAI, Vol. 2, pp. 1031–1036

Noam Chomsky. 1957. *Syntactic Structures*. The Hague: Mouton

Michael A. Covington. 1990. *A Dependency Parser for Variable-Word-Order Languages*. Research Report AI-1990-01, Artificial Intelligence Center, The University of Georgia

Michael A. Covington. 2001. *A fundamental Algorithm for Dependency Parsing*. In Proceedings of the 39th Annual ACM Southeast Conference. Eds. John A. Miller and Jeffrey W. Smith, pp. 95–102

Michael A. Covington. 2003. *A Free-Word-Order Dependency Parser in Prolog*. Prolog Natural Language Tools, The University of Georgia http://www.ai.uga.edu/mc/dparser/dparser.pdf

Haim Gaifman. 1965. Dependency Systems and Phrase-Structure Systems. *Information and Control*, 8:304–307

Eva Hajičová, Jan Hajič, Martin Holub, Petr Pajas, Veronika Kolářová-Řezníčková, Petr Sgall, Barbora Vidová Hladká. 2001. *The Current Status of the Prague Dependency Treebank*. In Proceedings of the 5th International Conference on Text, Speech and Dialogue, Železná Ruda-Špičák, Czech Republic, Springer-Verlag Berlin Heidelberg New York, pp. 11–20

Timo Järvinen and Pasi Tapanainen. 1998. *Towards an implementable dependency grammar*. In Proceedings of the Workshop "Processing of Dependency-Based Grammars", Quebec, Canada, pp. 1–10

Igor Mel'čuk. 1988. *Dependency Syntax: Theory and Practice*. Albany, N.Y.: The State University of New York Press

Mitchell P. Marcus, Beatrice Santorini and Mary Ann Marcinkiewicz. 1993. Building a large annotated corpus of English: The Penn treebank. *Computational Linguistics*, 19(2):313–330

Joakim Nivre. 2002. *What kinds of trees grow in Swedish soil? A comparison of four annotation schemes for Swedish*. In Hinrichs, E. and Simov, K. (eds) Proceedings of the First Workshop on Treebanks and Linguistic Theories (TLT2002)

Joakim Nivre, Jens Nilsson and Johan Hall. 2006. *Talbanken05: A Swedish Treebank with Phrase Structure and Dependency Annotation*. In Proceedings of LREC, pp. 1392–1395

Carl Pollard and Ivan A. Sag. 1994. *Head-Driven Phrase Structure Grammar*. Chicago: University of Chicago Press

Ferdinand de Saussure. 1966. *Course in General Linguistics*. New York: McGraw-Hill Book Company

Lucien Tesnière. 1959. *Éléments de syntaxe structurale*. Klincksieck, Paris

Martin Volk. 2006. *How bad is the problem of PP-attachment? A comparison of English, German and Swedish*. In Proceedings of ACL-SIGSEM Workshop on Prepositions, Trento

Wojciech Skut, Brigitte Krenn, Thorsten Brants and Hans Uszkoreit. 1997. *An Annotation Scheme for Free Word Order Languages*. In Proceedings of the Fifth Conference on Applied Language Processing (ANLP 1997) pp. 27–28

Using Danish as a CG Interlingua:
A Wide-Coverage Norwegian-English Machine Translation System

Eckhard Bick
Institute of Language and
Communication
University of Southern Denmark
Odense, Denmark
eckhard.bick@mail.dk

Lars Nygaard
The Text Laboratory

University of Oslo
Oslo, Norway
lars.nygaard@iln.uio.no

Abstract

This paper presents a rule-based Norwegian-English MT system. Exploiting the closeness of Norwegian and Danish, and the existence of a well-performing Danish-English system, Danish is used as an «interlingua». Structural analysis and polysemy resolution are based on Constraint Grammar (CG) function tags and dependency structures. We describe the semiautomatic construction of the necessary Norwegian-Danish dictionary and evaluate the method used as well as the coverage of the lexicon.

1 Introduction

Machine translation (MT) is no longer an unpractical science. Especially the advent of corpora with hundreds of millions of words and advanced machine learning techniques, bilingual electronic data and advanced machine learning techniques have fueled a torrent of MT-project for a large number of language pairs. However, the potentially most powerful, deep rule-based approaches still struggle, for most languages, with a serious coverage problem when used on running, mixed domain text. Also, some languages, like English, German and Japanese, are more equal than others, not least in a funding-heavy environment like MT.

The focus of this paper will be threefold: Firstly, the system presented here is targeting one of the small, «unequal» languages, Norwegian. Secondly, the method used to create a Norwegian-English translator, is ressource-economical in that it uses another, very similar language, Danish, as an «interlingua» in the sense of translation knowledge recycling (Paul 2001), but with the recycling step at the SL side rather than the TL side. Thirdly, we will discuss an unusual analysis and transfer methodology based on Constraint Grammar dependency parsing. In short, we set out to construct a Norwegian-English MT system by building a smaller, Norwegian-Danish one and piping its output into an existing Danish deep parser (DanGram, Bick 2003) and an existing, robust Danish-English MT system (Dan2Eng, Bick 2006 and 2007).

2 The MT system

The Bokmål standard variety of Norwegian is a language historically so close to Danish, that speakers of one language can understand texts in the

Joakim Nivre, Heiki-Jaan Kaalep, Kadri Muischnek and Mare Koit (Eds.)
NODALIDA 2007 Conference Proceedings, pp. 21–28

other without prior training - though the same does not necessarily hold for the spoken varieties. It is therefore a less challenging task to create a Norwegian-Danish MT system than a Norwegian-English or even Norwegian-Japanese one. Furthermore, syntactic differences are so few, that lexical transfer can to a large degree be handled at the word level with only part of speech (PoS) disambiguation and no syntactic disambiguation, allowing us to depend on the Danish parser to provide a deep structural analysis. Furthermore, the polysemy spectrum of many Bokmål words closely matches the semantics of the corresponding Danish word, so different English translation equivalents can be chosen using Danish context-based discriminators.

2.1 Norwegian analysis

As a first step of analysis, we use the Oslo-Bergen Tagger (Hagen et al. 2000) to provide lemma disambiguation and PoS tagging, the idea being to translate results into Danish, using a large bilingual lexicon, and feed them into the syntactic and dependency stages of the DanGram parser. However, though both the OBT tagger and DanGram adhere to the Constraint Grammar (CG) formalism (Karlsson 1990), a number of descriptive compatibility issues had to be addressed. Since categories could not always be mapped one-to-one, we had to also use the otherwise to-be-skipped syntactic stage of the OBT tagger in order to further disambiguate a word's part of speech. Thus, the Danish preposition-adverb distinction is underspecified in the Norwegian system where the 2 lexemes have the same form, using the preposition tag even without the presence of a pp. The same holds for about 50 words that in Danish are regarded as unambiguous adverbs, but in Norwegian as unambiguous prepositions.

2.2 The Norwegian-Danish lexicon

The complexity of a Norwegian-Danish dictionary can be compared to Spanish-Catalan language pair addressed in the open source Apertium MT project (Corbí-Bellot et al. 2005), where a 1-to-1 lexicon was deemed sufficient (with a few polysemous cases handled as multi-word expressions), avoiding the disambiguation complexity of many-to-many lexica necessary for less-related languages. Even without extensive polysemy mismatches, the productive compounding nature of Scandinavian languages, however, increases lexical complexity as compared to Romance languages - an issue reflected in the transfer evaluation in chapter 2.3.

In a project with virtually zero funding, like ours, it can be difficult to build or buy a lexicon, not to mention the general lack of wide-coverage Norwegian-Danish electronic lexica to begin with. So with only a few thousand words from terminology lists or the like available, creative methods had to be employed, and we opted for a bootstrapping system with the following steps:

(a) Create a large corpus of monolingual - Norwegian text and lemmatize it automatically. Quality was less important in this step, since frequency measures could be employed to weed out errors and create a candidate list of Norwegian lemmas.

(b) Regard Norwegian as misspelled Danish, and run a Danish spell checker on the lemma-list obtained from (a). Assume translation as identical, if the Norwegian word is accepted by a Danish spell checker. Use correction suggestions by spell checkers as translations suggestions. Because differences could be greater than Levenshtein distance 1 or 2, a special, CG-based spell checker (OrdRet, Bick 2006) was used, with a particular focus on heavy, dyslexic spelling deviations and a mixed graphical-phonetic approach.

(c) Produce phonetic transmutation rules for Norwegian and Danish spelling to generate hypothetical Danish words from Norwegian candidates, and than check if a word of the relevant word class was listed in either DanGram's parsing lexicon or its spell checker fullform list.

Methods (a-c) resulted in a list of 226,000 lemmas with translations candidates in Danish. Only 20,000 low-frequency words were completely unmatchable. In a first round of manual revision, all closed-class words, all polylexical matches were checked, and a confidence value from DanGram's spell checker module was used to grade suggestions into safe, unsafe and none. Next, a compound analyzer was written and run on all Norwegian words, accepting compound splits as likely if the resulting parts both individually existed in the word list, finally creating a Danish translation from the translations of the parts, and checking it and its epenthetic letters against the Danish lexicon. This step not only helped to fill in remaining blanks, but was also used to corroborate spell checker suggestions as correct, if they matched the translation produced by compound analysis - or replace them, if not. After this, 13.800 lemmas had no translation, 23.500 lemmas were left with an «unsafe» marking from the spell checker stage, and in 20.700 cases, compound analysis contradicted spell checker or list suggestions otherwise deemed safe. Allowing overrides in the latter case, and removing the two former cases, we were left with a bilingual lemma list of 188.500 entries.

Finally, a dual pass of manual checking was directed at all items with a frequency count over 10, corresponding to about 12.5%. In obvious cases, related low-frequency words in neighbouring positions on the alphabetical list were corrected at the same time.

In order to evaluate our method of lexicon-creation, we extracted all words with frequency 9 - the most frequent group without prior manual revision - and inspected all suggested translations (1544 cases).

type	*n*	*%*
non-word	33	2.1 %
wrong PoS	8	0.5 %
etymology =	161	10.4 %
transparent[1]	6	0.4
intransparent[2]	20	1.3 %
all corrected	**187**	**12.1 %**
all	228	14.8 %

Table 1

As can be seen from table 1, ignoring the 2.6 % of non-words from the corpus-based lemma-list, about 12% of the unrevised translations were wrong. However, in most of these cases (10.4%, over 4/5), the Danish translations were still etymologically - and thus spelling-wise - related to their Norwegian

---

[1] brise (blæse), spenntak (spændloft), stabbe, strupetak (strubelåg), villastrøk (villakvarter), vårluft (forårsluft)
[2] guttete (drengete), havert (slags sæl), hengemyr (hængedynd), kraftsektor (energisektor), koring, kvinneyrke, langdryg, låtskriver, lønnsnemnd, malingflekk, omvisning (rundvisning), purke (so), sauebonde, smokk (sut), strikkegenser, søppelbøtte (affaldsbøtte), tukle (fumle), tøyelig (fleksibel), vassdrag (vandløb), yrkesutdanning

counterparts, and should thus be accessible to improved automatic matching-techniques.

frequen cy	non- word	wrong PoS	correct ed
9 (all)	2.1 %	0.5 %	12.1 %
5	0.5 %	1.5 %	14 %
4	4 %	0.5 %	14 %
3	1 %	0.5 %	10.5 %
2	4 %	3 %	9.5 %
1	3.5 %	0.5 %	8.5 %
average	2.5 %	1.1 %	11.4 %

Table 2

Small checks were also conducted for other frequencies (200 words each), randomly extracting 1 out of 10 words. Results indicate that automatic translatability remains similar in general, though
there was a slight correlation between falling frequency and *less* need for correction. The proportion of non-words was high for low frequencies, possibly reflecting spelling errors and analysis problems with rare words in the corpus data. However, since having non-existing words in the SL-list, is only «noise» and not a problem for the MT system, we conclude from their translatability that low-frequency words are at least as safe a contribution to the lexicon as high-frequency words.

2.3 Norwegian-Danish transfer

Analysed input from the Oslo-Bergen-tagger is danified by substituting Danish base forms for Norwegian ones. Even with an extensive bilingual word list, the transfer program is not, however, a mere lookup procedure. Due to the compounding structure of the languages involved, compound analysis has to be performed both on the Norwegian and the Danish side - the

former to achieve a part-by-part translation for words not listed in the bilingual lexicon, the latter to permit assignment of secondary *Danish* information (valency, semantics) to Danish translations not covered by the DanGram monolingual lexicon.

The Norwegian-Danish transfer module was evaluated on 1,000 mixed-genre sentences from the Norwegian web part of the Leipzig Corpora Collection[3] and a 6.500 word chunk from the ECIcorpus[4].

	Web	Litterature
words	15,641	6,521
N, ADJ, V, ADV	8,976 (57.4%)	3,098 (47.5%)
not in noda-lex	991 (6.3%)	182 (2.8%)
compound s	458 (2.9%)	78 (1.2%)
not in dan-lex	127 (0.8%)	32 (0.5%)

Table 3

The failure rate for Norwegian words was 6.3% in the web corpus, in part compensated by the fact that almost half of these (2.9%) could still be compound-analyzed. The coverage rate of the Danish lexicon was very high - only 0.8% of suggested translations were not found. Figures for the literature corpus were almost twice as good - even when taking into account that the percentage of open-class inflecting words was 10 percentage points lower in this corpus.

2.4 Danish generation

Finally, Danish full-forms are generated from the translated base-forms, based

---

[3] http://corpora.uni-leipzig.de
[4] European Corpus Initiative, http://www.elsnet.org/resources/eciCorpus.html

both on the filtered OBT morphological tag string, and inflexional information from the Danish lexicon.

"*[hus] N NEU S DEF GEN*", for instance, will be inflected as *hus -> NEU DEF huset -> GEN husets.* Irregular forms are stored in full in a separate file, and compound stems are constructed, prior to inflexion, using rules for the insertion of epenthetic s or epenthetic e.

(1) *agurk+tid -> agurketid*
(2) *forbud+stat -> forbudsstat*

Alas, Danish and Norwegian morphology are not completely isomorphic, and in order to handle differences in a context-dependent way, a special CG grammar is run before generation. This grammar handles, for instance, the Norwegian phenomenon of double definiteness:

*(3) NOR: **den** store bil**en** -> DAN: **den** store bil*

Here, so-called substitution rules are used, replacing the tag DEF with IDF in the presence of definite articles (example below) or pre- or post-positioned determiners and attributes (syntactic tags @<ADJ, @<DET, @ADJ>, @DET>):

SUBSTITUTE (DEF) (IDF) TARGET (N)
IF (*-1 ART BARRIER NON-PRE-N/ADV) ;

2.5 Structural analysis

Syntactic-functional analysis was based not on the Norwegian OBT-analysis, but on a from-scratch analysis of the translated Danish text, in part because of the high syntactic accuracy of the Danish parser (Bick 2000), in part to ensure compatibility with the descriptive conventions used in the next syntactic stage, dependency analysis, and the Danish-English MT system itself. The Dependency grammar in question (described in Bick 2005) consists of a few hundred rules targeting CG function tags, supported by attachment direction markers and close/long-attachment markers from a special CG layer run as a last step before dependency.

2.6 Danish-English transfer

Though the Danish-English MT system (Dan2eng, fBick 2007) is not the focus of this paper, and used *as is* in a black box fashion, a short description is in order - not least because of the perspective of ultimately creating a similar system for direct Norwegian-English transfer.

The core principle of Dan2eng is to rely as much as possible on deep and accurate SL analysis. In this spirit, the selection of translation equivalents is based on lexical transfer rules exploiting *syntactic* relations in a semanticised way. The way in which Dan2eng semanticizes syntax, differs significantly from many older rule-based MT systems designed in the 80's and 90's. First, it uses dependency rather than constituent analyses, and second, it is the first MT system ever to be based on Constraint Grammar, a combination that provides it with a robust way of progressing from shallow to deep analyses (Bick 2005) without the high percentage of parse failures inherent to many generative systems when run on free text[5].

As an example, let us have a look at the translation spectrum Danish verb *at regne (to rain),* which has many other, non-meteorological, meanings *(calculate, consider, expect, convert ...)* as well. Here, Dan2eng simply uses *grammatical distinctors* to *distinguish* between translations, rather than *define* sub-senses.

---

[5] Even today, MT systems using deep syntax, may find it cautious to restrict their domain or structural scope, like the LFG- and HPSG-based LOGON system (Lønning et al. 2004).

Thus, the translation *rain (a)* is chosen if a daughter/dependent (D) exists with the function of situative/formal subject (@S-SUBJ), while most other meanings ask for a human subject. As a default[6] translation for the latter *calculate (f)* is chosen, but the presence of other dependents (objects or particles) may trigger other translations. *regne med (c-e),* for instance, will mean *include,* if *med* has been identified as an adverb, while the preposition *med* triggers the translations *count on* for human «granddaughter» dependents (GD = <H>), and *expect* otherwise. Note that the *include* translation also could have been conditioned by the presence of an object (D = @ACC), but would then have to be differentiated from (b), *regne for ('consider').*

regne_V[7]
(a) D=(@S-SUBJ) :rain;
(b) D=(<H> @ACC) D=("for" PRP)_nil :consider;
(c) D=("med" PRP)_on GD=(<H>) :count;
(d) D=("med" PRP)_on :expect;
(e) D=(@ACC) D=("med" ADV)_nil :include;
(f) D=(<H> @SUBJ) D?=("på" PRP)_nil :calculate;

The example shows how information from different descriptive layers is integrated in the transfer rules. Structural conditions may either be expressed in n-gram fashion (with P+n or P-n) positions, or dependency fashion (reference to daughters, mothers, granddaughters and grandmothers independent of distance). Semantic conditions can either be inferred with

---

[6] The ordering of differentiator-translation pairs is important - readings with fewer restrictions have to come last. The example lacks the general, differentiator-free default provided with all real lexicon entries.
[7] The full list of differentiators for this verb contains 13 cases, including several prepositional complements not included here *(regne efter, blandt, fra, om, sammen, ud, fejl ...)*

regular expressions from word or base forms, or exploit DanGram's semantic prototype tags in a systematic way, e.g. <tool>, <container>, <food>, <Hprof> etc. for nouns (160 types in all). Adjectives and verbs have fewer classes (e.g. psychological adjective, move, speech or cognitive verbs), but make up for this with a rich annotation of argument/valency tags.

The rule-based transfer system is supplemented by a dictionary of fixed expressions and a (so far sentence-based) translation memory. The Danish-English bilingual lexicon was built to match the coverage of the DanGram lexicon (100.000 words plus 40.000 names), but does not yet have the same coverage for compounds. In any case, compounds are productive, and therefore covered by a special back-up module that combines part-translations, affix-translations. Rules may be used to force a different translation for a lexeme if used as first or second part in compounds, e.g. *FN-styrke,* where *styrke* should be *'force',* not *'strength'.* The compound module is doubly important for our Nor2eng interlingua approach, since secondary Danish lookup-failures may be caused by Norwegian lookup-failures.

2.7 English generation and syntax

English generation is handled much like Danish generation, drawing on CG morphological tags, a lexicon of irregular forms and some phonetic/stress heuristics to inflect translated base forms - again supported by a special CG layer performing systematic substitutions (for instance plural translations of singular words) and insertions (certain modals, or articles). Differences in syntax are handled by successive transformation rules, which may move either words or whole dependency tree sections if certain tags, tokens or sequences are found.

In the following example, two movement rules were applied. The first changes the Scandinavian VS order into SV after a filled front field, placing the fronted adverbial between S and V. The other rule, classifying the adverbial, decides on a better place for it - between auxiliary and main verb.

NOR: *På 1980-tallet ble sammenhengen mellom sosiale faktorer og helse i stor grad avskrevet.*

DAN:

I	*PRP @ADVL*	*#1->13*
1980'erne	*N @P<*	*#2->1*
blev	*V @STA*	*#3->0*
sammenhængen	*N*	*@SUBJ #4->3*
mellem	*PRP @N<*	*#5->4*
sociale	*ADJ @>N*	*#6->7*
faktorer <cjt1>	*N @P<*	*#7->5*
og	*KC @CO*	*#8->7*
helse <cjt2>	*N @P<*	*#9->7*
i	*PRP @ADVL*	*#10->13*
stor	*ADJ @>N*	*#11->12*
grad	*N @P<*	*#12->10*
afskrevet	*V @AUX<*	*#13->3.*

ENG: *In the 1980s the connexion between social factors and health was largely written off.*

Note also the fact, that the preposition change is a difference between Norwegian and Danish, not between Danish and English, and that the subject movement acted on the *whole* NP, including its dependent PP, which again contained a coordination.

The necessary dependency links are marked in the Danish interlingua sentence.

Illustration 1

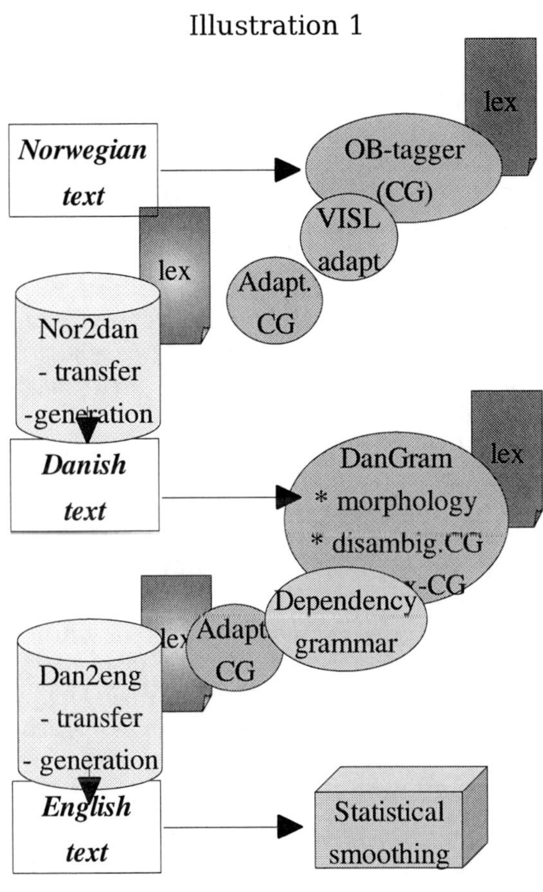

3 Perspectives: Statistical smoothing

In spite of the fact that Dan2Eng employs tens of thousands of hand-written lexical transfer rules, it is extremely difficult to cover all idiosyncrasies of, for instance, preposition usage or choice of synonym in a rule based way. Furthermore, mismatches are more likely when chaining two translations. On the other hand, statistical methods allow to check the probabilities of rule-suggested translations in a given context, smoothing out translational rough spots. Given the lack of large bilingual Norwegian-Danish or Norwegian-English corpora, it is an added advantage, that such methods work with *monolingual,* target language corpora - of which there are almost unlimited amounts availabe in the case of English. To prepare for an integration of TL smoothing, we performed dependency annotation of 1 billion words, and started extracting n-gram information as well as what we call dep-grams - hierarchical chains of dependency-linked words, the former with the perspective of preposition-smoothing, the latter for argument-smoothing.

Future evaluations, to be conducted after a more complete revision of the Norwegian bilingual lexicon and the construction of a polysemy-sensitive Norwegian-Danish transfer grammar, will have to address not only the overall quality of the MT system as a whole - optimally in comparison with other systems, like LOGON (Lønning et al. 2004) -, but also the relative contributions of rule based and statistical modules.

References

Bick, Eckhard. 2001. «En Constraint Grammar Parser for Dansk», in Peter Widell & Mette Kunøe (eds.), *8. Møde om Udforskningen af Dansk Sprog, 12.-13. oktober 2000*, pp. 40-50, Århus University

Bick, Eckhard. 2003, «A CG & PSG Hybrid Approach to Automatic Corpus Annotation», In: Kiril Simow & Petya Osenova (eds.), *Proceedings of SProLaC2003* (at Corpus Linguistics 2003, Lancaster), pp. 1-12

Bick, Eckhard. 2005 «Turning Constraint Grammar Data into Running Dependency Treebanks», In: Civit, Montserrat & Kübler, Sandra & Martí, Ma. Antònia (red.), *Proceedings of TLT 2005 (4th Workshop on Treebanks and Linguistic Theory, Barcelona, December 9th - 10th, 2005)*, pp.19-27

Bick, Eckhard. 2006. «A Constraint Grammar Based Spellchecker for Danish with a Special Focus on Dyslexics». In: Suominen, Mickael et al. (ed.) *A Man of Measure: Festschrift in Honour of Fred Karlsson on his 60th Birthday*. Special Supplement to SKY Jounal of Linguistics, Vol. 19 (ISSN 1796-279X), pp. 387-396. Turku: The Linguistic Association of Finland

Bick, Eckhard. 2007. «Fra syntaks til semantik: Polysemiresolution igennem dependensstrukturer i dansk-engelsk maskinoversættelse.» (forthcoming)

Corbí-Bello, Antonio M. et al. 2005. An open-source shallow-transfer machine translation engine for the Romance Languages of Spain. In *Proceedings of the European Association for Machine Translation, 10th Annual Conference*, Budapest 2005, p. 79-86.

Hagen, Kristin, Johannessen, Janne Bondi, Nøklestad, Anders. 2000. "A Constraint-Based Tagger for Norwegian". In: Lindberg, C.-E. and Lund, S.N. (red.): 17th Scandinavian Conference of Linguistic, Odense. Odense Working Papers in Language and Communication, No. 19, vol I.

Karlsson, Fred. 1990. Constraint Grammar as a Framework for Parsing Running Text. In: Karlgren, Hans (ed.), *COLING-90 Helsinki: Proceedings of the 13th International.* Conference on Computational Linguistics, Vol. 3, pp. 168-173

Lønning, Jan Tore, Stephan Oepen, Dorothee Beermann, Lars Hellan, John Carroll, Helge Dyvik, Dan Flickinger, Janne Bondi Johannessen, Paul Meurer, Torbjørn Nordgård, Victoria Rosén, and Erik Velldal. 2004. LOGON. A Norwegian MT effort. In *Proceedings of the Workshop in Recent Advances in Scandinavian Machine Translation*, Uppsala, Sweden,

Paul, Michael. 2001. Knowledge Recycling for Related Languages. *Proceedings of MT Summit VIII*. Santiago de Compostela, Spain. pp. 265-269.

An Advanced Speech Corpus for Norwegian

Janne Bondi Johannessen, Kristin Hagen, Joel Priestley and Lars Nygaard
The Text Lab, Univ. of Oslo,
P.O.Box 1102 Blindern, N-0317 Oslo, Norway
{jannebj, kristiha, joelp, larsnyg}@iln.uio.no

Abstract

This paper describes a new Norwegian speech corpus – The NoTa Corpus – that exhibits a variety of useful and advanced features. It contains 900 000 words of transcribed, lemmatised and POS tagged Oslo speech (carefully selected to cover many speech varieties), which is linked directly to audio and video. It has advanced search interfaces both for searches and results presentations. Since corpora of this kind are aimed at linguists and non-technical users, our guideline has been to keep user-interfaces maximally simple at all levels. The paper describes the contents of the corpus, and focuses on some nice features of its search interface. Some problems and solutions w.r.t. transcription are discussed, and the corpus is compared with five other speech corpora.

1 Introduction

In this paper, we will present the NoTa Corpus – a new speech corpus for Norwegian. It has been developed in order to serve non-technical linguists as well as developers in language technology. This means that it will be a valuable language resource for a wide range of users, for research problems in such diverse disciplines as lexicography, phonology, morphology, syntax, semantics, pragmatics, dialectology, socio-linguistics, psycholinguistics, speech synthesis, grammatical tagging and parsing, and artificial intelligence.

For linguist users, the search and results interfaces are developed in order to ensure a simple human-machine dialogue, a non-trivial task given the complex searches that can arise from the wide range of possible combinations of search variables, including multimodal options. Both the contents and interfaces for search and presentation of results have been planned in order to give maximal value for the user linguist at a minimum of effort and training.

For language and speech technologists we have focused on a high technical standard for various aspects of the contents, especially audio quality and standardised text markup.

With our aim at developing a high standard speech corpus, we have used a variety of off-the-shelf programs as well as tools and resources that we have developed ourselves, many of which will be available for the larger research community.

The corpus consists of 900 000 words that are transcribed, lemmatised and POS tagged. The transcriptions are linked to audio and video. A result concordance with video is illustrated below:

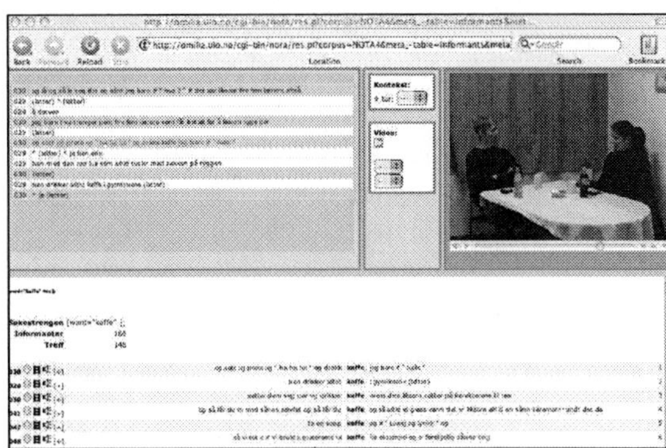

Figure 1. The main results page with video viewing.

Joakim Nivre, Heiki-Jaan Kaalep, Kadri Muischnek and Mare Koit (Eds.)
NODALIDA 2007 Conference Proceedings, pp. 29–36

Section 2 of the paper focuses on the contents of the corpus; annotation, multimedia representation, selection of informants and type of recordings, and transcription. Section 3 describes the search interface with special interest given to criteria regarding linguistic and informant selection. In section 4 we compare the corpus with five other speech corpora along some of the variables that have been highlighted in this paper.

2 Contents of the NoTa Corpus

2.1 Annotation and multimedia representation

The NoTa corpus is transcribed using standard orthography[1]. (The reason for this choice and some discussion about transcription is given in section 2.3.) The corpus is lemmatised and POS tagged by a TreeTagger trained on a manually corrected version of the Oslo-Bergen tagger, which is a written language tagger (for details, see Nøklestad and Søfteland, to appear).

The corpus is represented with video and audio recordings that are linked to the transcriptions[2]. The linking between transcription and audio/video makes it possible for the user to get a direct multimedia representation of any desired fragment of the corpus.

The corpus is searchable via the Internet site using the corpus explorer tool Glossa (Nygaard 2007), a very user-friendly interface built on top of the IMS Corpus Work Bench Query system. The results are shown as concordances linked to the multimedia representations. The Glossa system also allows further processing of the search results by exporting all or a subset of them to external file formats, and by viewing them in a variety of ways, such as frequency counts, collocations, statistical measures, pie charts etc.

All transcriptions of the speech occurring in the corpus are searchable, as are the specially annotated events such as laughter and coughing, plus a variety of interjections and exclamations, extralinguistic noises etc. It is also possible to do searches via grammatical tags. (Some examples will be given in section 3.)

2.2 Informants and recording situation

The corpus consists of the speech of 166 informants from the Oslo area, carefully divided to represent in equal numbers gender, age (three groups; 16–25, 26–50, 51–95), educational background and place of residence. The informants were recruited in a variety of ways, from actively contacting centres for elderly people, schools and work places, to using the press, students and the network of people we knew.

Each informant takes part in a semi-formal ten-minute interview with a project assistant, in which he or she is asked general questions about his or her life. In addition, each informant takes part in an informal 30-minute dialogue with another informant, at which point the informants get served drinks and snacks to add to the informal atmosphere. This way the corpus has two different speech styles from each informant.

Norwegian legislation requires a high level of anonymity and security (to the extent that this is possible when informants appear on audio and video). This has two consequences. First, the topics that are talked about must be "safe": the informants must be instructed not to talk about e.g. politics, religion, illness, criminality, and other people. Second, the informants must not be linked to the data by name or other identification, so the lists of their names and addresses have had to be destroyed.

The second consequence cannot be compensated, but the first consequence turns out not to be a serious problem. The informants get a list of possible topics (such as film, pets, travel, sports) to help them if the conversation goes dead. By comparing the two styles of each informant, it is clear that the limitation on topic is not generally inhibiting.

2.3 Transcription

The NoTa corpus has been transcribed by standard orthography (Norwegian Bokmål), in accord with the practice in other speech corpora, such as the Spoken Dutch Corpus (CGN). The benefits of such a choice over a more phonetic variant are numerous: Transcribers do not need special

---

[1] All speech is transcribed using the freely downloadable program Transcriber.

[2] We have used Quicktime Pro to convert from .wav-format to AAC in .mov-files, to be played by each user in Quicktime, via a central streamer.

training; inter-annotator agreement in transcriptions is more likely to obtain; fewer options will make transcribing quicker; the resulting transcription can readily be used for searching, reading it will be easier, and tagging and parsing will be easier.

However, speech will always contain linguistic as well as non-linguistic information that standard orthography – as it appears in standard dictionaries[3] – has no remedies for, and which corpus developers want to and sometimes need to cater for, so some concessions will have to be made. We shall mention a few of them here, and otherwise refer to Hagen (2005), Johannessen et al. (2005), Bødal et al. (to appear).

A first challenge is to decide what it means to use an orthographic standard. Should it only count at word-level? How about syntax? Consider the example below. In Norwegian, the standard norm says that 3p pl pronouns are inflected for case, so that nominative is used with subjects, and accusative with objects (example 1 below). However, many people violate that norm in various ways, as in (2).

```
(1a)   De           går
       they-NOM     walk
(1b)   Anne ser     dem.
       Anne sees    them-ACC.

(2a)   Dem          går.
       them-ACC     walk
 (2b)  Anne ser de.
       Anne sees    they-NOM.
```

We have chosen to follow the orthographic norms only at word-level, so that it is irrelevant whether a word is used "wrongly"; what is relevant is whether a given spoken word has an orthographic equivalent. Thus, the examples in (2) are acceptable transcriptions in the NoTa corpus. Also, maybe needless to say, "incorrect" word order will never be changed by the transcribers.

A second challenge is words that occur in spoken language only. One difficult type is words that are clearly variants of written ones, but where it is unclear of which particular word. Consider the Norwegian clitic (spoken) pronouns in (3), which are

unmarked for case. Choosing an orthographic form for them would be to either force a particular case onto them, something we have already seen can be very difficult due to inter-speaker variation, or to force a choice of animacy even when the context is ambiguous. Some choices of pronouns are given in (4).

```
(3a)   a       3p sg fem
(3b)   n       3p sg masc

(4a)   hun     3p sg fem nom
       henne   3p sg fem acc

(4b)   han     3p sg masc ani-
                           mate nom
       ham     3p sg masc ani-
                           mate acc
       den     3p sg inanimate
```

We have chosen to add these and other words that do not have a clear equivalent in the standard orthography, to a word-list that we ask the transcribers to use.

A second type of words not found in the standard dictionary are typically dialect words or borrowings. We simply use these as they are, and have chosen to tag them in the following way:

```
(5a)   den fisken ser gøllei
           [language=x] ut
       that fish looks "gøllei"
               (horrible)

(5b)   yes [language=x] det er fint
       "yes" that is good
```

Interjections are a third type of words that are not all found in the dictionary. Like with other non-standard words, we found that we had to add them to our word-list. Distinguishing between interjections and other noises is not necessarily easy, however. Our rule of thumb was to try to fit some constant meaning to the sound sequence. If possible, we treated the candidate as an interjection, and devised a uniform spelling for the word in question. This work was also necessary to distinguish these interjections from similar, but non-identical, ones that already existed in the dictionary. Some of our new interjections together with some old ones (marked with BMO) can be seen in (6):

____

[3] Standard orthography in the NoTa context is defined as that which can be found in Wangensteen (2005): *Bokmålsordboka*.

(6)

```
aha (surprised) BMO
e (hesitating - irrespective
of the vowel quantity)
eh (indicating distance)
ehe ("I see" - two syllables)
em (hesitation)
heh (impressed)
hm (inquiring, wondering) BMO
hæ (inquiring) BMO
jaha (strengthen "yes") BMO
m (hesitation, accepting)
m-m (benektende)
mhm ("I see" - two syllables)
mm (confirming - two syll.)
næ (surprised, wondering)
nja (doubting) BMO
næhei (strengthening "no")
ops (something went wrong)
u (impressed)
ææ (confirming - two syll.)
å-å (something went wrong)
å ja (suprised)
```

In addition to interjections, there are meaningful sounds that many speech corpora annotate, such as laughter. Their meaning is not as conventionalised as that of interjections, and we have chosen to have very coarse-grained categories, (7). They are annotated in the corpus as tags.

(7)

```
Front clicking sound
Back clicking sound
Sucking noise
Sibilant
Yawning
Laughter
Breathing
Special cough[4]
```

All transcriptions have been proof-read by other transcribers than those having done the original transcription, and regular transcription meetings were held between the half a dozen transcribers and the project management during the 18 months project period. The correctness and inter-annotator agreement ought therefore to be high, although we

have no numbers to show it, and must admit as well that we do still find mis-annotations.

Most of the corpus consists of dialogue. We have taken this genre seriously, and gone to great lengths to annotate turn taking, overlaps, interruptions etc. This choice has slowed down the transcription process considerably, but we think has also added to the general value of the corpus.

A picture of a dialogue sequence with informants is shown in figure 11.

3 The Search Interface

3.1 Limiting Search w.r.t. Informants

It is possible, and indeed easy, to limit the search to subgroups of informants. One main choice is between types of recording; free dialogue vs. semi-formal interview:

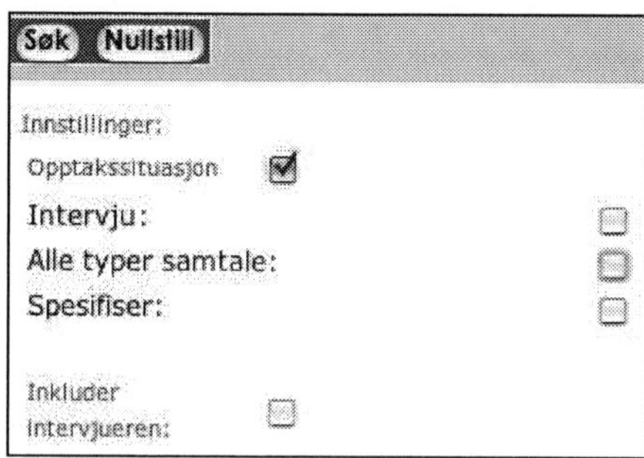

Figure 2. Limiting searches w.r.t. recording type.

Furthermore, it is possible to limit the subgroup of informants according to all the informant variables, such as gender, age, place of residence, place of birth, work, educational background:

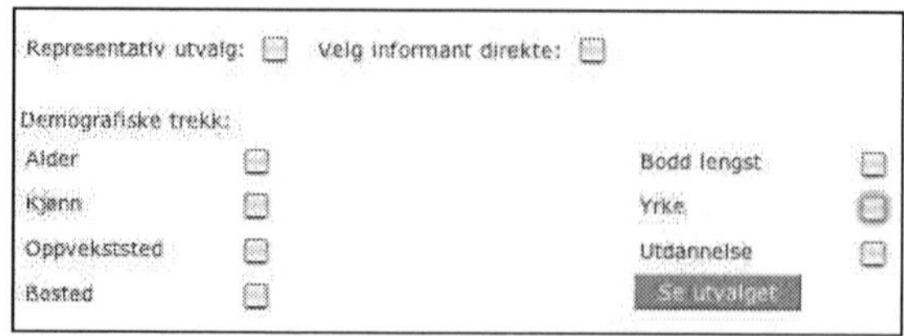

Figure 3. Choosing subgroups of informants.

Ticking off some of the boxes will lead to the popping up of new and more detailed ones. The idea behind the gradually more specific choices is to keep each interface no more complex than the user needs, while at the same time allowing even

---

[4] Ordinary cough resulting from illness is not annotated.

advanced, complex searches to have a user-friendly interface.

In the figure above, the various boxes expands into new menus (e.g. those that refer to place of birth or residence) or to new boxes for numbers (e.g. for age). Figure 4 shows how having ticked off the box for *yrke* ('work') – also found in the figure above – has expanded the choice with several more subcategories, for types such as *håndverk/yrkesfag* ('trade'), *service*, *kontor* ('office'), frie yrker ('free trades'). (The categories have been adopted from the state agency Statistics Norway.)

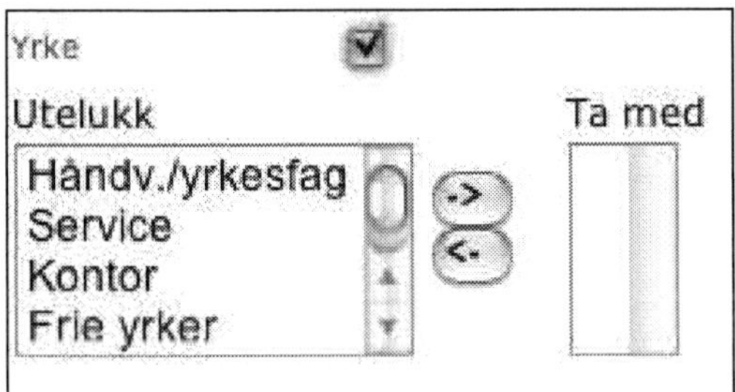

Figure 4. Ticking off a choice such as yrke *('work'), expands the choice into subtypes.*

3.2 Limiting Search w.r.t. Linguistic Criteria

A maximum level of user-friendliness has been attempted at all levels, given that the users will generally be non-technical linguists who are opposed to going through a long period of learning how to use such tools. We support the ideas advanced by Johannessen, Hagen and Nøklestad (2000), in which regular expressions for any kind of simple or complex search are to be avoided for non-technical users. User-interfaces for machine-human dialogue should be based on boxes and menus, not complicated query languages. Below is a search interface of the simplest kind – for just one or two words:

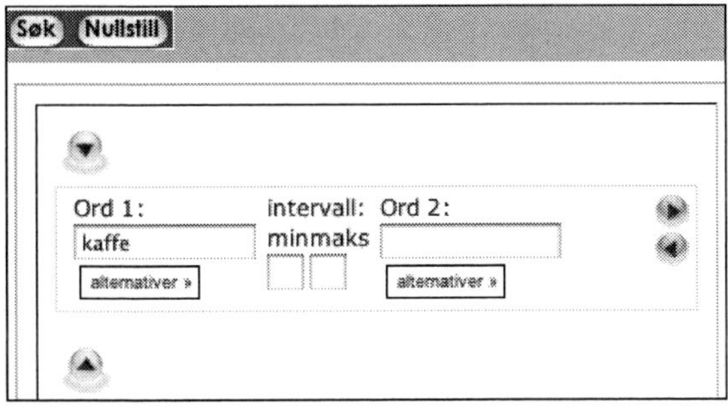

Figure 5. Search interface for linguistic strings.

In order to increase the number of search words, the user clicks on the arrow on the right hand side, and more boxes will appear. In order to search for alternative words, the user clicks on the arrows below, to get more boxes along that dimension.

By pulling down a menu at a word, more options will appear. Since the corpus is part-of-speech (POS) tagged, one option is to choose part of speech (*ordklasse*). It should be noted that POS can also be chosen without an accompanying specification of a word or part of word, giving the user a frequently wanted search option. In this respect it is superior to many other corpora, whether written or spoken language ones. Thus, a user can choose, for example, to get all the nouns in the corpus.

The advantage of this search option is unquestionable. For a linguist who studies the behaviour of a particular part of speech in its context, being able to get a concordance of all instances of that category, gives great opportunities for empirical exploration.

It is of course possible to specify only parts of words, such as the beginning, the middle, or the end. Given that the corpus is lemmatised, it also possible to specify a search for all words belonging to the same paradigm, by choosing 'lemma'. Below is an example of how to choose POS with no specified word or string of letters.

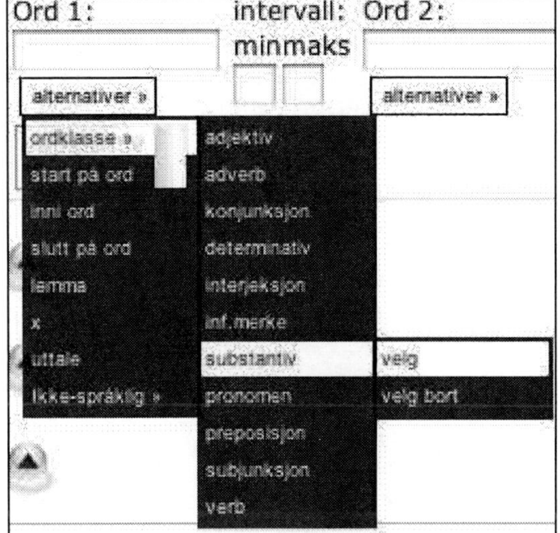

Figure 6. Searching for all nouns in the corpus.

Notice in Figure 6 that we have chosen the *velg* option ('choose'). We could also have chosen the negative *velg bort* ('exclude'), a useful feature to exclude a part of speech from a particular search context. Below are shown a very small subset of the resulting 85233 hits for this search.

nei nei på	**stadion**	
r) * oppå	**tribunen**	?
a jeg sto i	**mål**	da
de en bra	**jobb**	det var
et var litt	**forskjell**	fra # den d
en der m	**rævkampen**	mot Hviter
npen mot	**Hviterussland**	
or mange	**stadion**	tar jeg
ar det på	**stadion**	i hvert fall
e ord) en	**kompis**	av meg so

Figure 7. Results from a search on all nouns.

Below is an example where we have chosen to search for all instances of the irregular verb *være* ('be'), regardless of inflection, followed by a preposition. This time, we have written the infinitive form (the dictionary look-up form) of the verb in the first box, and made sure we have chosen the alternative *lemma* from the menu. The second box is empty, but the alternative POS *preposition* has been chosen from the menu.

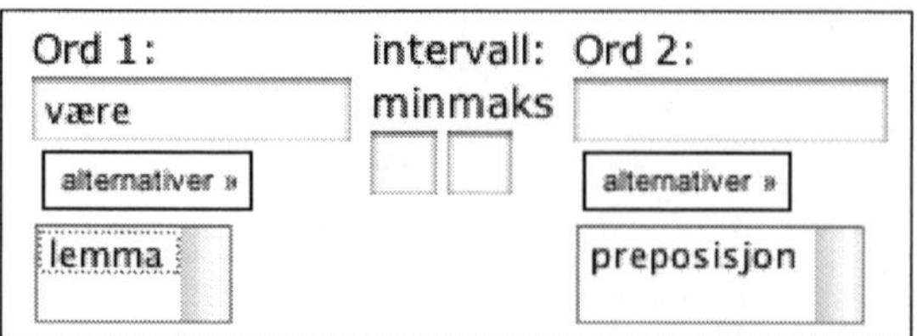

Figure 8. Search for all inflectional forms of the verb være *('be') followed by a preposition.*

The corpus yields 3135 results, some of which are shown below:

har du noen gang	**vært i**	Tromsø (u
jeg har	**vært i**	Tromsø ja
iksom alltid hadde	**vært der oppe**	jeg
r en kamerat som	**er fra**	Tønsberg
uten at Lyn	**var i**	finalen en
ja de # de	**er i**	semien de

Figure 9. Some results from searching for the lemma være *('be') followed by a preposition.*

4 Comparison with Other Speech Corpora

It is instructive to compare the NoTa corpus with other speech corpora. Such corpora are generally expensive to develop, and more so if they are to have a variety of different features. For this reason existing speech corpora do not necessarily have as many advanced features as their developers and users would have liked.

In this section, we will compare the NoTa corpus with three other Scandinavian speech corpora: the Swedish Gøteborg Spoken Language Corpus (GSLC), the Danish BySoc Corpus, and a small dialect corpus of Norwegian (Talesøk). We will also compare it with the British National Corpus (BNC), possibly the most widely known speech corpus available, and the Scottish Corpus of Text and Speech (SCOTS), a new speech corpus with many nice features. See the Reference section for all URLs.

The corpora vary somewhat in size (up to 2 million words, except for the BNC, which is 10 million words), but they have in common that they have been updated after 2000, and that they all aim at a wider audience of non-technical experts.

The table does not reflect reality in every detail: We have ticked off "yes" for multimedia representations in the SCOTS corpus, although the texts in that corpus vary w.r.t. this variable. Also, we have written "no" for tagged transcriptions in Talesøk, since the tagging that exists for that corpus are not available from the main search interface.

	NoTa	**Talesøk**	**GSLC**	**BySoc**	**BNC**	**SCOTS**
Transcription linked to audio	Yes	Yes	No	No	No	Yes
Transcription linked to video	Yes	No	No	No	No	Yes
User-friendly search without regular expressions	Yes	Yes	No	No	No	No
Possible to limit informant selection	Yes	Yes	Yes	Yes	Yes	Yes
Overlaps/ turntaking annotated	Yes	Yes	Yes	Yes	No	Yes
Transcription as standard orthography (or slightly modified)	Yes	Yes	Yes	Yes	Yes	Yes
POS tagged	Yes	No	No	No	Yes	No
POS tags can be used as the only search expressions	Yes	–	–	–	No	–

Figure 10. A comparison between the NoTa corpus and five other speech corpora.

The table shows that the NoTa corpus compares favourably with the other corpora w.r.t. the variables we have chosen. This is of course related to the fact that the NoTa corpus is the newest one, and we have been able to learn from the other corpora. Also, the general technical advances have made it possible to offer features that would have been unthinkable only a few years ago. We have chosen variables that have been important to us as developers. However, we think that these features are important to many other researchers, too.

5   Access

Corpus search via the corpus web site (see Reference section for URL) is available for all researchers. Information about how to get a password is also given there.

The corpus can also be downloaded to see the full transcriptions and view and listen to the full recordings. Furthermore, full-scale versions can be downloaded for other purposes, such as language technology research and development. Contact information is given on the web site.

6   Conclusion and Future Work

We believe that we have developed a speech corpus that will be valuable to linguists as well as technologists, both due to its technical features and its contents. Its main use will, we think, be the corpus with its user-friendly web interface, but the transcriptions, audio files, and tools and resources developed as part of the project will all be useful for other researchers.

There are mainly two paths that we plan to follow in the future. One is to syntactically parse the corpus. So far, some preliminary work has been done w.r.t. pre-processing (see Johannessen and Jørgensen 2006, Jørgensen 2007).

The other path we hope to follow is expanding the corpus. We are expanding it at the moment by adding more speech material of young urbans via cooperation with the project UPUS. We are also planning to add material from other big cities (Bergen, Trondheim, Tromsø), and dialect material from rural areas. The latter task has started in connection with cooperation within the Nordic Centre of Excellence in Microcomparative Syntax, NORMS, and the ScanDiaSyn network.

We also hope to evaluate the corpus.

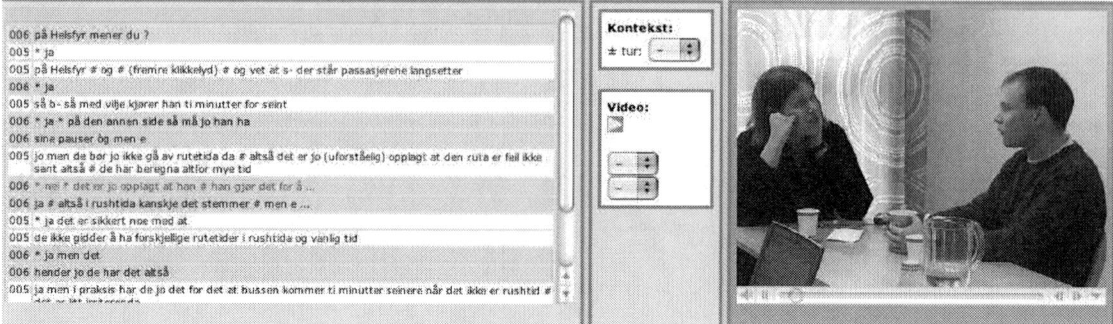

Figure 11. An example of dialogue in a multimedia window.

References

British National Corpus: http://www.natcorp.ox.ac.uk/

BySoc Corpus: Danish Vernacular – Dansk Talesprog. http://www.id.cbs.dk/~pjuel/cgi-bin/BySoc_ID/index.cgi?EeNnGg

Bødal, Anne Marit, Hilde Cathrine Haug, Ingunn Indrebø Ims and Signe Laake. To appear. Dilemma ved ortografisk transkripsjon. In Johannessen and Hagen (eds.).

Gøteborg Spoken Language Corpus: http://www.ling.gu.se/projekt/tal/index.cgi?PAGE=3

Hagen, Kristin. 2005. Transkripsjonsveiledning for NoTa-Oslo. Ms. The Text Laboratory, Univ. of Oslo. http://www.tekstlab.uio.no/nota/oslo/index.html

IMS Corpus Work Bench: http://www.ims.uni-stuttgart.de/projekte/CorpusWorkbench/OldDocus/FAQ.html

.Johannessen Janne Bondi, and Kristin Hagen (eds.). To appear: *Språk i Oslo*, Novus forlag, Oslo.

Johannessen, Janne Bondi, Lars Nygaard, Kristin Hagen, Hanne Gram Simonsen. 2005. Transkripsjon i et talespråkskorpus Paper presented at MONS 11, Bergen.

Johannessen, Janne Bondi, Kristin Hagen and Anders Nøklestad. 2000. A Web-Based Advanced and User Friendly System: The Oslo Corpus of Tagged Norwegian Texts. In Gavrilidou, M., G. et al. (eds.) *Proceedings, Second International Conference on Language Resources and Evaluation (LREC 2000)*, Athens, 1725-1729.

Johannessen, Janne Bondi and Fredrik Jørgensen. 2006. Annotating and Parsing Spoken Language. In Henrichsen, Peter Juel and Peter Rossen Skadhauge (eds.): *Treebanking for Discourse and Speech*. p. 83-103. Samfundslitteratur, København.

Jørgensen, Fredrik. To appear. Ytringer, setninger, fragmenter og feiltyper. In Johannessen and Hagen (eds.).

Nordic Centre of Excellence in Microcomparative Syntax, NORMS. http://norms.uit.no/

NoTa Norwegian Speech Corpus. The Text Laboratory, ILN, University of Oslo. http://www.tekstlab.uio.no/nota/oslo/index.html

Nygaard, Lars. 2007. *Glossa – The Corpus Explorer, Version.0.9.*http://www.hf.uio.no/tekstlab/glossa.html

Nøklestad, Anders and Åshild Søfteland, UiO. To appear. Manuell morfologisk tagging av NoTa-materialet med støtte fra en statistisk tagger. In Johannessen and Hagen (eds.).

Oslo-Bergen Tagger. http://omilia.uio.no/obt/

Scandinavian Dialect Syntax, ScanDiaSyn. http://uit.no/scandiasyn

Scottish Corpus of Text and Speech. http://www.scottishcorpus.ac.uk/

Spoken Dutch Corpus (CGN). http://lands.let.kun.nl/cgn/ehome.htm

Talesøk. http://helmer.aksis.uib.no/talekorpus/Hovedside.htm

Trascriber: http://trans.sourceforge.net/en/presentation.php

UPUS. http://www.hf.ntnu.no/hf/adm/forskning/prosjekter/UPUS

Wangensteen, Boye. 2005. Edited: *Bokmålsordboka: definisjons- og rettskrivningsordbok*. Kunnskapsforlaget, Oslo.

Time Extraction from Real-time Generated Football Reports

Markus Borg
Department of Computer Science
Lund University, LTH
d02mbr@student.lth.se

Abstract

This paper describes a system to extract events and time information from football match reports generated through minute-by-minute reporting. We describe a method that uses regular expressions to find the events and divides them into different types to determine in which order they occurred. In addition, our system detects time expressions and we present a way to structure the collected data using XML.

1 Introduction

Real-time football reports are an increasingly popular way to describe what happens during a football game. A reporter working on covering the match continually writes usually one or two sentences at a time. Whenever an interesting event happens (a goal scoring opportunity, an injury, a booking etc.), a brief description is presented and often the time is given. As the sentences are produced, people interested in what happens can for instance conveniently follow this on the Internet. Examples of such services include *Aftonbladet*[1], a Swedish newspaper and the *UEFA*[2] homepage, an example in English with so called minute-by-minute reporting.

There are also other ways to present the report. People can subscribe to a game and get text messages directly to the mobile phone. The Swedish newspaper *Helsingborgs Dagblad*[3] provides this, but there are numerous other examples. Traditionally many viewers have also followed the latest results through teletext using a normal TV set in a similar way.

The objective of this work is to discover the various events within the texts, analyze them, and order them. When submitted in addition to the text, this information could then be presented to the viewers in the form of chains of events. It would then be possible to use this data on an arbitrary platform according to user preferences. Some users may be interested in viewing a short graphical version of the action on the display of the mobile phone, while others might want to collect statistical data on a PC.

Section 2 discusses related work. In section 3, the corpus used in this project is described. In section 4, we describe how the output data is structured. Section 5 presents how the time expressions and events are found, section 6 shows how the links between those are determined. In section 7, we present the results of our evaluation. Finally, section 8 draws some conclusions and outlines directions for future work.

2 Previous work

There has been much research conducted on the representation of time and events and their temporal relations. Relevant recent papers include Lapata and Lascarides (2004), which like this paper focuses on ordering of events within sentences. They propose a data intensive approach to automatically capture im-

---

[1]The largest daily newspaper in Scandinavia with a sport section offering reporting in real-time. www.aftonbladet.se

[2]The administrative and controlling body for European football with a homepage offering minute-by-minute reporting. www.uefa.com

[3]A local newspaper in Swedish published in Helsingborg. Offers live football coverage via SMS. www.hd.se

Joakim Nivre, Heiki-Jaan Kaalep, Kadri Muischnek and Mare Koit (Eds.)
NODALIDA 2007 Conference Proceedings, pp. 37–43

plicit temporal information, relying on a probabilistic model. Machine learning techniques have been used by different groups to determine temporal relations in natural language texts. Mani et al. (2006) achieved comparably favourable results using decision trees.

There has also been research on extraction of time information in Swedish, Berglund et al. (2006) presents a way to detect time expressions and events from authentic newspaper articles in the traffic accident domain. It is part of the Carsim system (Johansson et al., 2005), which converts textual descriptions of accidents into animated three-dimensional scenes. Another project about information extraction in the domain of football is SOBA (Buitelaar et al., 2006). SOBA automatically extracts information from different sources on web pages, such as tables, texts, and image captions.

Our work presents a way to extract time information from one source of football reports generated through minute-by-minute reporting, which is the main novelty of this paper. The central claims are that regular expressions, although simple, still can be adequate for the task of extracting temporal information from limited closed-domain texts and that dividing events into types is instrumental in guessing in which order they occurred. A preliminary system was implemented to evaluate those claims.

3 Corpus description

The texts we worked with come from an online football management game called *Hattrick*[4]. It is currently the biggest game of its kind with close to one million active players in January 2007. Every player takes on the role as manager for a team and plays one or two games each week, which results in a huge amount of available reports in the database. At this time, the reports are available in 40 languages.

We have chosen these texts because of the availability and the fact that the variety of expressions fits very well to test the system. The texts are not too simple however, since sentences are generated as results from 170 various events. Each event has on average five different wordings, resulting in a vocabulary suitable for this project (Henriksson, 2007).

---

[4]An online, browser-based, football management game developed and based in Sweden. Has been running since August 30, 1997. www.hattrick.org

Table 1: Example of a match report

Efter 18 minuters spel bröt jublet lös då Nicolas Jullien kom igenom gästernas mittförsvar och dundrade in 1 - 0 för Rydebäcks. Daniel Fridquist i Rydebäcks tilldelades efter 20 minuter gult kort för osportsligt uppträdande. I den 22:e matchminuten fick gästernas mittförsvar se sig rundat av Mikael Martinsson som slog in 2 - 0 för Rydebäcks. I den 26:e minuten fick Östen Sörensson i Nynäshamns gult kort när han gick med dobbarna före in i en duell. Rydebäcks tvingades samtidigt till ett byte eftersom John Hörnsten inte kunde fortsätta efter den omilda behandlingen. Alex Lunenburg fick kliva in i hans position. 2 - 0 var ställningen i halvtid. Halvleken dominerades av Rydebäcks som övertygade med ett 55-procentigt bollinnehav.

English version of the same report:

In the 18th minute cheers broke out as Nicolas Jullien found his way through the guests' central defence, clipping the 1 - 0 goal in for Rydebäcks. Daniel Fridquist of Rydebäcks received a yellow card in the 20th minute for unsportsmanlike behaviour. In the 22nd minute of the match, the visitors' central line of defence had to look on as Mikael Martinsson dashed through, knocking home 2 - 0 for Rydebäcks. In the 26th minute, Nynäshamns's sten Sörensson received a yellow card for going into a challenge studs first. Rydebäcks were forced to a substitution as John Hörnsten couldn't continue playing due to the rough treatment, forcing Alex Lunenburg to come in from the sidelines. 2 - 0 was the halftime score. The forty-five minutes were dominated by Rydebäcks, with an impressive 55 percent possession of the ball.

Hattrick offers vivid texts. However, the limited variation in style made the hand crafting of football-related regular expressions tractable. An extract of a match report is shown in Table 1.

4 Annotation scheme

To get a useful information exchange, it is important to structure the data in a good way. For this task we have used a subset of TimeML (Pustejovsky et al., 2003) with some modifications. It is a robust specification language for events and temporal expressions in natural language. The full complexity of TimeML was not suitable at this stage of our project, therefore we have decided to work with the most useful parts and add a football-related attribute. Our system annotates absolute time expressions, events and time links to represent the necessary information.

The absolute time expressions are represented by `TIMEX3` elements. Each element contains two attributes: `tid` (unique ID number) and `type` (so far always `TIME`). As in this example:

```
<TIMEX3 tid="t3" type="TIME">
den 19:e matchminuten</TIMEX3>
```

The various events are annotated as `EVENT` elements. Each element has three attributes: `eid` (unique ID number), `class` (`OCCURRENCE` or `STATE`), and type (`IDLEBALL`, `PREFINISH`, `FINISH`, `SAVE`, or `OTHER`). The elements of class `STATE` have type `OTHER`. The elements of class `OCCURRENCE` have one of the other types, describing the event that took place on the field. As in this example:

```
<EVENT eid="e4" class="OCCURRENCE"
type="FINISH">skalla in</EVENT>
```

The links between time expressions and events are represented by `TLINK` elements (time links). Links between a time expression and an event have the attributes: `time` (`tid` of the `TIMEX3`), `event` (`eid` of the `EVENT`), and `type` (which is set to `DURING` in all cases, all events during the same minute of the game get this). Links between two events have the attributes: `sevent` (`eid` of source event), `tevent` (`tid` of target event), and `type` (so far always `BEFORE`). This means that the source event happens before the target event. Example:

```
<TLINK sevent="e5" tevent="e6"
type="BEFORE"/>
```

The root node is `<TimeML>` and the first child is `<Text>`. This element has one `<s>` child for each sentence in the report. Every `<s>` element contains text nodes and possibly `<TIMEX3>` and `<EVENT>` elements. The `<TLINK>` elements, if present, follow after the `<Text>` element. Table 2 shows an example of a short match report annotated with our scheme.

5 Detection of absolute time expressions and events

The test application has been implemented in Java and heavily uses the built-in package for regular ex-

Table 2: Example of XML output

```
<?xml version="1.0"?>
<TimeML>
 <Text>
  <s>Efter<TIMEX3 tid="t1" type="TIME">7
  minuters spel</TIMEX3> blev publiken som
  galen efter att Mats Aronsson <EVENT
  eid="e1" class="OCCURRENCE"
  type="PREFINISH"> kom igenom bortalagets
  backlinje</EVENT> och <EVENT eid="e2"
  class="OCCURRENCE" type="FINISH">dundrade
  in</EVENT> 1 - 0 for Fortuna. </s>
  <s>Daniel Malmsten i Fortuna tilldelades
  <TIMEX3 tid="t1" type="TIME">efter 12
  minuter</TIMEX3> gult kort efter farligt
  spel. </s>
  <s>I <TIMEX3 tid="t2" type="TIME">den 25
  :e matchminuten</TIMEX3> fick bortalagets
  mitt<EVENT eid="e4" class="OCCURRENCE"
  type="PREFINISH">forsvar se sig rundat
  </EVENT> av Jonas Storm som <EVENT
  eid="e3" class="OCCURRENCE" type="FINISH">
  slog in </EVENT> 2 - 0 for Fortuna. </s>
  <s>I <TIMEX3 tid="t3" type="TIME">den 29:e
  minuten</TIMEX3> fick John Evans i Klippan
  gult kort efter en vansinnig tackling.
  </s>
  <s>Fortuna tvingades samtidigt till ett
  byte eftersom Stefan Blomdahl inte kunde
  spela vidare efter den omilda
  behandlingen. </s>
  <s>Dieter Fieback fick kliva in i hans
  position. </s>
  <s><EVENT eid="e5" class="STATE"
  type="OTHER"> Det stod 2 - 0 i pausvilan
  </EVENT>. </s>
  <s>Halvleken dominerades av Fortuna
  som overtygade med ett
  55-procentigt bollinnehav. </s>
 </Text>

 <TLINK time="t1" event="e1" type="DURING"/>
 <TLINK time="t1" event="e2" type="DURING"/>
 <TLINK time="t2" event="e4" type="DURING"/>
 <TLINK time="t2" event="e3" type="DURING"/>
 <TLINK sevent="e1" tevent="e2"
 type="BEFORE"/>
 <TLINK sevent="e4" tevent="e3"
 type="BEFORE"/>

</TimeML>
```

pressions. In total, the regular expressions take less than 50 lines of code and there are probably many possible optimizations left to be done. The usage of regular expressions makes the program very fast, the analysis of the text can be made without noticeable delay.

5.1 Finding time expressions

The program finds absolute time expressions, for instance *"in the 16th minute"* in order to put those on a timeline. This linear dimensional conception of time is not necessarily the best choice for representing the time events (Moens and Steedman, 1987), but for the 90 minutes of a football game, we considered it suitable. Relative time expressions, for example *"5 minutes later"* are not considered at all. In our corpus, we observe only a limited number of ways to express absolute time. Two lines of code were required to get a very good recall. An example of a regular expression include:

```
(I|i) (den)? [0-9]+:e
(match|spel)?minuten
```

5.2 Finding events

Events on the football field are described in numerous ways to make the text interesting to the reader. Every reporter has one personal style of writing and since the texts in Hattrick have developed during many years and different people have been involved, the finding of the events proved to be more of a challenge. The diversity of the football language used demanded about 45 lines of regular expressions. By grouping those according to the different types described in section 4, the event is given its type at the same time as it is detected in the text. Three examples of regular expressions are shown below.

```
(reducera|kvittera) till
[0-9]+ - [0-9]+
(komma|tagit sig) igenom
drygade [\\w]+ ut (sin ledning|
ledningen till [0-9]+ - [0-9]+)
```

6 Time links

The detection of time links between events or between events and time expressions is of course critical to this application. If not an unquestionable majority of the time links are correct, the resulting out-put file cannot be considered useful. Links between time expressions and events are always inserted in the same way, but we have tried two different approaches between events.

6.1 Connecting time expressions and events

Since all absolute time expressions in the football reports we have observed have expressed a certain minute of the game and since the reports are generated in real-time, the following strategy is used. If the sentence contains a time expression, all events within the same sentence are considered to occur during this time. We have not encountered any examples contradicting this so far. Therefore, one TLINK of the type DURING is added for every event in the sentence. Cases of multiple absolute time expressions within the same sentence have not been encountered and are not treated in special ways.

6.2 Ordering events

The fact that the text is generated in real-time, means that the later the sentence was written, the later the contained events happened. Consequently, the task is to find the chain of events within the actual sentence being processed. The chronological order of a football report written after the final whistle is much harder to determine since this property seldom is the case.

In this project, it was assumed that the events involved with goal scoring opportunities always could be ordered in a linear fashion. If it is said that a striker scores a goal and the team got the equalizer, then the goal is considered to happen before the result changes. Other approaches could be used according to taste, but here those events are not thought as simultaneous and the time links are inserted accordingly. The first event is given a time link to the next one and so on until the last event has been reached.

The basic assumption used to implement the ordering was that the different events within a sentence appear in the text in the same order as they happened during the game. This very simple approach is used as the baseline in the evaluation in section 7.

The second strategy implemented, instead utilizes the divison into the six different types, described in section 5.2. The types are described in Table 1.

Table 3: Types of events

#	Type	Example
0	RESULT-CHANGE	Team taking the lead, scored another goal etc.
1	SAVE	Keeper saves, defender blocks etc.
2	FINISH	Shots, touches etc. towards the goal
3	PREFINISH	Passes, crosses, rushes etc.
4	IDLEBALL	Set pieces, keeper throwing the ball etc.
5	OTHER	All events of the class "STATE"

The types are then considered to always follow a certain order regarding each other. The types given high numbers happen before the lower ones. If multiple events of the same type are present, they get time links in the same order as they appear in the text.

7 Evaluation

This section contains the results of an evaluation of the system, aimed at testing the recall and precision of the regular expressions used. The two different strategies of inserting time links were also tested. Since the size of the experiment is small, the results can only be taken as indicative.

7.1 Experimental setup

To make our application able to handle enough football-related expressions, we used 25 different texts in the training set, from which we crafted the regular expressions. The following composition of reports was used: eight reports from league games in higher divisions, seven reports from leagues in the middle, five reports from lower divisions and five reports from matches between national teams. This should ensure that reports from teams of various levels are covered by the system.

Our test set contained three reports from different teams. We selected reports from matches with 4 goals, to be certain that enough goal scoring opportunities were described in the text. Then we annotated the texts by hand in what we consider to be the

correct way, by finding all expressions and detecting the correct order of events. In the end, we compared our results with the output from the system.

7.2 Results

We started by looking at the absolute time expressions. This proved to be an easy task and the system found all of them. We suspected this early while working with the training set. Absolute time appears to be expressed in limited ways in football reports.

As the next step, we measured how many of the events were found. The reports in total contained 53 and our system reached a recall of 79.4% with a precision of 87.5%. The recall level could be increased simply by adding more texts to the training set. The precision found however, was lower than expected and further analysis showed that some mistakes were repeatedly made. Some key words the system is looking for are used in various situations. A good example of this is the word hörna 'corner', which in Swedish is used both for the actual corner kick and when defenders or keepers save the ball by redirecting it and it passes the short line, resulting in a corner kick for the attacking team. Without a word sense disambiguation step, getting a perfect precision would be impossible. One way could be to first test if it appears after an event of the type `FINISH` or not.

Apparently, without considering parts of speech or other language characteristics, it was possible to quickly get an acceptable recall with a system entirely based on regular expressions.

The final part of the evaluation was about testing if our ideas of dividing events into certain types gave a better ordering. The three reports contained 18 sentences with multiple events, in total 47 events, suggesting that they seldom are alone in a sentence in a football report. They were divided the following way: 12 sentences had two events, one sentence had three events and five sentences had four events. Five of the events were wrongly detected, since the system treated some of the single events as two.

If the additionally found events were disregarded altogether, the baseline produced correct time links for 12 of the 18 sentences (66.7%). The strategy with the types gives a correct output between all the remaining events.

The additional events do not necessarily have to

be disregarded however, since they can be assumed to happen after the core event they were derived from. With this assumption, the result is as follows: the baseline still produced the correct result for 12 sentences (66.7%). The more complex strategy produced correct time links for 15 sentences (83.3%).

The result of the baseline shows that the events in a football report cannot be considered to happen in the same way as they appear within a sentence. We can also conclude that dividing events into those different types and assuming that passes happen before shots etc., gives a better result. The failed time links are produced in this evaluation because of failed event detection. Since some additional set pieces were introduced, they were treated as the starts of the event chains. Examples of this were shots from the penalty area (treated like penalty kicks) and the issue of corners as previously described. Still, the more complex strategy gave a significant increase in producing correct time links.

8   Conclusions

This paper described a way to extract time information from football reports, generated in real-time by the game engine in Hattrick. The evaluation of the system showed that if a sentence contains events, there are usually more than one. Those events cannot be expected to have happened in the same order as they appeared within a sentence written in Swedish. Although the limited set of data prevents any definitive conclusions, the work indicates that regular expressions together with type divided events can produce output well describing events on a football field. The methods should be possible to apply also on other domains with a somewhat limited vocabulary.

There are some limitations of the project. Firstly, we only consider events that have to do with goal scoring opportunities. Secondly, since the nature of real-time generated reports means that the events in the current sentence happen after the previously reported events in prior sentences, we only construct partial orderings. In this case, it means we only look at chains of events within sentences. Thirdly, no information about participants is extracted.

Further extensions could be to include also other types of events like injuries and substitutions, but we think that scoring events are more interesting to focus on at this stage. We also think it would make sense to add information about whether something actually happened or not, since this version of the system does not differentiate between "had a chance to shoot but did not" and "came through and shot". Both shots would now be treated as the same `FINISH` type.

The next step to make the system more robust could be to include a part of speech tagger. Handcrafting regular expressions is obviously possible for limited domains, but since natural language is neither regular nor context-free, the method is not scalable for future more complex texts. However, the system is probably already good enough to be tested for simple visualization purposes of Hattrick reports.

Acknowledgements

We would like to thank Richard Johansson and Pierre Nugues who supervised us during this project and Christian Henriksson, Language Administrator at Hattrick, for explaining internals of the report system and providing us with figures.

References

Anders Berglund, Richard Johansson, and Pierre Nugues. 2006. A machine learning approach to extract temporal information from texts in Swedish and generate animated 3D scenes. In *Proceedings of EACL-2006*, Trento, Italy, April 15-16.

Paul Buitelaar, Phipipp Cimiano, Stefania Racioppa, and Melanie Siegel. 2006. Ontology-based information extraction with SOBA. In *Proceedings of the International Conference on Language Resources and Evaluation (LREC)*, pages 2321–2324. ELRA, May.

Christian Henriksson. 2007. Personal correspondence by email. Language Administrator, Hattrick Limited (division of ExtraLives AB), Jan.

Richard Johansson, Anders Berglund, Magnus Danielsson, and Pierre Nugues. 2005. Automatic text-to-scene conversion in the traffic accident domain. In *Proceedings of the Nineteenth International Joint Conference on Artificial Intelligence*, pages 1073–1078. Edinburgh, Scotland.

Mirella Lapata and Alex Lascarides. 2004. Inferring sentence-internal temporal relations. In *Proceedings of the Human Language Technology Conference of the North American Chapter of the Association for Computational Linguistics*.

Inderjeet Mani, Marc Verhagen, Ben Wellner, Chong Min Lee, and James Pustejovsky. 2006. Machine learning of temporal relations. In *ACL '06: Proceedings of the 21st International Conference on Computational Linguistics and the 44th annual meeting of the ACL*, pages 753–760, Morristown, NJ, USA. Association for Computational Linguistics.

Marc Moens and Mark Steedman. 1987. Temporal ontology in natural language. In *Proceedings of the 25th annual meeting on Association for Linguistics*, pages 1–7. Stanford, California, July.

James Pustejovsky, JosCasta, Robert Ingria, Roser Saurand Robert Gaizauskas, Andrea Setzer, and Graham Katz. 2003. Timeml: Robust specification of event and temporal expressions in text. In *Fifth International Workshop on Computational Semantics*, pages 1073–1078.

Spoken Document Retrieval in a Highly Inflectional Language

Inger Ekman and Kalervo Järvelin
Department of Information Studies, University of Tampere
33014 University of Tampere
`inger.ekman@uta.fi,`

`kalervo.jarvelin@uta.fi`

Abstract

Being able to search for relevant information within a collection of documents is vital for the effective use of any kind of storage media. The main body of Spoken Document Retrieval research has concentrated on the English language, leaving other languages – and information produced in them – without the benefit of existing SDR systems. Especially the performance of vocabulary based speech recognition suffers from inflection. This also affects the usability of retrieval systems based on vocabulary-based recognition techniques. We discuss a method for rapid phoneme filtering to facilitate fast searches for words unknown by large vocabulary speech recognizers. The method is evaluated against a speech database in Finnish, which is a highly inflected language.

1   Introduction

With increasing storage capacity, providing audio information has become a common feature in many media systems. There are many sources of purely spoken documents, radio programs and voice messaging to name a few. Both education and research would benefit from effective storage and retrieval of audio material, such as lectures and interviews. Voice is also used to convey information in multimedia files.

Whereas some media file types (like pictures) are indifferent to language, speech is not. The main body of Spoken Document Retrieval (SDR) research has mainly focused on retrieval of English speech. Since English is a language with very limited inflection, current SDR has not adequately dealt with the implications inflection has on neither speech recognition nor its effects on the retrieval task.

Compared to English, Finnish is an exceptionally highly inflected language (Karlsson 1983). This does not, however, limit the value of this kind of research only to Finnish. In fact, looking at the languages spoken in Europe, English is one of the least inflectional languages (Lamel 2002). Current SDR methods developed for English do not take into account various difficulties in speech recognition and indexing that arise from inflection.

In this paper, we will examine the following questions: 1) How does inflection affect speech recognition and SDR? 2) What solutions are there to deal with inflection in SDR? 3) How to filter/retrieve spoken documents in a highly inflected language? And 4) what is the effectiveness of Spoken Document Filtering on a Finnish test database? How does it compare to text-based retrieval under the same conditions?

2   SDR methods

There are two main approaches to the SDR task: First one can transcribe the spoken material into words by means of a large vocabulary continuous speech recognizer (LVCSR). After recognizing the speech, text retrieval methods can be used to search through the produced transcripts. To enhance results, various methods of error-correction have been developed, e.g., using multiple recognizers (Jones et al. 1996; Ng 2000; Sanderson & Crestani 1998) or alternative recognitions of single words or phrases, also called n-best lists (Siegler 1999). Additionally, document expansion using a

Joakim Nivre, Heiki-Jaan Kaalep, Kadri Muischnek and Mare Koit (Eds.)
NODALIDA 2007 Conference Proceedings, pp. 44–50

text corpus has been used with some success to mitigate the effect of errors produced by the LVCSR (Singhal et al. 1998).

Because of the limited vocabulary of the recognizer, there will always be Out Of Vocabulary (OOV) words, which appear in the documents but not in their transcripts. This is especially problematic when the lost words are particularly descriptive, such as technical terms and names of people or places (Garofolo et al. 1998). Additionally OOV words tend to cause more than one error (Lamel 2002). Erroneous recognition of vocabulary words can also lead to terms disappearing from the documents.

Alternatively to recognizing words, documents can also be recognized at sub-word level as phones or phonemes. The recognition units can be single sounds (see Ng & Zue (1997) for results for various recognition categories) or sequences of several recognition units, but recognition is not restricted by a vocabulary of possible words. In these systems, retrieval is usually done by "translating" search words or phrases into their phonetic form and searching for appearances of similar-sounding slots.

The problem of OOV words does not occur with phone recognition. Phone recognition is also a magnitude faster than LVCSR. However, recognizing phones is more error prone than word-based recognition, because no higher-level information can be used to narrow down the number of possible interpretations. Another problem with phone-based recognition is the loss of word boundary information. Because of this, retrieval systems cannot use traditional indexing. The loss of word boundary information also further challenges the matching task. Phone retrieval methods therefore have to be able to deal with errors as well as managing the indexing task.

There are two major approaches to phone-recognized SDR, n-grams and word spotting. With n-grams, transcripts are split into n-length partially overlapping sequences, which are used in a similar fashion to words in the ordinary indexing approach (Wechsler & Schäuble 1995; Ng & Zue 1997, Ng & Zobel 1998). Since n-grams in effect examine words in separate small pieces it alleviates some of the problems of erroneous recognition as well as variations in inflection (to the extent that inflection occurs as suffixes). This error tolerant quality has also been used to deal with word variations e.g.

when searching for historical word forms (Robertson & Willett 1992). Other solutions for phone based SDR have focused on trying to develop faster scanning techniques for the search phase instead of new indexing techniques (Brown et al 1996; Ferrieux & Peillon 1999; James 1995).

3 The Effects of Inflection on SDR

The target language can affect the suitability of SDR methods. The effects are mainly due to the morphology of a language. Morphology deals with the structure of morphemes - roots, prefixes and suffixes - and rules for their combination. Inflection occurs when inflectional affixes are added to a word stem. The stem can remain unchanged, or change depending on the affix. The rate of inflection of a language can be considered a continuous scale: At one end we find languages such as Vietnamese that have no inflection. At the other extreme are languages like Inuit that combine multiple morphemes into whole sentences, confusing the distinction between word and sentence. (Pirkola 2001.)

Morphology affects SDR by making both recognition and retrieval harder. Since morphology is concerned with the structural variation of words, it affects only vocabulary-based, not phone/phoneme-based SDR. Morphology affects recognition in two ways. First is the issue of building a recognition vocabulary. Due to inflection, the necessary vocabulary size is much greater the more inflected a language is. For example, due to inflection Finnish has a cautious estimate of 2000 different possible noun and 12000 verb forms. (Karlsson 1883.) The presence of inflected words in documents requires being able to match them with query words in different form. This feature directly affects the retrieval phase and has already called for new indexing methods for text retrieval (Alkula 2001). All forms are naturally not as frequent. In text retrieval inflection can be dealt with rather well by converting search terms to only a handful of all the possible variations (Kettunen & Airio 2006). Nevertheless, achieving necessary vocabulary coverage for LVCSR in inflected languages would demand including at least some of the most common inflected forms for each word in the dictionary. With larger vocabularies, performance usually suffers and recognition becomes slower.

Another problem imposed by inflection is that most recognizers use Language Models (LM) based on word order to help decide which words of the vocabulary are likely to occur in the speech stream. Since the function of an inflected word is indicated by its ending, word order is liberated. This aspect has been shown to affect the usability of traditional LMs for Russian that similar to Finnish has very free word order (Whittaker & Woodland 2003). Another problem with language models is that the statistical model of word order assumes a certain genre of speech. Whereas phone recognition is mostly concerned with recording quality and speaker, LM:s restrict a certain recognition system to certain styles of spoken communication: models suitable for the recognition of formal news speech are not as such usable for telephone conversations or informal interviews.

Many of the problems posed by inflection can be solved by using smaller recognition units such as morphemes (Kurimo et al. 2005). However, even morpheme recognizers are restricted to using a vocabulary of sorts, albeit more flexible in this aspect than LVCSR.

4 Using Phone Filtering in SDR for Inflected Languages

As argued in the previous chapter, the word-based approach is strongly affected by inflection and thus not as such appropriate for dealing with inflected SDR. Phone-based recognition, on the other hand, does not suffer from inflection. Moreover, the problem with inflection in the retrieval phase is often solved by the approximate-matching nature of the retrieval algorithms. Phone-based systems thus seem to provide several benefits over the LVCSR approach with inflected languages.

Further, word-based retrieval limits the possible search words to those of the recognition vocabulary. The only way to guarantee unlimited vocabulary searches seems to be to recognize speech on the sub-word level. Thus there will be a need for methods capable of dealing with phone recognized speech even in systems designed for less inflected languages.

However, while phone based recognition of speech is faster than LVCSR, retrieval by phones usually is slow compared to the speed of traditional indexing. Although there are accurate algorithms for word spotting, these are quite time-

consuming. Filtering provides a faster way of processing phone-recognized transcripts, although perhaps not as accurate as more time-consuming methods.

In our view, filtering can benefit the system in three ways: First, the filtering process provides a rapid means of pre-processing and prioritizing documents for consecutive retrieval stages. Second, we hope to use filtering to provide the user with initial results. Listening to even a few speech documents will involve the user for some time. Meanwhile the system can use accurate but time-consuming matching algorithms to produce better results. Third, through immediate feedback, the system will be giving the user information based upon which they can rethink and evaluate their requests. Automatic relevance feedback based on the first few retrieved documents can be used to improve search performance.

4.1 Filtering with N-gram Signatures

The prototype retrieval system uses n-grams together with document signatures to make scanning the whole speech database as fast as possible. The underlying idea is to represent every document in the database by a standard-length bit-vector. After breaking down the phone-recognized speech document to n-grams (this is simply achieved by splitting document into partially overlapping n length subsequences), the content of the document is encoded in the vector. 1-bits are used to indicate that a certain n-gram exists in the document, whereas zero indicates non-existence. In the filtering phase, each request is put through the same procedure and compared to all the documents in the database with only a few bitwise operations per document signature. This method (also know as q-gram filtering) is a very fast way to scan for a certain sequence of characters compared to most known approximate string-matching algorithms (Navarro 2001).

4.2 The Finnish SDR Test Collection

To evaluate our filtering system, we used a test collection containing 288 news stories on different topics. The test collection is a subset of documents from a larger text database containing 55000 news documents and 35 test topics with relevance assessments. The documents are domestic, foreign and economic news, dating between 1988-1992

(Sormunen 2000). The 288 documents for the SDR collection were selected from among the relevant documents of 17 test topics (topics 2–18). Therefore we were able to use both the textual test topic and the relevance assessments. The documents were originally written newspaper articles, and were manipulated to resemble spoken news stories (elimination or rephrasing of numerical expressions, etc.). The stories were spoken by one single person and recorded in a studio environment. The resulting test database contains a total of 4h 47 min of speech, with individual stories about one minute each. Speech recognition used a phone recognizer developed at Tampere University of Technology. The recognizer produced a mixed transcript of phones and phone sequences with an average phone error of 42.0%.

Table 1 The Finnish test collection.

Nr of documents	288		
Total length	4h 47min		
Average length of speech documents	59.8s/ 93 words		
Average length of phone transcripts	712 phones		
Average phone error rate	42.0%		
Number of test topics	17		
Number of relevant documents/topic	Avg.	Min	Max
	16.9	4	39
Topic length (words)	Avg.	Min	Max
	13.9	3	27

Test requests were manually formed from the 17 topics, based on the textual requests by selecting informative words from a set of individually spoken words and word combinations (e.g. 'united nations' 'carl bildt'). Included were base forms of words appearing in the textual request, as well as words classified as possible to derive from the request with general information about the subject. The requests had on the average 13,9 words. On average, each topic had a recall base of 17 documents. The test collection is described in Table 1.

4.3 Evaluation of the filtering system

We tested the performance of n-gram filtering and compared different combinations of retrieval parameters. Tests were performed on n = 2, 3, 4 and 5. Additionally, signatures were formed both over whole news stories, as well as partially overlapping smaller story segments, or *windows*, of 10, 20, 50, 100, 200 and 500 phones. The total number of parameter combinations is 4*6=24.

To optimize processing time, all query words are combined before the matching phase by concatenating their transcripts. Each document is evaluated against the query and assigned a score $Sim(a,b) = |A \cap B| / \min \{|A|, |B|\}$, where A and B are the sets of n-grams of the current document and query, respectively. The windows are scored separately. The final document score is defined as the maximum of each document's window scores. Finally, all documents are ranked. For evaluation, the whole result list was inspected.

The filtering results are presented in Table 2. Comparisons to a text baseline are shown below, in Table 3. The text baseline used the parameter combination that gave the best results: 5-gram with 500 phone windowing.

Table 2 Average precision of multi-word topics (N=17). Highest values within each gram size in **bold**.

Window size	2-gram	3-gram	4-gram	5-gram
10	0.099	0.182	0.252	0.247
20	0.116	0.248	0.305	0.302
50	0.131	0.254	0.331	0.329
100	0.136	0.258	0.332	0.351
200	**0.152**	**0.281**	0.362	0.353
500	0.131	0.251	**0.384**	**0.381**
whole	0.109	0.217	0.335	0.362

Table 3 The average SDR effectiveness in relation to the baseline text search. The text baseline used 5-grams with 500 phone windowing.

Window size	2-gram	3-gram	4-gram	5-gram
10	10.9 %	20.1 %	27.8 %	27.3 %
20	12.9 %	27.4 %	33.7 %	33.4 %
50	14.4 %	28.1 %	36.6 %	36.4 %
100	15.1 %	28.5 %	36.7 %	38.8 %
200	16.8 %	31.1 %	40.0 %	39.1 %
500	14.4 %	27.7 %	42.5 %	42.1 %
whole	12.1 %	24.0 %	37.1 %	40.0 %

Table 2 shows filtering performance. At its best, filtering reaches an average precision of 0.384 for 4-grams using 500 phone windows.

Splitting the stories slightly improves performance. The ideal window size depends on *n* size. The effect is emphasized because queries are represented as one signature; multiple query words are unlikely to fit within smaller windows.

Table 3 shows relative precision for speech filtering compared to a text baseline using the same filtering methods. The results show performance as good as 42.5% of that of a text filtering.

4.4 Filtering Performance Across Recall Levels

In addition to knowing the average precisions, we are interested in how precision develops over recall levels. To save space, we will only consider the best approaches within each gram category, namely 2- and 3-grams with segment size 200 and 4- and 5-grams with 500 phone segments.

As can be seen from Figure 1, precision develops similarly for all top parameter combinations. For these approaches, one can see that precision drops in the usual way towards around or slightly above 10% precision at 100% recall.

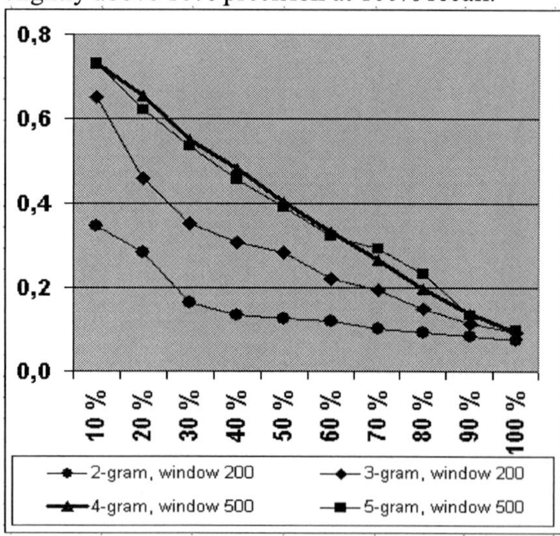

Figure 1 Precision over 10 recall levels. Precision on the y-axis, recall on the x-axis. The best approach (4-gram with window size 500) is shown in strong line.

The development of precision has implications for the use of filtering. In order to make the best of the filtering process' benefits, it is probably worth cutting off the document collection at recall levels lower than 100%. If a user would choose to inspect all the results, they will most likely also be spending more time with the system, which will allow the use of more time-consuming methods for maximal recall. However, for the typical user it is unlikely that poor precision at these levels would affect the user perception of the system, since few users can be assumed to inspect the result list this far.

More notable is the high precision obtained at the lower recall levels. The results are as high as 0.732 with 4-gram and 500 phone windowing. This means that the majority of the documents presented first in the result list are relevant, with roughly only one in four not containing relevant information. This suggests that the filtered document collection could indeed be used as a preliminary search result.

5 Conclusion and future work

The main focus of the international SDR research community has been on English. Since languages vary, it is important that research is carried out in other languages as well. The research presented in this paper aims at clarifying the effects of inflection on speech recognition and SDR and propose means to deal with SDR in highly inflected languages. One such language is Finnish, which we use as a test case to evaluate an n-gram filtering method for rapid SDR.

Morphology affects SDR on two levels: speech recognition and IR. The enormous number of words necessary for decent coverage makes LVCSR hard to implement for highly inflected languages. Less restricted word order, on the other hand, complicates the use of word order based language models. Morphology affects SDR also because request words may be in different forms than document words and thus provide less than expected evidence for retrieval – especially due to often short and sometimes variable inflectional stems.

We have examined the use of n-gram filtering for rapid scanning of a spoken document collection. The results presented in this paper suggest that this approach could be used to preprocess a database and thus shorten the retrieval phase for slower word-spotting algorithms. An average precision as high as 38.4 (42.6% relative to text filtering) was achieved with a very time-efficient parameter combination using 4-grams and a 500-phone window. Also, n-grams seem to be capable of matching words in different inflectional forms.

Comparing our results to earlier results on n-gram length for English (e.g. Ng et al. 2000) this study indicates reasonable performance on Finnish with 4- and 5-grams, whereas results for English have shown better results for smaller 3-grams. This result may be at least in part dependent on the type of phone recognizer used. Our recognizer used phone sequences, which to some extent raises the probability of longer matches in the transcripts. However, the text baseline produced best results with 5-grams. Notably, Finnish words are longer on the average than English, so longer grams may be found beneficial in Finnish phone based SDR.

Longer n-grams naturally mean more of the descriptiveness of words is maintained. On the other hand, optimal n-gram size is affected by the recognition system used, since this dictates what kind of errors can occur. The quality of recognition also has its effects on chosen n size; the performance of long grams depends on how frequently (or consistently) recognition errors occur. Longer n-grams also increase the risk that the individual n-gram becomes over specific with regards to inflection (i.e. matches only with a certain inflectional form), or that the n-gram involves phones from several words at once. However, based on our results, this did not seem to happen. Further investigation is needed to confirm, whether this is indeed the case.

One important step towards the development of SDR methods is the availability of a suitable test database for retrieval experimentation. Unfortunately, realistic databases of several hundreds of hours of speech are as yet unavailable for Finnish. In addition to examining retrieval methods, our project also created a test database consisting of 4,7 hours of speech. This speech database, along with the spoken query words and relevance assessments, are currently being shared with other researchers and research sites, to facilitate further exploration on approaches to Finnish SDR. Promising results have been made using morph-based recognition and retrieval (Kurimo et al. 2005). Further work includes investigating the combination of LVCSR and phone retrieval to find out how approaches are optimally combined to complement each other.

6   References

Alkula, R. 2001. From plain character strings to meaningful words: Producing Better Full Text Databases for Inflectional and Compounding Languages with Morphological Analysis Software. Information Retrieval (4). 195–208.

Brown, M.; Foote, J.; Jones, G. Spärck Jones, K. & Young, S. Open-Vocabulary Speech Indexing for Voice and Video Mail Retrieval. ACM Multimedia 1996. 307–316.

Ferrieux, A. & Peillon, S. Phoneme-level Indexing for Fast and Vocabulary-Independent Voice/Voice Retrieval. Proc. ESCA ETRW Workshop on Accessing Information in Spoken Audio 1999. 60–63.

Garofolo, J.; Voorhees, E.; Auzanne, C. & Stanford, V. Spoken Document Retrieval: 1998 Evaluation and Investigation of New Metrics. ESCA ETRW workshop on Accessing Information in Spoken Audio 1998. 1–7.

James, D. The Application of Classical Information Retrieval Techniques to Spoken Documents. PhD thesis. Cambridge University. 1995.

Jones, G.; Foote, J.; Spärck Jones, K. & Young, S. Retrieving spoken documents by combining multiple index sources. ACM SIGIR 1996. ACM Press. 30–38.

Karlsson, F. Suomen kielen äänne- ja muotorakenne. [Finnish Phonetic and Morphological Structure.] WSOY. 1983.

Kettunen, K. & Airio, E. Is a morphologically complex language really that complex in full-text retrieval? In T. Salakoski et al. (Eds.): Advances in Natural Language Processing, LNAI 4139, pp. 411 - 422, 2006. Springer-Verlag Berlin Heidelberg.

Kurimo, M.; Turunen, V. & Ekman, I. Speech Transcription and Spoken Document Retrieval in Finnish. In Machine Learning for Multimodal Interaction, Revised Selected Papers of the MLMI 2004 workshop. Lecture Notes in Computer Science, Vol. 3361 pp. 253-262, Springer, 2005.

Lamel, L. Some Issues in Speech Recognizer Portability. ISCA SALTMIL SIG Workshop at LREC 2002.

Navarro, G. A guided tour to approximate string matching. ACM Computing Surveys, 33, 1 (2001). ACM Press. 31–88.

Ng, C. & Zobel, J. Speech Retrieval using Phonemes with Error Correction. ACM SIGIR 1998. ACM Press. 365–366.

Ng, C.; Wilkinson, R. & Zobel, J. Experiments in Spoken Document Retrieval using Phoneme N-grams. Speech Communication, 32, 1–2 (2000). 61–77.

Ng, K. & Zue, W. Subword Unit Representations for Spoken Document Retrieval. Eurospeech 1997. 1607–1610.

Ng, K. Information Fusion for Spoken Document Retrieval. International Conference on Acoustics Speech and Signal Processing (ICASSP) 2000.

Pirkola, A. Morphological Typology of Languages for IR. Journal of Documentation, 57, 3 (2001). 330–348.

Robertson A. & Willett, P. Searching for historical word-forms in a database of 17th-century English text using spelling-correction methods. Proc. ACM SIGIR 1992. 256–265.

Sanderson, M. & Crestani, F. Mixing and Merging for Spoken Document Retrieval. European Conference on Research and Advanced Technology for Digital Libraries 1998. 397–407.

Siegler, M. Integration of Continuous Speech Recognition and Information Retrieval for Mutually Optimal Performance. PhD thesis. Carnegie Mellon University. 1999.

Singhal, A.; Choi, J.; Hindle, D.; Lewis, D. & Pereira, F. AT&T at TREC-7. TREC-7 1998. NIST Special Publications 500-242. 239–252.

Sormunen, E. A Method for Measuring Wide Range Performance of Boolean Queries in Full-Text Databases. PhD thesis. University of Tampere. 2000.

Wechsler, M & Schäuble, P. Speech Retrieval Based on Automatic Indexing. Final Workshop on Multimedia Information Retrieval 1995

Whittaker, E. & Woodland, P. Language modeling for Russian and English using words and classes. Computer Speech and Language 17 (2003). 87–104.

Inducing Baseform Models from
a Swedish Vocabulary Pool

Eva Forsbom

Department of Linguistics and Philology

Uppsala University/Graduate School of Language Technology

Box 635, SE-751 26 UPPSALA

`evafo@stp.lingfil.uu.se`

Abstract

In many language technology applications, we need to map wordforms to a citation form or baseform, or the other way around, e.g. for lexicon lookup or for representational purposes.

In this paper, we used a suffix trie mapper with suffix-change probabilities, and computed wordform-baseform and baseform-wordform models from eight subsets of a ranked Swedish vocabulary. All models were evaluated for both directions on a testset, and four of the models were also evaluated for wordform-baseform mapping on five unseen texts.

For wordform-baseform mapping, the best models performed on par with state-of-the-art systems. Most models were useful for some situation—given mapping direction, and time and space restrictions—but no model was best for all situations.

1   Introduction

In many language technology applications, such as machine translation or cross-language information retrieval, words are looked up in a lexicon where only one form of the word—the citation form (usually the baseform)—is present. Even for other applications, such as monolingual information retrieval or lexical cohesion analysis, it can be useful to conflate all forms of a word into one "concept" form.

Thus, there is a need for a wordform-baseform mapper.

Going in the other direction—from baseform to wordform—could also be useful for applications such as natural language generation, or query expansion in information retrieval. A mapper that can handle both directions reasonably well, perhaps with different underlying language models, would be an extra treat: two applications for the price of one.

But what kind of information, and how much, should such models contain? In this paper, we test two assumptions: 1) that irregular wordforms either are among the most top-frequent words in a vocabulary, or so rarely used that they are insignificant for a robust application, and 2) that rules for regular forms can be induced from a limited number of examples.

We describe the induction of various wordform-baseform mapping models (Section 3.3) from subsets of a Swedish vocabulary pool (Section 3.1), in the framework of Wicentowski's Base Model (Section 3.2). The models are evaluated both on a testset (Section 4.1) and on unseen texts (Section 4.2).

2   Background

For languages with little inflectional morphology, such as English, stemming can be adequate for finding most baseforms, but for morphologically richer languages, such as Swedish, more morphologic analysis is usually needed.

Several academic systems for morphologic analysis of Swedish words exist (for an overview, see e.g. Dura (1998)), but they are not always suited for simple wordform-baseform mapping and generally not publicly available. At least two commer-

Joakim Nivre, Heiki-Jaan Kaalep, Kadri Muischnek and Mare Koit (Eds.)
NODALIDA 2007 Conference Proceedings, pp. 51–58

cial systems with publicly available demos exist, SWETWOL (Karlsson, 1992) and Lexware (Dura, 1998), although the demos come with limited access. Both systems are rule-based. SWETWOL is based on two-level morphology, and outputs all possible analyses of a word. It is possible to retrieve a baseform from the analysis, but a disambiguator is needed to choose among the alternative analyses. Lexware is based on inflectional paradigm rules and word-formation rules, and outputs a single analysis (in the demo version). It is generally possible to retrieve the baseform from the analysis.

In Wicentowski's statistically based approach (Wicentowski, 2002), four mapping model types are used, where wordforms are stored in a suffix trie, with varying amount of morphological information in the nodes. In the simplest type, Base Model, the node annotations contain probability estimates for suffix transformations from wordform to baseform, optionally conditioned on a part-of-speech (PoS) tag. Suffix transformations are learnt from a list of ⟨wordform, baseform⟩ tuples (or ⟨wordform, PoS tag, baseform⟩ triples), which could be taken from a dictionary, collected from a corpus, or compiled manually. The probability estimates are also computed from that list.

As the Base Model only considers suffix changes, it is not appropriate for all languages. For suffigating languages like Swedish, however, it has proved to work well: 94.97% type accuracy for a model trained on Stockholm-Umeå Corpus (SUC 1.0) (Ejerhed et al., 1997), evaluated on a testset without part-of-speech tags (13,871 verb forms, 53,115 noun forms, and 53,115 adjective forms) (Wicentowski, 2002).

As a side effect, the mapper can also be used for wordform generation for a baseform given a part-of-speech tag, if the model is reversed and the tag contains enough information. Wicentowski considers this an easier task than wordform-baseform mapping, but did only a minor evaluation on verb forms for English, French and German, and using separate models for each part-of-speech tag. Accuracy ranges from 88.70 to 99.78%.

3 Experimental setup

As we cannot fit all the words in a language into a model, we have to choose the ones that are most useful. Our assumption is that we do not need all regular wordforms in the model, as the ones missing can be handled by analogy. On the other hand, we have to include all irregular wordforms, at least the most frequently used wordforms, or else the application would not be robust enough.

To test our assumptions of the kind and amount of data needed for a good mapper, we used various subsets from a frequency-ranked vocabulary, and our Perl implementation of Wicentowski's Base Model.

3.1 Vocabulary pool

The data used for induction in the experiments come from a Swedish lemma vocabulary pool (Forsbom, 2006) derived from version 2.0 of the 1-million word balanced corpora Stockholm-Umeå Corpus (SUC) (Ejerhed et al., 2006). SUC is compiled in a manner similar in spirit to that of the Brown (Francis and Kučera, 1979) corpus, and is meant to be representative of what a person might have read in a year in the early nineties. Each word is annotated with its baseform and its part-of-speech (mapped to the PAROLE tagset). The texts are also categorised in 9 major categories (genres) and 48 subcategories (domains).

The units of the vocabulary pool are "lemmas", or rather the baseforms from the SUC annotation disambiguated for part-of-speech, so that the preposition *om* 'about' becomes om.S and the subjunction *om* 'if' becomes om.CS. The lemmas are ranked according to relative frequency weighted with dispersion, i.e. how evenly spread-out they are across the subdivisions of the corpus, so that more evenly-spread words with the same frequency are ranked higher.

The total lemma vocabulary has 69,560 entries, but there is also a genre and domain independent base vocabulary, restricted to entries which occur in more than 3 genres, which has 8,554 entries.

For our experiments, we used only the original SUC baseform in ⟨wordform, PAROLE tag, baseform⟩ (or the reverse) triples as input for inducing the mapping models from various subsets of the vocabulary.

3.2 Base Model mapper

In our implementation of Wicentowski's Base Model, the suffix transformations are conditioned on a part-of-speech tag, to limit the number of possible transformations.

When using the mapper on seen words in our version, the mapper returns only the transformation(s) applicable to those words, i.e. a single transformation for non-ambiguous words, and a set of transformations ranked by their estimated probability for ambiguous words. For unseen words, the mapper follows the design of the original Base Model, and the mapper returns applicable transformations ranked by a weighted back-off probability based on the longest common suffix. The weight is static, and set to 0.1. Our mapper outputs the top-ranked baseforms, optionally with a confidence score.

3.3 Models

In the experiments, two sets of models were trained (see Table 1): one with all entries from the full vocabulary (105,815 entries), and one with only entries from the base vocabulary (28,050 entries). The set based on the full vocabulary is the same as in Wicentowski's experiments, apart from corpus version and the inclusion of PoS tags. Our hypothesis is that it contains all the frequent irregular forms, more than enough samples of regular forms, and some infrequent irregular forms that are not so useful. The set based on the base vocabulary, on the other hand, should contain all the frequent, but no infrequent, irregular forms, and enough samples of regular forms.

The full set obviously takes up more space, takes longer to load and takes longer to search in.

The PAROLE part-of-speech set is rather detailed (153 tags), and an automatic part-of-speech tagger is likely to make a few errors on the more detailed morphological information, while the actual part-of-speech most often is correct (cf. Megyesi (2002)). To see how the Base Model performed in circumstances with a less detailed tagset, we also conflated the PAROLE set to a smaller set (29 tags), i.e. the same set used for disambiguating lemmas in the vocabulary pool. For most words it is simply the part-of-speech, but for common nouns, for example, there is a distinction between neuter and non-neuter gender, as the same baseform could have two differing paradigms depending on gender.

Loading the models with shorter tags used roughly the same amount of time and space, but the lookup time for the evaluation testset (163,999 entries) was about three times longer than for the models with more detailed tags, as there were more alternatives for each node in the trie. For wordform lookup, the shorter tags were not expected to be very useful, as they give no clue about what wordform should be generated.

In addition, we used wordform filtering for four models, since many baseforms had several alternative wordforms connected to a part-of-speech. Wordform filtering was mainly intended for baseform-wordform mapping. Most of the alternatives were antiquated forms (e.g. *hwarandra* for *varandra* 'each other' and *hafva* for *ha(va)* 'have') or forms from reported speech (e.g. *e', e, ä', ä* for *är* 'is'), and some baseforms were not real lemmas, i.e. having the same inflectional paradigm (e.g. *vara* as auxiliary, 'be', or as main verb, 'be' or 'last').

In two of the wordform-filtered models, only wordforms occurring more than once were included, to get rid of wordforms for which statistic information was unreliable. This frequency-based filtering was very aggressive, in particular for the full vocabulary model; reducing its size by more than 50%.

Another filter was used in the two other models, to filter out alternative wordforms for a part-of-speech and baseform, i.e. if their frequency ratio (among all alternatives for that case) were less than or equal to 0.1, to remove the least plausible wordforms. This ratio-based filtering was rather modest for both vocabulary models.

4   Evaluation

We wanted to evaluate the theoretical bounds of the models on a testset which include many words not present in the models, and with many semi-regular and irregular forms, to see their limitations (see Section 4.1). But, as the models are to be used in real applications, mainly for baseform lookup, we also wanted to evaluate them on real, unseen, texts (see Section 4.2).

Model	Set	Filter	Tagset	Size	Loading		Lookup
					Memory	Time	Time
FullFull (bf)	Full	v=full,f=0,r=0	Full	105,815	156MB	24.79s	5m16s
FullFull (wf)	Full	v=full,f=0,r=0	Full	105,815	119MB	22.25s	5m18s
FullShort	Full	v=full,f=0,r=0	Short	105,815	155MB	25.10s	19m57s
FullFiltered1	Full	v=full,f=1,r=0	Full	44,918	66MB	9.77s	3m18s
FullFiltered01	Full	v=full,f=0,r=0.1	Full	105,289	155MB	24.60s	4m47s
BaseFull (bf)	Base	v=base,f=0,r=0	Full	28,050	40MB	5.64s	4m00s
BaseFull (wf)	Base	v=base,f=0,r=0	Full	28,050	23MB	4.34s	3m33s
BaseShort	Base	v=base,f=0,r=0	Short	28,050	39MB	5.30s	13m37s
BaseFiltered1	Base	v=base,f=1,r=0	Full	21,645	32MB	4.21s	2m59s
BaseFiltered01	Base	v=base,f=0,r=0.1	Full	27,540	39MB	5.26s	3m16s

Table 1: SUC baseform/wordform models. Filters: v=vocabulary, f=frequency, r=ratio. Time and memory usage was measured with `top` and `time` on a computer with 4 processors (Intel(R) Xeon(TM) CPU 2.80GHz), i686 Linux kernel 2.6.16-1.2115_FC4smp, 2070kB RAM ($k=2^{10}$, $M=2^{20}$).

4.1 In theory: Testset

In the absence of a standardised testset for Swedish morphology, we used the freely available DSSO (Westerberg, 2003)[1], which the Swedish spelling dictionary for `OpenOffice` is based upon.

DSSO contains some morphosyntactic information, such as part-of-speech, case, number, and tense, but misses information on, for example, gender for nouns. In some cases, it has a different view of what part-of-speech a word belongs to (e.g. no determiners, just pronouns, or no subjunctions, just conjunctions), or what the baseform of a word is (e.g. participles have the infinitive verb form as baseform, while in SUC they are mapped to the non-neuter, indefinite, participle form—an adjective form).

In order to make DSSO useful for evaluation of our models, we automatically transformed the DSSO morphosyntactic information into PAROLE tags. In the case of systematic differences, we used a set of rules to do the mapping, and in case of missing information, we used the statistical part-of-speech tagger TnT (Brants, 2000) with a model trained on SUC (Megyesi, 2002) to output all possible tags for each word and then heuristics to choose the right information (e.g. for noun gender, the gender of the most probable noun tag, and non-neuter as default). Obvious errors were corrected, and some erroneous entries in the original DSSO were filtered out, but a few errors may remain.

The transformed testset contains 163,999 entries of ⟨wordform, PAROLE tag, baseform⟩ triples

(19.80% in common with the FullFull model. More than half of the entries are common nouns (91,436).

In Table 2, the error rates for the various models on DSSO with only the top 1 alternative are given. The results cover both baseform lookup and, the reverse, wordform lookup. The lower bounds[2] for baseform lookups are given by two baselines: no change of form, and stemming by the freely available Snowball stemmer for Swedish (Porter, 2001). Upper bounds (or state-of-the-art performance) could not be computed for this testset, as we did not have access to state-of-the-art systems other than as demos with limited access. Performance has been reported for, for example, SWETWOL as 0.7 and 0.4% error rate, respectively, for baseform lookup on two texts (Karlsson, 1992): 1) 47,422 tokens (8,432 types) and 2) 54,542 (5,857).[3] The error rates were based on tokens rather than types, which makes comparison hard. Our models are way better than the lower bounds, but also a bit away from the upper bound, although the comparison is skewed, since our error rates are based on types and on the top 1 ranked alternative only.

Among our models, the FullFull model was the best, both for baseform and wordform lookup. And the frequency-filtered models did worse than the unfiltered models, even on wordform lookup, which

---

[2] Here, lower is used in the sense worst performance, although the numbers for the error rates are higher.

[3] In a list message summary on PoS-taggers 1993, Lingsoft reports on the performance ("recognised 99.3%", or an error rate of 0.7%) for a list of 300,000 wordforms (http://www.sfs.uni-tuebingen.de/~abney/taggers.html) The performance probably refers to recall rather than precision, and tokens rather than types.

Model	Baseform	Wordform
FullFull	4.35	5.52
FullShort	9.66	73.69
FullFiltered1	5.24	7.54
FullFiltered01	4.36	5.51
BaseFull	5.14	6.61
BaseShort	8.49	73.03
BaseFiltered1	5.64	8.42
BaseFiltered01	5.14	6.62
Snowball	57.38	-
NoChange	76.56	-

Table 2: Overall error rates for SUC models and baselines on DSSO (top 1 ranked).

they were supposed to boost performance for, while the ratio-filtered models did about the same as the unfiltered models. For baseform lookup, the models with conflated part-of-speech tags did worse than the models with the full tagset, but much better than the lower bounds. For wordform lookup, on the other hand, they were as lousy as expected.

In Figure 1, we show the error contribution by part-of-speech tag for baseform lookup with the FullFull model. The majority of errors come from genitive forms of common nouns (NC**G@**), where no applicable mapping was found at all and a non-changed form was used (e.g. *bärsens* 'the beers" for *bärs*), or the wordform was missing from the model and the majority regular mapping was used (e.g. *bevi* '(a) proof's" for *bevis*). As it turns out, there are very few genitive forms at all present in the model (1,052 plural forms and 2,619 singular forms), compared to the number of common noun baseforms (21,067). As baseforms ending in *s* or *x*, *z* are ambiguous for case, writers also usually avoid the synthetic form and use reformulation strategies instead, to be clearer. So, in real-life situations, the genitive errors might not be so important. They might also be possible to remedy in some respect by editing the model to include genitive forms for all baseforms in the model.

Other common errors originate from plural forms of common nouns (NC*P*@**) not found in the model, where the baseform should end with a vowel or have a vowel inserted before *l, n, r,* but the vowel is clipped (e.g. *backarna* 'the hills' to *back* instead of *backe*, or *fablerna* 'the fables' to *fabl* instead of *fabel*). Neuter adjectives (AQPNSNIS) where the baseform should end with *t*, but the *t* is clipped (e.g.

transparen 'transparent' instead of *transparent*) is another common error source. Deponential verbs (V@**SS) not in the model also have their *s*-suffix chopped off (e.g. *ända* 'to end' instead of *ändas*), an error which can be attributed to the tagset rather than the application, since the tagset does not distinguish between deponential verbs and passive verb forms.

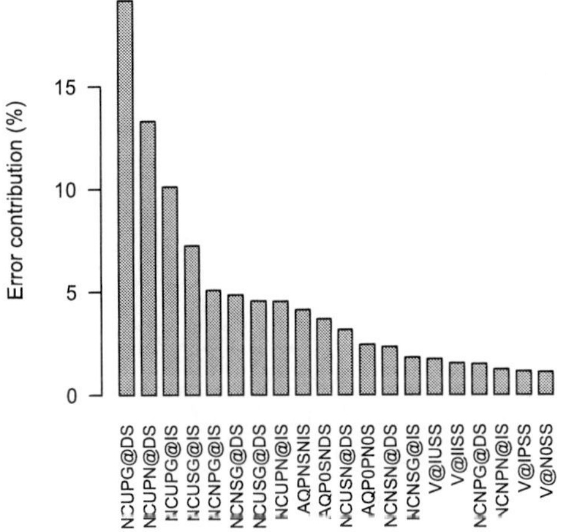

Figure 1: Error contribution by PAROLE tag for FullFull on DSSO baseform lookup (top 1 ranked, error contribution≥1).

As our models are based on statistics, wordforms (or baseforms) that are not in the models are usually assigned the analysis of the most regular mapping, although the correct mapping is also given, but as a lower ranked alternative. When looking at the top 2-10 ranked alternatives, the error rate for all models goes down drastically for the first 2-4 alternatives, and then levels out (see Figures 2 and 3). This is also a more fair comparison with SWETWOL (although the token-type discrepancy is still present).

For baseform lookup, the FullFull, FullFullFiltered01, FullShort and BaseShort models are at the same error rate level as SWETWOL from top 4 onwards, and BaseFull and BaseFullFiltered01 is close (0.8% error rate). The two models with the conflated tagset actually outperform the models with the full tagset from top 4 or 5. This indicates that the full tagset is better for disambiguating regular alternatives with the same suffix within the same part-of-

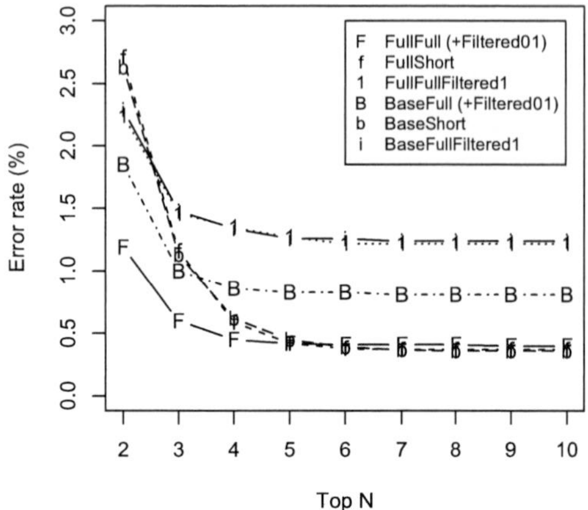

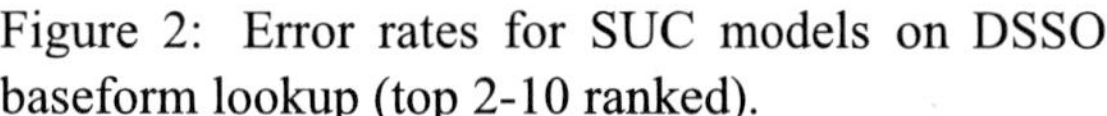

Figure 2: Error rates for SUC models on DSSO baseform lookup (top 2-10 ranked).

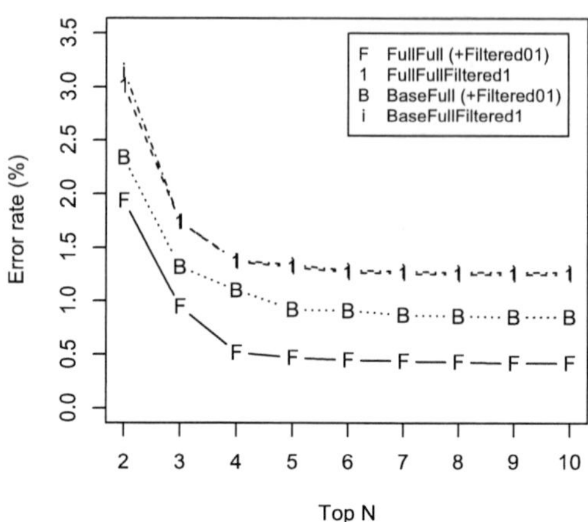

Figure 3: Error rates for SUC models on DSSO wordform lookup (top 2-10 ranked).

speech, while the conflated tagset is better at disambiguating alternatives where the more detailed morphosyntactic information in the full tagset gives too few data points. In those cases, the FullShort and BaseShort models rely more on the suffixes than the tags.

For wordform lookup, all models with the full tagset have error rates between 0.5 and 1.3% from top 5 onward. As mentioned before, the wordform filterings did not help much. On the other hand, the two models with the conflated tagset (not intended for wordform lookup and not shown in the figure) reach error rates of 13.6 (BaseFull) and 33.1% (FullFull) for the top 10 ranked alternatives.

4.2 In practice: Real texts

In the more real-life evaluation, we only used the unfiltered models: FullFull, FullShort, BaseFull, and BaseShort, and only used them for baseform lookup. The selected models were applied to five news texts, randomly sampled from the Scarrie corpus (Dahlqvist, 1999).

As input, we used corrected output from the tagger used for the testset. We corrected the tags as the evaluation should evaluate the models, not the tagger. We also used a single analysis as output, as in the following example for the wordforms *spårlöst*

'without a trace' and *industrikoncernen 'the industrial concern'*:

```
spårlöst            RG0S       spårlöst
industrikoncernen NCUSN@DS industrikoncern
```

For the comparison, the texts were also analysed with 2 other morphological analysers: SWETWOL and Lexware. The two analysers are not designed for baseform lookup as such, but can be used for the task if the output is post-processed.

SWETWOL is a commercial morphological transducer lexicon description of Swedish[4]. It is based on classical Swedish grammar and can analyse words by inflection, derivation and compounding. The SWETWOL analyser consists of a lexicon with more than 45,000 entries, mostly derived from SAOL[5] and a set of two-level rules compiled into run-time finite-state automata. The output is all possible analyses of the wordform, as in the following examples:

```
"<spårlöst>"
    "spår|lös"   A NEU INDEF SG NOM
    "spår#lös"   A NEU INDEF SG NOM
    "spår#lösa"  V ACT SUPINE
    "spår#lösa"  V PCP2 UTR/NEU INDEF SG NOM
    "spårlöst"   ADV
"<industrikoncernen>"
```

---

[4] http://www.lingsoft.fi/cgi-pub/swetwol
[5] Svenska Akademiens Ordlista 'Swedish Academy Wordlist'.

```
"industri#koncern"  N UTR DEF SG NOM
```

In the comparison, we used the analysis (or analyses) corresponding to the correct part-of-speech tag given the context. If there were more than one analysis with correct part-of-speech, the correct baseform for the word in context was used.

Lexware is a commercial "language engine" (Dura, 1998) with, *inter alia*, morphological analysis of Swedish wordforms. Its knowledge base is derived from the information in NEO[6], and it has 80,000 entries, inflectional patterns, and 400 word formation rules. For the comparison, we used the Nyckelord tagging demo[7], where the output is the baseform (including word ID and any segmentation), part-of-speech, and inflectional pattern ID, as in the following examples:

```
"spårlöst"
  spårlös(44004) ADVERB inflections=1
"industrikoncernen"
  industri(22508)_koncern(25765) NOUN
                          inflections=3
```

The texts used for evaluation were tokenised at major punctuation characters and white space (752 tokens in total), but not normalised (i.e. case-folded) before mapping. There were 398 normalised types, but 403 different analyses, in at least one analyser: 4 types differed in analysis due to capitalisation, and 3 types due to homonymity. Accuracy was therefore counted on the basis of the 403 "types".

As we were comparing morphological analysers implemented for different application purposes, and using slightly differing levels of analysis, we had to be a bit lenient in our evaluation. The pronoun *det* ('it', neuter), for example, could be treated as either an inflection of *den* (uter) or as a baseform. Other examples are adverbs (*spårlöst*) derived from adjectives (*spårlös*), which could be treated either as neuter inflectional forms of the adjective, derivations, or as baseforms. When there was no possible difference in analysis level, we therefore counted an analysis as correct if the analysis of an inflected word was correct, and as incorrect if an analysis of a non-inflected word was incorrect. Where there was a possible difference in analysis level, we counted an

___
[6]Nationalencyklopedins ordbok 'Swedish National Encyclopedia Wordlist'.

[7]http://www.nla.se/lexware/

analysis as acceptable if the analysis of an inflected word was one of the possible variants, and as unacceptable if the analysis of a possibly non-inflected word was none of the possible variants. As can be seen in Table 3, our models did a bit better (99.3%) than SWETWOL (98.3%), which in turn did better than Lexware (97.5%), but the differences are small.

However, Lexware was somewhat penalised since it uses its own tagger and some of the errors were tagging errors. Some words were also segmented correctly, but as Lexware uses baseforms also for the parts, it was not possible to derive the baseform from the parts, it was counted as an error, e.g. *20-|öre|valör* for *20-öresvalörerna* instead of the correct *20-öresvalör* 'value of 20 öre', i.e. the glueing *s* is missing. For some reason, probably because it was not in the lexicon, Lexware also messed up *O-listenoterade* 'listed on the O list (stock exchange)' while it did a perfect job on the almost identical *A-listenoterade*.

Case errors were not counted as errors here as normalisation was not the object of evaluation. SWETWOL always does lower-case conversion, but keeps record of initial capitals, so it is possible to restore it if necessary. Our Swedish models are case-normalised, so the input should really be normalised beforehand, so that any normalised forms that are in the models can be recognised. For example, the normalised wordform of *Aktier* 'stocks' is in the models, and correctly analysed if normalised beforehand, but incorrectly analysed if not normalised.

The BaseFull model also made a mistake on *rånarna* 'the robbers', which it analysed as *rån* 'robbery', and not the correct *rånare*. The word was not in the model, and *arna* is a common inflectional ending for definite plural nouns.

5 Concluding remarks

In this paper, we investigated the performance of a wordform-baseform mapper (or reverse), using various subsets of a Swedish frequency-ranked vocabulary pool as input models. We wanted to find out what kind of information, and how much, a good model should contain. The hypothesis was that a smaller model would fit two assumptions: 1) that irregular wordforms either are among the most top-frequent words in a vocabulary, or so rarely used that

	Analysis	Max	Full Full	Full Short	Base Full	Base Short	SWETWOL	Lexware
Non-	Incorrect	198	0	1	0	1	2	2
inflected	Unacceptable	44	0	0	0	0	0	1
Subtotal	Accurate	242	242	241	242	241	240	239
Inflected	Acceptable	13	13	13	13	13	13	13
	Correct	148	146	144	146	144	144	141
Subtotal	Accurate	161	159	157	159	157	157	154
Total	Accuracy (%)	100	99.3	98.8	99.3	98.8	98.3	97.5

Table 3: Results for baseform lookup for the 4 models, SWETWOL, and Lexware.

they are insignificant for a robust application, and 2) that rules for regular forms can be induced from a limited number of examples.

Eight subsets from the vocabulary pool were used as models, and were evaluated for both directions on a testset of mappings. Four of the models were also used for wordform-baseform mapping on 5 randomly selected texts from the Scarrie corpus.

For the corpus text evaluation, the smaller models performed as good as the larger ones, which indicates that our hypothesis is plausible.

Most models were useful for some situation, but no model was best for all situations, so when using the mapping application for either baseform or wordform mapping, one can choose a suitable setting for how many top-ranked alternatives should be returned and a suitable model, depending on the intended application of the baseform or wordform mapping, and requirements on accuracy, speed, and space limitations.

For wordform-baseform mapping, the best models also performed on par with state-of-the-art systems.

A demonstrator and the BaseModel package, with programs, models, and testset, are available from `http://stp.lingfil.uu.se/~evafo/ resources/baseformmodels/`.

Acknowledgements

This research was funded by the Swedish and Nordic Graduate School of Language Technology. We also wish to thank the reviewers for their comments.

References

Thorsten Brants. 2000. TnT - a statistical part-of-speech tagger. In *Proc. of the Sixth Applied Natural Language Processing Conference*, Seattle, Washington.

Bengt Dahlqvist. 1999. A Swedish text corpus for generating dictionaries. In Anna Sågvall Hein, editor, *The SCARRIE Swedish Newspaper Corpus*, Working Papers in Computational Linguistics & Language Engineering 6. Dep. of Linguistics, Uppsala University.

Elżbieta Dura. 1998. *Parsing Words*. Data Linguistica 19. Göteborg University, Göteborg. PhD thesis.

Eva Ejerhed, Gunnel Källgren, and Benny Brodda. 1997. Stockholm-Umeå corpus version 1.0, SUC 1.0. Dep. of Linguistics, Stockholm University and Dep. of Linguistics, Umeå University.

Eva Ejerhed, Gunnel Källgren, and Benny Brodda. 2006. Stockholm-Umeå corpus version 2.0, SUC 2.0. Dep. of Linguistics, Stockholm University and Dep. of Linguistics, Umeå University.

Eva Forsbom. 2006. A Swedish base vocabulary pool. Presented at the Swedish Language Technology Conference, Göteborg.

W. Nelson Francis and Henry Kučera, 1979. *Manual of information to accompany a Standard Sample of Present-day Edited American English, for use with digital computers*. Providence, R.I. Original ed. 1964, revised 1971, revised and augmented 1979.

Fred Karlsson. 1992. SWETWOL: A comprehensive morphological analyzer for Swedish. *Nordic Journal of Linguistics*, 15(1):1–45.

Beáta Megyesi. 2002. *Data-Driven Syntactic Analysis. Methods and Applications for Swedish*. TRITA-TMH 2002:7. Inst. for Speech, Music and Hearing, Royal Institute of Technology, Stockholm. PhD thesis.

Martin F. Porter. 2001. Snowball: A language for stemming algorithms. `http://snowball. tartarus.org`.

Tom Westerberg. 2003. Den stora svenska ordlistan [The large Swedish dictionary]. Version 1.13.

Richard Wicentowski. 2002. *Modeling and Learning Multilingual Inflectional Morphology in a Minimally Supervised Framework*. Ph.D. thesis, John Hopkins University, Baltimore, Maryland.

Achieving Goals in Collaboration:
Analysis of Estonian Institutional Calls

Olga Gerassimenko
Faculty of Philosophy
University of Tartu
Tartu, 50409
olga.gerassimenko@ut.ee

Mare Koit
Faculty of Mathematics and Computer Science
University of Tartu
Tartu, 50409
mare.koit@ut.ee

Andriela Rääbis
Faculty of Philosophy
University of Tartu
Tartu, 50409
andriela.raabis@ut.ee

Krista Strandson
Faculty of Philosophy
University of Tartu
Tartu, 50409
krista.strandson@ut.ee

Abstract

Estonian institutional calls are analyzed with the further aim to develop a dialogue system. The analysis is based on the Estonian Dialogue Corpus. Four types of dialogues are considered: calls to travel agencies and outpatients' offices, ordering a taxi, and directory inquiries. A customer's goal is either to get information or to trigger an action by the operator. This goal is achieved in collaboration with the operator. Sub-dialogues are initiated both by the customer and operator in order to achieve sub-goals of the initial goal. A stack is an appropriate data structure for saving goals and sub-goals.

1 Introduction

Communication between A and B is possible only if the partners have a *shared knowledge*: a common language and world knowledge, a common view of norms and rules of communication; A's knowledge about B should have a common part with B's knowledge about himself/herself, and conversely; the participants should share at least the goal to communicate one with another. In this sense, every communication is collaboration.

In task-oriented dialogues, the cooperative participants additionally have a common goal – to solve a task. A goal can be achieved through a sequence of sub-goals, i.e. setting up and solving subtasks. Solving of every subtask initiates a sub-dialogue.

A simple task-oriented dialogue arises when a customer calls an information center and asks a question. The operator cannot always give an answer immediately. She needs additional information in order to determine the customer's goal precisely, and initiates an *information-sharing* sub-dialogue. Similarly, a customer may start a *clarification* sub-dialogue if the answer does not satisfy his goal. Both partners can initiate *correction* sub-dialogues during a dialogue.

These three kinds of sub-dialogues are differently understood by researchers (Hennoste et al., 2005). Information-sharing is a transfer of knowledge from one participant to another. Sometimes this kind of sub-dialogue is called knowledge precondition sub-dialogue because they are initiated by the agent to satisfy the preconditions of a higher-level goal (Jurafsky and Martin, 2000: 748).

Joakim Nivre, Heiki-Jaan Kaalep, Kadri Muischnek and Mare Koit (Eds.)
NODALIDA 2007 Conference Proceedings, pp. 59–66

In this case, an agent tries to elicit knowledge from the partner (e.g. a travel agent asks details of a trip from a customer). On the other hand, a negotiation sub-dialogue can be initiated by an agent to evaluate a proposal of the partner (Chu-Carrol and Carberry, 1995), e.g. a dialogue system (DS) is transferring its own knowledge to the user to resolve its uncertainty regarding the acceptance of a user proposal. In their later publications, negotiation is called a correction sub-dialogue (Chu-Carrol and Carberry, 1998; Jurafsky and Martin, 2000: 748). Correction is considered as a plan change (e.g. a customer rejects a previous plan to travel on Friday and orders a ticket for Sunday), or error correction (Kirchhoff, 2001). Clarification is considered as specification of answer (e.g. after a customer gets the gate number from the operator, he in addition asks for the precise location of the gate), or as solving of communication problems (McTear, 2004). In conversation analysis (CA), solving of communication problems is called repair (Schegloff, 1986). Figure 1 illustrates the different kinds of sub-dialogues and their typical location (A, B – dialogue participants).

A: request/ question B: *information-sharing* A: -"- B: grant/answer	A: request/ question B: grant/answer A: *clarification/ (error) correction / repair* B: -"-	A: proposal B: *negotiation / correction* A: -"- B: accept/reject

Figure 1. Sub-dialogues of a dialogue

Our further aim is to develop a DS which performs the role of an information operator interacting with a user in Estonian. Therefore we studied Estonian human-human institutional calls in order to explain how a customer (A) achieves his goal in collaboration with an operator (B). Three kinds of sub-dialogues are considered in dialogues: 1) information-sharing initiated by B before giving answer, 2) clarification initiated by A after receiving answer, and 3) repairs initiated both by A or B for solving communication problems. Negotiations in sense of (Chu-Carrol and Carberry, 1995) are not considered here because there are few proposals in our analyzed dialogues.

The paper is organized as follows. In Section 2 we give an overview of our empirical material. Section 3 clarifies what do customers ask and which dialogue acts they use in order to set up their goals. In Section 4 we consider different kinds of sub-dialogues used by participants who collaborate for achieving a joint goal – information-sharing, clarification and repair. Section 5 investigates how to model the process of achieving goals by using a stack structure. In Section 6 we will make conclusions.

2 Corpus Used

Our current study is based on the Estonian Dialogue Corpus (EDiC)[1]. The corpus contains about 900 authentic human-human spoken dialogues, including over 800 calls. Dialogue acts are annotated in the corpus. A DAMSL-like typology[2] of dialogue acts is used for annotation (Gerassimenko et al., 2004). For this paper, 144 institutional calls (total 19,938 tokens) were selected from EDiC. Four situational groups are represented in the dialogues: calls to travel agencies, to outpatients' offices, for taxi, and directory inquiries (Table 1). The calls to travel agencies form the biggest part of the selected sub-corpus. The remaining dialogue types are considered for comparison. The dialogues are quite different but they still share an important feature – they all are collaborative. The Workbench[3] of EDiC was used for calculations and analyses.

Table 1. Overview of the corpus

Dialogue type	Number of		Average length: number of	
	dialo-gues	tokens	utter-ances	tokens
Travel agency	36	12,104	54	336
Directory inquiries	60	4,384	19	73
Outpa-tients' offices	26	2,422	24	93
Taxi	22	1,028	13	47
Total	**144**	**19,938**		

---

[1] http://math.ut.ee/~koit/Dialoog/EDiC.html

[2] The acts are divided into two big groups – adjacency pair (AP) acts (e.g. question–answer) and single (non-AP) acts (e.g. continuer). Names of dialogue acts consist of two parts separated by a colon: the first two letters give abbreviation of the name of act-group, e.g. QU – questions, VR – voluntary responses; the third letter is used only for AP acts – the first (F) or second (S) part of an AP act; 2) full name of the act, for example, QUF: WH (wh-question), QUS: GIVING INFORMATION, VR: CONTINUER. The act names are originally in Estonian.

[3] http://math.ut.ee/~treumuth/

In calls to travel agencies and directory inquiries, a customer wants to get information (and e.g. not to book a trip). When calling an outpatients' office or ordering a taxi, a customer expects an action by the operator in most cases (booking a reception time with a doctor, sending a taxi). Still, performing the action is accompanied with giving information (e.g. *yes, a taxi will come*).

In the following we will investigate how a customer achieves his goal, and how a collaborative operator assists him.

A typical call starts with a ritual part (greetings, identification, Schegloff, 1986). After that, a customer formulates a task starting the main part of the dialogue. During the main part, a task is solved in collaboration with an operator. A dialogue ends with a ritual part – thanking, leave-taking.

3 Customers' Goals

The main part of a dialogue begins with setting up of a goal by a customer.

3.1 What do customers ask

In our dialogues, a customer's goal is either 1) to get information (e.g. a phone number, address, etc.) or 2) to trigger an action by the operator (e.g. to send a taxi). In the latter case, the operator always informs the customer that either the action is performed or she is unable to perform it. Therefore, doing an action is accompanied with giving information.

In calls to *travel agencies* and *directory inquiries*, only information is asked for (phone numbers, bus schedules, opening hours of institutions, how to travel to a certain country, etc). There are no dialogues in our sub-corpus where a customer calling a travel agency books a trip.

Calling an *outpatients' office*, customers typically have a goal to book reception time with a doctor (21 dialogues), they seldom request information (about a certain patient, abatements, booking, following therapy – 5 dialogues in our data). Calling a *taxi company*, customers mostly want to order a taxi, i.e. they request an action (20 dialogues out of 22).

In majority of dialogues, customers achieve the goal. In directory inquiries, there are only two cases when a customer does not get the asked information (which is missing in a data base).

Calling an outpatients' office, a customer does not get information in one case because he is unable to describe the requested exploration. Booking a reception time succeeds in all cases.

Ordering a taxi succeeds in 18 cases out of 20. The 2 reasons of failure are that the taxi company does not have the requested mini-bus (one case), and a customer disclaims himself (one case).

In travel agency dialogues, the situation is different. A customer gets the requested information only in 12 dialogues out of 36. The typical reason of failure is that shared knowledge is missing – a customer does not have previous knowledge about the fields of activity of the agency (e.g. he asks how to travel to England but the agency offers only trips inside Estonia). In three dialogues, there are no more places available for the requested trip.

3.2 How do customers set up their goals

Customers use directives or questions in order to set up a goal.

In our typology, we make a difference between directives and questions (Gerassimenko et al., 2004). Questions have special explicit formal features in Estonian – interrogatives, intonation, specific word order. Other requests for information and directive-actions in sense of DAMSL are considered as directives (Ex 1)[4]:

(1)
```
.hh     olen     uvitatud     reisidest
Skandi`naaviamaadesse=h.  DIF: REQUEST
```
I'm interested in trips to Scandinavian countries

In *directory inquiries*, a customer typically asks one question or makes one request in order to set up his goal. In calls to *outpatient offices*, similarly one dialogue act is sufficient. If a customer expects information then he uses a question. If he expects an action of the operator then a directive is used. Ordering a *taxi*, a customer always uses a directive.

Calling a *travel agency*, customers use one dialogue act for setting up the initial goal in 22 dialogues (out of 36), and two acts (utterances) in one turn in 5 cases (mostly a question or a request together with specifying information). In the remaining 9 cases, a response of the operator (continuer or acknowledgement) follows to the customer's request which signals that the operator is waiting for adjustment of the initial request. After that, the

---

[4] Transcription of conversation analysis is used in examples, cf. http://math.ut.ee/~koit/Dialoog/EDiC.html and (Gerassimenko et al. 2004).

customer asks a question or adds specifying information to his request. This can be considered as a collaborative behavior because information comes to the partner step by step which makes understanding it easier (Ex 2, A – customer, B – operator):

(2)
```
A: .hh e sooviks: sõita Tallinnast
`Münhenisse lennukiga.   DIF: REQUEST
```
I'd like to travel from Tallinn to Munich by plain
```
B: jaa?     VR: NEUTRAL CONTINUER
```
yes?
```
A: ee `üliõpilasele kui=palju `mak-
sab.   QUF: WH
```
how much does it cost for a student?

4   Subdialogues

The simplest structure of the main part of a dialogue is as follows:

A: request/question
B: (action +) giving information/missing information

This structure is preferred in directory inquiries but impossible in calls to outpatients' offices where booking a reception time is expected. In this case, some personal data are needed, and it would be non-collaborative if a patient gave all the data in his/her first request (cf. Gricean maxim of quantity).

There are 14 directory inquiries (out of 60) with such simple structure. In additional 17 inquiries, the operator initiates an information-sharing subdialogue after which she is able to give the requested information or to tell that information is missing in the data base. In the remaining directory inquiries, there are more subdialogues.

Only one ordering of a taxi has the simplest structure. There are no calls to travel agencies with such simple structure. Thus, there are few dialogues without sub-dialogues.

Therefore, a typical collaborative task-oriented dialogue includes sub-dialogues. A sub-dialogue is a rule, not an exception in conversation, they express collaboration (Lochbaum, 1998).

4.1 Information-sharing

Information-sharing is mostly initiated by the operator after a customer's first request or question. The purpose of it is to get additional information which is needed for answering. In a previous work

(Hennoste et al., 2005), information-sharing sub-dialogues were studied in Estonian directory inquiries. It is typical that such a sub-dialogue consists of one question (offering an answer, yes/no or alternative question in most cases) followed by the answer or, more rarely, of one directive (offer) followed by agreeing (Ex 3, a subdialogue is marked with -->).

(3)
```
A: .hh `oskate te ehk `öelda Tar-
tus:=e mõnda telefoni`numbrit `kus
`tegeldaks vanurite `abistamisega,
aga et see=ei=oleks nagu `piirkonna:
(.) mingi number=aga (.) `üldine, £
QUF: OPEN YES/NO
```
could you give me a phone number in Tartu for help to older persons, not a district one but a general number
```
    (1.5)
--> B: tändab aga siis ma pakuks
teile äkki `linnavalitsuse sotsiaal-
abi `osakonna   DIF: OFFER    | ACF:
ADJUSTING CONDITIONS OF ANSWER
```
well then I can propose the social wellfare department of the municipality to you
```
--> A: £ .hh ee jah, nähtavasti
`küll=h. £    DIS: AGREEMENT | ACS:
ADJUSTING CONDITIONS OF ANSWER (4.0)
```
yes obviously yes

The adjusting conditions of B's answer are either obtaining details for the information retrieval or for the action (e.g. if A wants to book a reception time with a doctor then his personal data are needed), or to offer choices to A (e.g. registration office or information desk of an institution), or to make a choice by the information operator and ask an agreement of A (Ex 3).

In directory inquiries, information-sharing will specify an institution (its name, location, structural unit, fields of activity) or will expect a choice/approval of a phone number.

If a customer who is calling an outpatients' office needs information about a patient (another person) then an operator always asks the patient's name, department of the hospital, time of the operation, etc before giving information. If a customer needs to book a reception time then the operator asks his name, ID code, has he visited the doctor previously, which type the visit is (regular, or for a deficiency certificate). The task is not solved until the operator has got all the needed data. Therefore, booking a reception time is different from a directory inquiry – the operator offers a time before information-sharing but the patient's agreement does not mean that the goal is achieved (Ex 4).

(4)
```
B: .hh siis on kakskümend=kuus
ap'rill kell 'kuusteist kolm'kümend.
DIF: OFFER
```
April twenty six at 4.30 p.m.
```
A: jah, sobib 'küll. | DIS: AGREEMENT
```
yes, it's OK
```
--> B: ja kuidas lapse 'nimi on. QUF:
WH | ACF: ADJUSTING CONDITIONS OF
ANSWER |
```
and what's the name of the child?

In calls for a taxi, the customer's name, the flat number, and/or the phone number are asked by the operator if a customer orders a taxi to a block of flats with several entrances (the taxi operator is able to determine the house type on the basis of its address). After that, she confirms that a taxi will come. Therefore, sending a taxi is similar to booking a reception time at an outpatients' office – the task is solved only after the customer's data have been obtained.

The type of information needed by an operator determines the type of the dialogue act which initiates an information-sharing sub-dialogue. In calls to travel agencies, outpatients' offices or for a taxi, the operator typically asks wh-questions. Checking questions, yes-no questions and offers are the next more frequent dialogue acts. In calls to travel agencies, the operator typically requests the time and duration of the requested trip, the names and ages of travellers (Ex 5).

(5)
```
B: lennukiga? VR: NEUTRAL
ACKNOWLEDGEMENT
```
by plane?
```
--> kui=vana te 'olete.    QUF: WH |
ACS: ADJUSTING CONDITIONS OF ANSWER
```
how old are you?
```
--> A: mm (.) kakskümend='üks. QUS:
GIVING INFORMATION | ACS: ADJUSTING
CONDITIONS OF ANSWER
```
um twenty one
```
--> B: olete 'üliõpilane. | QUF:
OFFERING ANSWER | ACS: ADJUSTING
CONDITIONS OF ANSWER
```
are you a student?
```
--> A: jah. QUS:YES | ACS: ADJUSTING
CONDITIONS OF ANSWER
```
yes

The first part of an AP used by B in starting of a sub-dialogue determines the possible second parts which can be used by A. In our dialogues, A's agreement/*yes* mostly follows B's offer/yes-no question (80%). This means that B correctly recognized A's (sub)goal.

Information-sharing sub-dialogues typically consist of one AP in directory inquiries and ordering a taxi (an operator asks a question and a customer answers). The sub-dialogues are longer in calls to travel agencies and to outpatients' offices because more adjustments are needed here (personal data, different details of a trip, etc). Table 2 gives an overview of adjustments in different types of dialogues.

Table 2. Information-sharing sub-dialogues

Dialogue type	Number of adjustments	Typical information shared
Travel agency	73	time, duration of a trip, personal data of travellers
Directory inquiries	58	name, location, fields of activity of an institution, choices of phone numbers
Outpatients' offices	70	reception time, personal data of a patient
Taxi	18	customer's name, flat number
Total	**214**	

The main aim of an information-sharing sub-dialogue initiated by an operator is to specify a customer's goal and to collect information for answering.

4.2 Clarification

Clarification is untypical in directory inquiries – a customer initiates a clarification sub-dialogue only in 10 cases. Adjustments (mostly expressed by wh-questions) are related to the location of the institution which phone number was received, the fields of its activity, how to call the number, and presence of other phone numbers.

In calls to outpatients' offices, there are 7 clarifications: what weekday is it, how long time a consultation lasts, is it free of charge (wh-questions, alternative or yes/no questions are used).

When ordering a taxi, a customer initiates a clarification in 9 cases, typically asking how long it takes to a taxi to arrive (by a wh-question), Ex 6.

(6)
```
B: ja `tuleb teile auto.  DIS: OTHER
and a taxi will come to you
(.)
--> A: kui `kiiresti ta [jõuab.]
QUF: WH
how quickly it will arrive
--> B: [.hh] `saadan teile
`Anne`linnast auto.  QUS: GIVING
INFORMATION
I'll send a car from Anne district to you
(0.5)
A: ahah?  VR: NEUTRAL CHANGE OF STATE
I see
aitäh.    RIF: THANKING
thanks
```

In calls to travel agencies, there are 39 clarifications – much more than in other dialogue types. It is understandable because there are many details of trips which are needed to be specified. Customers ask for the price, duration of a trip, is a visa and/or insurance needed, are they included into the price, are there abatements, are there another possibilities to travel, etc (Ex 7). Table 3 gives an overview of adjustments initiated by customers. The aim of a clarification initiated by a customer is to specify the answer received. A customer's initial goal is achieved but he is adjusting some more details.

Table 3. Clarification sub-dialogues

Dialogue type	Number of adjustments	Typical information clarified by customer
Travel agency	39	price, accommodation, visa
Directory inquiries	10	location of an institution, presence of other phone numbers
Outpatients' offices	7	duration of a consultation, which weekday
Taxi	9	time to wait
Total	**65**	

(7)
```
B: hh < siis jääb vist > (0.5) kell
`kaheksa läheb tegelikult `välja (.)
ee katama`raan, (.) sõidab `tund ne-
likend=`viis. QUS: GIVING INFORMATION
a catamaran departs at 8 o'clock, the travel time is one
hour forthy five minutes
A: ahah, VR: NEUTRAL CHANGE OF STATE
I see
sellega isegi `peaaegu `jõuab
AI: INFERENCE
I will almost manage
```

```
--> ja see on sis `esimene laev=ve.
QUE: OPEN YES-NO
and is this the first boat?
```

4.3 Repair

We differentiate three types of repair initiations. The first two types are *checking* and *non-understanding:* the hearer initiates a repair and the partner carries it out. Both of these initiations indicate a perception problem by the hearer: non-understanding expects the partner to repeat, explain and/or specify the problematic part of his turn, and checking clarifies the problematic part thus expecting the partner either to confirm or to correct this repetition (Ex 8, a sub-sub-dialogue, and Ex 9). The third type is *reformulation* where the hearer initiates a repair and suggests her own interpretation of the problematic item. The partner may agree with or reject this interpretation (Ex 10). Thus the hearer is not correcting a mistake here but indicating an understanding problem.

(8)
```
A: sooviks taksot `Puurmanni `viis-
teist. DIF: REQUEST
(0.5)
a taxi to Puurmanni fifteen please
--> B: ja `kelle `nimele.  QUF: WH |
ACF: ADJUSTIBG CONDITIONS OF ANSWER
and what's the name?
--> A: Ülle? QUS: GIVING INFORMATION
| ACS: ADJUSTIBG CONDITIONS OF ANSWER
Ülle
(.)
----> B: `Ülle `nimele. QUF: OFFERING
ANSWER | RPF: CHECKING
Ülle is the name
----> A: jah. QUS : YES | RPS: REPAIR
yes
```

(9)
```
B: 0.5) `lennujaama vahe on `ka kuhu
te soovite. QUF: OPEN YES-NO | ACF:
ADJUSTING CONDITIONS OF ANSWER (.)
is there a difference between airports you want to arrive
to?
--> A: mis QUF: WH | RPF: NON-
UNDERSTANDING
sorry?
--> B: et kas on `lennujaama vahe ka
kas `Kätvik ((Gatwick)) või (.) [ei
ole] QUF: OPEN YES-NO | QUS: GIVING
INFORMATION | RPS: REPAIR
is there a difference between airports – Gatwick or not?
```

(10)
```
A: järgmine `teisipäev.   QUS: GIVING
INFORMATION | ACS: ADJUSTING
CONDITIONS OF ANSWER
next Tuesday
(1.0) ää `kaks üliõpilast.
AI: SPECIFICATION
um two students
(2.0)
--> B: * kuupäev=on * (1.0) kakskend=
`kolm jah.   QUF: OFFERING ANSWER |
RPF: REFORMULATION
the date is twenty third yes
--> A: jah. QUS: YES | RPS:
PERFORMING
yes
```

The repairing sub-dialogues are initiated in certain limited cases, e.g. with regard to information that must be exact (prices, concessions, e-mail addresses, actions that will be carried out next). The problems that cause correction can in principle be located in an arbitrary past turn. In our sub-corpus, repairs are initiated with regard to the immediately preceding turn in 90% of cases. Table 4 gives an overview of repair initiations in our corpus. The most frequent repair initiation is checking. As one can expect, calls to travel agencies include the most number of repairs. Calls to travel agencies are different from other types of dialogues – reformulations are used almost only here, both by customers and operators, very frequently. The reason is that there are many details of trips which have to be clarified in order to understand them correctly.

Table 4. Number of repair initiations by customer (A) and operator (B)

Dialogue type	Checking		Non-under-standing		Refor-mulation		Total
	A	B	A	B	A	B	
Travel agencies	8	16	5	3	19	12	63
Directory inquiries	10	11	3	2	2	6	34
Outpa-tients' offices	10	13	3	4	-	3	33
Ordering a taxi	1	12	-	10	-	3	26
Total	29	52	11	19	21	24	156

The aim of repairs is to solve communication problems and this way to work for solving the initial task, for achieving a communicative goal.

5 How to Model It?

Utterance	Dialogue act	Goal stack
A: (.) ee ma=oleks uvi-tatud informat-sioonist kuidas: reisida ´Inglismaale. I'm interested in how to travel to England	QUF: WH	
B: jaa? yes	VR: NEUTRAL CONTINUER	travel to England
A: et: (.) ilm-selt kas ´lennukiga: len-nukipileti: (1.2) või=või obviously by plane or or	AI: SPECIFICATION |	
B: lennukiga? by plane	VR: NEUTRAL ACKNOWLEDGEMENT	travel to England by plane
		~~travel to England~~
--> kui=vana te ´olete. how old are you	QUF: WH | ACF: ADJUSTING CONDITIONS OF ANSWER	age of the traveler
		travel to England by plane
--> A: mm (.) kakskümend=´üks. um twenty one	QUS: GIVING INFORMATION | ACS: ADJUSTING CONDITIONS OF ANSWER	
--> B: olete ´üliõpilane. are you a student	QUE: OFFERING ANSWER | ACF: ADJUSTING CONDITIONS OF ANSWER	status of the trav-eler
		~~age of the traveler~~
		travel to England by plane
--> A: jah. yes	QUS: YES | ACS: ADJUSTING CONDITIONS OF ANSWER	~~status of the trav-eler~~
		travel to England by plane

Figure 2. Goal stack (Example 5)

A stack is an appropriate data structure to describe the setting up and abandoning of goals, shared between a customer (A) and the DS (agent, B). A's first question/request sets up the main goal which is put at the bottom of the stack (Fig. 2). The following information-sharing questions set up new goals which go into the stack step by step. To achieve the main goal, all the goals in the stack that are located higher than the main goal must be achieved and removed. If the stack is empty then all the goals have been achieved (Jokinen 1996).

To start a repair after A's request, DS puts a goal into the stack only after the repair is performed. Similarly, if A starts a repair after getting an answer then the goal remains in the stack until the communication problem is solved. Information-sharing is " forward-looking", i.e. advances a theme, while repair is " backward-looking", i.e. solves a problem in the previous text.

6 Conclusion and Future Work

Estonian institutional calls were analysed with the further aim to develop a DS. A customer's first request or question sets up a goal which will be achieved in collaboration with an operator. Sub-dialogues are initiated in order to set up and achieve sub-goals. Information-sharing is a transfer of knowledge from one partner to another in order to achieve a common goal in a collaborative dialogue. Clarification is initiated by a customer after receiving an answer if he needs to adjust some details of the answer. Repair can be used for solving communication problems by both participants, regarding both a question (request) or an answer (grant). A typical repair is reformulation in calls to travel agencies and checking of a phone number in other types of dialogues.

The structure of a dialogue depends on its type. Calls for a taxi have the simplest structure while calls to travel agencies include the most number of sub-dialogues of various kinds. In any case, sub-dialogues express collaboration of both participants who are working for achieving of a common goal.

A simple DS is implemented which gives information about flights leaving from the Tallinn Airport[5]. Our future work concerns implementation of the stack structure in the DS.

---

[5] http://math.ut.ee/~treumuth

Acknowledgement

This work is supported by Estonian Science Foundation (grant No 5685).

References

Jennifer Chu-Carrol and Sandra Carberry. 1998. Collaborative response generation in planning dialogues. *Computational Linguistics*, 24(3): 355-400.

Jennifer Chu-Carrol and Sandra Carberry. 1995. Generating information-sharing subdialogues in expert-user consultation. *Proc. of IJCAI*. Retrieved February 13, 2005, from http://arxiv.org/abs/cmp-lg/9701003.

Olga Gerassimenko, Tiit Hennoste, Mare Koit, Andriela Rääbis, Krista Strandson, Maret Valdisoo, Evely Vutt. 2004. Annotated dialogue corpus as a language resource: an experience of building the Estonian dialogue corpus. *The first Baltic conference "Human language technologies. The Baltic perspective"*. Riga, 150–155.

Tiit Hennoste, Olga Gerassimenko, Riina Kasterpalu, Mare Koit, Andriela Rääbis, Krista Strandson, Maret Valdisoo. 2005. Information-Sharing and Correction in Estonian Information Dialogues: Corpus Analysis. *Proc. of the Second Baltic Conference on Human Language Technologies*. Tallinn, 249-254.

Kristiina Jokinen. 1996. Goal formulation based on communicative principles. *Proc. of the 16th International Conference on Computational Linguistics*. Copenhagen, Denmark. 598-603.

Daniel Jurafsky and James H. Martin. 2000. *An introduction to natural language processing, computational linguistics, and speech recognition*. Prentice Hall.

Katrin Kirchhoff. 2001. A comparison of classification techniques for the automatic detection of error corrections in human-computer dialogues. *Proc. of the NAACL Workshop on Adaptation in Dialogue Systems*, Pittsburgh, PA. Retrieved February 13, 2005, from http://ssli.ee.washington.edu/people/katrin/-Papers/naacl01.pdf

Karen E. Lochbaum. 1998. A collaborative planning model of intentional structure. *Computational Linguistics,* 24(4): 525-572.

Michael F. McTear. 2004. *Spoken dialogue technology: toward the conversational user interface*. London: Springer Verlag.

Emanuel Schegloff. 1986. The routine as achievement. - *Human Studies,* 9: 111-152.

Development of Text-To-Speech System for Latvian

Kārlis Goba
Tilde
Vienības gatve 75a, Riga, LV1004
Latvia
karlis.goba@tilde.lv

Andrejs Vasiļjevs
Tilde
Vienības gatve 75a, Riga, LV1004
Latvia
andrejs.vasiljevs@tilde.lv

Abstract

This paper describes the development of the first text-to-speech (TTS) synthesizer for Latvian language. It provides an overview of the project background and describes the general approach, the choices and particular implementation aspects of the principal TTS components: NLP, prosody and waveform generation. A novelty for waveform synthesis is the combination of corpus-based unit selection methods with traditional diphone synthesis. We conclude that the proposed combination of rather simple language models and synthesis methods yields a cost effective TTS synthesizer of adequate quality.

1 Introduction

This paper describes the development of the first text-to-speech (TTS) synthesis system for Latvian.

The Latvian language spoken by 1.6 million people is the only official language in Latvia and one of the working languages of European Union. Despite the important role of Latvian, until now there was no text-to-speech synthesizer for this language. As a result, there are no applications in use providing Latvian speech capabilities.

The population group with the most acute need for speech enabled technologies are visually impaired people. TTS is an essential technology enabling them to use computer applications, browse the internet and communicate via e-mail. Some of them are advanced computer users using English TTS, but majority do not have sufficient English skills. Attempts to use English TTS for reading and preparing Latvian texts have failed due to principal differences in Latvian and English pronunciation. Latvian text pronounced by English TTS is practically incomprehensible even by the most tolerant and striving users.

In late 1990s and the beginning of this century, a few experiments on Latvian TTS were carried out by the Institute of Informatics and Mathematics of the University of Latvia. These were experiments of speech generation by concatenation of individually recorded phonemes. It became clear quite soon that this approach cannot lead to human-like speech and the experimental system was never completed.

Ilze Auzina (2005) has summarized many of the aspects that need to be accounted for in speech synthesis of Latvian. Auzina proposes models for syllable boundary detection and a framework for grapheme-to-phoneme conversion.

Juris Grigorjevs has carried out research on Latvian speech analysis at Department of Philology of University of Latvia. In this research Grigorjevs (2005) carried out experiments on Latvian vowel generation using formant synthesis.

There has been an attempt to create a Latvian adaptation of the *WinTalker* system developed by a Czech company called *RosaSoft*. The pronunciation generated by pilot model was better than Latvian texts pronounced by non-Latvian TTS but still of a very low quality and barely recognizable. For this reason it was not accepted by users and was not further developed.

The current development project of Latvian TTS synthesizer was started in 2005. The project is carried out as part of a European Commission funded programme to facilitate accessibility for impaired people.

The following sections describe the general approach and the motivation behind the decisions made while creating the text-to-speech synthesizer.

Joakim Nivre, Heiki-Jaan Kaalep, Kadri Muischnek and Mare Koit (Eds.)
NODALIDA 2007 Conference Proceedings, pp. 67–72

2   TTS overview

The primary purpose of Latvian TTS is to address the needs of visually impaired people using computers in the Latvian language environment – browsing Latvian internet, reading and creating Latvian documents, enabling e-mail and chat communication in Latvian.

The requirements of this project include natural sounding text-to-speech synthesis in Latvian that can be integrated with screen-reading accessibility software for visually impaired people. The basic requirements of TTS engines, like the possibility to change voice pitch and speech rate, as well as support for user pronunciation dictionaries are included. Language processing within the TTS engine has to be robust and functional in order to provide stable and consistent output in different usage environments.

The system architecture covers the traditional text-to-speech transformation, performing text normalization, grapheme-to-phoneme conversion, prosody generation, and waveform synthesis.

Latvian in general can be considered a *phonetic language* – a language with relatively simple relationship between orthography and phonology as defined by Huang et al. (2001).

From the TTS synthesis perspective, Latvian has several specific properties:
- Short and long vowels and consonants
- Largely phonetic orthography
- Highly inflected language
- Uniform stress pattern
- Lexical syllable tones

These properties have to be taken into account in text normalization, grapheme-to-phoneme conversion and prosody generation. The following subsections describe their impact.

2.1   Language processing

Language processing consists of text normalization and the subsequent conversion to narrow phonetic transcription.

As a first step, text containing words, abbreviations, numbers, punctuation and other symbols is transformed to normalized orthography.

Latvian has a rich inflectional system. Nouns, adverbs, verbs and participles take different forms depending on gender, number, case, degree, definiteness, mood, tense and person. The constituents of sentence are required to be in agreement between each other. This influences the disambiguation of abbreviated text elements during text normalization.

Some Latvian abbreviations have fixed representations while others should be represented in the inflected form depending on the context:

u.tml.   *un tamlīdzīgi* ('and so on')
u.c.   *un citi / citiem / ...* ('and others')

The fixed representations are included in text processing rules. However, currently no processing is done to determine the inflection of inflected abbreviations.

Appropriate inflectional form should be also determined while transcribing measurement units and numbers:

5 g   *pieci grami / piecu gramu / ...*

Here simple contextual rules are used. The ending of the next word is used to determine the inflectional form of the numeral.

Pronunciation of acronyms depends on linguistic traditions. Acronyms traditionally are read letter by letter, though in some cases they are pronounced phonetically, in Latvian or in their original language:

ASV   */ā es vē/*
PVN   */pē vē en/*
LTV7   */el tē vē septiņi/*
NATO   */nato/*
SIA   */siā/*
KNAB   */knab/*
UNESCO */junesko/*
Reuters   */roiters/*

The pronunciation of acronyms has to be included in the user pronunciation dictionary.

In the Latvian orthography, the letters *e*, *ē* and *o* are homographs and can denote different phonetic values depending on the lexical properties of the word. In some cases the lexical information is not sufficient to distinguish:

vēlu   */ve:lu/* (verb 'to roll')
vēlu   */væ:lu/* (verb 'to wish' or adverb 'late')
robots   */ruobuots/* (adjective 'serrate')
robots   */robots/* (noun 'a robot')
aerobs   */aero:bs/* (adjective 'aerobic')

In these cases, part-of-speech tagging or morphologic analysis may be used for phonetic disambiguation. For efficiency reasons and since such homographs are not very frequent in Latvian, we include only the statistically most frequent forms in disambiguation rules.

Latvian orthography tries to retain the morphologic structure of words as much as possible, while observing a number of pronunciation rules. These rules have to be accounted for also in the grapheme-to-phoneme conversion, e.g. regressive assimilation between subsequent voiced and unvoiced consonants, which also occurs across word borders.

Language processing is performed by over 1,000 regular expression search-and-replace rules.

2.2 Prosody modelling

Latvian has several properties of tonal languages. Each word has an associated stress placement and tone pattern. Both the stress and the tone pattern are distinctive lexical features, e.g. the minimal pairs:

nêķur	((he)does not make fire)
nekúr	(nowhere)
māja	(house)
māja	((he) waved)

Syllables with a long nucleus (long vowel, diphthong or vowel and syllabic sonorant) have one of the three distinct tones present in Latvian. The tones are lexical features of morphologic constituents (the root and optional prefixes, suffixes and endings).

However, quantitative research on the usage of tones in Latvian is lacking. Laua (1997) describes the three tones in a qualitative way:

Tone	Description
Stretched	Pitch is rising steadily to high
Falling	Pitch is slowly falling from high
Broken	Pitch and intensity are rising until the break, when the intensity suddenly drops and resumes after the break

In modern spoken Latvian, two of the three long syllable tones merge together depending on regional dialect of the speaker. The three-tone system, being the richest and the oldest, is currently preserved only in certain regions (Laua 1997). Experiments suggest that it is acceptable to follow this tendency and to model only two distinct syllable tone patterns: stretched and non-stretched (combined rising and broken tone).

The tone pattern is most distinctive in stressed syllables. Experiments suggest that it is acceptable to model the tone of unstressed syllables with a neutral pitch contour. Stressed syllable tone has a lexical function in modern Latvian, while the tone distinction in unstressed syllables has a minor influence on understanding and perceiving of speech.

The syllable stress in Latvian is expressed by emphasizing the tonal contour and lengthening of the stressed syllable. In general, the syllable stress falls on the first syllable. Exceptions include a fixed list of words that have historically merged together (e.g. *labvákar < lábu vákaru*), as well as the superlative degree of adjectives and adverbs (e.g. *vislábākajam*).

The Fujisaki pitch model has been successfully adapted for many languages, including such tonal languages as Swedish and Chinese (Fujisaki 2004). Experiments with Fujisaki model showed that the syllable tone accents in Latvian can be sufficiently modelled with one or two accent commands near the nuclei of stressed syllables.

To model syllable and phrase level stress, discrete prosodic events are inserted in the narrow phonetic transcription. This processing is rule-based. To obtain F0 contour, the prosodic events are converted to accent and pitch commands.

The prosodic events are located at stressed syllable nuclei and the boundaries of prosodic phrase. Prosodic phrases are determined in a simplified way as indicated by text punctuation.

The vowel length is lexical and is marked in orthography with macron diacritics. The consonant length is denoted as double consonants. The length of plosives and fricatives is also influenced by the phonetic context.

Duration is also modelled in discrete steps. Special symbols denoting relative increase or decrease in duration are inserted in the narrow phonetic transcription according to manually written rules. The rules include only the well-known regular phenomena of the Latvian language: the lengthening of unvoiced plosives between two short vowels, the lengthening of stressed syllables and the shortening of short final syllables. Other prosodic factors (phonetic context, structure and position of words, metric feet and phrases) are not taken into account.

2.3 Waveform synthesis

According to Morais and Violaro (2005), corpus-based synthesis approach is the dominant trend in this decade in speech synthesis, which provides high naturalness, accuracy and intelligibility.

In corpus-based synthesis, pre-recorded speech units are concatenated and transformed to produce speech. At runtime, appropriate acoustic patterns and the prosody of a sentence are superimposed during concatenation by means of digital signal processing techniques.

Drawbacks of the corpus-based synthesis are the high development costs and the relatively high memory and processing requirements for running the system. Corpus-based synthesis using a large number of larger recorded units like sentences, words, phrases and morphemes, may produce higher quality speech, but requires a lot of processing power and memory for unit storage.

According to the traditional approach, only one recorded speech unit for each diphone is stored in the diphone synthesis system, and it is presumed that diphones are context-independent. This implies that each diphone has to be carefully selected and evaluated against other diphones that might precede or follow it in order to minimize the possible discontinuities.However, this is a very time-consuming task.Moreover, diphones are influenced by the context and the presumption does not quite hold true.

To improve the quality of Latvian TTS, it was decided to store multiple variations of most diphones and to select the appropriate variant during speech synthesis.

Initially, several variations of each diphone in different contexts were recorded to increase the represented variation of vowels and consonants.

Then, several subsequent diphones were marked in frequently occurring words, including weekdays, months, frequent country and city names etc. During synthesis, these subsequent diphones have minimal join costs during diphone selection, thus allowing use of effectively larger speech units.

The size of the phone set in Latvian is quite disputable and there is no agreement on this in literature. 30 consonant allophones, 2 glides and 6 short and 6 long vowels can be identified, as well as numerous diphthongs. Including all these phones in a phone set significantly increases the size of diphone set above 2000 diphones.

For diphone synthesis, the phone set has to be acoustically representative, i.e. covering the various spectrally steady regions (phone centres) for speech production. Thus experiments were done to decide on the possible size reduction of the acoustic inventory.

Grigorjevs (2005) has shown that the spectral properties of phonemically short and long vowels in Latvian are not distinctive, thus long vowels can be perceived as only differing in duration.

During the development of TTS, experiments of time-scale modification of recorded speech were carried out. Results suggested neither vowels nor unvoiced plosives and consonant sonorants of different length and duration show considerable spectral differences. This allows simplifying the diphone set by treating long and short phonemes uniformly.

The diphone set was further simplified and reduced in size by treating affricates as consecutive plosives and fricatives (/ts/ /tš/ /dz/ /dž/) and treating diphthongs as two consecutive vowels. To cover the possible allophonic and spectral variation of these component phones, multiple occurrences of diphones containing the subject phones in different contexts were recorded.

After the reduction, the acoustic phone set consists of 29 phones including 6 vowel phones, 22 consonant phones and a silence phone. That gives 841 phone pairs, of which about 750 diphones are possible in Latvian.

The speech material for diphones includes one or several words for each possible phone combination. These words are wrapped in carrier sentences to provide natural speech flow.

Several professional speakers were tested to select the most appropriate voice. Recorded sentences were phonetically segmented and manual selection of diphones was made from the recorded material.

The total size of the diphone database is ~2,200 diphones, on average containing 3 variations of each phone pair. Each diphone is divided into overlapping pitch-synchronous windows and the respective LPC coefficients and the residual signal are stored in the diphone database.

The LPC analysis is used for two purposes. First, it allows separating the source (excitation) from the filter (formants) within the limits of linear model. Applying pitch and duration modification to the LPC residual allows introducing less distortion in modified speech. Second, the LPC coefficients are used for evaluating the spectral distance between two diphones during diphone candidate selection at synthesis.

During synthesis, the diphone candidates are selected by dynamic programming algorithm that minimizes the cumulative sum of unit join costs. Currently only spectral distance estimate is used for join costs. The selected diphones are then pitch-synchronously concatenated and the LPC residual signal is modified to the target pitch and duration by overlap-add method. The waveform is generated by LPC synthesis.

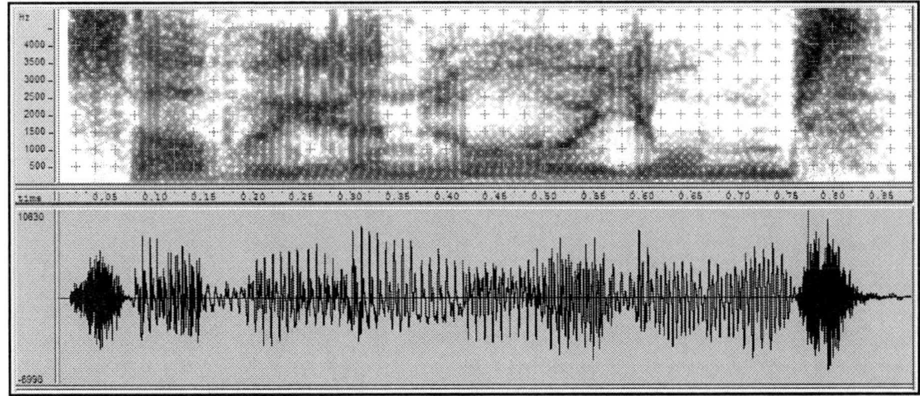

Figure 1. The spectrogram and waveform of a synthesized word /*savienuojums*/ (connection). Random diphone variations are chosen. Note the discontinuities.

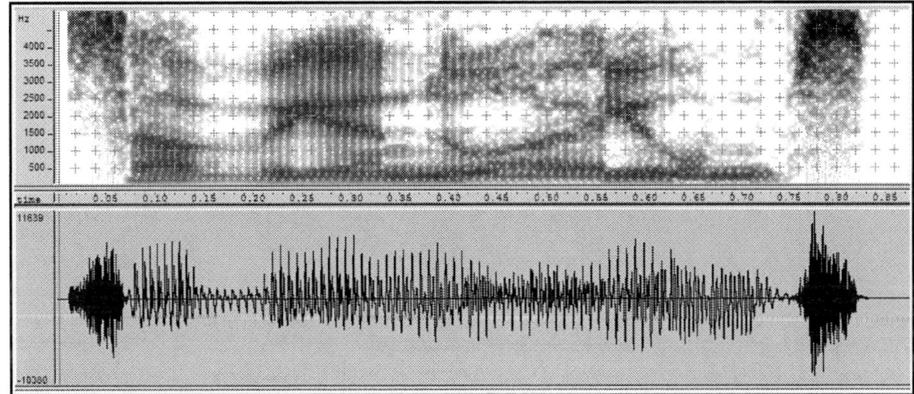

Figure 2. The spectrogram and waveform of a synthesized word /*savienuojums*/ (connection). LPC coefficient-based diphone selection is used. Note the smooth concatenation at diphthong /*ie*/ and the discontinuities at diphthong /*uo*/.

3   Conclusions and further work

The Latvian TTS system described in this paper currently is being beta tested in real usage scenarios. Feedback from the first users is very positive. They characterize generated speech as natural-sounding, with correct Latvian pronunciation of majority of phrases and efficient work even on relatively old systems (200 MHz Pentium processor). The project demonstrates applicability of diphone synthesis in combination with such speech quality improvements as usage of multiple diphone variations and LPC residual modification.

The combined approach of diphone synthesis and unit selection provides a good compromise between the speed and the effectiveness of speech synthesis, and the quality of the produced speech:

- Increasing the variety of vowel and consonant pronunciation,

- Decreasing the spectral discontinuity between adjacent diphones (for comparison, see Figure 1 and Figure 2),

- Enabling "reconstruction" of longer speech units what were adjacent in speech material used for diphone extraction.

However, Latvian prosody is not yet fully developed. The simplified phrase prosody model shows good results with relatively short sentences. Such sentences are frequent when screen reading software is used by visually impaired people for interface with computer. However, it is more difficult to follow such synthetic voice for longer and more complex sentences.

Further work will concentrate on development of the speech rhythm and intonation model, evaluation of the resulting system and the implemented improvements in comparison to the classical diphone synthesis, and integration of the speech synthesizer with different application scenarios.

Kārlis Goba and Andrejs Vasiļjevs

References

Ilze Auzina. 2005. *Computer Modelling of Latvian Pronunciation: synopsis of doctoral thesis*. Riga, Latvia.

Hiroya Fujisaki, 2004. *Information, Prosody, and Modelling with Emphasis on Tonal Features of Speech*. Speech Prosody 2004, Nara, Japan.

Juris Grigorjevs. 2005. *Acoustic and Auditory Characteristics of Latvian Vowel System: synopsis of doctoral thesis*. Riga, Latvia.

Xuedong Huang, Alex Acero, Hsiao-Wuen Hon. 2001. *Spoken Language Processing. A Guide to Theory, Algorithm, and System Development*. Prentice Hall.

Alise Laua. 1997. *Latviešu literārās valodas fonētika (Phonetics of literary Latvian), 4th edition*. Riga.

Edmilson Morais and Fĩbio Violaro. 2005. *Data-Driven Text-to-Speech Synthesis*. XXII Simpósio Brasileiro de Telecomunicações, Campinas, Brazil.

Evaluating Stages of Development in Second Language French: A Machine-Learning Approach

Jonas Granfeldt
Centre for languages and literature
Lund university
Box 201, S-221 00 Lund, Sweden
`jonas.granfeldt@rom.lu.se`

Pierre Nugues
Department of Computer science
Lund Institute of Technology
Box 118, S-221 00 Lund, Sweden
`Pierre.Nugues@cs.lth.se`

Abstract

This paper describes a system to define and evaluate development stages in second language French. The identification of such stages can be formulated as determining the frequency of some lexical and grammatical features in the learners' production and how they vary over time. The problems in this procedure are threefold: identify the relevant features, decide on cutoff points for the stages, and evaluate the degree of success of the model.

The system addresses these three problems. It consists of a morphosyntactic analyzer called Direkt Profil and a machine-learning module connected to it. We first describe the usefulness and rationale behind its development. We then present the corpus we used to develop the analyzer. Finally, we present new and substantially improved results on training machine-learning classifiers compared to previous experiments (Granfeldt et al., 2006). We also introduce a method to select attributes in order to identify the most relevant grammatical features.

1 Introduction

Since the beginning of systematic research in second language acquisition (SLA) in the 1970s, one line of investigation was to identify and analyze stages of development that learners pass through when acquiring a second or a foreign language. See Sharwood-Smith and Truscott (2005) for a re-cent discussion. Stage identification can be applied to data from all linguistic levels, but it is perhaps most interesting for the development of morphology and syntax. Within SLA, the learner's internal grammar is considered as its own system, an interlanguage grammar, that develops and restructures over time (Selinker, 1972). The objective of this research is to determine and model the growth of the learner's grammar, where the identification of relevant grammatical features, the definition of development stages, and their evaluation are complex tasks requiring a systematic methodology (Ellis and Barkhuizen, 2005), pp. 97–98.

In this paper, we describe and evaluate a system that has fully automated this process. As possible applications for it, we can think of diagnostic tools for assessing language development and we hope that both learners and teachers will find it useful in this respect. However, we focus here on how our system, and more generally the methodology we propose, can assist researchers when working with grammatical stages. In order to understand its relevance, we begin with a simplified description of how stage identification is commonly carried out in the field of SLA.

2 Background

2.1 Current methodology for identifying stages of development

The first step to identify stages of development is to determine and extract grammatical features in the production (oral or written) of a representative population of learners. The selection of features can

Joakim Nivre, Heiki-Jaan Kaalep, Kadri Muischnek and Mare Koit (Eds.)
NODALIDA 2007 Conference Proceedings, pp. 73–80

be theoretically or empirically motivated, the crucial point being that the selected features have a content validity, i.e. that they are features whose realizations can translate a qualitative change in the learner's grammar. A second step is to understand and model the development of these features over time. Some linguistic features show a straightforward linear development, i.e. the scores for adequate use of the feature increases steadily with time at some observable rate. Other features show a nonlinear, sometimes U-shaped, development where the scores initially are high and then decrease in a second phase, only to regain a high level of correctness in a third phase.

Once the developmental trajectories are known, a third step is to decide on cutoff points in the data where the learner has reached a new stage of development. Most researchers work on several grammatical features at the same time, a procedure sometimes referred to as grammatical profiling. This means that the establishment of a stage of development has to take into consideration the analysis of a large number of categories.

2.2 Some problems with the current methodology

A necessary component in the method described above is an in-depth morphosyntactic analysis of the language samples produced by the learners. In our case, these are written texts but they might also be transcriptions of oral productions. Most analysts working with first and second language acquisition have now access to relatively large amounts of machine-readable data (large in SLA terms). It is also common for widespread languages, like English and French, to use tools such as morphological parsers and part-of-speech taggers (MacWhinney, 2000). These tools can considerably reduce the otherwise very time-consuming analysis step.

But even so, a lot of manual analysis is left to be done. First there is currently no reliable automated tool to parse learner's data although there have been some attempts for English (Sagae et al., 2005). For French, some of the linguistic structures and features used in grammatical profiling can be captured using available part-of-speech taggers and morphological parsers. But other more complex structures such as the agreement between constituents can-

not. Another problem in grammatical profiling is that current tools usually work on one single feature at the time in a pipeline architecture, while one needs to analyze a large number of phenomena at the same time. A third problem concerns the artificiality in identifying stages (Ellis and Barkhuizen, 2005), p.98.

The result of the morphosyntactic analysis is typically a frequency analysis of certain features. For a particular linguistic phenomenon, say 3rd person agreement in the present tense, a typical procedure is to identify the different realizations of the phenomena and count them. The compiled data for all the features are then often inspected intuitively in order to identify suitable stages of development. In the SLA domain, there are currently multiple ways of dealing with this step and there has not been any principled evaluation of them. A possible reason for this is that there is currently no framework that has connected any sophisticated statistical treatment to the first two steps: the morphosyntactic analysis and the frequency count. If a fully automated processing pipeline were available, all steps in this tricky process could be evaluated more thoroughly.

We report here the current status of our system that aims at overcoming the methodological problems discussed above. The rest of the paper is organized as follows. We begin by summarizing briefly the previous work on the morphosyntactic development of second language French. Then we describe the corpus we are using to develop the analyzer to extract the grammatical features and constructions. The analyzer, called Direkt Profil, is also presented briefly. In the last sections, we discuss our machine-learning approach to identify the stages of development and select attributes and we present our current results.

3 Morphosyntactic development of second language French

Studies on the morphosyntactic development of second language French have to a large extent been empirically driven. One of their specific aims was the identification of a large number of developmentally related grammatical features and constructions along with hypotheses about their sequence of acquisition. The study by Bartning and Schlyter

Stages	1	2	3	4	5	6
% of finite forms of lexical verbs in obligatory contexts	50-75	70-80	80-90	90-98	100	100
% of 1st person plural S-V agreement (*nous V-ons*)	–	70-80	80-95	100	100	100
% 3rd pers plural agreement with irregular lexical verbs like *viennent, veulent, prennent*	–	–	a few cases	≈ 50	few errors	100
Object pronouns (placement)	–	SVO	S(v)oV	SovV app.	SovV prod	acquired (also *y* and *en*)
% of grammatical gender agreement	55-75	60-80	65-85	70-90	75-95	90-100

Table 1: Developmental sequences from Bartning and Schlyter (2004). Legend: – = no occurrences; app = appears; prod = productive advanced stage.

(2004) is an example of it for spoken French, where the authors identified some 25 different morphosyntactic features and proposed a definition of their development over time in adult Swedish learners. Taken together, these features delineate six stages of development in the shape of grammatical profiles – ranging from beginners to very advanced learners. Examples of features are shown in Table 1. As the language learner moves towards an increasing automation of the target language, the produced structures become more frequent, more complex, and more appropriate. Developmental sequences describe this process in linguistic terms.

4   The CEFLE Corpus

To develop our analyzer (see Sect. 5) and to test the machine-learning approach to stages of development, we used the Lund CEFLE Corpus (*Corpus Écrit de Français Langue Étrangère*) (Ågren, 2005). CEFLE consists of texts in French as a foreign language written by 85 Swedish students with different levels of proficiency. It contains approximately 400 texts and 100,000 words. It also features a control group of 22 French native speakers. CEFLE was compiled throughout the academic year 2003/2004. During this period, each student wrote four or five texts in French at two months intervals. The aim of this study was to analyze the morphosyntactic development in written production.

For the present study, we used a random selection of 317 texts from the CEFLE corpus, see Table 2.

A member of the team annotated one text from each learner using the criteria in Bartning and Schlyter (2004) and classified it according to the developmental stage the text was reflecting. For our current experiments (see below), we subsequently assigned the same classification to the three or four other texts of the same learner in the CEFLE corpus. The assumption behind the decision to propagate the stage of development from one annotated text to all the texts of the same learner is that a learner generally does not move up to the next stage during the short period under which the collection of the texts took place.

5   Direkt Profil

Direkt Profil (Granfeldt et al., 2005; Granfeldt et al., 2006) is a morphosyntactic analyzer designed for French as a second language. The initial aim was to implement the grammatical features and constructions in Table 1. In the current version of the system, a few features are still lacking but there is also a great number of additional ones that were not present from the beginning. The system has been presented in some detail in previous papers and we only give a brief description of the main parts.

Verb groups and noun groups represent the essential grammatical support of the profile classification. The majority of syntactic annotation standards for French take such groups into account in one way or another. However, in their present shape, these standards are insufficient to mark up constructions

CEFLE corpus			**Selection of CEFLE used** (averages)		
Task name	Elicitation type	Words		Text length	Sent. length
Homme	Pictures	17,260	Stage 1 (N=23)	78	6.9
Souvenir	Pers. Narrative	14,365	Stage 2 (N=98)	161	8.4
Italie	Pics	30,840	Stage 3 (N=97)	212	9.8
Moi	Pers. Narrative	30,355	Stage 4 (N=58)	320	11.6
Total		92,820	Control (N=41)	308	15.2

Table 2: General description of the CEFLE corpus and the selection used in the experiments reported in this paper.

of Table 1, many of which are specific to foreign language writers. On the basis of the linguistic constructions in Bartning and Schlyter (2004), we developed our own annotation scheme. The current version of Direkt Profil, v. 2.1, detects three types of syntactic groups, nonrecursive noun groups, verb groups, prepositional groups, and conjunctions, that it annotates using the XML format.

Direkt Profil applies a cascade of three sets of rules to produce the four layers of annotations. The first unit segments the text in words. An intermediate unit identifies the prefabricated expressions. The third unit annotates simultaneously the parts of speech and the groups. Finally, the engine creates a group of results and connects them to a profile. The analyzer uses manually written rules and a lexicon of inflected terms. The recognition of the group boundaries is done by a set of closed-class words and the heuristics inside the rules. It should be noted that the engine neither annotates all the words, nor all segments. It considers only those, which are relevant for the determination of the stage. The engine applies the rules from left to right then from right to left to solve certain problems of agreement.

The current version of Direkt Profil is available online from this address: http://www.rom.lu.se:8080/profil. The performance of Direkt Profil version 1.5.2 was evaluated in Granfeldt et al. (2005). The results showed an overall F-measure of 0.83 (precision and recall).

6   A machine-learning approach to evaluate stages of development

The frequency count of the grammatical constructions and features form a basis to establish general stages of development. In our system, the frequency analysis is obtained automatically as the output from Direkt Profil.

One core problem in this last step of the procedure is that the data from the frequency analysis show a gradual increase that looks more like a development through continua than a development in discrete stages. Any definition of a stage will be to some extent arbitrary. Currently, there are a variety of methods that are used in field, but there is no principled way of evaluating these procedures. In the work of Bartning and Schlyter (2004), six stages of development were defined, five of which were subsequently identified by a human annotator in the CEFLE corpus. In the following section, we evaluate the probability of the existence of five different stages using machine-learning techniques.

6.1   First experiment: Classification analysis using all features

As experimental setup, we used the texts from each of the 85 learners that were manually assigned with their stage of development. The classification was done using the criteria in Table 1. Then we reused the same classification for the learner's three or sometimes four other texts in the CEFLE corpus, resulting in 276 classified texts. An additional 41 texts came from the control group of native speakers, resulting in a total of 317 classified texts.

We then used three machine-learning algorithms: the ID3/C4.5 algorithm (Quinlan, 1986), support vector machines (Boser et al., 1992), and logistic model trees (Landwehr et al., 2003). The training phase automatically induces classifiers from the selection of texts in the CEFLE corpus and the features we extract with the analyzer. We did all our exper-

	C4.5			SVM			LMT		
Stage	Precision	Recall	F-score	Precision	Recall	F-score	Precision	Recall	F-score
1–2	0.66	0.70	0.68	0.70	0.71	0.71	0.76	0.75	0.75
3–4	0.70	0.68	0.69	0.71	0.72	0.71	0.76	0.79	0.77
Control	0.71	0.66	0.68	0.70	0.63	0.67	0.89	0.83	0.86

Table 3: Results of the classification of texts into three stages for the three classifiers. Each classifier used 142 attributes and was trained on 317 texts from the CEFLE corpus.

iments with the Weka collection[1] of machine learning algorithms (Witten and Frank, 2005) and we evaluated them using the embedded 10-fold cross-validation.

We first clustered the five stages into three larger stages, where stages 1 and 2 together with stages 3 and 4 were into two stages and we trained the classifiers on them. We then ran a second evaluation with the original five stages. The results for the 317 texts and a feature vector consisting of 142 features are shown in Tables 4 and 5.

These results can be compared to those we obtained with a previous version of Direkt Profil (1.5.4) using a smaller number of features (33) and a smaller training corpus (80 texts). Those results (Granfeldt et al., 2006) showed that the best classifier at that point, SVM, obtained an average precision and recall in the vicinity of 70% for the three-stage classification, and an average of 43% precision and 36% recall in the five-stage classification. The current results with more than 100 more features and a nearly four times bigger training corpus show an improvement of nearly 10 percentage points. The currently best classifying algorithm, LMT, obtains an average precision and recall of 79% for the three-stage classification (Table 3). For the five-stage classification, the improvement is even greater. LMT obtains 62% precision and 59% recall. In comparing the two best performing algorithms, SVM and LMT, one observation is that LMT outperforms SVM on the intermediate and advanced stages of development – 3, 4, and the control group of native speakers – but not on the first two stages of development. We have currently no explanation for this fact.

In conclusion of this first experiment, we can say that the increased number of attributes and the larger training corpus resulted in better overall performance for all three classifiers. But the improvement was not as great as we expected. We suspected that with the introduction of more than 100 new features compared to our previous experiments, we also introduced some irrelevant features for the classification. We ran an attribute selection procedure in order to identify the best features at this point. The results of this second experiment are presented in the next section.

6.2 Second experiment: Classification analysis using attribute selection

To evaluate the 142 attributes, we measured the information gain for each attribute with respect to the class. This method is derived from ID3 and is part of the Weka software. We used the ranker search method that ranks individual attributes according to their evaluation. Tables 5 and 6 show the results for the top 10 and top 20 attributes according to the information gain evaluation method.

In the next step, we ran a new classification experiment using the same three algorithms as in the first experiment and the same selection of 317 texts from the CEFLE corpus. We first evaluated the performance of the classifiers using the top 10 attributes. The results for the five-stage classification are shown in Table 7.

This experiment produced mixed results. On an average, the radical reduction of the number of attributes from 142 to 10 does not seem to affect the results very much. The average precision and recall figures for LMT are respectively 66% and 58%. This would suggest that there is a lot of noise in the remaining 132 attributes. On the other hand, the results for the lowest stage of development deteriorate. The SVM algorithm does not identify one single text as being on stage 1 using the top 10 attributes. This would suggest that within the remain-

---

[1] Available from: http://www.cs.waikato.ac.nz/ml/weka/.

Stage	C4.5			SVM			LMT		
	Precision	Recall	F-score	Precision	Recall	F-score	Precision	Recall	F-score
1	0.37	0.42	0.39	0.54	0.58	0.56	0.44	0.33	0.38
2	0.50	0.52	0.51	0.60	0.60	0.60	0.59	0.61	0.60
3	0.42	0.46	0.44	0.45	0.46	0.45	0.51	0.54	0.53
4	0.48	0.38	0.42	0.52	0.50	0.51	0.64	0.66	0.65
Control	0.71	0.66	0.68	0.70	0.63	0.67	0.89	0.83	0.86

Table 4: Results of the classification of texts into five stages for the three classifiers. Each classifier used 142 attributes and was trained on 317 texts from the CEFLE corpus.

Avg. merit	Avg. rank	Attribute name
0.405	1.4	Percentage of Determiner-Noun sequences with agreement (number and gender)
0.354	2.2	Percentage unknown words
0.33	3.2	Percentage NPs with gender agreement
0.313	3.9	Percentage prepositions (out of all parts-of-speech)
0.311	4.3	Average sentence length
0.208	6.2	Percentage Noun-Adjective sequences with agreement (number and gender)
0.198	7.4	Percentage subject-verb agreement with modals + infinitive
0.187	8.3	Percentage subject-verb agreement in passé composé structures
0.177	9.3	Percentage subject-verb agreement with être/avoir in 3rd person plural
0.176	9.8	Percentage subject-verb agreement with modal verbs and pronominal subjects

Table 5: The top 10 attributes. Attributes 1–10

Avg. merit	Avg. rank	Attribute name
0.168	11.4	Percentage verbs in present tense (out of all tenses)
0.165	11.8	Percentage verbs in Passé composé (out of all tenses)
0.15	14	Percentage subject-verb agreement with modal verbs (all subjects)
0.142	15.7	Percentage subject-verb agreement with modal verbs in sg
0.14	16.2	Percentage subject-verb agreement with modal verbs in present tense and 3rd person pronominal subject
0.136	16.7	Percentage finite lexical verbs in finite contexts
0.133	17.3	Percentage subject-verb agreement with finite lexical verbs
0.131	18.1	Percentage subject-verb agreement with sg pronominal subjects and modal verbs
0.125	19.3	Percentage subject-verb with lexical verbs in 3rd person plural
0.116	21.4	Percentage subject-verb with pronominal subjects and être/avoir

Table 6: The 10 next attributes. Attributes 11–20

Stage	C4.5			SVM			LMT		
	Precision	Recall	F-score	Precision	Recall	F-score	Precision	Recall	F-score
1	0.46	0.46	0.46	0.00	0.00	0.00	0.78	0.29	0.42
2	0.50	0.49	0.49	0.53	0.72	0.61	0.57	0.70	0.63
3	0.43	0.42	0.43	0.50	0.43	0.46	0.55	0.49	0.52
4	0.50	0.57	0.53	0.62	0.71	0.66	0.63	0.64	0.63
Control	0.84	0.76	0.79	0.94	0.76	0.84	0.78	0.78	0.78

Table 7: Results of the classification of texts into five stages for the three classifiers. Each classifier used the top 10 attributes evaluated with the InfoGain method in Weka and was trained on 317 texts from the CEFLE corpus.

ing 132 attributes there are some attributes that are very important for identifying texts in stage 1. In our next evaluation, we therefore included the next 10 attributes in the attribute ranking (attributes 11–20) resulting in a feature vector of 20 attributes. The results for a five-stages classifications are shown in Table 8

Arguably, the overall results are better but the average for LMT actually shows a slight decrease compared to the previous experiment with only the top 10 features. All three classifiers identify texts on stage 1 using a feature vector with the top 20 features. We also note a difference in precision and recall figures for stage 1 using the ranked attributes. While these figures were relatively close in the first experiment using all 142 attributes (see Table 3 and Table 4), they are wide apart in the two following experiments (with recall figures being considerably lower than precision figures). This means that the recall quality depends on a much larger set of attributes for the lowest stage of development than for the other stages. Since the precision and recall figures for the other stages are close throughout, this could in turn mean that the stage 1 is the most heterogeneous stage.

7 Conclusion and future work

There is an ongoing discussion in the field of second language acquisition on the existence of discrete "stages" and how to define them, see for instance Sharwood-Smith and Truscott (2005). We believe that language development is systematic but always gradual if one looks close enough at the data. Our view is that developmental stages should reflect this property.

In this paper, we have presented and evaluated a system that can assist researchers in working with stages of development in second language French. The system consists of a morphosyntactic analyzer called Direkt Profil and a machine-learning module connected to it. A set of 317 texts from the CEFLE corpus was classified according to the stage of development they were reflecting. In classifying the texts, we built on previous research on morphosyntactic development in French second language. We extracted vectors of 142 features from the texts using the morphosyntactic analyzer we constructed. We then trained three different classifiers to evaluate the hypothesis that there were five stages of development represented in the material.

The results from a first classification experiment using a feature vector containing all the 142 features showed a substantial improvement of more than 10 percentage points compared to our previous results. For a three-stage classification, the average precision and recall figure for the system is now 79%. In trying to identify the most relevant features for classification, we used an attribute selection method based on the information gain and we identified two sets of top ranked attributes: the top ten attributes and the top twenty attributes. The results showed that while the overall performance was surprisingly not affected by the radical reduction of the number of attributes (from 142 to 10 and 20 respectively), the results for the lowest stage of development were affected very negatively. One conclusion at this point is that the stage 1 texts are very heterogeneous constructs to the point that it has to be questioned if they have an independent status.

From the results on the morphosyntactic analysis

Stage	C4.5			SVM			LMT		
	Precision	Recall	F-score	Precision	Recall	F-score	Precision	Recall	F-score
1	0.56	0.38	0.45	0.60	0.38	0.46	0.53	0.38	0.44
2	0.51	0.53	0.52	0.61	0.62	0.62	0.61	0.61	0.61
3	0.49	0.47	0.48	0.54	0.57	0.56	0.56	0.59	0.57
4	0.45	0.55	0.50	0.61	0.69	0.65	0.61	0.62	0.62
Control	0.78	0.68	0.73	0.83	0.73	0.78	0.86	0.88	0.87

Table 8: Results of the classification of texts into five stages for the three classifiers. Each classifier used the top 20 attributes evaluated with the InfoGain method in Weka and was trained on 317 texts from the CEFLE corpus.

it is clear that there is room for improvement. We are currently looking into the possibility of using a statistical POS tagger and a chunker trained on an annotated corpus of native French. The preliminary results are encouraging despite the very different kinds of data (native and nonnative French).

Acknowledgments

The research presented here is supported by a grant from the Swedish Research Council, grant number 2004-1674 to the first author and by grants from the Elisabeth Rausing foundation for research in the Humanities and from Erik Philip-Sörenssens foundation for research.

References

Malin Ågren. 2005. Le marquage morphologique du nombre dans la phrase nominale. une étude sur l'acquisition du français L2 écrit. Technical report, Institut d'études romanes de Lund. Lund University.

Inge Bartning and Suzanne Schlyter. 2004. Stades et itinéraires acquisitionnels des apprenants suédophones en français L2. *Journal of French Language Studies*, 14(3):281–299.

Bernhard Boser, Isabelle Guyon, and Vladimir Vapnik. 1992. A training algorithm for optimal margin classifiers. In *Proceedings of the Fifth Annual Workshop on Computational Learning Theory*, pages 144–152, Pittsburgh. ACM.

Rod Ellis and Gary Barkhuizen. 2005. *Analysing learner language*. Oxford University Press, Oxford.

Jonas Granfeldt, Pierre Nugues, Emil Persson, Lisa Persson, Fabian Kostadinov, Malin Ågren, and Suzanne Schlyter. 2005. Direkt profil: A system for evaluating texts of second language learners of French based on developmental sequences. In *Proceedings of The Second Workshop on Building Educational Applications Using Natural Language Processing, 43rd Annual Meeting of the Association of Computational Linguistics*, pages 53–60, Ann Arbor, June 29.

Jonas Granfeldt, Pierre Nugues, Malin Ågren, Jonas Thulin, Emil Persson, and Suzanne Schlyter. 2006. CEFLE and Direkt Profil: A new computer learner corpus in French L2 and a system for grammatical profiling. In *Proceedings of the 5th International Conference on Language Ressources and Evaluation*, pages 565–570, Genoa, Italy, 22-28 May.

Niels Landwehr, Mark Hall, and Eibe Frank. 2003. Logistic model trees. In Nada Lavrac, Dragan Gamberger, Ljupco Todorovski, and Hendrik Blockeel, editors, *Proceedings of the 14th European Conference on Machine Learning (ECML)*, volume 2837 of *Lecture Notes in Computer Science*, pages 241–252. Springer.

Brian MacWhinney. 2000. *The CHILDES project: Tools for analyzing talk*. Lawrence Erlbaum, Mahwah, New Jersey.

John Ross Quinlan. 1986. Induction of decision trees. *Machine Learning*, 1(1):81–106.

Kenji Sagae, Alon Lavie, and Brian MacWhinney. 2005. Automatic measurement of syntactic development in child language. In *Proceedings of the 43rd Annual Meeting of the Association for Computational Linguistics 2005*, pages 197–2004, Ann Arbor, USA, June.

Larry Selinker. 1972. Interlanguage. *International Review of Applied Linguistics*, 10(3):209–231.

Michael Sharwood-Smith and John Truscott. 2005. Stages or continua in second language acquisition: A MOGUL solution. *Applied Linguistics*, 26(2):219–240.

Ian H. Witten and Eibe Frank. 2005. *Data Mining. Practical Machine Learning Tools and Techniques*. Elsevier, Amsterdam.

Clausal Coordinate Ellipsis in German:
The TIGER Treebank as a Source of Evidence

Karin Harbusch
University of Koblenz-Landau
Computer Science Department
Universitätsstraße 1
56070 Koblenz, GERMANY
`harbusch@uni-koblenz.de`

Gerard Kempen
Max Planck Institute for Psycholinguistics
PO Box 310
6500 AH Nijmegen
THE NETHERLANDS
`gerard.kempen@mpi.nl`

Abstract

Syntactic parsers and generators need high-quality grammars of coordination and coordinate ellipsis—structures that occur very frequently but are much less well understood theoretically than many other domains of grammar. Modern grammars of coordinate ellipsis are based nearly exclusively on linguistic judgments (intuitions). The extent to which grammar rules based on this type of empirical evidence generate all and only the structures in text corpora, is unknown. As part of a project on the development of a grammar and a generator for coordinate ellipsis in German, we undertook an extensive exploration of the TIGER treebank—a syntactically annotated corpus of about 50,000 newspaper sentences. We report (1) frequency data for the various patterns of coordinate ellipsis, and (2) several rarely (but regularly) occurring 'fringe deviations' from the intuition-based rules for several ellipsis types. This information can help improve parser and generator performance.

1 Introduction

Coordinate structures often license elision of all but one of a set of syntactic constituents that express the same conceptual structure. In example (1) (next page), the conceptual structure underlying *my sister* belongs to the meaning of both conjuncts but is expressed overtly only in the anterior conjunct. The presumed ellipsis site is indicated by dots. At that site, the elliptical conjunct 'BORROWS' its

overt counterpart from the parallel conjunct.

In this paper, we present frequency data for the various types of elliptical constructions in German—data extracted from the TIGER treebank (Brants *et al.*, 2004). The frequencies can help improve generator and parser performance by guiding the selection of elision sites (in generation) and the reconstruction of elided materials (in parsing).

In the course of this project, we observed rare but nevertheless systematic deviations from ellipsis rules reported in the literature. These observations necessitate amendments to these rules.

In Section 2, we present an overview of the main phenomena of coordinate ellipsis. Section 3 characterizes the TIGER treebank. In Section 4, we report the key results from our treebank exploration and discuss implications for the grammar and for sentence parsing and generating. Finally, Section 5 outlines options for future work.

2 Coordinate ellipsis: the main phenomena

In the linguistic literature on coordinate syntactic structures (for overviews, see Van Oirsow, 1987; Johannessen, 1998; Steedman, 2000; Sag, Wasow & Bender, 2003; Te Velde, 2006; and Kempen, in press), one often distinguishes four main types of coordinate ellipsis:[1]

---

[1]We will not deal with the elliptical constructions known as VP Ellipsis, VP Anaphora and Pseudogapping because they involve the generation of pro-forms instead of, or in addition to, the ellipsis proper. For example, *John laughed, and Mary did, too*—a case of VP Ellipsis—, includes the pro-form *did*. Nor do we deal with recasts of clausal coordinations as coordinate NPs (e.g., changing *John likes skating and Peter likes skiing* into *John and Peter like skating and skiing, respectively*). Presumably, such conversions involve a logical rather than a syntactic mechanism.

Joakim Nivre, Heiki-Jaan Kaalep, Kadri Muischnek and Mare Koit (Eds.)
NODALIDA 2007 Conference Proceedings, pp. 81–88

- Forward Conjunction Reduction (FCR),
- GAPPING, with three special variants called Long Distance Gapping (LDG), SUBGAPPING, and STRIPPING,
- Backward Conjunction Reduction (BCR; also known as Right Node Raising or RNR), and
- Subject Gap in clauses with Finite/Fronted verbs (SGF).

They are illustrated in the English sentences (1) through (7). The distinctions also hold for German.

(1) FCR: *My sister lives in Utrecht and ... works in Amsterdam*

(2) GAPPING: *Last year, John had an office in Leiden and ... Peter ... in Nijmegen*

(3) LDG: *My wife wants to buy a car and my son ... a motorcycle*

(4) SUBGAPPING: *The driver was killed and the passenger ... severely wounded*

(5) STRIPPING: *My sister lives in Utrecht and my brother ..., too*

(6) BCR: *Anne arrived before three ... and Susi left after four o'clock yesterday*

(7) SGF: *Why did you leave but didn't ... tell me?*

The main defining characteristics of these ellipsis types are as follows. Notice, in particular, the different borrowing patterns (described and empirically justified in detail by Kempen, in press).

- In FCR, the anterior and the posterior conjoined clauses each include an overt head verb (*lives* and *works* in (1)). Borrowing by the posterior conjunct is restricted to left-peripheral major constituents[2] shared by the conjuncts.
- In GAPPING, the posterior conjunct consists of one or more major constituents, each expressing a contrast with a major constituent in the anterior conjunct. The constituents of the posterior conjunct are often called REMNANTS. The posterior conjunct borrows obligatorily all and only those major constituents of the anterior conjunct that are non-contrastive, and this set must include the head verb (in (2): *last year*, *had* and *an*

---

[2] We use the term "major constituent" of a clause in a broad sense that includes head verb (main, copula or auxiliary), arguments (e.g. subject, direct and indirect object, and non-finite complement clause), adjuncts (adverbial modifier, including adverbial clause), and subordinating conjunctions (i.e. the complementizer in complement clauses—*that*, *whether*—or the subordinator in adverbial clauses—*while*, *although*, *when*, etc.

office). This characterization is also valid for LDG, Subgapping and Stripping (see below). An important exception applies to negation elements, which are not always borrowed and are usually repeated in the posterior conjunct:

(8) *Hans wohnt nicht in Paris und Peter <u>nicht</u>*
Hans lives not in Paris and Peter not
in Rom
in Rome
'Hans doesn't live in Paris and Peter doesn't in Rome'.

- In LDG, the posterior conjunct consists of constituents whose left-hand counterparts belong to different clauses. *My son* in (3) is the counterpart of *my wife* in the main clause whereas *a motorcycle* pairs up with *a car* in the infinitival complement clause.
- SUBGAPPING is a special case of simple Gapping: the posterior conjunct includes one major constituent in the form of a non-finite complement clause ("VP"; *severely wounded* in (4)).
- STRIPPING is Gapping with the posterior conjunct consisting of one constituent only. This remnant is not a verb, and it is often supplemented by a modifier (such *too* in (5), *in particular*, or Ger. *zwar* 'more precisely').
- In BCR, the anterior conjunct borrows one or more—complete or partial—right-peripheral constituents from the posterior one (*o'clock* and *yesterday* in (6)).
- SGF is a coordination of MAIN clauses where the anterior conjunct exhibits subject-verb inversion (*did you* instead of *you did* in (7)), and the posterior conjunct borrows the anterior clause's subject NP. The posterior clause starts with the finite head verb, optionally borrowing the clause-initial (left-peripheral) modifier (if any—an adverbial phrase or clause, or a prepositional phrase). No other constituents are borrowable.

Modern grammars of coordinate ellipsis are based nearly exclusively on linguistic judgments (intuitions). The extent to which grammar rules based on this type of empirical evidence generate all and only the structures that populate text corpora, is unknown. The recent availability of the TIGER treebank (Brants *et al.*, 2004) enabled us to explore this question as part of a project on the development of a grammar and a generator for coordinate ellipsis in German and Dutch (Kempen, in press; Harbusch & Kempen, 2006).

3 A corpus study of clausal coordinate ellipsis in German

3.1 TIGER: Characterization and annotation

The TIGER Treebank (Release 2) contains 50.474 German syntactically annotated sentences from a German newspaper corpus. As illustrated in Figures 1 and 2, TIGER's annotation scheme uses many clause-level grammatical functions (subject, direct and indirect object, complement, modifier, etc.; depicted as edge labels in the sentence diagrams). Important for present purposes, elided (i.e. borrowed) constituents in coordinate clauses are represented by so-called SECONDARY EDGES, also labelled with a grammatical function. This feature facilitates well-targeted automatic recognition and extraction of syntactic trees that embody various types of coordinate ellipsis. Secondary edges are represented by curved arrows in TIGER tree diagrams such as Figures 1 and 2.

In TIGER's syntactic trees, the following types of coordination are distinguished:

- CAC: coordinated adpositions,
- CAP: coordinated adjectival phrases,
- CAVP: coordinated adverbial phrases,
- CCP: coordinated complementizer phrases (subordinating conjunctions),
- CNP: coordinated noun phrases,
- CO: coordination of "unlikes", i.e. of different categories (e.g. an AP and a PP)
- CS: coordinated finite clauses,
- CVP: coordinated verb phrases (non-finite clauses), and
- CVZ: coordinated infinitival clauses (VPs) with the head verb preceded by *zu* 'to' (as in *zu tun* 'to do').

Within a coordinate structure, the conjuncts are dominated by a CJ edge, and the coordinating conjunction by a CD edge. In the current project, we focus attention on the three latter types: coordinated finite and non-finite (including infinitival) clauses.

The three bottom rows of Table 1 show that 7194 corpus sentences—about 14 percent—include at least one clausal coordination, and that in more than half of these (4046) one or more constituents have been elided and need to be borrowed from the other conjunct. According to Brants *et al.* (2004: p.

599), "secondary edges are only employed for the annotation of coordinated sentences and verb phrases"—CS, CVP and CVZ.[3] Nevertheless, secondary edges occasionally turn up as parts of non-clausal coordination types—see the shaded cells of Table 1. However, ellipsis in non-clausal coordinate structures is not annotated systematically.

We deployed the TIGERSearch tool (König & Lezius, 2003)

- to design queries that retrieve all clausal coordinations (whether elliptical or not), and
- to classify the elliptical ones (those including one or more secondary edges) into one of the seven (sub)types of clausal coordinate ellipsis.

We took into consideration all clausal coordinations, including asyndetic ones (lacking an overt coordinating conjunction), and those consisting of more than two conjuncts. To simplify the computational corpus explorations, we assume that the treebank does not contain sentences from which secondary edges are missing.

Table 1. Number of TIGER sentences that include one or more coordinations of the type mentioned in the first column. The two rightmost columns indicate how many sentences contain at least one secondary edge.

Coordination type	Total	With secondary edge	
		Forward	Backward
CAC	30	0	0
CAP	2170	2	1
CAVP	204	0	0
CCP	2	0	0
CNP	10282	0	3
CO	374	3	0
CPP	1250	5	2
CS	5607	3150	343
CVP	1564	466	86
CVZ	23	1	0

(9) *Monopole sollen geknackt und Märkte*
Monopolies should shattered and markets
getrennt werden
split be
'Monopolies should be shattered and markets split'

Figure 1 shows the tree diagram for example (9)—

---

[3]We brought the TIGER structures annotated as CS, CVP and CVZ together under the heading of (non-)finite coordinated clauses. The left- and right-peripherality patterns of CVP and CVZ coordinations were checked by hand.

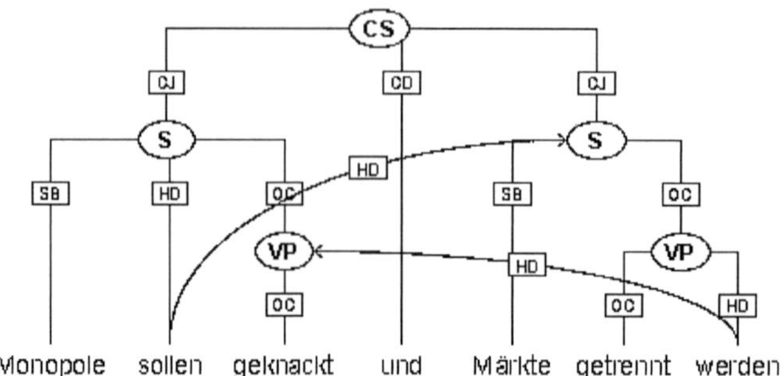

Figure 1. Tree diagram for example (9): Subgapping combined with BCR. The two remnants of the posterior clause are the NP *Märkte* and the VP (non-finite clause) *getrennt werden*. Abbreviations for edge labels: SB=subject, HD=head, OC=object complement, CD=coordinating conjunction, CJ=conjunct.

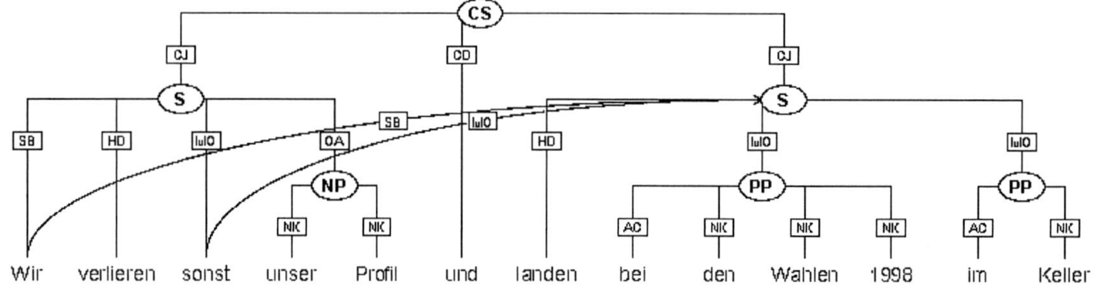

Figure 2. Tree diagram for FCR example (10): The posterior clause is headed by the overt finite verb *landen* and borrows its subject *wir* from the left. For the secondary edge dominating the adverbial modifier *sonst*, see the discussion in Section 3.2. Abbreviations: OA=direct object, NK=noun kernel/modifier, AC=adpositional case marker.

Table 2. Number of TIGER sentences with at least one clausal coordination, each sentence containing one or more secondary edges labelled with one of seven important grammatical functions. The total number of sentences with at least one clausal coordination (elliptical or non-elliptical) is shown within parentheses. Hence, the first number in a cell denotes a set of sentences that is a subset of the set denoted by the number in parentheses. The grey cells indicate borrowings that are either ruled out by the definition of the ellipsis type, or are entailed by the definition. E.g., SGF entails a secondary edge dominating the subject of the anterior clause, and rules out borrowings of constituents other than adverbial modifiers. The set of seven grammatical functions is not exhaustive because TIGER's annotation scheme distinguishes more grammatical functions than the seven listed here. As many TIGER sentences embody more than one clausal coordination, the numbers in a column do not add up to the total in the top row.

Borrowed (elided) constituent	Type of clausal coordinate ellipsis			
	FCR **N=2545**	**Gapping** **N=678**	**SGF** **N=384**	**BCR** **N=413**
Head verb of clause		678 (678)		22 (392)
Subject	1772 (2147)	208 (595)	384 (384)	27 (228)
Direct Object	10 (154)	6 (26)		1 (19)
Indirect Object	207 (1379)	55 (195)		24 (122)
Modifier	625 (1897)	197 (551)	157 (359)	73 (295)
Complementizer	433 (456)	9 (11)		0 (6)
Particle of separable verb	0 (193)	16 (22)		16 (21)

a clausal coordination which combines Subgapping with BCR. The forward pointing curved arrow emanating from the terminal node *sollen* 'should' indicates that the posterior clause is lacking its auxiliary and borrows it from the anterior clause. The backward pointing arrow is the secondary edge that denotes borrowing of the auxiliary *werden* 'be' by the anterior clause. Notice that secondary edges do not indicate the position of the borrowed constituent in the borrowing clause.

3.2 A methodological issue: Coordinate ellipsis vs. plausible conceptual inference

Figure 2 depicts FCR in sentence (10), which embodies a problematic aspect of the annotation in terms of secondary edges.

(10) *Wir verlieren sonst   unser Profil und*
    we lose   otherwise our   profile and
    landen bei den Wahlen 1998 im   Keller.
    end-up at the   elections 1998 in-the cellar
    'Otherwise, we lose our profile and end up in
    the cellar at the 1998 elections'

In FCR, borrowing is restricted to left-peripheral major constituents of the anterior clause (see the FCR borrowing rule in Section 2). In (10), the left periphery only includes the subject NP *wir* because the conjuncts start to deviate already at the position of the finite verbs (*verlieren* 'lose' versus *landen* 'end up'). Hence, borrowing of the post-verbal modifier *sonst* 'otherwise' seems to violate the FCR borrowing rule. However, borrowing should be distinguished from PLAUSIBLE CONCEPTUAL INFERENCE. The fact that readers of sentence (10) tend to interpret *sonst* as modifying the posterior conjunct, is based on semantic/pragmatic knowledge rather than on knowledge of syntax. There are no SYNTACTIC reasons to include *sonst* as part of the posterior conjunct: Without this modifier, the conjunct would not be ungrammatical. In contrast, the inclusion of *wir* IS needed to complete the clause headed by *landen*: Without a subject NP, this active finite clause would be ill-formed.

This calls for an evaluation of the status of secondary edges: If the syntactic well-formedness of a conjunct is not affected by removing such an edge, we consider it a case of plausible conceptual inference rather than borrowing licensed by coordinate ellipsis. (This holds for the borrowing of *sonst* in (10).) Only if removal of the edge would make the

conjunct ungrammatical (e.g., due to incompleteness of the subcategorization frame of a verb), we classify the edge as a case of genuine coordinate ellipsis (e.g., the borrowing of *wir* in (10)).

When classifying the secondary edges in each of the coordinate ellipsis types, we proceeded as follows.

GAPPING AND ITS SUBTYPES. The borrowing rule for these cases states that all non-contrastive major constituents are borrowed, except for negation elements (annotated by an NG edge). So we only needed to check whether the anterior clause included any non-contrastive major constituent that was not annotated as a secondary edge.

FCR. Left-peripheral borrowing of major constituents is mandatory here. Hence, in every FCR case, we determined the anterior clause's left-periphery, that is, the string from the leftmost major constituent up to and including the rightmost major constituent dominated by a secondary edge. If this string includes one or more major constituents without a secondary edge, this was counted as a potential violation of the borrowing rule. In Figure 2, the left-periphery consists of *wir verlieren sonst*, with *verlieren* indicating a potential borrowing violation. For all such patterns, we judged whether or not the secondary edges could denote plausible conceptual inferences. If so, the left periphery was readjusted by hand. For instance, as we judged *sonst* to be a plausible inference, the left periphery was reduced to *wir*, implying that the borrowing pattern in this sentence agrees with the rule.

BCR. For this ellipsis variant, we used the following definition of the right-periphery of the posterior clause: an uninterrupted string of major constituents dominated by secondary edges, extending backward from the end of the clause. We dealt with right-peripheral borrowings as if they were the mirror image of left-peripheral borrowing—though with an important exception: The leftmost constituent of the right-periphery need not be a complete major constituent (e.g. *o'clock* in (6)).

SGF. In addition to the subject NP, the posterior conjunct may only borrow—optionally—the clause-initial modifier of the anterior conjunct (e.g. *why* in (7)). So, the only possible violations of this rule are: borrowings of another type of major constituent, or of only a fragment of the clause-initial adverbial modifier, or of a constituent located to the right of the head verb. In such cases, we judged whether the corresponding secondary edge could be based on plausible conceptual inference rather than coordinate ellipsis.

We realize that the distinction between two types of secondary edges as well as the criteria we used to classify them, are 'friendly' to the rather strict intuition-based borrowing rules put forward in Section 2. The annotators seem to have made their secondary-edge decisions on the basis of a much more liberal borrowing regimen. However, we reasoned it is good methodology to start from a more restrictive, more parsimonious theory and to adopt a less parsimonious one only after the more restrictive theory has been falsified.

4 Results

As can be gleaned from Table 1 in Section 2, TIGER contains 7194 sentences that include at least one clausal coordination, and 4046 of them have been annotated with one or more secondary edges in coordinated clauses. We classified each of these edges as representing genuine coordinate borrowings or plausible inferences. In the course of this process, we removed 26 sentences, chiefly for one of two reasons: The sentence includes an annotation error, or all of its secondary edges were deemed to represent plausible conceptual inference rather than ellipsis. The remaining 4020 TIGER sentences exhibit at least one exemplar of a genuine coordinate elliptical clausal structure. Actually, all seven main and subtypes of coordinate ellipsis are represented in the corpus. See the first row of Table 2 for the number of sentences exhibiting one of the four main ellipsis types.

We used the set of 4020 sentences to try and answer the following two questions:

- How accurately do the borrowing rules postulated in linguistic grammars—and used in computational parsers and generators—mirror the borrowing patterns observable in real texts? (In the absence of a treebank for spoken corpora, our answer will be restricted to *written* texts.)
- How can the frequencies of the various borrowing patterns help parsers to reconstruct borrowed (elided) constituents more accurately, and generators to produce more natural sounding and more easily interpretable coordinations of elliptical clauses?

These questions are discussed in separate Sections.

4.1 Correctness of the borrowing rules

After removing secondary edges that we judged to represent plausible conceptual inference, and readjusting left- or right-peripheries, we observed that in about 99 percent of the sentences the borrowing patterns agree with the intuition-based rules. Hence, we may conclude that these rules are not far off the mark. Nevertheless, we spotted some 40 sentences that violate a borrowing rule but, according to our judgment, are at least marginally acceptable. We discovered four borrowing (elision) patterns that may be characterized as 'fringe deviations' from the intuition-based coordinate ellipsis rules. Each of the offending patterns that we report here, is embodied in several sentences, hence is unlikely to reflect bad writing or sloppy editing.

OVERREDUCTION: In Gapping, FCR or SGF, only part of a major constituent is elided. In examples (11) and (12), both combining Gapping with BCR, the head noun of one remnant (of the subject of the posterior conjunct) is elided (indicated by strikethroughs). Furthermore, TIGER includes at least four sentences where the head of the PP is missing from the posterior conjunct. In (13), this holds for *aus* 'from'.

(11) *...während bei der Sparkasse X Gebühren von 50 und bei der Bank Y sogar ~~Gebühren~~ von 60 Mark zu berappen sind*
'... whereas at Savings Bank X fees of 50 and at Bank Y even ~~fees~~ of 60 Mark have to be coughed up'

(12) *Dabei schrumpfte der Auftragseingang aus dem Inland um drei und ~~der Auftragseingang~~ aus dem Ausland um vier Prozent*
'Moreover, the number of domestic orders shrank with three and ~~the number of orders~~ from abroad with four percent'

(13) *Das Anzeigengeschäft trug dazu 36 Prozent bei, aus dem Vertrieb kamen 34 Prozent und ~~aus~~ dem Druck 21 Prozent herein*
'The Advertising Department contributed 36 percent, 34 percent came in from Sales and 21 percent from Printing'

PERIPHERALITY VIOLATIONS BY LITTLE WORDS. In at least 10 FCR sentences, the third-person reflexive pronoun *sich* ('himself, herself, themselves') is located within the left-periphery of the anterior conjunct. In (14), *sich* is 'too late' to be shared by the other conjunct. (The end of the left-peripheral region is indicated by slashes "//".) In (15), it is 'too early': It could be shared by the second conjunct, which however cannot use a reflexive pronoun. We also found a comparable case with pronominal NP *dies* 'this' and one with *niemals* 'never'.

The treebank contains one analogous example with BCR. In (16), the particle *an* causes a right-peripherality violation. The finite verb *berechnen* 'compute' is not a separable verb and does not have *an* as particle. However, it does need a direct object. This is elided here due to BCR, although its counterpart in the posterior clause is not right-peripheral.

(14) *... während // 78 Prozent <u>sich</u> für Bush und vier Prozent für Clinton aussprachen*
'... while 78 percent expressed themselves in favor of Bush and four percent for Clinton'

(15) *... daß <u>sich</u> weiß // davon am besten abhebt und von den Autofahrern am ehesten gesehen wird*
'... that [the color] white gives the better contrast and can be seen faster by the drivers'

(16) *[Sensoren ...] berechnen ~~die neue Position im Media-Land~~ und zeigen die neue Position im Media-Land <u>an</u>*
'[Sensors ...] compute and indicate the new position in Media-Land'

PERIPHERALITY VIOLATIONS BY CONTENT WORDS OR WORD GROUPS. In three sentences, a peripherality rule was violated by a content word, a word group, or even an entire subordinate clause. In FCR example (17), the posterior clause *noch immer gewährt* 'is still granting' borrows the direct object NP *Unterschlupf* 'shelter', implying that the left periphery is located to its right. This entails borrowing of PP *in der Vergangenheit* 'in the past', which however is semantically incompatible with the present tense of *gewährt* 'is granting'. In BCR sentence (18), the direct object NP *keine Garantie ...* 'no guarantee ...' borrowed by the anterior conjunct is not right-peripheral in the posterior conjunct but is followed there by the main verb *geben* and a complete extraposed complement clause. In BCR case (19), the passive auxiliary verb *werden* 'be' in the anterior conjunct is missing although a long extraposed PP follows its posterior counterpart. In TIGER, there are at least six BCR cases of the latter type (an extraposed constituent rightward of the presumed right periphery).

(17) *... das in der Vergangenheit so blutrünstigen Figuren [...] Unterschlupf // gegeben hatte bzw. noch immer gewährt*
'... which in the past had given shelter to bloodthirsty characters [...], resp. is still granting it'

(18) *Es gibt ~~keine Garantie dagegen daß [...]~~ und kann keine Garantie dagegen geben, daß [...]*
'There is ~~no guarantee~~ and there can be no guarantee that ...'

(19) *Nach und nach sollen dann auch Werke von exilierten Komponisten einbezogen ~~werden~~, der Aktionsradius erweitert werden auf Komponisten, die ...*
'By and by, works by exiled composers should be included, the radius of action extended to composers who ...'

SLOPPY GAPPING: remnants fulfilling a different grammatical function in the posterior conjunct than their counterpart in the anterior conjunct.[4] We found five cases (some perhaps intended as puns):

(20) *Es brachte [den SPD-Wirtschaftssprecher]_{direct object} [um seinen Job]_{modifier} und [der Öffentlichkeit]_{indirect object} [eine heftige Debatte]_{direct object}*
'It cost the SPD speaker for economy his job and brought the public a severe debate'

(21) *Auwälder dienen [dem Hochwasserschutz]_{indirect object} und [als Dschungel-Ersatz]_{modifier}*
'Riverside forests serve as protection against flooding and as jungle surrogate'

(22) Die Prinzessin erzählt im Fernsehen *[ihre Befindlichkeit]_{direct object}* und vielleicht auch *[von Männern]_{modifier}*
'On TV, the princess talks her sensitivities, and maybe also about men'

(23) *...1946 wurde er [Leiter ...]_{predicate} und [mit ... betraut]_{complement}*
'In 1946 he became head and was entrusted with ...'

---

[4] Sentences (20) through (24) cannot be analyzed as (non-clausal) 'coordinations of unlikes'. In such coordinations (a famous English example being *John is a Republican and proud of it*), the conjuncts are 'unlike' in that they embody constituents of different categories (NP and AP in the example). However, the unlike conjuncts should be adjacent AND fulfill the same grammatical function. This combination of criteria is not met by sentences (20) through (24).

(24) ... sie ... ziehen *[Grimassen]*_{direct object} und *[an den erkalteten Zigarillos]*_{modifier} ...
'... they make grimaces and draw on the dead cigarillos'

To conclude, although nearly all clausal elliptical coordinations obey the borrowing rules, the four groups of fringe deviations call for some relaxation.

4.2 Implications for grammar, parsing, and generation

An improved grammar rule for BCR seems to require a more general definition of 'end of clause': A clause ends not only after its last word but also at the position that serves as a receptacle for extraposed constituents (i.e. just before the word *yesterday* in (6)). Sentences (17) through (19) would be ruled in by this amendment. The borrowing rules for FCR and BCR may be allowed to overlook little words such as personal and reflexive pronouns, and verb particles. The other TIGER sentences cited in Section 4.1, however, seem to require more subtle finetuning.

Table 2 shows the borrowing (elision) frequencies of various grammatical functions in the four main types of clausal coordinate ellipsis. For example, the constituents most likely elided in FCR are the subject and the complementizer. This frequency information can help a chunker or shallow parser to reconstruct elided elements and thus to recover from parsing failure. This presupposes, of course, that the analyzer has been able to recognize the clausal coordination and the ellipsis type. Given the success of the strongly peripherality-oriented borrowing rules (Kempen, in press), they provide a sound basis for the design of efficient parsers for coordinate structures.

As for generation, elliptical coordinations figure prominently in several application domains, e.g. weather forecasting. More concise and more variegated texts can be produced if the generator is able to apply the various types of elision to non-reduced sentences which express the intended meaning (Harbusch & Kempen, 2006). In many sentences, for instance, Gapping and BCR form competing but mutually exclusive ways of avoiding unnecessary reduplication of sentence fragments. Frequency data such as those in Table 2 can help to select a natural sounding elision option.

5 Future work

Our evaluation study with the TIGER treebank revealed that the intuition-based borrowing (elision) rules summarized in Section 2 cover about 99 percent of the corpus sentences. One of our goals is to build an efficient parser that heavily relies on these rules in its treatment of coordinate structures. Another future project is to elicit from native speakers of German grammaticality judgments for sentences that embody the fringe deviations we discovered and reported in Section 4.1. The results will hopefully serve to finetune the borrowing rules.

References

Sabine Brants, Stefanie Dipper, Peter Eisenberg, Silvia Hansen-Schirra, Esther König, Wolfgang Lezius, Christian Rohrer, George Smith & Hans Uszkoreit (2004). TIGER: Linguistic Interpretation of a German Corpus. *Research on Language and Computation, 2,* 597-620.

Karin Harbusch & Gerard Kempen (2006). ELLEIPO: A module that computes coordinative ellipsis for language generators that don't. In: *EACL-2006: 11th Conference of the European Chapter of the Association for Computational Linguistics* (Trento, Italy; April 2006).

Janne B. Johannessen (1998). *Coordination.* Oxford: Oxford University Press.

Gerard Kempen (in press). Clausal coordination and coordinate ellipsis in a model of the speaker. *Linguistics.*

Esther König & Wolfgang Lezius (2003). The TIGER language – A Description Language for Syntax Graphs: Formal Definition. Tech. Rep. IMS, University of Stuttgart.

Ivan A. Sag, Thomas Wasow & Emily M. Bender (2003). Syntactic Theory: A formal introduction, Stanford: CSLI Publications, Second Edition.

Mark Steedman (2000). *The syntactic process.* Cambridge MA: MIT Press.

John R. te Velde (2006). *Deriving Coordinate Symmetries: A phase-based approach integrating Select, Merge, Copy and Match.* Amsterdam: Benjamins.

Robert R. van Oirsow (1987). *The syntax of coordination.* London: Croom Helm.

Widening the HolSum Search Scope

Martin Hassel and Jonas Sjöbergh
KTH CSC
{xmartin, jsh}@kth.se

Abstract

We investigate different areas of the high-dimensional vector space built by the automatic text summarizer HolSum, which evaluates sets of summary candidates using their similarity to the original text. Previously, the search for a good summary was constrained to a very limited area of the summary space. Since an exhaustive search is not reasonable we have sampled new parts of the space using randomly chosen starting points. We also replaced the simple greedy search with simulated annealing. A greedy search from the leading sentences still finds the best summary. Finally, we also evaluated a new word weighting scheme: the standard deviation of word distances, comparing it to the previously used $tf \cdot \log(idf)$ weighting. Different weighting schemes perform similarly, though the term frequency contributes more than other factors.

1 Language Independent Automatic Text Summarization

Today there is much research in automatic text summarization that is focused on knowledge-rich, and in practice language specific, methods. Methods using tools and annotated resources simply not available for many languages. Justifiably so, these knowledge-rich systems do in general perform better than earlier knowledge-poor approaches. It is however easy to see that there is a clear need for automatic summarization also for languages less in focus in this research area than the major European, Asian or Mid-Eastern languages.

One such attempt to develop a method for largely language independent automatic text summarization resulted in the HolSum summarizer (Hassel and Sjöbergh, 2005; Hassel and Sjöbergh, 2006), which can be implemented quickly using only a few very basic language resources. HolSum tries to capture the essence of a document being summarized by building a document space where a set of summary candidates can be evaluated against the original text. The HolSum summarizer thus takes the theoretically appealing approach of trying to optimize semantic similarity between the generated summary and the text being summarized, rather than lexical and syntactic similarity which many other systems and metrics do.

In this paper we evaluate several modifications to the HolSum approach, including changing the word space used and the search strategy for finding a good summary in the space of possible summary candidates.

2 Word Spaces

Word space models, most notably Latent Semantic Analysis (Deerwester et al., 1990; Landauer et al., 1998), enjoy considerable attention in current research on computational semantics. Since its introduction in 1990 Latent Semantic Analysis (LSA) has more or less spawned an entire research field. A wide range of word space models has since been developed, as well as numerous publications reporting exceptional results on many different tasks, such as information retrieval, various semantic knowledge tests, text categorization and word sense disambiguation.

The general idea behind word space models is to use statistics on word distributions in order to generate a high-dimensional vector space. In this vector space the words are represented by context vectors whose relative directions are assumed to indicate semantic similarity. The basis of this assumption is the *distributional hypothesis* (Harris, 1968), according to which words that occur in similar contexts also tend to have similar properties (meanings/functions). From this follows that if we repeatedly observe two words in the same (or very similar)

Joakim Nivre, Heiki-Jaan Kaalep, Kadri Muischnek and Mare Koit (Eds.)
NODALIDA 2007 Conference Proceedings, pp. 89–96

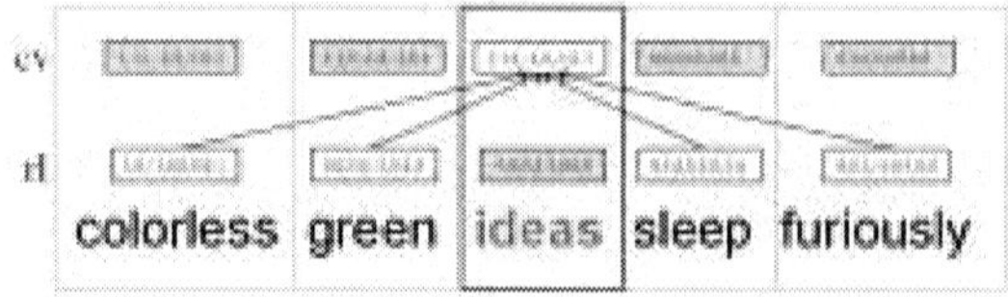

Figure 1: A Random Indexing context window focused on the token "ideas", taking note of the co-occurring tokens. The row marked as "cv" represents the continuously updated *context vectors* and the row marked as "rl" the static *random labels* (acting as addable meta words). Grayed out fields are not involved in the current token update.

contexts, then it is not too far fetched to assume that they also mean similar things (Sahlgren, 2006).

2.1 Random Indexing

In the HolSum summarizer the Random Indexing (Sahlgren, 2005) method is used to build a semantic vector space. This vector space is then used to choose a summary as close to the original text as possible from a set of summary candidates. Random Indexing (RI) presents an efficient, scalable and inherently incremental alternative to standard word space methods. As an alternative to LSA-like models that first construct a huge co-occurrence matrix and then perform the dimension reduction, Random Indexing instead accumulates context vectors continuously based on the occurrence of words (tokens) in contexts, without a need for a separate dimension reduction phase.

The construction of context vectors using RI can be viewed as a two-step process. First, each context (often each co-occurring word is considered a context) in the data is assigned a unique and (usually) randomly generated label. These labels can be viewed as sparse high-dimensional ternary vectors. [1] Their dimensionality (d) is usually chosen to be in the range of a couple of hundred up to several thousands, depending on the size and redundancy of the data you are working with. The labels consist of a very small number (usually about 1-2%) of randomly distributed +1s and -1s, with the rest of the elements of the vectors set to 0.

Next, the actual context vectors for the words are produced by scanning through the text and each time a token w occurs in a context (e.g. in a document or paragraph, or within a sliding context window), that

context's d-dimensional random label is added to the context vector for the token w. Thus, when using a sliding context window all tokens that appear within the context window contribute (to some degree) with their random labels to w's context vector. Words are then represented by d-dimensional context vectors that are the sums of the random labels of the co-occurring words, see Figure 1. When using a sliding context window it is also common to use some kind of distance weighting in order to give more weight to tokens closer in context.

One of the strengths of Random Indexing is that we can in a very elegant way fold the document currently being processed into the Random Index, thus immediately taking advantage of distributional patterns within the current document. This removes the problem of lack of data due to unknown words, since all words in the text will have been seen at least once (when the text itself was added to the Random Index). We also have a system that learns over time. Sparse data is still something of a problem though, since a never before seen word will only have as many contextual updates as the number of times it occurs in the current document. This is however better than no updates at all.

As with LSA-like models, for good performance Random Indexing needs large amounts of text (millions of words) when generating the conceptual representations. Since Random Indexing is resource lean and only requires access to raw (unannotated) text, this is generally not a problem.

3 The HolSum Summarizer

3.1 Evaluating Candidate Summaries

HolSum makes use of Random Indexing to differentiate between different summaries. Random Indexing gives each word a context vector that in some sense represents the semantic content of the word. We make use of these vectors when calculating a measure of similarity between two texts. Each text is assigned its own vector for semantic content, which is simply the (weighted) sum of all the context vectors of the words in the text. This can be seen as projecting the texts into a high-dimensional vector space where we can relate the texts to each other. Similarity between two texts is then measured as the similarity between the directions of the semantic vectors of the texts, in our case between the vector for the full text and the vectors for each of the candidate summaries.

When constructing the semantic vector for a text, the context vector for each word is weighted with the term frequency and some measure of topicality

---

[1] The extremely sparse random labels are handled internally as short lists of positions for non-zero elements and are generated on the fly whenever a never before seen token is encountered in the context during indexing.

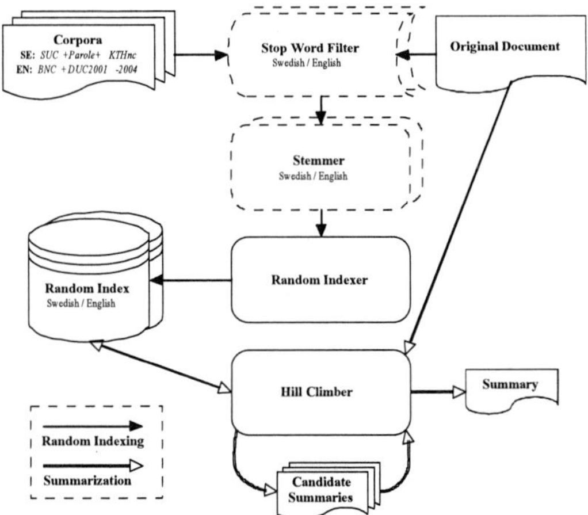

Figure 2: HolSum system layout. The candidate summaries are iteratively generated and evaluated (i.e. compared for semantic similarity against the original document).

(e.g. the inverse document frequency). If desired, other weighting criteria can easily be added, for instance for slanted or query based summaries where some words are deemed more important, or by giving words occurring early in the document, in document or paragraph headings etc. higher weight.

3.2 Finding a Better Summary

To find a good summary we start with one summary and then try to see if there is another summary that is "close" in some sense that is also a better summary. Better in this context means more similar to the original text, which is measured as described in the previous section. The reason we do not exhaustively pursue the best summary of all possible summaries is that there are exponentially many possible summaries. Comparing all of them to the original text would thus not be feasible.

It has been shown that the leading sentences of an article, especially within the news domain, are important and constitute a good summary (Edmundson, 1969; Brandow et al., 1995). Therefore, the "lead" summary, i.e. the first sentences from the document being summarized up to a specified length, was used in our experiments both as a baseline and as one of the starting points in our search for a better summary.

Using a standard hill climbing algorithm we then investigate all neighbors looking for a better summary. The summaries that are defined as neighbors to a given summary are simply those that can be created by removing one sentence and adding another. Since sentences vary in length we also allow removing two sentences and adding one new, or just adding one new sentence. This allows for optimizing the summary size for the specified compression rate.

When all such summaries have been investigated, the one most similar to the original document is updated to be the currently best candidate and the process is repeated. Any summary that is too short or too long (the wanted compression rate is given as a parameter to the program) is heavily penalized. Otherwise, the summaries tend to grow longer, since including more of the original text will make the summary more similar to it, and eventually include the whole text.

If no other summary is better than the current candidate the search is terminated. It is also possible to stop the search at any time if so desired and return the best candidate so far. A schematic layout of the complete system can be found in Figure 2.

In our experiments on the texts provided for the Document Understanding Conferences (DUC) the generated summaries are very short, about three sentences. This means that there are usually quite few, typically around four, search iterations. Some documents require quite many iterations before a local maximum is found, but these constitute a fairly small amount of the texts in the data set.

4 Evaluation

Even though the HolSum system was designed to be fairly language independent, here we only evaluate it on English. The reason is that large amounts of reference summaries and evaluation schemes have been developed for English. When large amounts of evaluation data is available it makes it easier to detect small effects of changes to a system, such as those we are investigating here. Several other summarization systems also exist for English, and can thus be used as reference points to see if the system performs well or not.

For English we build our conceptual representations for each word based on a large corpus, BNC – the British National Corpus (Burnard, 1995). We also add all the documents that are being summarized. The data used for building these representations is thus comprised of 100 million words from BNC and roughly 2 million words contained in 291 document sets provided for the Document Understanding Conferences 2001–2004 [2]. After stop word filtering and stemming this results in almost 290,000

---

[2]DUC, the Document Understanding Conferences, http://duc.nist.gov/

unique stems taken from 4,415 documents.

The HolSum summarization method has been evaluated in earlier experiments by Hassel & Sjöbergh (2006), showing promising results on manually written abstracts from the DUC.

For reasons of comparability we have chosen to evaluate using ROUGEeval (Lin, 2003) with the same data and model summaries. The evaluation was carried out by first using all manually created 100 word summaries provided for DUC 2004 as reference summaries, comparing our results to previous results on the same data set (Over and Yen, 2004; Hassel and Sjöbergh, 2006). Having reached a reasonable level of success we then compared against the complete set of human written 100 word summaries from DUC 2001–2004 in order to verify our method on a larger test set.

The evaluation has been carried out by computing ROUGE scores on the system generated summaries using the manual summaries from DUC as reference summaries. The ROUGE score is a recall based n-gram co-occurrence scoring metric that measures content similarity by computing the overlap of n-grams occurring in both a system generated summary as well as a set of model summaries. ROUGE scores have tentatively been shown to correlate with human evaluation (Lin and Hovy, 2003). As in DUC 2004, we have throughout the evaluations used ROUGEeval-1.4.2 with the following settings:

```
rouge -a -c 95 -b 665 -m -n 4 -w 1.2
```

In our experiments ROUGE scores are in the case of DUC 2004 calculated over 114 system generated summaries, one for each document set, and in the case of DUC 2001–2004 for 291 summaries. For reference, a human agreement score, see Table 1, has been calculated. For each document set ROUGE scores for each human written summary was calculated by treating the summary as a system summary and comparing it to the remaining human written ones. The mean value was then used. On average there are four human written summaries available for each set. Also, we evaluate a baseline (lead), which is the initial sentences in each text up to the allowed summary length.

We then generated a summary of each text in the data set and evaluated them compared to the 100 word reference abstracts provided. The length of these system generated summaries was allowed to vary between 75 and 110 words. We also evaluated the impact of the dimensionality chosen for the Random Indexing method by running our experiments for three different values for the dimensional-

ity, building semantic representations using 250, 500 and 1000 dimensions. Our results show little variation over different dimensionalities though. For each dimensionality we also calculated the mean performance using ten different random seeds, since there is a slight variation in how well the method works with different random projections.

4.1 Keywords Come in Bursts

When constructing the semantic vector for a text the context vector for each word is weighted with the importance of this word by simply making the length of the vector proportional to the importance of the word. The weight could for instance be something simple, such as making the length of the vector be $tf \cdot \log(idf)$ as used in previous HolSum evaluations, i.e. the term frequency and inverse document frequency. The term frequency is the frequency of the term within the given document and gives a measure of the importance of the term within that particular document. The inverse document frequency, on the other hand, is a measure of the general importance of the term, i.e. how specific the term is to said document (Salton and Buckley, 1987).

In addition to the highly traditional $tf \cdot \log(idf)$ weighting scheme, we have also experimented with utilizing the "burstiness" of a word for term weighting. Ortuño et al. (2002) have shown that the spatial information of a word, i.e. the way in which it is distributed in the text (independently of its relative frequency), is a good measure of the relevance of the word to the current text.

The burstiness of a word is here based on the standard deviation of the distance (in words) between different occurrences of this word in the text. Words that occur only with large distances between occurrences usually have a high standard deviation by chance, so the standard deviation is divided by the mean distance between occurrences. The final weight of a word is thus:

$$tf \cdot \frac{\sigma}{\mu}$$

where μ is the mean and σ the standard deviation of the distances between occurrences, in words.

Here too we have evaluated on three different dimensionality choices, 250, 500 and 1,000. Generally, as low dimensionality as possible is desirable, since processing time and memory usage is then lower. In Table 1 it can be seen that the variation between different dimensionalities is quite low. It is largest for $tf \cdot \log(idf)$, where the mean value for dimensionality 250 is 32.0 and the mean value for 1,000 is 32.4 in the DUC 2001–2004 data set. This is nice, since it seems

	DUC 2004	DUC 2001–2004
Baseline: lead	31.0	28.3
Human	42.6	39.7
$tf \cdot \log(idf)$, 1000	34.1	32.4
$tf \cdot \log(idf)$, 500	34.2	32.3
$tf \cdot \log(idf)$, 250	33.9	32.0
Burstiness, 1000	33.9	32.2
Burstiness, 500	33.7	32.1
Burstiness, 250	33.6	31.9

Table 1: ROUGE-1 scores for different dimensionality choices of the context vectors. There are 114 documents from DUC 2004 and 291 from DUC 2001–2004.

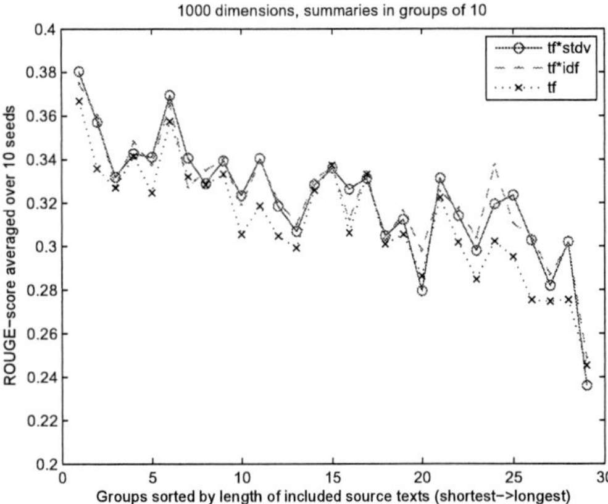

Figure 3: ROUGE-1 scores for three weighting schemes, divided into 29 groups of 10 summaries each sorted by compression rate. The leftmost group contains the summaries for the 10 shortest source texts while the rightmost group contains the summaries for the 10 longest.

to be unimportant to spend a lot of time optimizing the choice of this parameter.

For each choice of dimensionality the mean performance using ten different random seeds was calculated. The impact of the randomness of the method seems larger than the impact of the dimensionality choice. The largest variation was for the dimensionality 500, spanning 33.1–34.3 in ROUGE-1 scores for the DUC 2004 data set. Variations for the other dimensionalities were slightly less.

These results are unsurprisingly worse than those of the best systems of DUC 2004, which had ROUGE-1 scores of about 39. The top systems included summarizers using more advanced tools than those made available to HolSum, such as co-reference resolution or genre specific extraction patterns. Such tools seem to be quite useful, but since the HolSum system was meant to be language independent it uses only tokenization, stopword removal and stemming. The HolSum scores are however better than about half of the systems and well above the baseline.

One system (Jaoua et al., 2003; Jaoua et al., 2004) participating in the DUC 2004 used an approach similar to that of HolSum. A genetic algorithm was used to search through the space of possible extracts and coverage of high frequency words in the original text was used to rank summary candidates. The system achieved quite high ROUGE scores (higher than HolSum).

It can be noted that improving the ROUGE scores of HolSum is quite easy. Since the recall based measurements are never made worse by adding more words, simply making the summaries longer so as to fill up the allowed 100 words more fully gives higher scores. For ROUGE-1 using dimensionality 250 the scores are improved from 33.9 to 34.4 (DUC 2004) and from 32.0 to 32.7 (DUC 2001–2004) by simply always generating summaries of at least 100 words.

Since we were not particularly interested in generating higher ROUGE scores without making better summaries, we did not use such tricks in the evaluations, though.

The choice between $tf \cdot \log(idf)$ or burstiness seems to have very little impact, the results are nearly identical in ROUGE-1 scores. This is further supported when plotting a graph showing the ROUGE scores for three different weighting schemes. The first weighting scheme is burstiness weighting, the second is $tf \cdot \log(idf)$ and the third is weighting only by the term frequency. In Figure 3 we can see that it is the term frequency that is pulling the most weight and that the inverse document frequency and the standard deviation seem to add roughly the same improvement.

Removing the term frequency weighting lowers the performance substantially. A small test using dimensionality 250 and burstiness weighting but no term frequency weighting gave a ROUGE-1 score of 30.5 (DUC 2004) and 29.3 (DUC 2001–2004), compared to 33.6 and 31.9 using both term frequency and burstiness.

It should however not come as much of a surprise that the term frequency has the most impact during the accumulation of the context vectors. Since we apply stop word filtering prior to this step we have already filtered out most of the highly frequent function words. This means that the remaining high frequency words are content words and as such good descriptors of the document being summarized.

In Figure 3 we can also see that summarizer performs best at low compressions rates. This is due to the fact that the more of the source text that is included in the summary, the higher the chance of selecting sentences with words also used in the human written summaries in the gold standard.

4.2 Widening the Search Space

One thought that immediately strikes you is that there might be better summaries, according to the given criteria, out there in summary space. It might simply be the case that these remain unfound when going down the path of always choosing the best neighbor. What if beyond one of the lesser neighbors lies an even better summary?

The method we used for investigating this theory is simulated annealing (Kirkpatrick et al., 1983), augmented with back-off heuristics. Instead of in each step choosing the best neighbor as our next transition point we may go to a randomly chosen neighbor, as long as it is better than the current summary. However, in doing this we also keep track of the best neighbor so far, and in the case that we are lead too far down a garden path,[3] we can always go back to the best neighbor previously visited and start our search anew. A ban list containing all visited summaries, excluding the best summary so far, effectively hinders us from going down the same path again (not that it would have mattered much, bar computing time). This means that the annealing procedure will always perform at least on par with the greedy search regarding Random Indexing similarity scores.

With simulated annealing the cooling schedule is of great importance (Laarhoven and Aarts, 1987). The cooling schedule is the factor that in each transition governs the probability of choosing a random better neighbor instead of the best neighbor. Two common formulas for calculating the cooling factor were used in these experiments. The first schedule was calculated using the following formula:

$$T_i = T_0 \left(\frac{T_N}{T_0}\right)^{\frac{i}{N}}$$

In this formula T_i is the probability of choosing a random better neighbor in step i, where i increases from 0 to $N = 100$ transitions. The initial probability T_0 is set to 100% and the lowest allowed probability to $T_N = 5\%$. This schedule starts with a high probability for random behavior and then

	DUC 2004	DUC 2001–2004
Baseline: lead	31.0	28.3
Human	42.6	39.7
Original, 1000	34.1	32.4
Original, 500	34.2	32.3
Original, 250	33.9	32.0
Schedule 1, 1000	34.1	32.4
Schedule 1, 500	34.2	32.3
Schedule 1, 250	33.9	32.0
Schedule 2, 1000	34.2	32.4
Schedule 2, 500	34.2	32.3
Schedule 2, 250	34.0	32.0

Table 2: ROUGE-1 scores for the the two annealing schedules as well as the standard greedy search for reference.

rapidly reverts to a traditional greedy search. The second cooling schedule, using the same notation as above but with T_N set to zero, was designed to revert to a greedy search more linearly:

$$T_i = T_0 - i\frac{T_0 - T_N}{N}$$

The algorithm was in both cases set to break when no known neighbors are better than the current summary and no previous state or neighbor has been better, in terms of Random Indexing similarity, or the maximum number of 100 transitions has been reached. At this point the best state, current or previously visited, is returned. In most cases the maximum number of transitions was never reached.

As can be seen in Table 2 the resulting summaries were in almost all cases identical to the summaries generated using the bare greedy search algorithm. In the few cases (7 out of 2,910) where the summaries generated with a dimensionality of 500 differed, the second cooling schedule resulted in slightly higher ROUGE scores than the greedy search, but not enough to warrant the radically added computation time. For the same dimension the first schedule resulted in only one higher scoring summary.

Of course, a formula with a slower descent into a traditional greedy search could be used, but would probably lead to further increased run times. Simulated annealing using the two cooling schedules presented in this paper in general takes about three times as long to generate the 8,730 summaries evaluated in each run[4], compared to the standard greedy search.

---

[3]In our case ten transitions without finding a new summary that is better than best one seen so far.

[4]In each evaluation run the system generates summaries for 291 documents times 3 dimensionalities times 10 random projections (seeds).

	DUC 2004	DUC 2001–2004
Baseline: lead	31.0	28.3
Human	42.6	39.7
Original, 1000	34.1	32.4
Original, 500	34.2	32.3
Original, 250	33.9	32.0
Rand.sent., 1000	33.2	31.1
Rand.sent., 500	33.0	31.2
Rand.sent., 250	33.1	31.1
Rand.part, 1000	33.1	31.3
Rand.part, 500	33.2	31.3
Rand.part, 250	33.1	31.3

Table 3: ROUGE-1 scores for the two different random starting point strategies as well as the standard lead starting point for reference.

4.3   Different Points of Departure

Considering the approaches above, we have still only investigated a small fraction of the high-dimensional vector space representing all possible summaries. As stated in Section 3.2 it is simply not feasible to exhaustively search all possible summaries in pursuit of the best summary. Another option is to again put the greedy search to use, but this time giving it randomly chosen starting points. The idea here is that there may be better starting points than the leading sentences of the original text, thus taking other paths to possibly better summaries.

We have tried two approaches: the first simply chooses sentences randomly from the source text and concatenates them into an initial summary of desired length. The second, slightly less naive, approach picks a random sentence in the source text and extracts it and the following couple of sentences to use as the initial summary for that text. After this the algorithm proceeds as before, transforming the initial summary until no better summary is found.

As can be seen in Table 3, the results from both approaches are strikingly similar. Since they are also quite a lot worse than the original approach, this gives further support to the notion that the leading sentences of a document constitutes a stable starting point.

5   Conclusions

We have evaluated a new weighting scheme for the HolSum framework. Using the burstiness of a word instead of the $\log(idf)$ part of the standard $tf \cdot \log(idf)$ weighting gave results very similar to the original version. Further studies showed that the main contribution comes from the term frequency, while both the burstiness and the inverse document frequency add small improvements.

The standard HolSum method performs a greedy search starting with the leading sentences of the text. We examined if beginning the search with other summary candidates would perhaps lead to different local maxima. Indeed, this is the case, but starting with the leading sentences was much better than the considered alternatives. It is of course also possible to do several greedy searches starting from different summary candidates and then take the best result, but since the leading sentences perform much better than the other alternatives, this might not make much difference.

We also evaluated other search strategies than the original simple greedy search. Using simulated annealing to see if better results can be achieved when the risk of getting stuck early on in a local maxima is lowered was tested. There was no detectable improvement from using these more advanced search strategies.

All in all, using the leading sentences as a starting point and then finding better summaries using a simple greedy search seems to work quite well. If inverse document frequencies are not available, using the term burstiness instead (which can easily be calculated from the text itself) gives almost the same results.

While the HolSum framework does not perform quite as well as the most advanced summarization systems available for English, it has some merits. It is very easy to implement and requires only very basic resources. Only word and sentence tokenization, stemming and stopword removal, and access to large amounts of unannotated text was used. Thus, the system can be used on many other languages, as long as raw text and some form of tokenization (not necessarily into words) is available. If more advanced resources such as stemming are available these can also be added with almost no extra effort.

HolSum also has the intuitively appealing property of trying to optimize semantic similarity between the generated summary and the text being summarized, though this is not always what you want from a summary.

References

Ronald Brandow, Karl Mitze, and Lisa F. Rau. 1995. Automatic condensation of electronic publications by sentence selection. *Inf. Process. Manage.*, 31(5):675–685.

Lou Burnard. 1995. The Users Reference Guide for the British National Corpus.

Scott C. Deerwester, Susan T. Dumais, Thomas K. Landauer, George W. Furnas, and Richard A. Harshman. 1990. Indexing by Latent Semantic Analysis. *Journal of the American Society of Information Science*, 41(6):391–407.

H. P. Edmundson. 1969. New methods in automatic abstracting. *Journal of the Association for Computing Machinery*, 16(2):264–285.

Zelig S Harris. 1968. *Mathematical Structures of Language*. New York: Wiley.

Martin Hassel and Jonas Sjöbergh. 2005. A reflection of the whole picture is not always what you want, but that is what we give you. In *"Crossing Barriers in Text Summarization Research" workshop at RANLP'05*, Borovets, Bulgaria.

Martin Hassel and Jonas Sjöbergh. 2006. Towards holistic summarization: Selecting summaries, not sentences. In *Proceedings of the 7th International Conference on Language Resources and Evaluation*, Genoa, Italy.

Maher Jaoua, Fatma Jaoua Kallel, and Abdelmajid Ben Hamadou. 2003. Une méthode de condensation automatique des documents multiples: cas des dépêches de presse. In *proceedings of CIDE6*, Caen, France.

Fatma Kallel Jaoua, Maher Jaoua, Lamia Belguith Hadrich, and Abdelmajid Ben Hamadou. 2004. Summarization at LARIS laboratory. In *Proceedings of the Fourth Document Understanding Conference (DUC'04)*, Boston, Massachusetts, USA.

Scott Kirkpatrick, C. Daniel Gelatt, and M. P. Vecchi. 1983. Optimization by simulated annealing. *Science, Number 4598, 13 May 1983*, 220, 4598:671–680.

Peter J. M. Laarhoven and Emile H. L. Aarts, editors. 1987. *Simulated annealing: theory and applications*. Kluwer Academic Publishers, Norwell, MA, USA.

Thomas K. Landauer, Peter W. Foltz, and Darrell Laham. 1998. Introduction to Latent Semantic Analysis. *Discourse Processes*, 25:259–284.

Chin-Yew Lin and Eduard Hovy. 2003. The potential and limitations of automatic sentence extraction for summarization. In Dragomir Radev and Simone Teufel, editors, *HLT-NAACL 2003 Workshop: Text Summarization (DUC03)*, Edmonton, Alberta, Canada, May 31 - June 1. Association for Computational Linguistics.

Chin-Yew Lin. 2003. ROUGE: Recall-oriented understudy for gisting evaluation. http://www.isi.edu/˜cyl/ROUGE/.

M. Ortuño, P. Carpena, P. Bernaola-Galvan, E. Munoz, and A. Somoza. 2002. Keyword detection in natural languages and DNA. *Europhysics Letters*, 57:759–764.

Paul Over and James Yen. 2004. An introduction to duc 2004 intrinsic evaluation of generic new text summarization systems. http://www-nlpir.nist.gov/projects/duc/pubs/2004slides/duc2004.intro.pdf.

Magnus Sahlgren. 2005. An Introduction to Random Indexing. In *Methods and Applications of Semantic Indexing Workshop at the 7th International Conference on Terminology and Knowledge Engineering, TKE 2005)*, Copenhagen, Denmark, August 16.

Magnus Sahlgren. 2006. *The Word-Space Model: Using distributional analysis to represent syntagmatic and paradigmatic relations between words in high-dimensional vector spaces*. Ph.D. thesis, Department of Linguistics, Stockholm University.

Gerard Salton and Chris Buckley. 1987. Term weighting approaches in automatic text retrieval. Technical report, Ithaca, NY, USA.

Identifying Cross Language Term Equivalents Using Statistical Machine Translation and Distributional Association Measures

Hans Hjelm

CL Group, Department of Linguistics
Graduate School of Language Technology (GSLT) and Stockholm University
SE-106 91 Stockholm, Sweden
`hans.hjelm@ling.su.se`

Abstract

This article presents a comparison of the accuracy of a number of different approaches for identifying cross language term equivalents (translations). The methods investigated are on the one hand associative measures, commonly used in word-space models or in Information Retrieval and on the other hand a Statistical Machine Translation (SMT) approach. I have performed tests on six language pairs, using the JRC-Acquis parallel corpus as training material and Eurovoc as a gold standard. The SMT approach is shown to be more effective than the associative measures. The best results are achieved by taking a weighted average of the scores of the SMT approach and disparate associative measures.

1 Introduction

This article deals with the identification of cross language term equivalents, a topic interesting for its applicability in a number of language technology fields. The most obvious application is the automatic construction of domain-specific bilingual dictionaries. Such dictionaries are used in many different settings, including e.g., rule-based Machine Translation and Computer-Assisted Language Learning. Some approaches in Cross Language Information Retrieval also rely on the existence of bilingual dictionaries, for translating queries. The research pre-

sented in this article also integrates into Ontology Learning; this is described in section 3.

Many researchers have proposed various kinds of distributional association methods for the bilingual dictionary extraction task, see e.g., (Church and Gale, 1991), (Fung and Church, 1994) and (Smadja et al., 1996). Other researchers have tried to solve the task by using methods from SMT, see e.g., (Melamed, 2000) and (Tsuji and Kageura, 2004), though the focus there is word alignment rather than dictionary extraction.

This article presents a systematic comparison of these two main approaches on a variety of language pairs, using the JRC-Acquis parallel corpus (Steinberger et al., 2006) to train the models, and Eurovoc V4.2[1] to evaluate the results. Contrary to what is reported in (Sahlgren and Karlgren, 2005), the SMT approach here outperforms the associative measures. I also show that the results from the SMT approach can be improved by weighting them together with the results from the associative measures in an ensemble approach.

2 Background

This section gives a brief overview of related work using the associative measures and the SMT approach separately, followed by attempts to combine the two.

2.1 Distributional association measures

A number of articles have been published during the past two decades, where the distributional characteristics of words or terms in natural language texts

---

[1]http://eurovoc.europa.eu/

Joakim Nivre, Heiki-Jaan Kaalep, Kadri Muischnek and Mare Koit (Eds.)
NODALIDA 2007 Conference Proceedings, pp. 97–104

have been exploited in order to measure the semantic similarity between those same words or terms. In (Sahlgren, 2006), a major distinction is drawn between *syntagmatic* and *paradigmatic* relations. Words that stand in a syntagmatic relation to each other are words like *cradle – baby*; there is a thematic connection, but the two words do not necessarily share many semantic features. Conversely, the words *cradle – bed* are paradigmatically related, and many more semantic features are shared. Lund and Burgess (1996) refer to these relations as *associative* and *semantic*, respectively. Sahlgren also links syntagmatic relations to information contained in term-document co-occurrence models and paradigmatic relations to term-term co-occurrence models.

When dealing with large amounts of text, on the order of giga- or terabyte, calculations on co-occurrence matrices become very expensive, regarding both resources and time. To bypass this problem, different methods for reducing the dimensionality of the matrices have been proposed. In (Sahlgren and Karlgren, 2005), Random Indexing[2] is used for this very purpose, and the result is evaluated on a bilingual lexical acquisition task. Another widely used method for dimensionality reduction, the singular value decomposition (see e.g. (Golub and van Loan, 1996)), has yet to be evaluated on the dictionary extraction task. I hope to report on the results of ongoing experiments in this direction in the near future.

Regardless of whether dimensionality reduction has been performed or not, each word or term (row in the matrix) can be compared to each other word or term, using similarity measures defined for vectors. There is a plethora of such measures, many of which have been evaluated on the present task, or one similar to it. In (Ribeiro et al., 2000), a total of 28 different similarity measures are evaluated on extracting equivalents from aligned parallel texts. The task is similar to the one presented here, but they use one language pair (Spanish – Portuguese) for testing on a parallel corpus containing about 18,000 words. Two of the highest ranking measures in that evaluation, the cosine measure and the Mutual Information measure,[3] are compared in section 3.

How to exploit distributional models for solving the task at hand is described more closely in sections 3.3.1 through 3.3.3.

2.2 Statistical Machine Translation (SMT)

GIZA++,[4] which builds on IBM's translation models 1–5 (Brown et al., 1993), produces a bilingual dictionary file, where each source language word or term is listed with its possible translations and associated probabilities. The most probable translation of a particular source term can thus be found by sorting the possible translations in descending order based on their associated probabilities and then selecting the first translation in the sorted list. Melamed (2000) describes three statistically based approaches, all making use of co-occurrence information coupled with e.g., a noise model or statistical smoothing. Och and Ney (2003) propose extensions of IBM's translation models and show improvements on a word alignment task; the system is not evaluated on a dictionary extraction task.

2.3 Combining distributional association measures with SMT

Tiedemann (2003) proposes a method for word alignment which makes use of both distributional association measures[5] and the dictionary files produced by GIZA++ mentioned above. Note that the evaluations performed there are on a token level, rather than on a type level, which is what we are interested in here. Tiedemann also uses other information, such as string matching and part of speech, and so is able to boost the performance of GIZA++ by weighting the scores of the different sources together. However, in at least one of Tiedemann's evaluations, including information from any other source than GIZA++ resulted in a decrease in system performance.

3 Experimental setup and results

I compare the results for the distributional models when varying three different parameters:

1. Whether a matrix containing co-occurrence information based on shared neighbors (paradig-

---

[2]See the quoted article for a description of the Random Indexing methodology.

[3]Referred to as *Average Mutual Information* in Ribeiro's evaluation.

[4]http://www-i6.informatik.rwth-aachen.de/web/Software/

[5]He refers to these measures as *co-occurrence measures*.

matic) or shared documents/text segments (syntagmatic) is used.

2. Whether Random Indexing or no dimensionality reduction is used.

3. Whether cosine or Mutual Information is used as the similarity measure.

I describe each alternative further in sections 3.3.1 through 3.3.3.

3.1 Translating terms

Why translate terms rather than words? Consider e.g., ontologies and Ontology Learning (see e.g., (Cimiano, 2006)), a field growing in importance along with the emergence of the Semantic Web. In Ontology Learning, one of the main tasks is to identify all expressions that are of particular importance within the domain of interest, e.g., medicine or law. These expressions can consist of a single word or they can be multi-word units. When we are looking at a particular domain, these expressions are assumed to correspond to the terms in that domain. A lot of work in the field of Term Extraction has been carried out towards automating the term extraction process (see e.g., (Castellví et al., 2001; Jacquemin, 2001)).

After term extraction, the next question of interest for an ontology engineer would be whether some of the extracted terms refer to the same *concept*. A concept, as I use the term here, is compatible with the topmost point in Peirce's semiotic triangle (Ogden and Richards, 1923), connecting symbols (here terms) with objects or phenomena in the real world. Roughly, if we are dealing with terms from the same language that refer to the same concept, we say that these terms are *synonyms*. If the terms are from different languages, we call them *equivalents*. It is the latter that I am interested in identifying in this study. In the ontology learning application scenario, we are interested in finding equivalence relations between *terms* in the source and target languages – relations between terms and non-terms ("regular words") or relations purely between non-terms are only of secondary interest.

In my experiments, I assume that the term extraction has already been carried out correctly. This means two things:

1. The task for the systems consists in translating the Eurovoc terms.

2. The translation candidates are limited to the target language terms – no non-terms are allowed as translation candidates.

This may seem like a rigid restriction. However, if we assume that the term extraction process has been carried out correctly and we also assume that a *term* in the source language is always translated with a *term* in the target language, this restriction is needed for sake of consistency.

3.2 Data and gold standard

I used the JRC-Acquis parallel corpus for building the distributional models and for training the GIZA++ system. The corpus consists of legal texts concerning matters involving the EU. I have used all pairwise combinations of the following languages in my experiments: German, English, French and Swedish. This means that six language pairs have been evaluated and thus twelve directions of translation. The number of words per language varies between 6.5 million (Swedish) and 7.8 million (French).

The parallel corpora are distributed in a format where they have been aligned automatically on a paragraph level. The paragraphs are very short and usually only contain one sentence or even one part of a sentence. There are two alignment versions available for download;[6] I used the version produced by the Vanilla aligner[7] in my experiments. To ease some of the usual problems caused by sparse data (which is even worse when working with terms than with words), I lemmatized the texts using Intrafind's[8] LiSa system for morphological analysis (Hjelm and Schwarz, 2006). The Swedish texts, though, had to be left unprocessed, due to a lack of resources.

As a gold standard, against which to check the translations proposed by the system, I used Eurovoc V4.2, a freely available multilingual thesaurus existing in more than 20 languages and covering topics where the EU is active. The thesaurus con-

---

[6]http://wt.jrc.it/lt/Acquis/
[7]http://nl.ijs.si/telri/Vanilla/doc/ljubljana/
[8]http://www.intrafind.de

tains 6,645 concepts, each of which is given a *descriptor*, or recommended term, in each language. These descriptors constitute my gold standard; when the system translates the descriptor for a concept in the source language with the descriptor for the same concept in the target language, the translation is counted as correct, otherwise as incorrect. I also lemmatized the descriptors, in order for the gold standard to be on the same format as the corpora.

Next, I applied a very simple term spotting technique (for more on term spotting, see (Jacquemin, 2001)). Going through each text from left to right, I simply marked the longest matching string of complete words, that also is a descriptor for the language in question, as a term. I marked the terms so that they would be recognizable and so that the system would be able to treat them as single textual units. For example:

```
A new accounting system was installed. ⇒
a new ACTERM_accounting_system#4362 be
install .
```

3.3   Comparing the distributional models

Throughout all experiments, I use the log_2 of the frequencies in the models rather than using raw frequencies. The intuition behind this is that a word co-occurring twice with another word should be weighted higher than a word that co-occurs only once – but probably not *twice* as high. In Information Retrieval, using log frequencies, or the *logarithmic term frequency*, is a standard technique. It has also been applied successfully e.g., to the closely related problem of automatic thesaurus discovery (Grefenstette, 1994).

The matrix rows are then normalized so that the vectors are of unit length, in preparation for using the cosine measure.

3.3.1   Syntagmatic vs. paradigmatic models

When building the syntagmatic model, rows represent terms and columns represent documents, or in this case paragraphs. One model per language and language pair is needed, since the paragraph alignment is unique to each language pair.

When building a paradigmatic model, one usually makes use of a fixed-size sliding window

to determine which words are to be considered neighbors of the focus word. In these experiments, I use the target language part of the alignment unit as the window, as illustrated in figure 1. Nothing actually forces us to use the *target* language words as features, we might as well use the *source* language words as features, or use both. I will return to this point in section 3.3.4. I make no adjustment for the proximity of the words, since I do not wish to make any assumptions about the similarity of word order between the languages involved.

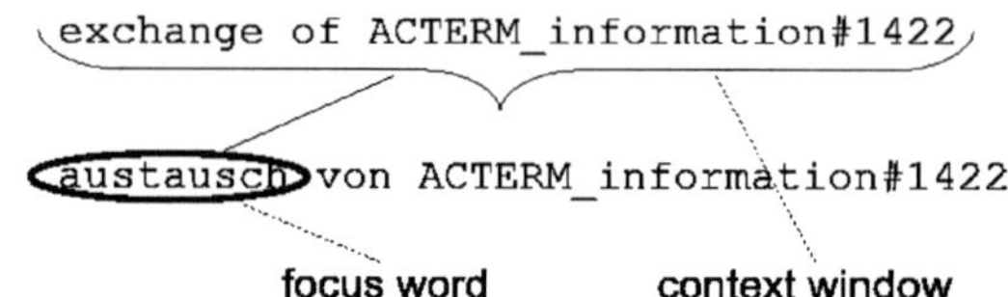

Figure 1: Constructing the paradigmatic model for translating from German to English. The focus word is circled.

3.3.2   Random indexing vs. full matrix

As mentioned previously, I wanted to compare the effects of using no dimensionality reduction with that of using Random Indexing. Of course, using a reduced matrix can give computational benefits (see section 2.1), especially when working with larger text collections. Here, I am mainly interested in the effects it might have on the *accuracy* of the system.

3.3.3   Cosine vs. Mutual Information

It would have been methodologically pleasing to try the different kinds of similarity measures with all combinations of syntagmatic vs. paradigmatic models, paired with both options for dimensionality reduction named previously. However, applying the Mutual Information measure does not make sense after the dimensionality reduction has been performed, since most or all vectors will be dense by then, containing few or no zeros. I use the following following formula to calculate Mutual Information:

$$\sum_{x,y} p(x,y) log \frac{p(x,y)}{p(x)p(y)}$$

This typically presupposes a binary representation, meaning that if the number of zero-entries in all vectors is very low or zero, the measure will judge most or all vectors to be equally similar to each other. I therefore refrained from evaluating the Mutual Information measure on models where dimensionality reduction had been performed. For the cosine measure, since the vectors are of unit length, I only have to calculate the dot product between the two vectors.

Given the great number of similarity measures available, it would have been possible to include many more in the evaluation. The cosine measure was chosen because of its widespread application in Information Retrieval and the Mutual Information measure because of its acceptance in the Information Theory community along with its giving the best results in the comparison in (Ribeiro et al., 2000).

3.3.4 Results for the comparison of the distributional models

For each combination of settings, I evaluated each of the twelve translation directions. Again, as mentioned in section 3, I only consider the descriptors of the target language as translation candidates. As input to the system, I use all source language descriptors that occur at least once in the source language text of the parallel corpus at hand. I also split the descriptors into eleven frequency classes (counted separately for each of the twelve directions of translation): 1, 2–5, 6–10, 11–50, 51–100, 101–500, 501–1000, 1001–5000, 5001–10000, 10001–50000 and 50001<=. I calculated the average accuracy for all twelve directions of translation, for each frequency class as well as the overall accuracy, regardless of frequency (displayed later in table 1). Figure 2 shows a comparison of all applicable combinations of settings when working with paradigmatic models. Figure 3 shows the same comparison for the syntagmatic models.

As mentioned in section 3.3.1, there is no inherent reason to choose the target language words as features when building a paradigmatic model. In fact, since four languages were involved in these experiments, I made an experiment where words from all four languages were used as features. As can be seen in table 1 (where this method is labeled "Paradigm-Full-Cosine-CL"), this brought a very moderate increase in performance, but still makes this the most effective paradigmatic model.

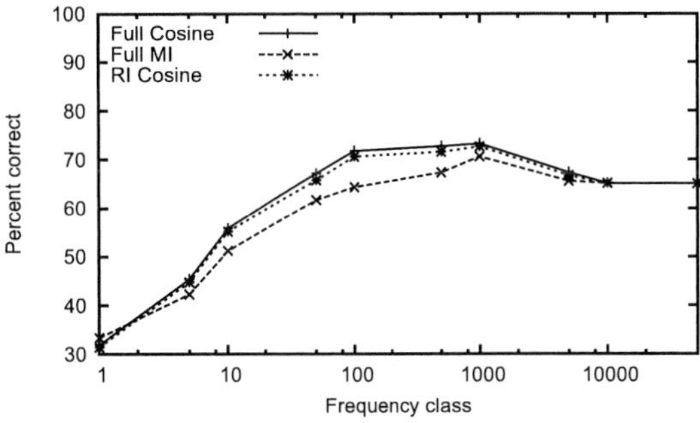

Figure 2: Paradigmatic models. "Full" stands for no dimensionality reduction, "MI" for Mutual Information and "RI" for Random Indexing

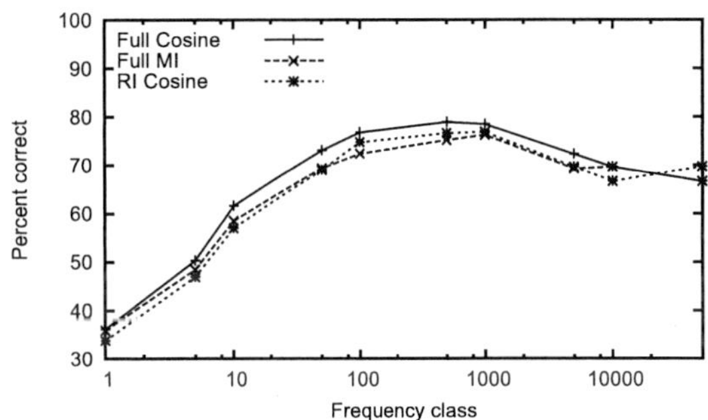

Figure 3: Syntagmatic models.

3.4 SMT vs. the distributional models

I ran the GIZA++ system with the standard settings provided in the publicly available distribution. Since all terms are treated as single words by the system, after the term spotting applied during preprocessing, we sidestep the problem of the lacking possibility in GIZA++ of capturing many-to-many relations. Figure 4 displays a comparison between the best performing syntagmatic and paradigmatic models with the results from GIZA++. "CL" in the figure stands for "Cross Language" and refers to the fact that words from all four languages involved were used as features when training that model.

3.5 Ensemble method

I combined the results of the top performing models, shown in figure 4, in an ensemble method. The idea here is that, even though the statistical model outperforms the other two, they may still contain useful information that the statistical model is missing. There are at least two factors one would

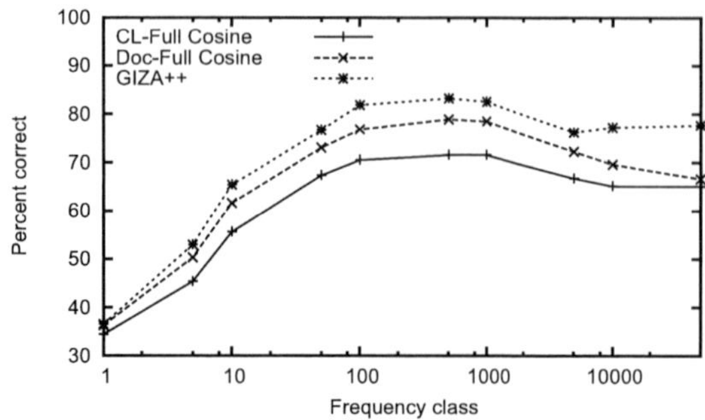

Figure 4: Top performing models compared: syntagmatic (labeled Doc-Full Cosine), paradigmatic (labeled CL-Full Cosine) and statistical (labeled GIZA++).

	Percent correct
Paradigm-Full-Cosine	56.0
Paradigm-Full-MI	52.4
Paradigm-RI-Cosine	55.1
Paradigm-Full-Cosine-CL	**56.2**
Syntagm-Full-Cosine	**61.4**
Syntagm-Full-MI	58.7
Syntagm-RI-Cosine	58.1
GIZA++	64.4 (64.0)
Ensemble	**65.8 (65.3)**

Table 1: Percent correct over all frequency classes, totally 37,316 translations evaluated. Numbers in parenthesis show results when German-French is not included (this direction of translation was used for parameter tuning in the ensemble method).

like to consider when combining the results of the different systems: how confident each system is of its decision (modeled in the S' function below) and how accurate the system has been in the past (modeled in the S'' function below). For each source language term, I look at the top ten translation candidates for each of the three models. The scores for each model are rescaled, so that the scores for the top ten translation candidates for a particular source term sum to one, or, equivalently:

$$S'(x,y) = \frac{S(x,y)}{\sum_{y_i} S(x,y_i)}$$

where x is the source term, y a translation candidate, S the scoring function and S' the rescaled scoring function. I then weight the scores from each model according to how accurately it performed on one direction of translation for one language pair,[9] which I set aside for testing during this particular experiment. The scoring function which is finally used to re-rank the top ten suggestions from the three models looks like this:

$$S''(x,y) = \alpha * S'_a(x,y) + \beta * S'_b(x,y) + \gamma * S'_c(x,y)$$

where α, β and γ are the accuracies of the respective models, normalized so that $\alpha + \beta + \gamma = 1$.[10] Basically, this amounts to the *average combination rule*, which is a standard way of combining multiple

classifiers (Tax et al., 2000). The results, displayed in figure 5, show a slight improvement when compared to using the statistical model alone. Finally, table 1 shows the percent correct for each method, regardless of frequency class.

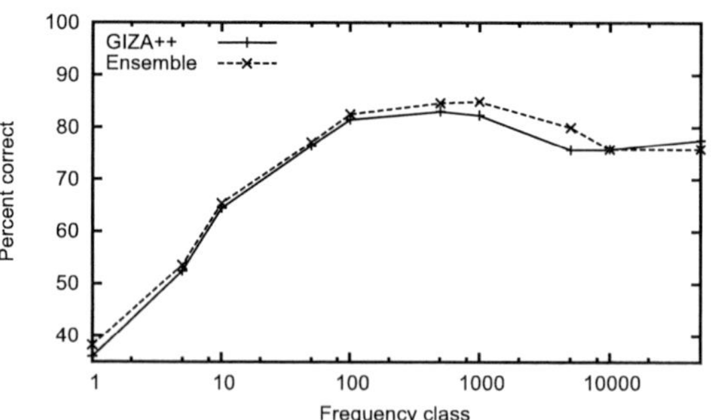

Figure 5: Comparing GIZA++ to the ensemble method.

4 Discussion and future work

Using the non-reduced matrix gives the highest correctness figures, both for the syntagmatic and the paradigmatic models, though the reduced version is trailing closely for the paradigmatic model, as seen in figure 2. There are possible computational benefits of using a reduced representation. However, since both data structures and algorithms designed for working with sparse matrices and vectors exist, one would have to investigate just where the breaking point lies. For the current experiments, using the non-reduced, sparse matrix proved more efficient

---

[9] I used German to French, to have one Germanic and one Romance language.

[10] This resulted in the following parameters, for the paradigmatic, syntagmatic and statistical models, respectively: $\alpha = 0.313$ $\beta = 0.334$ $\gamma = 0.353$.

both in terms of time and in terms of memory usage, since the reduced matrices have to work with dense representations. It should be noted that when using Random Indexing, the results will vary with the dimensionality of the matrix and the number of non-zero elements used in the random vectors. I used a dimensionality of 1800 and an average of eight non-zero elements (positive and negative), which lies in the range of what is suggested in (Sahlgren, 2006). We note a larger gap in accuracy between the reduced and the full matrix for the syntagmatic models than for the paradigmatic models (0.9% vs. 3.3%). From this we can hypothesize that the reduced syntagmatic model would have performed better using a higher dimensionality, considering that the non-reduced syntagmatic models have a higher dimensionality than the non-reduced paradigmatic models. This is left for future experiments to confirm.

The syntagmatic models consistently outperform the paradigmatic models in these experiments. I am not aware of another study which has directly compared these two approaches on the current task. Further, the cosine measure outperforms the Mutual Information measure in the cases where a direct comparison can be made. This is contrary to what Ribeiro (2000) reported, but the experiments described here have been conducted on a much larger corpus with a larger variability of languages – perhaps this could explain the differences in the results.

Further, the statistical approach clearly outperforms both the paradigmatic and the syntagmatic models. This is again contrary to what Sahlgren and Karlgren (2005) report. However, they claim an accuracy of "something less then 1/3" for the GIZA++ system, which lies far below the 64.4% measured here. The two evaluations can not be directly compared, due to several differences in the methodology of the experiments. The most important difference, which probably by itself explains the vast discrepancy when measuring the performance of GIZA++, is that this study uses texts aligned on a *paragraph* level, whereas Sahlgren and Karlgren used texts aligned on a *document* level. Sahlgren and Karlgren are also studying *words*, not *terms*, which makes their task harder, since they have to pick the correct word out of 40,000 to 70,000 translation candidates, whereas this study typically only has about 3,500 terms as translation candidates. On the other hand, the evaluation applied here is stricter, since only the descriptor in the target language is counted as correct, where Sahlgren and Karlgren also count partial matches in the target language part of a bilingual dictionary as correct.

The correctness for terms occurring only once seems low, at slightly below 40%. Consider, though, that there is no guarantee that the corresponding target language descriptor co-occurs *even once* with these terms. Such cases can arise from e.g., faulty sentence alignment or from the (human) translator choosing to use a different term than the descriptor in the target language translation.

Using the ensemble method described in section 3.5, the results are boosted with 1.3% points. Though the increase is relatively small, the difference is statistically significant beyond the 0.001 level according to McNemar's test. If we use a more lenient evaluation method, counting each result as correct if the corresponding descriptor occurs among the top three translation candidates, GIZA++ achieves 66.9% correct translations on average and the ensemble method reaches 68.6%. Extending this to the top ten candidates, we get 67.2% for GIZA++ and 70.3% for the ensemble method – a difference of 3.1% points. The rather small increases in correctness for GIZA++ using the lenient evaluation methods can most likely be explained by the internal thresholds in the system. Due to these thresholds, GIZA++ most often returns *less* than ten translation candidates for any given source term, which means that the system will not profit as much from using these lenient evaluation schemes.

5 Conclusions

I have compared two distributional models with a statistical method on the task of identifying cross language term equivalents. I have used all directions of translation between four European languages in the evaluation and I have used texts and a thesaurus covering European Union terminology to evaluate the methods. The paradigmatic distributional models were outperformed by the syntagmatic models and the cosine measure worked better than the Mutual Information measure. Both types of distributional models were outperformed by GIZA++, a SMT system. Combining the results of the top performing distributional models with the results of GIZA++ gives a statistically significant increase in accuracy.

References

Peter F. Brown, Stephen A. Della Pietra, Vincent J. Della Pietra, and Robert L. Mercer. 1993. The mathematics of machine translation: Parameter estimation. *Computational Linguistics*, 19(2):263–311.

M. Teresa Cabré Castellví, Rosa Estopà Bagot, and Jordi Vivaldi Palatresi. 2001. Automatic term detection: A review of current systems. In Didier Bourigault, editor, *Recent Advances in Computational Terminology*, chapter 3, pages 53–87. John Benjamins Publishing Company, Philadelphia, PA, USA.

Kenneth Church and William Gale. 1991. Concordances for parallel text. In *Proceedings of the Seventh Annual Conference of the UW Centre for the New OED and Text Research*, pages 40–62.

Philipp Cimiano. 2006. *Ontology Learning and Population from Text: Algorithms, Evaluation and Applications*. Springer-Verlag, New York, NY, USA.

Pascale Fung and Kenneth Church. 1994. K-Vec: A new approach for aligning parallel texts. In *Proceedings of COLING 94*, pages 1096–1102. COLING.

Gene H. Golub and Charles F. van Loan. 1996. *Matrix Computations*. Johns Hopkins University Press, Baltimore, MD, USA, 3 edition.

Gregory Grefenstette. 1994. *Explorations in Automatic Thesaurus Discovery*. Kluwer Academic Publishers, Boston, MA, USA.

Hans Hjelm and Christoph Schwarz. 2006. LiSa - morphological analysis for information retrieval. In Stefan Werner, editor, *Proceedings of the 15th NODALIDA conference, Joensuu 2005*, volume 1 of *University of Joensuu electronic publications in linguistics and language technology*. NoDaLiDa, Ling@JoY.

Christian Jacquemin. 2001. *Spotting and Discovering Terms through Natural Language Processing*. The MIT Press, Cambridge, Massachusetts, USA.

Kevin Lund and Curt Burgess. 1996. Producing high-dimensional semantic spaces from lexical cooccurrence. *Behavior Research Methods, Instruments, and Computers*, 28(2):203–208.

Dan Melamed. 2000. Models of translational equivalence among words. *Computational Linguistics*, 26(2):221–249.

Franz Josef Och and Hermann Ney. 2003. A systematic comparison of various statistical alignment models. *Computational Linguistics*, 29(1):19–51.

Charles Kay Ogden and Ivor Armstrong Richards. 1923. *The Meaning of Meaning*. Harcourt, Brace, and World, New York, NY, USA, 8th edition 1946 edition.

António Ribeiro, Gabriel Pereira Lopes, and João Mexia. 2000. Extracting equivalents from aligned parallel texts: Comparison of measures of similarity. In M. C. Monard and J. S. Sichman, editors, *Advances in Artificial Intelligence: International Joint Conference, 7th Ibero-American Conference on AI, 15th Brazilian Symposium on AI, IBERAMIA-SBIA 2000, Atibaia, SP, Brazil, November 2000. Proceedings*, Lecture Notes in Computer Science, pages 339–349. Springer-Verlag, Berlin Heidelberg, Germany.

Magnus Sahlgren and Jussi Karlgren. 2005. Automatic bilingual lexicon acquisition using random indexing of parallel corpora. *Natural Language Engineering*, 11(3):327–341.

Magnus Sahlgren. 2006. *The Word-Space Model: Using Distributional Analysis to Represent Syntagmatic and Paradigmatic Relations between Words in High-Dimensional Vector Spaces*. Ph.D. thesis, Stockholm University, Stockholm, Sweden.

Frank Smadja, Kathleen R. McKeown, and Vasileios Hatzivassiloglou. 1996. Translating collocations for bilingual lexicons: A statistical approach. *Computational Linguistics*, 22(1):1–38.

Ralf Steinberger, Bruno Pouliquen, Anna Widiger, Camelia Ignat, Tomaz Erjavec, Dan Tufis, and Dániel Varga. 2006. The jrc-acquis: A multilingual aligned parallel corpus with 20+ languages. In *Proceedings of the 5th International Conference on Language Resources and Evaluation (LREC'2006)*, Genoa, Italy.

David M. J. Tax, Martin van Breukelen, Robert P. W. Duin, and Josef Kittler. 2000. Combining multiple classifiers by averaging or by multiplying. *Pattern Recognition*, 33(9):1475 – 1485.

Jörg Tiedemann. 2003. *Recycling Translations: Extraction of Lexical Data from Parallel Corpora and their Application in Natural Language Processing*. Ph.D. thesis, Uppsala University, Uppsala, Sweden.

Keita Tsuji and Kyo Kageura. 2004. Extracting low-frequency translation pairs from japanese-english bilingual corpora. In Sophia Ananadiou and Pierre Zweigenbaum, editors, *COLING 2004 CompuTerm 2004: 3rd International Workshop on Computational Terminology*, pages 23–30, Geneva, Switzerland. COLING.

Extended Constituent-to-Dependency Conversion for English

Richard Johansson and **Pierre Nugues**
Department of Computer Science, LTH, Lund University, Sweden
{richard, pierre}@cs.lth.se

Abstract

We describe a new method to convert English constituent trees using the Penn Treebank annotation style into dependency trees. The new format was inspired by annotation practices used in other dependency treebanks with the intention to produce a better interface to further semantic processing than existing methods. In particular, we used a richer set of edge labels and introduced links to handle long-distance phenomena such as *wh*-movement and topicalization.

The resulting trees generally have a more complex dependency structure. For example, 6% of the trees contain at least one non-projective link, which is difficult for many parsing algorithms. As can be expected, the more complex structure and the enriched set of edge labels make the trees more difficult to predict, and we observed a decrease in parsing accuracy when applying two dependency parsers to the new corpus. However, the richer information contained in the new trees resulted in a 23% error reduction in a baseline FrameNet semantic role labeler that relied on dependency arc labels only.

1 Introduction

Labeled dependency parsing has become increasingly popular during the last few years. Dependency syntax offers a number of advantages from a practical perspective such as the availability of efficient parsing algorithms that analyze sentences in linear time while still achieving state-of-the-art results. It is arguably easier to understand and to teach to people without a linguistic background, which may be of use when annotating domain-specific data such as in medicine. Finally, some linguists argued that dependency grammar is universal whereas constituents would be more English-centric (Mel'čuk, 1988).

From a theoretical perspective, dependency syntax is arguably more intuitive than constituent syntax when explaining *linking*, i.e. the realization of the semantic arguments of predicates as syntactic units. This may also have practical implications for "semantic parsers", although this still remains to be seen in practice.

As statistical parsing is becoming the norm, syntactically annotated data, and hence the annotation style they adopt, plays a central role. For English, no significant dependency treebank exists, although there have been some preliminary efforts to create one (Rambow et al., 2002). Instead, the constituent-based Penn Treebank (Marcus et al., 1993), which is the largest treebank for English and the most common training resource for constituent parsing of this language, has been used to train most of the data-driven dependency parsers reported in the literature. However, since it based on constituent structures, a conversion method must be applied that transforms its constituent trees into dependency graphs.

The dependency trees produced by existing conversion methods (Magerman, 1994; Collins, 1999; Yamada and Matsumoto, 2003), which have been used by all recent papers on English dependency parsing, have been somewhat simplistic in view of original dependency treebanks such as the Danish Dependency Treebank (Trautner Kromann, 2003), in particular with respect to the set of edge labels and the treatment of complex long-distance linguistic relations such as *wh*-movement, topicalization, *it*-clefts, expletives, and gapping. However, this information *is* available in the Penn Treebank from version II when its syntactic representation was extended from bare bracketing to a much richer structure (Marcus et al., 1994), but with a few exceptions this has not yet been reflected by automatic parsers, neither constituent-based nor dependency-based.

This article describes a new constituent-to-dependency conversion procedure that makes better use of the existing information in the Treebank. The

Joakim Nivre, Heiki-Jaan Kaalep, Kadri Muischnek and Mare Koit (Eds.)
NODALIDA 2007 Conference Proceedings, pp. 105–112

idea of the new conversion method is to make use of the extended structure of the recent versions of the Penn Treebank to derive a more "semantically useful" representation. The first section of the article presents previous approaches to converting constituent trees into dependency trees. We then describe the modifications we brought to the previous methods. The last section describes a small experiment in which we study the impact of the new format on the performance of two statistical dependency parsers. Finally, we examine how the new representation affects semantic role classification.

2 Previous Constituent-to-Dependency Conversion Methods

The current conversion procedures are based on the idea of assigning each constituent in the parse tree a unique *head* selected amongst the constituent's children (Magerman, 1994). For example, the toy grammar below would select the noun as the head of an NP, the verb as the head of a VP, and VP as the head of an S consisting of a noun phrase and and a verb phrase:

```
NP  --> DT NN*
VP  --> VBD* NP
S   --> NP VP*
```

By following the child-parent links from the token level up to the root of the tree, we can label every constituent with a *head token*. The heads can then be used to create dependency trees: to determine the parent of a token in the dependency tree, we locate the highest constituent that it is the head of and select the head of its parent constituent.

Magerman (1994) produced a *head percolation table*, a set of priority lists, to find heads of constituents. Collins (1999) modified Magerman's rules and used them in his parser, which is constituent-based but uses dependency structures as an intermediate representation. Yamada and Matsumoto (2003) modified the table further and their procedure has become the most popular one to date. PENN2MALT (Nivre, 2006) is a reimplementation of Yamada and Matsumoto's method, and also defines a set of heuristics to infer arc labels in the dependency tree. Figure 1 shows the constituent tree of the sentence *Why, they wonder, should it belong to the EC?* from the Penn Treebank and Fig-

ure 2, the corresponding dependency tree produced by PENN2MALT.

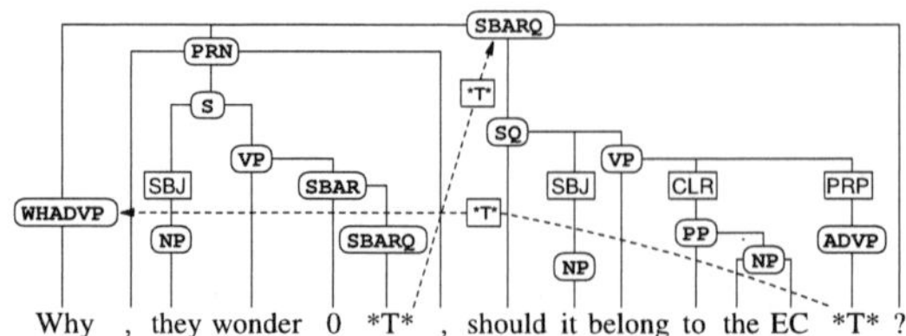

Figure 1: A constituent tree from the Penn Treebank.

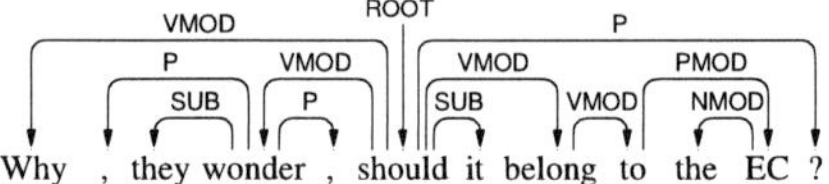

Figure 2: Dependency tree by PENN2MALT.

3 The New Conversion Procedure

As can be seen from the figures, the dependency tree that is created by PENN2MALT discards deep information such as the fact that the word *Why* refers to the purpose of the verb *belong*. It thus misses the direct relation between this question and a possible answer *It should belong to the EC because...* This relation is nevertheless present in the Penn Treebank II and is encoded in the form of a PRP link (purpose or reason) from the verb phrase to an empty node that is linked via a secondary edge to *Why* (Figure 1). In the new method, we link *wh*-words and topicalized phrases to their semantic heads, which we believe makes more sense in a dependency grammar.

In addition to the modification of dependency links, the new method uses a much richer set of dependency arc labels than PENN2MALT. The Penn annotation guidelines define a fairly large set of edge labels (referring to grammatical functions or properties of phrases), and most of these are retained in the new format. PENN2MALT only used SBJ, subject, and PRD, predicative complement. In addition, the number of inferred labels (i.e. the labels on the edges that carry no label in the Penn Treebank) has been extended.

Figure 3 shows the dependency tree that is produced by the new procedure. The benefit of retaining the deeper information should be obvious for applications that need to carry out some semantic processing, for example in question answering systems.

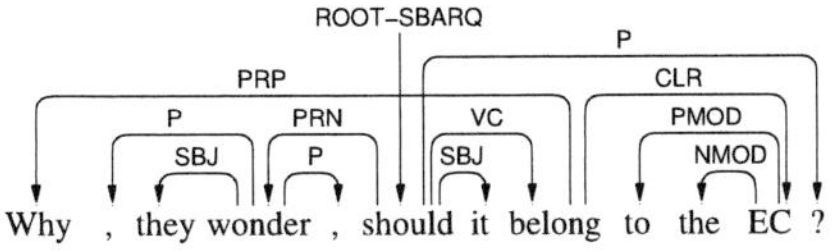

Figure 3: Dependency tree by the new procedure.

The next subsections detail the modifications of the previous methods.

3.1 Heuristically Deepening Noun Phrases

As a preprocessing step, the conversion method uses a few heuristic rules to add internal structure to some noun phrases. This is because a large number of noun phrases with a complex internal structure are annotated using a completely flat structure in the Penn Treebank. An extreme example is *other small apparel makers, button suppliers, trucking firms and fabric houses*. The main reasons for this are probably practical; it saves annotation time, and the internal structure may not be entirely clear to the manual annotators unless they are domain experts. However, the flat structure is very unappealing when the phrase is converted to a dependency structure, since this makes all words in the noun phrase direct dependents of the head word.

We used the following heuristics:

- Certain adverbs (such as *quite* or *too*) are joined with a consecutive adjective into an ADJP.

- Some common words in coordinated NPs (such as *& Co* and *and Sons*) provide a clue to how to bracket these coordinations.

- If there are two words with identical part-of-speech tags around a conjunction, they are assumed to be coordinated, such as in *a small and venomous snake*.

3.2 Head Rule Modifications

The fundamental task in a constituent-to-dependency conversion system is to find the head of each phrase, which is needed in order to create the dependency links. For the most part, we followed the earlier approach by using a set of head

percolation rules based on the phrase type, but our rules also made use of the context of the phrases and of grammatical functions. Table 1 shows the complete set of rules. In the table, NP-ε means NP with no function tag, ∗∗ means any phrase, and ∗-PRD means any phrase with a PRD function tag. The following subsections list the modifications of the rules used by Yamada and Matsumoto (2003).

ADJP	←	NNS QP NN \$ ADVP JJ VBN VBG ADJP JJR NP JJS DT FW RBR RBS SBAR RB
ADVP	→	RB RBR RBS FW ADVP TO CD JJR JJ IN NP JJS NN
CONJP	→	CC RB IN
FRAG	→	(NN∗ | NP) W∗ SBAR (PP | IN) (ADJP | JJ) ADVP RB
INTJ	←	∗∗
LST	→	LS :
NAC	←	NN∗ NP NAC EX \$ CD QP PRP VBG JJ JJS JJR ADJP FW
NP, NX	←	(NN∗ | NX) JJR CD JJ JJS RB QP NP-ε NP
PP, WHPP	→	(first non-punctuation after preposition)
PRN	→	(first non-punctuation)
PRT	→	RP
QP	←	\$ IN NNS NN JJ RB DT CD NCD QP JJR JJS
RRC	→	VP NP ADVP ADJP PP
S	←	VP ∗-PRD S SBAR ADJP UCP NP
SBAR	←	S SQ SINV SBAR FRAG IN DT
SBARQ	←	SQ S SINV SBARQ FRAG
SINV	←	VBZ VBD VBP VB MD VP ∗-PRD S SINV ADJP NP
SQ	←	VBZ VBD VBP VB MD ∗-PRD VP SQ
UCP	→	∗∗
VP	→	VBD VBN MD VBZ VB VBG VBP VP ∗-PRD ADJP NN NNS NP
WHADJP	←	CC WRB JJ ADJP
WHADVP	→	CC WRB
WHNP	←	NN∗ WDT WP WP\$ WHADJP WHPP WHNP
X	→	∗∗

Table 1: Head percolation rules.

Coordinated Phrases. The method of Yamada and Matsumoto (2003) analyzed coordinations inconsistently, although Collins (1999) had special rules for such constructions. In the new procedure, the leftmost conjunct is consistently regarded as the head of a coordinated structure, and all other conjuncts and conjunctions as children of the first conjunct. There is a considerable amount of literature on how to represent coordinations in dependency grammars. Treating the leftmost conjunct as the head introduces ambiguities when modifiers attach to the left. To have an unambiguous representation, the coordination should be represented using the conjunction as the head, but this is usually not preferred since it makes parsing more difficult.

PPs, Subordinate and Relative Clauses. In prepositional phrases, including *wh*-phrases such as *in which*, the preposition itself is regarded as a case marker and treated as a dependent. The same is true for other "linking words" such as subordinating conjunctions and relative pronouns.

Noun Phrases. For noun phrases, NX phrases (incomplete NPs) are moved to the highest priority. Similarly to the treatment of PPs above, possessive markers are regarded as dependents of the preceding noun. When trying to set a child NP as the head of an NP, the new conversion procedure skips NPs having a function tag (for instance, to avoid setting *tomorrow* as the head of *the meeting tomorrow*). In WHNP phrases (such as *what cat*), the noun instead of the *wh*-word is considered head.

Main Clauses (S, SQ, and SINV). In some rare cases, a main clause may lack a verb or a verb phrase. In those cases, we look for a constituent with a PRD edge label.

3.3 Modification of Arc Labeling Rules

3.3.1 Grammatical Functions from Penn

In addition to phrase labels such as NP and VP, Penn Treebank II uses a set of 21 property labels such as subject, SBJ, location, LOC, or manner, MNR. The properties may be combined, such as LOC-PRD-TPC. Of these labels, all were used to label dependency relations except four which reflect a structural property rather than a grammatical function: HLN (headline), TTL (title), NOM (non-NP acting as a nominal), and TPC (topicalization). The final one, topicalization, represents a property of a phrase that is arguably more semantically relevant than the three others, e.g. when analyzing the rhetorical structure. However, we think that this property is independent from grammatical functions – an object is an object whether fronted or not – and it is probably not relevant to a dependency grammar. For the treatment of the CLF (cleft) tag, which is also a structural property, see Sect 3.3.3.

Regarding a few of the function tags from Penn, we introduced minor modifications. The adverbial tag, ADV, was extended to all unmarked ADVP and PP nodes in verb phrases. According to Penn annotation conventions, ADV is implicit in these cases. The logical subject in passive clause tag, LGS, was moved to the edge between the verb phrase and *by*, rather than the edge between *by* and the noun phrase.

3.3.2 Inferred Labels

Most of the edges in the Treebank have no label. For these edges, we used heuristics to infer a suitable function tag. These rules are to a large extent based on corresponding rules in PENN2MALT.

The treatment of objects is somewhat different from previous approaches: we included clause complements (SBAR and S) into this category, whereas PENN2MALT includes NPs only. To filter out some frequent annotation errors (SBARs which should carry an edge label), we excluded SBARs starting with *as*, *for*, *since*, or *with*. Arguably, the clause complements should not use the same label as noun phrase objects. On the other hand, it is quite intuitive that the same label is used in *I told him that...* as in *I told him a message*.

In addition, we used a distinction between direct objects (OBJ) and indirect objects (IOBJ). Adding the IOBJ labels is not problematic if there is more than one object, in which case the IOBJ label is assigned to the first of them. However, if we make a distinction between direct and indirect object, it is not clear that there won't occur cases where there is only a single object, but that object should have an IOBJ function tag (such as in *Tell me!*). To have an idea of the number of such cases, we inspected a large set of instances of the verbs *give*, *tell*, and *provide*. Fortunately, the Treebank annotates most of those cases with an empty node to denote a missing object, although there are a few annotation errors that make the rule fail.

The function tag on the root token was used to express the type of sentence. We used four root labels: ROOT-S when the root constituent was S or SINV, ROOT-SBARQ and ROOT-SQ for SBARQ and SQ respectively, and ROOT-FRAG for everything else.

Algorithm 1 shows the complete set of rules that were used to assign labels to the edges that were not labeled by the Penn annotators.

Algorithm 1 Rules to label unlabeled arcs

---

let c be a token, C the highest phrase that c is the head of,
and P the parent of C
returns The label on the dependency arc from c to its parent

if C is the root node
  if C is S or SINV **return** ROOT-S
  if C is SQ **return** ROOT-SQ
  if C is SBARQ **return** ROOT-SBARQ
  else return ROOT-FRAG
else
  if C is the first of more than one object **return** IOBJ
  if C is an object **return** OBJ
  if C is PRN **return** PRN
  if c is punctuation **return** P
  if C is coordinated with P **return** COORD
  if C is PP, ADVP, or SBAR and P is VP **return** ADV
  if C is PRT and P is VP **return** PRT
  if C is VP and P is VP, SQ, or SINV **return** VC
  if P is VP, S, SBAR, SBARQ, SINV, or SQ **return** VMOD
  if P is NP, NX, NAC, or WHNP **return** NMOD
  if P is ADJP, ADVP, WHADJP, or WHADVP **return** AMOD
  if P is PP or WHPP **return** PMOD
  else return DEP
end if

3.3.3 Structural Labels

Although it is preferable that the dependency relations reflect function rather than structure, structural labels were still needed for a proper representation of a small set of complex constructions. We used three such labels: EXP (expletive), CLF (cleft), and GAP (gapping).

Expletive constructions and cleft sentences are rhetorical transformations that usually result in a fronted *it*. Although superficially similar, expletives and clefts are handled rather differently in the Penn conventions. In an expletive construction, the referent S node is linked via a secondary edge to the preceding *it*, while for clefts the main clause carries the function tag CLF and the referent is unlabeled. In the converted format, these constructions were treated similarly: we attached the referent to the main verb and put the CLF or EXP label on that link. Figures 4 and 5 show examples of an expletive and a cleft, respectively, and their corresponding representations as dependency trees.

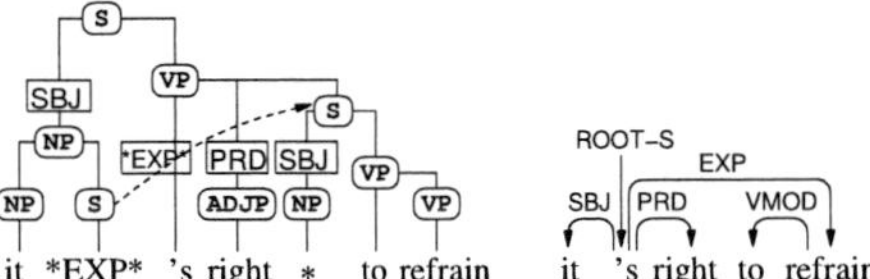

Figure 4: An expletive construction and its dependency representation.

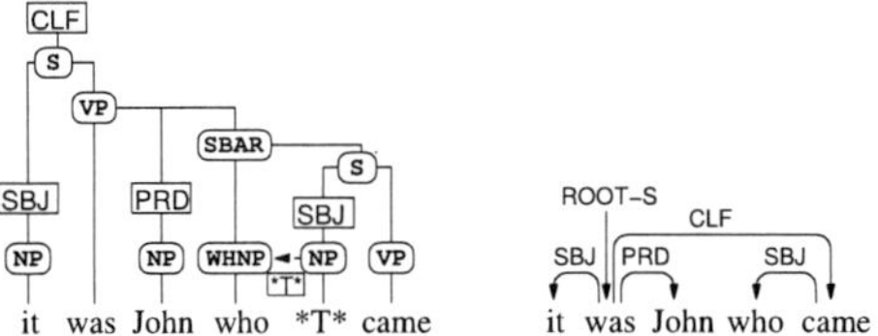

Figure 5: A cleft sentence and its dependency representation.

The phenomenon of gapping, i.e. when some part of a coordinated structure is ellipsed, is difficult to handle for any grammatical formalism, and a number of idiosyncratic solutions have been proposed. The approach used in Penn Treebank II is based on "templates." A coordinated structure with ellipsed constituents is assumed to be structurally identical to the first, and secondary edges (=) are used to identify corresponding constituents. In the dependency representation, we used the secondary edges as dependency links. Figure 6 shows an example of a constituent tree with gapping, and Figure 7 its corresponding dependency tree.

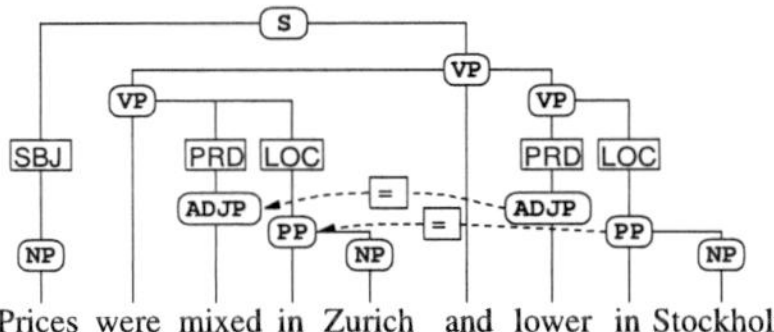

Figure 6: Example of gapping in the Penn Treebank.

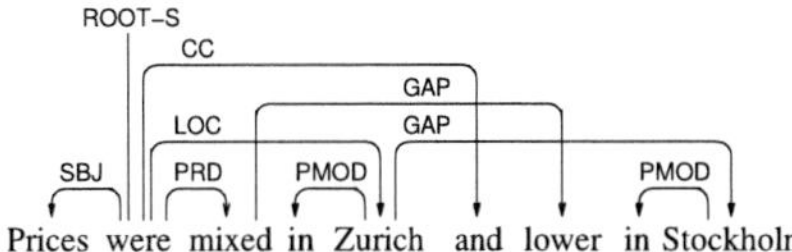

Figure 7: Dependency representation of gapping.

3.4 Relinking of Secondary Edges

Penn Treebank II defines seven kinds of secondary edges, which are listed in Table 2 along with their frequencies in WSJ sections 2–21 in the Treebank.

In many cases, the secondary edge represents a "deep governor", and is thus more useful as a dependency arc than the constituent attachment. In those cases, we relinked the heads of the constituents

Type	Description	#
T	Trace of *wh* and topicalization	15943
*	Other trace	18398
ICH	Discontinuous constituent	1000
RNR	Right node raising	345
=	Gapping	599
EXP	Expletive	557
PPA	Permanent predictable ambiguity	20

Table 2: Secondary edges in the Penn Treebank.

pointed to by the secondary edges. This was done for all *T* and *ICH* edges, unless the relinking causes the dependency graph to become cyclic (such as the link between the empty node and the root node in Figure 1). For right node raising, *RNR*, as for instance in *a U.S. and a Soviet naval vessel*, there are usually two secondary edges, of which only the first one is used. The treatment of the *EXP* and = links was described previously in Sect. 3.3.3.

The constituents pointed to by the "other trace" edges, of which traces of object movement in passive clauses seem to be the most frequent, could not be relinked since their original constituent attachments in most cases seem to be more meaningful as the dependency relation. For instance, we think the subject of a passive clause should not be relinked as an object of the passive verb. However, if the formalism were extended to allow for multiple heads, it could be useful to include those links as well.

The *PPA* (permanent predictable ambiguity) edges refer to cases where there is a structural ambiguity that cannot be resolved by the annotator, such as in *I saw a man with a telescope*. These links were not used in the conversion.

The relinking of constituents makes some trees *nonprojective*, i.e. the dependency tree cannot be drawn without crossing links. An example of this can be seen in Figure 3. In WSJ sections 2–21, the number of resulting nonprojective sentences was 2459 out of 39832, that is 6.17% of the sentences.

4 Experiments

4.1 Impact on Parsing Performance

The new format introduces more complexity in the dependency trees and and a practical issue is to determine how "parsable" they are. For instance, nonprojective trees makes parsing more complicated for some dependency parsers. To quantify this, we trained and evaluated two statistical dependency parsers on the new treebank.

MALTPARSER (Nivre et al., 2006) is based on a greedy parsing procedure that builds a parse tree incrementally while proceeding through the sentence one token at a time. By using a greedy strategy, a rich history-based feature set for the SVM classifier that selects the actions can be used. The parser produces projective trees only, but can handle nonprojectivity if a preprocessing step is used before training and a postprocessing step after parsing ("pseudo-projective parsing").

MSTPARSER (McDonald and Pereira, 2006) predicts a parse tree by maximizing a scoring function over the space of all possible parse trees. The scoring function is a weighted sum of features of single links or, if the "second-order" feature set is used, pairs of adjacent links. The parser can handle nonprojectivity, although the search then becomes NP-hard and has to be approximated.

Following convention, we trained the parsers on sections 2–21 of the WSJ part of the treebank. The training step took a few hours for MALTPARSER using a 64-bit AMD processor running at 2.2 GHz and roughly two days for MSTPARSER using a 32-bit Intel processor at 3.0 GHz.

To test the parsers, we ran the parser on Section 23 of the treebank and measured the labeled and unlabeled accuracy excluding punctuation. The gold-standard part-of-speech tags were used. Table 3 shows the results of the evaluation. For the new format, the relative increase in the number of errors is shown in brackets.

As can be expected, the new format is more difficult for parsers. For the labeled accuracy, this can partly be attributed to the richer set of function tags. For instance, PENN2MALT does not distinguish between temporal and locative adjuncts, but labels them all as verb modifiers. The difference in unlabeled accuracy is probably partly due to the fact that links can now be nonprojective, although this does not explain the whole difference. In addition, the feature sets used by the parsers may be suboptimal for the new way to represent some constructions. For instance, the large decrease in labeled accuracy by MSTPARSER can probably be explained by the fact that "linking words" such as prepositions and subordinating conjunctions do not attach to the verb (see Sect. 3.2). Since the feature set of MST-

	MALTPARSER		MSTPARSER	
	Labeled	Unlabeled	Labeled	Unlabeled
PENN2MALT	90.30%	91.36%	92.04%	93.06%
New conversion	87.63% (28%)	90.54% (9%)	86.92% (64%)	91.64% (20%)

Table 3: Parsing accuracy. Relative error increase in brackets.

PARSER cannot use features of grandchildren (because of independence assumptions needed to make search tractable), the lexical information about attachment behavior is lost in those cases. This is especially clear for the LGS label, which is assigned by MSTPARSER to many PPs not starting with *by*. MALTPARSER, on the other hand, can use this lexical information and performs better for those cases.

Function	R (MST)	P (MST)	R (MALT)	P (MALT)
CLF	0	0	0	0
CLR	50%	46%	70%	51%
COORD	69%	78%	82%	84%
EXP	45%	52%	35%	45%
GAP	16%	50%	20%	45%
IOBJ	54%	89%	63%	87%
LGS	64%	67%	90%	93%
OBJ	91%	78%	90%	90%
PRN	57%	72%	66%	40%
TMP	77%	80%	81%	86%

Table 4: Precision and recall results for a subset of the relations.

Table 4 shows the precision and recall results for the two parsers for some of the dependency relation types added in this conversion. The structural links (cleft, expletive, and gap) are difficult, which is hardly surprising since these phenomena result in long-distance dependencies and are comparatively rare in the Treebank.

4.2 Impact on Semantic Role Classification

To assess the semantic usefulness of the new dependency representation, we created a baseline semantic role labeler that we applied to the FrameNet example corpus (Baker et al., 1998), version 1.3, and compared its accuracy using the old and the new dependency treebanks. All sentences having a verb as target word were used and we tagged them using the MXPOST tagger (Ratnaparkhi, 1996). We then ran MALTPARSER using the statistical models obtained from both dependency treebanks. As input, the labeler received sentences where the semantic arguments were segmented but not labeled. For each argument that was not null-instantiated, we located the dependency node that was closest to the target in terms of the dependency tree. For most cases, this node was a direct dependent of the target verb.

The baseline role classifier considered the grammatical function of the argument node and assigned the semantic role label that was most frequently associated with this grammatical function for each verb in each frame. For instance, for the verb *tell* in the frame TELLING, we mapped the subject to the semantic role SPEAKER, the direct object to MESSAGE, and, for the new format, the indirect object to ADDRESSEE.

Method	Accuracy
PENN2MALT	64.3%
New conversion	72.5% (23%)

Table 5: Semantic role classification results.

Table 5 shows the accuracy of this baseline classifier when using the PENN2MALT and the new conversion, respectively. The new format gives a 23% error reduction for classification. Clearly, the improved performance is a result of the increased granularity of the set of edge labels that is gained by using Penn's edge labels and by distinguishing between direct and indirect objects. Table 6 shows an example of this: for the verb *receive* in the frame RECEIVING, the grammatical functions can express twice as many semantic roles. For this frame, the error reduction was 37.5%.

FN Role	PENN2MALT	New conversion
COUNTERTRANSFER	∅	∅
DEPICTIVE	∅	∅
DONOR	VMOD	CLR, DIR
MANNER	∅	∅
MEANS	∅	∅
MODE_OF_TRANSFER	∅	MNR
PATH	∅	∅
PLACE	∅	LOC
PURPOSE_OF_DONOR	∅	∅
PURPOSE_OF_THEME	∅	PRP
RECIPIENT	SUB	LGS, SBJ, VMOD
ROLE	∅	∅
THEME	OBJ	ADV, OBJ
TIME	∅	TMP

Table 6: FrameNet semantic roles and their corresponding grammatical functions for the verb *receive* in the frame RECEIVING.

5   Conclusion and Future Work

This paper presented a new method to convert English constituent structures in the Penn Treebank format into dependency trees. The aim was that the resulting trees should make more sense semantically than those produced by previous approaches. The new procedure relied on the extended representation that is available in the recent versions of the Treebank. The set of arc labels used by previous methods was enriched by using Penn's own set of labels and by creating a set of rules to infer some other.

The new format is structurally more complex; for instance, some sentences now have nonprojective links. This is reflected in the performance of two statistical parsers: the error rate increased by 28% for the best system. It would be interesting to examine in detail which constructions are problematic for the parser, and how complex phenomena such as coordination should be represented for best parsing performance. Possibly, better parsing results could be achieved by first predicting a parse tree in the PENN2MALT style or some other surface-oriented format, and then applying a (possibly statistically trained) transformation to arrive at the richer dependency structure.

A further step could be to extend the dependency structures to allow multiple-headed graphs, for which a practical parsing algorithm was recently proposed (McDonald and Pereira, 2006). This work was restricted to conventional single-headed dependency trees, which might be inadequate in some cases, such as right node raising and verbs of control and raising. Multiple-headed dependency parsing is also relevant for semantic interpretation of parse trees; ideally, all semantic arguments of a predicate verb would be direct dependents of that verb.

Finally, the motivation for this research is that we believe that a semantically oriented dependency structure will make automatic semantic analyses, such as FrameNet-based predicate argument structure analysis, more robust and easier to implement. While we see a large gain in semantic role classification accuracy with a baseline technique using only grammatical functions, it remains to be seen which impact the new formalism has on semantic role labeling in general. A well-designed dependency structure would ideally allow us to get rid of the very sparse and brittle *Path* feature that has been used in most contituent-based semantic role labelers to date.

References

Collin F. Baker, Charles J. Fillmore, and John B. Lowe. 1998. The Berkeley FrameNet Project. In *Proceedings of COLING-ACL'98*.

Michael J. Collins. 1999. Head-driven statistical models for natural language parsing. Ph.D. thesis, University of Pennsylvania, Philadelphia.

David M. Magerman. 1994. Natural language parsing as statistical pattern recognition. Ph.D. thesis, Stanford University.

Mitchell P. Marcus, Beatrice Santorini, and Mary Ann Marcinkiewicz. 1993. Building a large annotated corpus of English: the Penn Treebank. *Computational Linguistics*, 19(2):313–330.

Mitch Marcus, Grace Kim, Mary Ann Marcinkiewicz, Robert MacIntyre, Ann Bies, Mark Ferguson, Karen Katz, and Britta Schasberger. 1994. The Penn treebank: Annotating predicate argument structure. In *ARPA Human Language Technology Workshop*.

Ryan McDonald and Fernando Pereira. 2006. On-line learning of approximate dependency parsing algorithms. In *Proceedings EACL-2006*.

Igor A. Mel'čuk. 1988. *Dependency Syntax: Theory and Practice*. State University Press of New York, Albany.

Joakim Nivre, Johan Hall, and Jens Nilsson. 2006. Malt-Parser: A data-driven parser generator for dependency parsing. In *Proceedings of LREC2006*.

Joakim Nivre. 2006. *Inductive Dependency Parsing*. Springer Verlag.

Owen Rambow, Cassandre Creswell, Rachel Szekely, Harriet Tauber, and Marilyn Walker. 2002. A dependency treebank for English. In *Proceedings of LREC2002*.

Adwait Ratnaparkhi. 1996. A maximum entropy part-of-speech tagger. In *Proceedings of EMNLP-1996*.

Matthias Trautner Kromann. 2003. The Danish Dependency Treebank and the DTAG treebank tool. In *Proceedings of the Second Workshop on Treebanks and Linguistic Theories (TLT)*.

Hiroyasu Yamada and Yuji Matsumoto. 2003. Statistical dependency analysis with support vector machines. In *Proceedings of 8th International Workshop on Parsing Technologies*.

Comparison of the Methods of Self-Organizing Maps and Multidimensional Scaling in Analysis of Estonian Emotion Concepts

Toomas Kirt
Tallinn University of Technology
Tallinn
Estonia
Toomas.Kirt@mail.ee

Ene Vainik
Institute of the Estonian Language
Tallinn
Estonia
ene@eki.ee

Abstract

Self-organizing map (SOM) and multidimensional scaling (MDS) are the methods of data analysis that reduce dimensionality of the input data and visualize the structure of multidimensional data by means of projection. Both methods are widely used in different research areas. In the studies of emotion vocabulary and other psycho-lexical surveys the MDS has been prevalent. In this paper both of the methods are introduced and as an illustration they are applied to a case study of Estonian emotion concepts. There is a need to introduce some new methods to the field because exploiting only one analytical tool may tend to reveal only specific properties of data and thus have an unwanted impact on the results.

1 Introduction

Human's ability to perceive the structure of multidimensional data is limited and some methods are needed to reduce the dimensionality of data and to reveal its structure. Several methods and techniques of data analysis are used to project multidimensional data into a lower two- or three-dimensional space and to visualize the structure of it. In this paper the methods of self-organizing map (SOM) and multidimensional scaling (MDS) are under discussion.

Some of the researchers have compared the methods of SOM and MDS earlier and outlined both their similarities and dissimilarities (e.g.,

Kaski, 1997; Duda et al., 2001). Kaski has emphasized their general similarity in respect that both methods tend to reduce dimensionality of observed data and reveal its hidden structure. The two methods differ in the strategy applied to the data. The SOM tries to preserve local neighborhood relations and MDS the interpoint distances between samples.

A hypothesis could be formulated that the way the data are handled in an analytical tool might have an impact on the layout of the results. In order to test this hypothesis the data of present case study – a study of the Estonian concepts of emotion – was analyzed by both SOM and MDS. In the following we will demonstrate the layout of data on both cases and discuss their compatibility.

One of the purposes of the comparison of the two methods is to introduce the method of SOM as relatively unexploited in psycho-lexical studies. Although there are some examples of applying SOM to linguistic data (e.g., Honkela, 1997; Lagus et al., 2002) there are no references to other studies of emotion concepts by the self-organizing maps, yet. In the field of psycho-lexical studies MDS has prevailed so far (e.g., the MDS based Geneva Emotion Wheel (Scherer, 2005)), despite SOM's great popularity in several areas of data analysis (Kohonen, 2000).

In the first part of the paper the two methods are introduced. In the second part of the paper the survey of Estonian emotion concepts is used as an example to demonstrate the similarities and differences of the methods.

Joakim Nivre, Heiki-Jaan Kaalep, Kadri Muischnek and Mare Koit (Eds.)
NODALIDA 2007 Conference Proceedings, pp. 113–120

2   The Self-Organizing Map

The self-organizing map (Kohonen, 1982; 2000) is a tool for the visualization of high-dimensional data. It projects nonlinear relationships between high-dimensional input data into a two-dimensional output grid, named also a map. The self-organizing map is an artificial neural network that uses an unsupervised learning algorithm – it means there is no prior knowledge how input and output are connected.

To describe how the process for creating the self-organizing map works let assume, that we have input data as a set of sample vectors x. It is also called an input space. The output of the self-organizing map is a grid of vectors m_i that have the same number of elements as the sample vector x. Initially all the vectors of the output grid are initialized randomly.

The algorithm of SOM has two main basic steps that are repeated a number of times. First a random sample vector x(t) is chosen and compared with all the output vectors m_i to find closest unit c on the output grid that has a minimum distance $d(x - m_i)$ with a sample vector x. Secondly this best matching or winning vector and its neighborhood are changed closer to the sample vector. The formula for learning process is as follows:

$m_i(t+1) = m_i(t) + a(t)\ h_{ci}(t)(x(t) - m_i(t)).$

Where a(t) is learning rate factor and $h_{ci}(t)$ – neighborhood function at the time step t. During the learning process the learning rate and the neighborhood function are shrinking. The learning process results in an ordered output where similar sample vectors are projected as closely located units on the map.

For visualization of the self-organizing map an Unified distance matrix (U-matrix) is used (Ultsch, 1993). The U-matrix presents the distances between each map unit by color coding. The light color corresponds to a small distance between two map units and the dark color presents a bigger difference between the map units. The points on the output map that are on the light area belong to the same group or cluster and the dark area shows the borders between the clusters.

To illustrate the behavior of the SOM the matrix of distances between Estonian cities is used. The input data consists of distances between 59 Estonian cities. The initial distance matrix is downloaded from the web page of the Estonian Road Administration[1]. From the distance matrix the relative coordinates are calculated. The coordinate matrix is two-dimensional and therefore it is useful to see, how a method transforms the original data. The analysis is performed by the SOM toolbox ver 2.0 for Matlab[2].

The output of the SOM is presented in Figure 1. The map retains Estonian original topological structure in general terms, despite the fact that the eastern side of Estonia is projected on the top of the map. The cities that are close to each other in the real map are projected on the close map units. The color coding also gives some insight into distances between the cities and it is possible to identify regions where the density of population is higher. The local neighborhood is retained, but it is difficult to fully identify the map with the real map of Estonia.

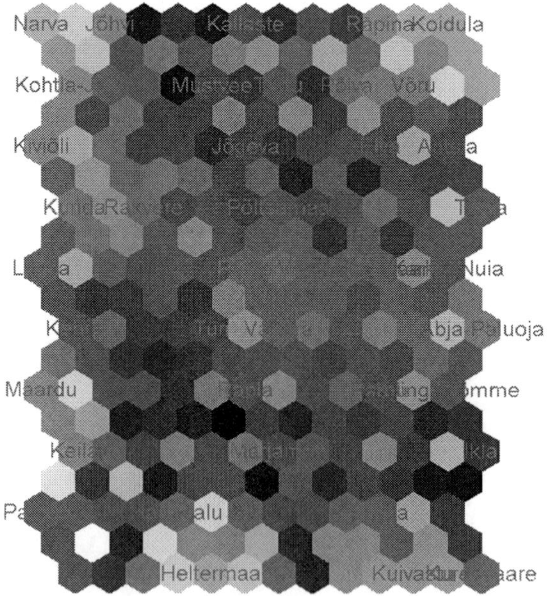

Figure 1. The SOM of Estonian Cities.

3   Multidimensional Scaling

The method of multidimensional scaling (MDS) is a set of related statistical techniques often used in data visualization for exploring proximities in data. The goal of the method is to project data points as points in some lower-dimensional space so that the

[1] Downloaded from http://www.mnt.ee/
[2] Downloaded from http://www.cis.hut.fi/projects/somtoolbox/

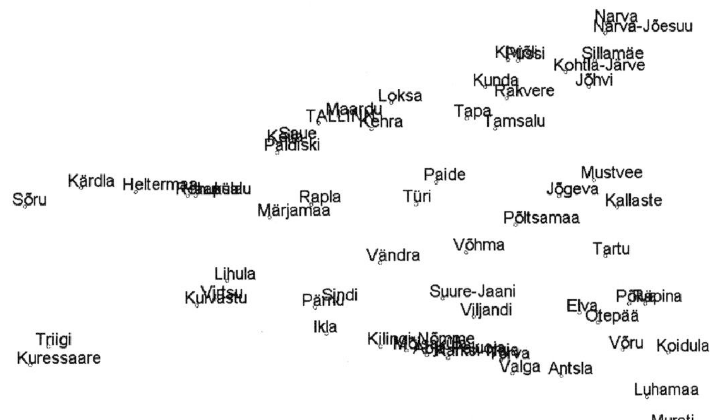

Figure 2. The MDS of Estonian Cities.

distances between the points correspond to the dissimilarities between the points in the original space as closely as possible. Such representation is valuable for gaining insight into the structure of data. MDS can be used as a method of reducing the dimensionality of the data and revealing the dissimilarity between the samples.

MDS is said to be metrical if it based on measured proximities and nonmetrical when the proximities are based on judgment (Jobson, 1992). The original method of MDS was metric (Torgerson, 1958). In current paper the analysis is based on nonmetrical data and therefore the nonmetric MDS is used. The data is analyzed by the statistical software package SPSS and the ALSCAL algorithm created by Takane et al. (1977).

There are n sample vectors $x_1,...,x_n$ and the distance between original samples i and j is g_{ij}. The y_i is the lower-dimensional representation of x_i and the distance between projected samples i and j is d_{ij}. The aim of the MDS method is to find a configuration of image points $y_1,...,y_n$ in a lower dimensional space for which the distances d_{ij} between the samples are as close as possible to the corresponding original distances g_{ij} so that the dissimilarities between the samples are retained as well as possible. Because it is impossible to find a configuration for which $d_{ij} = g_{ij}$ for all i and j, certain criteria are needed whether the result is good enough.

The interdistance matrix of Estonian cities is used again to illustrate the method of MDS (Figure 2). As it can be noticed the result resembles Estonian map despite the fact that some cities in the Northwest and Southwest are projected closer than they are in the real map. It can be caused by the well known "horseshoe effect" that is common to the multidimensional scaling (Buja and Swayne, 2002).

As we can see from the initial example (Figures 1 and 2) the two methods have their preferences. The SOM is good, if the data is represented as coordinates and local relations between the samples are important. The MDS is oriented to reveal the structure of metric distances between the samples and it reveals the overall picture of the data.

4   Study of Estonian Emotion Concepts

The purpose of the case study was to discover the hidden structure of the Estonian emotion concepts and whether it depended on how the information about concepts was gathered. According to the theory of conceptual spaces (Gärdenfors, 2000), the level of conceptual representations of emotions is assumed to be intermediate in abstractness between the levels of purely linguistic (symbolic) and subconceptual representation which is related to emotional experience. In the experiment these two levels of emotion knowledge (lexical and experiential) were used to approach the intermediate level of concepts. Two lexical tasks were designed that provided information about emotion concepts either through their relation to the episodes of emotional experience or through semantic interrelations of emotion terms (synonymy and antonymy).

4.1 Subjects and Procedures

The inquiry was carried out in written form, in 2003, in Estonia. The number of respondents was 100 (50 men and 50 women), aged from 14 to 76 (M = 40.2, SD = 18.61), all native speakers of Estonian. The selection of concepts to be included in the study (N=24) was based on the results of tests of free listings (Vainik, 2002), word frequencies in the corpora, and a comparison with word lists used by some earlier studies of Estonian emotion terms. We believe that the selected lexical items form a small but representative set of the core of the emotion category of Estonian lexicon, sufficient for comparing the structures of emotion concepts, which emerge from the two different lexical tasks.

In the first task the participants had to evaluate the meaning of every single word against a set of seven bipolar scales, inspired by Osgood's method of semantic differentials (Osgood et al., 1975). The "semantic features" measured with polar scales drew qualitative (unpleasant vs. pleasant), quantitative (strong vs. weak emotion, long vs. short in duration), situational (increases vs. decreases action readiness, follows vs. precedes an event), and interpretative distinctions (felt in the mind vs. body, depends mostly on oneself vs. others). The original bipolar scales were transformed from having +/- values into positive scales of 7–1, starting from 7 as the maximum value of the dominant or default feature, over 4 pointing to the irrelevance of the scale, and up to 1 as the minimum value (corresponding to the maximum of the opposite feature).

The second task was a free listing task (Corbett and Davies, 1997). Participants were provided with a blank space to write down as many synonyms and antonyms as came to mind for every presented item. The task eliciting similar concepts resulted in 4068 lexical items and the task eliciting opposite concepts resulted in 3694 lexical items. Before the analysis with SOM and MDS the information was first quantified. The words listed as similar or opposite were characterized by their indices of relative cognitive salience (Sutrop, 2001). The index which takes into account both frequency and mean position of a term was calculated for every word mentioned by at least three persons. Out of total 488 relations only 219 with indices greater than or equal to the average (S_{ave} = .07), were subsequently processed with SOM and MDS

4.2 Results of Task 1 and Task 2

In the first task the data pool of all answers to the 24 concepts on the 7 joint scales was processed. So a vector consisting of 700 answers represented each word. In the second task the words were described by a vector in length of 219 representing values of the index of relative cognitive salience.

Figure 3 and 4 present the structure of Estonian emotion concepts according to the results of the first task. The translations and locations of words on the SOM are given in the following Table 1. The MDS was created with translations only.

The SOM of the first task appears as a bilaterally symmetrical representation. The positive emotion concepts tend to gather to the upper part of the graph and the words referring to negative emotions to the lower part of the graph. Thus, the main organizing dimension of the representation, which extends the shape of the SOM map in one direction, appears to be negativeness and positiveness of the concepts. There is a darker area in the middle, which clearly separates these two clusters. One concept, *ärevus* 'anxiety', is located outside of these two clusters. Apparently it is identifiable neither as positive nor negative or having conflicting specifications in respect of affiliation. As the anticipatory states (*hirm* 'fear', *erutus* 'excitement', *mure* 'concern') are gathered to the right edge of the graph, the scale follows vs. precedes an event seems to function as an additional less important dimension. There is, however, no darker area on the SOM separating the extremes of this dimension.

The MDS represents concepts on the circle. By shape it resembles the circumplex model proposed by Russell (Russell, 1980; Russell et al., 1989). The MDS presents also a clear distinction between the positive and negative concepts on the horizontal scale – the more negative the concepts the more left they are situated and the positive concepts are situated on the right-hand side, accordingly. In MDS, too, the concept of *ärevus* 'anxiety' occurs as ambivalent between positive and negative concepts, and so does *kaastunne* 'pity, compassion'.

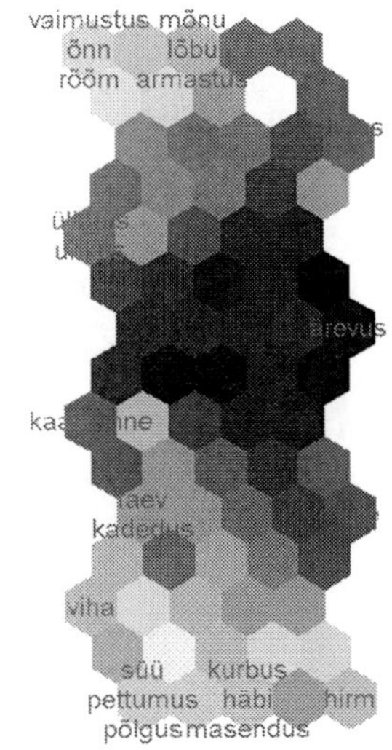

Figure 3. The SOM of the First Task.

Table 1. Location of Words on the SOM of the First Task.

enthusiasm	pleasure	passion
happiness	fun	
joy	love	
		excitement
		desire
surprise		
pride		
		anxiety
pity		
rage		concern
envy		
anger		
guilt	sadness	fear
disappointment	shame	
contempt	oppression	

There is another dimension that distinguishes the concepts on vertical scale: the states perceived as event preceding are situated on the upper part of the circle and the states perceived as following some event are situated in the bottom. According to the MDS presentation the concept *masendus* 'oppression' can be regarded as not clearly preceding nor following its eliciting event.

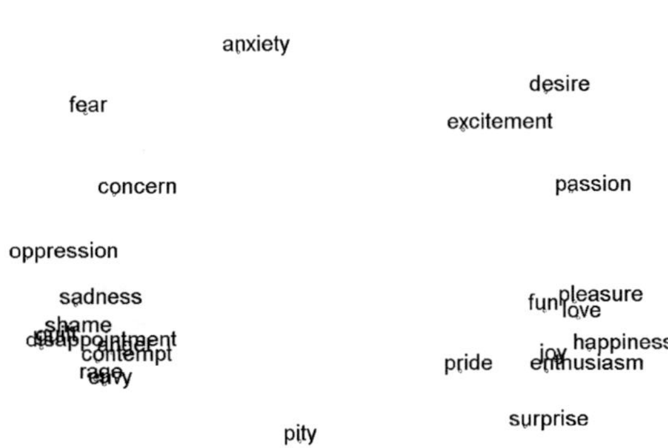

Figure 4. The MDS of the First Task.

The results of the first task characterize how the conceptual organization of emotion emerged from subconceptual and experiential level of knowledge in Gärdenfors's model (2000). It can be seen, that the two methods resulted in very similar layouts, except the orientation of the dimensions and the way of discriminating the groups.

Figures 5 and 6 (and Table 2) present the structure of the Estonian emotion concepts according to the results of the second task of the survey. This task addressed the most abstract and symbolic level of representation of emotion knowledge, according to the Theory of conceptual spaces (Gärdenfors, 2000), which was accessed through the semantic interrelations of emotion terms in our task.

On the SOM of the second task also a general vertical alignment of positive (bottom) versus negative (top) concepts is observable. There is a remarkably darker row of nodes aligned horizontally, separating those two categories of unequal size. The concepts have self-distributed into three clusters, though, as in the upper part of the graph there is a diagonally located darker area excluding the cluster of concepts in the uppermost right corner. One node containing two concepts *iha* 'desire' and *kirg* 'passion' are standing outside the clusters not belonging to any of them.

This SOM does not coincide with the SOM of the Task 1. Instead of two we have three clearly distinguishable clusters here. This lets us to conclude that the organization of emotion concepts is slightly different while emerging from the data about the relations of similarity and oppositeness. The SOM layouts thus occur to support the hypothesis of the case study about the plausibility of differences in conceptual organization due to the way the data about concepts is gathered.

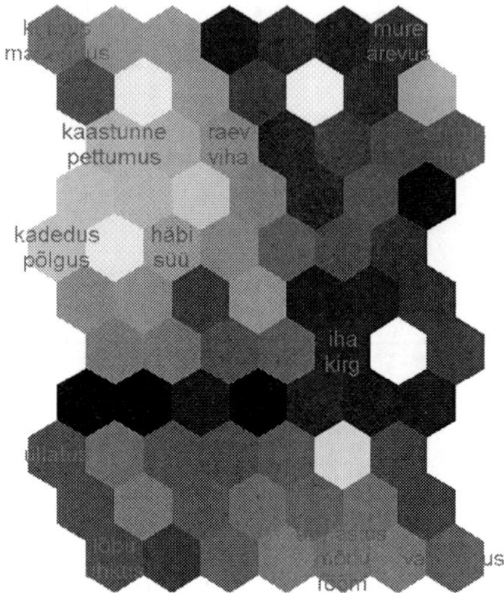

Figure 5. The SOM of the Second Task.

Table 2. Location of Words on the SOM of the Second Task.

| sadness | | concern | |
oppression		anxiety	
pity	rage	excitement	
disappointment	anger	fear	
envy	shame		
contempt	guilt		
		desire	
		passion	
surprise			
fun	happiness	love	enthusiasm
pride		pleasure	
		joy	

The MDS of the second task, on the other hand, retained the circular structure and there might be seen the horizontal alignment of positive (right-hand side) versus negative (left-hand side) concepts on the graph, as well as the vertical alignment of event preceding states (the upper part) versus the event following states (the lower part of the graph).

At the first glance the result of Task 2 as analyzed by MDS is very similar to the result of Task 1 except that the locations of *kaastunne* 'pity' and *vaimustus* 'enthusiasm' do not fit. This result leads us to two possible conclusions. First, we can conclude that the way the information about emotion concepts was gathered had no or only nonsignificant impact on their emergent structure, which proves the invalidity of our hypothesis of the case study. On the other hand, we can conclude that the method of MDS tends to generalize the results to fit a circular solution best presented by two crossing dimensions.

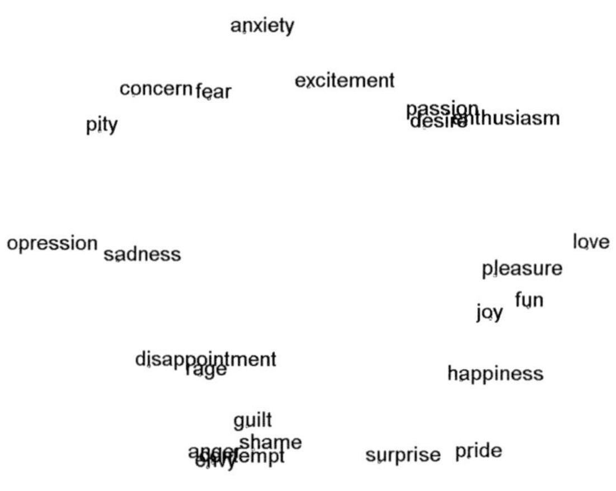

Figure 6. The MDS of the Second Task.

However, even on the circular arrangement there are actually three groups of concepts visible, especially with the prior knowledge from the SOM analysis. On the bottom right there is a cluster of positive concepts, the cluster of negative ones is situated on the bottom left and on the top there are concepts that might be described mostly by their quality as event preceding states. These three clusters are partly compatible with these three described on the SOM of the Task 2 (Figure 5).

5 Discussion

In previous section two tasks of differently accessed semantics of the Estonian emotion terms were compared and two methods of data analysis were applied. As a result, both methods gave us a general understanding what are the main dimensions that distinguish emotion concepts and revealed that there is clear distinction between positive and negative concepts. In the first task both methods distinguished two groups of concepts and in the second task one additional cluster emerged. The level of abstractness at which emotion knowledge was accessed in the tasks (subconceptual and experience-related vs. symbolic and lexicon-related) turned out as critical while SOM was used and nonsignificant while MDS was used. The hypothesis of the case study was thus proven only in the case of using SOM. With this conflicting result, however, is proven the main hypothesis of our present study. Namely, the way the data was handled in an analytical tool turned out to have an impact on the layout of the results.

Comparing the results of analysis of linguistic data SOM formed clearly separable clusters and MDS projected data on the circle. Supposedly, MDS presented the overall distances between the samples and therefore the extremity of dominant positive negative scale became dominant in both cases and the overall layout of the results occurred as the same - circular. At the same time the SOM gives an overview of local relations between concepts and forms local clusters. However, even the projection of local relationships between the samples gave us the insight that there is the division between the positive and negative concepts.

In the case the data was gathered from the task relying on the procedure of the Osgood's semantic differential or alike, the two methods revealed very similar results. In the case the data was gathered by assessing concept similarity and oppositeness the layouts of MDS and SOM seem somehow differently. It is probably the point where the different strategies used in the analytical tools turn out as critical. MDS uses a strategy to keep most dissimilar samples as apart as possible (it preserves the distances) and SOM uses the strategy to keep the most similar samples together (it preserves the neighborhood relations). The data of the Task 2 contained data about both assessed concept similarity (a tendency to interpret similar concepts as situated close to each other) and about oppositeness (a tendency to interpret most dissimilar samples as most apart in a hypothetical conceptual space (Gärdenfors, 2000)). Thus the construal of the Task 2 might have made it sensitive to the procedures used in the analytical tool.

While analyzing linguistic data containing information about concept similarities and dissimilarities it might be useful not to be grounded in just one analytical tool, because MDS gave similar circular structure as a result of both tasks. When some additional knowledge was acquired from the SOM analysis, a more complicated structure within the data was revealed. The interpretation of the results may depend on the interpreter – his or her thoroughness and in more general what he or she wants or supposes to see.

6 Conclusions

In the present paper the results of analysis of Estonian emotion concepts by two methods — the self-organizing maps and multidimensional scaling — were compared. Both methods gave us a general understanding what are the main dimensions distinguishing emotional concepts and revealed a clear distinction between positive and negative ones. Both methods also demonstrated their peculiarities due to the different strategies used in their procedures of data handling. Although both methods reveal the dominant dimensions describing the data, SOM stresses more on the local similarities and distinguishes clearly groups within the data. MDS reveals global dissimilarities between the samples and some background information is needed to distinguish groups. Our conclusion would be that exploiting only one analytical tool may tend to reveal only specific properties of data and thus have an unwanted impact on the results.

Acknowledgement

The study was supported by ETF grant 7149.

References

Buja A. and Swayne D. F. 2002. Visualization Methodology for Multidimensional Scaling. *Journal of Classification*, 19: 7-43.

Corbett G. G. and Davies I. R. L. 1997. Establishing basic color terms: Measures and techniques. In C. L. Hardin & L. Maffi (Eds.), *Color categories in thought and language* (pp. 197–223). Cambridge University Press, Cambridge.

Duda R. O., Hart P. E. and Stork D. G. 2001. *Pattern classification* (2nd ed.). John Wiley & Sons, New York.

Gärdenfors P. 2000. *Conceptual Spaces: The Geometry of Thought*. The MIT Press, London.

Honkela T. 1997. Learning to understand—General aspects of using self-organizing maps in natural language processing. In D. Dubois (Ed.), *Computing anticipatory systems* (pp. 563–576). American Institute of Physics, Woodbury, NY.

Jobson J. D. 1992. *Applied multivariate Data Analysis*, Vol. II. Springer, New York.

Kaski S. 1997. Data exploration using self-organizing maps. *Acta Polytechnica Scandinavica, Mathematics, Computing and Management in Engineering Series No. 82*. Helsinki University of Technology, Finland.

Kohonen T. 1982. Self-organized formation of topologically correct feature maps. *Biological Cybernetics*, 43: 59–69.

Kohonen T. 2000. *Self-organising maps* (3rd edition), Springer, Berlin.

Lagus K., Airola A. and Creutz M. 2002. Data analysis of conceptual similarities of Finnish verbs. In W. D. Gray and C. D. Schunn (Eds.), *Proceedings of the 24th Annual Conference of the Cognitive Science Society* (pp. 566–571). Lawrence Erlbaum, Hillsdale, NJ.

Osgood C. E., Suci G. J. and Tannenbaum, P. H. 1975. *The Measurement of Meaning*. University of Illinois Press, Urbana and Chicago.

Russell J. A. 1980. A circumflex model of affect. *Journal of Personality and Social Psychology*, 39: 1161–1178.

Russell J. A., Lewicka M. and Niit T. 1989. A cross-cultural study of a circumplex model of affect. *Journal of Personality and Social Psychology*, 57: 848–856.

Scherer K. R. 2005. What are emotions? And how should they be measured? *Social Science Information*, 44(4): 695–729.

Sutrop U. 2001. List task and a cognitive salience index. *Field Methods*, 13: 289–302.

Takane, Y., Young, F. W., and de Leeuw J. 1977. Nonmetric individual differences multidimensional scaling: an alternating least square method with optimal scaling features. *Psychometrika*, 42: 7-67.

Torgerson, W. S. 1958. *Theory and methods of scaling*. Chapman & Hall, London.

Ultsch, A. 1993. Knowledge extraction from self-organizing neural networks. In O. Opitz, B. Lausen, & R. Klar (Eds.), *Information and Classification* (pp. 301–306). Springer, Berlin.

Vainik, E. 2002. Emotions, emotion terms and emotion concepts in an Estonian folk model. *Trames*, 6(4): 322–341.

The Extraction of Trajectories from Real Texts Based on Linear Classification

Hanjing Li
Harbin Institute of Technology MOE-MS Key Laboratory of Natural Language Processing and Speech, Harbin, 150001

`hjlee@mtlab.hit.edu.cn`

Sheng Li
Harbin Institute of Technology MOE-MS Key Laboratory of Natural Language Processing and Speech, Harbin, 150001

`lisheng@hit.edu.cn`

Tiejun Zhao
Harbin Institute of Technology MOE-MS Key Laboratory of Natural Language Processing and Speech, Harbin, 150001

`tjzhao@mtlab.hit.edu.cn`

Jiyuan Zhao
Harbin Institute of Technology MOE-MS Key Laboratory of Natural Language Processing and Speech, Harbin, 150001

`jyzhao@mtlab.hit.edu.cn`

Abstract

Text-to-scene conversion systems need to share the spatial descriptions between natural language and the 3D scene. Such applications are the ideal candidates for the extraction of spatial relations from free texts, in which the extraction to trajectories that are focus objects in spatial descriptions is an essential problem. We present an analysis of how the space relations are described in Chinese. Based on this study, we propose a method where the extraction of trajectories is modeled as a binary classification problem and resolved based on a linear classifier with syntactic features. Moreover, experimental results are analyzed in detail to demonstrate the effectiveness of the linear classifier to the extraction problem of the trajectory concept.

1 Introduction

Text-to-scene conversion systems are systems where a static 3D scene or a cartoon is generated from text. How to extract spatial relations from texts is an essential problem for sharing the spatial information between natural language and 3D scene in such systems. A spatial relation is composed of a spatial expression and a trajectory according to cognitive linguistics. Furthermore, a trajectory is the focus object to be described in a spatial relation. Therefore, it is an essential problem to extract trajectories from a text for a text-to-scene system.

Until now, there are some researches done to resolve the extraction of the trajectory. It is resolved based on dependency relationship in *Wordseye* system (Coyne and Sproat, 2001), and case grammar in *SWAN* system (Lu and Zhang, 2002). But two points must be clarified in these two systems. First, the input of them was restricted to a simple subset of English or Chinese consisting of simple sentences without complex grammar phenomena such as clauses, ellipsis of the object or subject, and spatial focus shifts. Also, only one or zero spatial relation is and should be described clearly in one simple sentence, such as *The store is under the large willow.* (Coyne and Sproat, 2001). Second, they do not refer to the term trajectory and tasks of the extraction of the spatial relation and the trajectory. Although the *Carsim* system, which is another text-to-scene system, refers to the term trajectory and the task of the extraction of the trajectory on IDA method (Johansson, 2006), a trajectory means the route of every event in the animation which does not refer to the same meaning as in this paper.

Joakim Nivre, Heiki-Jaan Kaalep, Kadri Muischnek and Mare Koit (Eds.)
NODALIDA 2007 Conference Proceedings, pp. 121–127

The task considered here is to acquire the corresponding trajectories of a spatial expression at the text level, and then every trajectory and the spatial expression can compose a special spatial relation. For example, see the fable in Figure 1, "鹰" (the eagle) and "乌龟" (the tortoise) that should be extracted, match exactly with the spatial expression of "到高空" (in the clouds) separately and result in two spatial relations, "鹰到高空" (the eagle in the clouds) and "乌龟在高空" (the tortoise in the clouds) that can be acquired exactly. In the paper, we focus on the extraction from real texts. Based on an analysis of spatial descriptive Chinese language, we have developed a binary classifier that can identify trajectories and compose spatial relations.

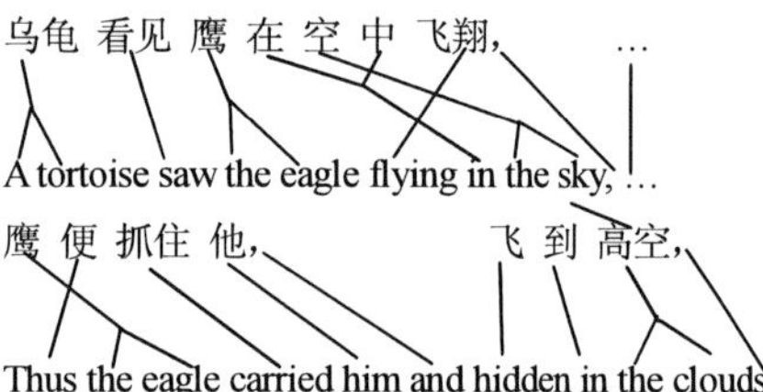

Figure 1: 'The Eagle and the Tortoise' in "Aesop's Fables"

To study the characteristics of descriptive spatial language, we analyzed the descriptions by cataloguing the relations between trajectories and their corresponding spatial expressions respectively on Chinese grammar. The combination style of a trajectory and the corresponding spatial expression is referred to as a descriptive strategy including three types of the mapping, the spatial focus shift and the syntactic location.

We propose a set of computational mechanisms that correspond to the most commonly used descriptive strategies. The related terms are formally defined first. Also the extraction of trajectories is modeled as a binary classification problem. Based on those formalizations, we deal with the extraction with Winnow being a linear classification algorithm on syntactic features at the text level.

To evaluate the method, we created an evaluation corpus of "Aesop's Fables", and used three evaluation measures including precision P (the percentage of all correct results in the all results identified by the method), recall R (the percentage of all correct results identified by the method in all really correct results), and F-score ($F=(P*R*2/(P+R))$).

The method has three advantages. First, it showed that the shallow syntactic features are effective for the extraction of the cognitive concept of a trajectory. Second, it did work in a range of linguistic phenomena that make use of really complex compositions of spatial semantics. Last, it was effective without a parser which is domain dependence for Chinese.

The paper is organized as follows. In Sect. 2, we analyze descriptive strategies in Chinese, and then give the definitions of terms. Also, we review SNoW. In Sect. 3, we first formalize the problem considered in this paper, and then we discuss the linear classifier to extract the trajectory. Experimental results are given in Sect. 4. Finally, we make some concluding remarks in Sect. 5.

2 The Resource Creation

2.1 The Definitions of Relevant Terms

We define formally terms including trajectory, landmark, spatial expression and spatial description. Trajectory and landmark are all from Langacker's Cognitive Grammar Framework (Langacker, 1987). Trajectory TR enclosed by a particular bound presents the focus object represented in a spatial description. The bound is called Landmark LM.

A spatial expression SE limits the location of the trajectory, and is formalized as ($[Pre]$, Loc, LM), in which [] means that the part can be omitted, Pre denotes preposition, and Loc denotes localizer (explained in (Zou, 1989)). For example "在空中" (in the sky) is formalized as (在, 中, 空) (in, ,sky).

A Spatial description describes the spatial configuration of a trajectory with respect to a landmark. In this paper, we define spatial description formally as a spatial relation. A spatial relation is composed of two parts including a spatial expression and trajectory and taken as a binary (($[Pre]$, Loc, LM), TR), which represents relative or absolute position and orientation. For example, the description of "鹰在空中" (the eagle in the sky) in Figure 1 is formalized as ((在, 中, 空), 鹰) ((in, , the sky), the eagle).

2.2 The Corpus Creation

As there are no publicly available evaluation corpora, we selected "Aesop's Fables" as a corpus for this task where 10 volumes and 434 texts in Chinese are available at http://www.white-collar.net/child/fable/yisuo/index.html.

The "Aesop's Fables" was annotated with spatial expressions, landmarks and trajectories successively, and turned into the evaluation database for the extraction of spatial relations. The texts annotated separately by every annotator were merged into the final corpus according to the all-passed rule. There were six annotators including 2 undergraduate students, 3 graduate students and 1 PhD student, who all take part in the project "Research on Visualization of Spatial Descriptions in text".

The "Aesop's Fables" was first segmented and part-of-speech (POS) annotated with the tool described in (Lv, 2003), anaphora resolved by hand, (for example, [AR乌龟/ng] is an anaphora resolution of "他/r" (it) in Figure 2), and then called initial corpus. Afterwards, the initial corpus was annotated on spatial relations by hand with the rules presented following.

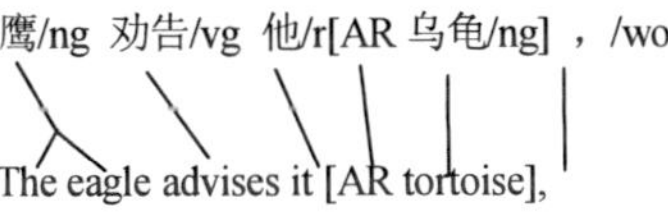

Figure 2: The sample of initial corpus with POS and anaphora resolution

Spatial Expression: Participants recognized a spatial expression according to the definition presented in Sect. 2.1, and annotated it with the following notations: the beginning symbol of a spatial expression #l, the end symbol #r, the spatial expression notation SE, and the sequence number of the spatial expression. For example in Figure 3, the string of "#l 空中/s #r[SE1]" means "空中" (in the sky) is the first spatial expression in the text. In addition, when there were two spatial expressions in one phrase of the definition they were all annotated separately at the same time like "#l在/p #l空中/s #r[SE1]#r[SE2]" in Figure 3.

Landmark: The landmark was annotated with *LM* and the same sequence number as its corresponding spatial expression in every annotated spatial expression. For example, the string of "#l空[LM1]中/s #r[SE1]" in Figure 3 shows that the landmark of "空" (the sky) corresponds to the first spatial expression of "空中" (in the sky). Moreover, when a landmark matched with two or more spatial expressions, it was annotated twice or more times. So, "空" (the sky) in Figure 3 was annotated with [LM1] and [LM2], meaning it is the

landmark not only for "空中" (in the sky) but also "在空中" (in the sky) at the same time.

Trajectory: The definition in Sect. 2.1 was not sufficient to annotate a trajectory for the participants, because there may be more than one word expressing the same object in the context. Thus, we proposed the nearest and right-most rule, which selects the sixth "乌龟" (the tortoise) as the corresponding trajectory of the third spatial expression in the text in the Figure 3. The trajectory notation is TR, and its sequence number is the same as its corresponding spatial expression.

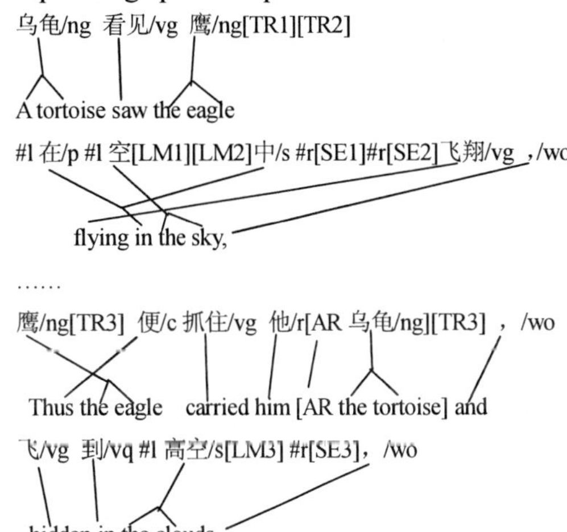

Figure 3: The sample of final corpus with spatial relations annotations[1]

Spatial Relation: All spatial relations were explicit as soon as the spatial expressions, landmarks and trajectories were all annotated. A spatial expression, a landmark and a trajectory with the same sequence number compose a specific spatial relation, like "空[LM1] 中/s #r[SE1]", "空[LM1]" and "鹰/ng[TR1]" in Figure 3 compose a spatial relation of ((在, 中, 空), 鹰) ((in, , the sky), eagle).

2.3 Analysis of the Descriptive Strategies

We distinguish two subsets of our development corpus, 1) a set containing 325 fables selected randomly from the corpus as the 'training database', 2) a set that containing the rest 109 fables of the corpus as the 'testing database'. Based on this corpus, how the spatial relations are expressed in Chinese is analyzed in detail.

---

[1] Some sentences are omitted because of the paper space, where four tortoise words are included.

Mapping: The mapping between trajectories and their corresponding spatial expression is the quantity ratio between them. There are four possible mappings in the corpus. 0:1 means that there is zero trajectory matching one spatial expression. 1:1, 2:1 or 3:1 means there are one, two or three trajectories matching one spatial expression which result in one, two or three spatial relations. The statistical data are shown in Table 1.

Spatial Focus Shift: The spatial focus is the current entity or group of entities (and its/their associated spatial location) that the reader is attending to in space (Maybury, 1990). In Figure 4(a), there is a spatial relation "农夫在墙下" (the farmer under a wall) between the trajectory "鹰" (the eagle) and its spatial expression "朝下" (down). In this case the current spatial focus shifts from "鹰" (the eagle) to "农夫" (the farmer), and back to "鹰" (the eagle).

There are three types of spatial focus shift. The first type is *typeSI* when there is no other spatial relation between a trajectory and its corresponding spatial expression. The second type is *typeSII* when there are other spatial expression(s), but no complete spatial relation between them, which means there is not any spatial focus shift too. In Figure 4(b), there is a spatial expression "画板上" (in the wall) between the trajectory "鸽子" (the pigeon) and its another corresponding spatial expression "地上" (onto the ground), which is the grammar ellipsis of a trajectory raised by the ellipses of the object or subject. Lastly, there is type *typeSIII*, in which there are complete spatial relation(s) between a trajectory and its corresponding spatial expression, such is the case in Figure 4(a). This type means there is a semantic interruption by the spatial focus shift. We show the statistical data for the spatial focus shift for 1:1 spatial relations in Table 2.

Syntactic Location Relation: There are three types of syntactic location relations between a trajectory and its corresponding spatial expression depending whether they are in the same sentence ended by full stop, question mark or excalmatory mark, or not. The first is called *typeLI* that means the trajectory and its spatial expression are in the same sub-sentence that is the sentence without punctuations. The second is *typeLII* – they are in the same full sentence, not sub-sentence. The last is *typeLIII* meaning they are in the different sen-

tences. The statistic data on the corpus is shown in Table 3.

Data base	Amount of 0:1	Amount of 1:1	Amount of 2:1	Amount of 3:1
Training	5 (8%)	539 (86.94%)	58 (9.35%)	18 (2.90%)
Testing	2 (8.85%)	203 (89.82%)	18 (7.96%)	3 (1.46%)

Table 1: Mapping between *TR* and *SE*

Data base of 1:1	Amount of *TypeSI*	Amount of *TypeSII*	Amount of *TypeSIII*
Training	523(97.03%)	14 (2.6%)	2 (0.37%)
Testing	190(93.60%)	11(5.42%)	2(0.99%)

Table 2: Spatial Focus Shift in 1:1 of *TR* and *SE*

Data base	Amount of *TypeLI*	Amount of *TypeLII*	Amount of *TypeLIII*
Training	439(71.38%)	158(25.69%)	18(2.93%)
Testing	159(70.98%)	63(28.13%)	2(0.89%)

Table 3: Syntactic Location Relations

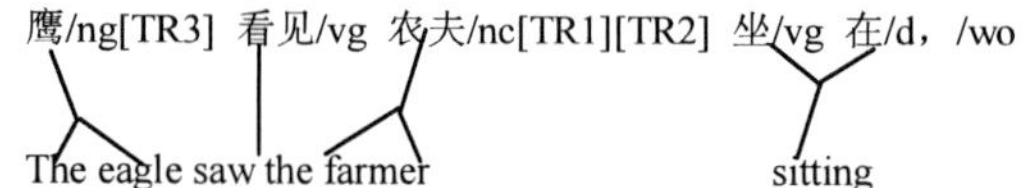

(a) A Sentence from 'The Eagle and the Farmer'

(b) A Sentence from 'The Pigeon and the Painting'

Figure 4: The sample for spatial focus shift

Those descriptive strategies are not mutually exclusive. Moreover, the phenomena of n:1 mapping, *typeSII*, *typeLII* and *typeLIII* are all produced by the ellipses of the object or subject. In addition, trajectories of 0:1 and *typeSIII* must be understood from the background of a text, so these two descriptive strategies are not the subjects in this paper.

2.4 Winnow

We choose SNoW as the classifier tool and Winnow as the learning algorithms. SNoW is an architecture consisting of a Sparse Network of linear separators utilizing three learning algorithm including Winnow (Littlestone, 1988). Winnow is used at each target node to learn its dependence on nodes in the first layer. Its input can be formalized as $(w_1, \alpha, \beta, \theta)$: an initial vector $w_1 \in Rn$ which is positive, promotion factors α and $\beta \in [1, \infty]$, and a threshold $\theta \in [0, \infty]$. The algorithm proceeds in a series of trials and predicts in each trial according to the threshold function $w_k \cdot X \geq \theta$ given $X \in Rn$. If the prediction is correct, then no update is performed; otherwise the weights are updated as follows:

- On a false positive prediction for all k set
  $w_k \leftarrow \alpha w_k$

- On a false negative prediction for all k set
  $w_k \leftarrow \beta w_k$

3 Extraction of the Trajectory

3.1 The Binary Classification

We model the problem of extracting trajectories from a text as a binary classification problem. The text has been initially tagged using a POS tagger and a spatial expression tagger. The text is taken as the set *Stext* where there are two parts: the spatial expression *sexp_tr* being matched with trajectories and words excluding those in *sexp_tr*, which compose the set *Stext_w*. Every word of the set *Stext_w* is a candidate *ctr*. A predicate p taking values in C = {-1, 1} asserts whether a *ctr* is a trajectory ($p(ctr)=1$), or is not ($p(ctr)=-1$). The task then is to find the classifier function h that maps every word in *Stext_w* to a single value in C, h: *Stext_w->C*. The classifier h, moreover, is found by Winnow.

3.2 Features of the trajectory Classifier

Based on the studies of the descriptive strategies, the features are selected on shallow syntax, and then are modeled as a unit vector $f\{pun,$ $pos\_ctr_1,..., pos\_ctr_m, pos\_verb_1,..., pos\_verb_n,$

$dis\_verb_1,..., dis\_verb_o, dis\_SE_1,..., dis\_SE_q,$ $dis\_SEL_1,..., dis\_SEL_p, dis\_SEN_1,..., dis\_SEN_h,$ $dis\_by_1,..., dis\_by_u, dis\_with_1,..., dis\_with_i, hby,$ $hwith\}$.

The value of the feature *pun* is 1 as the candidate is punctuation and the others are 0, otherwise, the value is 0 and the others are decided on the following discussion.

pos_ctr_i presents the candidate's POS. The used POS tool has 52 part-of-speech tags which are numbered. For example a candidate's POS is *noun*, and then the value of pos_ctr_1 is 1, and the others are 0.

When there is a verb in the same sentence with candidate, pos_verb_i is assigned 1. The number of pos_verb_i assigned 1 means the number of verbs which are in the same sentence with the candidate.

There are three classes of distance features. The first dis_verb_i is distances between a candidate and verbs *ph* which are in the same full sentence. The second is distances between a candidate and phrases *ph*. The phrases include the spatial expression *sexp_tr*, the last spatial expression and the next which are relative to *sexp_tr* according to the sequence in the context. These features are denoted by dis_SE_i, dis_SEL_j and dis_SEN_k. The third dis_by_i and dis_with_i are distances between a candidate and function words denoted by *fw* including 被 ('by') and 把 ('with') which are in the same sub-sentence.

The first and second distances are calculated with Equation 1. The third distances are calculated according to Equation 2. When *ctr* is before *ph* or *fw*, *sign* is 1, otherwise is -1. n represents the number of words between *ctr* and *fw*. n_0 is 1 when *ctr* and *ph* are in the same sub-sentence, otherwise it is 0. n_1 means the number of sub-sentences between *ctr* and *ph*. n_2 or n_3 means the number of full sentences or paragraphs between *ctr* and *ph*. Every one of distance values maps a distance feature.

$$dis(ctr, ph) = sign * \sum_{i=0}^{3} (n_i * 10^i) \quad (1)$$
$$dis(ctr, fw) = sign * n \quad (2)$$

It is an important feature identifying a trajectory whether 被('by') or 把('with') appears in the same sub-sentence with it. If 被('by') or 把('with') and *ctr* appear in the same sub-sentence, the value of the feature *hby* or *hwith* is 1, otherwise it is 0.

4 Experiments

4.1 Qualification of the Values of the Parameters

Before the experiments, we determined the parameters of Winnow: the promotion factors α and β, and the threshold θ, using the enumeration method. The values of these three parameters for one experiment were selected when the *F*-score was maximal at all runs in the numeric area and on the changing step of every parameter in Table 4 confirmed according to our experience.

4.2 Experiments with the Different Feature Spaces

The following experiments were done separately according to four different feature spaces defined in Table 5 according to features in Sect. 3.2. The values of the three parameters of following experiments are shown in Table 6.

Parameter	Min	Max	Step
α	1.0	2.0	0.1
β	0.0	0.9	0.1
θ	1	6	1

Table 4: The Numeric Areas and Steps on the Parameters

Features in the feature space	Name
Parts-of-speech of candidates	*Fea*00
POS of candidates and distances between a candidate and spatial expressions	*Fea*01
All features mentioned in Sect. 3.2	*Fea*10

Table 5: The Definitions of Feature Spaces

Feature Space	α	β	θ
*Fea*00	1.2	0.2	2
*Fea*01	1.6	0.3	2
*Fea*10	1.7	0.5	2

Table 6 Values of the Parameters

First, the performance of *Fea*01 being much better than *Fea*00 in Figure 5 shows that the feature of spatial expressions is effective, and a trajectory and a spatial expression are bounding.

Second, Figure 6 shows that the performance of *Fea*10 is much stronger than that of *Fea*01. The *F*-score on the testing database is much lower than on training dataset, but the precision is much higher for *Fea*01. In contrast, the performances of *Fea*10 between training database and testing database fall at the same degree. Therefore, the features on function words and verbs are effective.

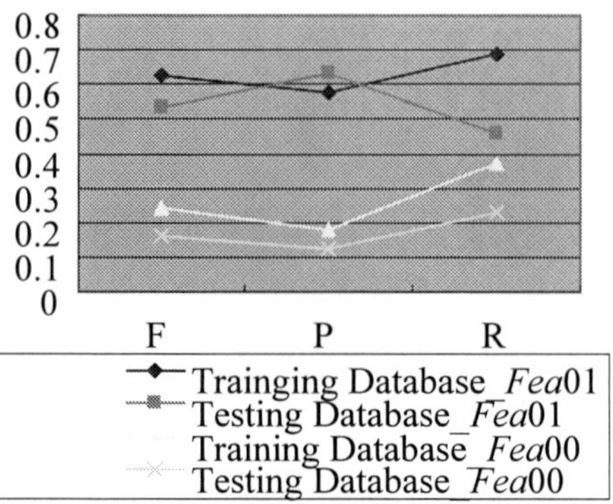

Figure 5: The Results on the Feature Spaces *Fea*01 and *Fea*00

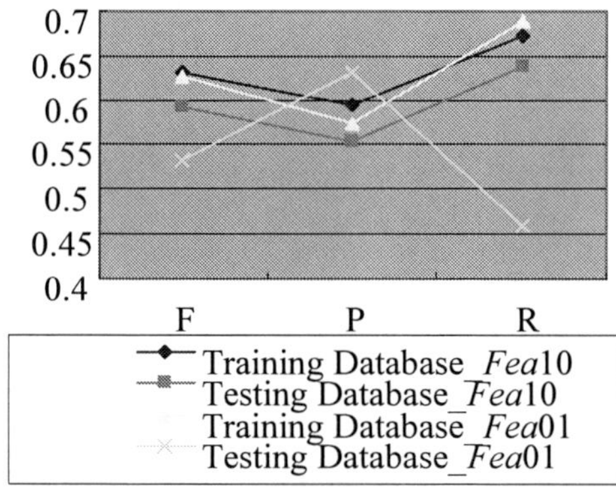

Figure 6: The Results on the Feature Spaces *Fea*10 and *Fea*01

We calculated the recalls on different mappings on *Fea*10 as shown in Figure 7. The method is most effective to 1:1 mapping, and can resolve the ellipsis of the object or subject in some degree.

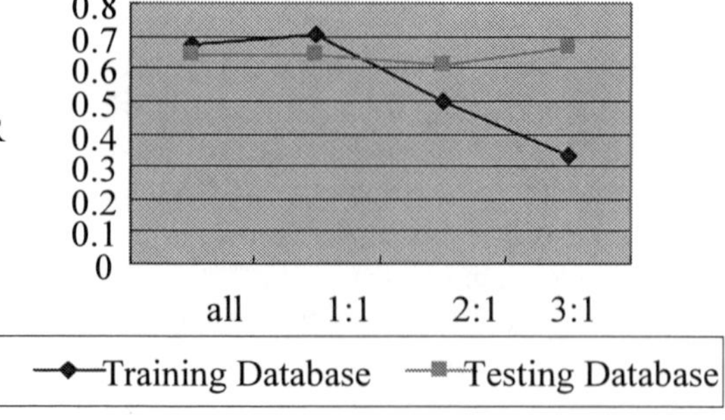

Figure 7: The Results on the Different Mappings

The recalls of syntactic locations are showed in Figure 8 for *Fea*10. The performance for the sub-sentence relation is over 85%. It is critical to resolve the data sparseness in the other two situations in the future.

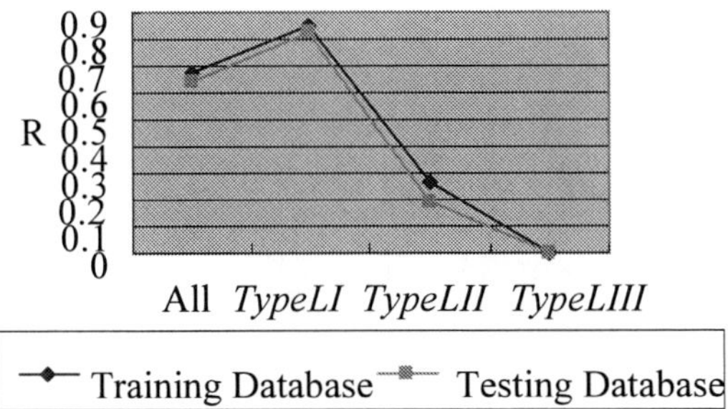

Figure 8: The Results on the Different Syntactic Location Relations

5   Conclusion

We showed the concepts of the spatial relation and trajectory and the descriptive strategy in Chinese texts. Based on these studies, we proposed that the extraction of the trajectory is a binary classification problem. We also proposed the method to extract the trajectories at the text level with a linear classifier. In the end, we presented experiments from different points of view to show that it is effective with a binary classifier with shallow syntactic features to extract a cognitive concept of a trajectory.

Further studies on the feature selecting in the semantics and at the text level are needed to improve the results and resolve the grammar and the semantic ellipsis of a trajectory, furthermore, to resolve the data sparseness. Moreover, we have found that about 94% words as trajectories are included in HowNet, which is a common sense knowledge base (Dong and Dong, 2002). Therefore, it is essential to take advantage of HowNet for better results in the next phases.

6   Acknowledgements

The authors gratefully acknowledge the suggestion and help of Dr. Lars Ahrenberg, director of the Natural Language Processing Library at the Linköping University, and the support from Natural Science Foundation in China (Project Number: 60575041). Finally, we thank blind reviewers for their thoughtful feedback.

References

Bob Coyne, Richard Sproat. 2001. *WordsEye: An Automatic Text-to-Scene Conversion System*. Proceedings of the SIGGRAPH 2001 Annual Conference on Computer graphics, Los Angeles, CA USA.

Zhengdong Dong, Qiang Dong. 2007. *HowNet*. http://www.keenage.com/

Richard Johansson. 2006. *Natural Language Processing Methods for Automatic Illustration of Text*. ISSN 1652-4691, Licentiate Thesis, LU-CS-LIC. Lund, Sweden.

Ronald W. Langacker. 1987. Foundations of Cognitive Grammar (2 Vols). Stanford, Calif.: Standford University Press.

Nicholos Littlestone. 1988. *Learning Quickly when Irrelevant Attributes Abound: A New Linear-threshold Algorithm*. Machine Learning 2:285–318

Ruqian Lu, Songmiao Zhang. 2002. *From Story to Animation – Full Life Cycle Computer Aided Animation Generation* (in Chinese). Acta Automatica Sinica, 28(3): 322-348

Yajuan Lv. 2003. *Research on Bilingual Corpus Alignment and Automatic Translation Knowledge Acquisition*. Dissertation for the doctoral degree in engineering, Harbin Institute of Technology, Harbin, China.

Mark T. Maybury. 1990. *Using Discourse Focus, Temporal Focus, and Spatial Focus to Generate Multisentential Text*. Proceedings of the Fifth International Workshop on Natural Language Generation: 70-78, Dawson, PA.

Dan Roth. 1998. *Learning to Resolve Natural Language Ambiguities: A Unified Approach*. Proceedings of AAAI-98, 15th Conference of the American Association for Artificial Intelligence: 806-813.

Shaohua Zou. 1989. *The Grammar Function of Spatial Function Words in Chinese* (in Chinese). ZHONG-GUO WUWEN, 3:173-178

IceParser: An Incremental Finite-State Parser for Icelandic

Hrafn Loftsson
Department of Computer Science
Reykjavik University
Reykjavik, Iceland
`hrafn@ru.is`

Eiríkur Rögnvaldsson
Department of Icelandic
University of Iceland
Reykjavik, Iceland
`eirikur@hi.is`

Abstract

We describe and evaluate an incremental finite-state parser for Icelandic – the first parser published for the language. Input to the parser is POS tagged text and it generates output according to a shallow syntactic annotation scheme, specifically designed for this project. The parser consists of a phrase structure module and a syntactic functions module. Both modules comprise a sequence of finite-state transducers, each of which adds syntactic information into substrings of the input text. F-measure for constituents and syntactic functions is 96.7% and 84.3%, respectively. These results are good, because Icelandic has a relatively free word order which can be difficult to account for in a parser. Moreover, of the various morphological features available in the rich POS tags, the transducers only use the case feature in their patterns.

1 Introduction

Syntactic analysis for natural languages is often divided into two categories: *full parsing*, in which a complete analysis for each sentence is computed, and *shallow parsing*, where sentence parts or chunks are analysed without building a complete parse tree.

One problem with full parsing is that the set of solutions can grow exponentially, because, generally, the parser considers all possible analysis of a given sentence. Moreover, since the goal is to build a complete parse tree for each sentence, the parser sometimes rejects a correct analysis of a sentence part on lower levels in the parse tree, on the ground that it does not fit into a global parse. Shallow parsing techniques do not have these problems because their aim is "to recover syntactic information efficiently and reliably from unrestricted text, by sacrificing completeness and depth of analysis" (Abney, 1996).

In many natural language processing (NLP) applications, it can be sufficient to analyse sentence parts or phrases. This can be the case, for example, in applications like information extraction, text summarisation and some types of grammar checking, in which identification of phrases is more important than a global parse. Additionally, in cases of low quality input or spoken language, a shallow parsing method can be more robust than a full parsing method, because of noise, missing words and mistakes in the input (Li and Roth, 2001).

In this paper we describe a shallow parser, *Ice-Parser*, for parsing Icelandic text – the first parser published for the language[1]. *IceParser* is based on the incremental finite-state approach, in which a parser comprises a sequence of finite-state transducers. The transducers add syntactic information into the text in an incremental manner.

The input to *IceParser* is part-of-speech (POS) tagged text, using the detailed *IFD* tagset (Pind et al., 1991). It produces output according to a shallow annotation scheme, specifically designed for

---

[1]This work was partly supported by the Icelandic Research Fund, grant "Shallow parsing of Icelandic text".

Joakim Nivre, Heiki-Jaan Kaalep, Kadri Muischnek and Mare Koit (Eds.)
NODALIDA 2007 Conference Proceedings, pp. 128–135

this project. The scheme consists of descriptions for annotation of both constituent structure and syntactic functions. Accordingly, the parser comprises two main modules: a phrase structure module and a syntactic functions module.

Evaluation shows that *IceParser* is both effective and efficient. F-measure for constituents and syntactic functions is 96.7% and 84.3%, respectively. These results are good, because the free word order in Icelandic can be difficult to account for in a parser. The parser is implemented in Java and processes about 11,300 word-tag pairs per second.

The remainder of this paper is organised as follows. In Section 2, we describe finite-state parsing in more detail. In Section 3, the main relevant features of Icelandic morphology and syntax are briefly described. Our annotation scheme is described in Section 4. We describe the design of *IceParser* in Section 5, and, in Section 6, we present the evaluation results. In Section 7, we analyse some of the errors, and we conclude in Section 8.

2 Finite-state parsing

Non-recursive language models, like finite-state grammars, have been used successfully to produce shallow parsers from the early 1990's.

The *reductionist* method by Koskenniemi et al. (1992) was influenced by the Constraint Grammar approach (Karlsson et al., 1995), in which syntactic tags are associated with words, instead of using phrase tree structures to represent parses. The main idea is to reduce all possible readings of a sentence (represented by finite-state automata) to one correct reading by a set of elimination rules.

A contrasting method is the *constructive* approach, which is based on a lexical description of a collection of syntactic patterns. The use of finite-state transducers to introduce syntactic labels into the input sentences is one example of the constructive approach.

A common constructive approach is to string together a sequence of transducers to build incremental (or cascading) shallow parsers (Grefenstette, 1996; Abney, 1997). Each transducer adds syntactic information into the text, such as brackets and names for grammatical functions. The hybrid method by (Aït-Mokhtar and Chanod, 1997) merges the con-

structive and the reductionist approaches by defining chunks (core phrases) by constraints rather than syntactic patterns.

The Xerox Finite-State Tool (XFST) (Karttunen et al., 1996) is often used to develop finite-state parsers. The XFST includes extensions to the standard regular expression calculus, which simplify the creation of finite-state transducers for syntactic processing.

Finite-state parsing methods have been used to develop a number of shallow parser for different languages, e.g. Spanish (Molina et al., 1999), Swedish (Megyesi and Rydin, 1999; Kokkinakis and Johansson-Kokkinakis, 1999), German (Müller, 2004), and French (Aït-Mokhtar and Chanod, 1997). Parsers built using finite-state methods are usually robust and fast, because they are, in fact, just a pipeline of lexical analysers.

3 Icelandic

Compared to its closest relatives (i.e. the other Nordic languages), Icelandic is a heavily inflected language, with nouns belonging to one of three genders, inflecting for four cases and two numbers. Additionally, nouns sometimes have a suffixed definite article. Adjectives inflect for four cases, three genders, three degrees, and two numbers, besides having both a "strong" (indefinite) and "weak" (definite) form; verbs inflect for three persons, two (main) moods, two tenses, and two voices; and so on.

Thus, the main Icelandic tagset, constructed in the compilation of the *IFD* corpus, is large (about 660 tags) compared to related languages. In this tagset, each character in a tag has a particular function. The first character denotes the *word class*. For each word class there is a predefined number of additional characters (at most six), which describe morphological features, like *gender*, *number* and *case* for nouns; *degree* and *declension* for adjectives; *voice*, *mood* and *tense* for verbs, etc.

To illustrate, consider the word *"hestarnir"* (horses). The corresponding tag is *"nkfng"*, denoting noun (n), masculine (k), plural (f), nominative (n), and suffixed definite article (g).

Due to the rich inflections which serve to indicate sentence-internal relationships and dependencies, Icelandic word order is rather free, especially in many styles of written language. This freedom mainly concerns the relative order of major syntactic constituents, such as noun phrases (subjects and objects), preposition phrases, and adverb phrases, but also, to a certain extent, phrase-internal word order.

If we were aiming at full parsing and wanted to build a complete hierarchical parse tree, we would be faced with many difficult practical and theoretical questions. However, our annotation scheme is shallow in the sense that its syntactic structures are rather flat and simple, i.e. the main emphasis is to annotate core phrases without showing a complete parse tree. Therefore, the relatively free word order does not necessarily pose a problem for our syntactic annotation by itself, even though it may in many cases make it difficult for our parser to correctly identify certain syntactic constituents and especially syntactic functions.

4   The annotation scheme

Our annotation scheme follows the dominant paradigm in treebank annotation, i.e. it is "the kind of theory-neutral annotation of constituent structure with added functional tags" (Nivre, 2002).

Two labels are attached to each marked constituent. The first one denotes the beginning of the constituent, the second one denotes the end (e.g. *[NP . . . NP]*). The main labels are *AdvP*, *AP*, *NP*, *PP* and *VP* – the standard labels used for phrase annotation (denoting adverb, adjective, noun, preposition, and verb phrase, respectively). Additionally, we use the labels *CP*, *SCP*, *InjP*, and *MWE* for marking coordinating conjunctions, subordinating conjunctions, interjections, and multiword expressions, respectively. Furthermore, we use the labels *APs* and *NPs*, for marking a sequence of adjective phrases (agreeing in gender, number and case) and noun phrases (agreeing in case), respectively.

Our scheme subclassifies VPs. A finite verb phrase is labelled as *[VP . . . VP]* and consists of a finite verb, optionally followed by a sequence of AdvPs and supine verbs. Other types of VPs are labelled as *[VPx . . . VPx]*, where x can have the following values: *i*, denoting an infinitive VP; *b*, denoting a VP which demands a predicate nominative (i.e primarily a verb phrase consisting of the verb *"vera"* (be)); *s*, denoting a supine VP; *p*, denoting

a past participle VP; *g*: denoting a present participle VP.

We use curly brackets for denoting the beginning and the end of a syntactic function (as carried out by Megyesi and Rydin (1999)). Special function tags are used for labels: **QUAL*, **SUBJ*, **OBJ*, **OBJAP*, **OBJNOM*, **IOBJ*, **COMP*, **TIMEX*, denoting a genitive qualifier, a subject, an object, an object of an AP, a nominative object, an indirect object, a complement, and a temporal expression, respectively.

Additionally, for some of the syntactic function labels (see table 2), we use relative position indicators ("<" and ">"). For example, **SUBJ>* means that the verb is positioned to the right of the subject, **SUBJ<* denotes that the verb is positioned to the left, while **SUBJ* is used when it is not clear where the accompanying verb is positioned or when the verb is missing. The motivation behind using the indicators is to simplify grammar checking at later stages. A thorough description of the annotation scheme can be found in (Loftsson and Rögnvaldsson, 2006).

We have constructed a *grammar definition corpus* (GDC), a corpus consisting of 214 sentences (selected from the *IFD* corpus), representing the major syntactic constructions in Icelandic. The purpose of the GDC is to "provide an unambiguous answer to the question how to analyse any utterance in the object language" (Voutilainen, 1997). Furthermore, this corpus has been used as the development corpus for *IceParser*.

To illustrate the annotation scheme, consider the following sentence parts (shown without POS tags), obtained from the GDC.

- {*SUBJ> [NP vagnstjórinn NP] *SUBJ>} [VP sá VP] {*OBJ< [NP mig NP] *OBJ<}
  (driver-the saw me)

- {*SUBJ> [NP systir NP] {*QUAL [NP hennar NP] *QUAL} *SUBJ>} [VPb var VPb]
  (sister her was)

- [VPb er VPb] {*SUBJ< [NP ég NP] *SUBJ<} {*COMP< [VPp fædd VPp] [CP og CP] [VPp uppalin VPp] *COMP<}
  (am I born and raised)

- {*SUBJ> [NP ég NP] *SUBJ>} [VPb er VPb] {*COMP< [AP bundin AP] *COMP<} {*OBJAP< [NP Reykjavík NP] *OBJAP<} (I am bound [to] Reykjavik)

5 IceParser

IceParser is designed to produce annotations according to the annotation scheme described in Section 4. The parser, which is purely constructive, consists of two main components: a phrase structure module (14 transducers) and a syntactic functions module (8 transducers). The purpose of the modular architecture "is to facilitate the work during development, to allow different uses of the parser and to reflect the different linguistic knowledge that is built into the parser" (Megyesi and Rydin, 1999). In both modules, the output of one transducer serves as the input to the following transducer in the sequence.

The transducers include numerous syntactic patterns, written to account for the relatively free word order of Icelandic. Apart from relying on *word class* or *subclass* information in the POS tags, the patterns only use the grammatical *case* feature.

The reason for not using to full extent the morphological information available in each POS tag, is that we want our parser to be utilised as a grammar checking tool, among other things. If the parser, for example, uses feature agreement to a great extent to mark phrases then it will not be possible for the grammar checking tool to point out feature agreement errors inside phrases. This is because the corresponding words would not have been recognised as one phrase by the parser, due to the lack of feature agreement!

The parser is implemented in Java and the lexical analyser generator tool JFlex (http://jflex.de/). Each transducer is written in a separate file, which is compiled into Java code using JFlex. The resulting Java code is a deterministic finite-state automaton (DFA), along with actions to execute for each recognised pattern. The actions add syntactic information into the text.

The reason for not using the XFST for implementation is that *IceParser* is part of a NLP toolkit for Icelandic, all of which is implemented in Java.

5.1 The phrase structure module

The purpose of the phrase structure module is to add brackets and labels to input sentences to indicate constituent structure. The syntactic annotation is performed in a bottom-up fashion, i.e. the deepest constituents are analysed first. For example, AdvPs are marked before APs, which are in turn marked before NPs.

To illustrate, consider the *Phrase_AdvP* transducer, which marks AdvPs, consisting of a single adverb, by putting the markers *[AdvP ... AdvP]* around it. An adverb in the input text is recognised using the regular expressions:

```
Adv={WordSpaces}{AdvTag}
```

The pattern *{WordSpaces}* denotes a sequence of word characters (all possible characters except white space) followed by one or more spaces. *{AdvTag}* is a pattern which matches an adverb POS tag. An *{Adv}* is thus a word tagged as an adverb.

The action associated with the *{Adv}* pattern is responsible for putting the appropriate brackets and labels around the recognised substring. For example, the word-tag pair *mjög aa* (very) is annotated as *[AdvP mjög aa AdvP]* by this transducer.

Consider the *Phrase_AP* transducer (slightly simplified), which marks APs, (using *[AP ... AP]*), consisting of a single adjective optionally preceded by an AdvP. It uses the following regular expressions:

```
Adj={WordSpaces}{AdjTag}
OpenAdvP="[AdvP"
CloseAdvP="AdvP]"
AdvPhrase={OpenAdvP}~{CloseAdvP}
AdjPhrase={AdvPhrase}?{Adj}
```

Here *{Adj}* is a pattern which matches a word tagged as an adjective. In JFlex, the regular expression ~*a* matches everything up to (and including) the first occurrence of a text matched by *a*. Thus, an *{AdvPhrase}*, to be included in an *{AdjPhrase}*, consist of a bracket and a label denoting the start of an adverb phrase followed by everything up to a label and a bracket denoting the end of the AdvP. For example, the substring *[AdvP mjög aa AdvP] góður lkensf* (very good) is annotated as *[AP [AdvP mjög aa AdvP] góður lkensf AP]* (henceforth, we do not show the POS tags in the examples).

The most complicated of all the transducers is the *Phrase_NP* transducer, which marks noun phrases (the resulting DFA consists of about 50,000 states). This is due to the various ways a NP can be generated – from a single pronoun (e.g. *[NP hann NP]* (he)), to a sequence of an indefinite pronoun, a demonstrative pronoun/article, a numeral, an adjective phrase and a noun (e.g. *[NP allir þessir þrír [AP stóru AP] strákar NP]* (all these three big boys)).

For example, the substring *[AP [AdvP mjög AdvP] góður AP] kennari* (very good teacher) is annotated as *[NP [AP [AdvP mjög AdvP] góður AP] kennari NP]* by this transducer.

5.2 The syntactic functions module

The purpose of the syntactic functions module is to add tags to denote grammatical functions. The input to the first transducer in this module is the output of the last transducer in the phrase structure module.

To illustrate, consider the *Func_SUBJ* transducer, which annotates subjects. This transducer uses various patterns to recognise subjects, depending on whether the subject appears to the left of the finite verb phrase, to the right of the verb phrase, precedes a relative conjunction, etc. Here, we only discuss (a simplified version of) the main case, in which the subject appears to the left of the finite verb phrase:

```
NomSubj={NPNom} | {NPsNom}
VPorVPBe={VP} | {VPBe}
SubjVerb=({NomSubj}{WS}+{VPorVPBe} |
    {DatSubj}{WS}+{VPDat} |
    {AccSubj}{WS}+{VPAcc}
```

{WS}+ denotes one or more white spaces. *{NomSubj}*, *{AccSubj}* and *{DatSubj}* match a single nominative NP, or a sequence of NPs, in the nominative, accusative, or dative case, respectively. *{VPorVPBe}* matches a finite verb phrase or a verb phrase containing the verb *"vera"* (be), and *{VPDat}* and *{VPAcc}* match verbs that demand oblique case subjects (this list of verbs is implemented as regular expressions). The action, associated with the pattern *{SubjVerb}*, finds out where the VP starts (using string searches) and puts the appropriate markers *{*SUBJ> ... *SUBJ>}* around the subject.

As another example, consider the *Func_COMP* transducer, whose main function is to annotate complements of the verb *"vera"*. A part of the patterns used by this transducer is (slightly simplified):

```
Compl={APSeqNom} | {NPSeqNom}  |
```

```
    {VPPastSeq}
SubjVerbBe={Subject}{WS}+{VPBe}{WS}+
SubjVerbCompl={SubjVerbBe}{Compl}
```

According to this pattern a *{Compl}* is a sequence of nominative APs or NPs, or a sequence of past participle VPs. A *{SubjVerbBe}* is a *{Subject}*, followed by a verb phrase containing the verb *"vera"*. The action, associated with the pattern *{SubjVerbCompl}*, finds out where the VP ends and puts the appropriate markers *{*COMP< ... *COMP<}* around the complement.

For example, for the substring *[NP hann NP] [VPb er VPb] [NP [AP [AdvP mjög AdvP] góður AP] kennari NP]* (he is very good teacher), the application of the *Func_SUBJ* and *Func_COMP* transducers results in the string *{*SUBJ> [NP hann NP] *SUBJ>} [VPb er VPb] {*COMP< [NP [AP [AdvP mjög AdvP] góður AP] kennari NP] *COMP<}*.

6 Evaluation

IceParser has been evaluated on 509 sentences (8281 tokens), randomly selected from the *IFD* corpus. Since this corpus is only POS tagged, two annotators manually annotated the sentences (after the parser had been developed) with constituent structure and syntactic functions, according to our annotation scheme. The resulting treebank is our *gold standard*.

We used the *Evalb* bracket scoring program (Sekine and Collins, 1997) for automatic evaluation. For the evaluation of labelled constituent structure, we carried out two experiments. In the first one, we used the tags from the *IFD* corpus, i.e. we assumed correct tagging (see column 2 in table 1). In this case, the overall F-measure ($2 * precision * recall/(precision + recall)$) is 96.7%.

As can be deduced from table 1, *VP*, *CP*, *SCP* and *InjP* are "easy" to annotate. These phrase types constitute 28.6% of the phrases in the gold standard, and, thus, help to make the overall accuracy quite high. On the other hand, the accuracy for the more "difficult" phrase types, like *AP*, *NP* and *PP* (which constitute 58.7% of the phrases), is about 95%-97%, according to our results.

In the second experiment, we used the tagger *IceTagger* (Loftsson, 2006) to tag the sentences in the gold standard, before *IceParser* was run. The POS

Phrase type	F-measure using correct POS tags	F-measure using *IceTagger*	Freq. in test data
AdvP	91.8%	85.1%	8.2%
AP	95.1%	86.3%	8.1%
APs	87.0%	68.6%	0.5%
NP	96.8%	93.0%	37.6%
NPs	80.4%	74.3%	1.5%
PP	96.7%	91.3%	13.0%
VPx	99.2%	93.8%	19.3%
CP	100.0%	99.6%	5.7%
SCP	99.6%	97.6%	3.4%
InjP	100.0%	96.3%	0.2%
MWE	96.9%	92.6%	2.5%
All	96.7%	91.9%	100.0%

Table 1: Results for the various phrase types.

Function type	F-measure using correct POS tags	F-measure using *IceTagger*	Freq. in test data
SUBJ	68.2%	47.6%	4.7%
SUBJ>	92.7%	89.4%	30.3%
SUBJ<	83.7%	75.1%	12.3%
OBJ	0.0%	0.0%	0.2%
OBJ>	43.5%	20.0%	0.8%
OBJ<	90.2%	78.2%	19.7%
OBJAP>	71.4%	57.2%	0.2%
OBJAP<	75.0%	46.2%	0.4%
OBJNOM<	30.8%	16.7%	0.6%
IOBJ<	73.3%	51.9%	0.9%
COMP	56.9%	40.0%	2.8%
COMP>	91.3%	91.3%	1.3%
COMP<	75.1%	70.0%	12.7%
QUAL	87.7%	77.9%	10.4%
TIMEX	74.7%	55.9%	2.7%
All	84.3%	75.3%	100.0%

Table 2: Results for the various syntactic functions.

tagging accuracy for these sentences is 91.1% (unknown word ratio is 7.8%). In this case, the overall F-measure for constituent structure drops from 96.7% to 91.9% (see column 3 in table 1), which is equivalent to about 5.0% reduction in accuracy. The POS tagging accuracy is relatively low, compared to related languages, and this has substantial effect on the overall parsing accuracy.

Unfortunately, we can not compare our results to other parsers for Icelandic, since this evaluation is the first parser evaluation published for the language. For the sake of a comparison with a related language[2], Swedish, Knutsson et al. (2003) report 88.7% F-measure for all phrases, and 91.4% for NPs, when using a tagger to preprocess the text and a shallow (not finite-state) rule-based parser. Using a finite-state parser, Kokkinakis and Johansson-Kokkinakis (1999) report higher numbers, 93.3% for all phrases and 96.2% for NPs, despite using a tagger for preprocessing. The tagger used, however, obtains very high accuracy when tagging the test data, i.e. 98.7%. We believe that this comparison indicates our parser performs well when annotating constituents.

For the evaluation of syntactic functions, we also carried out experiments with and without correct tagging. When using the correct tags from the *IFD* corpus, the overall F-measure is 84.3% – see column 2 of table 2. When considering subjects and objects, the highest accuracy is obtained for the functions *SUBJ>* and *OBJ<*, i.e. a subject whose accompanying verb is to the right, and an object whose accompanying verb is to the left. This was to be expected, because the normal word order is SVO. If the relative position indicator is ignored (many shallow parser do not include such an indicator), thus, for example, combining the three subject functions into one, F-measure for *SUBJ* and *OBJ* is 90.5% and 88.2%, respectively.

When *IceTagger* is used to produce tags, the overall F-measure for syntactic functions drops from 84.3% to 75.3% (see column 3 in table 2), which is equivalent to about 10.7% reduction in accuracy. Thus, the accuracy of the syntactic functions module is more sensitive to tagging errors than the constituent module. This can be explained by the fact that the former component relies to a much higher extent on the case feature, which is often responsible for the errors made by the tagger.

Again, we are not in a position to compare our results to another Icelandic parser. For German (a

---

[2]Note that comparison between languages is questionable, because of different language characteristics, parsing methods, annotation schemes, test data, evaluation methods, etc.

related language), Müller (2004), for example, has presented the following results of syntactic function annotation using a finite-state parser (and POS tags from a corpus): 82.5% F-measure for all functions, and 90.8%, 64.5% and 81.9%, for subjects, accusative objects and dative objects, respectively. If these results are used for comparison, *IceParser* seems to obtain good results for syntactic functions.

In the first version of *IceParser*, the output file of one transducer is used as an input file in the next transducer in the sequence. This version processes about 6,700 word-tag pairs per second (running on a Dell Optiplex GX620 Pentium 4, 3.20 GHz). We have implemented another version of the parser which, instead of reading and writing to files, reads from and writes directly to memory (using the Java classes *StringReader* and *StringWriter*). This version annotates about 11,300 word-tag pairs per second, which is equivalent to about 75% speed increase compared to the previous version.

7 Error analysis

In this section, we show examples of the errors made by *IceParser*.

The only type of error in adverb phrase annotation occurs when the parser incorrectly groups together two (or more) adjacent adverbs. Consider the incorrect output:

[PP um [NP það NP] PP] [VP vissi VP] [NP stelpan NP] [AdvP ekki þá AdvP] (about that knew girl not then).

The two adverbs at the end should form two distinct AdvPs, because *"ekki"* is a sentence adverb which does not modify the temporal adverb *"þá"*.

Adverbs are also the source of some of the errors made in then annotation of adjective phrases. Consider the incorrect output:

[CP og CP] [VP tóku VP] [NP [AP [AdvP fram AdvP] eigin AP] dósir NP] (and took out own cans). In this sentence part, the adverb *"fram"* is a particle associated with the verb *"tóku"* (take out), but not a modifier of the adjective *"eigin"*.

A frequent noun phrase error made by the parser is exemplified by the incorrect output *[NP árin NP] [AP gullnu AP]* (years golden). Here, the correct annotation is *[NP árin [AP gullnu AP] NP]*, because the adjective *"gullnu"* is a post-modifier of the noun

"árin". *IceParser* makes this type of error, because it does not include a pattern for noun-adjective word order.

The *Phrase_NPs* transducer groups together a sequence of noun phrases agreeing in case. Consider the incorrect output:

[AP sterkur AP] [VPb var VPb] [NPs [NP hann NP] [CP og CP] [NP íþróttamaður NP] NPs] [AP ágætur AP] (strong was he and athlete fine).

Here, the parser groups the noun phrases *[NP hann NP]* and *[NP íþróttamaður NP]* together, because the phrases agree in case. The correct annotation, however, is:

[AP sterkur AP] [VPb var VPb] [NP hann NP] [CP og CP] [NP íþróttamaður [AP ágætur AP] NP].

To give an example where *IceParser* annotates a subject without a correct position indicator, consider the output:

*[VPb er VPb] [AdvP ekki AdvP] [VPi að koma VPi] {*SUBJ [NP matur NP] *SUBJ}?* (is not to come food?).

The correct annotation for the subject is *{*SUBJ< [NP matur NP] *SUBJ<}*, because *"matur"* is the subject of the verb *"er"* at the beginning of the sentence. *IceParser* does include patterns to match the order VP-AdvP-SUBJ, but, in this case, the infinitive verb phrase *[VPi að koma VPi]* is positioned in between the AdvP and the SUBJ. The parser, however, marks all stand-alone nominative NPs as *{*SUBJ … *SUBJ}*, and therefore the *[NP matur NP]* phrase does receive subject marking, albeit incomplete.

Finally, note that some of the errors in syntactic function annotation are due to errors made in the phrase structure annotation. For the incorrect phrase structure output (discussed above) *[CP og CP] [VP tóku VP] [NP [AP [AdvP fram AdvP] eigin AP] dósir NP]*, the parser will produce the syntactic function:

*{*OBJ< [NP [AP [AdvP fram AdvP] eigin AP] dósir NP] *OBJ<}*.

This object is incorrect, because it includes the adverb phrase *[AdvP fram AdvP]*.

8 Conclusion

We have described and evaluated the incremental finite-state parser *IceParser*, for parsing Icelandic text. The parser comprises two modules: a phrase structure module and a syntactic functions module. Both modules consist of a sequence of transducers, which add syntactic information into the input strings, according to our shallow syntactic annotation scheme.

Evaluation shows that F-measure for phrases and syntactic functions is 96.7% and 84.3%, respectively. We have argued that these results are good, because Icelandic has a relatively free word order, which is difficult to account for in a parser. Moreover, of the various morphological features available in the rich POS tags, the transducers only use the case feature in their patterns.

In future work, we would like to improve individual components of our parser, and build a version of it which utilises to a greater extent the morphological information available in the POS tags.

9 Acknowledgements

Thanks to the Institute of Lexicography at the University of Iceland, for providing access to the *IFD* corpus.

References

S. Abney. 1996. Part-of-Speech Tagging and Partial Parsing. In K. Church, S. Young, and G. Bloothooft, editors, *Corpus-Based Methods in Language and Speech*. Kluwer Academic Publishers.

S. Abney. 1997. Partial Parsing via Finite-State Cascades. *Natural Language Engineering*, 2(4):337–344.

S. Aït-Mokhtar and J-P. Chanod. 1997. Incremental Finite-State Parsing. In *Proceedings of Applied Natural Language Processing*, Washington DC, USA.

G. Grefenstette. 1996. Light Parsing as Finite State Filtering. In *Proceedings of the ECAI '96 workshop on "Extended finite state models of language"*, Budapest, Hungary.

F. Karlsson, A. Voutilainen, J. Heikkilä, and A. Anttila. 1995. *Constraint Grammar: A Language-Independent System for Parsing Unrestricted Text*. Mouton de Gruyter, Berlin, Germany.

L. Karttunen, J-P. Chanod, Grefenstette, G., and A. Schiller. 1996. Regular expressions for language engineering. *Natural Language Engineering*, 2(4):305–328.

O. Knutsson, J. Bigert, and V. Kann. 2003. A Robust Shallow Parser for Swedish. In *Proceedings of NoDaLiDa 2003*, Reykjavik, Iceland.

D. Kokkinakis and S. Johansson-Kokkinakis. 1999. A Cascaded Finite-State Parser for Syntactic Analysis of Swedish. In *Proceedings of the 9th Conference of the European Chapter of the ACL (EACL)*, Bergen, Norwsay.

K. Koskenniemi, P. Tapanainen, and A. Voutilainen. 1992. Compiling and using finite-state syntactic rules. In *Proceedings of the 14th International Conference on Computational Linguistics*, Nantes, France.

X. Li and D. Roth. 2001. Exploring Evidence for Shallow Parsing. In *Proceedings of the 5th Conference on Computational Natural Language Learning*, Toulouse, France.

H. Loftsson and E. Rögnvaldsson. 2006. A shallow syntactic annotation scheme for Icelandic text. Technical Report RUTR-SSE06004, Department of Computer Science, Reykjavik University.

H. Loftsson. 2006. Tagging a Morphologically Complex Language Using Heuristics. In T. Salakoski, F. Ginter, S. Pyysalo, and T. Pahikkala, editors, *Advances in Natural Language Processing, 5th International Conference on NLP, FinTAL 2006, Proceedings*, Turku, Finland.

B. Megyesi and S. Rydin. 1999. Towards a Finite-State Parser for Swedish. In *Proceedings of NoDaLiDa 1999*, Throndheim, Norway.

A. Molina, F. Pla, L. Moreno, and N. Prieto. 1999. APOLN: A Partial Parser of Unrestricted Text. In *Proceedings of SNRFAI99*, Bilbao, Spain.

F-H. Müller. 2004. Annotating Grammatical Functions in German Using Finite-State Cascades. In *20th International Conference on Computational Linguistics*, Geneva, Switzerland.

J. Nivre. 2002. What kinds of trees grow in Swedish soil? A Comparison of Four Annotation Schemes for Swedish. In *Proceedings of the 1st Workshop on Treebanks and Linguistic Theories*, Sozopol, Bulgaria.

J. Pind, F. Magnússon, and S. Briem. 1991. *The Icelandic Frequency Dictionary*. The Institute of Lexicography, University of Iceland, Reykjavik, Iceland.

S. Sekine and M.J. Collins. 1997. The Evalb Software. http://nlp.cs.nyu.edu/evalb/. Site visited November 2006.

A. Voutilainen. 1997. Designing a (Finite-State) Parsing Grammar. In E. Roche and Y. Schabes, editors, *Finite-State Language Processing*. MIT Press.

The Swedish-Turkish Parallel Corpus
and Tools for its Creation

Beata B. Megyesi & Bengt Dahlqvist
Department of Linguistics and Philology
Uppsala University
(beata.megyesi|bengt.dahlqvist)@lingfil.uu.se

Abstract

We present a Swedish-Turkish parallel corpus and the automatic annotation procedure with tools that we have been using in order to build the corpus efficiently. The method presented here can be transferred directly to build other parallel corpora.

1 Introduction

Parallel corpora containing texts and their translations have been a popular research area within natural language processing during the last decade. This is due to the fact that parallel corpora are very useful in language research allowing empirical studies, and various applications in natural language processing. In the past years, methods have been developed to build parallel corpora by automatic means, and to re-use translational data from such corpora for several applications, such as machine translation, multi-lingual lexicography, and cross-lingual domain-specific terminology.

In this paper, we describe a Swedish-Turkish parallel corpus, and the method and tools used for building it. Our primary goal is to build a representative language resource for Swedish and Turkish to be able to study the relations between these languages. The components of the language resource are texts that are in translational relation to each other and are analyzed linguistically. More specifically, our goal is to build a Swedish-Turkish parallel corpus with contrastive studies in focus.

We build the corpus automatically by using a basic language resource kit (BLARK) for the involved languages and appropriate tools for the automatic alignment and correction of data. We choose tools that are user-friendly, understandable and easy to learn by people with less computer skills, thereby allowing researchers and students to align and correct the corpus data by themselves.

The corpus is part of the project "Supporting research environment for minor languages" aiming at building various types of language resources for Turkish, Hindi and Classic languages. The Swedish-Turkish corpus serves as a pilot project for building corpora for other language pairs dissimilar in language structure. Therefore, efforts are put on developing a general method and using tools that can be applied to other language pairs easily.

The Swedish-Turkish parallel corpus is intended to be used in teaching, research, and applications such as machine translation.

The paper is organized as follows: Section 2 gives an overview of parallel corpora; Section 3 describes the corpus data while Section 4 presents the method for building the corpus and the tools used. In Section 5, we suggest some further improvements and lastly, in Section 6, we summarize the paper.

2 Parallel Corpora

A parallel corpus is usually defined as a collection of original texts translated to another language where the texts, paragraphs, sentences, and words are typically linked to each other.

One of the most well-known and frequently used parallel corpora is Europarl (Koehn, 2002) which is a collection of material including 11 European languages taken from the proceedings of the European Parliament. Another parallel corpus is the JRC-Acquis Multilingual Parallel Corpus (Steinberger et al., 2006). It is the largest existing parallel corpus of today concerning both its size and the number of languages covered. The corpus consists of above 20 languages and 8,000 docu-

Joakim Nivre, Heiki-Jaan Kaalep, Kadri Muischnek and Mare Koit (Eds.)
NODALIDA 2007 Conference Proceedings, pp. 136–143

ments of legislative text, covering a variety of domains. Another often used resource is the Bible translated to a large number of languages and collected and annotated by Resnik et al. (1999). The OPUS corpus (Tiedemann and Nygaard, 2004) is another example of a freely available parallel language resource.

There are, of course, many other parallel corpus resources that contain sentences and words aligned in two languages only. Such corpora often exist for languages in Europe, for example the English-Norwegian Parallel Corpus (Oksefjell, 1999) and the IJS-ELAN Slovene-English Parallel Corpus (Erjavec, 2002). It is especially common to include English as one of the two languages in the pair. Parallel corpora for languages other than European or that exclude English are rare. There is therefore a need to develop language resources in general, and parallel corpora in particular for other language pairs as well.

Next, we describe the development of a Swedish-Turkish parallel corpus. To our knowledge, there is no similar or comparable resource such as the corpus we present in this paper.

3 Corpus Content

The corpus consists of original texts and their translations from Turkish to Swedish and from Swedish to Turkish with the exception of one text which is a translation to both languages.

We collected written texts to build a balanced corpus with respect to translational direction. The corpus contains both fiction and technical documents. The fiction part consists of one full novel "The White Castle" by Orhan Pamuk, and the first chapter of "Sofie's world" by Jostein Gaardner. As for the non-fiction, a book "Islam and Europe" by Ingmar Karlsson, a booklet "Information from the Swedish Migration office" and a number of short information brochures for Turkish immigrants from Swedish governmental agencies are included.

In Table 1, the corpus material is summarized. In total, the corpus consists of approximately 150,000 tokens in Swedish and 126,000 tokens in Turkish. Divided into text types, the fiction part of the corpus includes 59,720 tokens in Swedish, and 41,484 tokens in Turkish. The technical documents

are larger and contain 90,901 tokens in Swedish, and 85,171 tokens in Turkish.

The current material presented here serves as pilot linguistic data for the Swedish-Turkish parallel corpus. We intend to extend the material to other texts, both technical and fiction, in the future.

Table 1. The corpus data divided into text categories with number of tokens and types.

Document	# Token	# Type
Fiction		
The White Castle - Swe	53232	7748
The White Castle - Tur	36684	12472
Sofie's world - Swe	6488	1466
Sofie's world - Tur	4800	2215
Non-fiction		
Islam and Europe - Swe	55945	10977
Islam and Europa - Tur	48893	14128
Info about Sweden - Swe	24107	4576
Info about Sweden - Tur	23660	7119
Retirement - Swe	3417	818
Retirement - Tur	3664	1188
Dublin - Swe	392	169
Dublin - Tur	394	230
Pregnancy - Swe	949	409
Pregnancy - Tur	1042	567
Psychology - Swe	347	193
Psychology - Tur	281	220
Movement - Swe	543	300
Movement - Tur	568	369
Social security - Swe	5201	846
Social security - Tur	6669	2025

4 Corpus Annotation Procedure

The corpus material is processed automatically by using various tools making the annotation, alignment and manual correction easy and straightforward for users with less computer skills. This is necessary, as our ambition is to allow researchers and students of particular languages to enlarge the corpus by automatically processing and correcting the new data by themselves.

The following steps below give an overview of the annotation procedure and the involved tools.

1. **Preprocessing** for cleaning up the original files, partly manually.
2. **UplugConnector** for markup, linguistic analysis and alignment in a graphical interface to the **Uplug toolkit** (Tiedemann, 2003).
3. **ISA** (Tiedemann, 2006) for visualization of sentence alignment and manual correction.
4. Visualization of the material with the linguistic analysis without showing the structural markup using **Hpricot**.
5. **ICA** (Tiedemann, 2006) for visualization of the word alignment.

4.1 Preprocessing

First, the original materials received from the publishers in various formats are cleaned up. For example, rtf, doc, and pdf documents are converted to plain text files. In the case of the original pdf-file, we scanned and proof-read the material and, where necessary, corrected it to ensure that the plain text file is complete and correct.

Then, the texts are encoded according to international standards by using UTF-8 (Unicode). The plain text files are then processed by various tools. The sentences of the formatted texts in the source and target language are linguistically analyzed and aligned automatically, and the words are linked to each other in the two languages. Next, the corpus architecture and tools used to build the corpus is presented in more detail.

4.2 Corpus Markup

The clean plain text files are processed to markup the data, to annotate it with morpho-syntactic features, and to align the texts on the paragraph, sentence and word level. For this purpose, we use the Uplug toolkit which is a collection of tools for processing corpus data, created by Jörg Tiedemann (2003). Uplug was developed for word alignment in parallel corpora and utilizes BLARKs where possible. Uplug can be used for sentence splitting, tokenization, tagging by using external taggers, and paragraph, sentence and word alignment. Figure 1 gives an overview of the main modules in the corpus annotation procedure with Uplug.

All tools included are freely available for research purposes and are built in as components in the Uplug toolkit.

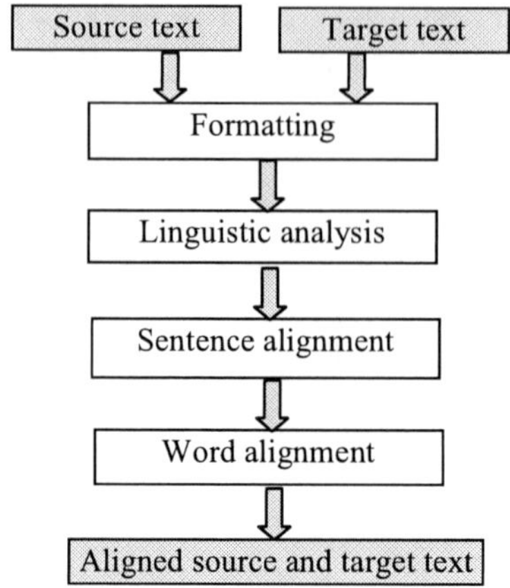

Figure 1. Modules of Uplug

The Uplug package consists of a number of perl scripts accessible by line commands with a large number of options and sometimes utilizing piping between commands. To facilitate easier access and usage of these scripts, a graphical user interface, UplugConnector, was developed in Java for the project. Here, the user can in a simple fashion choose a specific task to be performed and let the graphical user interface (GUI) set up the proper sequence of calls to Uplug and subsequently execute them. The figure below illustrates the Uplug Connector interface.

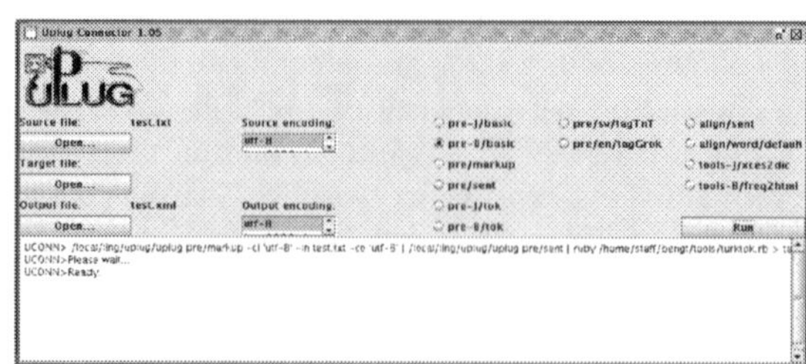

Figure 2. The Uplug Connector

The user can optionally give the location of the source and target files, decide where the output should be saved, and specify the encoding for the input and output files. For the markup, basic structural markup, sentence segmentation, and tokenization are available. In the toolkit, the user can also call for the sentence and word aligners and their visualization tool.

Further, the Uplug Connector GUI has been constructed to give the possibility to include calls to new scripts outside Uplug for complementary analysis, when such needs arise. The user can easily access to another resource if the available ones do not fit his/her needs, for example an external tokenizer, sentence splitter, or tagger.

4.2.1 Formatting

Each part of the corpus is clearly marked and annotated. We use the international XML Corpus Encoding Standard (XCES) for the annotation format.

The plain text files are processed by various tools in the BLARKs of the two languages. The sentence splitter is used to break the texts into sentences, and the texts are tokenized for both languages. Since the default tokenizer in Uplug (to our knowledge) does not handle character entities and hyphens in Turkish words correctly, an alternative tokenizer was developed in the project, loosely based on the Penn Treebank tokenizer by Robert MacIntyre (1995).

The sentences and words are then marked as s and w respectively, and receive an identification number. An example taken from Orhan Pamuk's book "The White Castle" is shown below for the sentence "Some other title did not exist" first in Swedish "Någon annan titel fanns inte.",

```
<s id="s11.4">
<w id="w11.4.1">Någon</w>
<w id="w11.4.2">annan</w>
<w id="w11.4.3">titel</w>
<w id="w11.4.4">fanns</w>
<w id="w11.4.5">inte</w>
<w id="w11.4.6">.</w>
</s>
```

then in Turkish "Başka bir başlık yoktu." :

```
<s id="s10.5">
<w id="w10.5.1">Başka</w>
<w id="w10.5.2">bir</w>
<w id="w10.5.3">başlık</w>
<w id="w10.5.4">yoktu</w>
<w id="w10.5.5">.</w>
</s>
```

4.2.2 Linguistic analysis

Once the sentences and tokens are identified, the data is analyzed linguistically. For the linguistic annotation, external morphological analyzers and part-of-speech taggers are used for the specific languages.

The Swedish texts are annotated with the Trigrams'n'Tags PoS tagger (Brants, 2000). The tagger was trained on Swedish (Megyesi, 2002) using the Stockholm-Umeå Corpus (SUC, 1997). For the labels, we use the PAROLE annotation scheme developed for Swedish (Ejerhed and Ridings, 1995). The tokens are annotated with part-of-speech and morphological features and are disambiguated according to the syntactic context with an accuracy of approximately 96% (Megyesi, 2002). An example of the morphological annotation for the same sentence as previously is shown below.

```
<s id="s11.4">
<w pos="DI@US@S" id="w11.4.1">Någon</w>
<w pos="AQPUSNIS" id="w11.4.2">annan</w>
<w pos="NCUSN@IS" id="w11.4.3">titel</w>
<w pos="V@IISS" id="w11.4.4">fanns</w>
<w pos="RG0S" id="w11.4.5">inte</w>
<w pos="FE" id="w11.4.6">.</w>
</s>
```

The Turkish material is analyzed linguistically by using an automatic morphological analyzer developed for Turkish (Oflazer, 1994). Each token in the text is segmented and annotated with morphological features including part-of-speech. The morphological analyzer does not disambiguate the tokens. Preliminary results show on part of the Turkish material that 74% of the tokens were correctly and completely analyzed with morphological features. The rest of the tokens are either ambiguous, or are unknown, often foreign words.

4.2.3 Sentence alignment, visualization and correction

Aligning the translated segments with source segments are essential for building parallel corpora. We use standard techniques for the establishment of links between source and target language segments. Paragraphs and sentences are aligned by using the length-based approach developed by Gale and Church (1993).

The aligned sentences are stored in XML format, as shown in the example below.

```
<cesAlign toDoc="vt.xml" version="1.0"     from
       Doc="vs_tnt.xml">
  <linkGrp targType="s" toDoc="vt.xml"     from
       Doc="vs_tnt.xml">
  <link certainty="8" xtargets="s1.1;s1.1" id="SL0.1"/>
  <link certainty="111" xtargets="s2.1;s2.1" id="SL0.2"/>
  <link    certainty="-1287"    xtargets="s3.1;s2.2    s3.1"
       id="SL0.3"/>
  <link certainty="340" xtargets="s3.2;s3.2" id="SL0.4"/>
  <link certainty="114" xtargets="s3.3;s3.3" id="SL0.5"/>
...
```

As the XML representation of the linking result is not user friendly even for people used to this kind of annotation, an interface for the visualization of the alignment result is required. In addition, since the automatic alignment generates some errors, we also need an interface for the manual correction of these.

As a tool for the correction of the sentence alignment, we choose the system ISA (Interactive Sentence Alignment) developed by Tiedemann (2006). ISA is a graphical interface for automatic and manual sentence alignment which uses the alignment tools implemented in Uplug. It handles the manual correction of the sentence alignment in a user-friendly, interactive fashion. Figure 3 shows ISA with the aligned sentences taken from Orhan Pamuk's book "The White Castle".

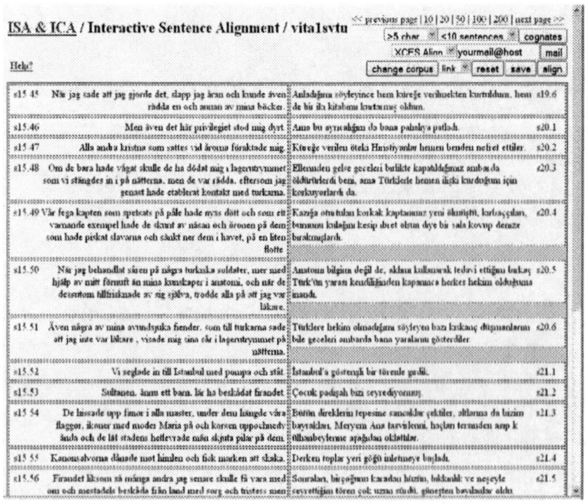

Figure 3. ISA showing the aligned sentences from "The White Castle".

Once the sentences are aligned in the source and target language, we send it for manual correction to a student who speaks both languages. With the help of ISA, the manual correction is easy and fast.

The results we present below are based on the sentence alignment results for the first chapter of the novel "The White Castle" by Orhan Pamuk.

The manually corrected alignment resulted in 178 sentence pairs after merges and splits. The distribution of the alignment types after the manual alignment is shown in column two in Table 2.

Table 2. Distribution of *manual* alignment for various link types and the result of the automatic sentence alignment.

Link type: Swedish-Turkish	Manual Number	Automatic	
		Number	Correct (%)
1-0	9	0	0
1-1	144	126	110 (87.3)
1-2	3	3	3 (100)
2-1	15	39	12 (33.0)
3-1	7	0	0
Total	**178**	**168**	**125 (74.4)**

The Uplug automatic sentence alignment produced 168 sentence pairs. The correctness of these compared with the manual alignment is presented in column three and four in Table 2. Our results show that 74.4% of the sentences were correctly aligned by the automatic aligner. All one-to-two links and 87.3% of the one-to-one mappings are correct. The lowest score are the two-to-one alignments, where 33% are correctly aligned.

For displaying the corrected sentence output from ISA after manual correction of the alignment together with the linguistic analysis, a script utilizing the structural XML-parser Hpricot (2006) was developed. It takes as input the tagged XML-files for the language pair together with the XML file containing the sentence alignment results produced by ISA and generates an HTML-file which is displaying the sentences aligned together with the linguistic information for each word shown in pop-up windows.

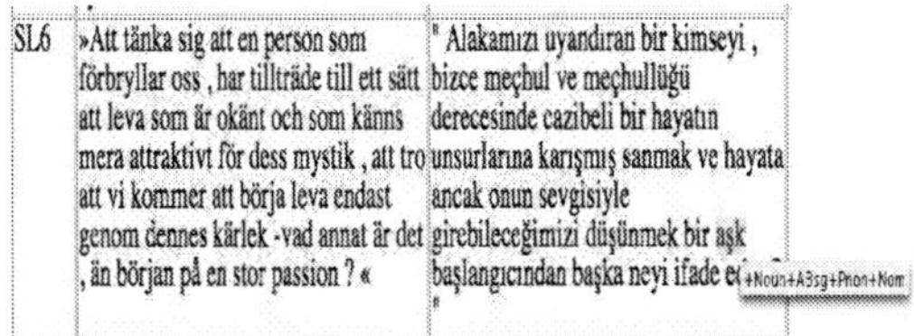

Figure 4. Visualization of aligned sentence pairs with linguistic annotation shown in the pop-up window.

The visualization tool makes it easier for students and researchers to study the grammatical annotation for the words and chosen structures for translation than the structurally marked up version of the corpus.

4.2.4 Word alignment and visualization

As the next step, words and phrases are aligned using the clue alignment approach (Tiedemann, 2003), and the toolbox for statistical machine translation GIZA++ (Och and Ney, 2003), also implemented in Uplug.

Results show that the word aligner aligned approximately 69% of the words correctly. For a pilot evaluation of the results, we investigated the error level on 7,077 word pairs in Swedish and Turkish sorted by decreasing frequency taken from "The White Castle".

Of the incorrectly aligned pairs that appeared at least twice in the material, 61% of the errors can be considered due to grammatical differences between the two languages. Often, Swedish has an expression of several tokens while Turkish expresses the same in one token. For example, the aligner often fails to attach the preposition (till, 'to') in prepositional phrases in Swedish (till sultanen, 'to the sultan') to the single Turkish word (padişaha). The aligner also fails to attach the subordinate conjunction (som, 'that') and the 3rd person pronoun (han, 'he') in the Swedish utterance (som han ville, 'that which he wanted') to the Turkish segment expressed as one single word, the verb (istediğini, 'that what he wanted') since Turkish is a pro-drop language and can leave out the pronominal subject and the relative clause is constructed as various participial forms with verbal suffixes.

The remaining errors, which constitute approximately 39% of the wrongly aligned material,

cannot be explained by grammatical differences between the two languages. Rather, these might appear as a consequence of the previously occurring errors in the sentence alignment.

To visualize the word alignment result in a simple way, a new script for HTML-visualization of the word alignment result was included in the UplugConnector. This takes as input the text file with word link information produced by Uplug, see Figure 5, and shows the word-pair frequencies. This visualization in fact serves as a bilingual lexicon created from the source and target language data.

Sofies värld

Nr	Frekvens	Svenska	Turkiska
1	62	"	"
2	58	.	.
3	58	?	?
4	34	,	,
5	29	och	ve
6	23	Sofie	Sofie
7	18	Men	Ama
8	17	en	bir
9	14	!	!
10	14	:	:

Figure 5. HTML-visualization of word alignment.

5 Further Developments

In the near future, we would like to extend the linguistic analysis with syntactic features for both languages, and apply a better morphological analysis for Turkish sentences. Also, we plan to use these annotations to improve the automatic word alignment, and use an appropriate tool for visualizing the syntactic annotation. In this way, we easily can build a parallel treebank. Finally, manual corrections of all materials in the corpus are carried out.

6 Conclusions

We presented a Swedish-Turkish parallel corpus − a less processed language pair − containing approximately 150,000 tokens in Swedish, and 126,000 tokens in Turkish. The corpus is automatically created by re-using and adjusting existing tools for the automatic alignment and its visualization, and basic language resource kits for the automatic annotation of the involved languages. The corpus is already in use in language teaching, primarily in Turkish.

Acknowledgments

We are grateful to Jörg Tiedemann for his kind support with Uplug, and Kemal Oflazer and Gülşen Eryiğit for the morpho-syntactic annotation of the Turkish material. Also, we would like to thank the publishers for allowing us to use the texts in the corpus. The project is financed by the Swedish Research Council and the Faculty of Languages at Uppsala University.

References

Thorsten Brants. 2000. TnT − A Statistical Part-of-Speech Tagger. In *Proceedings of the 6th Applied Natural Language Processing Conference*. Seattle, USA.

Kenneth W. Church. 1993. Char align: A program for aligning parallel texts at the character level. In *Proceedings of the 31st Annual Conference of the Association for Computational Linguistics*, ACL.

Eva Ejerhed and Daniel Ridings. 1995. *Parole ->SUC and SUC -> Parole*. http://sprakdata.gu.se/lb/sgml2suc.html

Tomaž Erjavec. 2002. The IJS-ELAN Slovene-English Parallel Corpus. *International Journal of Corpus Linguistics, 7(1)*, pp.1-20, 2002.

William A. Gale, and Kenneth W. Church. 1993. A Program for Aligning Sentences in Bilingual Corpora. *Computational Linguistics, 19(1)*, 75-102.

Hpricot. A Fast, Enjoyable HTML and XML Parser for Ruby http://code.whytheluckystiff.net/hpricot/ 2006.

Nancy Ide, and Greg Priest-Dorman. 2000. *Corpus Encoding Standard − Document CES 1*. Technical Report, Dept. of Computer Science, Vassar College, USA and Equipe Langue et Dialogue, France.

Philip Koehn. 2002. *Europarl: A Multilingual Corpus for Evaluation of Machine Translation*. Information Sciences Institute, University of Souther California.

Robert MacIntyre. 1995. *Penn Treebank tokenization on arbitrary raw text*. University of Pennsylvania, http://www.cis.upenn.edu/~treebank/tokenization.html

Beata Megyesi. 2002. *Data-Driven Syntactic Analysis − Methods and Applications for Swedish*. PhD Thesis. Kungliga Tekniska Högskolan. Sweden.

Beata B. Megyesi, Anna Sågvall Hein, and Eva Csato Johanson. 2006. Building a Swedish-Turkish Parallel Corpus. In *Proceedings of the Fifth International Conference on Language Resources and Evaluation (LREC'06)*. Genoa, Italy.

Kemal Oflazer. 1994. Two-level Description of Turkish Morphology, Literary and Linguistic Computing, Vol. 9, No:2.

Franz Josef Och, and Hermann Ney. 2003. A Systematic Comparison of Various Statistical Alignment Models. *Computational Linguistics*, volume 29:1, pp. 19-51, March 2003.

Signe Oksefjell. 1999. A Description of the English-Norwegian Parallel Corpus: Compilation and Further Developments. *International Journal of Corpus Linguistics*, 4:2, 197-219.

Philip Resnik, Mari Broman Olsen, and Mona Diab. 1999. The Bible as a Parallel Corpus: Annotating the "Book of 2000 Tongues". *Computers and the Humanities, 33(1-2)*, pp. 129-153, 1999.

John Sinclair. (Ed.) 1987. *Looking Up: An Account of the COBUILD Project in Lexical Computing*. London: Collins.

Ralf Steinberger, Bruno Pouliquen, Anna Widiger, Camelia Ignat, Tomaž Erjavec, Dan Tufiş, Dániel Varga. 2006. The JRC-Acquis: A multilingual aligned parallel corpus with 20+ languages. In *Proceedings of the 5th International Conference on Language Resources and Evaluation (LREC'2006)*. Genoa, Italy, 24-26 May 2006.

SUC. Department of Linguistics, Umeå University and Stockholm University. 1997. SUC 1.0 Stockholm Umeå Corpus, Version 1.0. ISBN:91-7191-348-3.

Jörg Tiedemann. 2003. *Recycling Translations − Extraction of Lexical Data from Parallel Corpora and their Applications in Natural Language Processing*. PhD Thesis. Uppsala University.

Jörg Tiedemann. 2004. Word to word alignment strategies. In *Proceedings of the 20th International Conference on Computational Linguistics* (COLING 2004). Geneva, Switzerland, August 23-27.

Jörg Tiedemann and Lars Nygaard. 2004. The OPUS corpus − parallel & free. In *Proceedings of the Fourth International Conference on Language Resources and Evaluation (LREC'04)*. Lisbon, Portugal, May 26-28, 2004.

Jörg Tiedemann. 2005. Optimisation of Word Alignment Clues. In *Journal of Natural Language Engineering, Special Issue on Parallel Texts*, Rada Mihalcea and Michel Simard, Cambridge University Press.

Jörg Tiedemann. 2006. ISA & ICA – Two Web Interfaces for Interactive Alignment of Bitext. In *Proceedings of the Fifth International Conference on Language Resources and Evaluation (LREC'06)*. Genoa, Italy.

Multivariate Cepstral Feature Compensation on Band-limited Data for Robust Speech Recognition

Nicolas Morales
HCTLab
Univ. Autónoma Madrid
Madrid. Spain
nicolas.morales@uam.es

Doroteo T. Toledano
ATVSLab
Univ. Autónoma Madrid
Madrid. Spain
doroteo.torre@uam.es

John H. L. Hansen
CRSS
Univ. of Texas at Dallas
Richardson, TX. USA
john.hansen@utdallas.edu

Javier Garrido
HCTLab
Univ. Autónoma Madrid
Madrid. Spain
javier.garrido@uam.es

Abstract

This paper describes a new method for compensating bandwidth mismatch for automatic speech recognition using multivariate linear combinations of feature vector components. It is shown that multivariate compensation is superior to methods based on linear compensations of individual features. Performance is evaluated on a real microphone-telephone mismatch condition (this involves noise compensation and bandwidth extension of real data), as well as on several artificial bandwidth limitations. Speech recognition accuracy using this approach is similar to that of acoustic model compensation methods for small to moderate mismatches, and allows keeping active a single acoustic model set for multiple bandwidth limitations.

1 Introduction

Noise robustness is a major issue in current research on Automatic Speech Recognition (ASR). Systems trained and tested under laboratory conditions reach high accuracy rates. However, when there is a mismatch between training and test conditions accuracy is severely affected.

This work studies the problem of mismatch between training and test in terms of available frequency bandwidth. Speech recognition systems are typically trained on full-bandwidth data (for speech recognition systems this is normally 0-8kHz). However, in real implementations part of the spectrum of input data could be missing; for example, this situation could be created by a channel distortion or sampling frequency below 16kHz.

Clearly, a simple solution to this problem is retraining new models for the specific type of channel. However, it may well be the case that not enough training data is available from the new environment. Also, when a wide range of possible band-limitations exists for a particular application training of acoustic models for each of them is not appropriate.

Our approach is to compensate band-limited feature vectors to generate pseudo-full-bandwidth features that can be passed to a speech recognizer trained on full-bandwidth speech. The advantages are twofold: first, it is easy to train and requires only small amounts of data. Second, the recognizer module keeps a single acoustic recognizer active at all times, a desirable situation for small devices where memory limitation and energy consumption are relevant.

Feature compensation has been used in the past, especially for speech affected by noise (Moreno, 1996; Droppo et al., 2001). In other cases, compensation is introduced in the decoder module (Deng et al., 2005).

For the case of bandwidth mismatch feature compensation has recently been used in the form of univariate linear and polynomial correction (Seltzer et al., 2005; Morales et al., 2005). These studies proposed compensation directly in the domain of Mel Frequency Cepstrum Coefficients

Joakim Nivre, Heiki-Jaan Kaalep, Kadri Muischnek and Mare Koit (Eds.)
NODALIDA 2007 Conference Proceedings, pp. 144–151

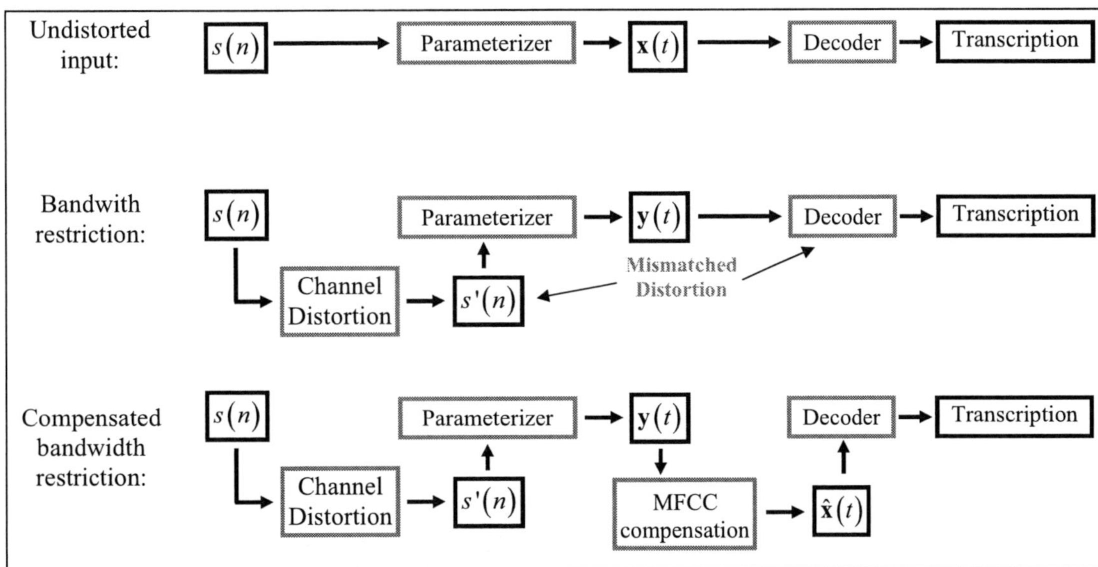

Figure 1. Modification of a basic speech recognizer system for MFCC feature compensation. The ideal working environment is noted as "Undistorted input". However, in many cases, some kind of distortion, affects the input signal, producing a mismatch between the characteristics of speech and the acoustic models of the decoder (in our case a bandwidth restriction). In this study mismatch is reduced by introducing an MFCC compensation module between the parameterizer and decoder modules.

(MFCC), the parameterization of choice for most speech recognizers. Thus, the compensator module may be easily inserted between the parameterizer and recognizer modules of already working ASR engines (Figure 1).

In this work we propose the use of multivariate linear correction for bandwidth compensation. Each individual MFCC is compensated using a linear combination of a selection of other coefficients in the same frame. The previously referenced univariate compensation algorithms corrected each MFCC coefficient independently based on the assumption that MFCCs are highly uncorrelated. However, as we show in Section 3, this assumption is less valid when data is band-limited. Experiments show that by discarding this assumption, better compensation and ASR performance may be achieved.

Band-restricted speech can be found in historical spoken document retrieval (Hansen et al., 2004). In broadcast news' transcription it may also occur that the channel conditions change abruptly and rapidly, for example when the studio presenter talks to an anchor in a foreign country. Other cases where multiple band-limiting distortions may be found are on-board systems, such as those in cars,

or in airplanes (Abut et al., 2005; Denenberg et al., 1993). In these cases using multiple acoustic model sets for the different conditions could be costly and complicated. On the contrary, feature compensation generalizes seamlessly to such aggressive environments; for example, it has been shown that multiple band-limitations may be automatically classified and successfully compensated using a single compensation system, and also that data from a sufficient number of environments allows for compensation of unseen distortions (Morales et al., 2007). These properties are related to the method employed for partitioning the limited-bandwidth MFCC space (Section 4) and are independent of whether univariate or multivariate compensations are applied. Thus, they hold true for multivariate compensation.

The rest of the paper is organized as follows: Section 2 introduces MFCC compensation and Section 3 discusses on the need of multivariate compensation for band-limited speech. Section 4 describes practical issues and Section 5 presents experimental results. In Section 6 conclusions are presented.

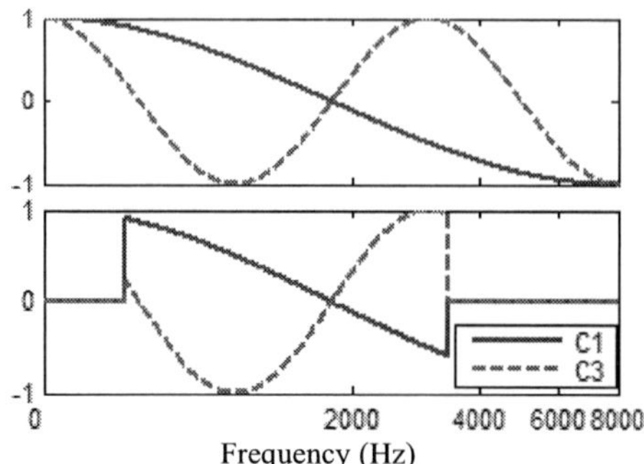

Figure 2. Cepstral transforms of orders 1 and 3 for full-bandwidth (top) and limited-bandwidth speech (bottom; 300-3400Hz band-pass filter). Band-limited transforms are no longer orthogonal.

2   MFCC Compensation

Previous works have studied in detail the effect of band-limiting distortions on the MFCCs (Huang et al., 2001; Morales et al., 2005). Here, we present their main conclusions.

The band-limited MFCC space may be modeled as a mixture of K Gaussian classes:

$$p(\mathbf{y}) = \sum_{k=1}^{K} N\left(\mathbf{y}; \boldsymbol{\mu}^k, \boldsymbol{\Sigma}^k\right) \cdot P(k), \qquad (1)$$

where $\mathbf{y}$ is the band-limited feature vector and $N\left(\Box; \boldsymbol{\mu}^k, \boldsymbol{\Sigma}^k\right)$ is the Gaussian distribution with mean vector $\boldsymbol{\mu}^k$ and covariance matrix $\boldsymbol{\Sigma}^k$ associated to class k. The full-bandwidth space is modeled similarly and assuming that both spaces are jointly Gaussian for each class k, the expectation of the full-bandwidth vector $\mathbf{x}$ is:

$$\hat{\mathbf{x}}(\mathbf{y}, k) = E\{\mathbf{x}|\mathbf{y}, k\} = \boldsymbol{\mu}_{\mathbf{x}}^k + \boldsymbol{\Sigma}_{\mathbf{xy}}^k \left(\boldsymbol{\Sigma}_{\mathbf{y}}^k\right)^{-1} \left(\mathbf{y} - \boldsymbol{\mu}_{\mathbf{y}}^k\right) = \\ = \mathbf{B}^k \mathbf{y} + \mathbf{b}^k \qquad (2)$$

where $\mathbf{B}^k$ and $\mathbf{b}^k$ are the compensation matrix and offset vector for class k, and sub-indexes $\mathbf{x}$ and $\mathbf{y}$ indicate full-bandwidth or limited bandwidth speech, respectively. Generally, the importance of non-diagonal terms was assumed negligible and $\mathbf{B}^k$ was diagonalized (Droppo et al., 2001; Morales et al., 2005). Thus, an expression for individual full-bandwidth MFCC coefficients may be simplified from (2) as:

$$x_i \approx \hat{x}_i\left(y_i|k\right) = B_i^k \cdot y_i + b_i^k, \qquad (3)$$

where i is the order of the MFCC coefficient, b_i^k is element i of vector $\mathbf{b}^k$ and B_i^k the diagonal element (i, i) in matrix $\mathbf{B}^k$.

As will be shown in the following section, the diagonal simplification in (3) that is acceptable on full-bandwidth speech corrupted by noise could be harmful when it is applied to band-limited speech.

3   On MFCC Uncorrelation and Band-limiting Distortions

MFCC features are generally assumed uncorrelated. In fact, this is one of the key points for their extended use in ASR systems – they allow using diagonal covariance matrices in Gaussian mixture models without significant performance loss. In the past, this assumption led to the use of diagonal compensation matrices for MFCC feature compensation. However, we recently observed that MFCC features coming from band-limited speech showed a higher degree of correlation than those coming from full-bandwidth speech.

In order to compare the degree of correlation between MFCC parameters we defined the following measure of non-diagonality for the covariance matrix:

$$nonDiag = \sum_{i}^{staticMFCCs} \sum_{j, j \neq i}^{MFCCs} \delta_{ij},$$

$$\delta_{ij} = \begin{cases} 1 & if \ \sqrt{\text{cov}(i,i) \cdot \text{cov}(j,j)} \leq \tau \cdot \text{cov}(i,j) \\ 0 & otherwise \end{cases}. \qquad (4)$$

Using $\tau = 5$ we obtained a nonDiagonality of 51 for full-bandwidth features, 108 for their corresponding 4kHz low-pass filtered features and 110 for a band-pass filter 300-3400Hz (similar results are found with other values of τ). This shows that filtered MFCCs are more correlated than full-bandwidth MFCCs. Thus, the general assumption of uncorrelation seems less valid for band-limited MFCCs and the use of a non-diagonal compensation matrix is justified.

From (2) we can establish the relationship between the covariance matrices of band-limited and full-bandwidth MFCCs as:

$$\boldsymbol{\Sigma}_{\mathbf{x}}^k = \mathbf{B}^k \cdot \boldsymbol{\Sigma}_{\mathbf{y}}^k \cdot \left(\mathbf{B}^k\right)^t. \qquad (5)$$

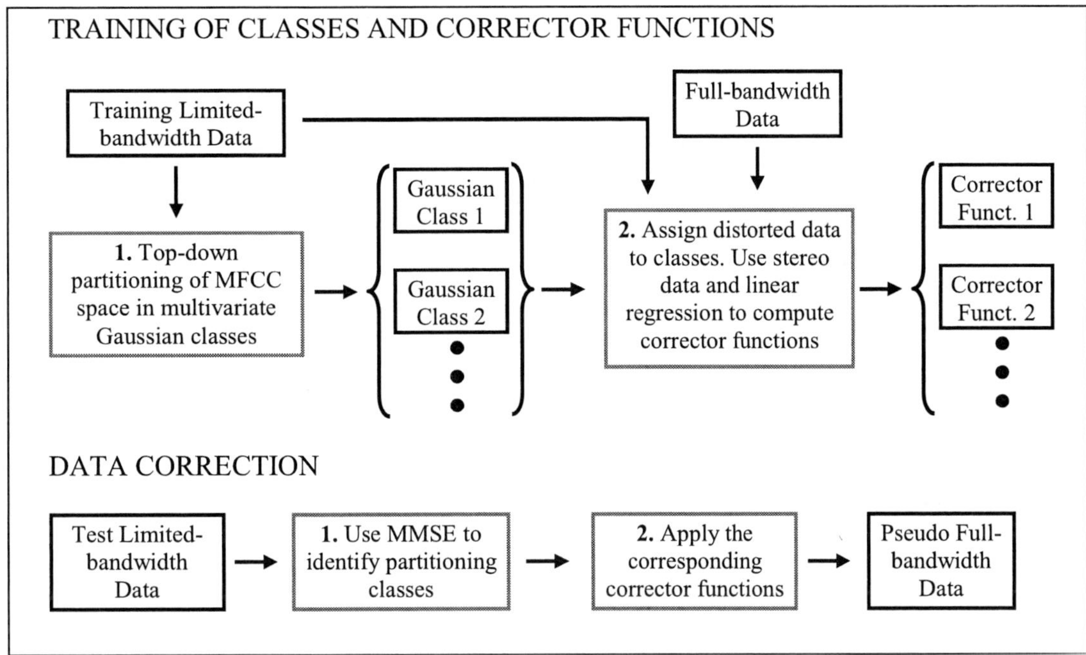

Figure 3. Schematic representations of the proposed architectures for training of classes and corrector functions and for compensation of band-limited MFCCs to generate pseudo-full bandwidth MFCCs.

Assuming that the covariance matrix of full-bandwidth MFCCs, Σ_x^k, is diagonal and that of band-limited features, Σ_y^k, is non-diagonal, then the compensation matrix, $\mathbf{B}^k$ needs to be non-diagonal, in order to satisfy (5).

The approximately uncorrelated nature of MFCCs has been empirically observed on speech data and is associated with the fact that the Discrete Cosine Transform (DCT) on filterbank energies and Principal Component Analysis (PCA) on the correlation matrix generate very similar transformations (Pols, 1977). However, as seen in Figure 2, using the DCT on band-limited frames is effectively a different transformation of that over full-bandwidth speech. The vectors in the basis are no longer orthogonal (on the contrary DCT on full-bandwidth data as well as PCA are orthogonal transforms) and empirical evidence suggests that this could increase correlation of band-limited MFCCs compared to full-bandwidth features (though more experiments should be done for better comprehension of this phenomenon).

Because our compensation framework does not require matrix inversions or expensive calculations

the computational cost of non-diagonal compensation matrices may be assumed if, as will be shown later, significant performance gains may be achieved.

4 Class and Corrector Function Training

The proposed framework is shown in Figure 3. Training consists of two steps. First, the partitioning classes from each environment are created and second, a corrector function is computed for each class and MFCC feature. When a system needs to be deployed in an environment where different types of bandwidth limitations may exist, classes and corrector functions are created independently for each of the existing conditions. Classes trained with data from the different distortions will be able to identify the type of distortion of incoming data and will then apply the appropriate compensation functions. Also, if the need to create classes for new distortions arises, these can be added to the existing framework without any further modification (Morales et al., 2007).

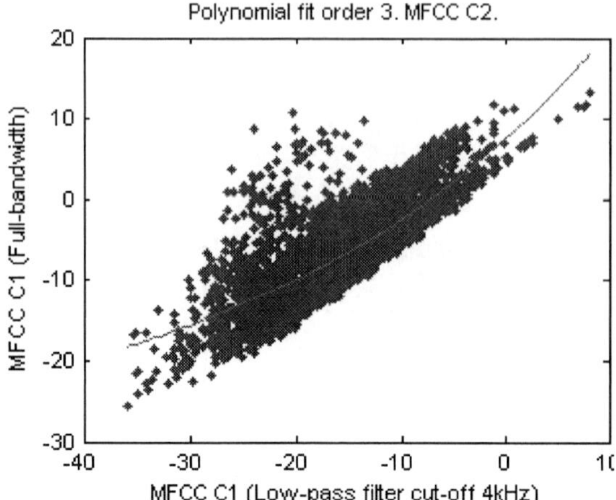

Figure 4. Mapping of low-pass filter 4kHz data to full-bandwidth for MFCC parameter C2 in a particular class k. The plot also shows a third order polynomial fit.

4.1 Class Creation

For each target distorting environment a different set of Gaussian classes is generated using a top-down approach: an initial multivariate Gaussian distribution with mean and diagonal covariance computed from all the training data is divided into two classes. Data are then re-assigned to either class and their mean vector and covariance matrix are re-estimated. The process is repeated introducing new classes in successive iterations until the number of final mixtures is reached.

4.2 Corrector Function Training

Separate correction matrices and offset vectors are trained for each compensation class defined in the restricted-bandwidth space as explained in Section 4.1. In our experiments we use stereo data to compute the coefficients in the corrector functions (here stereo data refers to speech recorded simultaneously under the full-bandwidth and limited bandwidth environments. Alternatively, when a good characterization of the distortion is available it is possible to generate pseudo-distorted data).

Band-limited speech frames from the training set are assigned to one of the corrector classes previously defined based on a maximum likelihood criterion:

$$\hat{k}(t) = \max_{k} \left(N\left(\mathbf{y}_t ; \boldsymbol{\mu}^k, \Sigma^k\right) \cdot P(k) \right), \quad 1 \le k \le K, \quad (6)$$

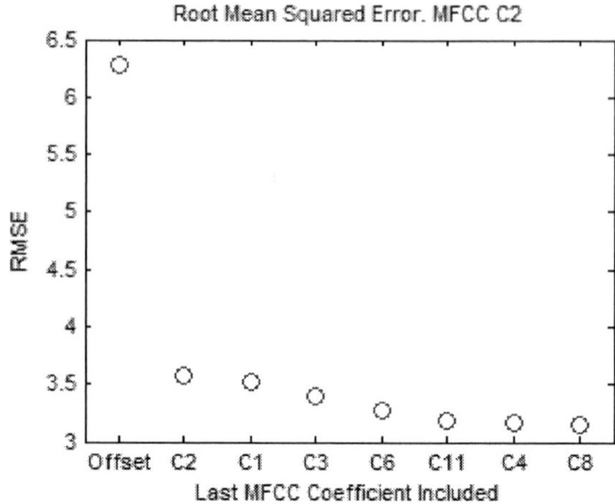

Figure 5. Root Mean Squared Error (RMSE) for multivariate fit of full-bandwidth MFCC C2 in a particular class k of the limited bandwidth space (for a low-pass filter, cut-off frequency 4kHz). RMSE improves as more coefficients are included in the fit. Ticks in the x-axis show the best coefficient to add in each step (C2, C1, etc. indicate static MFCC coefficients of orders 2, 1, etc., respectively).

where K is the total number of classes. For univariate polynomial correction, each MFCC value in the band-limited space is mapped to its equivalent in the full-bandwidth space. In Figure 4 each point represents the value of a given MFCC in the band-limited space (x-axis) and full-bandwidth space (y-axis). Then, for each corrector class the corresponding $\mathbf{B}^k$ and $\mathbf{b}^k$ are computed using linear regression (the green curve in Figure 4). For multivariate linear correction a similar approach is followed identifying feature vectors from stereo frames in the full-bandwidth and limited-bandwidth spaces and employing multivariate linear regression. Multivariate linear regression follows an incremental form, starting from a simple offset and adding successively the coefficient for which a higher decrease of Mean Squared Error (MSE) is achieved until no significant decrease is found. In this way, it is possible to determine the ideal number of MFCC coefficients to use for the compensation of a particular component. In figure 5 we show explicitly the evolution of the Root Mean Squared Error (RMSE) after inclusion of each individual coefficient in the regression. The target coefficient is full-bandwidth MFCC C2 and not surprisingly the first coefficient inserted is limited-bandwidth MFCC C2. Going from a simple offset to compensation with a single coefficient reduces RMSE from 6.28 to 3.58. This is equivalent to univariate linear compensation. However, the inclusion of the next 6 coefficients (C1, C3, C6, C11 and C4) further reduces RMSE to 3.14, which seems to indicate that significant benefits may be obtained by applying multivariate compensation. On the contrary inclusion of additional coefficients offers very little improvement, which indicates that in this case, compensation may be truncated after the best 7 coefficients.

Data compensation uses an MMSE version of (2) for multivariate and (3) for univariate compensation.

5 Results and Discussion

Experiments are based on two measures: first, direct reconstruction quality is assessed by computing the average Mahalanobis distance between real full-bandwidth data and estimated pseudo-full-bandwidth data (generated by compensation of limited-bandwidth data); second, ASR accuracy is evaluated using full-bandwidth acoustic models on pseudo-full-bandwidth data.

5.1 Measuring Reconstruction Quality

The quality of feature compensation may be directly measured in terms of a distance metric between the real full-bandwidth vectors and their corresponding reconstructed vectors. The ultimate goal being ASR performance, perfect reconstruction of feature vectors may be unnecessary as long as speech recognition decoding performs satisfactorily. However, a direct measure is useful because it is fast and independent of external elements such as grammar, phoneme list or other tunable parameters.

The quality measure used in this work is the average Mahalanobis distance. Table 1 shows a comparison between univariate linear compensation (*Univar*) and multivariate linear compensation (*Multivar*). As can be seen, multivariate linear compensation offers better performance for each group of MFCC parameters (this holds for each individual parameter, though a full table is not presented here for lack of space). We also compare reconstruction of dynamic parameters using feature compensation (*Multivar dynamic*) or computation with the typical definition of dynamic features, i.e. using linear regression on reconstructed static fea-

Mahalanobis Dist. (x10^{-2})	Univar static	Multivar dynamic	Multivar static
Static MFCCs	0.7848	0.7091	0.7091
Δ MFCCs	0.8180	0.7193	0.7234
ΔΔ MFCCs	0.8582	0.7393	0.7526
Total	**2.461**	**2.168**	**2.185**
ASR accuracy	66.97	68.22	68.46

Table 1. Mahalanobis distance between real full-bandwidth data and reconstructed data from low-pass filtered data with cut-off frequency 4kHz.

tures (*Multivar static*). Not surprisingly, the distance is smaller using *Multivar dynamic* compensation, because feature compensation minimizes MSE between the actual full-bandwidth data and pseudo-full-bandwidth data. However, from the point of view of speech recognition accuracy we have observed that dynamic features computed by regression of static features (*Multivar static*) is better. Thus, it seems that even if the actual MSE is minimized using feature compensation for dynamic features, this may cause incongruence between static and dynamic features producing a loss in accuracy (for example, in the case of low-pass filter with cut-off frequency 4kHz, regression obtains a relative 0.76% accuracy gain compared to dynamic feature compensation).

5.2 Measuring Speech Recognition

Speech recognition of reconstructed speech is evaluated using a phonetic recognition engine based on 51 Hidden Markov Models (HMM) and a phone bigram. The front-end uses pre-emphasis filtering (α=0.97) and 25ms Hamming windows with a 10ms window shift. Thirteen MFCC coefficients including C0 and their respective first and second order derivatives (39 total features) are computed from a filter-bank of 26 Mel-scaled filters distributed in the region 0-8 kHz. HMM models are trained using TIMIT (Fisher et al., 1986). For training we use all 4680 files in the training partition and evaluation is made on all the 1620 files in the test partition.

Comparison of Different Approaches

In this section different approaches are considered for the problem of band-limited input speech. Table 2 shows results for artificial filters applied on TIMIT: Low-Pass 6kHz, Low-Pass 4kHz and Band-Pass 300-3400Hz, the last one simulating a

Test Set	Correction	Percent Correct	Percent Accuracy
Full-Band	None	75.40	71.18
Low- Pass 6kHz	None	64.32	58.30
	Matched	75.45	71.03
	Model Adapt	74.97	70.35
	Univariate-32	74.88	70.65
	Multivariate-32	75.22	70.95
Low- Pass 4kHz	None	55.93	44.67
	Matched	74.73	69.33
	Model Adapt	73.30	68.38
	Univariate-32	72.41	66.97
	Multivariate-32	73.16	68.46
Band- Pass 300-3400 Hz	None	41.13	32.67
	Matched	71.86	65.73
	Model Adapt	70.04	64.25
	Univariate-32	65.63	58.46
	Multivariate-32	69.29	63.44
Real tele- phone data	None	30.98	21.23
	Matched	69.10	61.80
	Model Adapt	66.86	61.22
	Univariate-32	56.03	49.14
	Univariate-256	60.32	53.38
	Multivariate-32	62.53	56.78
	Multivariate-256	64.67	58.79

Table 2. Band-limited speech recognition results. In Univariate and Multivariate the number that follows indicates the amount of classes employed for band-limited space partitioning.

noise-free telephone channel. In addition, performance on real telephone data is given: the whole TIMIT database was passed through the telephone line in a single call. This is similar to NTIMIT (Jankowski et al., 1990), but in our case all data is distorted by the same channel; a desirable condition in stereo-data compensation.

For comparison, results are given in the first row for the case of full-bandwidth training and test data, setting the upper limit performance. Recognition with full-bandwidth models and restricted-bandwidth test data incurs in a significant accuracy loss even for small distortions like a 6kHz low-pass filter (accuracy goes from 71.18% to 58.30%, a relative 45% error increase; see Table 2). Thus, some compensation (either on the feature or the model side) needs to be applied.

The new multivariate linear correction approach clearly and significantly outperforms polynomial correction showing the convenience of a non-diagonal matrix for feature compensation (i.e. multivariate compensation). Also, the performance achieved is similar to that of model compensation approaches, even for the real telephone distortion,

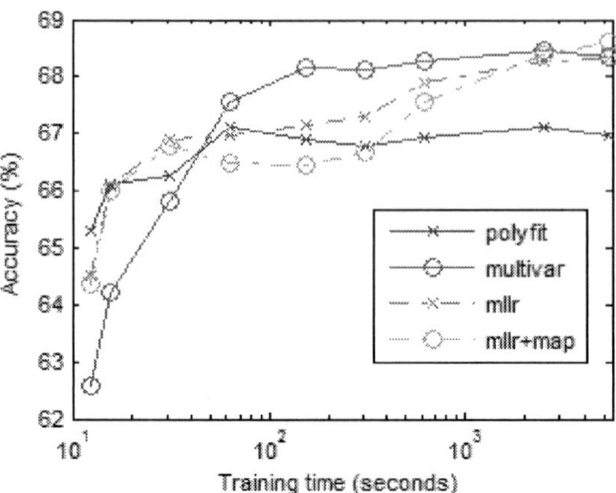

Figure 6. Accuracy for different feature compensation and model-based approaches for 8kHz-4kHz mismatch vs. available training data (in seconds).

were multivariate compensation is only 2.4% absolute worse than with model adaptation.

An important consideration is the number of corrector classes to be used. Previous experiments showed how compensation performance saturates for a *large* number of classes. Dealing with artificial filters, saturation appears for a number of classes around 25 (in our experiments, only 32 classes were used). On the contrary, for the more complicated situation of real telephone data, where noise is also present, a larger number of classes produced a very substantial improvement (compare results for 32 and 256 classes for this case).

Limited Amounts of Training Data

In real applications it could be difficult to produce sufficient amounts of training material for feature compensation or model adaptation. Figure 6 shows performance relative to the amount of training data available. *MLLR* denotes global MLLR adaptation followed by 32-class MLLR adaptation. *MLLR+MAP* uses MAP adaptation on previously MLLR-adapted models (this is also used for model adaptation in Table 2). When the amount of training material is very limited, model adaptation outperforms multivariate compensation, showing the effectiveness of global MLLR (the first stage applied in model adaptation). However, the learning slope in multivariate feature compensation is steeper and from ~50 seconds of training material, multivariate linear correction obtains better results than model adaptation methods, remaining so for as much as ~40 minutes of speech. Thus, it seems that at least for this particular case of filtering distortions and limited data, feature compensation could be a better approach than model adaptation.

6 Conclusions

A new feature compensation framework based on multivariate linear correction was presented. Feature compensation for robust ASR under multiple distorting environments is desirable because it allows using a single acoustic model set independent of the number of distorting environments, and keeps memory load and computation requirements low.

ASR accuracy with the proposed algorithm is similar to that of model-compensation approaches if large amounts of training material are available. In addition, when the amount of training data is small, multivariate linear correction shows better accuracy than all the other approaches considered. Experiments on real telephone data where also conducted showing very promising results (only ~2% absolute loss compared to model adaptation).

The new approach clearly outperforms our previous polynomial compensation with very small increase in computation time. This shows the great advantage of a full compensation matrix over a diagonal one for the case of band-limited data and is in agreement with the practical observations in Sections 3 and 4.2.

In the future, the need of stereo data should be overcome to allow straightforward application to a variety of new practical situations.

Acknowledgments

This research is supported in part by an MCyT project (TIC 2006-13141-C03).

References

H. Abut, J.H.L Hansen and K. Takeda (eds.). 2005. *DSP for in-vehicle and mobile systems.* Kluwer/Springer-Verlag.

L. Denenberg, H. Gish, M. Meteer, T. Miller, J.R. Rohlicek, W. Sadkin and M. Siu. 1993. Gisting conversational speech in real time. *Proceedings ICASSP, 2: 131-134.*

L. Deng, J. Droppo and A. Acero. 2005. Dynamic compensation of HMM variances using the feature enhancement uncertainty computed from a parametric model of speech distortion. *IEEE Speech and Audio Processing, 13(3):412-421.*

J. Droppo, L. Deng and A. Acero. 2001. Evaluation of the SPLICE algorithm on the Aurora2 database. *Proceedings EuroSpeech, 217-220.*

W. M. Fisher, R. Doddington and K. M. Goudie-Marshall. 1986. The DARPA Speech Recognition Research Database: Specifications and Status. *Proceedings DARPA Workshop on Speech Recognition, 93-99.*

J. H. L. Hansen, R. Huang, P. Mangalath, B. Zhou, M. Seadle, M. and J. Deller. 2004. SPEECHFIND: spoken document retrieval for a national gallery of the spoken word. *NORSIG, 1-4.*

X. Huang, A. Acero and H. W. Hon. 2001. *Spoken language processing.* Prentice Hall.

C. Jankowski, A. Kalyanswamy, S. Basson and J. Spitz. 1990. NTIMIT: A Phonetically Balanced, Continuous Speech, Telephone Bandwidth Speech Database. *Proceedings of ICASSP, 1:109-112 .*

N. Morales, D. T. Toledano, J. H. L. Hansen, J. Colas and J. Garrido. 2005. Statistical class-based MFCC enhancement of filtered and band-limited speech for robust ASR. *Proceedings EuroSpeech, 2629-2632.*

N. Morales, D. T. Toledano, J. H. L. Hansen and J. Colas. 2007. Blind feature compensation for time-variant band-limited speech recognition. *IEEE Signal Processing Letters, 14(1):70-73.*

P. Moreno. 1996. *Speech recognition in noisy environments.* PhD. Thesis in Electrical and Computer Engineering. Carnegie Mellon University, Pittsburgh.

L. C. W. Pols. 1977. *Spectral analysis and identification of Dutch vowels in monosyllabic words.* Ph.D. Thesis. Free University of Amsterdam.

M. Seltzer, A. Acero and J. Droppo. 2005. Robust bandwidth extension of noise-corrupted narrowband speech. *Proceedings EuroSpeech, 1509-1512.*

Theoretically Motivated Treebank Coverage

Victoria Rosén
University of Bergen and Unifob
victoria@uib.no

Koenraad de Smedt
University of Bergen and Unifob
desmedt@uib.no

Abstract

The question of grammar coverage in a treebank is addressed from the perspective of language description, not corpus description. We argue that a treebanking methodology based on parsing a corpus does not necessarily imply worse coverage than grammar induction based on a manually annotated corpus.

1 Introduction

The need for treebanks as an empirical basis for research on the grammar of a language is well established. While it is often stated that treebanks are useful for linguistic research as well as for language technology (Nivre et al., 2005), linguistic research with treebanks seems underrepresented in the literature (Nivre, 2005). Despite extensive research on the relation between treebanks and grammars, we think that theoretical issues in the relation between treebank annotation and grammar coverage have been underexposed.

Automatic grammar induction from manually annotated treebanks has been explored for over a decade (Krotov et al., 1994; Charniak, 1996; Burke et al., 2004; Cahill et al., 2004). Often, the quality of these grammars is discussed mainly as the percentage of coverage of the corpus by the grammar. There are, however, two obvious problems for inducing grammars from treebanks: one is the existence of annotation errors in the treebank (Dickinson and Meurers, 2005), and the other is the large

number of rules that are obtained. For the *Wall Street Journal* part of the Penn Treebank "approximately 17,500 rules are required to analyze just under 50,000 sentences — or about one distinct rule for every three sentences" (Gaizauskas, 1995). According to Gaizauskas, one "possible explanation for the large number of rules is that in contexts where the annotators were unsure of the syntactic structure they created long rules that avoided issues of the internal structure of constituents." Such rules have little empirical content. Even if the number of rules can be dramatically decreased by means of compaction (Dickinson, 2006), the question remains to what extent an induced grammar captures linguistic generalizations about the language or rather describes a particular annotation in a particular corpus.

Grammar induction approaches evaluate the accuracy of the grammar by "measuring the degree to which parser output replicates the analyses assigned to sentences in a manually annotated test corpus" (Carroll et al., 2003), which is thereby treated as a gold standard. Even if some annotation errors can be detected and corrected (Dickinson and Meurers, 2005; Dickinson, 2006), any natural corpus will undoubtedly also include typos and other errors. From the viewpoint of theoretical linguistics, it is undesirable to end up with a grammar that overgenerates (Charniak, 1996) while not capturing the necessary linguistic generalizations.

The problematic status of automatically induced grammars shows that despite the apparent advantage of automatic acquisition, a theoretically motivated handwritten grammar should not be dismissed as a valuable starting point in treebank construction.

Joakim Nivre, Heiki-Jaan Kaalep, Kadri Muischnek and Mare Koit (Eds.)
NODALIDA 2007 Conference Proceedings, pp. 152–159

Parsebanking (a term we heard first from Ron Kaplan) is an approach to treebanking by parsing a corpus with a wide coverage grammar which has been advocated and practiced in recent years. In this paradigm, the question of coverage in the relation between the grammar and the treebank must be explicitly addressed. Treebanks as parsed corpora can be used to evaluate the performance of a parser or track its performance over different versions (Van der Beek et al., 2002; Oepen et al., 2004b).

In the context of the TREPIL project, we are developing a tool called LFG PARSEBANKER for incremental and interactive parsebanking (Rosén et al., 2005b; Rosén et al., 2005a; Rosén et al., 2006) which is compatible with any LFG grammar (Bresnan, 2001) implemented in XLE (Maxwell and Kaplan, 1993). We are therefore not committed to any particular grammar, although we are committed to the LFG formalism. In our approach, manual annotation is still necessary if the correct analysis has to be chosen among a number of possibilities. Much of our current research effort is in fact aimed at maximizing the efficiency of the disambiguation process.

Not every item that is passed to the parser as a 'sentence' can be expected to obtain an analysis (let alone a correct analysis). There may however be several reasons for this. In the following we will examine various coverage issues. It is useful to distinguish clearly between different types of non-coverage. In the first place we draw a distinction between input that one may not expect the grammar to cover and input that one would expect it to cover. The former is treated under sections 2 and 3. Input that ideally should be covered is discussed in sections 4 and 5. The examples given here will be mainly from the Norwegian grammar NorGram (Butt et al., 2002) but the points made are of a more general nature.

2 Non-syntactic input

Not everything in a corpus that typographically looks like a sentence (starts with an uppercase letter, ends with a period) is necessarily actually a sentence in the grammatical sense. Especially in corpus material such as newspaper text, many text chunks will be headlines, headers, lists, etc.

The PARC 700 Dependency Bank (King et al., 2003) contains dependency structures for 700 sentences randomly extracted from section 23 of the UPenn *Wall Street Journal* treebank (Marcus et al., 1994). The sentences were parsed with PARC's LFG grammar for English and the f-structures were converted into dependency structures. Many of the sentences received more than one parse, and example (1) is cited as an example of a sentence for which "the best parse was far from the desired parse" (King et al., 2003).

(1) *8 13/16% to 8 11/16% one month; 8 13/16% to 8 11/16% two months; 8 13/16% to 8 11/16% three months; 8 3/4% to 8 5/8% four months; 8 11/16% to 8 9/16% five months; 8 5/8% to 8 1/2% six months.*

It is not surprising that the grammar did not produce the desired parse for this item, since it doesn't have the structure of an English sentence. An alternative view would be to consider this a non-sentential item of some sort. It is in fact far from clear how it should be analyzed, if at all. It seems to be a list of some sort, and the readers of the *Wall Street Journal* may know how to process it. But grammatical analysis is not obviously appropriate for sundry lists. Although the *Wall Street Journal* may have a standard way of listing this information, it is clear that this is not a part of the grammar of the English language. We argue that items that have no true syntactic structure should not be annotated as such (but see the possibility of fragment parsing discussed below).

3 Performance phenomena

Performance errors are particularly salient in spoken language corpora, but they are also a feature of written language corpora which cannot be ignored. We will examine these in turn.

3.1 Spoken language corpora

The syntactic annotation of spoken language corpora is complicated by the fact that spoken language is characterized by numerous dysfluencies: false starts, repetitions, repairs, etc. There is no widespread consensus on how dysfluencies should be handled with respect to syntactic annotation.

Victoria Rosén and Koenraad De Smedt

Johannessen and Jørgensen (2006) discuss different strategies that various researchers have taken to the syntactic annotation of spoken language, ranging from ignoring any performance features in spoken language to including all of them, for instance speech repairs, in the annotation. The example in (2) from Sampson (2003), here in labeled bracket notation, illustrates the latter strategy.

(2) *and that [$_{NomCl}$ [$_{NP}$ any bonus [$_{RelCl}$ he] # anything [$_{RelCl}$ he gets* obj *[$_{PP}$ over that]]] is [$_{NP}$ a bonus]]*

Sampson discusses the difficulties involved in indicating "what is going on in a 'speech repair'". In this case, he says that "a speaker embarks on a relative clause modifying *any bonus* and then decides instead to use *anything* as the head of the phrase and to make *bonus* the predicate". He uses the crosshatch symbol to indicate the point at which there is an interruption. He states that "we need rules for deciding how to fit that symbol, and the words before and after it, into a coherent structure[. . .]" and subsequently asks the question "Where in the tree do we attach the interruption symbol?" He doesn't go into detail on how such questions are answered, but says: "[This analysis] is based on explicit decisions about these and related questions, and the variety of speech management phenomena found in real-life spontaneous speech is such that these guidelines have had to grow quite complex; but only by virtue of them can thousands of individual speech repairs be annotated in a predictable, consistent fashion."

A consistent method of annotating speech repairs is certainly a good thing if one is interested in studying speech repairs. At the same time, it is not necessarily a good choice to mix this annotation with the annotation of syntactic structure. A phrase structure tree is normally used to indicate the constituent structure of a phrase or sentence, but the noun phrase indicated in this tree is not a recognizable pattern for a well-formed noun phrase. A better approach would be to let the dysfluency annotation and the syntactic annotation be done on separate levels.

In our approach to syntactic annotation of spoken language, only parts of utterances that have clear constituent structure will be annotated syntactically. For the example in (2), this would be the noun phrase *any bonus* and the clause *anything he gets over that*

is a bonus. The rest of the utterance could of course be part of speech tagged, but a syntactic analysis in addition to tagging does not seem warranted when the syntactic structure is unclear.

Even though the problem of identifying grammatical and nongrammatical parts of spoken utterances is nontrivial, it is possible, with the help of the LFG PARSEBANKER, to achieve as good and rich an annotation for the grammatical parts of spoken language as for written language (Rosén, submitted).

3.2 Written language corpora

Performance errors are common in all text types. They are especially frequent in certain types of texts, such as newspapers, which are quickly written and typically proofread cursorily or not at all. For this reason it is somewhat surprising that so many corpora are heavily based on newspaper texts. This question seems to have been given little attention in the literature, although Becker et al. (2003) developed an error typology for a German newspaper corpus.

If one is interested in robustness, performance errors should not be corrected. Since our focus is on grammar, we are, however, not interested in trying to treat ungrammatical input as if it were grammatical. In contrast to some automatically induced grammars, we want to avoid building a grammar that covers ungrammatical input. There are then several possibilities for dealing with ungrammatical input. While one possibility consists of simply rejecting such items, another consists of correcting the errors but retaining information about what actually occurred in the corpus, and a third of assigning partial parsing, which is basically the same approach we adopt for speech performance phenomena, as discussed above.

In the LOGON Norwegian–English machine translation project (Oepen et al., 2004a), the problem of performance errors was dealt with through the "careful copy editor" principle, which may be formulated: "if there is a typographical error in the test corpus which a careful copy editor would have corrected, the test corpus item should be corrected". A treebank built in the LOGON project contained sentences corrected according to this principle because these sentences were important for coverage in this specific application.

It is however not always easy to determine what kind of performance errors should be corrected if this approach is chosen. Clear typographical errors like misspellings are unproblematic. Grammatical performance errors are more difficult to decide on. What would a careful copy editor do with the sentence in (3)?

(3) *He wants to among other things to go fishing.*

Most editors would probably consider this an unintentional repetition of the infinitival marker, and would delete one of them. In the LFG PARSE-BANKER, we can comment out one (or the other) and get a parse, retaining the information on what was actually in the corpus. Consider however the partial sentence in (4) from the LOGON development corpus.

(4) *[...] med innlagt   solnedgang og*
     [...] with included sunset   and
     flott   utsyn mot   Nesjøen,
     beautiful view   towards Nesjøen,
     Nordskardsfjellet og   ikke minst opp
     Nordskardsfjellet and not least   up
     mot   Sylmassivet.
     towards Sylmassivet.
     "[...] including a sunset and beautiful view out over Nesjøen, Nordskardsfjellet and of course up toward the Syl massif."

The problem in (4) is that there is a coordination of unlike constituents, a PP, an NP and another PP. Note that the professional idiomatic translation exhibits a parallel construction in English. A really careful copy editor would have corrected this, for instance by adding the preposition *mot* before *Nordskardsfjellet*, thus making a phrase of three coordinated PPs. This kind of construction, on the borderline of grammaticality, is a difficult problem, but not only for us. What do manually constructed treebanks do with this kind of sentence? Perhaps such language use is one reason why there are so many once-only rules in hand-annotated treebanks.

Some may want to consider the language in (4) more or less acceptable, whereas others do not want to include in the grammar. It is of course possible to maintain different versions of the grammar, one that includes it (for instance for robust parsing) and

one that does not (for instance for generation). Our point is that providing an analysis or not for such an example must be a conscious choice. One should not contrive an analysis for a single example (thereby raising it from instance to type) if it is not motivated in terms of a linguistic generalization.

If one chooses to exclude borderline constructions from the grammar, one may still obtain *fragment* analyses for the parts that are covered. The simpler example in (5), with a similar pattern, may serve as an illustration. The Norwegian grammar produces the fragment analysis in Figure 1.

(5) *Petter går   til butikken, parken   og til*
     Petter goes to store-the, park-the and to
     slottet.
     castle-the
     "Petter goes to the store, the park and to the castle."

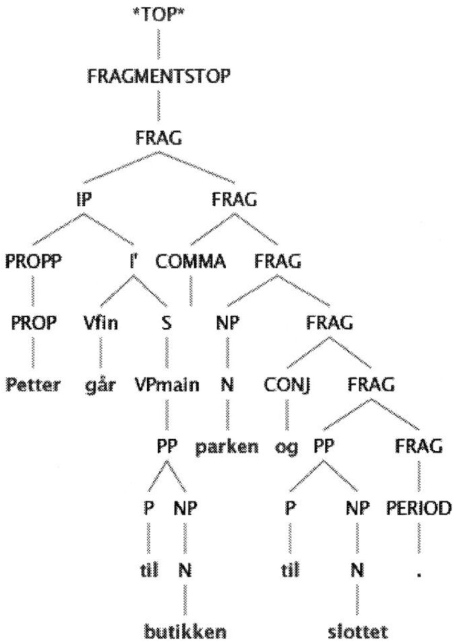

Figure 1: Fragment analysis for (5).

Summing up, we aim at a methodology for treebank construction based on linguistically motivated grammars and therefore ungrammatical input is rejected. In some applications, for instance for the purpose of compiling an error corpus, one might want to parse a corrected version of an item. In other applications that prioritize robustness over grammatical correctness, a more tolerant grammar may be used. If one doesn't want to alter the sentence and doesn't want to include the construction in the grammar, there is the option of producing a fragment analysis. Fragment analyses have proved useful for machine translation in the LOGON project.

4   Open-endedness of language

A handwritten grammar will always miss some constructions, not only by accidental omissions, but also because language is creative and open-ended. As an example of this class of coverage issues, we may consider resultatives, as in (6).

(6)   a. *He wiped the table clean.*
      b. *She hammered the metal flat.*

A resultative analysis presupposes that the verb subcategorizes for a predicate adjective complement, in addition to a subject and an object. This is not a problem for verbs like those in the examples in (6), where it is well known that they take such complements. Common resultative verbs may be expected to be present in the lexicon with the appropriate subcategorization frame. The problem with this construction is that it is quite creative. Example (7) from a Norwegian newspaper article about a man who threw garbage into his neighbor's yard illustrates this creativity well.

(7)   *Det   trekker   til   seg   store   mengder*
      it   draws   to   self large   quantities
      fugler   som   deretter   skiter
      birds   that   subsequently   poop
      eiendommen   full.
      property-the   full
      "This attracts large quantities of birds who subsequently poop the property full."

If the appropriate subcategorization frame for the verb *skite* is added to the lexicon, the sentence will get the intended analysis. This particular resultative use of this verb is impossible to predict, but with an interactive and incremental approach to parsebanking, it is not difficult to incorporate even such unexpected usages into the grammar and lexicon and thereby include them in the treebank.

Some constructions on the borderline of grammaticality were initially kept outside our Norwegian grammar, but were later included based on insights derived from the LOGON corpus. Example (8) consists of two independent clauses separated by a comma. In school teacher jargon, it would be called a run-on sentence.

(8)   *Her   går   bjørka   over   1200   meter,*
      here   goes birch-the   over   1200   meters,
      det   er   høyest   i   landet.
      that   is   highest   in   country-the
      "Here birches grow over 1200 meters, that is the highest in the country."

According to the normative rules of writing, both in Norwegian and English, independent clauses in the same sentence must be conjoined by a conjunction or a semicolon, not just a comma.

If this type of sentence is to be considered outside of the scope of the grammar, a high quality fragment analysis may still be produced. The c-structure representation of a fragment analysis for (8) is provided in Figure 2.

Our corpus work so far suggests however that authors quite often write sentences like this. Therefore the grammar has been modified to allow the comma to function in the same way as a conjunction in the grammar rules. In that case the sentence may be fully analyzed, as in Figure 3.

Parsebanking is a suitable methodology for tackling these coverage issues due to its incremental nature, so that the treebank is a gradually refined product of testing in the grammar construction process. The parsebanking approach benefits from advanced tools for supporting the communication between annotators and grammar developers (Rosén et al., 2006), for regression testing (Oepen et al., 2004b), etc.

5   Difficult syntactic problems

In the previous section we have demonstrated how some coverage problems, whether syntactic or lexical, come to light when the grammar is confronted with a corpus. Such coverage problems can be remedied by revising the grammar or lexicon and reparsing, for which we are developing efficient tools.

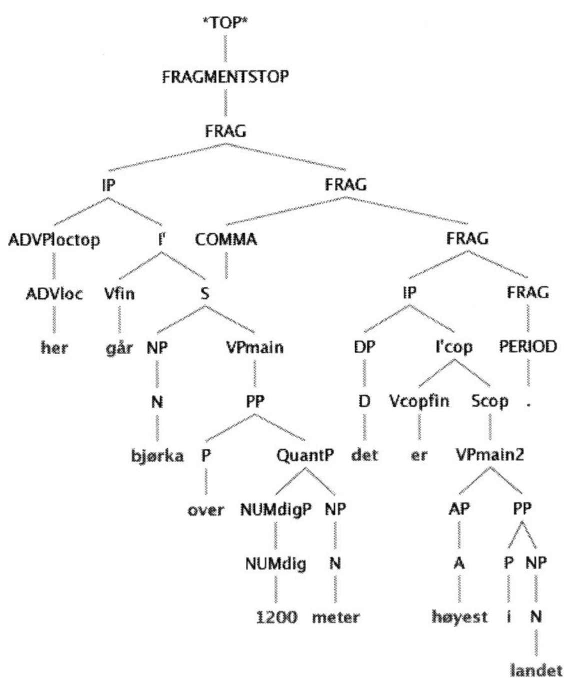

Figure 2: Fragment analysis for (8).

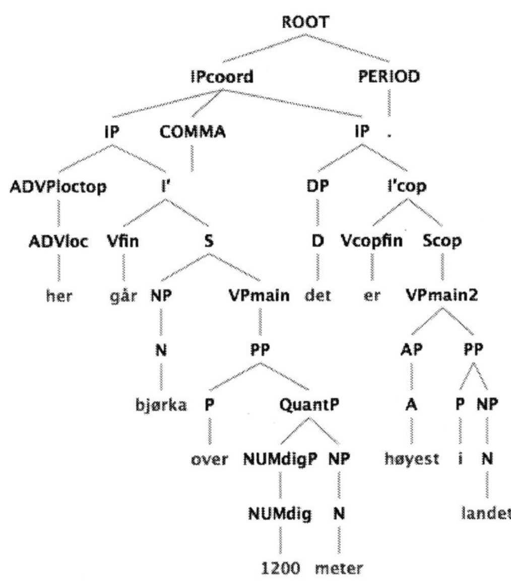

Figure 3: Full analysis for (8).

This is not to say that there are not real coverage problems for a handwritten grammar. There are genuinely difficult syntactic problems for all approaches to syntactic annotation.

A construction that has been the subject of much debate is the so-called "the more the merrier" construction (also called the "covariational conditional construction" (Goldberg and Casenhiser, 2006) and "correlative *the*-clauses"), examples of which are given in (9)–(11).

(9) *The more the merrier.*

(10) *The more chips you eat, the more you want.*

(11) *The bigger they come, the harder they fall.*

Among other issues, it has been debated how the definite article should be analyzed here, since it is not clear that it is a determiner in this construction. In the Penn Treebank II's *Bracketing Guidelines* (Bies et al., 1995), we find an overview of bracket labels for annotating phrases. This explanation is

provided for how the label *X* is to be used: "Unknown, uncertain or unbracketable. X is often used for bracketing typos and in bracketing *the... the*-constructions (see section 10 [Subordinate Clauses] and section 25 [Correlative *the*-Clauses])." In section 10.7 we read: "There is no definitive policy for handling these cases. Most analyses involve the use of SBAR." Then some sample analyses are provided for this construction. The analysis of the sentence in (12) is given in (13).

(12) *The more he muzzles his colleagues, the more leaks will pop up all around Washington.*

(13)
```
(S (SBAR-ADV (X the more)
             (S (NP-SBJ he)
                (VP muzzles
                    (NP his
                        colleagues))))
    '
    (X the more)
    (NP-SBJ leaks)
    (VP will
        (VP pop
            (PRT up)
            (PP-LOC all around
                    (NP Washington)))))
```

Here the *X* is used to label a part of the tree for which the analysis is undecided. Although in a sense a tree has been drawn, it's a bit paradoxical to bracket a constituent with a label that means "unknown, uncertain or unbracketable". Furthermore, it is strange that the same annotation is used for both typos and challenging constructions. The question is whether this can be considered meaningful coverage. An alternative view would be that this is analogous to our fragment parsing, and that it only partially provides an analysis for the sentence.

If the treebank were to consist only of trees, it would be possible to construct a tool which would allow an annotator to edit a fragment analysis, erasing all the fragment nodes and creating new nodes and branches. However, manipulating the output of the grammar would mean that the treebank no longer was in sync with the grammar. Rather than devising ad hoc structures, we think it is fairer to admit that certain constructions are simply not covered yet.

Moreover, in our multilevel framework based on LFG, manual editing is not a desirable solution, since the c-structure is co-described by the grammar with the f-structure and the mrs-structure. Thus, manipulation of one structure would cause the different levels to no longer correspond, and since this correspondence is grammar dependent, it is not possible to make a tool that assures these correspondences for items that fall outside of the grammar.

6   Conclusion

In our work on treebanking as automatic parsing of a corpus, we have met criticism that not everything in the corpus is analyzed, or even can be analyzed. It might however be counterproductive to analyze everything just for the sake of the analysis. We have suggested that building a treebank is not just a matter of assigning some analysis to everything, but also of making grammaticality judgments. Analyses that contribute nothing to a linguistically motivated grammatical description are at best superfluous and increase grammar size. For items outside of the coverage of the grammar, a fragment analysis will often be useful. The parser then assigns structures to the largest chunks that it can analyze. This makes it easy for annotators and grammar developers to see what is covered and what is not. Legitimate analyses that are missing will be detected in our incremental and interactive approach linking treebanking

to grammar development (Rosén et al., 2006), and their detection will lead to better coverage after revision of the grammar. Our aim is to develop treebanking methods that provide a correct and theoretically motivated account of a *language*, not of a corpus. With this aim, automatic parsing yields better quality by avoiding inconsistencies and other errors associated with a manual approach and eliminates complicated postprocessing steps for error detection and compaction.

References

Markus Becker, Andrew Bredenkamp, Berthold Crysmann, and Judith Klein. 2003. Annotation of error types for German Newsgroup Corpus. In Anne Abeillé, editor, *Treebanks: Building and Using Parsed Corpora*, chapter 6, pages 89–100. Kluwer Academic Publishers.

Ann Bies, Mark Ferguson, Karen Katz, Robert MacIntyre, Victoria Tredennick, Grace Kim, Mary Ann Marcinkiewicz, and Britta Schasberger. 1995. Bracketing guidelines for Treebank II style Penn Treebank Project. Technical report, University of Pennsylvania.

Joan Bresnan. 2001. *Lexical-Functional Syntax*. Blackwell, Malden, MA.

Michael Burke, Aoife Cahill, Ruth O' Donovan, Josef Van Genabith, and Andy Way. 2004. Treebankbased acquisition of wide-coverage, probabilistic LFG resources: Project overview, results and evaluation. In *The First International Joint Conference on Natural Language Processing (IJCNLP-04), Workshop "Beyond shallow analyses – Formalisms and statistical modeling for deep analyses", March 22-24, 2004 Sanya City, Hainan Island, China.*

Miriam Butt, Helge Dyvik, Tracy Holloway King, Hiroshi Masuichi, and Christian Rohrer. 2002. The Parallel Grammar project. In *Proceedings of COLING-2002 Workshop on Grammar Engineering and Evaluation, Taipei, Taiwan.*

Aoife Cahill, Michael Burke, Ruth O'Donovan, Josef Van Genabith, and Andy Way. 2004. Long-distance dependency resolution in automatically acquired widecoverage PCFG-based LFG approximations. In *Proceedings of the 42nd Meeting of the Association for Computational Linguistics.*

John Carroll, Guido Minnen, and Ted Briscoe. 2003. Parser evaluation: Using a grammatical relation annotation scheme. In Anne Abeillé, editor, *Treebanks: Building and Using Parsed Corpora*, chapter 17, pages 299–316. Kluwer Academic Publishers.

Eugene Charniak. 1996. Tree-bank grammars. Technical Report CS-96-02, Dept. of Computer Science, Brown University, Providence, Rhode Island, January.

Markus Dickinson and W. Detmar Meurers. 2005. Prune diseased branches to get healthy trees! In *Proceedings of the Fourth Workshop on Treebanks and Linguistic Theories (TLT 2005)*.

Markus Dickinson. 2006. Rule equivalence for error detection. In Jan Hajič and Joakim Nivre, editors, *Proceedings of the Fifth Workshop on Treebanks and Linguistic Theories*.

Robert Gaizauskas. 1995. Investigations into the grammar underlying the Penn Treebank II. Technical Report Research Memorandum CS-95-25, University of Sheffield.

Adele E. Goldberg and Devin Casenhiser. 2006. English constructions. In Bas Aarts and April McMahon, editors, *The Handbook of English Linguistics*, Blackwell Handbooks in Linguistics, chapter 15. Blackwell.

Janne Bondi Johannessen and Fredrik Jørgensen. 2006. Annotating and parsing spoken language. In Peter Juel Henrichsen and Peter Rossen Skadhauge, editors, *Treebanking for Discourse and Speech: Proceedings of the NODALIDA 2005 Special Session on Treebanks for Spoken Language and Discourse*, pages 83–104, Copenhagen. Samfundslitteratur.

Tracy Holloway King, Richard Crouch, Stefan Riezler, Mary Dalrymple, and Ronald M. Kaplan. 2003. The PARC 700 dependency bank. In *Proceedings of the 4th International Workshop on Linguistically Interpreted Corpora, held at the 10th Conference of the European Chapter of the Association for Computational Linguistics (EACL'03)*, Budapest.

Alexander Krotov, Robert Gaizauskas, and Yorick Wilks. 1994. Acquiring a stochastic context-free grammar from the Penn Treebank. In *Proceedings of Third Conference on the Cognitive Science of Natural Language Processing*, pages 79–86.

Mitchell Marcus, Grace Kim, Mary Ann Marcinkiewicz, Robert MacIntyre, Ann Bies, Mark Ferguson, Karen Katz, and Britta Schasberger. 1994. The Penn Treebank: Annotating predicate argument structure. In *Proceedings of the ARPA Human Language Technology Workshop*.

John Maxwell and Ronald M. Kaplan. 1993. The interface between phrasal and functional constraints. *Computational Linguistics*, 19(4):571–589.

Joakim Nivre, Koenraad De Smedt, and Martin Volk. 2005. Treebanking in Northern Europe: A white paper. In Henrik Holmboe, editor, *Nordisk Sprogteknologi 2004. Årbog for Nordisk Sprogteknologisk*

Forskningsprogram 2000-2004, pages 97–112. Museum Tusculanums Forlag, Copenhagen.

Joakim Nivre. 2005. Book review of Anne Abeillé, editor, Treebanks: Building and using parsed corpora, Kluwer AP, 2003. *Machine Translation*, 18:373–376.

Stephan Oepen, Helge Dyvik, Jan Tore Lønning, Erik Velldal, Dorothee Beermann, John Carroll, Dan Flickinger, Lars Hellan, Janne Bondi Johannessen, Paul Meurer, Torbjørn Nordgård, and Victoria Rosén. 2004a. Som å kapp-ete med trollet? Towards MRS-based Norwegian–English Machine Translation. In *Proceedings of the 10th International Conference on Theoretical and Methodological Issues in Machine Translation*, Baltimore, MD, October.

Stephan Oepen, Dan Flickinger, Kristina Toutanova, and Christopher D. Manning. 2004b. LinGO Redwoods, a rich and dynamic treebank for HPSG. *Research on Language & Computation*, 2(4):575–596, December.

Victoria Rosén, Koenraad De Smedt, Helge Dyvik, and Paul Meurer. 2005a. TREPIL: Developing methods and tools for multilevel treebank construction. In Montserrat Civit, Sandra Kübler, and Ma. Antònia Martí, editors, *Proceedings of the Fourth Workshop on Treebanks and Linguistic Theories (TLT 2005)*, pages 161–172.

Victoria Rosén, Paul Meurer, and Koenraad De Smedt. 2005b. Constructing a parsed corpus with a large LFG grammar. In *Proceedings of LFG'05*, pages 371–387. CSLI Publications.

Victoria Rosén, Koenraad De Smedt, and Paul Meurer. 2006. Towards a toolkit linking treebanking to grammar development. In *Proceedings of the Fifth Workshop on Treebanks and Linguistic Theories*, pages 55–66.

Victoria Rosén. submitted. Mot en trebank for talespråk. In Janne Bondi Johannessen and Kristin Hagen, editors, *Språk i Oslo. Ny forskning omkring talespråk*. Novus forlag, Oslo.

Geoffrey Sampson. 2003. Thoughts on two decades of drawing trees. In Anne Abeillé, editor, *Treebanks: Building and Using Parsed Corpora*, chapter 2, pages 23–41. Kluwer Academic Publishers.

Leonoor Van der Beek, Gosse Bouma, Robert Malouf, and Gertjan Van Noord. 2002. The Alpino dependency treebank. In *Computational Linguistics in the Netherlands (CLIN) 2001*, Twente University.

Utterance-initial duration of Finnish non-plosive consonants

Tuomo Saarni
Department of Information Technology

University of Turku
FI-20014 TURKU
tuomo.saarni@utu.fi

Jussi Hakokari
Department of Information Technology/
Phonetics Laboratory
University of Turku
FI-20014 TURKU
jussi.hakokari@utu.fi

Olli Aaltonen
Phonetics Laboratory
University of Turku

Jouni Isoaho
Dept. of Information Technology
University of Turku

Tapio Salakoski
Dept. of Information Technology
University of Turku

Abstract

We have investigated utterance-initial duration of non-plosive consonants in two qualitatively different Finnish speech corpora. The goal has been to identify any possible lengthening or shortening effects the domain edge (here, the beginning of an utterance) might have on segmental duration. Duration was observed at phone level. The results indicate that cases of lengthening, shortening, and absence of any effect all occur. Those are determined by the speech sounds phonemic identity, and the results were similar in both corpora. For instance /s/ and /r/ are lengthened while /j/ and /m/ are shortened. Contrasted with previous research on various languages, the phonetic universality associated with final lengthening does not apply for initial duration processes.

1 Introduction

Several domains (levels of phrase or utterance) have been credited to show initial domain-edge processes in various languages. These processes have mainly been referred to as either initial lengthening or shortening. Lengthening refers to cases in which speaking rate is briefly decelerated right as the speaker commences articulation. Shortening is the opposite; the speaker accelerates (producing relatively short segments) before re-suming normal pace. Final lengthening, a domain-edge process involving considerable slowing down at the ends of utterances, has been found in practically all languages investigated. Yet initial effects have produced contrasting results depending on the language in question and the methodology used.

Initial lengthening has been reported in Chinese (Zu & Chen 1998, Cao 2004; syllable duration). Languages with reported shortening include Swedish (Hansson 2003; syllable duration at word level), Japanese (Kaiki et al. 1990), and Eskimo (Nagano-Madsen 1992). Venditti & van Santen (1998; phone duration) report initial lengthening of consonants and shortening of vowels in Japanese. White (2002) has found differences between various English consonant sounds.

The phenomenon is likely to be related to initial strengthening, a stronger contact between associated articulators such as the tongue and palate. These two effects, however, have been connected in no uniform fashion. For instance, Fougeron & Keating (1997) found that while for American English /n/ there is spatially greater linguo-palatal contact initially than medially, the acoustic duration is in fact shorter. The opposite was found in Korean by Cho & Keating (2001); in Korean initial strengthening and lengthening appear to correlate. Fougeron (2001) has suggested strengthening may be language-specific. Fougeron also (2001) claims articulatory variations in initial position are not conditioned by pauses but occur also internally at boundaries. In another tradition of terminology, boundary-adjacency is the common name for finality and initiality.

Joakim Nivre, Heiki-Jaan Kaalep, Kadri Muischnek and Mare Koit (Eds.)
NODALIDA 2007 Conference Proceedings, pp. 160–166

Previous investigation (Saarni et al. 2006) into the matter has revealed what could be considered initial domain-edge effect on segmental duration. Lengthening was found in all utterance-initial vowels (diphthongs included) in syllables such as V or VC. The lengthening did not extend to the entire first syllable (such as CV or CVC); cf. Byrd (2000) for similar observation in English. There was also shortening of phonologically long plosives, but the general category of non-plosive consonants was hardly affected. The category contains many articulatorily diverse sounds, however. Since edge effects in them has been documented in other languages (cf. White 2002), we decided to examine them phoneme by phoneme to find out if there are contrasting qualities that were neutralized in the former categorical examination.

The potential of corpus studies and phone-level approach have been mostly overlooked in previous research. Syllable-level studies, mainly on traditional elicited laboratory speech, have dominated duration research. Our previous results have led us to believe a syllable-level examination will miss some of the finer details of domain-edge processes. Not only can the observed phenomenon operate on a finer time scale than the syllable, but phonemically specific behaviors do not show if syllables consisting of different sounds are treated equally.

The study at hand covers the native Finnish consonants with the exception of plosives and any phonemically long consonants. Plosives are usually impossible to measure in initial position since the sound signal carries no trace of the initiation of the implosive phase. Long consonants, on the other hand, are geminates and may not occur in initial position.

This study is limited to the paradigm of corpus-based speech acoustics, and cannot as such address the question of initial strengthening. However, acoustic duration of speech segments will be carefully examined, allowing us to contribute to the controversy around the seemingly language-dependent domain-initial edge effects.

At this point, when little conclusive has been presented on the subject, we need to recognize the possibility of two different kinds of initial edge effects. First, the first position is articulatorily peculiar in that there is no excitation sound until the contact between articulators is already made. For instance, plosives usually do not have audible implosion phases. Fricatives and approximants may

also start out "half-way", at the point when a constriction of the vocal tract is already reached. Second, a longer lasting compression or expansion may take place (cf. Hansson 2003) independently of the above-mentioned effect, just like final lengthening usually increases segmental duration over a number of phones. White (2002) also points out that utterance-initial syllable onsets are shorter than word-initial onsets utterance-medially.

First, the speech corpora used in the study are briefly described. Second we explain the way in which the statistical analysis was run on the corpora. Both the numerical results and some description of the figures follow third.

2 Speech Material

Two kinds of Standard Finnish speech corpora were studied. The first one ('single-speaker', or SS) consisted of sentences picked from a periodical and read aloud by an adult male speaker. The reading was done with intent to prepare a corpus for research use. SS is comprised of 967 utterances with 41 306 phones. Of these 14 170 are non-plosive consonants and thus investigated here.

The second ('multi-speaker', or MS) consisted of television news reading, field and weather reports, and oral presentations by 9 men and 6 women, all of whom were professional speakers. Unlike the individual in SS, these speakers were not aware their speech would be used for research purposes. There were a total of 1 148 utterances and 31 414 phones including 10 584 short consonants.

All in all, there were about one and a half hours of continuous speech with any and all pauses eliminated. The corpora were annotated by hand and improved and rechecked several times both by a trained human annotator and by computer scripts designed to detect suspicious annotation. Scripts were designed for preparing the corpus information for phone-level statistical analysis, as ~73 000 phones cannot be entered manually.

3 Methods

To examine how duration in utterance-initial environment develops as closely as possible, we chose a phone-level approach. It is our conviction that researchers should not restrict themselves to syllable and word-level measuring exclusively, as has been the trend. Our previous research has shown that not all phenomena of segmental duration operate on syllable level. Conversely, some information may actually be overlooked unless phone-by-phone calculations are run on the test material. We organized all the phones into separate data sets by their phonemic identity and their distance from the beginning of the utterance. For instance, 22 utterances in SS and 34 utterances in MS began with the phoneme /r/. All these were then put into their respective slot "position 1" (see graphs 1-8 in the results section). In 30 and 39 of the utterances the second phone was /r/, and all these were assigned into "position 2". This was done to the first 15 positions and all the phonemically short non-plosive consonants, /s, r, m, j, n, h, ʋ, ŋ, l, ɾ/. The few and far between non-native sounds (such as /ʃ/ and /f/) were not studied, and neither at this point the phonologically long variants (/sː, nː, .../) of native consonants. As geminates, the latter may occur at the earliest between the first and the second syllable (i.e. position 2). Finally, the mean duration and 95 % confidence interval were calculated for all positions. The confidence intervals are shown as error bar graphics; if two error bars do not overlap, their difference is statistically significant at p<0.05 level. For comparison, there is a horizontal line indicating the mean duration of the phoneme in question. It is the mean calculated from the entire corpus, not just the first fifteen positions in the figures.

A caveat on terminology is in order. We prefer to use the word utterance in the purely phonetic sense of a single, continuous flow of speech internally uninterrupted by pauses. There is no reference to a syntactic unit, such as sentence, made here. Terminal and non-terminal intonation units are treated equally, which is not necessarily the most informative alternative.

4 Results

The results show there is both significant lengthening and shortening in utterance-initial consonants, depending on what phoneme is examined. In the figures, the vertical axis shows the mean duration of applicable segments in milliseconds and their 95 % confidence intervals; the horizontal axis describes the position from the beginning of the utterance. The horizontal line is the mean duration of all the phonemes in question that can be

found in the corpus, even those that are beyond the 15 phone scope of the graph. Please bear in mind that the overall mean is somewhat high due to segments that have been significantly affected by final lengthening (Hakokari et al. 2005).

The phonemes can be divided roughly into four groups. First, the sounds /s/ and /r/ are significantly lengthened in both corpora. Second, the sounds /m/ and /j/ are significantly shortened in both corpora. Third, the sounds /n/, /h/, and /ʋ/ are shortened to some degree in MS but not in SS. Fourth, the sounds /ŋ/ and /l/ are not affected in either one. The latter are not shown in the figures below.

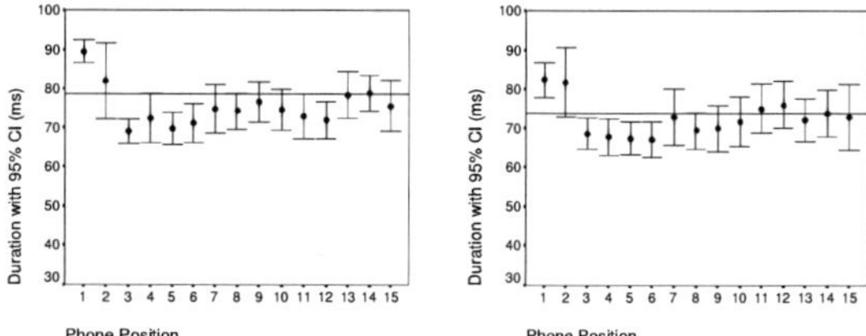

Figure 1. /s/ in SS (left) and MS (right) corpora.

The alveolar fricative /s/, of which there are distinct rounded and unrounded allophones, is lengthened initially in the first position and to some degree in the second. In both corpora there is a gentle shortening (of dubious significance, though) after the lengthening before the mean line is reached. There were a total of 177 utterance-initial items in both corpora combined, but only 38 in the second position.

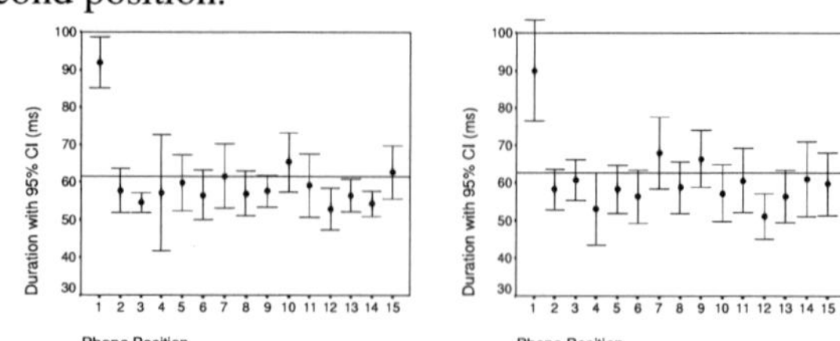

Figure 2. /r/ in SS (left) and MS (right) corpora.

The medioalveolar trill /r/ shows similar behavior in both corpora. It is considerably lengthened in the initial position, after which there is no effect. There were a total of 56 utterance-initial items in both corpora combined, and 64 in the second position.

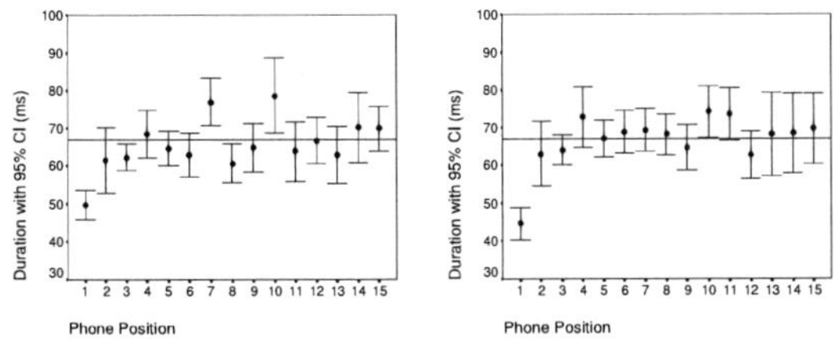

Figure 3. /m/ in SS (left) and MS (right) corpora.

The results for the bilabial nasal /m/ are near-identical for the three first positions in both corpora. Unlike with /s/ and /r/, the first position is significantly shorter than the following ones. There were a total of 199 utterance-initial items in both corpora combined, but only 16 in the second position.

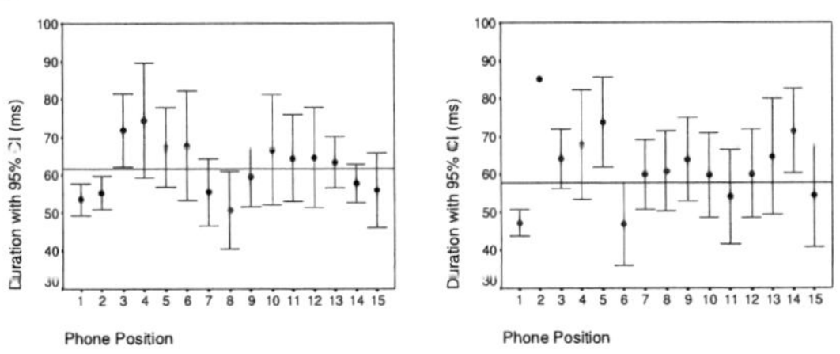

Figure 4. /j/ in SS (left) and MS (right) corpora.

The palatal approximant /j/ is shortened to some degree in SS for both initial and second position, but only for the initial MS. However, the second position has only one item in MS and three in SS, making it impossible to hypothesize anything. All in all, there is much variation in the sound's duration beyond the initial position, and the sound is very hard to segment objectively. Furthermore, /j/ may only occur syllable-initially and its sample size is relatively low. The first position has 257 items in both corpora combined; we can only conclude those are significantly shorter than the mean.

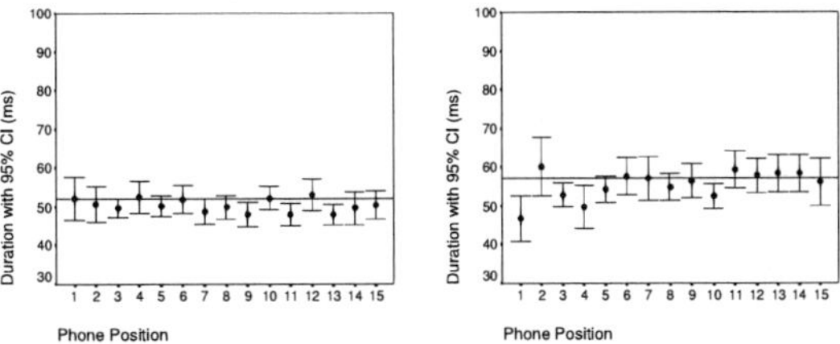

Figure 5. /n/ in SS (left) and MS (right) corpora.

The alveolar nasal /n/ is slightly shorter initially in MS than the rest, but its statistical significance is not clear. In SS corpus there is no shortening what-

soever. There were a total of 112 utterance-initial items in both corpora combined, and 62 in the second position.

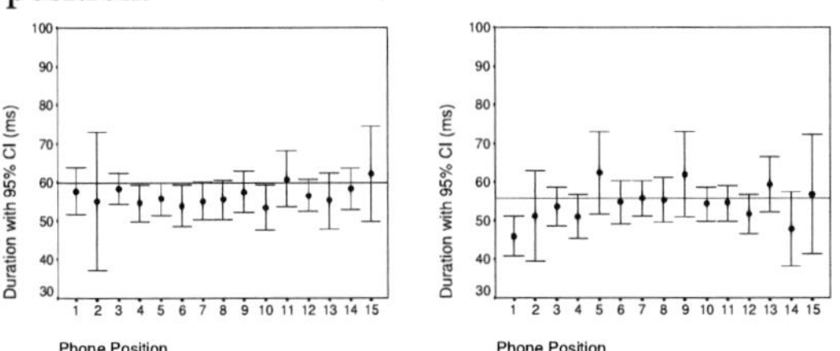

Figure 6. /ʋ/ in SS (left) and MS (right) corpora.

The initial labiodental approximant /ʋ/ is again slightly shorter than the rest in MS (significance unclear), but not in SS. There were a total of 144 utterance-initial items in both corpora combined, but only 12 in the second position. Also /ʋ/ can only occur in syllable-initial position.

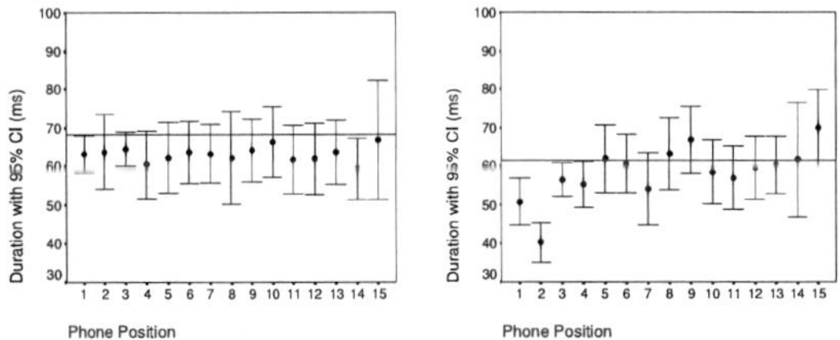

Figure 7. /h/ in SS (left) and MS (right) corpora.

Also /h/ shows no shortening in SS but some in MS. The second position is particularly pronounced. The sound is frustratingly difficult to segment accurately due to the variety of strategies that can be used to produce it, including a variety of non-modal phonations.

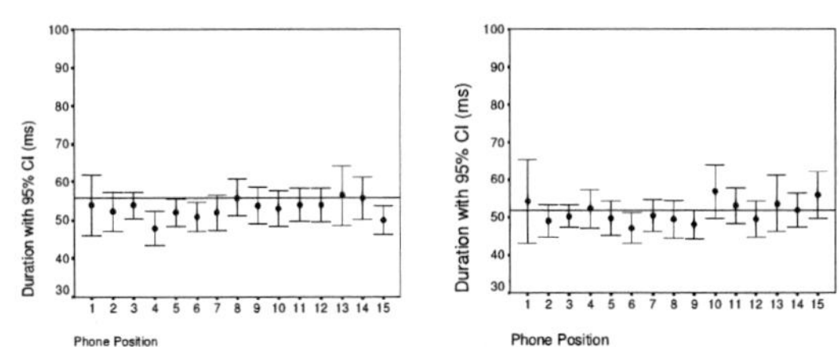

Figure 8. /l/ in SS (left) and MS (right) corpora.

The lateral approximant /l/ (fig. 8) showed no effect on duration in either of the corpora.

There was a slight downward trend for /ŋ/ in MS, though, which might marginally contribute to initial shortening in a word level examination. /ŋ/

does not occur in the initial position in Finnish due to phonotactic restrictions. In educated Standard Finnish /ɾ/ is mostly realized as a single trill (flap), but it cannot occur word-initially or finally. It is very often credited to be a voiced alveolar plosive /d/ mainly for orthographical reasons. It may be produced as a true voiced plosive by some speakers, especially in foreign names and recent loan words, but that is uncommon. In vernaculars it is either omitted or it has become assimilated with other sounds; consequently, a variety of strategies are used to produce the phoneme (see Suomi 1980 for a detailed account). In any case it is marginal in frequency (only ~2,9 % of all the non-plosive consonants in the material) and does not produce very reliable results. There were 6 counts of initial /ɾ/ in the material showing a high mean duration but little consistency.

5 Discussion

As described in the results section, many of the phonemes displayed deviant duration in the first (onset) or the first two positions within an utterance. The question of stress must be addressed first, as stressed syllables are generally expected to undergo lengthening. Unstressed utterance-initial speech sounds are next to impossible to study for reference, since Finnish has an invariable first syllable stress. Unlike in some other first syllable-stressing languages, such as the closely related Estonian, even foreign loan words are forced into the same stress pattern in Finnish. Furthermore, the lengthening as witnessed in /r/ applies to the first position only (syllable onset) while the second position represents overwhelmingly the syllable coda (syllable-initial consonant clusters are not native to Finnish). Thus, lengthening can be expected in words such as /ro.po/ ('a coin, mite') but not in words such as /or.po/ ('an orphant'). Obviously, the fact that some phonemes are shortened and other lengthened is equally difficult to explain away in terms of stress or accent. On the other hand, a future study should be done on the corpora to determine whether any of these effects can be reproduced with a word-initial instead of an utterance-initial examination.

Another issue is segmentation. The corpora had different annotators, but the results are still mostly comparable. However, certain speech sounds are more difficult to objectively segment than others. The trill /r/ makes the following vowel r-colored making it often a subjective task to determine where the sound ends. The true approximants /ʋ/ and /j/, well described as glides, are notoriously difficult to segment, especially in a medial position. Neither has any fricative noise in Finnish. However, the shortening of /j/ and the lengthening of /r/ are so clear in both corpora it is fairly safe to say they are not solely products of segmentation strategies. /ʋ/ and /j/, being phonotactically restricted in Finnish, are unfortunately very rare in position two and not that common elsewhere either (in fact may only occur syllable-initially); hence the great variation in both corpora. The sample size for the first-position /j/ is considerably greater for the multi-speaker corpus; being of more informal a nature, it contains many utterances beginning with the word /jɑ/ ('and').

Nasal coarticulation may affect adjacent sounds as well, much depending on the speaker. True nasal articulation is still easy to tell apart from nasalized vowels because the oral closure and release may be pinpointed accurately in the speech signal. The shortening of /m/ is especially significant, since the two other nasal phonemes /ŋ/ and /n/ show little or no shortening. White (2002) has reported very similar results for /m/ in his English test material.

/h/ was slightly affected by shortening in multi-speaker but not to a slightest degree in the single-speaker corpus. Since segmenting the sound is an extremely subjective task, we hesitate to draw any conclusions on the subject. There is a variety of allophones and articulatory variation in how the sound is realized, ranging from breathy phonation to fricative noise.

The alveolar fricative /s/ was significantly lengthened initially. The sound also underwent an exceptional amount of final lengthening as both phonologically short and long in a past study by Hakokari et al. (2005). That suggests the sound is more liable to vary in duration according to its position in prosodic structure. Shadle & Scully (1995) have suggested the exact opposite; the fricative is presumably insensitive to vowel context. Fougeron (2001) has found the sound fairly insensitive to prosodic context as well, and characterized it as having "few degrees of articulatory and acoustic freedom". The reason for such differences between languages cannot be answered at the moment. Differences in method alone do not feel adequate to count for the discrepancy. On the other hand, in English, there is no such allophonic variance (cf. "articulatory freedom") in /s/ as in Finnish. In Finnish the labialized allophone [sʷ] is acoustically very distinct, with energy at relatively low frequencies; it is easily interpreted as /ʃ/ by English speakers. In the absence of a voiced/voiceless distinction of consonants in the language it may be produced voiced.

Given that all vowels have been found to undergo lengthening in initial position (Saarni & al. 2006), it is worth noting that either lengthening or shortening are more common than no modification of duration at all.

6   Conclusion

This study has observed the duration of short consonants (plosives excluded) in two qualitatively different Standard Finnish speech corpora. The goal has been to identify any possible durational effects an utterance-initial position has on these speech sounds. Previous studies have indicated both language-specific and, within language, phoneme-specific initial manipulations of segmental duration.

The results suggest there is no reason to posit either a feature initial shortening or lengthening in Finnish, as both kinds of durational patterns occur. Lengthening or shortening seems governed by the phonemic identity of the segment occupying the initial position in an utterance. The voiceless sibilant and voiced trill were lengthened, while nasals and approximants showed various amounts of shortening. The lateral approximant was the only sound unaffected in both corpora, although there was considerable variation in its initial position that sample size alone does not explain.

The results are not all similar to those obtained in other languages, which supports the view that initial duration is not based on strictly universal premises. Some level of individual variation may be expected as well, since 2 of the consonants were, on average, shortened by the 15 speakers of the multi-speaker corpus, but not by the individual in the single-speaker corpus.

The instantly visible lengthening and shortening affect only the first or the first two phones of the utterance. Word-level examinations were not run on the corpora at this point, but none of the results rule out the possible shortening or lengthening of the entire first word or so. Statistically significant compression or expansion of the beginning of the utterance (as in narrow confidence intervals) may be established only with a great amount of data, since the intrinsic durations of speech sounds will induce variation.

Perhaps the greatest contribution of this study is pointing out that the most common approach used today, limiting oneself to the syllable level and making no distinction between different speech sounds (operating on "syllable duration"), is prone to miss even the most robust characteristics of duration near the edge of the domain. The results presented in this paper may be useful for instance in speech synthesis. On the other hand, the methods and analysis may be used by researchers in speech technology to produce viable speech scientific information (provided they have a corpus readily available), even when their primary concern is technological development.

References

Dani Byrd. 2000. Articulatory Vowel Lengthening and Coordination at Phrasal Junctures. Phonetica 57, pp. 3-16.

Jianfen Cao. 2004. Restudy of segmental lengthening in Mandarin Chinese. Proceedings of Speech Prosody 2004 (SP-2004), Nara, Japan, pp. 231-234.

Taehong Cho & Keating. 2001. Articulatory and acoustic studies on domain.initial strengthening in Korean. Journal of Phonetics 29 (2), pp. 155-190

Cécile Fougeron. 2001. Articulatory properties of initial segments in several prosodic constituents in French. Journal of Phonetics 29 (2), pp. 109-135.

Cécile Fougeron and Patricia A. Keating. 1997. Articulatory strengthening at edges of prosodic domains. Journal of the Acoustical Society of America 101 (6), pp. 3728-3740.

Jussi Hakokari, Tuomo Saarni, Tapio Salakoski, Jouni Isoaho, Olli Aaltonen. 2005. Determining prepausal lengthening for Finnish rule-based speech synthesis. Proceedings of Speech Analysis, Synthesis and Recognition, Applications of Phonetics (SASR 2005), Kraków, Poland.

Petra Hansson. 2003. Prosodic phrasing in spontaneous Swedish. An academic dissertation. Travaux de l'institut de linguistique de Lund 43. Lund University.

Nobuyoshi Kaiki, Kazuya Takeda, Yoshinori Sagisaka. Statistical analysis for segmental duration rules in Japanese speech synthesis. Proceedings of the 1990 International conference on Spoken Language Processing, Kobe, Japan, pp. 17-20.

Yasuko Nagano-Madsen. 1992. Temporal characterristics in Eskimo and Yoruba: a typological consideration. In Huber (ed.): Papers from the Sixth Swedish Phonetics Conference held in Gothenburg. Technical Report No. 10, Department of Information Theory, School of Electrical and Computer Engineering, Chalmers University of Technology, Gothenburg. pp. 47-50.

Tuomo Saarni, Jussi Hakokari, Jouni Isoaho, Olli Aaltonen, Tapio Salakoski. 2006. Segmental duration in utterance-initial environment: evidence from Finnish speech corpora. Advances in Natural Language Processing: 5th International Conference on NLP, Fin-TAL 2006, Turku, Finland. Published as a volume in Springer series "Lecture notes in Artificial Intelligence". pp. 576-584.

Christine H. Shadle and Celia Scully. 1995. An articulatory-acoustic-aerodynamic analysis of [s] in VCV sequences. Journal of Phonetics 23, pp. 53-66.

Kari Suomi. 1980. Voicing in English and Finnish stops. A typological comparison with an interlanguage study of the two languages in contact. Publications of the Department of Finnish and General Linguistics of the University of Turku 10.

Jennifer J. Venditti and Jan P.H. van Santen. 1998. Modeling segmental durations for Japanese text-to-speech synthesis. Proceedings of the Third ESCA Workshop on Speech Synthesis 1998.

Laurence S. White. 2002. English Speech Timing: a Domain and Locus Approach. University of Edinburgh PhD dissertation.

Yiqing Zu and Xiaoxia Chen. 1998. Segmental durations of a labeled speech database and its relation to prosodic boundaries. Proceedings of the 1st International Symposium on Chinese Spoken Language Processing (ISCSLP 1998).

Comprehension Assistant for Languages of Baltic States

Inguna Skadiņa
Tilde
Vienības gatve 75a, Riga, Latvia
LV1004

inguna.skadina@tilde.lv

Andrejs Vasiļjevs
Tilde
Vienības gatve 75a, Riga, Latvia
LV1004

andrejs@tilde.lv

Daiga Deksne
Tilde
Vienības gatve 75a, Riga, Latvia
LV1004

daiga.deksne@tilde.lv

Raivis Skadiņš
Tilde
Vienības gatve 75a, Riga, Latvia
LV1004

raivis.skadins@tilde.lv

Linda Goldberga
Tilde
Vienības gatve 75a, Riga, Latvia
LV1004

linda.goldberga@tilde.lv

Abstract

This paper presents results of a pilot project for the development of a foreign text comprehension assistant. This tool provides word, phrase and simple sentence translation between the languages of the Baltic countries (Estonian, Latvian and Lithuanian) and widely used European languages (English, German, French and Russian). The paper presents the general architecture of the system, describes its main constituents and outlines difficulties in multilingual phrase translation. The system demonstrates original adaptation of rule based techniques and statistical methods to deal with language specificities, such as inflectional word forms, free word order, and the lack of sizeable, sufficiently representative parallel corpora.

1 Introduction

For relatively small languages such as languages of the Baltic countries, electronic dictionaries and comprehension assistance tools play an important role in communication. Until now, several commercial desktop electronic dictionaries have been developed. Most of them are bilingual (different bilingual dictionaries of Fotonia, Festart English-Latvian dictionary, English-Estonian dictionary by Filosoft, and others), some are multilingual (MOT GlobalDix by Kielikone, multilingual dictionaries of Tilde).

Although electronic dictionaries are useful for communication, they are insufficient to overcome language barriers. Even after finding a translation of each word in a sentence, the user is still left unaided to figure out which translations to choose and how to form a sentence from them. Translation of text units out of context is the main drawback of electronic dictionaries. The role of the word in a sentence or its part of speech are important in determining the right translation. Electronic dictionaries are also of little assistance in detecting idiomatic expressions. Even if an expression is provided in the dictionary, the user usually is not able to detect it in a source text and is mislead by a confusing word-by-word translation.

On the other hand, Machine Translation (MT) systems for larger languages are rapidly gaining global popularity. However, they are not able to approach the quality of human translation. There-

Joakim Nivre, Heiki-Jaan Kaalep, Kadri Muischnek and Mare Koit (Eds.)
NODALIDA 2007 Conference Proceedings, pp. 167–174

fore MT systems are appropriate for users with no or very limited language skills as a fast way of grasping the basic subject matter of the content.

An alternative solution is a comprehension assistant, which assists user in understanding foreign language text (Feldweg and Breidt, 1996; Prószéky and Balázs, 2002; Deksne et al 2005). This approach addresses a usage scenario where the user has some knowledge of the target language but occasionally needs assistance in understanding unknown words or phrases. Users with intermediate language skills prefer to read the original text and use translation assistance only when it is necessary. The comprehension assistant provides possible translations of a phrase or a word in context, helps to understand the structure of the sentence or the phrase and find relations between words, detects and translates idiomatic expressions. Translation of phrases as well as possible translations of individual words are provided.

The translation is provided as a screen tip in the context of the source text. Users are not disturbed from the source text, they see the translation context, are involved in the translation process by translating incomprehensible phrases only and interpreting the text themselves.

We have generalized the above mentioned approach from a single language pair to multilingual approach, covering languages of the Baltic countries and the most popular European languages. The developed system architecture allows simple inclusion of new language pairs – since the major constituents are language independent, only the language dependent content needs to be filled for a new language pair.

2   System Architecture

The aim of the comprehension assistant is to identify individual phrases in the text and provide the user with full translation of the whole phrase, as well as separate translations of the words constituting the phrase.

The comprehension assistant is built from separate components, each of them having their own functionality. (See Figure 1).

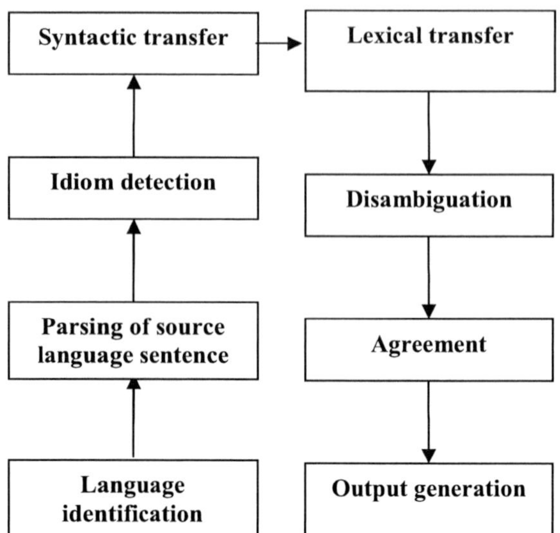

Figure 1. The chain of the comprehension assistant components.

During the translation process, components are executed successively. It means that the input data for each subsequent component are the internal structures created or processed by the previous component. At first, the system tracks the mouse pointer and retrieves text under it. Then it detects the language, analyzes the text, finds translation of the phrase containing the word under cursor and finds all translations for each word in the phrase. Finally, all results are presented to the user. Output contains both - the phrase translation and the translations of each word of the phrase. If the system cannot identify a phrase, translations of individual words are provided.

2.1   Language identification

Language identification module is developed to relieve the user from the need to select the translation source and target languages every time the language of the text changes. This module automatically identifies the language of the text and provides the appropriate source and target language information to the system. Currently the system identifies the following languages: English, Estonian, French, German, Latvian, Lithuanian and Russian.

For language identification, the character n-gram approach is used (Grefenstette, 1995; Bashir Ahmed et al, 2004). The *language reference model* is based on the most frequent character n-grams of sizes 1, 2, 3 and 4. For this purpose the text corpus of every supported language is analyzed, most frequent sequences of one, two, three and four character long text strings are determined and probabilities of those n-grams are calculated.

During language identification of a particular text, we calculate frequency scores of character n-grams in this text to get the *text model*. The resulting text model is compared to the language reference models for all supported languages. The closest matching is based on 600 most characteristic n-grams of the language.

2.2 Parser

The aim of the parser component is to obtain a fully or partially parsed sentence. As the parsers differ from language to language, a wrapper component is developed, which transforms the output of different parsers to a unique format necessary for further processing. For widely spoken European languages, parsers are licensed from third party software vendors: Connexor[1], Dictum[2].

Parsers for Baltic languages have been developed within the project and have two constituents: the language independent parsing engine and the language dependent set of syntax rules.

The formal grammar we use for syntax rules is derived from unification grammar. Since Baltic languages are highly inflective languages, the syntax of the parsing rules needs to have attributes allowing inclusion of morphological information.

A parsing rule consists of two parts: description of the syntactic structure (a context free grammar rule) and usage conditions which describe constraints as well allow to assign or pass morphological and syntactic features between nodes.

In Figure 2, a simplified parser rule is shown. The rule describes the structure of a noun phrase (NP) consisting of an attributive adjective phrase (AP), the head noun (N) and an optional prepositional phrase (PP). The double equation mark '==' is used to describe conditions, i.e., the rule will be executed only if there will be agreement in case, gender and number between the adjective phrase (AP) and the noun (N). The single equation mark '=' is used to assign properties to the nodes. In the sample below, the noun phrase will inherit case, gender and number from the main noun.

```
NP -> attr:AP main:N (mod:PP)
    attr:AP.Case==main:N.Case
    attr:AP.Gender==main:N.Gender
    attr:AP.Number==main:N.Number
    NP.Case=main:N.Case
    NP.Gender=main:N.Gender
    NP.Number=main:N.Number
```

Figure 2. A simplified noun phrase parsing rule.

The parsing engine is based on CYK (Cocke-Younger-Kasami) algorithm (Cocke and Schwartz, 1970; Younger, 1967; Kasami, 1965). It uses bottom-up approach which allows partial parse of input sentence.

Original CYK algorithm supports context-free grammars written in Chomsky normal form (CNF). The developed rule formalism differs from CNF. Therefore parsing rules are transformed to CNF which is extended with attributes. The CYK parsing algorithm also was improved to handle attributes both for constraints and for assigning or passing attribute values between nodes.

Currently parsing rules are developed for Latvian and Lithuanian languages; for Estonian, a small demo grammar is being developed.

The output of the parser component is a syntax tree, or parts of the syntax tree of the sentence (see Figure 3) in case when full sentence parsing fails. Currently parsers for languages of the Baltic countries have no disambiguation constituent, therefore the first full parse tree, if it exists, is chosen for transfer. For the widely used European languages, parsers return a single parse tree.

---

[1] www.connexor.com
[2] http://www.dictum.ru/?main=products&sub=dictascope

```
ministri nolēma piešķirt līdzekļus vētras seku novēršanai
nolēma Base form:nolemt Morphology:vs0000300i000000000000000010
    ministri:subj Base form:ministrs Morphology:n0mpn030000000n0000000000010
    piešķirt:obj Base form:piešķirt Morphology:v00000000n000000000000000010
        līdzekļus:obj Base form:līdzeklis Morphology:n0mpa030000000n0000000000010
        novēršanai:dat Base form:novēršana Morphology:n0fsd030000000n0000000000010
            seku:mod Base form:sekas Morphology:n0fpg030000000n0000000000010
            vētras:mod Base form:vētra Morphology:n0fsg030000000n0000000000010
```

NT	BASEFORM	MORPHOLOGY ATTRIBUTES
N	sekas	n0fpg000000000n0000000000010
N	seka	n0fpg000000000n0000000000010
N	seka	n0fsa000000000n0000000000010

N, N, N ministri	V nolēma	V piešķirt	N līdzekļus	N, N, N, N vētras	N, N, N seku	N novēršanai
SENT	VP	**VP**		**NP** NP NP	NP	
SENT	VP			**NP** NP		
SENT	SENT					
		VP VP				
	VP VP					
SENT SENT						

Figure 3. A parsed Latvian sentence in the form of the dependency tree (above) and as the matrix of the chunk parser (below).

2.3   Idiom processing

There are many cases in real texts where the meaning of a collocation of words is not based on the meaning of its parts. Baltic languages are not an exception and are rich in idiomatic expressions. For example, the literal translation of the Latvian expression *Gāž kā ar spaiņiem* (*It rains cats and dogs*) would be *Pouring like with buckets*.

Such idioms should be identified and treated as a whole in translation. In the comprehension assistant tool they are identified comparing adjacent words in the text to the stored list of idioms. If a matching idiomatic expression is found then the corresponding nodes in the parse tree are located and the translated idiom is attached to them. The information of the syntactic tree of the whole sentence is not used in idiom translation, however, the translated idiom is integrated into the tree to use it later in transfer, agreement and other processes.

Another specific case is translation of software interface elements. If the mouse pointer is located on menu items, the windows title bar, a dialog box message or other user interface elements, to increase quality of translation, specific dictionaries of pre-translated user interface strings and computer terminology are used.

The third case is English phrasal verbs which are language dependent (they are not typical for Latvian, Lithuanian and Russian) and are therefore handled in the syntactic transfer component.

2.4   Syntactic transfer

In the transfer phase, the syntactic tree in the source language is transformed into the corresponding syntactic tree for the target language. Syntactical transformations are made to map one tree structure to another by applying transfer rules. The developed rule formalism allows to:

- change word order,
- delete or hide nodes,
- insert new nodes,
- transfer or assign syntactic, morphological or lexical properties,
- change type of syntactic relations between words.

Usually the transfer is applied to two or three syntactically related nodes, the order of which could be arbitrary in the text. Although transfer rules analyse syntactic relations between words, the word order could be changed during transfer. The following example shows a transfer rule for the transformation of a genitive phrase during translation from English into Latvian:

```
TransferRule(N<-mod-PREP<-pcomp-N)
{
        Child.SourceSpelling == "of";
        Grandchild.Case = genitive;
        MakeLink(Child – hidden -> Parent);
        Swap(GrandChild, Parent);
        MakeLink(GrandChild - mod -> Parent);
}
```
Figure 4. Transfer rule sample.

Applying this rule to the tree representing the English noun phrase 'team of scientists', the word 'scientists' will be moved to the position before the main word 'team' and the case of the word will be changed to the possessive case (genitive) and the preposition 'of' will be discarded.

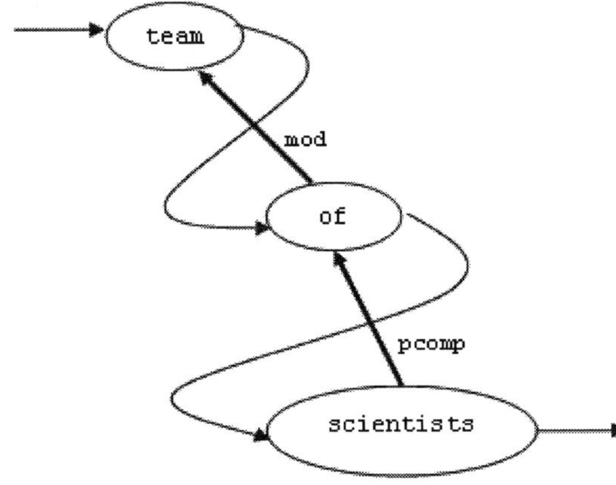

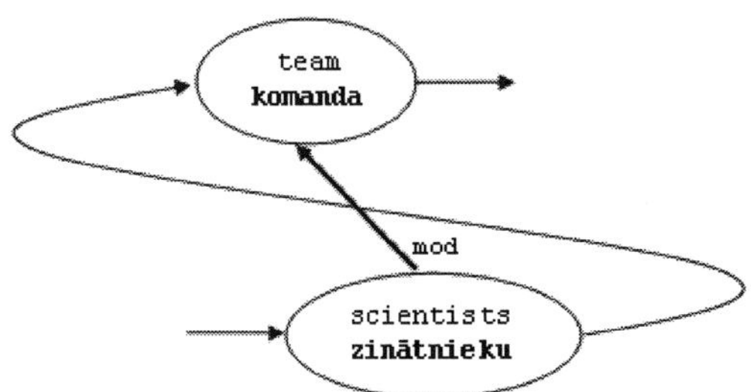

Figure 5. Sample syntactic tree before applying syntactic transfer rule (Figure 4) and after it. Light arrows show word sequence.

2.5 Lexical transfer

The lexical transfer component finds translations of the word in a bilingual dictionary based on the part of speech identified by the parser component. For example, for the English word *rest* in sentence *we need a rest*, noun translations (for Latvian: *atpūta, miers, pauze, pārtraukums*) will be selected and verb translations (for Latvian: *palikt, atpūsties, balstīties, gulties*) will be dismissed.

If there is no translation for the word in the required part of speech, the dictionary lookup is attempted for alternate classes. For instance, instead of a participle, the translation of adjective could be selected.

Usually, dictionaries include only translations of primary words without translations of derivations. For example, dictionaries usually have entries for words like 'assume', but less often they have entries for 'assumption', 'assumed' (adverb) or 'assuming' (noun), and they usually do not have entries for words like 'assumer' and 'assumingly'. For such cases, if the translation of a word is not in the dictionary, specific suffixes and prefixes are cut off at the end and the beginning of the word during dictionary lookup and added to the translated word of the target language. For example, a participle can be translated as the infinitive of the corresponding verb and then the required participle form is synthesized from the translation. Nouns can be cut off suffixes: *–tion, -er, -or*, then translated as verbs and the translations synthesized into the required nouns.

The obtained translations are arranged by their significance (score). Each translation has a label attached identifying whether it can be used in the translation of the phrase. Specific translations are not used in phrase translation, they appear only in the list for each word. In case when a single word is translated, the translations are taken from a richer dictionary where translations are grouped by meanings, including comments on usage.

2.6 Disambiguation

The task of the disambiguation phase is to choose the most appropriate target language word from the several words selected in the lexical transfer phase. We use statistical methods for disambiguation. Traditionally bilingual corpus is used to get statistical data for disambiguation. For Baltic languages the available bilingual corpus is very limited, so we combined two approaches – using a monolingual corpus and multiword expressions with their translation equivalents extracted from the multilingual dictionary.

We applied different approaches for Latvian and Lithuanian. For Latvian disambiguation, we decided to take into account statistical data about the probability of syntactic pairs - two words being syntactically related in a phrase or sentence. This is a more advanced approach compared to bigram probability - probability of two words appearing next to each other in a sentence. We use several syntactic relations such as *subject(noun, verb)*, *object(verb, noun)*, *attribute(adjective, noun)* and *attribute(noun, noun)*.

We gathered a large corpus of Latvian texts from web content. We applied a shallow parser on this corpus to get pairs of syntactically related words. The frequency of each unique pair was calculated. Frequency data were normalized to get probability of syntactic pairs. We call the resulting data the *syntactic language model* (SLM) and use it for disambiguation.

In the syntactic tree of the target language we have one or more Latvian language words mapped to every node (source language word). For every connected Latvian word pair in the tree we find probability from the Latvian SLM. Now we can disambiguate the syntactic tree by selecting those translations that give the highest probability for the whole tree representing the phrase or the sentence.

This SLM based disambiguation improves the quality of the translation compared to the most primitive method of using just the first translation from the dictionary. But the drawback of this method is usage of target language data only and ignoring the source language text in disambiguation.

For Lithuanian disambiguation, we tried a more advanced approach. We used an English-Lithuanian dictionary with a large number of phrase translations. We applied shallow parsing

to it and aligned Lithuanian syntactic bigrams with the corresponding English syntactic bigrams. Again the frequency and probability of such bilingual pairs were calculated. We call the resulting data the *syntactic translation model* (STM).

For English-Lithuanian translation, we find probability in the Lithuanian syntactic tree for every combination of English source and Lithuanian target words at one node connected with the same combination at other node. Probability for this bilingual pair (EN/LT –EN/LT) is found in the English-Lithuanian STM.

Usage of the STM model should potentially provide better disambiguation quality than the SLM model. But we realized that for quality improvements we need much larger bilingual corpus of phrase translations than we have from the English-Lithuanian dictionary we used. Currently, the SLM model demonstrates better results but another comparison should be performed after creating a larger bilingual corpus and rebuilding STM.

As seen in Figure 6, different translations of the verb "pick" are chosen when it is used with nouns 'berries', 'gift' and 'nose'.

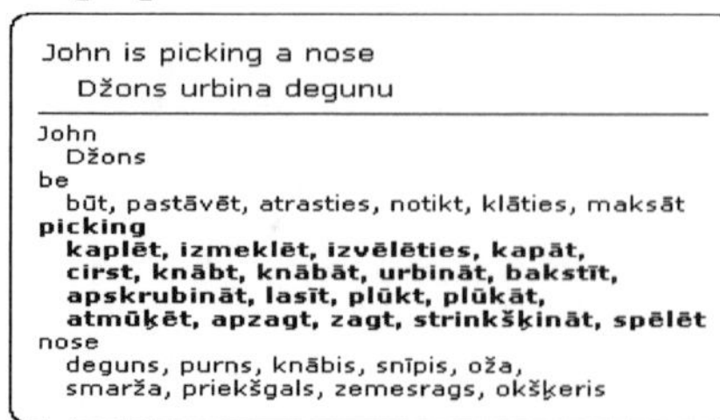

Figure 6. Disambiguation of meanings of the word 'pick' in English-Latvian translation.

2.7   Agreement

At the end of the disambiguation process, the target language syntactic tree contains only one target language word at each tree node. Tree nodes have some morphological properties (e.g., tense for verbs, case and number for nouns) set during parsing and transfer phases. But there are just target language dependent properties which must be set depending on the properties of other words and syntactic relations of words in the target language. For example, in the Baltic languages, the noun and the adjective must agree in case, number and gender. This agreement is established by agreement rules.

```
Rule(N<-attr-A)
        {
        Child.Number = Parent.Number;
        Child.Case = Parent.Case;
        Child.Gender = Parent.Gender;
        }
```

Figure 7. Agreement rule which assigns adjective (A) child node properties of parent noun node (N): gender, case and number.

Through agreement rules, the agreement module passes properties from one word to other and sets the missing morphological properties so that all morphological properties are set and all words in the phrase are in agreement.

Finaly, word form generation is applied according to the morphological properties of the word.

2.8   Output generation

The last phase is formatting of the resulting phrase or sentence.

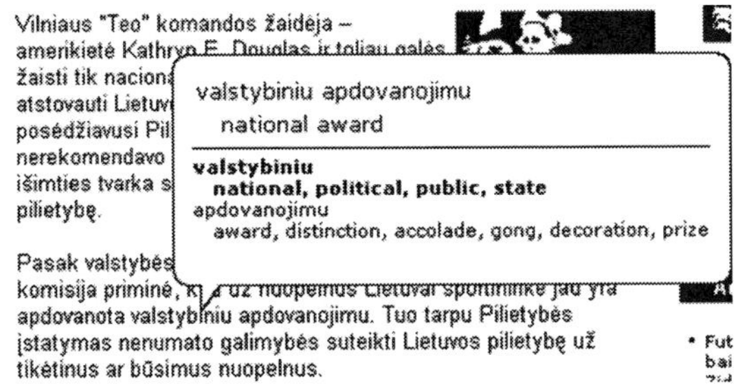

Figure 8. Translation from Lithuanian into English.

The module returns translation results to the user according to the current position of the mouse pointer on the source text. The largest translated phrase related to the selected source word is returned together with translations of separate words of the phrase.

3   Achieved results and future work

Currently the comprehension assistant is at the stage of a pilot project – all system components are implemented and dictionaries for all language pairs are included. However, the level of phrase/sentence translation differs for different language pairs – currently it is better developed for Baltic languages (Latvian, Lithuanian) and less developed for Estonian. For Estonian, currently only a small grammar has been developed, and a rich set of Estonian syntax rules for this system is being currently implemented. Also the English and Russian translation directions are more developed while for German and French only the basic syntactic constructions are currently implemented.

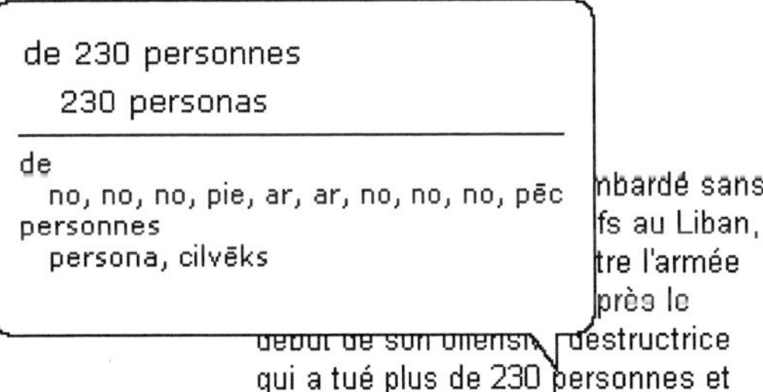

Figure 8. French-Latvian phrase translation.

Quality of translation of phrases varies depending on the complexity of the text. The system can handle relatively simple phrases, but fails dealing with texts from specific domains or dealing with texts with complex grammar and idiomatic meaning, like news headlines.

For test purposes, the gold standard for each language pair is developed. It contains main syntactic constructions for each language pair, as well as some typical cases of word sense disambiguation are included. Tests of the system have shown several weaknesses of the system. This is the basis for future work on improvement of the system.

One of the problems is proper nouns which are not distinguished, therefore, they sometimes are translated with a standard dictionary and the obtained translation does not match the context. In future, we should improve the functionality of proper noun recognition and they should be identified and translated using special dictionaries.

There is still a lot of work to be done to improve the quality of the dictionaries. To improve translation quality, a revised dictionary is necessary which would meet usage-specific criteria.

Quality of dictionaries is important but dictionaries alone can not solve ambiguity issues. The disambiguation algorithm should be improved and statistical data (syntactic translation model) for disambiguator should be gathered from a large scale parallel corpus.

During development, system tests on the gold standard are performed; in future, evaluation of the whole system is planned.

References

Ahmed Bashir, Cha Sung-Hyuk, and Charles Tappert. 2004. Language Identification from Text Using N-gram Based Cumulative Frequency Addition, *Proceedings of Student/Faculty Research Day, CSIS, Pace University*.

John Cocke, Jacob T Schwartz. 1970. Programming languages and their compilers: Preliminary notes. *Technical report, Courant Institute of Mathematical Sciences*, New York University.

Gregory Grefenstette. 1995. Comparing two Language Identification Schemes, *JADT 1995, 3rd International conference on Statistical Analysis of Textual Data, Rome, Italy*.

Daiga Deksne, Inguna Skadiņa, Raivis Skadiņš, Andrejs Vasiļjevs. 2005. Foreign language reading tool – first step towards English-Latvian commercial machine translation system. *Proceeding of the Second Baltic Conference on Human Language Technologies*, 113-118, Tallinn, Estonia.

Helmut Feldweg, Elisabeth Breidt. 1996. COMPASS - An Intelligent Dictionary System for Reading Text in a Foreign Language. *Papers in Computational Lexicography (COMPLEX 96)*, Linguistics Institute, HAS, Budapest, 53-62.

T. Kasami. 1965. An efficient recognition and syntax-analysis algorithm for context-free languages. *Scientific report AFCRL-65-758*, Air Force Cambridge Research Lab, Bedford, MA.

Gábor Prószéky. 2002. Comprehension Assistance Meets Machine Translation. Tomaš Erjavec; Jerneja Gros (eds) *Language Technologies*, 1–5. Institut Jošef Stefan,Ljubljana, Slovenia.

Gábor Prószéky, Kis Balázs. 2002. Development of a Context-Sensitive Dictionary. *Proceedings of the 10th International Congress of the European Association for Lexicography (EURALEX)*, Vol. I, 281–290. Copenhagen, Denmark.

Daniel H Younger. 1967. Recognition and parsing of context-free languages in time n^3. *Information and Control 10(2)*, 189–208.

Andrejs Vasiļjevs, Jana Ķikāne, Raivis Skadiņš. 2004. Development of HLT for Baltic languages in widely used applications. *Proceedings of First Baltic Conference „Human Language Technologies – the Baltic Perspective"*, 198-201, Riga, Latvia.

Combining Contexts in Lexicon Learning for Semantic Parsing

Richard Socher
Saarland University
richard@socher.org

Chris Biemann
University of Leipzig
Ifi, NLP Department
Johannisgasse 26
04103 Leipzig, Germany
biem@informatik.uni-leipzig.de

Rainer Osswald
FernUniversität in Hagen
Department of Mathematics
and Computer Science, IICS
rainer.osswald@fernuni-hagen.de

Abstract

We introduce a method for the automatic construction of noun entries in a semantic lexicon. Using the entries already present in the lexicon, semantic features are inherited from known to yet unknown words along similar contexts. As contexts, we use three specific syntactic-semantic relations: modifying adjective, verb-deep-subject and verb-deep-object. The combination of evidences from different contexts yields very high precision for most semantic features, giving rise to the fully automatic incorporation into the lexicon.

1 Introduction

Advanced tasks such as text summarization and question answering call for tools that support the semantic analysis of natural language texts. While syntactic parsers have been intensively studied for decades, broad coverage semantic parsing is a relatively recent research topic. Semantic parsing aims at constructing a semantic representation of a sentence, abstracting from the syntactic form and allowing queries for meaning rather than syntax. That is, semantic relations between concepts are in the focus of interest rather than syntactic relations between words and phrases.

A major current line of research for extracting semantic structures from texts is concerned with semantic role labeling. The FrameNet database (Baker et al., 1998) provides an inventory of semantic frames together with a list of lexical units associated with these frames. Semantic parsing then

means to choose appropriate semantic frames from the frame inventory depending on the lexical concepts present in the given sentence and to assign frame-specific roles to concepts. A related task has been defined as part of CoNLL 2004 (Carreras and Màrques, 2004). Here, machine learning methods are used to learn a semantic role labeler from an annotated text to extract a fixed set of semantic relations.

If one aims at deep semantic parsing, a lexicon containing semantic information about words and concepts is a prerequisite. Building such a lexicon is a time-consuming and expensive task. The acquisition bottleneck is extremely thin in this area, as lexicon entries tend to be rather complex. Therefore, methods that are capable of automatically or semi-automatically extending semantic lexicons are highly needed to overcome the bottleneck and to scale the lexicon to a size where satisfactory coverage can be reached. In this paper, we present a method that enlarges the number of noun entries in the lexicon of a semantic parser for German.

1.1 Related Work

Extending a given lexicon with the help of a parser relying on this lexicon can be viewed as a step of a bootstrapping cycle: Lexicon entries of known words are used to obtain entries for previously unknown words by exploiting a parsed corpus.

Early bootstrapping approaches such as (Riloff and Shepherd, 1997) were based on few seed words of a semantic category and their nearest neighbor contexts. Higher precision was achieved by separating extraction patterns into two groups by (Roark

Joakim Nivre, Heiki-Jaan Kaalep, Kadri Muischnek and Mare Koit (Eds.)
NODALIDA 2007 Conference Proceedings, pp. 175–182

and Charniak, 1998): Conjunctions, lists and appositives being one and noun compounds being the other. Since bootstrapping single categories often leads to category shifts in later steps, (Thelen and Riloff, 2002) use an un-annotated corpus, seed words and a large body of extraction patterns to discover multiple semantic categories like *event* or *human* simultaneously.

Another related research line is distributional clustering to obtain semantic classes via similar contexts, e.g. (Pereira et al., 1993; Lin, 1998; Rooth et al., 1999). Here, semantic classes are created by the clustering method rather than assigned to predefined classes in the lexicon; these works also employ the distributional hypothesis, i.e. that similar semantic properties are reflected in similar (syntactic) contexts.

Our setup differs from these approaches in that we use a conceptual framework that covers all sorts of nouns rather than concentrating on a small set of domain-specific classes or leaving the definition of the classes to the method. Moreover, we combine three different context types; see (Hagiwara et al., 2006) for a discussion on context combination for synonym acquisition.

2 Semantic Lexicon and Parser

This section gives a brief outline of the semantic parsing framework with respect to which our learning task is set up. The task is to automatically extend a semantic lexicon used for semantic parsing by exploiting parses that have been generated on the basis of the already existing lexicon. From these parses we extract three types of syntactic-semantic noun contexts which are then employed to classify unknown nouns on the basis of classified nouns, as explained in more detail in Section 3.

2.1 The MultiNet Formalism

The semantic parses we exploited for our experiments comply with the MultiNet knowledge representation formalism (Helbig, 2006). MultiNet represents the semantics of natural language expressions by means of semantic networks, where nodes represent concepts and edges represent relations between concepts. Each concept node is labeled by an element from a predefined upper-domain hierarchy of

object [o]	
concrete object [co]	
discrete object [d]	house, apple, tiger
substance [s]	milk, honey, iron
abstract object [ab]	
attribute [at]	
measurable attribute [oa]	weight, length
non-measurable attribute [na]	form, trait, charm
relationship [re]	causality, similarity
ideal object [io]	justice, category
abstract temporal object [ta]	Easter, holiday
modality [mo]	necessity, permission
situational object [abs]	
dynamic situational object [ad]	race, robbery
static situational object [as]	equilibrium, sleep
quantity [qn]	
unit of measurement [me]	kg, meter, mile
...	

Table 1: Part of the MultiNet sort hierarchy relevant to concepts expressed by nouns

45 *ontological sorts* such as 'discrete object' (*d*), 'attribute' (*at*), and 'situational object' (*abs*) (see Table 1) and various so-called layer features indicating facticity, quantification, and referential determination among other things. In addition, MultiNet comprises about one hundred *semantic relations* including a set of *semantic case roles* such as AGT (agent), AFF (affected object), MEXP (mental experiencer) as well as relations for expressing causation, implication, temporality, and so on. The reader is referred to (Helbig, 2006) for a detailed account of the MultiNet paradigm.

2.2 Semantic Parser

The parsed German corpora used in our experiments have been produced by the syntactic-semantic parser described in (Hartrumpf, 2003). This parser, which has been successfully employed for information retrieval and question answering tasks (Hartrumpf, 2005), relies on the computational lexicon HaGenLex (see below) and has components for word sense disambiguation, compound analysis, and coreference resolution. In addition to MultiNet structures, the parser also generates syntactic dependency trees.

The semantic structures produced by the parser depend essentially on the semantic roles specified in the valency frames of the HaGenLex entries. Working with these semantic parses enables us to investigate specific syntactic-semantic contexts of nouns with respect to their potential to act as indicators for

Name	Meaning	Examples	
		+	−
ANIMAL	animal	*fox*	*person*
ANIMATE	living being	*tree*	*stone*
ARTIF	artifact	*house*	*tree*
AXIAL	object with distinguished axis	*pencil*	*sphere*
GEOGR	geographical object	*the Alps*	*table*
HUMAN	human being	*woman*	*ape*
INFO	(carrier of) information	*book*	*grass*
INSTIT	institution	*UNO*	*apple*
INSTRU	instrument	*hammer*	*lake*
LEGPER	juridical or natural person	*firm*	*animal*
MENTAL	mental object or situation	*pleasure*	*length*
METHOD	method	*procedure*	*book*
MOVABLE	object being movable	*car*	*forest*
POTAG	potential agent	*motor*	*poster*
SPATIAL	object with spatial extension	*table*	*idea*
THCONC	theoretical concept	*category*	*fear*

Table 2: Set of 16 binary semantic features

the semantic sort of the nouns. In the experiments described in the following, we focus on the *argument position* a noun takes in the valency frame of a verb, thereby abstracting from the specific semantic role of the argument. Though attractive in principle, preliminary investigations have indicated a sparse-data problem for specific semantic roles.

2.3 The Lexicon HaGenLex

In our experiments, we use part of the computational lexicon HaGenLex (Hagen German Lexicon) as training data. HaGenLex contains about 25,000 German lexical entries (13,000 nouns, 7,000 verbs) with detailed morphological, syntactic, and semantic specifications (Hartrumpf et al., 2003). The semantic specification of HaGenLex entries rests on the MultiNet formalism, that is, every entry is assigned with an ontological sort of the MultiNet sort hierarchy and all valency frames are equipped with MultiNet case roles.

In addition, the noun entries in HaGenLex are classified with respect to 16 *binary semantic features* such as ANIMATE, HUMAN, ARTIF(ICIAL), and INFO(RMATION); see Table 2 for the full list. The features and ontological sorts are not independent of each other; e.g., HUMAN:+ implies ANIMATE:+, ARTIF:−, and sort *d* (discrete object). To prevent inconsistencies, the possible combinations of semantic features and ontological sorts are explicitly combined into *complex semantic sorts*. Figure 1 shows two examples of such combined

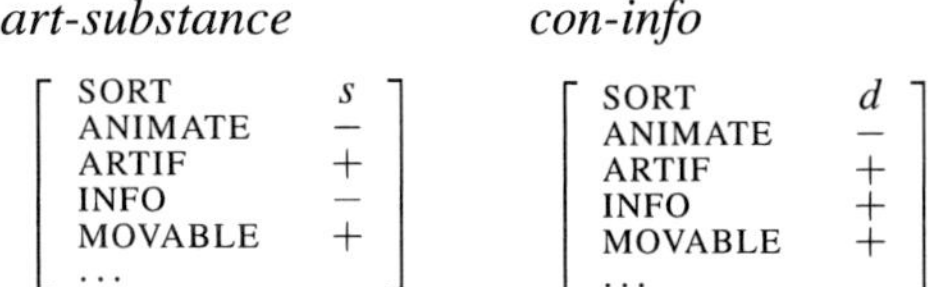

Figure 1: Two examples of complex semantic sorts: *art-substance* (artifical substance) and *con-info* (concrete information object).

sorts: *art-substance* (artifical substance), e.g., *paper*, *beer*, and *con-info* (concrete information object), e.g., *poster*, *certificate*. In total, there are 50 complex semantic sorts; Table 7 lists the 15 most frequent of them in our training data. Since not all of the complex semantic sorts are specified with respect to every feature and because of the ontological sort hierarchy, there is a natural *specialization hierarchy* on the set of complex sorts.

3 Method

The goal of our experiments is to assign complex semantic sorts to unknown nouns. To this end, we separately train binary classifiers for the ontological sorts and semantic features and combine their results in a second step to a complex semantic sort, if possible. Since we use 16 features (Table 2) and 17 sorts (Table 1), this leads to 33 binary classifiers. It should be mentioned that certain classifiers show a fairly strong bias with respect to their distribution within the noun entries of HaGenLex, which in turn gives rise to some unwelcome effects for the respective training results. The *bias* is here defined as the proportion of the more frequent of the two classes.

3.1 Data and Data Structure

Following the distributional hypothesis (Harris, 1968), nouns in a similar context can be assumed to share semantic properties. In our experimental setup, the context of each noun consists of one co-occurring word in a specific relation. These *context elements* are adjectives or verbs in their respective base form. They are automatically disambiguated by the parser if multiple polysemous meanings are present in the lexicon. (The different meanings are indicated by numbers attached to the base form; cf. Figure 2.) In the case of verbs we further distinguish between the different argument positions taken by

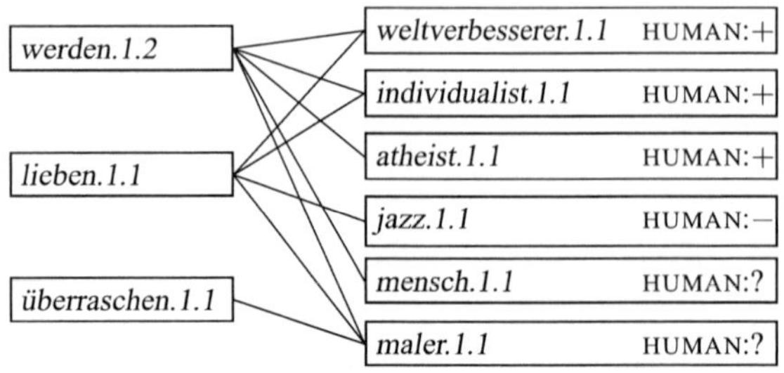

Figure 2: Small sample data for German verb-deep-object relations. Connections indicate co-occurrence in the data.

the noun in the valency frame of the verb. For simplicity, we restrict ourselves to the first two argument positions, henceforth referred to the *deep-subject* and the *deep-object* position, respectively. Notice that according to this terminology, the grammatical subject in passive voice coincides with the deep object.

Pairs of context elements and nouns are aligned in a bipartite graph where known nouns are connected to their context elements which in turn are connected to unknown words, as shown in Figure 2. Before the algorithm starts, a profile of context elements for each noun is extracted from a corpus, which was parsed with the semantic parser described in Section 2.2. It states how often a noun co-occurs with its context elements. We used a corpus of 3,068,945 sentences obtained from the Wortschatz project (Biemann et al., 2004), consisting mainly of contemporary newspaper texts. The parser has a coverage of 42% on this corpus.

3.2   Algorithm

After initialization, the algorithm runs with one specific context type (adjective, deep-subject, or deep-object) at a time. For each context type the process is carried out for all 33 classifiers. (The combination of all context types into one bipartite graph produced worse results in preliminary experiments.) The algorithm's core loop alternates between two phases:

1. *Training*: Each context element gets assigned probabilities that express how indicative this word is for both the positive and the negative class of the classifier in this run. The probability is calculated by dividing the frequency dis-

tribution of each class by the total number of nouns in that class, followed by a normalization step per context element.

2. *Classification*: New classes are assigned to unclassified nouns by multiplying the normalized class probabilities of all context elements class-wise from their profiles of context elements. Class probabilities are multiplied only from context elements that had occurred in a profile of a known noun. New nouns get the class with the highest resulting probability.

This alternation of profile calculation and classification is iterated in a bootstrapping fashion. A difference to other bootstrapping methods like those mentioned in the introduction is that the algorithm only iterates about five times, classifying about 95% of all new nouns during the first iteration. The class profiles are updated based on the new classifications and the cycle starts again unless no new nouns are classified. Figure 3 shows the algorithm in pseudo code.

```
Initialize the training set;
While (new nouns get classified){
   Calculate context element profiles;
   For (each unclassified noun n){
      Multiply class probabilities
         class-wise;
   Assign class with highest
      probability to noun n;
   }
}
```

Figure 3: Algorithm for noun classification in pseudo code

Modification of the algorithm is possible by introducing a threshold α for the minimum number of context elements a noun has to co-occur with in order to be assigned their class. Several experiments proved $\alpha = 5$ to be a good heuristics. With fewer evidence precision drops significantly and with higher numbers recall drops without a gain in precision. In the next section, we will illustrate the algorithm with an example classification.

3.3   Example

For a small demonstration we use the data depicted in Figure 2. First the distribution of classes per context element is calculated as shown in Figure 4a.

a)

Context element	HUMAN:+	HUMAN:−
werden.1.2	3	0
lieben.1.1	2	1

b)

werden.1.2	3/3	0/1
lieben.1.1	2/3	1/1

c)

werden.1.2	1	0
lieben.1.1	0.4	0.6

Figure 4: Stepwise calculation of class probabilities per context element for classifier HUMAN.

Then the distribution is divided by the total number of nouns in that class (Figure 4b). Finally, the relative frequencies are normalized to one per context element; e.g., for *lieben.1.1*:

$$P(\text{HUMAN}:+) = \frac{2/3}{2/3+1/1} = 2/5 = 0.4$$

Figure 4c shows the resulting probability vectors. Now the other nouns get classified by combining the probabilities of co-occurring context elements: For *mensch.1.1* the probabilities are: $P(\text{HUMAN}:+) = 1$ and $P(\text{HUMAN}:-) = 0$, so *mensch.1.1* is HUMAN:+ with high confidence. The case for *maler.1.1* is a bit more difficult because it co-occurs with two different context elements, whose probabilities are multiplied class-wise: $P(\text{HUMAN}:+) = 1 \cdot 0.4 = 0.4$ and $P(\text{HUMAN}:-) = 0 \cdot 0.6 = 0$. So *maler.1.1* also gets the class HUMAN:+ because *werden.1.2* does not occur with a HUMAN:− noun. Notice here that the verb *berraschen.1.1* could not be used since it has not yet appeared in any profile of a known noun. This changes in the next iteration, as now *berraschen.1.1* appears in the profile of the newly classified *maler.1.1*. Further notice that *werden.1.2* with probability 0 for HUMAN:− prevents *maler.1.1* to ever get this characteristic. Smoothing, i.e. assigning small minimum probabilities for all classes did, however, not affect the results much in previous experiments and was therefore not undertaken.

3.4 Building Complex Semantic Sorts

After bootstrapping the 33 binary classifiers, their outcomes can be used to build complex semantic sorts. Previous experiments showed significantly better results for single characteristics than executing the method directly on the 50 complex semantic

sorts introduced in Section 2.3. The results of the binary classifiers for a given noun are combined as follows:

(1) Determine all complex semantic sorts whose semantic features and ontological sorts are compatible with the results of all binary classifiers.

(2) From the results of (1) select those sorts that are minimal with respect to the specialization relation defined on the set of complex semantic sorts (see Section 2.3).

(3) If the set determined in (2) contains exactly one element, then assign this semantic sort to the given noun, otherwise refuse a classification.

3.5 Combination of Context Types

While past experiments on extending HaGenLex (Biemann and Osswald, 2006) have solely been conducted with modifying adjectives as context elements of nouns, the present study also investigates verb-deep-object and verb-deep-subject relations. It is thus possible to combine the results of different context types. In our experiments, the combination is carried out two ways: In a *lenient* setting, only those nouns are left in, which were assigned the same class (positive or negative) of the same classifier at least twice during the experiments with adjective, deep-subjects and deep-objects. In a *strict* setting, classifications in all three context types had to agree.

By combining the results from different context types we gain stronger evidence for each characteristic, possibly at the cost of losing recall. Since we aim rather at producing correct entries in the lexicon than a bulk of wrong ones, precision is the primary measure to optimize here.

4 Experiments

After parsing the corpus with the semantic parser, we extracted the following numbers of different co-occurrences for each context type:

430,916 verb-deep-subject

408,699 verb-deep-object

450,184 adjective-noun

Context type	Bias	Prec.	Rec.	max.Rec.
adjective-noun	0.841	0.927	0.122	0.390
verb-d-subject	0.850	0.967	0.111	0.339
verb-d-object	0.837	0.973	0.094	0.292

Table 3: Average bias, precision, recall and maximally possible recall of three context types ($\alpha = 5$).

Context type	Precision	Recall
adjective-noun	0.845	0.319
verb-d-object	0.891	0.292
verb-d-subject	0.878	0.248

Table 4: Results with $\alpha = 1$ as a preparation for context type combination.

For evaluation we used 10-fold-cross-validation on 11,100 HaGenLex nouns, where the partition was ensured to retain class distribution.

4.1 Experiments

Table 3 shows the arithmetic means of all 33 characteristics and their respective bias, precision, recall and maximally possible recall for each context type. Note that the maximal recall is bounded by the relatively small intersection of known nouns in the database and nouns in the particular part of the corpus.

The results clearly demonstrate the superiority of verbal contexts in this approach, improving precision by 5% as compared to adjective modifiers and not supporting the findings of (Hagiwara et al., 2006), where the modifier relation was reported to perform best on a related task. Bootstrapping on pairs of verb-deep-object co-occurrences shows a precision of 97.3% averaged over all characteristics.

Nevertheless it seems promising to combine the classifier results from different context types by the methods described in Section 3.5 to classify new nouns more correctly. In this setting, the parameter α was reduced from 5 to 1, that is, only one context element is sufficient for new nouns to be classified. The average results for these single context bootstrapping runs are listed in Table 4. Precision is much lower in these experiments because of the parameter setting. The main objective is a high recall, since high precision is supposed to be created by the combination of these results as described in Sec-

Sem. feature or ontol. sort	Strict comb.		Lenient comb.	
	Prec.	Rec.	Prec.	Rec.
HUMAN	0.997	0.143	0.969	0.273
GEOGR	0.982	0.136	0.908	0.257
SPATIAL	0.988	0.123	0.943	0.263
LEGPER	0.997	0.141	0.970	0.275
INSTIT	0.995	0.172	0.972	0.289
ANIMAL	0.996	0.179	0.985	0.298
POTAG	0.995	0.138	0.969	0.274
MOVABLE	0.967	0.120	0.900	0.249
ANIMATE	0.996	0.141	0.970	0.274
INFO	0.967	0.129	0.874	0.243
THCONC	0.944	0.115	0.849	0.238
METHOD	0.997	0.179	0.983	0.300
AXIAL	0.964	0.123	0.904	0.251
MENTAL	0.986	0.159	0.948	0.278
INSTR	0.981	0.143	0.918	0.263
ARTIF	0.926	0.092	0.817	0.217
d	0.980	0.121	0.927	0.257
na	0.996	0.176	0.977	0.297
abs	0.970	0.117	0.907	0.253
mo	0.998	0.182	0.988	0.304
ta	0.989	0.157	0.959	0.279
co	0.988	0.123	0.943	0.263
ab	0.989	0.124	0.945	0.262
s	0.992	0.165	0.965	0.288
oa	0.996	0.176	0.980	0.295
io	0.927	0.096	0.825	0.224
o	1.000	0.191	0.998	0.316
me	1.000	0.191	0.998	0.316
qn	1.000	0.191	0.998	0.316
ad	0.960	0.120	0.891	0.251
at	0.991	0.164	0.956	0.283
re	1.000	0.197	1.000	0.322
as	0.947	0.125	0.860	0.242
Average	0.982	0.147	0.939	0.273

Table 5: Precision and Recall for the combination of classifications using different context types.

tion 3.5. The outcome of this process is displayed in Table 5, yielding mostly higher precision and higher recall values than the results of using only a single context type.

Evaluating the combination to complex semantic sorts, the verb-deep-subject contexts gives the best results, as Table 6 indicates. The lenient combination's recall is almost twice as high, but falls short on precision. Notice that in this case average values are not obtained by the arithmetic mean of all semantic sorts, but by the total number of correctly and falsely identified nouns.

Table 7 shows the cross-validation results for assigning complex semantic sorts for the 15 most frequent sorts in the 11,100 noun sample. Examples

Context type	Recall	Precision
adjective	0.039	0.684
deep-object	0.049	0.758
deep-subject	0.057	0.872
lenient combination	0.113	0.772
strict combination	0.059	0.752

Table 6: Recall and precision of complex semantic sorts, with $\alpha = 5$ for single context types and $\alpha = 1$ for combinations

Complex sort	#	%Rec.	%Prec.
nonment-dyn-abs-situation	2752	12.83	88.92
human-object	2359	20.26	94.65
prot-theor-concept	815	1.23	62.50
animal-object	593	0.84	100.00
ax-mov-art-discrete	568	1.06	60.00
plant-object	445	0.22	25.00
nonment-stat-abs-situation	378	1.32	62.50
nonmov-art-discrete	191	3.14	40.00
nonax-mov-art-discrete	174	0.57	16.67
mov-nonanimate-con-potag	159	1.89	50.00
abs-info	148	4.73	53.85
art-substance	147	1.36	50.00
tem-abstractum	143	1.40	100.00
art-con-geogr	138	1.45	28.57
nat-substance	130	1.54	25.00

Table 7: Complex semantic sorts, number of nouns in the initial set, recall and precision.

for the largest group of non-mental dynamic situations are *wettbewerb.1.1* ('competition'), *zusamme-narbeit.1.1* ('co-operation'), *apokalypse.1.1* ('apocalypse') or *aufklï¿½ung.1.2* ('elucidation'). Only four semantic sorts have a precision above 75%. Recall is only satisfactory for two sorts. In total, 1,041 new nouns (i.e. not listed in the lexicon before) were classified. Various sorts cannot successfully be identified with this method or the used settings. The following list shows all semantic sorts that have not been assigned to any nouns, even though they occurred more than 100 times in the initial set of 11,100 nouns: *nonoper-attribute*, *ment-stat-abs-situation*, *nat-discrete* and *prot-discrete*.

While the number of new nouns for which a combination to complex semantic sorts was possible is not very satisfying, there seems to be room for improvement by exploiting the binary characteristics in a more sophisticated way than by the straightforward algorithm described in Section 3.5. The

combined run on the three context types, on which this combination to semantic sorts is based, created 125,491 new single binary characteristics for 3,755 nouns not in the lexicon. It should be possible to improve this number by using a larger corpus.

4.2 Discussion of Results

The presented experiments use fine grained binary features rather than complex semantic sorts as in most other works. Evidence from different relations improves results to an average of 98.2% precision for binary characteristics, with most characteristics above 99% (see Table 5). If the time consuming work of creating a reasonably small lexicon of nouns and their binary characteristics is done once, our algorithm can then be used effectively to increase the lexicon size.

However, some classes with a skewed distribution (bias above 0.8) have the problem of not assigning the smaller class correctly. Almost half of the 33 characteristics have this problem in bootstrapping runs over single context types. With the strict and lenient combination the problem is alleviated since the few wrong classifications rarely occur twice.

In an environment where incomplete semantic specifications are allowed in the lexicon some characteristics can be incorporated without supervision. If precision is the only concern and a small recall is acceptable then only nouns with three identical values (98.2% precision, 14.7% recall) should be used, whereas results with two identical values return more new nouns (27.3%) with a slightly lower precision of 93.9%. These results cannot be used successfully in the subsequent combination to complex semantic sorts. This is due to the fact that for each separate characteristic, many classified nouns are different, not producing enough overlap. Thus, the recall for some characteristics drops in both the lenient and the strict combination. The same accounts for the newly defined nouns and their binary characteristics.

Lastly, in case complex semantic sorts are required for the lexicon, the best results can be obtained by using the outcome of bootstrapping on verb-deep-subject relations as Table 6 indicates. Here, an average precision of 87.2% for all kinds of semantic sorts is still an improvement over previous methods.

5   Conclusion

This paper investigates the extension and improvement of the lexical acquisition approach as presented in (Biemann and Osswald, 2006). New relations such as the ones between a verb and its arguments have been utilized as input and have shown a significantly higher precision than modifying adjectives.

By using only nouns that were identified as having the same class in three different context types, we got a precision of 98.2% averaged over all binary semantic characteristics, with a recall of 14.7%. However, the maximally possible recall is bounded by the corpus and is at around 36% for the single context types.

We showed that by creating complex semantic sorts with the help of binary characteristics, new nouns from different kinds of sorts can be identified with a precision of about 87%. Finally, the high amount of single characteristics obtained for yet unknown nouns renders this approach very useful for lexical acquisition.

Acknowledgments

We would like to thank Sven Hartrumpf for helping us with parsing the corpus.

References

Collin F. Baker, Charles J. Fillmore, and John B. Lowe. 1998. The Berkeley FrameNet project. In *Proceedings of COLING/ACL'98*, Montréal, Canada.

Chris Biemann and Rainer Osswald. 2006. Automatic extension of feature-based semantic lexicons via contextual attributes. In *From Data and Information Analysis to Knowledge Engineering – Proceedings of the 29th Annual Conference of the Gesellschaft für Klassifikation*, pages 326–333. Springer.

Christian Biemann, Stefan Bordag, Gerhard Heyer, Uwe Quasthoff, and Christian Wolff. 2004. Language-independent methods for compiling monolingual lexical data. In *Proceedings of CicLING 2004*, LNCS 2945, pages 215–228, Berlin. Springer.

Xavier Carreras and Lluís Màrques. 2004. Introduction to the CoNLL-2004 shared task: Semantic role labeling. In *Proceedings of CoNLL-2004*, pages 89–97.

Masato Hagiwara, Yasuhiro Ogawa, and Katsuhiko Toyama. 2006. Selection of effective contextual information for automatic synonym acquisition. In *Proceedings of COLING/ACL 2006*, Sydney, Australia.

Zelig Harris. 1968. *Mathematical Structures of Language*. New York, Wiley.

Sven Hartrumpf, Hermann Helbig, and Rainer Osswald. 2003. The semantically based computer lexicon HaGenLex – Structure and technological environment. *Traitement automatique des langues*, 44(2):81–105.

Sven Hartrumpf. 2003. *Hybrid Disambiguation in Natural Language Analysis*. Der Andere Verlag, Osnabrück, Germany.

Sven Hartrumpf. 2005. Question answering using sentence parsing and semantic network matching. In *Multilingual Information Access for Text, Speech and Images: 5th Workshop of the Cross-Language Evaluation Forum, CLEF 2004*, LNCS 3491, pages 512–521. Springer.

Hermann Helbig. 2006. *Knowledge Representation and the Semantics of Natural Language*. Springer, Berlin.

Dekang Lin. 1998. Automatic retrieval and clustering of similar words. In *Proceedings of the 17th international conference on Computational linguistics*, pages 768–774.

Fernando Pereira, Naftali Tishby, and Lillian Lee. 1993. Distributional clustering of english words. In *Proceedings of the 31st annual meeting on Association for Computational Linguistics*, pages 183–190.

Ellen Riloff and Jessica Shepherd. 1997. A corpus-based approach for building semantic lexicons. In *Proceedings of the Second Conference on Empirical Methods in Natural Language Processing*, pages 117–124.

Brian Roark and Eugene Charniak. 1998. Noun-phrase co-occurence statistics for semi-automatic semantic lexicon construction. In *Proceedings of COLING/ACL'98*, Montréal, Canada, pages 1110–1116.

Mats Rooth, Stefan Riezler, Detlef Prescher, Glenn Carroll, and Franz Beil. 1999. Inducing a semantically annotated lexicon via EM-based clustering. In *Proceedings of the 37th Annual Meeting of the ACL*.

Michael Thelen and Ellen Riloff. 2002. A bootstrapping method for learning semantic lexicons using extraction pattern contexts. In *Proceedings of the 2002 Conference on Empirical Methods in Natural Language Processing*.

Polynomial Charts for Totally Unordered Languages

Anders Søgaard
Center for Language Technology
Njalsgade 80
DK-2300 Copenhagen
anders@cst.dk

Abstract

Totally unordered or discontinuous composition blows up chart size on most set-ups. This paper analyzes the effects of total unordering to type 2 grammars and simple attribute-value grammars (s-AVGs). In both cases, charts turn exponential in size. It is shown that the k ambiguity constraint turns charts polynomial, even for s-AVGs. Consequently, tractable parsing can be deviced.

1 Introduction

It is common knowledge among linguists that in many languages, the daughters of syntactic constituents can be locally reordered with little or no effect on grammaticality. Certain languages – of which Dyirbal and Warlpiri are often-cited members, but that also include Estonian and Finnish – exhibit a much more radical form of unordering, the kind of unordering that has made linguists propose "crossed brances" analyses, e.g.

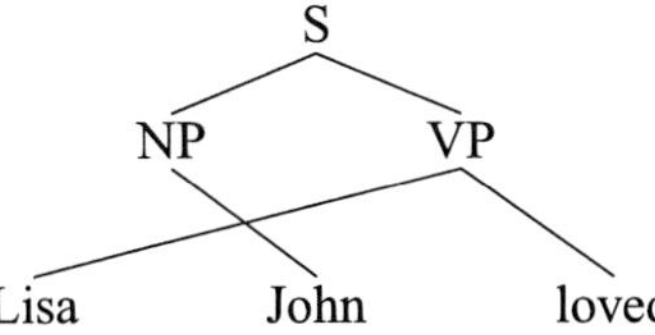

yielding **love**(**John**, **Lisa**). The Finnish translation is *Liisaa Jussi rakasti*. All six permutations of this sentence are grammatical.

Unordered grammars have been suggested in face of intra-constituent free word order. Similarly, a few authors have proposed *totally* unordered grammars in face of free word order phenomena that involve discontinuous constituents. Dowty (1995), originally published in 1989, is often cited as the original source.

This paper is structured as follows: Sect. 2 defines type 2 grammars and s-AVGs, and their totally unordered pendants. Sect. 3 establishes bounds on chart size for these kinds of grammars. Charts for totally unordered grammars are shown to be worst case exponential. In reply to this, Sect. 4 introduces the k-ambiguity constraint, which turns totally unordered charts polynomial again. Of course this means that polynomial time parsing can be deviced.

2 Grammars and total unordering

Our first task is to properly define the grammars in question:

2.1 Type 2 grammars

Definition 2.1 (Type 2 grammars). $G = \langle N, T, P, \{S\} \rangle$ is a type 2 grammar iff every production rule in P is of the form

$$A \rightarrow \omega$$

where $A \in N$ and $\omega \in \{N \cup T\}^{+}$.

Definition 2.2 (Derivability). For a type 2 grammar G and $\omega_1, \omega_2 \in (N \cup T)^*$, $\omega_1 \Longrightarrow_1 \omega_2$ iff there is a $A \rightarrow \phi \in P$ and there are $\psi_1, \psi_2 \in (N \cup T)^*$ such that $\omega_1 = \psi_1 A \psi_2$ and $\omega_2 = \psi_1 \phi \psi_2$. $\stackrel{*}{\Longrightarrow}_1$ (the derivability relation) is the reflexive transitive closure of $\Longrightarrow_1$.

Definition 2.3 (Type 2 languages). The language of a type 2 grammar G is defined as

Joakim Nivre, Heiki-Jaan Kaalep, Kadri Muischnek and Mare Koit (Eds.)
NODALIDA 2007 Conference Proceedings, pp. 183–190

$$L(G) \;=\; \{x \in T^* : S \overset{*}{\Longrightarrow}_1 x\}.$$

Definition 2.4 (Chomsky normal form). A type 2 grammar $G = \langle N, T, P, \{S\} \rangle$ is in Chomsky normal form iff each production has one of the following forms:

- $A \to BC$

- $A \to a$

- $S \to \epsilon$

where $a \in T$ and $B, C \in N - \{S\}$.

Example 2.5. Consider the type 2 grammar with rules $S \to aXb|ab, X \to aXb|ab$. The Chomsky normal form of this grammar is obtained by adding the rules $A \to a, B \to b$ and by reducing the length of the S, X-rules. Consequently, P' now includes:

$$
\begin{aligned}
S &\to AT|AB & T &\to XB \\
X &\to AT|AB & A &\to a \\
B &\to b
\end{aligned}
$$

Lemma 2.6 (Equivalence of normal forms). *Say $G = \langle N, T, P, \{S\} \rangle$ is a type 2 grammar. There is an algorithm to construct a grammar $G' = \langle N', T, P', \{S'\} \rangle$ in Chomsky normal form that is weakly equivalent to G.*

Proof. See Sudkamp (2005, 122–3). □

2.2 Totally unordered type 2 grammars

Definition 2.7 (Totally unordered type 2 grammars). $G = \langle N, T, P, \{S\} \rangle$ is a type 2 grammar iff every production rule in P is of the form

$$A \;\to\; \omega$$

where $A \in N$ and $\omega \in \{N \cup T\}^*$.

Definition 2.8 (Derivability). If $A \overset{*}{\Longrightarrow}_1 \omega$ and $\omega' \in permute(\omega)$, then $A \overset{*}{\Longrightarrow}_2 \omega'$.

Definition 2.9 (Totally unordered type 2 languages). The language of a totally unordered type 2 grammar G is defined as

$$L(G) \;=\; \{x \in T^* : S \overset{*}{\Longrightarrow}_2 x\}.$$

2.3 s-AVGs

s-AVGs are defined over simple attribute-value structures (s-AVSs):

Definition 2.10 (s-AVS). An s-AVS A is defined over a signature $\langle \mathsf{Attr}, \mathsf{Atms}, \rho \rangle$, where $\rho : \mathsf{Attr} \to 2^{\mathsf{Atms}}$, such that $A \in \mathsf{Attr} \to 2^{\mathsf{Atms}}$ and $\forall a \in \mathrm{DOM}(A).A(a) \in \rho(a)$.

Definition 2.11 (s-AVG). An s-AVG is a 5-tuple $G = \langle \langle \mathsf{Attr}, \mathsf{Atms}, \rho \rangle, \mathsf{AttrPerc}, T, P, \{S\} \rangle$, where $\mathsf{AttrPerc} \subseteq \mathsf{Attr}$, $\rho : \mathsf{Attr} \to 2^{\mathsf{Atms}}$, S is an s-AVS, and every production rule in P is of the form $\alpha \to \omega_i$ or $\alpha_0 \to \alpha_1 \ldots \alpha_n$ where $n \geq 2$, α_i is an s-AVS, and

$$(1) \quad \forall a \in \mathrm{DOM}(\alpha_0) \cap \mathsf{AttrPerc}.\forall 1 \leq i \leq n.f \in \mathrm{DOM}(\alpha_i) \wedge \alpha_i(a) = \alpha_0(a)$$

where $\alpha(a)$ is the value of a in the s-AVS α with $\alpha(a) \in \rho(a)$.

Intuitively, the AttrPerc features are agreement features whose values percolate up the tree if defined for every level of it.

Example 2.12. Consider the grammar $G_1 = \langle \langle \{\mathrm{CAT, PLU, PER}\}, \{s, vp, np, v, n, 1, 2, 3, +, -\}, \rho \rangle, \{\mathrm{PLU, PER}\}, \{I, men, John, sleep, sleeps\}, P, S \rangle$ where ρ is the specification of appropriate values of attributes:

$$
\begin{aligned}
\rho(\mathrm{CAT}) &= \{s, vp, np, v, n\} \\
\rho(\mathrm{PER}) &= \{1, 2, 3\} \\
\rho(\mathrm{PLU}) &= \{+, -\}
\end{aligned}
$$

and P is the set of production rules:

$$
\begin{bmatrix} \text{CAT } s \end{bmatrix} \to \begin{bmatrix} \text{CAT } np \end{bmatrix}, \begin{bmatrix} \text{CAT } vp \end{bmatrix} \qquad \begin{bmatrix} \text{CAT } vp \end{bmatrix} \to \begin{bmatrix} \text{CAT } v \end{bmatrix}
$$

$$
\begin{bmatrix} \text{CAT } np \end{bmatrix} \to \begin{bmatrix} \text{CAT } n \end{bmatrix} \qquad \begin{bmatrix} \text{CAT } n \\ \text{PER } 1 \end{bmatrix} \to I
$$

$$
\begin{bmatrix} \text{CAT } n \\ \text{PLU } + \end{bmatrix} \to men \qquad \begin{bmatrix} \text{CAT } n \\ \text{PLU } - \\ \text{PER } 3 \end{bmatrix} \to John
$$

$$
\begin{bmatrix} \text{CAT } v \\ \text{PLU } + \end{bmatrix} \to sleep \qquad \begin{bmatrix} \text{CAT } v \\ \text{PLU } - \\ \text{PER } 3 \end{bmatrix} \to sleeps
$$

(1) applies to the subset of attributes $\{\mathrm{PLU, PER}\}$. The start symbol is $S : \begin{bmatrix} \text{CAT } s \end{bmatrix}$. The grammar generates exactly the sentences:

(2) I sleep.

(3) Men sleep.

(4) John sleeps.

Definition 2.13 (Subsumption). An s-AVS α subsumes an s-AVS β ($\alpha \sqsubseteq \beta$) iff $\forall a.\text{DOM}(a).\alpha(a) = \beta(a)$.

Definition 2.14 (Derivability). Say $G = \langle\langle\text{Attr}, \text{Atms}, \rho\rangle, \text{AttrPerc}, T, P, \{S\}\rangle$ is an s-AVG. If P contains a production $A \rightarrow \omega$, then for any ϕ_1, ϕ_2, $\phi_1 A' \phi_2 \Longrightarrow_3 \phi_1 \omega' \phi_2$ if $A \sqsubseteq A'$ and $\omega \sqsubseteq \omega'$. $\overset{*}{\Longrightarrow}_3$ is the reflexive, transitive closure of $\Longrightarrow_3$.

Definition 2.15 (s-AVG languages). The language of an s-AVG G is defined as

$$L(G) \;=\; \{x \in T^* : \exists S'. S' \sqsupseteq S \wedge S' \overset{*}{\Longrightarrow}_3 x\}.$$

2.4 Totally unordered s-AVGs

Call totally unordered s-AVGs u-AVGs.

Definition 2.16 (u-AVG). A u-AVG is a 5-tuple $G = \langle\langle\text{Attr}, \text{Atms}, \rho\rangle, \text{AttrPerc}, T, P, \{S\}\rangle$.

Definition 2.17 (Derivability). If $A \overset{*}{\Longrightarrow}_3 \omega$ and $\omega' \in permute(\omega)$, then $A \overset{*}{\Longrightarrow}_4 \omega'$.

Remark 2.18. (1) means that no Chomsky normal form can be obtained for s-AVG or u-AVG.

3 Bounds on chart size

3.1 Type 2 grammars

Lemma 3.1 (Size of derivation structure). *Say $D = \langle V, e \rangle$ is a derivation structure for ω, G where G is a type 2 grammar in Chomsky normal form. It now holds that $|V| \leq (3n - 1)$.*

Proof. Since G is in Chomsky normal form, there are only two kinds of production rules: Any derivation of ω of length n needs $n - 1$ binary applications, and n unary ones, i.e. of non-branching rules. There are n many terminals. Consequently, the derivation structure is at most $3n - 1$. $\qquad\square$

Definition 3.2 (ω-grammar). Say you have a type 2 grammar in Chomsky normal form $G = \langle N, T, P, \{S\}\rangle$ and some string $\omega_1 \ldots \omega_n$. Construct $G_\omega = \langle N_\omega, T_\omega, P_\omega, \{{}_1 S_n\}\rangle$ such that

$$T_\omega \;=\; \{\omega_1, \ldots, \omega_n\}$$

and, recursively

(a) $(\omega_i \in T_\omega$ and $A \rightarrow \omega_i \in P) \Rightarrow ({}_i A_i \in N_\omega$ and ${}_i A_i \rightarrow \omega_i \in P_\omega)$

(b) $({}_i B_{j,j+1} C_k \in N_\omega$ and $A \rightarrow BC) \Rightarrow ({}_i A_k \in N_\omega \wedge {}_i A_k \rightarrow {}_i B_{jj+1} C_k \in P_\omega)$

Example 3.3. Consider $aabb$-grammar of the Chomsky normal form grammar in Example 2.5. First $T_\omega = \{a_1, a_2, b_3, b_4\}$. By (a), the terminal rules are constructed: ${}_1 A_1 \rightarrow a_1$, ${}_2 A_2 \rightarrow a_2$, ${}_3 B_3 \rightarrow b_3$, and ${}_4 B_4 \rightarrow b_4$. Nonterminal binary rules can now be constructed:

$$\begin{aligned}
{}_2 S_3 &\rightarrow {}_2 A_{23} B_3 & {}_2 X_3 &\rightarrow {}_2 A_{23} B_3 \\
{}_2 T_4 &\rightarrow {}_2 X_{34} B_4 & {}_1 X_4 &\rightarrow {}_1 A_{12} T_4 \\
{}_1 S_4 &\rightarrow {}_1 A_{12} T_4
\end{aligned}$$

$$N_{aabb} \;=\; \{{}_1 A_1, {}_2 A_2, {}_3 B_3, {}_4 B_4, {}_2 S_3, {}_2 X_3, {}_2 T_4, {}_1 X_4, {}_1 S_4\}.$$

Our construction of G_ω gives us two sets of possible interest, N_ω and P_ω. It is easy to see that

$$|N_\omega| \;\leq\; |N| \times \left(\frac{n^2 + n}{2}\right)$$

where $|\omega| = n$. In our example above this amounts to $|N_{aabb}| = 9 \leq 4 \times \frac{4 \times 5}{2} = 40$.

The chart size is bounded by $|P_\omega| + n$.

Lemma 3.4 (Chart size). *Say G is a type 2 grammar in Chomsky normal and $\omega \in T^*$. It now holds that $|C_{G,\omega}| \leq (|N_\omega| \times n \times |N|^2) + (|N| \times n) + n$.*

Proof. Each ω-nonterminal ($|N_\omega|$ many) has at most two daughters, and $n \times |N|$ nonterminals are non-branching. Since there are at most n ways to split up the span of a branching terminal in two, and at most $|N|^2$ variable combinations for the two daughters, $((|N_\omega|) \times n \times |N|^2 + (n \times |N|))$ is clearly an upper bound on $|P_\omega|$. In fact, the result is suboptimal, since the ${}_i X_i$-nonterminals count twice. $\qquad\square$

The number of trees with n leafs is C_{n-1} (the Catalan number).

3.2 Totally unordered type 2 grammars

Lemma 3.5 (Size of derivation structure). *Say $D = \langle V, e \rangle$ is a derivation structure for ω, G where G is a totally unordered type 2 grammar in Chomsky normal form. It now holds that $|V| \leq (3n - 1)$.*

Proof. Similar to the proof of Lemma 3.1. $\qquad\square$

Definition 3.6 (ω-grammar). Say you have a totally unordered type 2 grammar in Chomsky normal form $G = \langle N, T, P, \{S\}\rangle$ and some string $\omega_1 \ldots \omega_n$. Construct $G_\omega = \langle N_\omega, T_\omega, P_\omega, \{S\}\rangle$ such that

$$T_\omega \;=\; \{\omega_1, \ldots, \omega_n\}$$

and, recursively

(a) $(\omega_i \in T_\omega$ and $A \to \omega_i \in P) \Rightarrow (A_{\{i\}} \in N_\omega$ and $A_{\{i\}} \to \omega_i \in P_\omega)$

(b) $(B_\Sigma, C_{\Sigma'} \in N_\omega$ and $\Sigma \cap \Sigma' = \emptyset$ and $A \to BC) \Rightarrow (A_{\Sigma \cup \Sigma'} \in N_\omega \wedge A_{\Sigma \cup \Sigma'} \to B_\Sigma C_{\Sigma'} \in P_\omega)$

Lemma 3.7 (Chart size, upper bound). *Say G is a totally unordered type 2 grammar in Chomsky normal and $\omega \in T^*$. It now holds that $|C_{G,\omega}| \leq |N_\omega|^2 \times n^2 \times |N|^2) + (n \times |N|) + n$.*

Proof. There are n^2 ways to split up a sequence in two discontinuous parts. $\qquad\square$

Lemma 3.8 (Chart size, lower bound). *Say G is a totally unordered type 2 grammar in Chomsky normal and $\omega \in T^*$. It now holds that $|C_{G,\omega}| \notin \mathcal{O}(n^k)$, i.e. chart size is exponential.*

Proof. It is easy to see this. You only need to consider the upper bound on $|N_\omega|$ in the totally unordered case:

$$|N_\omega| \;\leq\; |N| \times 2^n$$

$\qquad\square$

3.3   s-AVGs

Lemma 3.9 (Size of derivation structure). *Say $D = \langle V, e \rangle$ is a derivation structure for ω, G where G is an s-AVG. It now holds that $|V| \leq 3n - 1 \times (|\mathsf{Attr}| + 1)$.*

Definition 3.10 (ω-grammar). Say you have an s-AVG $G = \langle\langle \mathsf{Attr}, \mathsf{Atms}, \rho\rangle, \mathsf{AttrPerc}, T, P, \{S\}\rangle$ and some string $\omega_1 \ldots \omega_n$. Construct $G_\omega = \langle\langle \mathsf{Attr}, \mathsf{Atms}_\omega, \rho\rangle, \mathsf{AttrPerc}, T_\omega, P_\omega, \{_1 S_n\}\rangle$ such that

$$T_\omega \;=\; \{\omega_1, \ldots, \omega_n\}$$

and, recursively

(a) $([\omega]_i \in T_\omega$ and $\alpha \to [\omega]_i \in P) \Rightarrow (_i[\alpha]_i \in N_\omega$ and $_i[\alpha]_i \to [\omega]_i \in P_\omega)$

(b) $(_i[\alpha_1]_{j,j+1} [\alpha_2]_k, \ldots, _{m-1}[\alpha_n]_m \in N_\omega$ and $[\alpha_0] \to [\alpha'_1][\alpha'_2] \ldots [\alpha'_n] \in P$ and $\forall 1 \leq i \leq n.[\alpha_i] \sqsubseteq [\alpha'_i] \vee [\alpha'_i] \sqsubseteq [\alpha_i]) \Rightarrow (_i[\alpha_0]_m \in N_\omega \wedge {}_i[\alpha_0]_m \to_i [\alpha_1]_{j,j+1} [\alpha_2]_k, \ldots, _{m-1}[\alpha_n]_m \in P_\omega)$

I introduce square brackets to enhance readability, i.e. to separate daughter tags from positions. Positions are outside brackets.

We no longer have a set $|N|$ to measure chart size. The set of possible category structures is $\mathsf{Atms}^{\mathsf{Attr}}$. However, by inspection of our definition of ω, a tighter bound is obtained:

$$|N_\omega| \;\leq\; |P| \times \left(\tfrac{n^2+n}{2}\right)$$

Unfortunately, no such bound can be placed on $|P_\omega|$. The reason is, of course, that productions $_i[\alpha_0]_m \to {}_i[\alpha_1] \ldots [\alpha_n]_m$, and not $_i[\alpha_0]_m \to {}_i[\alpha'_1] \ldots [\alpha'_n]_m$ are recorded in Definition 3.10.

Lemma 3.11 (Chart size). *Say G is an s-AVG and $\omega \in T^*$. It now holds that $|C_{G,\omega}| \leq (|N_\omega| \times n \times |\mathsf{Atms}|^{|\mathsf{Attr}| \times k}) + (|P| \times n) + n$, if G do not contain m-ary rules such that $m > k$.*

Proof. Compare the situation to Lemma 3.4. $|\mathsf{Atms}|^{|\mathsf{Attr}| \times k}$ is the number of combinations of daughter categories in k-ary productions. $\qquad\square$

3.4   Totally unordered s-AVGs

The upper bound on derivation structions in the totally unordered case is the same as for s-AVGs. ω-grammars for u-AVG are built analogously to ω-grammars for totally unordered type 2 grammars. It is easy to see that:

$$|N_\omega| \;\leq\; |P| \times 2^n$$

It now holds:

Lemma 3.12 (Chart size). *Say G is an u-AVG and $\omega \in T^*$. It now holds that $|C_{G,\omega}| \leq (|N_\omega| \times n \times |\mathsf{Atms}|^{|\mathsf{Attr}| \times k}) + (|P| \times n) + n$, if G do not contain m-ary rules such that $m > k$.*

In sum,

Theorem 3.13. *Totally unordered 2 grammars, s-AVGs and u-AVGs have worst case exponential charts.*

This leads us to consider complexity and generative capacity.

3.5 Complexity and generative capacity

Consider the universal recognition problem:

Definition 3.14 (Universal recognition). Universal recognition is the decision problem:

> INSTANCE: A grammar $\mathcal{G}$ and a string ω.
> QUESTION: Is ω in the language denoted by $\mathcal{G}$?

Lemma 3.15 ((Barton, 1985)). *The universal recognition problem for totally unordered type 2 grammars is NP-complete.*

Proof. The vertex cover problem involves finding the smallest set V' of vertices in a graph $G = \langle V, E \rangle$ such that every edge has at least one endpoint in the set. Formally, $V' \subseteq V : \forall \{a, b\} \in E : a \in V' \vee b \in V'$. The problem is thus an optimization problem, formulated as a decision problem:

> INSTANCE: A graph G and a positive integer k.
> QUESTION: Is there a vertex cover of size k or less for G?

Say $k = 2, V = \{a, b, c, d\}, E = \{(a, c), (b, c), (b, d), (c, d)\}$. One way to obtain a vertex cover is to go through the edges and underline one endpoint of each edge. If you can do that and only underline two vertex symbols, a vertex cover has been found. Since $|V| = 4$, this is equivalent to leaving two vertex symbols untouched. Consequently, the vertex cover problem for this specific instance is encoded by the totally unordered type 2 grammar, where δ is a bookkeeping dummy symbol:

$$
\begin{aligned}
S &\rightarrow \rho_1 \rho_2 \rho_3 \rho_4 u u \delta \delta \delta \delta \\
\rho_1 &\rightarrow a \mid c \\
\rho_2 &\rightarrow b \mid c \\
\rho_3 &\rightarrow b \mid d \\
\rho_4 &\rightarrow c \mid d \\
u &\rightarrow aaaa \mid bbbb \mid cccc \mid dddd \\
\delta &\rightarrow a \mid b \mid c \mid d
\end{aligned}
$$

ρ_i captures the ith edge in E. The input string $\omega = aaaabbbbccccdddd$. Generally, the first production has as many ρ_i as there are edges in the graph, $|V| - k$ many u's and $|E| \times |V| - |E| - |E| \times (|V| - k)$ many δ's, i.e. the length of the string minus the number of edges and the extension of $|V| - k$ many u's. The ρ_i productions are simple, u extends into $|E|$

many a's or b's or so on, and δ extends into all possible vertices. Since the grammar and input string can be constructed in polynomial time from an underlying vertex cover problem $\langle k, V, E \rangle$, universal recognition of UCFG must be at least as hard as solving the vertex cover problem. Since the vertex cover problem is NP-complete (Garey and Johnson, 1979), the universal recognition problem for totally unordered type 2 grammars is accordingly NP-hard. It is easy to see that it is also in NP. Simply guess a derivation, polynomial in size by Lemma 3.5, and evaluate it in polynomial time. $\qquad\square$

Lemma 3.16. *The universal recognition problem for s-AVGs is NP-complete.*

Proof. The 3SAT problem is a variant of the satisfiability problem of propositional logic for conjunctions of clauses of three literals, e.g. $p \vee p \vee p \wedge \neg p \vee \neg p \vee \neg p$ is *not* satisfiable in any model. Its complexity is the same as its older sister's: It is NP-complete. It is relatively easy to code this problem up in s-AVG. The details are left for the reader. *Hint:* Introduce agreement features for truth assignments and build ternary phrases that ensure at least one propositional variable in the original problem is true. Since AttrPerc must percolate by (1), you need four rules for each propositional variable (true and false for with and without negation). It follows that the universal recognition problem for s-AVGs is NP-hard. It is easy to see that it is also in NP. Simply guess a derivation, polynomial in size by Lemma 3.9, and evaluate it in polynomial time. $\qquad\square$

Lemma 3.17. *The universal recognition problem for u-AVGs is NP-complete.*

Proof. Similar to the proof of Lemma 3.16. Extra features can be used for clause bounds. $\qquad\square$

Remark 3.18. It is cheap to add linear precedence constraints to totally unordered type 2 grammars and u-AVGs, e.g. to ensure that all verbs precede nouns. Such constraints can be resolved in time $\mathcal{O}(n^2)$ on even the most naïve set-up.

If linear precedence constraints are added, it holds that

Lemma 3.19. *The totally unordered type 2 languages and the totally unordered simple attribute-value languages both are not included in the type 2 languages.*

Proof. Both the totally unordered type 2 languages and the totally unordered simple attribute-value languages include $\{a^m b^n c^m d^n\}$. The simplest way to encode it is to let some rule $S \rightarrow abScd|abcd$ interact with some precedence rule that requires all a's to precede all b's, and so on. Similarly, with s-AVSs. It is just as easy to code up the MIX language, for instance. $\square$

4 k-ambiguity

Our strategy to obtain polynomial charts in the totally unordered cases is to restrict ambiguity. A rigid lexicon is first imposed. In a rigid lexicon every phonological string is associated with at most one lexical entry.

Remark 4.1. Rigidity is a strong constraint in the absence of inheritance. Inheritance provides an alternative to lexical ambiguity, namely underspecification. Such use of inheritance seems necessary for realistic applications of k-ambiguous grammars. Rigidity needs only to apply to open class items. There seems to be some evidence from cognitive neuropsychology that people actually underspecify open class items wrt. morphological features, valence and even syntactic category.

The next step is to restrict ambiguity in parsing.

Definition 4.2. A sign is horizontally k-ambiguous if it only combines with k signs in a sentence. A grammar is horizontally k-ambiguous if all signs are k-ambiguous. A grammar is vertically k-ambiguous if signs are combined unambiguously after k steps.

It is important to remember that our unordered grammars allow signs to combine non-locally. The notion of k-ambiguity can be illustrated by an example from Icelandic:

Example 4.3. Icelandic has nominative objects. Consider, for instance:

(5) *Hún spurði hvort sá*
    she asked whether the.NOM

    grunaði væri örugglega
    suspected.NOM was.3SG.SUBJ surely

þú.

you.SG.NOM

'She asked whether the suspect surely was you.'

In addition, both SVO and OVS constructions occur. So in many cases, a verb that seeks to combine with an object has more than one candidate for doing so, even in sentences with only three constituents:

$$\text{NP.NOM} \quad \text{V.} \quad \text{NP.NOM}$$

The V constituent is said to be horizontally 2-ambiguous in this case.

For simplicity, the notion of the order of an s-AVS is introduced:

Definition 4.4. An s-AVS α is said to be of order l iff $|\text{DOM}(\alpha)| = l$. If all s-AVSs in a grammar G are of order l, G is itself said to be of order 1.

Lemma 4.5. *Type 2 grammars are equivalent to s-AVGs of order 1. Totally unordered type 2 languages are equivalent to u-AVGs of order 1.*

Proof. Trivial. $\square$

Say s-AVSs are of order 1, and vertical ambiguity 1 (i.e. horizontal ambiguity k). We then have:

$$|C_{G,\omega}| \ \leq \ (\tfrac{n^2-n}{2} + \sum_{1<i}^{i<n}(kn(n-i))) + n$$

First all initial combinations $\frac{n^2-n}{2}$ are checked. At this point, there can be at most kn candidate models. For each candidate model, the next set of combinations is checked. Since vertical ambiguity is 1, the set of candidate models remains at most kn.

If we fix vertical ambiguity to k (i.e. horizontal ambiguity n):

$$|C_{G,\omega}| \ \leq \ (\tfrac{n^2-n}{2} + \sum_{1<i}^{i<n}(n^k(n-i))) + n$$

which is in $\mathcal{O}(n^{k+2})$. Since the order of s-AVSs is bound by $|\text{Attr}|$, it holds that:

Theorem 4.6. *k-ambiguous totally unordered 2 grammars, k-ambiguous s-AVGs and k-ambiguous u-AVGs have polynomial charts.*

Proof. See above. The result for s-AVGs is subsumed by the result for u-AVGs. $\square$

Remark 4.7. For unordered type 2 grammars, and possibly for totally unordered ones too, it is an alternative to say that all totally unordered productions in a chart have a yield of at most k. This gives a bound on chart size:

$$\sum_{i<k}^{0\leq i}(|N| \times (n-i) \times \sum_{j<(k-i)}^{0\leq j}(|N|^{k-j} \times (k-i) \times (n-j)))$$
$$+ \sum_{i<n}^{k<i}(|N|^3 \times (n-i))$$

This fragment no longer generates the MIX language. Such a constraint is obviously not enough for u-AVG, since s-AVG is NP-complete. A third possibility is to restrict the arity of productions.

5   Conclusions and related work

In last year's conference, Søgaard and Haugereid (2006) presented, in a rather informal fashion, a restrictive typed attribute-value structure grammar formalism $\mathcal{T}_f$ for free word order phenomena, equipped with a polynomial parsing algorithm. In $\mathcal{T}_f$, horizontal $k = 1$. The purpose of their paper was mostly philosophical, i.e. in favor of underspecification rather than ambiguity, but many details were left unclear. In a sense, this paper provides a formal basis for some of the claims made in that paper. In particular, types are easily added to s-AVG and u-AVG, and more flexible attribute-value structures can be employed (as long as they are at most polynomial in the size of strings). Unlike $\mathcal{T}_f$, k-ambiguous grammars also admit fixed ambiguity.

Other researchers have tried to single out tractable attribute-value grammars:

Seki et al. (1993) operate in the context of LFG. For a start, they restrict the expressive power of LFG by restricting the syntax of LFG-style functional schemas to:

$$(\uparrow \texttt{attr} = \texttt{val}) \text{ or } (\uparrow \texttt{attr} =\downarrow)$$

Call this fragment non-deterministic copying LFG (nc-LFG). They then proceed to define two tractable fragments of nc-LFG:

Definition 5.1. An nc-LFG is called a dc-LFG (deterministic ...) if each pair of rules $r_1 : A \to \alpha_1$ and $r_2 : A \to \alpha_2$ whose left-hand sides are the same is inconsistent in the sense that there exists no f-structure that locally satisfies both of the functional schemata of r_1 and r_2.

Definition 5.2. An nc-LFG is called a fc-LFG (finite ...) if it contains only a finite number of so-called "subphrase nonterminal" (SPN) multisets, i.e. a multiset of nonterminals N such that there exists consistent productions $A_1 \to \alpha_1 \ldots A_n \ldots \alpha_n$ and an attribute $\texttt{attr}$ such that $N = \{\alpha_i \in \{\alpha_1 \ldots \alpha_n\} | (\uparrow \texttt{attr} =\downarrow)$ is the FS of $\alpha_i\}$.

A nice example of an nc-LFG that is not an fc-LFG is mentioned in (Seki et al., 1993):

Example 5.3. Let G be an nc-LFG where $N = \{S\}$, $T = \{a\}$, $\texttt{Lbls} = \{\texttt{log}\}$, e the only value, and productions are:

$$S \quad \to \quad S \qquad S$$
$$(\uparrow \texttt{log} =\downarrow) \quad (\uparrow \texttt{log} =\downarrow)$$
$$S \quad \to \quad a$$
$$(\uparrow \texttt{log} = e)$$

G is *not* an fc-LFG, since the SPN multisets in G include

$$\{\{S\}\}, \{\{S,S\}\}, \{\{S,S,S,S\}\}, \ldots .$$

Both fragments are tractable, and the weak generative capacity of dc-LFG is equivalent to that of finite-state translation systems, while the weak generative capacity of fc-LFG is equivalent to that of linear indexed grammars. It follows that fc-LFG is also equivalent to one-reentrant attribute-value grammar (Feinstein and Wintner, 2006).

Keller and Weir (1995) go beyond linear indexed grammars on their way toward attribute-value grammar. The first step on this path is to replace the stacks of indeces in linear indexed grammars with trees. Tractability is ensured by the requirement that subtrees of any mother that are passed to daughters that share subtrees with one another must appear as siblings in the mother's tree. The following such grammar generates $\{a^n b^n c^n\}$:

$$\begin{aligned}
S_1[\sigma_0] &\to A[x]S_2[\sigma(x,x)] \\
S_2[\sigma(x,y)] &\to B[x]S_3[y] \\
S_3[x] &\to C[x] \\
A[\sigma_2(x)] &\to aA[x] \\
B[\sigma_2(x)] &\to bB[x] \\
C[\sigma_2(x)] &\to cC[x] \\
A[\sigma_1] &\to a \\
B[\sigma_1] &\to b \\
C[\sigma_1] &\to c
\end{aligned}$$

In a sense, this is much like s-AVG, except that reentrancies replace (1) and roots cannot be reentered. Keller and Weir argue this is no problem if the entire structure is seen as the derivational output, rather than just the AVS of the mother. In addition, reentrancy is interpreted intensionally in their set-up, rather than extensionally. This is similar to ours.

Both formalisms are stronger than k-ambiguous u-AVG in some respects. This is easy to see. Both nc-LFG and Keller and Weir's richer fragment of attribute-value grammar are superfinite, i.e. they generate all finite languages. k-ambiguous u-AVG doesn't. It holds that:

Lemma 5.4. *The k-ambiguous u-AVG languages do not include (all of) the regular languages.*

The proof is omitted, but consider the simpler proof of:

Lemma 5.5. *The 1-ambiguous u-AVG languages do not include (all of) the regular languages.*

Proof. Consider the language

$$\underset{\text{but not } j}{a\{b|\ldots|n\}} \quad \cup \quad \underset{\text{but not } i}{p\{b|\ldots|n\}} \quad \cup \quad \{b|\ldots|n\}$$

in which ab, ai, pj, b are strings, while aj, pi, bb are not. This language is regular, but cannot be generated by a 1-ambiguous u-AVG. $\qquad\square$

It should be relatively easy to see how this generalizes to k-ambiguous u-AVG.

In sum, it was shown that the exponential worst case complexity of totally unordered charts is drammaticaly reduced by the k-ambiguity constraint. In particular k-ambiguous charts are in $\mathcal{O}(n^{k+2})$. Since subsumption is linear time solvable, the recognition problem for k-ambiguous u-AVGs is also solvable in polynomial time. Efficient algorithms and their complexity are the topic of future publications. k-ambiguous u-AVG differs in significant ways from other polynomial time attribute-value grammars. In particular, k-ambiguous u-AVG was designed for analyses of discontinuous constituency. It provides the formal machinery needed for "crossed branches" analyses. In addition, k-ambiguous u-AVG is not superfinite. It is conjectured – also by one of the reviewers – that this has interesting consequences for learnability.

References

Edward Barton. 1985. The computational difficulty of ID/LP parsing. In *Proceedings of the 23th Annual Meeting of the Association for Computational Linguistics*, pages 76–81, Chicago, Illinois.

David Dowty. 1995. Toward a minimalist theory of syntactic structure. In Harry Bunt and Arthur van Horck, editors, *Discontinuous constituency*, pages 11–62. de Gruyter, Berlin, Germany.

Daniel Feinstein and Shuly Wintner. 2006. Highly constrained unification grammars. In *Proceedings of the 21st International Conference on Computational Linguistics and 44th Annual Meeting of the Association for Computational Linguistics*, pages 1089–1096, Sydney, Australia.

Michael Garey and David Johnson. 1979. *Computers and intractability*. W. H. Freeman & Co., New York, New York.

Bill Keller and David Weir. 1995. A tractable extension of linear indexed grammars. In *Proceedings of the 7th European Chapter of the Association for Computational Linguistics*, pages 75–82, Dublin, Ireland.

Hiroyuki Seki, Ryuichi Nakanishi, Yuichi Kaji, Sachiko Ando, and Tadao Kasami. 1993. Parallel multiple context-free grammars, finite-state translation systems, and polynomial-time recognizable subclasses of lexical-functional grammars. In *Proceedings of the 31st Annual Meeting on the Association for Computational Linguistics*, pages 130–139, Columbus, Ohio.

Anders Søgaard and Petter Haugereid. 2006. Functionality in grammar design. In Stefan Werner, editor, *Proceedings of the 15th Nordic Conference of Computational Linguistics*, pages 180–189, Joensuu, Finland.

Thomas Sudkamp. 2005. *Languages and machines*. Pearson, Boston, Massachusetts, 3rd edition.

Comparing French PP-attachment to English, German and Swedish

Martin Volk and Frida Tidström
Stockholm University
Department of Linguistics
106 91 Stockholm, Sweden
`volk@ling.su.se`

Abstract

The correct attachment of prepositional phrases (PPs) is a central disambiguation problem when parsing natural languages. This paper compares the baseline situation for French as exemplified in the Le Monde treebank with earlier findings for English, German and Swedish.

We perform uniform treebank queries and show that the noun attachment rate for French prepositions is strongly influenced by the preposition *de* which is by far the most frequent preposition and has a strong tendency for noun attachment. We therefore also compute the noun attachment rate for the other prepositions separately as well as for the many complex prepositions that are explicitly marked in this treebank.

1 Introduction

Any computer system for natural language processing has to struggle with the problem of ambiguities. If the system is meant to extract precise information from a text, the ambiguities must be resolved. One of the most frequent ambiguities arises from the attachment of prepositional phrases (PPs). Simply stated, a PP that follows a noun (in French as in English, German or Swedish) can be attached to the preceding noun or to the verb of the same clause.

In the last decade various methods for the resolution of PP attachment ambiguities have been proposed. The seminal paper by Hindle and Rooth (1993) started a sequence of studies for English. Volk (2001; 2002) has investigated similar methods for German. Recently other languages such

as Dutch (Vandeghinste, 2002), Swedish (Kokkinakis, 2000; Aasa, 2004), and French (Gaussier and Cancedda, 2001; Gala and Lafourcade, 2005) have followed.

Volk (2006) investigated the attachment tendencies of prepositions in English, German and Swedish. He found that English had the highest overall noun attachment rate followed by Swedish and German. He also showed that the high rate in English was highly influenced by the preposition *of*. From this study he derived a list of criteria for profiling data sets for PP attachment experiments. In the current paper we have applied this list of criteria to French. We have obtained a French treebank and converted it into TIGER-XML so that we can use the same approach as for the other treebanks investigated earlier.

In the PP attachment research for other languages there is often a comparison of the disambiguation accuracy with the results for English. But are the results really comparable across languages? Volk (2006) showed that disambiguation efforts start from very different baselines in English, German and Swedish. In this paper we investigate how French fits into this picture.

2 Background

In their pioneering work Hindle and Rooth (1993) did not have access to a large treebank. Therefore they proposed an unsupervised method for resolving PP attachment ambiguities. A year later Ratnaparkhi et al. (1994) published a supervised approach to the PP attachment problem. They had extracted quadruples V-N-P-N[1] (plus the accompanying attachment decision) from both an IBM computer manuals treebank (about 9000 tuples)

---

[1] The V-N-P-N quadruples also contain the head noun of the NP within the PP.

Joakim Nivre, Heiki-Jaan Kaalep, Kadri Muischnek and Mare Koit (Eds.)
NODALIDA 2007 Conference Proceedings, pp. 191–198

and from the Wall Street Journal (WSJ) section of the Penn treebank (about 24,000 tuples). The latter tuple set has been reused by subsequent research, so let us focus on this one.[2] Ratnaparkhi et al. (1994) used 20,801 tuples for training and 3097 tuples for evaluation. They reported on 81.6% correct attachments.

But have they solved the same problem as (Hindle and Rooth, 1993)? What was the initial bias towards noun attachment in their data? It turns out that their training set (the 20,801 tuples) contains only 52% noun attachments, while their test set (the 3097 tuples) contains 59% noun attachments. The difference in noun attachments between these two sets is striking, but Ratnaparkhi ct al. (1994) do not discuss this (and we also do not have an explanation for this). But it makes obvious that Ratnaparkhi et al. (1994) were tackling a problem different from Hindle and Rooth (1993) given the fact that their baseline was at 59% guessing noun attachment (rather than 67% in the Hindle and Rooth experiments).

Of course, the baseline is not a direct indicator of the difficulty of the disambiguation task. We may construct (artificial) cases with low baselines and a simple distribution of PP attachment tendencies. For example, we may construct the case that a language has 100 different prepositions, where 50 prepositions always introduce noun attachments, and the other 50 prepositions always require verb attachments. If we also assume that both groups occur with the same frequency, we have a 50% baseline but still a trivial disambiguation task.

In reality the baseline puts the disambiguation result into perspective. If, for instance, the baseline is 60% and the disambiguation result is 80% correct attachments, then we will claim that our disambiguation procedure is useful. Whereas if we have a baseline of 80% and the disambiguation result is 75%, then the procedure can be discarded.

So what are the baselines reported for other languages? And is it possible to use the same extraction mechanisms for V-N-P-N tuples in order to come to comparable baselines across languages?

For English, Volk (2006) had used sections 0 to 12 of the WSJ part of the Penn Treebank (Marcus et al., 1993) with a total of 24,618 sentences for his experiments. He computed a noun attachment rate

of 75% over all common nouns (see section 5 for a definition of the noun attachment rate, NAR). This is a surprisingly high number. One reason for this high baseline stems from the fact that he queried for all sequences noun+PP as possibly ambiguous whereas previous research looked only at such sequences within verb phrases. Since he has done the same for all other languages, this is still worthwhile.

For German he had mainly used the large NEGRA and TIGER treebanks with a total of 60,000 trees. He computed a 60% noun attachment rate for common nouns over these treebanks. And for Swedish he had looked at a part of the Talbanken treebank with 6100 trees, which also resulted in a rate of 60% for regular nouns (while he computed significantly higher values for deadjectival nouns (69.5%), and deverbal nouns (77%). Taken together this results in a NAR of 64%.

Now we want to compare these results with a French treebank. We have obtained the French newspaper treebank Le Monde developed at Université Paris 7. The development and the major annotation decisions are described in (Abeillé et al., 2003). The treebank is accompanied by guidelines detailing the annotation decisions concerning the morpho-syntactic annotation (Abeillé and Clément, 2003), the constituent structure annotation (Abeillé et al., 2004) and the functional labels.

The Le Monde treebank consists of two parts. Part one contains 20,500 trees with constituent structure nodes but no functional information. In contrast, part two does contain functional information added to 9,300 trees. The treebank is distributed in a proprietary XML format. We have converted the treebank into TIGER-XML for use with the query tool TIGER-Search.

TIGER-Search is a powerful treebank query tool developed at the University of Stuttgart (König and Lezius, 2002). Its query language allows for feature-value descriptions of syntax graphs. It is similar in expressiveness to tgrep (Rohde, 2005) but it comes with graphical output and highlighting of the syntax trees plus nice frequency tables.

3 Conversion of the Le Monde Treebank to TIGER-XML

TIGER-XML allows the declaration of all annotation features (and the sets of possible values) which will be checked during the import of

---

[2]The Ratnaparkhi training and test sets were later distributed together with a development set of 4039 V-N-P-N tuples.

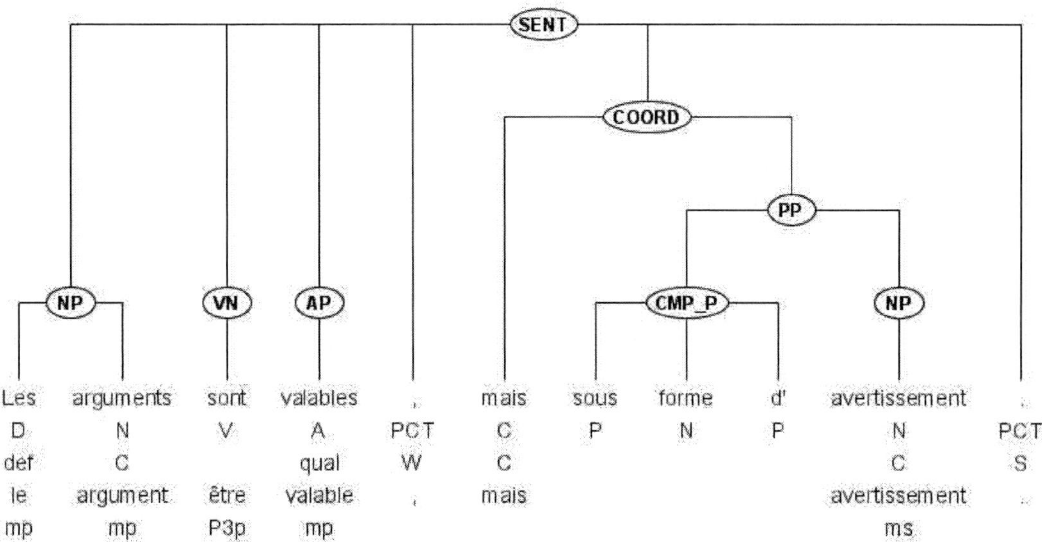

Figure 1: Tree from the Le Monde Treebank with coordination and a compound preposition (CMP_P)

the treebank into the TIGER-Search query tool. Therefore we first collected all word level features and all syntactic features from the French treebank files and compared them against the treebank documentation.

3.1 Word level features

The Le Monde treebank comes with the following word level information: Part-of-Speech tags (main classes and subclasses), morphology information and lemmas.

The developers have made some interesting tokenization decisions. Contracted word forms lead to the insertion of empty tokens (e.g. the preposition *du* gets the lemma *de* and leads to the insertion of an empty token with the lemma *le*). This is an elegant solution to explicitly represent the determiner.[3] Apostrophe contractions are split into two tokens (e.g. *d'un, l'on, c'est*). But in order to capture multi-token units, compounds are specially marked. For example *jusqu'au* is first split into two tokens and then annotated as compound preposition. (Other compounds are annotated accordingly: e.g. *premier ministre* as compound noun and *au contraire* as compound adverb.)

It was particularly difficult to preserve the compound information in the conversion, since TIGER-XML does not provide a representation level between tokens and syntactic nodes. We have therefore decided to use category nodes for grouping compounds. We have introduced the special node label CMP for such compounds (compare to the compounded preposition CMP_P in figure 1).

During the conversion it became clear that the treebank authors have not performed domain checks for the values of the various linguistic features. The treebank contains some undefined and undocumented feature values. For example, we found 13 documented PoS tags: the usual A, N, V, P tags, two pronoun classes (clitic and others), plus a tag each for adverbs, conjunctions, determiners, foreign words, interjections, and punctuation symbols. Finally there is a special tag for prefixes which is used for the first part of hyphenated compounds (for example in *vice-présidente* and in *franco-américain*).[4] But we also found two undocumented PoS tags: "PC" which we suspect stands for Préposition-Conjonction, and "X" for which we have no good guess. In addition there were 11 occurrences of erroneous PoS tags (e.g.

---

[3] Similar to French, German also has a set of contracted prepositions, e.g. German *im* stands for *in dem*. Sometimes a complex lemma is used for marking such contractions: *in-dem*.

[4] These hyphenated compounds are actually split into two tokens but they are not explicitly marked as compounds. This is strange since so many other types of compounds are explicitly marked in the Le Monde treebank.

ADVP, CC, W, PRE) which we have turned into the undefined tag label "–".

Similar problems of out-of-domain labels occurred also for the PoS subclassification tags. The Le Monde treebank uses 18 tags to subclassify the PoS tags. For example the general pronouns are subclassified into demonstrative, interrogative, possessive, and relative pronouns. In addition to erroneous labels, the SubPoS tags have the unfortunate complication that two of them have double meanings: For example "C" stands for both "Common noun" in combination with nouns (PoS tag = N), and it stands for "Coordination" in combination with conjunctions (PoS tag = C).

The Le Monde treebank comes with complex morphology tags (person, gender, number, tense). We represent them as complex features in TIGER-XML (e.g. "S3p" stands for "3rd person plural, present tense, subjunctive"). This means that one needs to use a regular expression search over the complex features when looking for a specific atomic feature (like person or tense).

TIGER-XML allows us to associate features with non-terminals (i.e. nodes) in the tree. In fact a node label (like NP or CMP_P) is just a feature like any other. Since compounds are represented as non-terminals, we have added the Part-of-Speech subclass, the morphology and the lemma as features. For example, the compound noun *banques centrales* comes with the additional information that it is a common noun (subclass) in feminine plural (morphology) and has the lemma *banque centrale*. Compound prepositions are not divided into subclasses and have no associated morphology information, but they do have a lemma which sometimes differs from the surface form, as for *au profit du* which has the lemma *à le profit de*.

3.2 Syntax level features

The Le Monde treebank comes with 13 documented node labels (e.g. NP, PP, SENT). Most of the constituent grouping follows the traditional strategies. Two deviations are noteworthy: First, there is no VP label for finite verb phrases but rather a label for the verb nucleus. This helps to avoid crossing branches in cases where the subject is located between the verb and the objects. However, infinitive and participle verb phrases are marked.[5]

---

[5]The avoidance of finite VPs is similar to the annotation in the German TIGER treebank.

preposition	freq	percentage
de, d', des, du	39188	53.2%
à, au, aux	10683	14.5%
en	4779	6.5%
dans	3569	4.8%
par	3091	4.1%
sur	2675	3.6%
pour	2508	3.4%
avec	1573	2.1%
entre	733	1.0%

Table 1: The most frequent French prepositions

Second, the annotation of coordinated structures is strange in that the first conjunct is superior to the second which is introduced with a node labeled COORD (e.g. NP[Christian Blanc COORD[and NP[Eric Frey]]]). The coordination in figure 1 is an example of sentence coordination.

As mentioned above, part two of the treebank contains additional functional information for subject, modifier, and different types of objects. Only constituents with these functions get a functional label. All others are left empty. For example, there is no explicit head information. In this paper we focus on the larger part of the treebank (i.e. the part that lacks the functional information), and we will refer to this first part as the Le Monde treebank hereafter.

4 Prepositions in the Le Monde Treebank

In the Le Monde treebank, there are 73,650 atomic preposition tokens directly dominated by a PP (rather than as part of a compound preposition or some other constituent). They account for 46 preposition types (counted via their lemmas, i.e. *d', des, du* and *de* count as the same preposition)[6]. We present the 9 most frequent prepositions in table 1. These comprise 93.2% of the atomic preposition tokens. As we can see, the preposition *de* strongly dominates the list.

The 46 preposition types are a relatively low number compared to, for instance, German which usually counts around 100 atomic preposition types (Volk, 2001). But a comparison with other French preposition lists confirms this number. For

---

[6]Note that the query [cat="PP"] > [pos="P"] leads to 64 different preposition types. But manual inspection shows that 18 of them are spelling errors (e.g. *ee* instead of *en*), mathematical symbols (+-/) or compound prepositions.

example the French PrepLex Database[7], which contains the merged information from a number of sources (including the syntactic part of Prep-Net (Saint-Dizier, 2006)), lists 49 "simple" prepositions (in contrast to multi-word prepositions). 40 of them also occur as prepositions in the Le Monde treebank. The nine remaining ones either do not occur at all in the Le Monde treebank (*circa, confer, versus*) or they occur only with other PoS labels (*dixit, passé, sitôt, touchant, vu, ès*). On the other hand, there are six simple prepositions in the Le Monde treebank which are not listed in PrepLex (*autour, courant, environ, plein, plus, près*). Two of them occur only once as preposition but many times with other PoS labels (*autour* is adverb in 79 cases, and *plein* is adjective 28 times) which leaves some doubt about their status as preposition. The two sentence contexts do not force this interpretation either in our judgement.

In addition to prepositions dominated directly by PPs, the Le Monde treebank contains 21,570 atomic preposition tokens dominated by other categories. Table 2 lists the most frequent categories that dominate prepositions. Column 2 gives the frequency for how often the category contains a preposition, and column 3 gives the percentage relative to the sum of all frequencies in column 2 (including some rare categories not listed in the table).

Not surprisingly compound prepositions lead the list, but also infinitive and participle verb phrases are frequently introduced by a preposition. For example: *un moyen simple VPinf[de prouver cette intention]* (a simple way to prove this intention). Furthermore there are different compounds that contain prepositions: compound adverbs (*à tout prix, aujourd'hui*) , compound nouns (*arrêts de travail, sac à main*), compound verbs (*être en train, rappeler à l'ordre*), and even compounded conjunctions (*pour que, à mesure que*).

There are 5266 compound prepositions in the French treebank. These range from two-token compounds (e.g. *près de*) to seven-token compounds (*d' un bout à l' autre de*). The two-token compounds are mostly combinations with *de* or *à* on the second position. Also *d'ici, d'après, d'abord* with the preposition on the first position are regarded as compound prepositions in this treebank. The three-token compounds are mostly

category	P freq	P percentage
compound preps	6896	32.0%
infinitive VPs	6817	31.6%
compound adverbs	3868	17.9%
compound nouns	2324	10.8%
participle VPs	583	2.7%
NPs	502	2.3%
compound conj.	202	0.9%
compound verbs	125	0.6%

Table 2: Categories with prepositions

frozen prepositional phrases like *par rapport à, en raison de, à partir de*. The same is true for four-token and longer compounds with the restriction that almost all of them have *de* on the final position *à la fin de, dans le cadre de, au – sein de, de l' autre côté de*. In total there are 460 (!) compound preposition types. The most frequent ones are *par rapport à, il y a* and *près de*. This compares to 206 multi-word prepositions in PrepLex.

It might be surprising that *il y a* is listed as a compound preposition since none of its parts is a preposition. But the annotators of the Le Monde Treebank are not alone in this categorization. It is mentioned by (Grevisse, 1993) and also listed in PrepLex.

Compound prepositions function as heads in PPs in the majority of cases (4665 or 88.6%), but - like atomic prepositions - they also introduce infinitive VPs (in 7.8% of the cases; e.g. as in *[de peur de] s'attirer certaines foudres syndicales*) and NPs (in 3.3% of the cases). Such NPs are mostly introduced by *près de, plus de* and *moins de* as for example in *[près de] 1 million de tonnes*.

Unfortunately the treebank authors have not performed rigid consistency checks over the annotation of compound prepositions. For example, the sequence *en début de* as in *en début de semaine* is annotated once as a compound preposition, but 9 times it is annotated as a nested PP *[en NP[début PP[de NP[semaine]]]]*. In one case it is even annotated as a part of a compounded adverb in *en début de matinée*.

Interestingly coordination of PPs is relatively rare. The treebank contains only 27 cases of a preposition which is dominated by the COORD category. About half of them are comparative constructions with the preposition *comme* like in *au Royaume-Uni comme en Allemagne*.

According to (Pedersen et al., 1989), there is a

---

[7]The French PrepLex can be found at http://loriatal.loria .fr/Resources/PrepLex.txt

clear distinction between a PP attribute and a PP verb complement in French. The PP *i klubben* in the Swedish sentence "*Hon deltog aktivt i diskussionerna i klubben*" is ambiguous since it can be attached either to the verb *deltog* or to the noun *diskussionerna*. However, the French preposition *de* is principally used for PP attributes: *Elle participait activement aux discussions du club* (She participated actively in the discussions of the club).

A different preposition would be used for a PP adverbial: *Elle participait activement aux discussions au club* (She participated actively in the discussions in the club). The prepositions *de* (noun attachment) and *à, dans, sur* (verb attachment) accent different aspects in the examples in table 3.

5 Computing Noun Attachment Rates

Now we would like to determine the attachment tendency for the various French prepositions and the overall attachment tendency for French prepositions. We do that by computing the noun attachment rate (NAR) according to the following formula:

$$NAR = \frac{freq(noun + PP, noun\_attachm)}{freq(noun + PP)}$$

We assume that all PPs in noun+PP sequences which are not attached to a noun are attached to a verb. This means we ignore the very few cases of such PPs that might be attached to adjectives (as for instance the PP in *tard dans la soirée* (late in the evening)).

We compute the frequencies with TIGER-Search queries over the Le Monde treebank. Our experiments for determining attachment tendencies proceed along the following lines. We first query for all sequences of a noun immediately followed by a PP. With the dot being the precedence operator, we use the query:

```
[pos="N"] . [cat="PP"]
```

This query gives us the frequency of all ambiguously located PPs. We find that 35,787 out of 79,011 PPs (45.3%) in this treebank are in such an ambiguous position. These numbers include both common and proper nouns and PPs with all kinds of prepositions. We disregard the fact that in certain clause positions a PP in such a sequence cannot be verb-attached and is thus not ambiguous. For example, a French noun+PP sequence in subject position is not ambiguous with respect to PP attachment since the PP cannot attach to the verb.

Similar restrictions apply to Enlish, German and Swedish.

Since we distinguish common nouns and proper nouns in our investigations, we used a refined version of the above query which includes the Sub-PoS value with either "C" or "P".

In order to determine how many of these sequences are annotated as noun attachments, we query for noun phrases that contain both a common noun and an immediately following PP. This query looks like:

```
#np:[cat="NP"] > #pp:[cat="PP"] &
#np >* #n:[pos="N" & subpos="C"] &
#n . #pp
```

All strings starting with # are variables and the > symbol is the dominance operator. So, this query says: Search for an NP (and call it #np) that directly dominates a PP, and the NP also dominates (directly or indirectly) a noun which is immediately followed by the PP.

6 NAR Results for French

The first query finds that there are 34,476 occurrences of a PP immediately following a common noun in the Le Monde treebank. The second query results in 28,294 cases of a noun phrase dominating both the PP and the noun. In addition we find 395 cases of a (higher) PP which dominates the noun and the (lower) PP. So we add these two numbers (395 + 28,294) and divide by the number of all occurrences.

This leads to a NAR for common nouns followed by atomic prepositions of 83.2%, which is very high. French clearly has a tendency to attach the PP to the preceding noun. One reason must be that French produces genitive-like structures, compounds and measures with the help of the preposition *de*. Let us have a closer look at the attachment tendencies of the different prepositions in table 4.

Column 1 lists the lemmas of the 9 most frequent French prepositions. Column 2 contains the frequency of the preposition being the head of a PP in a (common) noun attachment context (like in query 2), while column 3 contains the frequency (being the head of a PP) in an ambiguous position (like in query 1). The rightmost column lists the NAR for each preposition (i.e. the ratio of the two previous columns given as percentage).

Clearly the high NAR for French is mainly due to the preposition *de* which accounts for more

	Verb attachment	Noun attachment
(1)	*Elle a construisit un hôpital à Nice*	*Elle mourut dans un hôpital de Nice*
	She constructed a hospital in Nice	She died in a hospital in Nice
(2)	*Il avait fait une tache sur le mur*	*Il se rappela la tache du mur*
	He had made a spot on the wall	He remembered the spot on the wall
(3)	*Cela a causé un scandale dans les années trente*	*Le livre décrit un scandale des années trente*
	This caused a scandal in the thirties	The book describes a scandal of the thirties

Table 3: Examples of noun vs verb attachments (taken from (Pedersen et al., 1989))

prep.	freq P N-att	freq P	NAR
de	23726	24387	97.3%
entre	202	282	71.6%
sur	537	930	57.7%
avec	190	375	50.7%
à	1308	2668	49.0%
par	289	618	46.7%
pour	341	768	44.4%
en	656	1502	43.7%
dans	291	855	34.0%

Table 4: The NAR for the most frequent French prepositions (relative to common nouns)

than half of the preposition tokens in the treebank. Only two more of the frequent prepositions show a clear noun attachment tendency: *entre* and *sur*. If we omit *de* from the computation of the NAR, we end up with a balanced situation, i.e. a NAR of 50% for all the remaining prepositions. We should also mention that there are some rarer prepositions with high NARs (an example is *sans* which occurs 75 times as preposition in the treebank and has a NAR of 73.3%).

This situation is very similar to English where the preposition *of* has a noun attachment rate of 99% and is very frequent. If *of* is omitted from the calculation, English in fact shows a tendency towards verb attachment.

Furthermore we find that the NAR for proper nouns followed by atomic prepositions is 42% in the French treebank. This is also in line with Volk's (2006) findings in the other languages. Proper nouns don't take prepositional complements and attributes as often as common nouns. For example, for German he found a NAR of around 20% for proper nouns.

If we look at French compound prepositions, the picture changes. We find a NAR of only 37.7% for compound prepositions which follow common nouns in the Le Monde treebank. We don't have any comparative figures for English, German and Swedish since compound prepositions are not marked in the treebanks for these languages.

7 Conclusions

Our findings put other results for French PP attachment resolution into perspective. If our NAR of 83.2% is a fair assessment of the attachment tendency of French PPs in ambiguous positions, then any lower accuracy scores based on automatic disambiguation are meaningless. A simple program can achieve 83.2% correct attachments by always predicting noun attachment for all ambiguously located PPs (that are headed by atomic prepositions).

Consider for example (Gaussier and Cancedda, 2001) who have tested their disambiguation method "against 900 manually annotated sequences of nuclei from the newspaper Le Monde". Since they give no reference to the Le Monde treebank, we assume that they used different annotated material, accidentally from the same newspaper. They report on results of 73.5% correct PP attachments. But they have only looked at V N P sequences which is different from our approach. Unfortunately they do not give the NAR for their data.

Our results are also interesting for general linguistic insights into the behavior of French prepositions. Second language learners could profit as well. The profiling of the prepositions with respect to their attachment tendencies tells a lot about the usage options.

In future work we would like to test the methods proposed in (Volk, 2001; Volk, 2002) for the resolution of German PP attachment ambiguities against the French treebank. Furthermore we would like to make contrastive studies on prepositions based on parallel treebanks. This will lead to an increased understanding of cross-language prepositional correspondences and help in building machine translation systems.

8 Acknowledgements

We would like to thank Anne Abeillé for making the French Le Monde treebank available to us. Part of this research was done while the first author was a visiting researcher at Macquarie University in Sydney. We gratefully acknowledge financial support through the Australian HCSNet.

References

Jörgen Aasa. 2004. Unsupervised resolution of PP attachment ambiguities in Swedish. Master's thesis, Stockholm University. Combined C/D level thesis.

Anne Abeillé and Lionel Clément. 2003. Annotation morpho-syntaxique. Les mots simples - les mots composés. Corpus Le Monde. Technical report, LLF, UFRL, Paris 7.

Anne Abeillé, Lionel Clément, and Francois Toussenel. 2003. Building a Treebank for French. In Anne Abeillé, editor, *Building and Using Parsed Corpora*, volume 20 of *Text, Speech and Language Technology*, chapter 10, pages 165–187. Kluwer, Dordrecht.

Anne Abeillé, François Toussenel, and Martine Chéradame. 2004. Corpus Le Monde. Annotations en constituants. Guide pour les correcteurs. Technical report, LLF, UFRL, Paris 7.

Nuria Gala and Mathieu Lafourcade. 2005. Combining corpus-based pattern distributions with lexical signatures for PP attachment ambiguity resolution. In *Proc. of SNLP-05, 6th Symposium on Natural Language Processing*, Chiang Rai, Thailand.

Eric Gaussier and Nicola Cancedda. 2001. Probabilistic models for PP-attachment resolution and NP analysis. In *Proc. of ACL-2001 CoNLL-2001 Workshop*, Toulouse. ACL.

Maurice Grevisse. 1993. *Le Bon Usage (Refondu par André Goose)*. Editions Duculot, Paris.

D. Hindle and M. Rooth. 1993. Structural ambiguity and lexical relations. *Computational Linguistics*, 19(1):103–120.

Dimitrios Kokkinakis. 2000. Supervised PP-attachment disambiguation for Swedish. *Nordic Journal of Linguistics, Special Issue on Cognitive Approaches to Language*, 23(2):191–213.

Esther König and Wolfgang Lezius. 2002. The TIGER language - a description language for syntax graphs. Part 1: User's guidelines. Technical report.

Mitchell P. Marcus, Beatrice Santorini, and Mary Ann Marcinkiewicz. 1993. Building a large annotated corpus of English: The Penn treebank. *Computational Linguistics*, 19(2):313–330.

John Pedersen, Ebbe Spang-Hanssen, and Carl Vikner. 1989. *Fransk Universitetsgrammatik*. Esselte Studium, Akademiförlaget. Translated by Olof Eriksson and Lars Lindvall.

A. Ratnaparkhi, J. Reynar, and S. Roukos. 1994. A maximum entropy model for prepositional phrase attachment. In *Proceedings of the ARPA Workshop on Human Language Technology*, Plainsboro, NJ, March.

Douglas L. T. Rohde, 2005. *TGrep2 User Manual*. MIT. Available from http://tedlab.mit.edu/~dr/Tgrep2/.

Patrick Saint-Dizier. 2006. PrepNet: a Multilingual Lexical Description of Prepositions. In *Language Resources and Evaluation Conference (LREC)*, pages 877–885, Genova. European Language Resources Association (ELRA).

Vincent Vandeghinste. 2002. Resolving PP attachment ambiguities using the WWW (abstract). In *Computational Linguistics in the Netherlands*, Groningen.

Martin Volk. 2001. *The automatic resolution of prepositional phrase attachment ambiguities in German*. Habilitationsschrift, University of Zurich.

Martin Volk. 2002. Combining unsupervised and supervised methods for PP attachment disambiguation. In *Proc. of COLING-2002*, Taipeh.

Martin Volk. 2006. How bad is the problem of PP-attachment? A comparison of English, German and Swedish. In *Proc. of ACL-SIGSEM Workshop on Prepositions*, Trento, April.

Interview and Delivery: Dialogue Strategies for Conversational Recommender Systems

Pontus Wärnestål, Lars Degerstedt and **Arne Jönsson**
Department of Computer Science
Linköping University, Sweden
{ponjo,larde,arnjo}@ida.liu.se

Abstract

In our work with conversational recommender systems we have derived two dialogue strategies called interview and delivery. We explore the symmetry between preferential interview and traditional clarification questions, and arrive at basic interview and delivery strategies suitable for conversational recommender system implementations. The strategies are based on a corpus analysis of recommendation dialogues in the movie domain. We illustrate the strategies in a conversational music recommender system called CORESONG.

1 Introduction

Recommender systems aim at assisting users in searching, sorting, and selecting items from large information repositories. They differ from traditional information search engines in that they provide *personalized* service, and the key issue is to correctly construct, update and utilize individual records of user preferences. We employ a conversational approach to preference modeling and recommender system interaction in order to achieve a collaborative dialogue, which is likely to improve system prediction accuracy and user interaction quality (Carenini et al., 2003). Users can explain preferences in a qualitative way as opposed to only rely on the standard nominal 1-5 rating of items (Burke et al., 1997); and the dialogue structure can be used as a tool for detecting variations in preference strength depending on the user's dialogue act and the conversational circumstance in which it occurs (Carberry et al., 1999).

The successful dialogue systems to date are typically implemented in well-known domains and exhibit standardized dialogue strategies (e.g. flight ticket bookings, hotel reservations, etc.) rather than having a completely free and human-like language interaction (Pieraccini and Huerta, 2005). The goal of this paper is to advance our knowledge on recommendation dialogues. We have studied recommendation dialogues in media domains, such as music and movies, and present two *dialogue strategies* found in such dialogues.

For the purpose of describing the strategies, we view them as genres (Erickson, 2000), each with a specific purpose, form, and participatory structure. We illustrate the different strategy instances with a conversational music recommender system called CORESONG.

Note that the these two strategies cover all possible forms of the studied interaction, including utterances within and outside of the domain as well as e.g. questions where the user asks for help on how to use the system. How to differentiate between these and correctly provide relevant information is a technical issue presented in section 3.

2 Recommendation Dialogue Strategies

First we turn to the case to be studied: recommendation dialogue in media domains. For this purpose we have conducted a study where a human-human dialogue corpus study was collected (Johansson, 2003). Twenty-four dialogues were recorded in a living room environment with two participants, one acting as a recommender and one as a customer looking for movie recommendations. The participants did not know each other's movie preferences previously, since one goal was to examine how humans go about assessing preferences from scratch. As information resource the recommender had access to a laptop with a large movie information database with the attributes title, actor, director, genre, plot, and year for over 6.3 million individual film/TV credits. In total, 2,684 utterances (mean 112 utterances per dialogue) were transcribed and analyzed using the dialogue distilling method (Larsson et al., 2000) for systematic rewriting into human-machine dialogue. In the distilled corpus, the recommender is referred to as the "system" and the customer as the "user". The distilled corpus was then examined and by clustering re-occurring patterns in the dialogue two principal *dialogue strategies* emerged: **interview**, and **delivery**. Our hypothesis is that a recommendation dialogue model suitable for implementing

Joakim Nivre, Heiki-Jaan Kaalep, Kadri Muischnek and Mare Koit (Eds.)
NODALIDA 2007 Conference Proceedings, pp. 199–205

conversational recommender systems can be seen as a combination of interview and delivery strategy instances of varying complexity.

2.1 The Interview Strategy

The purpose of the interview is to collect information about opinions on domain entity types (e.g. genres, directors or actors in the movie domain) and specific items (i.e. specific movies). We refer to this information as *preferences*, which form the base for deliveries (e.g. product recommendations, or database search results). There are two roles in the interview: an *interviewer* that asks an *interviewee* to constrain or, in some cases, relax attribute values.

The interviewee is assumed to respond cooperatively, and is also free to volunteer preferences not explicitly asked for. The question-selection strategy (i.e. the order in which entity type and value preferences are requested by the interviewer) follows an order based on the interviewer's idea of importance in the domain and usually ends in "open" preference requests (e.g. utterance S4a in Figure 1). Our corpus analysis suggests a question-selection strategy that moves from generics to specifics (i.e. asking about genre preferences before asking about actor preferences). Note however, that the default order can be revised since interviewees may volunteer preferences in a different order and inform the interviewer of specific importance of certain attributes. Recommender systems that implement this kind of interviewer strategy are said to have a *dynamic* question-selection strategy (cf. (Bridge, 2002)), since the questions are chosen at run-time depending on what preferences have been given by the interviewee. As the dialogue progresses it may

S1a	Hello. Let's set up your music preferences.
S1b	Is there a particular genre you like?
U1	I like *techno*
S2a	These are the artists and albums that belong to the genre *Techno*: `[list]`
S2b	Any of these you like in particular?
U2	I like the artist *Flexter*
S3a	These albums are made by the artist *Flexter*: `[list]`
S3b	Any of these you like in particular?
U4	The first one is good
S4a	Ok. Do you have any other preferences?
U4	What *metal* bands are there?
S4a	These artists belong to the genre *Metal*: `[list]`

Figure 1: Preference question selection strategy in the constrain interview. Example from the music domain. Entity values are in *italics*. S = system, U = user.

become impossible to provide more deliveries based on the current preference model. The deliverer then takes on the interview strategy, but tries to relax the constraints. When asking for relaxations, the interviewer uses the inverse order in which attributes were requested in the constrain strategy. Figure 2 shows a sample relaxation interview used in the movie domain. When the preference

S1a	There are no more movies matching the current criteria.
S1b	Would you like to ignore any director preferences?
U2	Yes, skip all directors
S2a	Ok, I have a recommendation ready for you.
S2b	I think you will like the movie *The Usual Suspects*.

Figure 2: Relaxing a specific constraint in a preference interview (S1b), which is followed by a delivery (S2b). Example from the movie domain. S = system, U = user.

requests on the interviewer's agenda have been fulfilled and some *external resource*[1] responsible for reaching a solution, a delivery can be made. This depends on the task and the nature of the resource. In some cases the interviewer has a fixed agenda stating which attributes that need values supplied by the interviewee. The dialogue then progresses with repeated constrain requests in a "slot-filling" fashion. When all slots have been filled a delivery (typically in the form of a database result set) can be made. This strategy is standard for information-providing dialogue systems.

In other cases the requests for constraints are more dynamic. For instance, in recommender systems the number and nature of the "slots" that need to be filled depends on the interviewee's preferences. For one interviewee (the user) it might be enough for the interviewer (the system) to ask for a handful constraints[2] if her preferences are narrow enough to quickly reach high-quality predictions to be used for recommendations. For another interviewee (e.g. one with "too normal" preferences that does not make her easy to place in a *collaborative filtering neighborhood*) the interviewer might have to keep constraining for several turns until the recommendation engine is ready to provide a recommendation.

---

[1]Such as a recommender engine, or database back-end resource.

[2]This depends on the nature of the recommendation engine. "Low" might mean a dozen or more items in a collaborative filtering engine; or perhaps one or two genre preferences and a few actor preferences in a content-based movie recommender engine.

2.2 The Delivery Strategy

Ensuing an interview is a *delivery*. The goal of a delivery is to present the *result* of the preceding interview. The roles in the delivery strategy are: a *deliverer* and a *receiver*.

In the basic case, a delivery simply consists of presenting a solution to the deliverer in one go. This is called a *direct delivery*. However, a delivery can be more elaborate. For instance, a deliverer could motivate her choice of recommendation with a motivation for it, as well as follow-up questions regarding the quality of the given recommendation. Typically, deliveries such as recommendations are delivered when the system is ready (i.e. has collected enough user preferences); and not necessarily at the turn immediately following a user request for a recommendation. Therefore, we call such deliveries *indirect*. Motivations are central for building trust (Swearingen and Sinha, 2002) and help explaining the inner workings of the recommendation algorithm (Höök, 2000). They are frequently used in recommendation situations and therefore desirable in recommender system interaction. Asking the receiver for feedback on the delivered item is also considered part of the delivery strategy, and could be used in both recommendations and more traditional information delivery, such as in information-providing dialogue systems. The initiative is mainly on the deliverer (i.e. the system in an implementation). Figure 5 exemplifies the resulting dialogue of the two kinds of delivery in the CORESONG system.

Deliveries may consist of *exceptional results*. Exceptional results arise when the user has provided too little, ambiguous, or erroneous information; and needs guidance in order to achieve her goal. The amount and quality of such information depends on what background resources the deliverer has at her disposal. A dialogue system that employs an ontological model of the domain can, for instance, "know" that certain concepts are not covered by an underlying database (out-of-domain concepts). Other examples of exceptional results are empty result sets, or under-specified queries.

In our view of recommendation and information-providing dialogue, exceptional results is what drives the interview strategy. There is a symmetry between under-specified queries and resulting clarification dialogues, and preference acquisition for recommendation delivery. This similar structure makes it possible to use the interview strategy for both preference interviews, and for clarification strategies for poorly understood database requests. The generality of the interview and delivery strategies makes them suitable to use for both phenomena, as exemplified in Section 3.

It is important to note that the occurrences of exceptional results increase in human-computer dialogue compared to human-human ditto. A typical example is infor-

mation about out-of-domain concepts which is a direct consequence of the limited domain descriptions in information systems to date.

3 Recommendation as Dialogue Behaviors

This section presents the model for the interview and delivery strategies that is used in the conversational music recommender system CORESONG. The model is based directly on results from the corpus analysis. It is presented as *dialogue behavior diagrams* based on UML activity diagrams which also makes it computationally attractive[3].

CORESONG is a conversational recommender system implemented as a web application with typed chat-style interaction. The purpose of the system is to help users build music play lists for various situations, such as exercising or driving the car. CORESONG uses a relational database with song, genre, artist, album, and year information for over 8,000 songs (with more than 50 genres, 2,000 artists, and 650 albums). In order to produce recommendations the system also employs a content-based[4] recommendation engine (Burke, 2002).

3.1 The Dialogue Behavior Model

CORESONG's dialogue strategy is realized using a set of dialogue behavior automata. Each automaton describes the computational behavior of the dialogue strategy manager of the system in a (mathematically) precise and accurate way.

The model is defined as *strata* (i.e. layers) of dialogue behavior diagrams. Each such diagram formalizes a coherent behavior of the system, in terms of an activity diagram with enhanced notation for this purpose.

In particular, to formalize user and system utterances the dialogue behavior diagrams use the Preference Conversational Query Language, PCQL (Wärnestål et al., 2007). PCQL action statements are used for representation of both user and system acts and treat questions and statements in a symmetric way, both in and out of the system.

A PCQL action statement has the form

$$\langle \text{TAG} \rangle \; [\![\, \langle \mathit{fp} \rangle \,]\!] \; \{ \text{VALUES} \; [\![\, \langle \mathit{vlist} \rangle \,]\!] \, \}^?$$

where $\langle \text{TAG} \rangle$ is an action tag, $\langle \mathit{fp} \rangle$ is an FP state formula and the third argument $\langle \mathit{vlist} \rangle$ is an optional argument that holds a map of entity values (normally used for system

---

[3]Since activity diagrams naturally relate to state diagrams, the emerging standard of W3C's State Chart XML should be suitable for specifying dialogue behavior diagrams.

[4]A version utilizing a hybrid engine that mixes collaborative filtering and content-based recommendations is under development.

answers only)[5].

The FP state formula describes some aspects of the factual and preference state (the FP state) of the dialogue agent. The action tag expresses an *action* performed by the dialogue participant, a dialogue act, where the acting agent is doing something that will result in a response from the dialogue partner. For example, the utterance *"What do you think about the genre techno?"* can be represented as a the PCQL statement: ASK ⟦ ⊙ Genre = Techno ⟧[6]. PCQL makes no assumption on the constituents of the action tag set, since they are highly application-dependent. PCQL statements and FP states can express fragmented utterances, which (naturally) are common in on-going dialogue. A basic fragment resolution module, responsible for resolving anaphoric expressions, validates and completes PCQL statements prior to the dialogue behavior strata. This means that each dialogue behavior instance operates on complete PCQL statements.

Each dialogue behavior diagram can be used to produce one or several running dialogue behavior instances in the running system. A key point of the proposed model is to have several instances of the same behavior for different external resources (e.g. a database of products), where each behavior instance contributes to the complete dialogue system behavior.

3.2 Basic Behaviors

Figures 3 and 4 define two dialogue behaviors, interview and direct delivery. For a first version of CORESONG, these dialogue behaviors are instantiated for each of the two external resources, a music information database and a recommender engine.

The core symbol of the dialogue behavior diagram is an activity state where an action is carried out in the dialogue and labeled arrows are conditional transitions (*guards*) between states. Guards operate on FP state formulas that in turn may be manipulated by calls to back-end resources. Each **call** returns a result in the form of a PCQL action statement (stored in the % variable) that can be used by successive activities and guard functions.

Consider the direct delivery behavior in Figure 4. As the basic interview behavior it awaits input (the **in** node 21) and checks whether it is a request/ask move by using the is-ask function. If the check passes, the external resource connected to this particular diagram is queried (the **call** to the LookUp in node 24). The result of the query is presented to the user—if the size of the result set is within a pre-defined range—as a PCQL statement in node 25. The dialogue behavior diagram then informs the

---

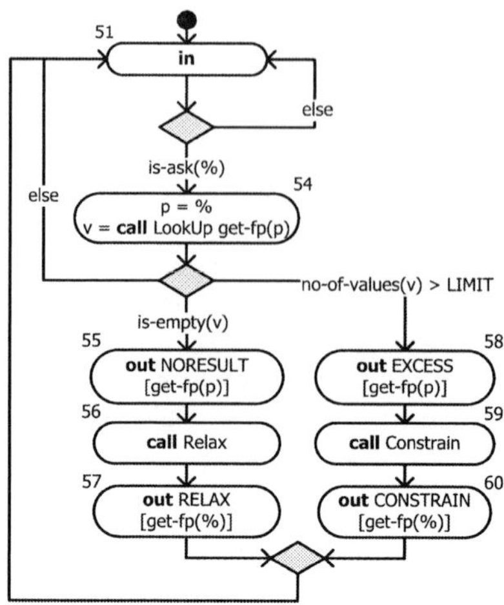

Figure 3: The interview dialogue behavior.

user that it is ready for a new turn (node 26), awaiting a new user move in node 21.

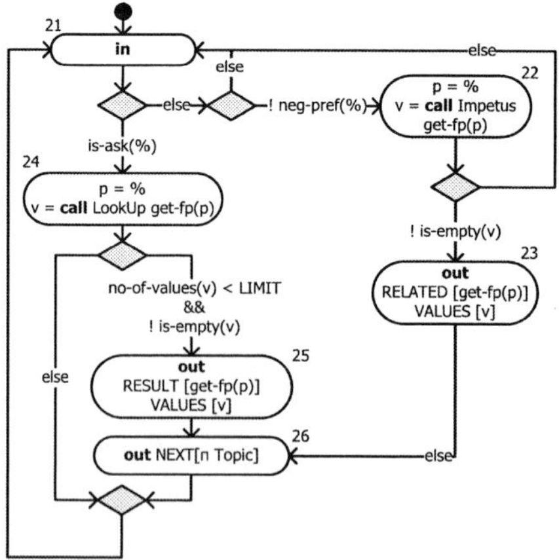

Figure 4: The direct delivery dialogue behavior.

Preferences are detected and recorded, annotated with user-defined *situations* (e.g. exercise, driving, work) in a preference model. Preference strengths are calculated (Carberry et al., 1999) and used by the external recommender engine resource, which in turn trigger node transitions in its connected dialogue behavior instances.

Figure 5 exemplifies how the interview and direct delivery dialogue behaviors of a database and a recommender engine resource collaborate in the dialogue. Utterance S1a is generated because the database has a valid result set based on the user's *preference* statement in U1. The result set is created by a tailored **call** to the database (node 22 in Figure 4) which retrieves related information to encourage the user to react on domain informa-

Action Tag	Sample Output Database	Recommender Engine
RESULT	These artists belong to the genre *techno*:	You might like the song x
MOTIVATE		You might like song x because it is liked by others who like y
RECOMMEND		Have you heard the song x?
NORESULT	There were no matches to your query	There are no products that match your preferences
RELAX	Do you want to disregard artist constraint?	Do you have any other preferences? [a]
EXCESS	There were too many matches to your query	I need more preferences in order to give you recommendations
CONSTRAIN	Please provide a genre	Are there any albums you like in particular?

[a] The utterance needs to be tailored depending on the recommender engine type.

Table 1: Examples of action tags and sample output from CORESONG's two back-end resources (the music database and the recommender engine). MOTIVATE and RECOMMEND are part of the indirect delivery behavior described in section 3.3 and only valid for the recommender engine.

tion (state 23). Since the preference model needs to be fleshed out with more preferences before the recommendation engine is ready to produce recommendations (transition 54 $\Rightarrow$ 58 in Figure 3), additional constraints are needed. When accessing the preference model (transition 59 $\Rightarrow$ 60 in Figure 3) the system is informed of which attribute that should be constrained (realized as a CONSTRAIN action in S1c). Constrain and Relax are back-end resources that keep track of the order in which domain entity types should be requested, depending on the content of the user's preference model. U2 is a *factual* query that

U1   I like the artist *Audioslave*.
S1a   These are the albums that belong to the artist *Audioslave*: [list]
S1b   I need more preferences in order to give you recommendations.
S1c   Please provide a genre that you like.
U2   What albums have the genre *Alternative*?
S2a   These albums belong to the genre *Alternative*: [list]
S2b   You might like the song *Original Fire*.
S2c   What else do you want to know?

Figure 5: Multiple deliveries from two back-end resources (database and recommender engine) and two dialogue behaviors (interview and direct delivery). S = system, U = user.

yet again renders the database with a valid result set, resulting in the S2a delivery (corresponding to node 25 in Figure 4). Since we model information requests as preferences (Carberry et al., 1999) the user's utterance in U2 is also interpreted as a proper response to S1c in the behaviors connected to the recommendation engine. This turn, we find that the recommender engine has a recommendation ready (due to the additional genre preference

in U2). S2b and S2c are thus part of the direct delivery behavior connected to a recommender engine (nodes 34 and 35).

3.3 Extending the Recommendation Behavior

As the dialogue excerpt in Figure 5 shows, the direct delivery instances in Figure 4 accommodate basic deliveries of both recommendations and database results. Recommendations, according to the corpus study, are often not as "blunt" as the direct delivery version of Figure 5, however. To enhance CORESONG's recommendation strategy and make it more human-like, we connect a new *indirect* delivery dialogue behavior to the recommender engine resource (see Figure 6). However, we leave the direct delivery dialogue behavior for the database resource intact, since it is still used as-is for factual questions, and conversational impetus.

By running this new dialogue behavior in parallel with the interviews and direct delivery dialogue behaviors we achieve dialogues such as the one exemplified in Figure 7 in cases when the recommender engine's status is ready to deliver recommendations. This complete behavior mimics the distilled corpus more closely. The system appears more "modest" in its recommendations, since it states a *motivation* before presenting the actual recommendation (S1b/S3a). Since the system cannot know whether the suggestion is previously familiar to the user, it delivers the recommendations in the form of questions (S1c/S3b). A set of new action tags are needed for the **out** activity states (utterance examples are found in Figure 7 and Table 1): MOTIVATE (S1b), RECOMMEND (S1c), and ASKRATE (S2a).

4   The Emergent Dialogue Strategy

In CORESONG, seamless integration of factual and preference aspects of the dialogue is achieved by having the individual dialogue behaviors combine their resulting

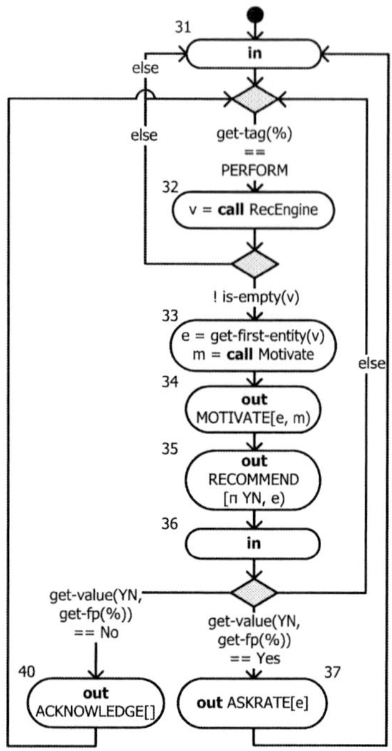

Figure 6: CORESONG's indirect recommendation delivery dialogue behavior.

U1   What albums belong to the genre *Alternative*?
S1a   These albums belong to the genre *Alternative*:
        [list]
S1b   You might like the song *Original Fire* because it is a song by Audioslave that belongs to the genre *Alternative*.
S1c   Have you heard it?
U2   Yes
S2a   Ok. What do you think about that song?
U3   It's great
S3a   You might like the song *One* by Creed because it is liked by others who like Audioslave.
S3b   Have you heard it?

Figure 7: Two recommendation deliveries in a dialogue strategy following the direct database delivery (in Figure 4) and the indirect recommendation delivery (in Figure 6).

outputs. Thus, the resulting dialogue strategy emerges from such combinations in a robust way.

Factual dialogues use instances of the interview and direct delivery dialogue behaviors (Figures 3 and 4). *Preferential* (and recommendation) dialogues also use the interview dialogue behavior, but instances of the indirect recommendation delivery behavior instead of the direct delivery behavior (compare Figure 6).

As the corpus suggests, the dialogue has a distinct exploratory flavor where preference eliciting goes hand in hand with a gradually increasing understanding of the domain (Swearingen and Sinha, 2002; Wärnestål, 2005). It is therefore important that factual interviews from the user's perspective are seamlessly blended with the preferential system interview as well as recommendation delivery.

Combining the behaviors' output into a coherent system utterance is by no means trivial. In CORESONG the solution is pragmatic and divided into two constructs: *behavior priority* and *action tag heuristics*.

Priority   We index behaviors with a priority and order the **out** PCQL statements accordingly (ascending order). For example, the indirect delivery has a higher priority than direct delivery. Technically, the interview has a higher priority than delivery, but in cases where a delivery and interview behavior are *connected to the same resource*, they are naturally mutually exclusive. However, if a delivery and an interview are connected to different resources, the higher interview priority comes into play.

Heuristic   Secondly, we employ a simple heuristic when surface realizing the output. It states that informing action statements always precedes action statements that hold ask/requesting tags, and that the ask/request action with the highest priority is chosen. For example, this guarantees that utterance S1c always occurs *after* S1a in Figure 7 even though they origin from different behaviors.

Conversational Impetus   On a final note, since most users are not aware of all their preferences at the outset of a dialogue session, it is important to trigger preference volunteering. It is mostly when exposed to information that the user brings her preferences into play (Carberry et al., 1999). This triggering we call *conversational impetus* since this is what drives the preference dialogue forward (Wärnestål, 2005). Conversational impetus in CORESONG is reached by accessing the database for all user input–not only information queries. The user is thus presented with related information that can encourage her to provide more preferences in a reactive manner (see U1 and S2a in Figure 1).

Our behavior-based approach supports such conversational impetus naturally since it is a direct consequence of running behavior instances for all background resources (i.e. both recommender engine and database resources), and how we combine the output from several sources.

5 Summary

In this paper we have presented the dialogue strategies interview and delivery for conversational recommender systems. The strategies were revealed from an analysis of a distilled corpus of dialogues collected in a movie recommendation task situation.

A behavior-based model of the strategies has been designed. The strategies lead to three different forms of dialogue behavior. The interview and direct delivery behaviors are suitable both for clarification questions in information-providing situations, as well as for preference interview in recommendation situations. Both factual information-providing and preferential interview strategies occur frequently in the studied recommendation dialogues.

We also presented an extension in the form of an indirect delivery behavior tailored for recommender engine resources. This extended behavior is based on the strategies revealed in the corpus analysis.

The resulting emergent dialogue strategy is accurately presented as strata of dialogue behavior diagrams and are effective computational artifacts that have been implemented in the CoreSong recommender system.

Acknowledgments

This work is supported by the Swedish National Graduate School for Language Technology (GSLT), and Santa Anna IT Research.

References

Derek Bridge. 2002. Towards Conversational Recommender Systems: A Dialogue Grammar Approach. In D.W.Aha, editor, *Proceedings of the Workshop in Mixed-Initiative Case-Based Reasoning, Workshop Programme at the Sixth European Conference in Case-Based Reasoning*, pages 9–22.

Robin D. Burke, Kristian J. Hammond, and Benjamin C. Young. 1997. The findme approach to assisted browsing. *IEEE Expert*, 12(4):32–40.

Robin D. Burke. 2002. Hybrid Recommender Systems: Survey and Experiments. *User Modeling and User-Adapted Interaction*, 12:331–370.

Sandra Carberry, Jennifer Chu-Carroll, and Stephanie Elzer. 1999. Constructing and Utilizing a Model of User Preferences in Collaborative Consultation Dialogues. *Computational Intelligence*, 15(3):185–217.

Giuseppe Carenini, Jocelyin Smith, and David Poole. 2003. Towards More Conversational and Collaborative Recommender Systems. In *Proceedings of the International Conference of Intelligent User Interfaces*, pages 12–18, Miami, Florida, USA.

Thomas Erickson. 2000. Making sense of computer-mediated communication (cmc): Conversations as genres, cmc systems as genre ecologies. In J. F. Nunamaker and Jr. Jr. R. H. Sprague, editors, *Proceedings of the 33rd Hawaii International Conference on System Sciences*, January.

Kristina Höök. 2000. Steps to take before IUIs become real. *Journal of Interacting with Computers*, 12(4):409–426, February.

Pontus Johansson. 2003. MadFilm - a multimodal approach to handle search and organization in a movie recommendation system. In *Proceedings of the 1st Nordic Symposium on Multimodal Communication*, pages 53–65, Helsingör, Denmark.

Staffan Larsson, Lena Santamarta, and Arne Jönsson. 2000. Using the Process of Distilling Dialogues to Understand Dialogue Systems. In *Proceedings of 6th International Conference on Spoken Language Processing (ICSLP2000/INTERSPEECH2000), Beijing, China*.

Roberto Pieraccini and Juan Huerta. 2005. Where do we go from here? Research and commercial spoken dialog systems. In *Proceedings of the 6th SIGdial Workshop on Discourse and Dialogue*, Lisbon, Portugal.

Kirsten Swearingen and Rashmi Sinha. 2002. Interaction Design for Recommender Systems. In *Interactive Systems (DIS2002)*, London, June.

Pontus Wärnestål, Lars Degerstedt, and Arne Jönsson. 2007. PCQL: A formalism for human-like preference dialogues. In *Proceedings of the 5th IJCAI Workshop on Knowledge and Reasoning in Practical Dialogue Systems*, Hyderabad, India, January.

Pontus Wärnestål. 2005. User evaluation of a conversational recommender system. In Ingrid Zukerman, Jan Alexandersson, and Arne Jönsson, editors, *Proceedings of the 4th IJCAI Workshop on Knowledge and Reasoning in Practical Dialogue Systems*, pages 32–39, Edinburgh, Scotland U.K.

III Student Papers

Linguistically Fuelled Text Similarity

Björn Andrist
KTH CSC
Stockholm
andrist@kth.se

Martin Hassel
KTH CSC
Stockholm
xmartin@kth.se

Abstract

This paper describes TEXTSIM, a system for determining the similarity between texts. Further, we show the results of a comparison between two various configurations of TEXTSIM; one with and one without any deeper linguistic analysis. To evaluate and compare the two models of TEXTSIM we used two sets of examples: a set of automatically generated examples and a set of examples acquired from two assessors. Depending on the type of documents, we found the model using linguistic analysis to perform equally well or better than the model not using linguistic analysis.

1   Introduction

Many NLP systems utilize statistics for various tasks, and in many cases it is not desirable that several instances of the same text are represented in these statistics. In order to detect similar texts a similarity system named TEXTSIM has been implemented and evaluated. We aimed to develop TEXTSIM in such a way that it mirrors the human perception of similarity between documents. Examples of such systems have successfully been implemented with the use of two mathematical notions called *resemblance* and *containment* (Broder, 1997).

Since the context in which TEXTSIM is to operate is restricted to documents written in natural language, the use of linguistic analysis is quite intuitive in an attempt to improve the technique.

In this project we have focused on texts written in Swedish. For linguistic analysis the grammar checker Granska (Domeij et al., 1999) has been utilized for *tokenizing, lemmatizing* and *part-of-speech tagging*.

Our hypothesis is that a system based on tokens, lemmas, and tags would outperform a system based solely on lexical tokens. This applies principally when comparing documents where lemmas and tags would provide additional information e.g. when documents are modified by synonyms or by tense.

2   Similarity between texts

We are interested in finding the document y in a document set D which is most similar to some document x, i.e.:

$$y = \underset{d \in D}{\mathrm{argmax}}\, sim(x, d)$$

where sim is some arbitrary function that quantifies the similarity between two documents. In order for our similarity function sim to be useful, we claim that a *transitive* relation $\mathcal{R}$ on a document set D, given by $a\mathcal{R}_x b \Leftrightarrow sim(x, a) > sim(x, b)$ where $a, b \in D$, must exist for every document $x \in D$. The transitive property of $\mathcal{R}$ implies that if $a\mathcal{R}_x b$ and $b\mathcal{R}_x c \Rightarrow a\mathcal{R}_x c$. This property was of great importance when designing TEXTSIM, because it enabled us to construct reliable training data.

2.1   Training data

In order to mirror human perception of similarity between documents the training and evaluation data

Joakim Nivre, Heiki-Jaan Kaalep, Kadri Muischnek and Mare Koit (Eds.)
NODALIDA 2007 Conference Proceedings, pp. 207–211

should preferably be comprised of examples from human subjects. Furthermore, the training data ought to be reliable and preferably easy to generate. In this context, reliable data is data from a subject who produces approximately the same results when repeating a test. We used the following method for generating training examples. Give a subject three documents: a reference document R and two other documents A and B. Thereafter the subject specifies which of the documents A or B that he/she considers to be most similar to R.

This method generated reliable data and it was also possible to automatically generate large amounts of training examples by using hypotheses about the similarity between documents.

2.2 Resemblance and containment

Resemblance and containment quantify the similarity between two documents. The degree of resemblance and containment is represented by a real number $x \in [0, 1]$. A resemblance value close to 1 indicates a high level of similarity between two documents. A containment value close to 1 indicates that one of two documents nearly contains the other document. Resemblance and containment are clearly defined in (Broder, 1997). However, a short summary is given below.

Consider a document as a sequence of tokens. A token could be a word, a punctuation mark, etc. We call a subsequence of a document a *shingle*. Further, a shingle of a specific size w will be referred to as a *w-shingle*.

Let $S(A, w)$ represent the multiset of w-shingles for a document A. Given two documents A and B and a fixed shingle size of w, the resemblance can be computed by dividing the number of w-shingles in common with the total number of distinct w-shingles:

$$r_w(A, B) = \frac{|S(A, w) \cap S(B, w)|}{|S(A, w) \cup S(B, w)|}.$$

To compute the containment of A in B, divide the number of w-shingles in common, with the number of w-shingles in A:

$$c_w(A, B) = \frac{|S(A, w) \cap S(B, w)|}{|S(A, w)|}.$$

Computing the resemblance and containment is a very time consuming task for large document sets and therefore we make an unbiased estimate of the resemblance and the containment. The estimate is performed by comparing sketches of documents, created by hashing a subset of the sequences of strings contained in the documents.

2.3 Features, weighting and learning

When comparing two documents, A and B, the following features are of interest: i) the resemblance of A and B, $r(A, B)$, which determines to what degree the documents resemble one another. ii) the containment of A in B $c(B, A)$, which is required to detect those documents which are contained in previously processed documents. iii) the containment of B in A, $c(B, A)$, which is required to detect documents which contain previously processed documents.

In order to build a system capable of learning from the training instances comprised of the three documents, R, A, and B, a perceptron (Mitchell, 1997) is used. When solely using tokens for document comparison, the perceptron needs six input nodes: $r(R, A)$, $c(R, A)$, $c(A, R)$, $r(R, B)$, $c(R, B)$, and $c(B, R)$. When using tokens, lemmas and tags for document comparison, the perceptron needs a total of 18 input nodes (six for each type). In either case, the perceptron only has one output node, where a positive output node indicates that document R is more similar to A than B.

Given a document R and a document set D, the document in D which is most similar to R can be found by iterating over D. In each iteration, the output of the perceptron determines the most similar document.

3 Evaluation of the text similarity system

We have evaluated two configurations of TEXTSIM: one based solely on tokens and one based on tokens, lemmas, and PoS tags. In order to evaluate and compare the models we used two sets of examples. First a set of automatically generated examples, and second, a set of examples acquired from two assessors. Furthermore, two evaluation experiments were conducted. The first experiment used a generated example set for training as well as testing.

The second experiment used the generated example set for training and the assessor example set for testing.

3.1 System configurations

Using TEXTSIM, two models for determining the similarity between documents were configured:

Model 1 was based on the perceptron with 6 input nodes. The input was collected from the resemblance and the containment of documents in token form.

Model 2 was based on the perceptron with 18 input nodes. The input was collected from the resemblance and the containment of documents using token, lemmas, and tags.

Both models were configured using 3-shingles where every fourth shingle formed the sketches. The learning rate and the number of maximum epochs was determined by evaluating various values of these parameters. The evaluation was conducted by means of one representative example set containing 400 examples.

3.2 Data sets

The reference documents that were used during training and testing were collected from two sources. The first was KTH News Corpus (Hassel, 2001), a digital corpus containing news articles from the web sites of widely spread Swedish newspapers. The second being the results from an experiment using Trace-it (Severinson-Eklundh & Kollberg, 1996) where a group of writers were asked to write short essays. Trace-it is a revision analysis tool that automatically stores a revision of a text after every modification of the text.

To automatically generate variants of the reference documents we substituted words with synonyms using Synlex and replaced words with misspellings using Missplel.

Missplel is a program for generating human like spelling errors (Bigert et al., 2003). It can be configured to produce a great variety of spelling errors. One can also configure Missplel to only substitute words so that the PoS tag of a word is changed and vice versa.

Synlex is an on-line Swedish dictionary of synonyms constructed by having people vote for the synonymity of possible synonym pairs (Kann & Rosell, 2005). We automatically replace a certain amount of the words in a document by synonyms in Synlex. Most likely this will lead to a lot of inappropriate replacements due to the ambiguity of many words. However, this method was deemed sufficient for generating training data.

3.3 Example types

The data used for training and evaluation was divided into the following five main types:

Type 1.a: A and B were generated from R with Missplel using the same type of errors, but with different amounts of misspelled words.

Type 1.b: A and B were generated from R with Synlex using different amounts of synonyms.

Type 2: A and B were generated from R by Missplel using different types of errors though the total sum of errors in A and B was equal.

Type 3: A was generated from R by substituting a certain amount of words with synonyms fetched from Synlex. B was generated from R with rearranged paragraphs and sentences.

Type 4: A was generated from R by introducing spelling errors with Missplel. B was generated from R by replacing a certain amount of words with synonyms from Synlex.

Type 5: A was generated from R by introducing spelling errors and/or by replacing words with synonyms from Synlex. B originated from R but was expressed in another tense.

Examples of types 1.a, 1.b, and 4 were not difficult to generate while examples of the types 2, 3, and 5 required manual editing.

3.3.1 The generated example set

The generated example set was created in order to acquire large amounts of training and evaluation data. It contained examples of the types 1.a, 1.b, and 4. Documents were sampled from the KTH News Corpus. The samples contained documents containing 200–300 tokens each. 1000 reference documents were used to generate 5850 examples.

3.3.2 The assessor example set

The assessor example set was acquired from two assessors and contained examples of all types, i.e. 1.a, 1.b, 2, 3, 4, and 5. We aimed to find test data that was both difficult to classify and reliable. This is an inconsistency since the less difficult the documents are to classify the more reliable the test data ought to be.

The test was carried out with two assessors. The examples were randomly ordered prior to giving them to the assessors. The assessors were only informed about the context in which the examples would be used. The assessors were given 25 examples, five of each main type. Each example was comprised of a document triple (R, A, B). For each example the assessors were asked to read the documents R, A, and B in order to determine which of the documents A or B that they thought was most similar to R.

3.4 Performance

The performance of the two systems was evaluated and compared with each other using the generated example set as well as the assessor example set. However, consideration should be taken to the fact that not every type of the examples in the assessor example set was included in the training examples. Preferably, all example types should be properly represented in both the training set as well as the test set.

3.4.1 Performance on generated examples

The reported error rates are the mean values of 10-fold cross-validations repeated ten times using the generated example set. Table 1 presents the error rates for each type and the overall error rate when evaluating the entire example set.

Type	Model 1	Model 2	Examples
Type 1.a	14.5%	13.3%	1970
Type 1.b	0.4%	0.4%	1940
Type 4	29.4%	5.6%	1940
All types	14.2%	8.0%	5850

Table 1: Error rates for each type of text for Model 1 (tokens) and Model 2 (tokens, lemmas and PoS tags) respectively.

The most significant difference between Model 1 and Model 2 appears in the examples of Type 4. This corresponds well with our hypothesis. Model 1 has shown not to be efficient in separating document pairs with the same amount of token overlap. Further, the differences in performance between Model 1 and Model 2 are negligible on the examples of types 1 and 2. Changes that have been initiated in the examples of types 1 and 2 are mirrored equally in the token representation, the lemma representation and the tag representation of the documents. Thus the tags and lemmas are superfluous and do not improve the performance of Model 2.

The reason for the substantial differences between Type 1 and Type 2 is a result of the more accurate data obtained from the method using Synlex compared to the method using Missplel. However, our attention is not drawn to the differences in values between the various types but to the differences between Models 1 and 2.

Finally, a significant difference between Models 1 and 2 was apparent when using the entire set of generated examples.

3.4.2 Performance on the assessor example set

Model 1 and Model 2 were trained on the generated example set and thereafter compared with the assessors perception of similarity. The assessors agreed on 19 of the 25 examples. As in the evaluation using the generated example set our attention is drawn to the differences between Models 1 and 2, and not the absolute error rates. By using the examples that the assessors agreed upon, the error rate for Model 1 is 6/19 while the error rate on Model 2 is 4/19.

Type	Assessors	Model 1	Model 2
Type 1	4/5	1	0
Type 2	5/5	1	1
Type 3	1/5	0	0
Type 4	5/5	2	0
Type 5	4/5	2	3
Total	19/25	6	4

Table 2: The number of errors for each type of text for Model 1 and Model 2 respectively. The assessors column indicates the agreement between the assessors.

4 Conclusions

The system using tokens, lemmas, and PoS tags outperformed the system using only tokens, both when evaluation was performed on the generated example set and the examples acquired from assessors. However, this is at the cost of performance with respect to memory and speed. The most obvious differences between the systems appeared on documents with the same amount of token overlap but with different types of variations.

The evaluation was performed on a small amount of assessor examples. A more reliable method would have been to acquire a substantially larger amount of assessor examples in order to facilitate the performance of a stratified k-fold cross-validation on the assessor examples without the generated example set.

References

J. Bigert, L. Ericson, and A. Solis. 2003. Missplel and AutoEval: Two generic tools for automatic evaluation. *Proc. of NODALIDA 2003.*

A. Z. Broder. 1997. On the resemblance and containment of documents. In *Compression and Complexity of Sequences (SEQUENCES 97)*, 21–29. IEEE Computer Society, 1998.

R. Domeij, O. Knutsson, J. Carlberger, and V. Kann. 1999. Granska – an efficient hybrid system for Swedish grammar checking. *Proc. of NODALIDA 1999.*

M. Hassel. 2001. Automatic construction of a Swedish news corpus. *Proc. of NODALIDA 2001.*

V. Kann and M. Rosell. 2005. Free Construction of a Free Swedish Dictionary of Synonyms. *Proc. of NODALIDA 2005.*

T. Mitchell. 1997. *Machine Learning.* McGraw Hill.

K. Severinson-Eklundh, P. Kollberg. 1996. A computer tool and framework for analysing on-line revisions. *Levy, C. M. and Ransdell, S. (eds), The science of writing: Theories, Methods, Individual Differences, and Applications, 163–188, Lawrence Erlbaum Ass.*

Using Parallel Corpora to Create a Greek-English Dictionary with Uplug

Konstantinos Charitakis

Department of Computer and Systems Sciences (DSV)

KTH-Stockholm University

164 40 Kista

Stockholm, Sweden

`kcha@kth.se`

Abstract

This paper presents the construction of a Greek-English bilingual dictionary from parallel corpora that were created manually by collecting documents retrieved from the Internet. The parallel corpora processing was performed by the Uplug word alignment system without the use of language specific information. A sample was extracted from the population of suggested translations and was included in questionnaires that were sent out to Greek-English speakers who evaluated the sample based on the quality of the translation pairs. For the suggested translation pairs of the sample belonging to the stratum with the higher frequency of occurrence, 67.11% correct translations were achieved. With an overall 50.63% of correct translations of the sample, the results were promising considering the minimal optimisation of the corpus and the differences between the two languages.

1 Introduction

Due to the diversity of the known languages and the vast amount of resources required to produce a bilingual dictionary, people have turned their efforts towards the automation of the task. The emergence of statistical methods has shown promising results and they have given results accurate enough, with less effort and resources required that could be used for the task of automated dictionary extraction (Brown et al., 1990). Parallel corpora, which are texts aligned together with their translation in one or more languages, are extensively used in statistical translation methods as they contain a vast amount of bilingual lexical information (Veronis, 2000). After the emergence of statistical translation methods many corpora processing systems and tools have been implemented and have been applied to parallel corpora of most of the popular natural languages. However there are not many projects on automated creation of a dictionary between the Greek and English language pair.

Similar work of extraction of Greek-English dictionary was performed by Piperidis et al. (1997; 2005), although in both cases the approach was different as it employed statistical techniques coupled with linguistic information for better results and it was applied on a corpus in software domain and on a corpus consisting of official EU documents respectively.

Related work with the use of the same system is the work described by Dalianis et al. (2007) where they used Uplug on Scandinavian and English parallel corpora and obtained 71% and 93% for precision and recall respectively, for Swedish-English dictionaries.

The primary focus of this paper is on the extraction and evaluation of a Greek-English dictionary created from parallel corpora using the Uplug system. The task was performed without the use of linguistic information and without the use of optimised sentence aligned corpora for the Greek-English language pair.

2 Dictionary Extraction and Evaluation

2.1 The Uplug System

For the processing of the corpora, the Uplug word alignment system was used. Uplug origins from a project in Uppsala University and provides a collection of tools for linguistic corpus processing, word alignment and term extraction from parallel corpora (Tiedemann, 1999).

Joakim Nivre, Heiki-Jaan Kaalep, Kadri Muischnek and Mare Koit (Eds.)

NODALIDA 2007 Conference Proceedings, pp. 212–215

Uplug uses language-specific pre-processing modules if available. In other case Uplug uses the basic pre-processing modules that run the general tokenizer, the sentence splitter and add simple XML markup.

The word aligner implemented in the Uplug system is the *Clue Aligner* which is based on the combination of word alignment clues. The idea is that features like frequency, part-of-speech, parsing and word form, together with similarity and frequency measures are taken into account and are considered as association clues between words. All these association clues are then combined together in order to find links between words in the source and target languages (Tiedemann, 2003). Uplug uses the word Clue Aligner to iterative size reduction and alignment of the corpora.

2.2 Collection of Parallel Corpora

There are many available public corpora over the web. One of the most interesting attempts is the OPUS corpus (Tiedemann and Nygaard, 2004). However the corpora provided in most cases are already aligned, most often at sentence level and tagged using XML format. There were concerns about the optimised corpora available, in the way that optimised corpora would give optimised results while our intention was to work with as realistic input elements as possible. In order to test the full potential of the Uplug system including its sentence alignment process, it was thought necessary the use of raw text parallel corpora. Therefore a manually created corpus was used.

The English and Greek translated documents included in the corpus were mainly collected from the web site of the European Union.

All web documents were stripped from their HTML format and were included in plain unformatted text in one single text source file. Documents available in PDF format had to be included also in unformatted text in the text source file, after they have been manually aligned at document and paragraph level to their original state.

Corpus	Size	Words	Unique words
English	1.23 MB	196,048	10,450
Greek	2.46 MB	204,043	18,117

Table 1. Characteristics of parallel corpora.

The final bilingual corpus created constituted the Greek text, which contained 204,043 words, and the English text which contained 196,048 words. The Greek text contained 18,117 different

unique words while the English text 10,450 unique words (see Table 1 above).

2.3 Processing of Parallel Corpora

All processes after the input of the parallel corpora from pre-processing to dictionary extraction were performed automatically by Uplug. The result of the sentence alignment was used as is, without any corrections. The result was neither filtered nor altered. Pre-processing of the parallel corpora was performed using the basic preprocessing modules due to lack of language specific tools for the Greek language. Word alignment was performed by the Clue Aligner.

2.4 Extraction of Sample Data

The system extracted many translation pairs with frequency of occurrence (f) less than three (f=2 and f=1). These translations were not considered worth evaluating as they were not containing any sign of consistency. The majority of these translations were incorrect although there are exceptions of a few correct ones.

For the evaluation of the results a sample of the output data was used. The sample was extracted using the stratified sampling method. In this method the population is divided into non overlapping categories (stratums). Then random sampling is used to select a sufficient number of elements from each stratum.

The results had to be filtered and only the translation pairs with frequency of occurrence (f) above a threshold included in the evaluation, in order to avoid evaluation of pairs with occurrence that might be based on chances. That threshold was decided to be a frequency of occurrence above or equal to three (f≥3). Therefore translation pairs with frequency of occurrence less than three were excluded from the process of extraction of the sample and evaluation.

Following this method the population of translation pairs with frequency of occurrence above three was divided in five stratums. The five stratums consisted of pairs with frequency of occurrence:

- f equal to 3 (f=3)
- f equal to 4 (f=4)
- f equal to 5 (f=5)
- f equal to 6 and up to 10 ($6 \leq f < 11$)
- f equal to 11 and up to maximum ($11 \leq f$)

Then a random sample of approximately 100 suggested translation pairs from each stratum was drawn and five different tables were created. Each table contained the translation pairs that were collected randomly from one of the five categories mentioned earlier.

The total number of pairs with frequency of occurrence above or equal to three ($f \geq 3$) was 1,276 pairs and 498 of them comprised the sample included in the questionnaires.

2.5 Evaluation of Results

There are different ways to evaluate extracted dictionaries. Some of the most common metrics used are precision and recall calculations. However, the use of the above metrics is difficult when the alignments are not just one-to-one (Merkel and Ahrenberg, 1998) like it happens in the extracted dictionary as a result of this project. Therefore the evaluation method used was based on the judgment of fluent Greek-English speakers on the quality of extracted translation pairs. This is a quite common way to evaluate automatically created bilingual dictionaries (Sjöbergh, 2005).

The results of the dictionary were evaluated by classifying suggested translation pairs of the sample into categories depending on their translation quality. It was performed by 12 fluent Greek-English speakers who classified each translation pair of the sample according to one of the five following choices.

1. Accurate – suggested translation is an accurate translation of the source word.
2. Somewhat correct – correct but not accurate translation where someone will understand the meaning of the original word.
3. Undecided – person evaluating is undecided or not familiar with a term.
4. Somewhat incorrect – suggested translation is not correct but can still be useful for a reader to understand the general meaning of a word in a text.
5. Wrong – suggested translation is just plain wrong.

The evaluation rules were left open and the tables containing the randomly collected pairs from the respective stratums were included in the questionnaire in random order regarding the frequency of occurrence, so the evaluation would be as unbiased as possible and reviewers would not realise a pattern in the quality of the translation pairs.

2.6 Results

The results of the analysis of the questionnaires are given in the Tables 2 and 3 below.

	$11 \leq f$ (%)	$6 \leq f < 11$ (%)	$f=5$ (%)	$f=4$ (%)	$f=3$ (%)
Accurate	42.98	43.27	30.51	23.29	20.06
Somewhat Correct	24.12	19.69	18.72	16.21	14.29
Undecided	2.08	2.28	2.25	1.70	1.58
Somewhat Incorrect	7.84	8.79	10.70	10.92	13.04
Wrong	22.95	25.95	37.79	47.86	51.00

Table 2. Analytical distribution of the evaluation results for each stratum of the sample.

The sum of the percentages of the categories "Accurate" (42.98%) and "Somewhat correct" (24.12%) from the stratum of the sample with the higher frequency ($11 \leq f$) of occurrence is a total of 67.10% of correct translations. Based on the results presented in table 2 above, the overall distribution of the suggested translations based on their quality is given in Table 3 bellow.

	Average (%)
Accurate	32.02 %
Somewhat Correct	18.61 %
Undecided	1.98 %
Somewhat Incorrect	10.26 %
Wrong	37.11 %

Table 3. Overall distribution of translations of the extracted sample based on their quality.

Table 3 contains the calculation of the average of each row from table 2. It shows the average for each category (accurate, somewhat correct, etc.) for all stratums ($11 \leq f$, $6 \leq f < 11$ etc.).

Therefore the correct translations could be summed up to 50.63% of the extracted sample of suggested translations, calculated by adding the percentages of categories "Accurate" (32.02%) and "Somewhat correct" (18.61%).

Table 4 below contains some random examples of suggested translations as appeared in the final output.

96 Commission	Επιτροπή
58 may	μπορεί
4 ensure	εξασφαλίζει

Table 4. Random examples of the suggested translations with their frequency of occurrence.

3   Conclusion

The objective of the project was to use parallel corpora for automated extraction of a bilingual Greek-English dictionary using the Uplug system without the use of linguistic information. The corpora used contained documents in English and Greek retrieved from the Web. The resulted translations of the dictionary were evaluated by Greek-English speakers in order to assess the quality of the suggested translations.

For the suggested translation pairs of the sample belonging to the stratum with the higher frequency (f >11) of occurrence, 67.10% correct translations were achieved.

It was interesting to notice that characteristics such as the quality and the frequency of occurrence of translation pairs are directly proportional (see table 2). In other words one can notice a decrease of the percentage of correct translations as the frequency of occurrence of translation pairs decreases and on the other hand one can notice an increase of the percentage of wrong translations as the frequency of occurrence decreases.

This implies that larger corpora with a bigger collection of documents in the same domain that use the same vocabulary and have a high frequency of usage of the same words, are more appropriate in order to achieve better word alignment quality.

From the analysis of the evaluation of the extracted dictionary sample, it can be concluded that 50.63% of accurate and correct translations has been achieved. This is a respectful percentage of correct translations if someone considers the minimal optimisation of the corpora used, the relatively small size of corpora (400,091 words) and the difference in morphology between the language pair. Of course the different alphabet used by the two languages is also an issue, having in mind that String Similarity measures are used to identify translation equivalents.

Acknowledgments

Many thanks to associate professor Hercules Dalianis for his guidance and enthusiastic supervision and also special thanks to Martin Rimka for introducing me to Uplug.

References

F. Peter Brown, John Cocke, A. Stephen Della-Pietra, J. Vincent Della-Pietra, Frederick Jelinek, D. John Lafferty, L. Robert Mercer and S. Paul Roossin. 1990. *A Statistical Approach to Machine Translation*. Computational Linguistics, 16(2):79-85.

Hercules Dalianis, Martin Rimka and Viggo Kann. 2007. TvärSök - Using Uplug and Site-Seeker to construct a cross language search engine for Scandinavian. Presented at the Workshop of the Nordisk Netordbog, Copenhagen, Denmark, April 26, 2007

Magnus Merkel and Lars Ahrenberg. 1998. *Evaluating Word Alignment Systems. PLUG report*. Department of Computer and Information Science, Linköping university, Sweden.

Stelios Piperidis, Sotiris Boutsis and Iason Demiros. 1997. *Automatic translation lexicon generation from multilingual texts*. In Workshop on Multilinguality in the Software Industry: the AI Contribution (MULSAIC'97), In 15th International Joint Conference on Artificial Intelligence (IJCAI'97), (pp 57-62). Nagoya, Japan.

Stelios Piperidis, Panagiotis Dimitrakis and Irene Balta. 2005. *Lexical Transfer Selection Using Annotated Parallel Corpora*. In Fifth International Conference on Recent Advances in Natural Language Processing – RANLP 2005, 25 September 2005, Borovets, Bulgaria.

Jonas Sjöbergh. 2005. *Creating a free digital Japanese-Swedish lexicon*. In proceedings of PACLING '05, (pp 296-300). Meisei University, Japan.

Jörg Tiedemann. 1999. *Uplug - a modular corpus tool for parallel corpora*. In the Parallel Corpus Symposium (PKS99). Uppsala University, Sweden.

Jörg Tiedemann. 2003. *Combining clues for word alignment*. In Proceedings of the 10th Conference of the European Chapter of the ACL (EACL03) Budapest, Hungary.

Jörg Tiedemann and Lars Nygaard. 2004. *The OPUS corpus - parallel & free*. In Proceedings of the 4th International Conference on Language Resources and Evaluation (LREC'04). Lisbon, Portugal.

Jean Veronis. 2000. *From the Rosetta stone to the information society: A survey of parallel text processing*. Parallel Text Processing, Jean Veronis (editor), Kluwer Academic Publishers, pp. 1-25.

Unmediated Data-Oriented Generation

Dave Cochran
Cognitive Systems Group
School of Computer Science
University of St. Andrews
Fife, KY16 9SX, Scotland
davec@cs.st-andrews.ac.uk

Abstract

We present the first extension of the Data-Oriented Parsing paradigm (Bod 1998a) to Natural Language Generation: Unmediated Data-Oriented Generation, or UDOG. It is "unmediated" because instead of using a logic-like amodal representation of meaning as a basis for semantics (Van den Berg *et al* 1994), it exploits direct connections between exemplars in linguistic and non-linguistic (in this case visual) modalities as the basis for meaning.

1   Introduction

Since Data-Oriented Parsing (DOP) was first proposed (Scha 1990) and implemented (Bod 1992) as a method for statistical parsing by directly exploiting the statistical regularities present in a training corpus without requiring any abstract representations to be generated, no equivalent system for language generation has been developed. This paper presents the first Data-Oriented Generation algorithm: Unmediated Data-Oriented Generation, or UDOG. Whereas previous attempts to represent meaning in DOP models have relied on node-label annotations in a formal language, such as First Order Predicate Logic (Bod *et al* 1996), or the OVIS Update Language (Veldhuijzen van Zanten 1996; Bod 1998b) to provide amodal representations of meaning, UDOG exploits direct connections between exemplars in linguistic and non-linguistic (in

this case visual) modalities as the basis for meaning.

The model presented here offers a very simple first pass at UDOG, using a toy corpus and an extremely simple set of visual stimuli consisting of one-dimensional arrangements of lines and dots. Section 2 gives background information on the DOP paradigm, and Section 3 describes the task the present implementation of UDOG was designed to perform. The algorithm itself is described in Section 4, and the evaluation criteria are described and evaluation results given in Section 5. In Section 6, some cognitive implications of the results are considered and the overall significance of the model is assessed.

2   Background

2.1   Data-Oriented Parsing

The simplest manifestation of DOP is DOP1, as described in Bod (1998a pp 12-23 and 40-50), though more sophisticated versions exist. The parser uses a large parsed corpus divided into a training corpus and a smaller corpus against which the parser is tested. The parser breaks every tree in the training corpus down into all its possible subtrees, according to the wellformedness rules below.

- Every subtree must be of at least depth 1.

- Every connection must have a node on either end.

- Sister relationships must be preserved.

Joakim Nivre, Heiki-Jaan Kaalep, Kadri Muischnek and Mare Koit (Eds.)
NODALIDA 2007 Conference Proceedings, pp. 216–223

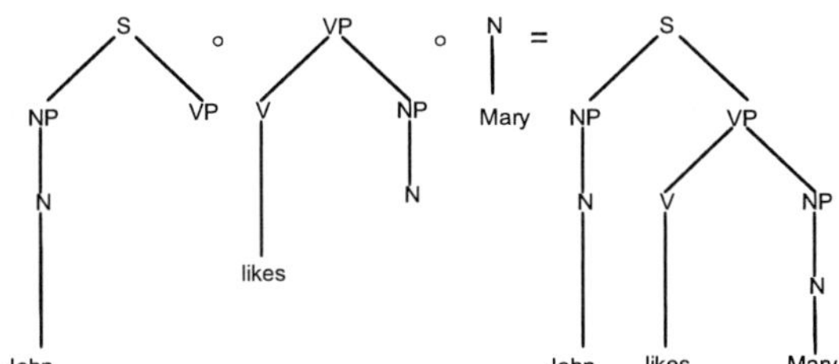

Figure 1: A derivation of "John likes Mary".
"∘" is the tree-substitution operator.

The parser is given test corpus strings and builds up new parse-trees for these using fragments of arbitrary depth extracted from the training corpus, starting with a fragment with an S-node at the top, and then, for each nonterminal leaf-node, working rightwards, substituting in additional subtrees, the topmost node of which must carry the same label as the node to be substituted. (see fig. 1).

In DOP research it is necessary to distinguish between *parses* and *derivations*. A parse is the tree structure expressed over a string, and a derivation is the particular sequence of subtree substitutions by which it was constructed. When parsing with probabilistic context-free grammars (PCFG's, see Manning and Schütze (1999, pp.381-405). Note that a PCFG is equivalent to a DOP grammar in which subtree depth has been restricted to 1), there is a one-to-one mapping between parses and derivations, because all non-terminal nodes *must* be substitution sites. In DOP, subtrees can be of any depth, and so in any given derivation, any subset of the non-terminal nodes could have been substitution sites, while the remainder will not have been. As such, if a parse contains N many non-terminal nodes, it will have 2^N many derivations.

For each subtree substitution t, its probability $P(t)$ is calculated as its total frequency of occurrence $|t|$ in the training corpus over the summed corpus frequency of subtrees with the same root node; $P(t) = |t| / \Sigma_{\{t':r(t')=r(t)\}}|t'|$, where $r(t)$ and $r(t')$ are the node-labels on the root-nodes of subtrees t and t'. The probability of a derivation is the product of the probabilities of its subtrees, $P(t_1 \circ \dots \circ t_n) = \Pi_i P(t_i)$: And the probability of a parse T is the sum of the probabilities of its possible derivations D, $P(T) = \Sigma_{\{D:D\ derives\ T\}} P(D)$.

The output of the parser is, in theory, the most probable parse. In practice, there are issues of computational complexity that prevent this from being calculated directly; instead, Monte-Carlo sampling may be employed to approximate the most probable parse (Bod 1993)

Bod (1998a p.54) reports accuracies of 85% on the ATIS[1] corpus for DOP1. Bod (2005) reports accuracies of 91.1% for a more sophisticated form of DOP, DOP+.

3   The Task

3.1   Training Data

UDOG differs from existing DOP algorithms in that the items in the training data are not single trees over a string, but *pairs* of trees, one over a linguistic string, the other over content in some other cognitive modality, connected at particular nodes by crossmodal linkages. Figure 2 shows an example of a tree pair used in the present simulations: both the visual and verbal content are annotated with labeled tree-structures, and additionally a few of the crossmodals are shown.

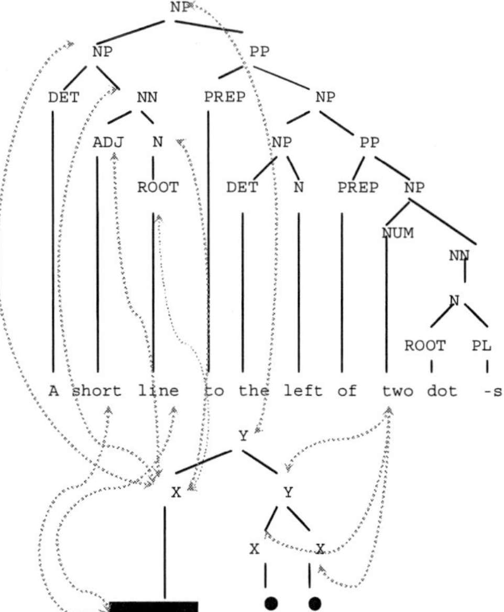

Figure 2: Paired image and description trees, with crossmodal connections; note that some crossmodals have been omitted for clarity.

A training corpus of image-description pairs such as this was generated from templates using a script, "CorpusMonkey". CorpusMonkey generated all 120 possibilities for images consisting of either one group of one, two or three dots, dashes, short lines or long lines[2], paired with a description of the form "X", "two X-s" or "three X-s"; or two such groups, provided each group is comprised of different types of basic object, paired with descriptions of either the form "X to the left of Y", or "Y to the right of X". Which form of description was employed was selected at random, with equal probabilities.

3.2   Tests

Two tests were used to evaluate UDOG's performance. The General Test was run in six parts; the CorpusMonkey training data was divided into six blocks, and in each part a different block was selected to be test data, while the rest was used as training data, so that it was only ever tested on unseen data. The test data was presented as unparsed visual stimuli alone, of which the system was required to produce descriptions. In the second test, the Wug Test, the complete CorpusMonkey corpus was presented, plus twelve identical tokens of the form shown in Figure 3[3], introducing a new type of object (a seven-pixel line) and a new vocabulary item, a "wug".

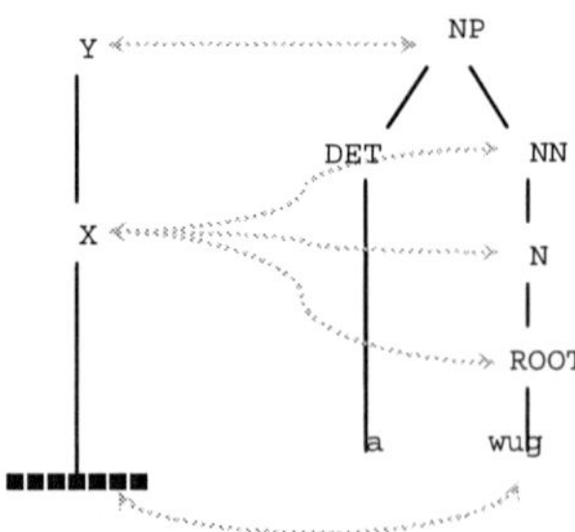

Figure 3: A novel item of vocabulary

The system was then tested using images comprising a group of one, two, or three wugs to the left or right of one, two or three dots, dashes, short lines or long lines. Thus, UDOG was required to extract syntactic patterns from the CorpusMonkey data, and redeploy them with a vocabulary item that it had not encountered in such contexts; this was therefore A direct test of UDOG's ability to generalize syntactic patterns beyond the training data.

4   The UDOG algorithm

4.1   Substitutions

Like DOP1, UDOG derivations are constructed from arbitrary-depth fragments extracted from the training data; unlike DOP, the fragments are in fact groups of crossmodally connected subtrees (exactly one non-linguistic (visual) and one or more linguistic), which, if possible, should be connected at their root nodes, and correspondingly, the substitution sites are not single nodes, but groups of nodes, (again, one non-linguistic and one or more linguistic), which should also, if possible, be crossmodally connected.

Thus, at each step of the derivation, exactly one substitution site on the image tree is chosen at random; if this substitution site is crossmodally connected to any of the potential substitution sites on the verbal tree[4], it can in theory substitute subtrees at *all* of these sites. The wellformedness criteria are as follows:

1) All of the component unimodal subtrees are well-formed by the normal standards of DOP1.
2) All unimodal subtrees should originate from the same tree-pair P.
3) Each verbal subtree should contain only nodes which either:
   a) Have no crossmodal connections at all, or
   b) Have crossmodal connections, at least one of which is to a node in the visual subtree.
4) The root node of each verbal subtree should be crossmodally connected to the root node of the visual subtree.

---

[2] A dot was always a single pixel, a dash was a three-pixel line, a short line five pixels, and a long line ten.

[3] The decision to use twelve tokens was arbitrary, but it was felt that in order to cut down the noise in the Monte Carlo sample, the prevalence of wugs in the corpus should be in the same order of magnitude as that of other basic objects. As it was there were a quarter as many wugs as any other basic object.

[4] In the case of the first substitution in a derivation, a substitution site of a crossmodally connected NP node and Y node is assumed. All tree pairs in the training data are rooted in crossmodally connected NP and Y nodes.

5) No root node of a verbal subtree can be an ancestor or descendant of the root node of any other: that is to say, if nodes n_1 and n_2 are in an ancestor-descendant relationship *in the verbal tree W of the originating corpus tree-pair*, they cannot both be selected to be the head-nodes of subtrees in the same bimodal subtree.
6) The set of verbal subtrees in a well-formed bimodal subtree cannot be a proper subset of the set of verbal subtrees in any other well-formed subtree.
7) For each node-label L represented x many times in the set of possible substitution sites, there should be no more than x many verbal subtrees in the bimodal subtree with root-nodes labelled L.

The algorithm exhaustively checks all possible subsets of the set of nodes in the verbal tree connected to the root node of the visual subtree for validity, according to the standards of (5), (6) and (7). A subset is chosen at random, at a probability modelled by the equation:

$$P(S) = \frac{\sum_{node_i \in S} subtrees_{node_i}}{\sum_{S_i \in V} \sum_{node_j \in S_i} subtrees_{node_j}} \quad (1)$$

Where S and S_i are sets of nodes, V is the set of valid sets of nodes according to criteria (5), (6) and (7) above, and $subtrees_{node_x}$ is the total number of subtrees rooted in $node_x$. The total number of subtrees of any node *node* can be found using equation 2:

$$subtrees_{node} = \prod_{\{node_i : node = mother(node_i)\}} (subtrees_{node_i} + 1) \quad (2)$$

For each node n in the chosen set, a subtree t for which $n = root(t)$ is chosen at a probability modeled by equation 3 below:

$$P(t) = \frac{1}{subtrees_{t(root)}} \quad (3)$$

If it is either not possible to find a substitution site, or a bimodal subtree, that meets the above criteria, the system backs off to a simpler system, whereby a well-formed exemplar fragment comprises one visual and one verbal tree, and must otherwise only meet criteria (1)-(3) of the normal wellformedness criteria.

4.2 From derivations to final outputs

Substitutions continue until *either* the visual *or* the verbal tree is completed: that is to say, has no non-terminal leaf nodes. There is no guarantee that the two trees will be completed together, and indeed, since the verbal trees in the training data have far more nodes than the visual trees, it almost always happens that the visual tree is completed first. Thus, because of the high prevalence of incomplete verbal trees in the output from derivations, instead of simply gathering the outputs of many derivations and polling them as a Monte-Carlo set for the most frequent output, an algorithm, the details of which are not relevant here, was used to find the largest unifiable subset of the trees in the sample. Two trees are taken to be unifiable if there is at least one possible (not necessarily complete) tree of which both trees are co-racinous[5] legal subtrees according to the unimodal wellformedness criteria of DOP1. The unification of the two trees, then, is the smallest tree that meets this description, if any tree can. Two unifiable trees and their unification are shown in Figure 4. The system's output, then, is the unification of the largest unifiable subset of the sample.

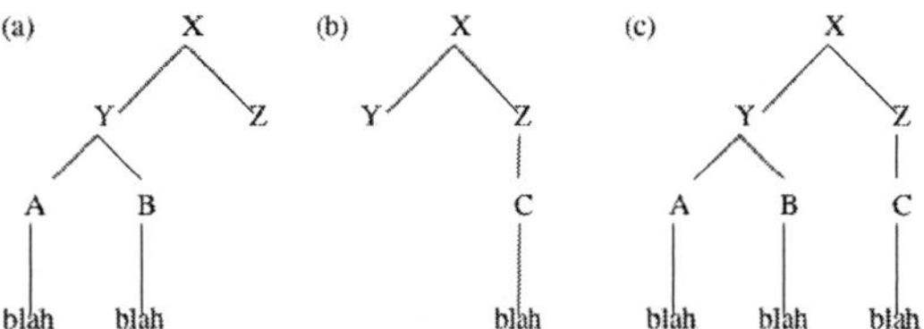

Figure 4: two unifiable trees (a, b) and their unification, (c)

The working assumption here is that, although the trees output by UDOG are incomplete, they will tend, if the algorithm is working, to be fragments of correct outputs: therefore unifying them allows complete (or at least, closer to complete) trees to be made. If fragments of correct trees are indeed the most frequent output, the largest unifiable set should unify into a correct complete output

4.3 Naïve UDOG

For comparison, a naïve version of the algorithm was also tested; this version used the "backoff" behaviour described at the end of §4.1 as it's de-

---

[5] Subtrees t^1 and t^2 are co-racinous iff $root(t^1) \equiv root(t^2)$.

fault behaviour. Thus the full version of UDOG ("Smart" UDOG) used wellformedness criteria (4)-(7) as a way of "binding" meaningfully related subparts of paired trees, whereas Naïve UDOG relies on frequency of co-occurrence alone.

5   Results and Discussion

5.1   Evaluating the outputs

In both tests the output for each stimulus of both models was manually scored as the average of four measures: Object (O), Number (N), Relation (R) and Grammaticality (G). The measures used are tabulated in Table 1. All measures were taken as percentages.

(O)	Judged on the identification of the correct type or types of basic object[6] in the stimulus. Because, in some outputs, the number of types named did not match with the number of types present in the stimulus, this was judged as an F1-score: that is to say, as the harmonic mean[7] of precision (the proportion of correct elements in the output) and recall (the proportion of elements in the input correctly named in the output).
(N)	Judged according to whether the named objects were correctly numbered. Again, this was expressed as an F1-score.
(R)	If the image contained only one group of same-type basic objects, or a single basic object, full marks on this measure were awarded for naming only one object type, and no "to the left of" or "to the right of" term, and zero marks are awarded otherwise. If two types of basic object are present in the stimulus, full marks are awarded if only the two types are named and the left/right relationship between them is correctly described. Partial marks are given if a correct relationship description is present but more than two tokens of object-

(G)	A purely subjective measure of grammaticality and intelligibility.

group namings are present, because in this case the system has in such a case had extra chances to get it right.

Table 1: scoring criteria

5.2   General Test

The results of the general test on both systems are summarised in Table 2 below.

	O	N	R	G	Overall
Naïve	54.48 %	33.88 %	22.70 %	28.42 %	36.62%
Smart	76.51 %	71.70 %	53.99 %	57.60 %	68.52%

Table 2: Performances of the Naïve and Smart-UDOG systems on the general test.

Eyeballing the data, the overwhelming impression is that the smart system far outperforms the naïve system on all measures; overall, the smart performance is almost double the naïve, and on individual measures the smart system more than doubles the naïve score on all counts except Object, where it is still approximately 40% better. It is notable that Object is the only metric for the most part not dependent on word-ordering considerations. It is also of interest that, in comparing the three non-subjective scoring criteria (Object, Number and Relation), for both systems, the easiest, Object, was that which depended on the shortest-distance syntactic/semantic relations (between noun and adjective within an NN group, if any syntactic relation was present at all), and the hardest was that which depended on the longest-distance syntactic/semantic relationship, spanning the whole noun phrase. A 2x4 mixed-design ANOVA was conducted to test the significance of the differences in Table 3.

	F	Sig. at p
System	67.71	<0.001
System * Scoring Criterion	11.31	<0.001
Scoring Criterion	93.79	<0.001

Table 3: 2x4 mixed design ANOVA

The differences between the two systems, four scoring criteria, and their interaction, were all found to be highly significant at p <0.001. This finding was investigated in more detail, comparing

---

[6] "Dot", "dash", etc...

[7] The harmonic mean or x and y is given by the equation

$$M = \frac{2xy}{x + y}$$

the individual scoring criteria (within systems) using pairwise t-tests (Table 4) and the systems performance on each scoring criterion individually using independent samples t-tests (Table 5).

		t	Sig. at p
Naïve	O–N	5.92	<0.001
	O-R	10.88	<0.001
	O-G	9.15	<0.001
	N-R	6.31	<0.001
	N-G	5.10	<0.001
	R-G	-2.62	0.01
Smart	O-N	-5.14	<0.001
	O-R	6.51	<0.001
	O-G	5.45	<0.001
	N-R	9.07	<0.001
	N-G	8.84	<0.001
	R-G	-1.31	0.193

Table 4: Pairwise t-tests for significance of difference between types of measure

	t	Sig. at p
O	7.143	<0.001
N	11.124	<0.001
R	5.656	<0.001
G	5.489	<0.001

Table 5: Independent samples t-tests, for significance of difference between systems

All differences between types of measure proved highly significant, at p<0.001, except for between Relation and Grammaticality, which remains significant at p<0.05 for Naïve UDOG, and does not attain significance for Smart-UDOG. All these results were double-checked using non-parametric tests (Friedman tests for the pairwise t-tests, a Kruskal-Wallis test for the independent samples t-test).

5.3   Wug Test

The results of the Wug test on both systems are summarised in Table 6 below

	O	N	R	G	Overall
Naïve	50.65%	29.31%	8.01%	14.54%	25.62%
Smart	79.45%	94.62%	69.06%	66.00%	77.28%

Table 6: Results from the Wugs test

Eyeballing the data, the difference between the two systems seems to be even more marked, most notably in Relation, where Naïve UDOG performs at a fraction of its score on the general test, whereas Smart-UDOG has actually improved. Indeed, the pattern is found across the board, that Naïve UDOG becomes less accurate faced with a vocabulary item for which it has no context, whereas Smart-UDOG performs better than in the general test.

Theoretically speaking, what is of greatest interest here is effect of the "wug" condition on performance, as compared to the general test (or, here, the "no-wug" condition), in relation to the Relation score, since the binding of elements into correct semantic relations was quite explicitly what the smart system was formulated to do, and to the Overall score. A 72-item random sample was taken at random from the general test dataset, so that 2x2 mixed ANOVAs could be performed, between "system" and "wugs/no-wugs", for the Relation score (Table 7), and the Overall score (Table 8).

	F	Sig. at p
System	237.861	<0.001
System * Wugs	6.422	0.12
Wugs	0.483	0.488

Table 7: 2x2 mixed design ANOVA on Overall scores

	F	Sig. at p
System	124.054	<0.001
System * Wugs	0.194	0.047
Wugs	93.79	0.66

Table 8: 2x2 mixed design ANOVA on Relation scores

No main effect, in either case, was found for Wugs, which is unsurprising given that the difference between wugs and no-wugs in the two systems pull in opposite directions. In both cases, significant interaction effects were found for System and Wugs, at p<0.05, and highly significant results were found for System, at p<0.001. The effect of the Wugs condition was investigated in greater detail using independent t-tests (Table 9).

		t	Sig. at p
Rela-tion	Naïve	3.446	0.01
	Smart	-2.217	0.028
Overall	Naïve	3.15	0.002
	Smart	168.395	0.027

Table 9: independent t-tests on the effect of the "wugs" condition on relation scores and overall scores for both models.

In all cases, the effect of the Wugs parameter is found to be significant at $p < 0.05$. It is no surprise that the naïve version suffered in the wug test; it relies wholly on the contexts given in exemplars to bind syntactic elements within semantic relations, which it was expressly denied in the wug test. The surprising result is that the improvement in performance in Smart-UDOG also proved significant.

6 Discussion & Conclusions

First of all, Smart-UDOG shows, for the first time, that the Data-Oriented approach can be applied to generation tasks, and that a Data-Oriented model can integrate more than one cognitive modality.

6.1 Why did Wugs *help* Smart UDOG?

One outcome of the tests performed on the two UDOG systems was that Smart UDOG would actually perform better on the Wug Test than on the General Test; I had instead expected that it would either show no significant effect, or that its performance would be decremented, either to the same degree as the Naïve system, indicating that the "Smart" welformedness conditions should be seen as a technological fix for sparse data, or to a significantly less degree, indicating that they should be seen as essential to the success of the algorithm. However, it is easy to figure out just how the Wug condition helped Smart-UDOG along. One common type of error is illustrated in a real example taken from Smart-UDOG's performance on the General Test:

Input = ■■■■■　　■　　■　　■
Output = a dot *PL* to the right *PREP* a short line to the line of two *NN*

A correct output here would have been "Three dots to the right of a short line" or "A short line to the left of three dots".

What has happened here is that structure for the relation expression has been imported into the output from two separate sources: one coming with material contributing to the description of the single short line, the other coming with the what I presume to be an abortive attempt at describing two of the three dots. In both cases, the object-and-number describing material came bound up with relation-describing material, and these together caused a confused and ill-formed output. In the Wug Test, the description of the wug cannot come with such extraneous material, since the only exemplars associating the word "wug" with images of wugs contain nothing more than a single wug, described as "a wug" (see Figure 3).

This suggests an interesting hypothesis regarding First Language Acquisition, to be followed up if further work on UDOG proves successful. Smart-UDOG benefits notably from having access to isolated examples of words paired with their referents. Bates *et al* (1988) outline a "two-strand" theory of individual differences in First Language Acquisition, wherein two main learning strategies employed by infant language learners: "Strand two" is characterised by slow vocabulary growth and a tendency towards holophrases in which multi-word utterances are used as unanalysed wholes, but of greater interest here is "Strand one". Below is Bates *et al*'s (ibid.) full tabulation of the key features of "Strand one" semantic learning:

- High proportion of nouns in first 50 words
- Single words in early speech
- Imitates object names
- Greater variety within lexical categories
- Meaningful elements only
- High adjective use
- Context-flexible use of names
- Rapid vocabulary growth

Bates *et al*, ibid.

If some mechanism like Smart-UDOG does indeed form the basis of human linguistic production, might it be that the comparatively rapid vocabulary learning of "Strand one" learners, and their ability to use names context-flexibly, owes to their creation of exemplars of a noun linked to its referent, isolated from context, just like the "wug" exemplars in the Wug Test in §§5.2 and 6.3, which are then available to the child as part of her exemplar-base. This suggests a direction for the empirical testing of the UDOG model against human subjects.

6.2 Conclusion

The achievement of the model itself is small, but what it has shown to be possible – generation and the integration of multiple cognitive modalities under a Data-Oriented framework, represent considerable advances for Data-Oriented approaches to Cognitive Science and Artificial Intelligence. On the webpage for the new Cognitive Systems research group at the University of St. Andrews, Bod (2006) proposes the goal of the new group to be "to develop one system that *unifies* different modalities" (author's emphasis): certainly the models of language, music and reasoning in Bod (2005) show that unimodal DOP models can be used to unify cognitive modalities under a single *formalism*; but the programme of multimodal Data-Oriented research that the present work warrants, offers a potential way to *integrate* different modalities within a single *model*.

Acknowledgements

Thanks to Rens Bod, Hannah Cornish, and several anonymous reviewers for helpful comments and discussion, and especially to Simon Kirby, who had several very good reasons not supervise for this project, but did anyway, and to great effect. This work was supported by the AHRC.

References

Elizabeth Bates, Inge Bretherton, and Lynn Snyder. 1988. *From first words to grammar: Individual differences and dissociable mechanisms*. Cambridge University Press. New York, NY.

Rens Bod. 1992. A Computational Model of Language Performance; Data-Oriented Parsing. *Proceedings COLING-92*, Nantes, France.

- 1993. Applying Monte Carlo Techniques to Data Oriented Parsing. *Computational Linguistics in the Netherlands*, Tilburg, The Netherlands.

- 1998a. *Beyond Grammar; An Experience-Based Theory of Language*. Centre for the Study of Language and Information, Stanford, CA.

- 1998b. Spoken Dialogue Interpretation with the DOP Model. *Proceedings COLING-ACL-98*, Montreal, Canada.

- 2005. Towards Unifying Perception and Cognition: The Ubiquity of Trees. Prepublication.

- 2006. Cognitive Systems Group: The DOP Approach to Language and Cognition. http://cogsys.dcs.st-and.ac.uk/ (Accessed 28th August 2006).

Rens Bod, Remco Bonnema and Remco Scha. 1996. A Data-Oriented Approach to Semantic Interpretation. *Proceedings Workshop on Corpus-Oriented Semantic Analysis,* ECAI-96, Budapest, Hungary.

Chris Manning and Hinrich Schütze. 1999. *Foundations of Statistical Natural Language Processing*. The MIT Press. Cambridge MA.

Remco Scha. 1990. Taaltheorie en Taaltechnologie: Competence en Performance. In Q. de Kort and G. Leerdam (eds.), *Computertoepassingen in de Neerlandistiek*, Landelijke Vereniging van Neerlandici (LVVN-jaarboek). Almere, The Netherlands.

Van den Berg, M., R. Bod, and R. Scha. (1994). A Corpus Based Approach to Semantic Interpretation. *Proceedings Ninth Amsterdam Colloquium*, Amsterdam, the Netherlands.

Gert Veldhuijzen van Zanten. 1996. Semantics of update expressions. *Technical Report 24*. NWO Priority Programme Language and Speech Technology, The Hague, The Netherlands.

Decomposing Swedish Compounds
Using Memory-Based Learning

Karin Friberg

Department of Swedish Language

Göteborg University

Sweden

`karin.friberg@svenska.gu.se`

Abstract

Swedish morphology differs significantly from English in several ways. This is something which makes natural language processing based on the English language not always applicable for Swedish material. One area where there is a difference is compounding. The word-forming process of compounding is very productive in Swedish. The compounds are mostly written as one word, without the segmentation point marked in any way. Thus segmentation has to be done in order to interpret the compounds.

In this study I have implemented a decomposer which finds the segmentation point in Swedish compounds, making it easier to handle compounds in natural language processing. Brodda's algorithm for heuristic compound segmentation guided the work. The decomposer is implemented in TiMBL, a memory-based learner.

1 Introduction

Compounding is, in Swedish, a very productive process. The number of possible compounds is huge, and it is not possible to list them. The use of compounds and the coining of new compounds is also significant. 10% of the words in Swedish newspaper text have been found to be compounds after removal of stopwords (Hedlund, 2002). The frequency and the structure of Swedish compounds poses problems in natural language processing tasks which have to be dealt with.

Areas where this is important are for example information retrieval, machine translation and speech synthesis. In information retrieval a search query may contain a term which in a certain document only occurs hidden in a compound. Or it can be the other way around. The query may contain a compound but the concepts of any or both of the constituents may in a certain document only occur as simplex words.

In order to make use of the constituents of Swedish compounds, one must first determine which they are. One problem for languages where compounds are written with no white space between the parts, as in Swedish, is to find the parts, that is to determine the compound segmentation point.

In this paper I describe an experiment using memory-based learning for compound segmentation. The hypothesis is that this should work because n-grams around a segmentation point tend to contain grapheme clusters that do not occur in simplex words (Brodda, 1979). The learner is thus trained to distinguish clusters appearing around segmentation points from other clusters.

2 Background

There are different approaches for constructing systems that deal with segmentation of Swedish compounds, including the use of word lists, manually written rules or machine learning. The simplest approach would be to list the compounds in a word list with the segmentation point marked. However, since the process of compounding is so productive, it would be difficult to get sufficient coverage with

Joakim Nivre, Heiki-Jaan Kaalep, Kadri Muischnek and Mare Koit (Eds.)

NODALIDA 2007 Conference Proceedings, pp. 224–230

such a system.

2.1 Previous work

Sjöbergh and Kann (2006) present a successful segmentation system which uses word lists, although not with whole'compounds. The system consists of a *first part list*, a *last part list*, and an *individual word list*. Sjöbergh and Kann report 99% success for both precision and recall.

A well-known system for analyzing Swedish words, including compounds, is SWETWOL (Karlsson, 1992). SWETWOL is based on manually written rules, and uses the Two Level formalism. SWETWOL gives several alternative interpretations if found, and the analyses include part of speech of all segments. Lexicalized compounds and derivations have been listed in SWETWOL and the system regards these as wholes in order to avoid incorrect decomposition.

Witschel and Biemann (2005) present a segmentation system for German compounds using Compact Patricia Tries, a type of classifier which they themselves present as something between a rule-based and a memory-based learner. They report results around 96% for the F-value.

In his thesis Kokkinakis (2001) mentions a rule-based segmentation tool based on Brodda's segmentation algorithm describing clusters at compound segmentation points. (See section 2.2.) Kokkinakis reports 96% precision.

2.2 Brodda's Segmentation Algorithm

The present study presents a compound segmentation system that, as Kokkinaki's system, is inspired by Brodda's segmentation algorithm, but instead of manually written rules uses memory-based learning.

Brodda's algorithm concerns Swedish grapheme combinations. Like other languages, the Swedish language has rules stating which combinations of consonants and vowels can appear at the beginning of a word, at the end or internally. In his algorithm, Brodda (1979) states that when two Swedish words are combined together in a compound, the result is often a consonant cluster in the segmentation point that is not allowed internally in simplex words, for example the cluster '**rkskr**' in '*korkskruv*' ('*corkscrew*'). Brodda describes a six level hierarchy of clusters, from those that say noth-

ing about the probability of a segmentation point, like '**ll**', to those that always signal a segmentation point, like '**ntst**'. Brodda's algorithm identifies 50% of tested compounds uniquely with the correct segmentation and another 40% with multiple segmentation points. 10% of the compounds are missed (Brodda, 1979).

2.3 TiMBL

TiMBL (Daelemans et al., 2004) is a memory-based learner used here to classify positions in presumed compounds as being segmentation points or not.

A memory-based learner stores classified instances in memory and later, given test instances, compares these to the stored instances by calculating the distance or similarity between them. It then assigns the class of the majority of the nearest neighbors to the instance to be classified.

The properties of the instances are described in feature vectors in the form of a list of an arbitrary number of features, separated by commas, followed by a class label and ended by a period. (See Example 1 in section 3.1.)

After testing for optimal settings for the learner, I chose 'Overlap', which counts the number of features that coincide between two vectors, and 'MVDM' (Modified Value Difference Metric) which considers some values to be more alike than others, making the distance smaller. For example, an 'n' can be considered to be more similar to an 'm' than to a 'p'. The parameter feature weighting concerns how much weight each feature is given. For this I used the setting 'Gain Ratio' which normalizes the weight considering the number of values the feature may take. Finally, there is class voting which is about how much influence each neighbor has. Here I chose 'Majority Voting' where the class with the largest part of the k nearest neighbors is chosen regardless of the distance.

3   Method

The aim of this study is to have TiMBL learn to classify every position in a string as a compound segmentation point or not.

To train a memory-based learner, data is needed to supply instances of all classes. In this case the classes are: segmentation point = Y, no segmentation point = N. To this end I used compounds from the on-line medical lexicon MedLex (Kokkinakis, 2004). I had at my disposal a list of 5 786 compounds with the segmentation point marked. Since MedLex is a medical lexicon constructed by adding medical terms to a learners' dictionary, a great part of these compounds, but far from all, are from the medical domain. I put aside one tenth of the compounds for testing and used nine tenths for training.

3.1 Feature vectors

The starting point of this study is, as mentioned, Brodda's segmentation algorithm (Brodda, 1979), which tells us that clusters not allowed in simplex words signal probable compound segmentation points. With this in mind I created feature vectors representing the graphemes around a supposed compound boundary.

The feature vector I used as baseline had the following components: the word in question (ignored in training and testing), four graphemes before and four graphemes after the supposed segmentation point, three graphemes before and three graphemes after the segmentation point, two graphemes before and two graphemes after the segmentation point, and finally the class label.

> abstinens~besvär,nens,besv,ens,bes,ns,be,Y.
> abstinens~besvär,inen,sbes,nen,sbe,en,sb,N.

Example 1. A positive (Y) and a negative (N) example of the baseline feature vector.

The graphemes closest to the segmentation point are repeated in several features in order to give graphemes closer to the compound boundary more weight and also to catch cases where the cluster around the segmentation point is smaller than four graphemes on either side.

I limited the negative cases of training instances to represent points one and two positions to the right and to the left of the predetermined compound boundary. For the batch testing below, the test cases were limited to testing five positions in each word, the supposed segmentation point and two positions to the left and two to the right of the boundary.

3.2 Experiments

I did some experimenting with the feature vector, ignoring a varying number of features. No combi-

nation of ignored features gave a positive result. I went on trying to group similar graphemes. Since the clusters Brodda mentioned were mostly consonant clusters, I replaced all vowels with one and the same symbol, hoping to get more matching of close neighbors. This had a devastating result. I tried the same approach with the so called heavy vowels '$\mathring{a}$', '$\ddot{a}$', '$\ddot{o}$', 'y', 'u' and 'i' which are mostly found in stems (Brodda, 1979). This gave a somewhat better result, but again worse than with no vowel substitution.

I also tried a case of consonant substitution. Swedish phonotactics tells us that if a word starts with a cluster of three consonants the first one has to be 's', the second a voiceless plosive, 'p', 't' or 'k', and the last one 'r', 'l', 'j' or 'v' (Lundström-Holmberg and af Trampe, 1987). With this in mind I replaced all voiceless plosives with a common symbol. This did not have as bad result as the vowel substitutions, but was still no improvement to the baseline.

I finally tried extending the feature vector with features representing graphemes across the segmentation point. First, a feature consisting of one grapheme on each side (1+1). I then added another one with varying numbers of graphemes on either side of the segmentation point (2+2, 1+2, 3+1, etc.). This, finally, gave results improving on the original vector. (See Table 1 below.)

> abstinens~besvär,nens,besv,ens,bes,ns,be,sb,ensb,Y.
> abstinens~besvär,inen,sbes,nen,sbe,en,sb,ns,nens,N.

Example 2. The feature vector giving the best results, with boundary features 1+1 and 3+1.

4 Results

The outcome important in this case is 'positive recall', that is the procentage of found segmentation points and 'positive precision', the procentage of true segmentation points among the declared segmentation points. Positive recall is a measure that mirrors the procentage of missed positives and positive precision mirrors the procentage of false positives. In many cases having high recall is more essential than having high precision since a user getting superfluous results easily can discard the incor-

Feature properties	Missed positives	Recall (positive)	False positives	Precision (positive)
Baseline	41	92.9	40	93.1
Ignore feature 6	41	92.9	40	93.1
Ignore features 5 and 6	42	92.7	52	91.2
Ignore features 4 and 6	46	92.1	47	91.9
Ignore feature 2	57	90.2	57	90.2
Ignore feature 3	64	88.9	61	89.4
Vowel substitution	94	83.8	107	81.9
Heavy vowel substitution	64	88.9	71	87.9
Voiceless plosive substitution	47	91.9	51	91.3
Boundary feature 1+1	38	93.4	43	92.6
Boundary feature 1+1, 2+2	40	93.1	38	93.4
Boundary feature 1+1, 2+1	35	94.0	37	93.6
Boundary feature 1+1, 1+2	35	94.0	40	93.2
Boundary feature 1+1, 3+1	**32**	**94.5**	**36**	**93.8**
Boundary feature 1+1, 3+2	40	93.1	34	94.1
Boundary feature 1+1, 4+1	41	93.8	36	93.0

Table 1: The effect on precision and recall, when experimenting with the feature vector, testing on five positions in a total of 579 words.

rect ones. Furthermore, there are often multiple correct answers. Declared false positives are not seldom morpheme boundaries or alternative or even additional compound boundaries.

Looking at the false positives in this case, it is clear that the learner has not been able to detect all forbidden clusters. No Swedish words begin with 'ttk', 'tst', 'lk', 'tg', 'rs or end with 'rnskl' 'sn' or 'mk'. The fact that these clusters are missed follows from never explicitly having stated which the forbidden clusters are. Among the false positives is also the case of '*Bricker+-blåsa*' which has been declared to have its segmentation point before the hyphen, as well as after. One way to go from here might be to combine this learner with a filter removing false positives containing forbidden start or end clusters and segmentation points before hyphens.

The results of the false positives also reveals a well-known problem in decomposing Swedish compounds. It is the handling of the link morpheme. In in the process of compounding a link morpheme, most often an 's', is sometimes inserted between the parts of a compound. The problem is to determine whether an 's' in the vicinity of a segmentation point, belongs to the component to the right, or if it is in fact a link morpheme, which is closer bound to the component to the right.

The results from experimenting with the feature vector can be seen in Table 1 above. The best result, with the vector including boundary features 1+1 and 3+1, gave 94,5% recall, which means that almost 19 out of 20 segmentation points were found. This is somewhat better than the 90% reported by Brodda (1979). The precision in the tables above are not quite comparable to Brodda's results since tests have not been done in every position of the words, only the compound boundary and two positions preceding and following it.

To see how well the learner manages to decompose whole compounds, I tried the best feature vector (boundary feature 1+1 and 3+1) on 12 randomly selected words. (See Appendix A.) All 12 segmentation points were found, that is 0% failure. 3 words, 25%, were unambiguously decomposed correctly, and 9 words, 75%, had multiple segmentation. This can be compared to Brodda's 10% failure, 50% unambiguous segmentation and 40% multiple segmentation (Brodda, 1979). However, 8 out of 15 false positives have been decomposed at morpheme boundaries. In other words, there are only 7 instances of completely false positives, that is segmentation within a morpheme.

5   Conclusion

A conclusion that can be drawn from the experiments above is that it is possible to state that some features are more alike than others, hence the good results of the MVDM setting. Considering the fact that no improvements could be reached by ignoring features, it appears correct to assume that substrings up to the length of four graphemes on either side of the segmentation point give information about permissible clusters. It is also important to consider information across the segmentation point. However, replacing groups of graphemes with a common substitute is not successful, which tells us that every grapheme has its own way of behaving.

The performance of the TiMBL decomposer must be considered satisfactory. Several of the failures are proposed boundaries at morpheme borders, which could be of use in some applications. Finally, the precision could be further improved by simple filters, removing forbidden start and end clusters and compound boundaries before hyphens.

A   Results testing all positions in 12 randomly selected words

Below is the result of running 12 randomly selected words through the decomposer, testing in every position of the words. The strings in **boldface** are correctly decomposed. A plus sign (+) represents segmentation at a morpheme boundary. A minus sign (-) represents an incorrect decomposition within a morpheme.

anti+klimax

abort+rådgivning
abor-trådgivning
abortråd+givning

elektroretino+grafi
el-ektroretinografi
elektro+retinografi
elektrore-tinografi

folk+bokföring
folkbok+föring

immuno+logi
im-munologi

kommun+fullmäktige
kommunfull+mäktige

millimeter+rättvisa
milli+meterrättvisa
millimeterrätt+visa

overhead+projektor
o-verheadprojektor
over+headprojektor
overheadproj-ektor

senare+lägga
sen+arelägga

sommar+stuga
som-marstuga

tid+rymd

värme+bölja

B   Missed positives using boundary features 1+1 and 3+1

an+fordran
bak+åt
bockhorns+klöver
cerebro+spinal
del+ta
dos+ekvivalent
döds+trött
hov+tång
in+jaga
kontant+insats
kull+kasta
land+sätta
Medel+svensson
mot+åtgärd
nefr+ektomi
nor+adrenalin

pappers+tiger
prust+rot
rep+övning
rid+sår
rök+dykare
silver+nitrat
skräm+skott
slät+struken
tinning+lob
tviste+mål
ur+skog
utom+kved
vak+natt
varnings+triangel
ved+bod
vid+öppen

lång‖s-ökt
löne‖an+språk
mikrovåg+s‖ugn
mot‖åt+gärd
pastor+s‖expedition
prus-t‖rot
rid‖s-år
rätte‖sn-öre
sjuk‖av+drag
skörbjugg+s‖ört
spö-rs‖mål
strepto‖my-cin
stru-p‖lock
tallko-tt‖körtel
tillhand+a‖hålla
tvis-te‖mål
tätt‖be+byggd
utom‖k-ved

C False positives using boundary features 1+1 and 3+1

The correct segmentation point is marked by two vertical bars (‖). A plus sign (+) represents an incorrect segmentation by the learner at a morpheme boundary. A minus sign (-) represents an incorrect segmentation by the learner within a morpheme. In the string Bricker+-‖blåsa the minus sign is a grapheme which belongs to the compound that is decomposed.

abor-t‖rådgivning
akter‖se-glad
ben‖s-tomme
bockhorn+s‖klöver
bockhorns‖kl-över
Bricker+-‖blåsa
elektro‖en-cefalogram
hop-p‖lös
hydro‖ne-fros
hög+t‖stående
konsument‖om+budsman
kontan-t‖insats
kort‖s-lutning
kul-l‖kasta
land+s‖kamp
lek‖s-kola
luft‖om+byte
lång+t‖gående

References

Benny Brodda. 1979. Något om de svenska ordens fonotax och morfotax: Iakttagelse med utgångspunkt från experiment med automatisk morfologisk analys. *PILUS nr 38.* Institutionen för lingvistik, Stockholm University. (Also in: "I huvet på Benny Brodda" Festskrift till densammes 65-årsdag.)

Walter Daelemans, Jakub Zavrel, Ko van der Sloot, Antal van den Bosch. 2004. *TiMBL Memory-Based Learner, version 5.1. Reference Guide.* ILK Technical Report – ILK 04-02.

Hedlund, Turid. 2002. Compounds in dictionary-based cross-language information retrieval. *Information Research*, volume 7 No.2. 2002. Department of Information Studies. University of Tampere, Finland.

Fred Karlsson. 1992. SWETWOL: A Comprehensive Morphological analyser for Swedish. *Nordic Journal of Lingusitics 15*, pages 1-45.

Dimitrios Kokkinakis. 2001. *A Framework for the Acquisition of Lexical Knowledge: Description and Applications.* Department of Swedish Language, Språkdata, Göteborg University.

Dimitrios Kokkinakis. 2004. *MEDLEX: Technical Report.* Department of Swedish Language, Språkdata, Göteborg University. [www] <http://demo.spraakdata.gu.se/svedk/pbl/MEDLEX _work2004.pdf>. The reference created February 7, 2007.

Eva Lundström-Holmberg, Peter af Trampe. 1987. *Elementär fonetik*. Studentlitteratur, Lund.

Jonas Sjöbergh, Viggo Kann. 2006. Vad kan statistik avslöja om svenska sammansättningar. *Språk & stil 16*.

Hans Friedrich Witschel, Chris Biemann. 2005. *Rigorous dimensionality reduction through linguistically motivated feature selection for text categorization*. Proceedings of the 15th NODALIDA conference, Joensuu, 2005.

Memory-based learning of word translation

Maria Holmqvist
Department of Computer and Information Science
Linköpings universitet
`marho@ida.liu.se`

Abstract

A basic task in machine translation is to choose the right translation for source words with several possible translations in the target language. In this paper we treat word translation as a word sense disambiguation problem and train memory-based classifiers on words with alternative translations. The training data was automatically labeled with the corresponding translations by word-aligning a parallel corpus. Results show that many words were translated with accuracy above the baseline.

1 Introduction

A problem in machine translation (MT) is choosing the right translation of a word or phrase with several equivalents in the target language. This problem of choosing the right translation of a source word in context is closely related to the well-researched problem of word sense disambiguation (WSD) which is the task of identifying the correct sense of a semantically ambiguous word in context.

In this paper we describe an experiment with machine learning of word translation from English to Swedish within a corpus-based approach to machine translation: direct (word-based) translation (Ahrenberg and Holmqvist, 2004). In the experiment we used lexical and grammatical correspondence information derived from parallel texts and a memory-based learning algorithm (Daelemans, 1999) to learn which translation should be used in a certain context during automatic translation.

Memory-based learning and similar machine learning techniques[1] have been successfully applied to the related problem of word sense disambiguation (Mihalcea, 2002; Ng and Lee, 1996; Hoste et al., 2002). Several other machine learning approaches used for word sense disambiguation have had similar success with the word translation task, including support-vector machines (Murata et al., 2001) and maximum entropy (Vickrey et al., 2005). The benefits of using a dedicated WSD/machine learning algorithm over a typical MT method like statistical MT, is that the WSD algorithm can take advantage of many types of contextual information not just a window of surrounding word forms. Recent attempts to combine the benefits of WSD and statistical methods include Carpuat and Wu (2005) and Vickrey et al. (2005).

2 Background

2.1 Word translation variation

Although the word translation task is a challenge for most MT systems, it is especially challenging for corpus-based methods that rely on information from real-world translation examples. Translations made by professional translators contain more variation in syntax and word choice than what is strictly necessary to produce fluent and accurate translations. This variation is one of the challenges when we try to learn word translation directly from parallel corpora.

The following translation ambiguities from English–Swedish corpus data illustrate the range of variation in word translation:

chair	*ordförande* (person)
chair	*stol* (furniture)

---

[1] E.g., exemplar-based or instance-based learning.

Joakim Nivre, Heiki-Jaan Kaalep, Kadri Muischnek and Mare Koit (Eds.)
NODALIDA 2007 Conference Proceedings, pp. 231–234

select	*välj* (choose)
select	*markera* (a choice on the file menu)
You can	*du* kan (you can)
It tells *you*	Det beskriver *NULL* (it describes)

Only the first example, *chair*, is a pure WSD problem dealing with sense. For the other words it is less obvious why a translation is used instead of another. In the last example, the deletion of *you* is a result of a change of the sentence from active to passive mode. Perhaps a translation system will not have to handle all of these translation ambiguities. However, there is also a real possibility that this variation in the corpus reflects the translator's knowledge of the subject domain, and language specific text norms within this domain. For translation scholars, extracting such knowledge from a translation can be as rewarding as extracting knowledge about lexical and structural correspondences (Merkel et al., 2003).

2.2   Memory-based learning

In our word translation experiment we used memory-based learning to train classifiers (Daelemans, 1999). A memory based classifier avoids overgeneralization by storing all training examples as feature vectors in memory without pruning exceptional instances. At run time a new instance is compared to the stored examples and gets a classification according to the closest match (nearest neighbors) in the database. All learning was done using the TiMBL software package [2] and the associated Paramsearch tool was used to optimize the parameter settings for the learning algorithm (Daelemans et al., 2004).

3   Learning word translation: An experiment

We conducted an experiment to find out to what extent correct translation of ambiguous words from the source context can be predicted using memory-based learning (Daelemans, 1999). We define the learning task as follows: for a lemma a and its context in the source language S, find the correct translation (lemma) in the target language T. The source context was represented by automatically selected contextual features based on a set of features used successfully in word sense disambiguation (Mihalcea, 2002).

3.1   The parallel corpus

The translation data was extracted from parallel texts from the English–Swedish translation of a database software manual. Both source and target texts are linguistically annotated with a dependency parser [3] that provides each word with lemma, part-of-speech, morphology and dependency relations (Tapanainen and Järvinen, 1997). The corpus is relatively small, consisting of 5382 aligned sentence pairs. To extract lexical correspondences (words and their translations) the corpus was word aligned with a combination of manual and automatic alignment. The first 1000 sentences were word aligned manually and the remaining 4382 sentences were aligned using the automatic word alignment tool I*Trix (Merkel et al., 2003).

3.2   Word types

We trained translation classifiers on 34 ambiguous word types that were selected from the corpus based on two criteria:

1. Their frequency in the manually aligned part of the training corpus.
2. Word alignment quality.

Instances of each word were extracted from the entire corpus and randomly assigned to train and test data containing 2/3 and 1/3 of the instances respectively. Afterwards, word alignments of instances in the test data were manually corrected in order to obtain gold standard translations for the evaluation of our classifiers. The manual correction showed that the alignment accuracy of the 34 selected words ranged from 78% to 100%. The number of target alternatives ranges from 2 to 11 and the most frequent target baseline ranged from 27% to 98%. Table 1 shows a sample of selected words.

Word	Targets
change (verb)	använda, byta, ändra
in (prep)	på, med, i

Table 1. Two of the selected words.

3.3   Filtering noisy training data

Since training data was extracted from automatic word alignment of a parallel corpus the classifications (targets) in training data contained noise. We therefore decided to try and filter the data by

---

removing instances with targets that did not occur in the manually aligned portion of the data.

The effects of filtering noisy data were investigated by comparing classifiers based on the original training data with classifiers based on the filtered data.

3.4 Feature selection

Careful selection of features and tuning of algorithm parameters are vital for machine learning performance. Tuning must be performed individually for each word classifier and in this experiment we used the feature selection procedure *forward selection* to optimize the features for each word. Starting with an empty set of features and another set of candidate features, each feature was tested using "leave one out"-testing on the training data. The candidate feature which improved the classification the most was selected and added to the feature set. This process of trying out candidate features was repeated until there was no more improvement in classification accuracy.

The set of candidate features in Table 2 was inspired by the ones used by Mihalcea (2002) for the WSD task, but we included features that use dependency information, such as properties of the head and daughter word. If a feature was not present in the context it was replaced with a default value, MISS. The features Col (collocations) and SK (sense specific keywords) are binary features that represent whether the collocation/keyword is present in the current sentence context or not. Following Ng and Lee (1996), the keywords and collocations for each word type are those that (1) occur at least 5 times with a target, and (2) have a conditional probability above 0.8, where the conditional probability is the number of times a keyword/collocation occurs with a word w with target word t divided with all occurrences of word w. For the noun *data* this produced the following set of collocations:

```
data access, data sources, data ac-
cess page, offline data, data in a,
data in, data from
```

and keywords:

```
sources, report, fields, list,
form, PivotTable
```

3.5 TiMBL parameter settings

The TiMBL parameter settings were also individually set for each word learning task. Ideally, parameter and feature optimization should be interleaved and exhaustive. As a decent compromise, we ran the Paramsearch utility to optimize the parameter settings (feature weighting, number of k-nearest neighbors and distance metric) each time a new feature was selected from the set of candidate features.

Dependency features					
	Form	Base	PoS	Morf.	Dep. rel
Current word	x		x	x	x
Head	x	x	x	x	x
Right daughter	x	x	x	x	x
Left daughter	x	x	x	x	x
Head of NP		x		x	
Surface features					
	N	V	NE	Prep	Pron	Det
Before	x	x	x	x	x	x
After	x	x	x	x	x	
Other features					
CF	Words and PoS in window size -1, +2				
Col	Collocations (Ng and Lee, 1996) (max. 5)				
SK	Sense specific keywords (max. 5)				

Table 2. Candidate features.

3.6 Results

Table 3 shows the average results of training and testing on all word types using filtered and unfiltered training data. The results are compared against a baseline of applying the most frequent translation found in training data. Results show that on average, the memory-based classifiers did better on the word translation task than the simple baseline. However, for both types of training data only about 60% of the words were more accurate than the baseline. By filtering the noisy training data we also achieved better results. However, this improvement was rather modest and was not consistent over all word types.

	Original	**Filtered**	**Baseline**
Accuracy	67.2%	70.7%	63.3%

Table 3. Average accuracy for all word types with original and filtered data.

It is also clear from comparing the memory-based classifiers to the baseline in Figure 1, that the classifiers have considerable difficulties competing with high baseline accuracy. For the majority of words with a baseline accuracy over

60% the memory-based method achieved an accuracy equal to or less than baseline.

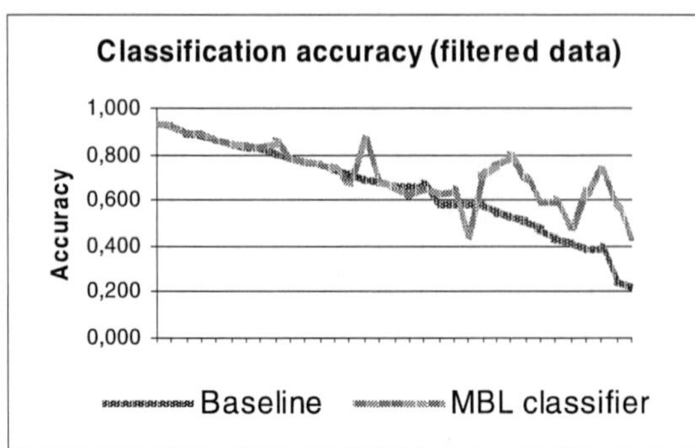

Figure 1. Classification accuracy compared to baseline accuracy (most frequent target).

The best contextual features for classification were automatically selected for each word type. For example, the classifier for preposition *on* selected features RightDaughterLemma and NounBefore to compare instances. The classifier for the word type *you* trained on the original data set used the Keyword feature. Here the presence or absence of the keywords: *move, drag, ID, indexes*, and *spreadsheet* turned out to be useful contextual features for deciding on the correct translation.

Interestingly, many of the selected features were features that we derived from the relations in the dependency parsetree. Table 4 presents the surrounding words used as contextual features for the nouns in the experiment.

Nouns	Features
argument	CurrentNode
custom	Head
data	LeftDaughter VerbBefore
item	NamedEntityAfter PronounAfter
view	Head LeftDaughter NamedEntityBefore

Table 4. Contextual features selected for nouns.

4 Conclusion

We have carried out an experiment with memory-based learning of word translation to see if we can train useful classifiers for this task, despite the noisy data produced by automatic word alignment. Results show that our memory-based classifier in many cases will be more accurate in predicting translations than a baseline classifier, especially on words with a baseline accuracy of

less than 60%. We also showed that dependency type features were found to be useful contextual cues for deciding the correct translations of words.

References

Lars Ahrenberg and Maria Holmqvist. 2004. Back to the future? The case for English–Swedish direct machine translation. In *Proc. of RASMAT'2004*.

Marine Carpuat and Dekai Wu. 2005. Word sense disambiguation vs. statistical machine translation. In *Proc. of ACL'2005*, pp. 387–394.

Walter Daelemans. 1999. Memory-based language processing. *Journal for Experimental and Theoretical Artificial Intelligence,* 11(3), pp. 287–467.

Walter Daelemans, Jakub Zavrel, Ko Van der Sloot, and Antal Van den Bosch. 2004. *TiMBL: Tilburg Memory Based Learner, version 5.1, Reference Guide*.

Véronique Hoste, Iris Hendrickx, Walter Daelemans, and Antal van den Bosch. 2002. Parameter optimization for machine learning of word sense disambiguation. *Natural Language Engineering,* 8(4), pp. 311–325,

Magnus Merkel, Michael Petterstedt, and Lars Ahrenberg. 2003. Interactive Word Alignment for Corpus Linguistics. In *Proc. from Corpus Linguistics 2003*.

Rada Mihalcea. 2002. Instance based learning with automatic feature selection applied to word sense disambiguation. In *Proc. of COLING 2002*, pp. 1–10.

Masaki Murata, Kiyotaka Uchimoto, Qing Ma, and Hitoshi Isahara. 2001. Using a support-vector machine for Japanese-to-English translation of tense, aspect, and modality. In *Proc. of ACL'2001 Workshop on Data-Driven Methods in Machine Translation,* pp. 1–8.

Hwee Tou Ng and Hian Beng Lee. 1996. Integrating multiple knowledge sources to disambiguate word-sense: An exemplar-based approach. In *Proc. of the 34th Annual Meeting of the ACL*, pp. 40–47.

Pasi Tapanainen and Timo Järvinen. 1997. A non-projective dependency parser. In *Proc. of ANLP'1997*, pp. 64–71.

David Vickrey, Luke Biewald, Marc Teyssier, and Daphne Koller. 2005. Word-sense disambiguation for machine translation. In *Proc. of EMNLP'2005*, pp. 771–778.

Clause Boundary Detection in Transcribed Spoken Language

Fredrik Jørgensen
Department of Linguistics and Scandinavian Studies
University of Oslo
`fredrik.jorgensen@iln.uio.no`

Abstract

We argue that finite clauses should be regarded as the basic unit in syntactic analysis of spoken language, and describe a method that automatically detects clause boundaries by classifying coordinating conjunctions in spoken language discourse as belonging to either the syntactic level or the discourse level of analysis. The method exploits the special role that coordinating conjunctions play in organizing spoken language discourse, and that coordinating conjunctions at discourse level mark clause boundaries.

1 Introduction

Syntactic analysis of written language rests on the *sentence* as the object of analysis, and aims at describing the inner structure of a sentence. The Cambridge Encyclopedia of Language (Crystal, 1987) states this explicitly:

"A sentence is the largest unit to which syntactic rules apply."
(Crystal, 1987, p. 94)

But do sentences exists *per se* in spoken language? Capitalized first words and full stops, which are used to identify sentences in written language, are parts of the writing system. For spoken language, we need to investigate properties of the spoken language systems, e.g. in terms of intonation units (Chafe and Danielewicz, 1987). But the notion of intonation units is problematic:

"Speakers are sloppy in this respect, often producing a sentence-final intonation before they mean to, or neglecting to produce one when they should." (Chafe and Danielewicz, 1987, p. 103)

Looking at spoken language data, it is hard to find evidence that sentences, as we find them in written language, are the basic units of syntactic analysis. Miller and Weinert (1998) argue extensively that sentences are found in written language only, and that they should be treated as a low-level discourse unit rather than syntactic units. Instead, the *clause* should be regarded as the basic syntactic unit of spoken language (Miller and Weinert, 1998, p. 71). Levelt (1989) also treats clauses as the basic grammatical units, where speaker utterances are partitioned into finite clauses, which in turn may be partitioned into one or more basic clauses (finite or non-finite).

We adopt the view that clauses are the natural building blocks of a spoken language discourse, and that clauses also should be the starting point for syntactic analysis of spoken language. This view can be summarized by rephrasing The Cambridge Encyclopedia of Language: *For spoken language, the finite clause is the largest unit to which syntactic rules apply.*

Note that although we want to treat the finite clause as the *largest unit* to which syntactic rules apply, this does not mean that the finite clause is the *only unit* to which syntactic rules apply, neither is the finite clause the only unit corresponding to a complete utterance. Utterances may consist of single words or phrases, which may or may not be ellip-

Joakim Nivre, Heiki-Jaan Kaalep, Kadri Muischnek and Mare Koit (Eds.)
NODALIDA 2007 Conference Proceedings, pp. 235–239

tical from a syntactic or broader communicational or informational perspective. When we speak of clause boundaries in this paper, what we mean is boundaries between segment units or topic units which are maximally a finite clause, but which may consist of smaller syntactic units.

Turning now to coordinating conjunctions, we find that in written language, a coordinating conjunction is a word that links words, phrases, or clauses into compound elements. This is also true for spoken language. But conjunctions have another important role in spoken language, namely organizing the clauses of the discourse, or having other pragmatic functions, e.g. to avoid turn shifts, to mark questions, to express modality etc. Schiffrin (1987) explicitly discusses the English conjunctions *and, but* and *or*, and their role as what she calls "Discourse connectives" These "discourse connectives" or "discourse conjunctions" are better understood at the discourse level, rather than at the syntactic level. Conjunctions also relate larger parts of the discourse, which are not necessarily adjacent to the conjunction (Webber et al., 2006). For instance, the Norwegian and Swedish conjunction *men* ('but') can be used to signal a shift from a digression and back to the main topic of the conversation (Svennevig, 1999; Horne et al., 2001).

As coordinating conjunctions organize the clauses of the discourse, they also turn out to be potential indicators of clause boundaries within an utterance. Detecting clause boundaries may be important for several linguistic disciplines, such as morpho-syntax (e.g. Part of Speech tagging), syntax (e.g. parsing and (semi-)automatic treebank construction) and semantics (in dialogue systems, where e.g. propositions, events or speech acts are necessary for semantic representations).

In this paper, we propose a method to automatically identify clause boundaries in a spoken language corpus of Norwegian. The method described is a supervised machine learning method, where we propose a partial solution to clause boundary detection by reducing the task to a classification problem, classifying conjunctions as either belonging to the discourse level (clause boundaries) or the syntactic level (linking sub-clausal elements). The clauses may in turn be combined into larger discourse structures, or used to define discourse relations, based

on the discourse conjunctions and any other feature of the discourse or insight from pragmatic theory. However, these tasks are beyond the scope of this paper.

2 Clause Boundary Detection

The clause boundary detection experiment is structured as follows:

1. Assign a category type (discourse or syntactic) to a set of coordinating conjunctions in a spoken language corpus
2. Extract a set of features from the context of the conjunctions
3. Apply a machine learning method (memory based learning/TiMBL)
4. Evaluate the results (using ten-fold cross validation)

2.1 Data: The NoTa Corpus

The NoTa corpus[1] is an on-line corpus of approximately 1 million words of transcribed spoken Norwegian. Approximately 80.000 words have been manually Part of Speech-tagged, and the current experiment has been run on this part of the corpus.

The discourse in NoTa is divided into *turns* and *segments*, where segments are the lowest discourse units, corresponding to single utterances. Segments in NoTa correspond quite closely to the intonation units of Chafe and Danielewicz (1987), but are based on a combination of intonation, pauses and length of the utterance. Segment may include several clauses, and in some cases clauses are spread throughout more than one segment.

2.2 Annotation of Conjunctions

We have already described two of the conjunction types in this experiment; *Discourse* and *Syntactic* conjunctions. In addition to these two main categories of conjunctions, I've included a third category, *Indeterminable* conjunctions. This is due to the discourse particle *sånn* ('like', 'you know', 'stuff', 'that' etc.), which is very frequent in spoken Norwegian (ranked 12 in spoken Norwegian and 575 in written Norwegian). *Sånn* may function as a pro-word for a number of phrase types, and phrases

---

[1]http://www.tekstlab.uio.no/NoTa/Oslo/index.html

starting with *sånn* belong to the syntactic level. But the attachment site if *sånn* phrases is often difficult or even impossible to determine. In (1), *sånn* may be conjoined to the VP (*lekte sisten*/'played tag') or the NP (*sisten*/'tag').

> (1) fløy etter hverandre og lekte sisten og
>   *ran after each other and played 'tag' and*
>   sånn
>   *stuff*

Due to these complications, any conjunction followed by a phrase where the first word is *sånn* is classified as an *Indeterminable* conjunction. Thus, all conjunctions in the training data are annotated belonging to one of the three categories:

Syntactic Conjunctions: Conjunctions that combine two syntactic constituents below the finite clause. This category is assigned to all conjunctions where two or more conjuncts are identified in the context. Whenever the conjuncts are not identifiable in the context, the conjunction will *not* be annotated as a Syntactic Conjunction, even though the missing conjunct may be due to e.g. self-interruption. This in order to avoid speculations and arbitrary decisions about the speakers' intentions.

Indetetminable Conjunctions: Conjunctions followed by a phrase where *sånn* is the first word.

Discourse Conjunctions: All other conjunctions. These conjunctions may combine clauses, may be discourse fillers etc. These conjunctions all share the property that they do not disrupt a syntactic constituent below the clause level.

In total, 853 conjunctions in the NoTa were assigned one of these three categories.

2.3   Feature Set

Decision on and extraction of the feature set is the core of any application using machine learning methods. The feature set used in this experiment is grouped into one basic feature set, which is incremented with new features, as described below:

Basic: Word form of the conjunction and word form, lemma and part of speech for ± 4 tokens (tag set size = 17). (Features 1-25).

+Match: Binary value stating if the PoS tags and/or word forms of the preceding and succeeding tokens are identical. (Features 26-27).

+Filter: Filter out tokens which does not fill any syntactic role (pragmatic and spoken language words: *interjections, conjunctions, unknown words, pauses, punctuation*. (Features 28-35).

+RelFreq: Relative frequencies for the previous word-form and/or PoS ending a segment, and the next word form and/or PoS starting a segment (after applying filtering). Inclusion of relative frequencies has been proved useful for sentence boundary detection in written language (See e.g Stevenson and Gaizauskas (2000)). (Features 36-41).

Number	Feature Set	Description
1	*Basic*	word form of the conjunction
2-9	*Basic*	window of ± 4 word forms
10-17	*Basic*	window of ± 4 lemmas
18-25	*Basic*	window of ± 4 PoS
26	*+Match*	prev word and next word identical?
27	*+Match*	prev PoS and next PoS identical?
28-33	*+Filter*	filtered, ⊥1 word, PoS and word/PoS
34	*+Filter*	filtered, prev word and next word identical?
35	*+Filter*	filtered, prev PoS and next PoS identical?
36	*+RelFreq*	filtered, rel. freq. for prev PoS ending a segment
37	*+RelFreq*	filtered, rel. freq. for next PoS starting a segment
38	*+RelFreq*	filtered, rel. freq. for prev word ending a segment
39	*+RelFreq*	filtered, rel. freq. for next word starting a segment
40	*+RelFreq*	filtered, rel. freq. for prev word/PoS ending a segment
41	*+RelFreq*	filtered, rel. freq. for next word/PoS starting a segment

Table 1: Feature Set for Conjunction Classification

3   Results

All experiments were run with the memory based learning application TiMBL (Daelemans et al., 2004), using 'modified value difference' as similarity metric and k-value = 3. The results were evaluated using ten-fold cross validation.

For each feature set, *forward search* was applied, an algorithm for automatic feature selection. *For-*

ward search, implemented as follows:

1. Run the classifier and rank the features by a information gain metric.

2. Run the classifier with only the highest ranked feature. For every feature, starting from the top of the ranked list, add this to the feature set and run the classifier again. If the accuracy increases, keep the feature. Otherwise, lose it.

The results with the different feature sets are shown in Table 2. The columns show the feature set, number of features before ($n(all)$) and after ($n(fwd)$) forward search, and accuracy before ($acc(all)$) and after ($acc(fwd)$) forward search.

Baseline is the most frequent class (Discourse conjunctions), and gives an accuracy of 71.16%. The basic feature set gives 89.09%, while the maximum feature set gives 90.85% before forward search and 94.37% after forward search.

The accuracy without forward search increase for each feature set added, in total an accuracy gain of 1.76%. It is interesting to note that after forward search, the basic feature set is the second best, and the total accuracy gain with the maximum feature set is only 0.47%.

In the maximum feature set, the following 13 features were kept after the automatic feature selection (ranked by information gain):

1. *PoS match (filtered)*
2. *PoS match (unfiltered)*
3. *conjunction word form*
4. *relative frequency for next PoS beginning a segment*
5. *relative frequency for previous PoS ending a segment*
6. *+1 PoS (filtered)*
7. *+2 PoS*
8. *-1 PoS*
9. *-3 PoS*
10. *+3 PoS*
11. *+1 word form*
12. *+2 word form*
13. *+3 word form*

The maximum feature set after forward search has several advantages. Not only does this feature set

Feature set	n(all)	acc(all)	n(fwd)	acc(fwd)
Baseline	-	71.16%	-	-
Basic	25	89.10%	4	93.90%
+Match	27	89.68%	6	93.08%
+Filter	35	90.27%	11	93.79%
+RelFreq	41	90.86%	13	94.37%

Table 2: Results for Conjunction Classification

give better accuracy, it is half the size as the basic feature set, which means less processing time, and it requires fewer training instances. Figure 1 shows the learning curve for the basic feature set before forward search, and the maximum feature set after forward search. Figure 1 implies that for the basic feature set, approximately 600 training instances are needed, while for the maximum feature set after (forward search), 400 training instances are sufficient.

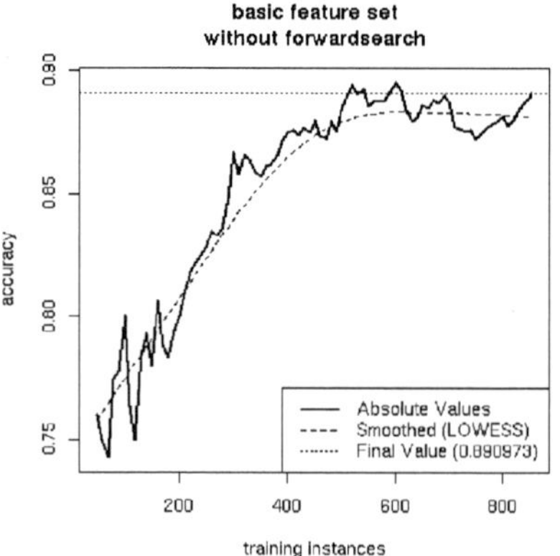

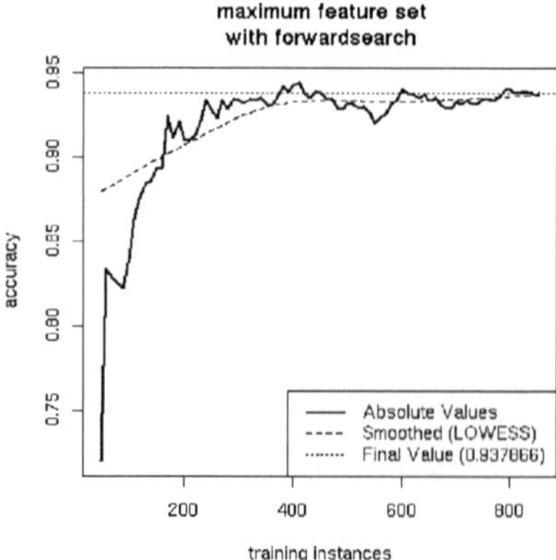

Figure 1: Learning curves for Basic Feature Set and Maximum Feature Set

An example of output of the system is given in (2), where conjuncts marked **D**(iscourse) are interpreted as belonging to the discourse level, and at the same time functioning as clause boundaries. In this example, the three units are (i) a clause containing a repair, (ii) an interrupted clause or a fragment, and (iii) a finite clause.

(2)   **og/D**   der   bodde jeg til   jeg var   like
      ***and*/D** *there lived   I   until I   was just*

      før   jeg fylte   seks år   **for/D**   jeg
      *before I   turned six   years **because*/D** I*

      hus- **og/D**   det husker   jeg veldig godt
      *re-   **and*/D** that remember I   very   well*

      'And I lived there until I was just before I turned six. Because I re-. And I remember that very well'

The partitioning into clauses, as shown in (2), may prove useful both for parsing and for detecting so-called "disfluencies" (see e.g. Shriberg (1994)), as the three segments to be analyzed are shorter and simpler than the original segment.

Note that the results reported in this paper only states how many of the conjunctions are classified correctly. It does not state anything about the proportion of clause boundaries correctly identified in the data, as the NoTa corpus is not currently annotated with this information. The proportion of clause boundaries detected in the corpus is crucial to evaluating the usefulness of the method described. Thus, the method described above is only claimed to be a partial solution to the problem of spoken language clause boundary detection.

4   Conclusion

This experiment describes a method for partially solving the clause boundary detection by exploiting the special role coordinating conjunctions play in structuring a discourse, and reducing clause boundary detection to a classification problem. The method gives promising results with relatively few training instances.

References

Wallace Chafe and Jane Danielewicz. Properties of written and spoken language. In S. Jay Samuels and Rosalind Horowitz, editors, *Comprehending Oral and Written Language*, pages 83–113. Academic Press, 1987.

David Crystal. *The Cambridge Encyclopedia of Language*. Cambridge University Press, New York, 1987.

Walter Daelemans, Jakub Zavrel, Ko van der Sloot K, and Antal van den Bosch A. *TiMBL: Tilburg Memory Based Learner, version 5.1, Reference Guide. ILK Technical Report 04-02*, 2004.

Merle Horne, Petra Hansson, Gösta Bruce, Johan Frid, and Marcus Filipsson. Cue words and the topic structure of spoken discourse: The case of swedish men 'but'. *Journal of Pragmatics*, 33(7): 1061–1081, July 2001.

Willem J. Levelt. *Speaking*. The MIT Press, 1989.

Jim Miller and Regina Weinert. *Spontaneous Spoken Language*. Oxford University Press, 1998.

Deborah Schiffrin. *Discourse Markers*. Cambridge University Press, 1987.

E.E. Shriberg. *Preliminaries to a Theory of Speech Disfluencies*. PhD thesis, University of California at Berkeley, 1994.

M. Stevenson and R. Gaizauskas. Experiments on sentence boundary detection. In *Proceedings of the sixth conference on Applied natural language processing table of contents*, pages 84 – 89, Seattle, Washington, 2000.

Jan Svennevig. Talespråket - mellom pragmatikk og grammatikk. In M. Engebretsen and J. Svennevig, editors, *Mediet teller! Tverrfaglige perspektiver på skrift og tale*, pages 101–116. Høgskolen i Agder, 1999.

Bonnie Webber, Aravind Joshi, Eleni Miltsakaki, Rashmi Prasad, Nikhil Dinesh, Alan Lee, and Katherine Forbes. A short introduction to the penn discourse treebank. In Peter Juel Henrichsen and Peter Rossen Skadhauge, editors, *Treebanking for Discourse and Speech*, volume 32 of *Copenhagen Studies in Language*, pages 9–28. Samfundslitteratur Press, Copenhagen, 2006.

The Effects of Disfluency Detection in Parsing Spoken Language

Fredrik Jørgensen
Department of Linguistics and Scandinavian Studies
University of Oslo
`fredrik.jorgensen@iln.uio.no`

Abstract

Spoken language contains disfluencies that, because of their irregular nature, may lead to reduced performance of data-driven parsers. This paper describes an experiment that quantifies the effects of disfluency detection and disfluency removal on data-driven parsing of spoken language data. The experiment consists of creating two reduced versions from a spoken language treebank, the Switchboard Corpus, mimicking a speech-recognizer output with and without disfluency detection and deletion. Two data-driven parsers are applied on the new data, and the parsers' output is evaluated and compared.

1 Introduction

Spoken language data differs from written language data in several respects. Spoken language is less "well-behaved" or well-formed than written language in the sense that in spoken language, all editing is performed real-time. There is no possibility of deleting what has been said, and utterances often contain repetitions, corrections and interruptions, or are left unfinished. These phenomena are often referred to as disfluencies, and their status in syntax is unclear. However, in syntactically annotated spoken language corpora (i.e., treebanks), disfluencies are often retained as unconventional syntactic patterns, in contrast with the rest of the annotation, which is solely syntactically motivated.

This experiment seeks to quantify data-driven parser performance on spoken language data with and without disfluencies. The hypothesis for the experiment is that because data-driven parsers generalize over regularities in language, and because language containing disfluencies is expected to be less regular than more well-formed or grammatical language, the detection and removal of disfluencies will improve parser performance.

The result of this study indicates to what degree of magnitude disfluencies affect parser performance, and what kind of performance gain can be expected when removing disfluencies prior to parsing. The study may also be used as a partial basis for deciding when disfluency detection is more effective, either prior to or during parsing.

For this experiment, I have chosen data-driven parsers as opposed to manually written, rule-based parser, because most rule-based parsers have no way of handling disfluencies. It is very difficult to formulate general rules about the syntactic structure of disfluencies, and it is not clear whether these rules actually are syntactic rules or merely generalizations over how we communicate or perform online editing of utterances. This in turn means that disfluency detection may be crucial for a rule-based parser applied on spoken language.

2 The Experiment

2.1 Experiment Outline

The main idea of this experiment is to take a treebank, transform it into versions with and without disfluencies, and apply data-driven parsers on the new versions.

The treebank chosen in this experiment is the

Joakim Nivre, Heiki-Jaan Kaalep, Kadri Muischnek and Mare Koit (Eds.)
NODALIDA 2007 Conference Proceedings, pp. 240–244

Data Set	Sentences	Words	Files
Training	46104	604967	sw2005 - sw3993
Test	6998	81787	sw4004 - sw4936
Total	53102	686754	sw2005 - sw4936

Table 1: Description of Training and Test Data

Switchboard Corpus. This treebank has a consistent annotation of disfluencies, which makes the disfluencies easy to identify and remove, without taking any particular view on the status of disfluencies in relation to syntactic theory. We transform the treebank into three different versions. One *Original* version for comparison, one *No Markup* version, where all punctuation and disfluency markup is removed, and one *No Disfluency* version, where all disfluencies are removed. This is described in more detail in Section 2.3.

After the transformation, two data-driven parsers (one constituency-based and one dependency-based) have been trained and tested on the new versions of the treebank. Finally, the parser performance on the different versions are evaluated and compared.

2.2 Prerequisites

2.2.1 Data: The Switchboard Corpus

The Switchboard Corpus, a part of the Penn Treebank (Marcus et al., 1993), consists of recorded telephone dialogs. The corpus is annotated syntactically, with specific node labels and Part of Speech (PoS) tags for speech related phenomena. These include:

- Fillers and discourse markers (UH)

- Unfinished nodes (XP-UNF)

- Edited sections (EDITED) Following the terminology of Shriberg (1994), an EDITED node consists of the *reparandum*, and is immediately followed by a *repairs*, the string replacing the reparandum.

An example of a tree from the Switchboard Corpus is given in Figure 1.

The data used for training and testing is from the parsed version of the Switchboard Corpus, as described in Table 1.

2.2.2 Parsers

Two parsers were trained and tested on the three versions of the treebank: Dan Bikel's Parser (constituency-based) and the MaltParser (dependency-based). The choice of *particular* parsers is not central to this experiment, as we are comparing different data, and not different parsers. But by including one constituency-based and one dependency-based parser, we are able to see if the same tendencies apply to both *types* of parsers.

Dan Bikel's parser[1] is based on the parsing algorithm of Michael Collins' head-driven lexicalized statistical parser (Collins, 1999).

The MaltParser[2] reduces the parsing process to a classification task, using a machine learning method of choice (memory-based learning or support vector machines) for classification. For details, see Nivre and Hall (2005). Before applying the MaltParser on the data, it had to be converted from constituency annotation (labeled bracketing) to dependency relations (labeled relations between words). This was done using the Penn2Malt[3] converter.

2.3 Treebank Transformation

As mentioned above, the Switchboard Corpus was transformed into three different versions:

1. An *Original* version. Nothing is removed.

2. A *No Markup* version, where all non-word markup is removed. This includes punctuation, traces and disfluency markup (e.g. interruption points, start and end tags of repair sequences etc.). This transformation is intended to mimic the output from a speech recognizer.

   Removed: -DFL- -NONE- : , . "

3. A *No Disfluencies* version, where all repairs, unfinished nodes and parenthenticals are removed. In addition, all sentences ending in an unfinished node are considered unfinished sentences, and are also removed:

   Removed: *xp*-UNF EDITED PRN

---

[1]http://www.cis.upenn.edu/~dbikel/software.html
[2]http://www.vxu.se/msi/~nivre/research/MaltParser.html
[3]http://w3.msi.vxu.se/~nivre/research/Penn2Malt.html

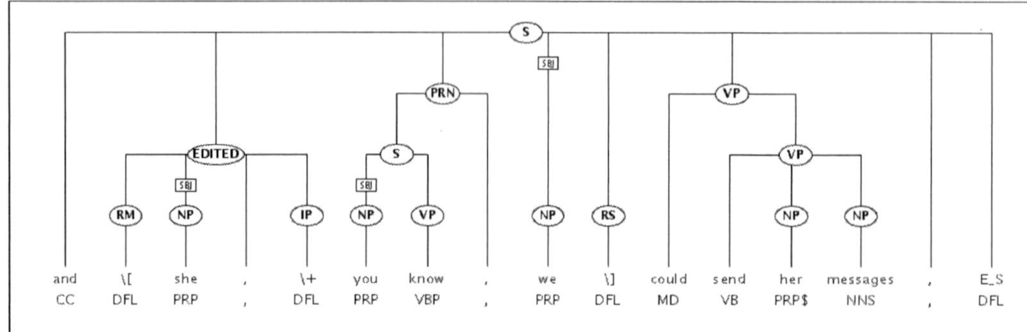

Figure 1: Original sentence from the Switchboard Corpus

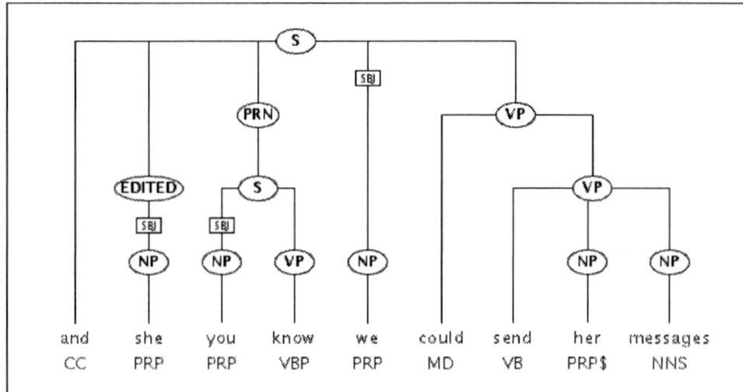

Figure 2: Sentence from the Switchboard Corpus, *No Markup* version

Figure 3: Sentence from the Switchboard Corpus, *No Disfluencies* version

Corpus Version	Avg. Words per Sentences
Original	11.69
No Markup	9.93
No Disfluencies	9.12

Table 2: Avg. sentence length after transformation

In addition, all sentences consisting of 2 or less words were removed from the corpus. The average sentence length after filtering is shown in Table 2.

The transformation was performed by a perl script, available at `folk.uio.no/fredrijo/software`. The *Original* sentence in Figure 1 can be seen as *No Markup* in Figure 2 and *No Disfluencies* in Figure 3.

2.4 Running the Experiment

The experiment consists of the following steps:

1. **Transformation:** Transform the treebank into three different versions.

2. **Filtering:** Filter out sentences with two words or less in the *No Disfluencies* version from all versions of the treebank.

3. **Conversion:** Convert the treebank to Malt Tab format, using Penn2Malt (for the MaltParser only).

4. **Training:** Train the parser on each of the three versions.

5. **Parsing:** Parse the test collection, using the three different "versions" of the parser.

6. **Evaluation:** Evaluate the parser output against the manually annotated gold standard test set. For the constituency parser, the evaluation metrics are precision, recall and F score for labeled and unlabeled bracketing. The scores are generated using `evalb`[4]. For the dependency

---

[4] http://nlp.cs.nyu.edu/evalb/

parser, the evaluation metrics are labeled and unlabeled attachment (of dependency relations) and label accuracy (for the edge labels), using the CONLL evaluation script `eval.pl`[5].

3   Results

The test set of 6998 sentences was divided into 10 partitions or samples. The results for Dan Bikel's Parser and the MaltParser are shown in Table 3 and Table 4, respectively. The results are given as sample means with standard error.

As we see from the results for Dan Bikel's Parser, there are statistically significant differences in results between the three versions of the corpus. A comparison of the *No Markup* and the *No Disfluencies* versions is shown below, with p values:

Lbl. Precision	+1.71	$(p < 0.0001)$
Unlbl. Precision	+1.63	$(p < 0.0001)$
Lbl. Recall	+1.68	$(p = 0.0003)$
Unlbl. Recall	+1.60	$(p = 0.0001)$
Lbl. F Score	+1.70	$(p < 0.0001)$
Unlbl. F Score	+1.62	$(p < 0.0001)$

The results for the MaltParser are somewhat different, as the results for the *Original* version are better than for the *No Markup* version. But if we compare the *No Markup* and *No Disfluencies* versions, we see that the improvement here is also significant, as shown below:

Labeled attachment	+2.16	$(p < 0.0001)$
Unlabeled attachment	+1.71	$(p < 0.0001)$
Label accuracy	+1.90	$(p < 0.0001)$

Note also the MaltParser's decrease in performance from the *Original* version to the *No Markup*, shown in Table 4. I have no explanation why the MaltParser shows a decrease while Dan Bikel's Parser shows an increase here.

4   Discussion

Before investigating the results, it is worthwhile considering the nature of the experiment for a moment. We are not comparing different systems on the same data set, but rather different data sets. Thus, we are in a sense comparing apples and pears. There are

two points to be made here. First, one could imagine trying to evaluate the parsers only on the shared part of the sentence in the *No Markup* and *No Disfluencies* versions, i.e. evaluating the results only on the parts of the sentence that do not contain disfluencies. But as we find crossing brackets into the disfluency sections, it is not clear how this could be done practically. Second, it actually does make sense to compare apples and pears in this experiment. The results also give an indication of how well parsers identify disfluencies, and one way of using the results is to argue for or against passing the sentences to the parser as they are as opposed to detecting and removing disfluencies prior to parsing.

We see, in accordance with the hypothesis, that parsing performance increases significantly (in terms of sample means with standard error intervals) when disfluencies are detected prior to the parsing. It has not been tested here if the improvement is due to the data being more grammatical, and consequentially more regular and predictable, in the *No Disfluencies* version, but this seems a plausible explanation.

One factor that may influence the results, by increasing parser performance, is the fact that the average sentence length is reduced by 2.57 words from the *Original* to the *No Disfluencies* version. I have not tested the significance of sentence length in this study, but this should be investigated.

This experiment mimics change in parsing performance on the output of a "perfect" disfluency detection system. A natural extension to this experiment is to compare the results from a pipe-line system consisting of a disfluency detection system and a parser, to a system where the parser itself is responsible for detecting the disfluencies. Charniak and Johnson (2001) reports one such experiment, concluding that disfluency detection prior to the parsing does not improve parsing significantly. This of course depends on the quality of the disfluency detection as well as how the disfluency detection and the parser integrate. This study, however, states that disfluency detection, when combined with *disfluency removal* prior to the parsing, does have a significant impact on parser performance.

---

[5]http://nextens.uvt.nl/conll/software.html

Corpus	Precision		Recall		F Score	
version	Lbl.	Unlbl.	Lbl.	Unlbl.	Lbl.	Unlbl.
Original	82.70 ± 0.26	84.94 ± 0.23	82.53 ± 0.29	84.76 ± 0.26	82.62 ± 0.27	84.85 ± 0.25
No Markup	88.45 ± 0.23	89.89 ± 0.21	87.91 ± 0.26	89.34 ± 0.24	88.18 ± 0.24	89.61 ± 0.22
No Disfluencies	90.17 ± 0.22	91.52 ± 0.19	89.59 ± 0.27	90.94 ± 0.24	89.88 ± 0.24	91.23 ± 0.21

Table 3: Results for Dan Bikel's Parser, Sample Means with Standard Errors

Corpus	Labeled	Unlabeled	Label
version	attachment	attachment	accuracy
Original	85.99 ± 0.35	88.79 ± 0.32	87.71 ± 0.32
No Markup	85.06 ± 0.27	88.35 ± 0.22	86.65 ± 0.21
No Disfluencies	87.20 ± 0.18	90.06 ± 0.15	88.55 ± 0.16

Table 4: Results for Malt Parser, Sample Means with Standard Errors

5 Conclusion

In this paper, I have quantified the effects disfluency detection and disfluency removal have on data-driven parsing of spoken language data, using two different parsers, Dan Bikel's Parser and the Malt-Parser, applied on various versions of the Switchboard Corpus. The experiment shows that parsing performance is increased when disfluencies are removed prior to parsing.

References

Eugene Charniak and Mark Johnson. Edit detection and parsing for transcribed speech, 2001.

Michael Collins. *Head-Driven Statistical Models for Natural Language Parsing*. PhD thesis, University of Pennsylvania, 1999.

Mitchell P. Marcus, Beatrice Santorini, and Mary Ann Marcinkiewicz. Building a large annotated corpus of english: The penn treebank. *Computational Linguistics*, 19(2):313–330, 1993.

J. Nivre and J. Hall. Maltparser: A language-independent system for data-driven dependency parsing. In *Proceedings of the Fourth Workshop on Treebanks and Linguistic Theories*, Barcelona, 9-10 December 2005.

E.E. Shriberg. *Preliminaries to a Theory of Speech Disfluencies*. PhD thesis, University of California at Berkeley, 1994.

Tagging a Norwegian Speech Corpus

Anders Nøklestad
The Text Laboratory
University of Oslo
P.O. Box 1102 Blindern
0317 Oslo, Norway
`anders.noklestad@iln.uio.no`

Åshild Søfteland
Department of Linguistics and Scandinavian Studies
University of Oslo
P.O. Box 1102 Blindern
0317 Oslo, Norway
`ashildso@hfstud.uio.no`

Abstract

This paper describes work on the grammatical tagging of a newly created Norwegian speech corpus: the first corpus of modern Norwegian speech. We use an iterative procedure to perform computer-aided manual tagging of a part of the corpus. This material is then used to train the final taggers, which are applied to the rest of the corpus. We experiment with taggers that are based on three different data-driven methods: memory-based learning, decision trees, and hidden Markov models, and find that the decision tree tagger performs best. We also test the effects of removing pauses and/or hesitations from the material before training and applying the taggers. We conclude that these attempts at cleaning up hurt the performance of the taggers, indicating that such material, rather than functioning as noise, actually contributes important information about the grammatical function of the words in their nearest context.

1 Introduction

In this paper we describe a number of experiments on tagging a Norwegian speech corpus. The corpus, called NoTa (*Norsk talespråkskorpus* "Norwegian Speech Corpus"), contains 900,000 words of present-day Norwegian speech from informants located in the Oslo area. The corpus has a web-based search interface that enables queries to be restricted by a wide variety of informant properties, and the search results are linked to audio and video recordings of the informants.

The corpus is transcribed in standard orthography, and is tagged using a modified version of the tag set used by the Oslo-Bergen tagger (Hagen et al., 2000), a rule-based tagger for written Norwegian. In addition to part-of-speech, the tagset encodes detailed information about morphosyntactic features (e.g. gender, number, definiteness, tense) and certain lexical features (e.g. whether or not a certain pronoun is used to denote human beings). Because of this high level of detail, the tagset is relatively large, counting a total of 302 different tags. For more information about the NoTa corpus, see Johannessen and Hagen (to appear).

2 The taggers

In our experiments, we have used three different data-driven taggers. The first is the Memory-Based Tagger (MBT)[1] (Daelemans et al., 2003), which uses memory-based learning and is built on top of the Tilburg Memory-Based Learner (TiMBL) (Daelemans et al., 2004). The second one is the TreeTagger (Schmid, 1994)[2], which is based on decision tree technology. We used the TreeTagger in its default setting as a trigram tagger (running it as a bigram tagger yielded slightly inferior results). Finally, QTag (Tufis and Mason, 1998) is a trigram Hidden Markov Model (HMM) tagger. HMM tag-

---

[1] The Memory-Based Tagger can be downloaded from `http://ilk.uvt.nl/mbt/`.
[2] The TreeTagger is available from `http://www.ims.uni-stuttgart.de/projekte/corplex/TreeTagger/DecisionTreeTagger.html`.

Joakim Nivre, Heiki-Jaan Kaalep, Kadri Muischnek and Mare Koit (Eds.)
NODALIDA 2007 Conference Proceedings, pp. 245–248

gers are probably the most widespread type of part-of-speech tagger, and is the technology that was used, for instance, to tag the Swedish Gothenburg Spoken Language Corpus, as described by Nivre and Grönqvist (2001).

3 Creating the training corpus

All of the taggers we have tested make use of supervised learning, meaning that they need to be trained on a manually tagged corpus. We used the Memory-Based Tagger to create such a corpus using an iterative procedure which is commonly employed in cases where no pre-tagged material is available.

We started by tagging a small part of the corpus completely by hand, and trained a first version of the tagger on this material. We then ran the tagger on a different part of the corpus, manually corrected the tagger output, and added the corrected material to the training corpus. We were then in a position to re-train the tagger on this bigger training corpus, so that it could be applied to yet another part of the corpus, yielding slightly better results than it did the first time. By repeating this process, we simultaneously obtained an increasingly better tagger and an increasingly larger manually corrected corpus, which now contains approx. 190,000 tokens.

4 Cross-validation experiments

We have run 10-fold cross-validation experiments (Weiss and Kulikowski, 1991) with the different taggers on the manually tagged corpus of 190K tokens. In 10-fold cross-validation, 90% of the data is used for training and the remaining 10% for testing, and this procedure is repeated ten times, using a diffent 10% for testing each time. The data were shuffled before the distribution into training and test data began.

The MBT and QTag require a training corpus where each token is accompanied by its manually disambiguated tag, and a test corpus consisting only of tokens (however, if disambiguated tags are given in the test corpus as well, the MBT will report on its accuracy rate at the end of testing).

The TreeTagger accepts the same kinds of files, but also requires a lexicon that lists the set of possible tags for each known word, as well as a set of open class tags that can be used for unknown words.

Assuming that the lexicon is only supposed to contain known words, i.e., words that occur in the training data, we create a different lexicon for each fold by extracting all tags that occur for each word in the training corpus used in the fold. The set of open class tags includes all noun, verb, and adjective tags[3] that occur in the manually tagged corpus, reaching a total of 112. This presents the tagger with a fairly high number of choices for unknown words—compare this number, for instance, to the mere 17 tags that are suggested for the Penn Treebank tagset by the documentation for the TreeTagger.

Table 1 shows the averages and standard deviations for the 10-fold cross-validation experiments with the Memory-Based Tagger and the TreeTagger. The TreeTagger shows the best performance, while the performance of the HMM-based QTag lags far behind the other two taggers. Using McNemar's test, we have found all differences between the taggers to be statistically significant at the 0.01 level.

TreeTagger's superior performance over the HMM tagger agrees with Schmid's (1994) findings for written English, where TreeTagger outperformed the HMM tagger presented by Kempe (1993). In Megyesi's (2002) experiments on written Swedish, on the other hand, an HMM tagger (Brants, 2000) outperformed all other taggers, including one that used memory-based learning, thus showing results that differ considerably from those obtained here (she did not test any decision tree tagger). Our TreeTagger results are better than the best results obtained in either of these studies (which were 96.36% and 93.55%, respectively), and better than the 95.29% accuracy obtained by the HMM tagger in Nivre and Grönqvist's (2001) experiments on spoken Swedish with their largest tagset of 23 tags.

5 Removing pauses and hesitations

One of the properties that characterize spoken as opposed to written language is the presence of pauses and hesitations, as illustrated in (1), where e represents a hesitation sound and # represents a pause:

(1)   men i hvert fall # det er e
       "but anyway # it is e"

---

[3]In NoTa, all traditional adverbs that may be inflected are treated as adjectives (in accordance with Faarlund et al. 1995); hence, adverb is not counted among the open classes.

	Avg. accuracy	Standard deviation
TreeTagger	96.89	0.56
MBT	95.19	0.15
QTag	89.96	0.30

Table 1: Average accuracy and standard deviation for the 10-fold cross-validation experiments using the TreeTagger, the Memory-Based Tagger, and QTag.

We wanted to examine the effect of such phenomena on the performance of a statistical tagger for Norwegian spoken language. If pauses and hesitations tend to occur more or less randomly throughout an utterance, we would expect them to have a negative impact on the tagger. This is so because a pause or a hesitation occurring between two words will reduce the confidence of the tagger with respect to the propensity of these words to occur together. If, on the other hand, they tend to occur at certain structural positions in the sentence, they may actually contribute important information about the grammatical properties of the surrounding words.

In order to investigate this question, we have created versions of the cross-validation data in which we remove either pauses or hesitations or both, and we have re-run the 10-fold cross-validation experiments on these data. The results are shown in Table 2. For each tagger, the first row repeats the performance given in Table 1 on the original corpus; the second row shows the performance when hesitations are filtered out; the third row lists the performance with pauses removed, and the fourth row shows the results when both hesitations and pauses are filtered out.

Interestingly, removal of hesitations and pauses deteriorates the performance of the MBT and the TreeTagger, indicating that this material does not in fact function as noise for these taggers, but rather provides useful information about the grammatical status of surrounding words. This is particularly true for pauses, where removal leads to the largest drop in performance. Removing pauses is detrimental for QTag as well, but deleting hesitations actually improves the performance of this tagger. The indication that pauses in particular may provide important grammatical information supports the findings

by Strangert (1993) that pauses tend to occur at positions that are relevant to the underlying message, including syntactic boundaries.

	Accuracy (std.dev.)
TreeTagger	96.89 ($\pm$ 0.56)
TreeTagger **-hesitations**	96.86 ($\pm$ 0.58)
TreeTagger **-pauses**	96.67 ($\pm$ 0.60)
TreeTagger **-both**	96.61 ($\pm$ 0.61)
MBT	95.19 ($\pm$ 0.15)
MBT **-hesitations**	95.10 ($\pm$ 0.18)
MBT **-pauses**	94.78 ($\pm$ 0.19)
MBT **-both**	94.68 ($\pm$ 0.17)
QTag	89.96 ($\pm$ 0.30)
QTag **-hesitations**	90.11 ($\pm$ 0.28)
QTag **-pauses**	89.10 ($\pm$ 0.36)
QTag **-both**	89.19 ($\pm$ 0.31)

Table 2: Average accuracy and standard deviation for the experiments involving removal of hesitations and pauses. See the text for explanation.

6 Problematic words and tags

Table 3 lists the words that are most often mistagged by the TreeTagger, along with the proportion of the total number of errors that these errors constitute. The most problematic word is *så* (eng.: "so"), which may be either verb, conjunction, subjunction, or adverb, and which often occurs at the end of an utterance, making it hard to determine its correct category, as can be seen in (2):

(2)   nå er det jo in å bo på østkanten da # altså # *så* ...
        "now it is in to live on the east side, you know # then # so ..."

Interestingly, the words in Table 3 are also among the words that are most difficult for the human annotators to disambiguate.

Table 4 lists the most common tag confusions made by the TreeTagger. The table shows the erroneous tag produced by the tagger along with the correct tag. The clearest tendency to be extracted from this table seems to be that adverbs, prepositions, and subjunctions are easily confused by the tagger. Also,

word	error (%)	word	error (%)
så	13.1	som	3.3
det	9.4	de	3.0
noe	5.8	da	2.7
den	3.6	noen	2.0
for	3.4	jo	1.9

Table 3: The ten words that are most commonly mistagged by the TreeTagger in the cross-validation experiments.

it is worth noting that all of the words in Table 3 except *jo* exhibit one or more of the ambiguities listed in Table 4.

Output tag	Correct tag
pron_nøyt_ent_pers_3	pron/det
adv	konj/sbu/adv
adj_nøyt_ub_ent_pos	adj_ub_m/f_ent_pos
adv	konj
sbu	prep
konj	adv
adj_ub_m/f_ent_pos	adj_nøyt_ub_ent_pos
prep	sbu
adv	sbu
pron/det	pron_nøyt_ent_pers_3

Table 4: The most common tag confusions made by the TreeTagger.

7   Conclusions and future work

We have described experiments on Norwegian speech data with three data-driven taggers and found that the best performing one is the decision tree-based TreeTagger. This tagger is now being used to tag the rest of the 900,000 word corpus. We have also found that hesitations, and in particular pauses, seem to provide useful information for the taggers. In the future, we would like to modify the Oslo-Bergen rule-based written language tagger (Hagen et al., 2000) to become better suited for spoken language and compare its performance to that of the data-driven taggers.

References

T. Brants. 2000. TnT - A Statistical Part-of-Speech Tagger. *Proceedings of the 6th Applied Natural Language Processing Conference (ANLP-00)*, Seattle, Washington, USA.

W. Daelemans, J. Zavrel, A. Van den Bosch, and K. Van der Sloot. 2003. *MBT: Memory-Based Tagger, version 2.0, Reference Guide*. ILK Technical Report Series 03-13.

W. Daelemans, J. Zavrel, K. Van der Sloot, and A. Van den Bosch. 2004. *TiMBL: Tilburg Memory Based Learner, version 5.1, Reference Guide*. ILK Technical Report Series 04-02.

J.T. Faarlund, S. Lie, and K.I. Vannebo. 1995. *Norsk referansegrammatikk*. Universitetsforlaget, Oslo.

K. Hagen, J.B. Johannessen, and A. Nøklestad. 2000. A Constraint-Based Tagger for Norwegian. *17th Scandinavian Conference of Linguistics*, Volume I, no. 19. Odense Working Papers in Language and Communication.

J.B. Johannessen and K. Hagen. To appear. *Språk i Oslo*. Novus forlag, Oslo.

A. Kempe. 1993. *A probabilistic tagger and an analysis of tagging errors*. Technical report, Institut für Maschinelle Sprachverarbeitung, Universität Stuttgart.

B. Megyesi. 2002. *Data-Driven Syntactic Analysis. Methods and Applications for Swedish*. Doctoral dissertation, Departement of Speech, Music and Hearing, KTH, Stockholm.

J. Nivre and L. Grönqvist. 2001. Tagging a Corpus of Spoken Swedish. *International Journal of Corpus Linguistics* 6(1), 47-78.

H. Schmid. 1994. Probabilistic part-of-speech tagging using decision trees. *Proceedings of the International Conference on New Methods in Language Processing*.

E. Strangert. 1993. Clause Structure and Prosodic Segmentation. *FONETIK -93 Papers from the 7th Swedish Phonetics Conference*, Uppsala May 12-14 1993.

D. Tufis and O. Mason 1998. Tagging Romanian Texts: a Case Study for QTAG, a Language Independent Probabilistic Tagger. *Proceedings of the First International Conference on Language Resources & Evaluation (LREC)*, Granada (Spain), 28-30 May 1998, p.589-596.

S. Weiss and C. Kulikowski 1991. *Computer systems that learn*. Morgan Kaufmann, San Mateo, CA.

Initial Experiments with Estonian Speech Recognition

Anton Ragni

Department of Physics
University of Tartu
51010 Tartu, Estonia
`ragni@ut.ee`

Abstract

This paper presents a short description of work recently done at University of Tartu to construct a word–based speech recognition system. Simple bigram and trigram language models with cross–word triphone acoustic models are used by a one–pass best hypothesis recognizer to perform decoding of test data. The lowest word error rate of 37.5% reported in this paper is a common figure for word–based speech recognition of languages like Estonian.

1 Introduction

Estonian belongs to a family of inflectional and agglutinative languages which received a particular attention in recent years (Maučec et al., 2003; Kurimo et al., 2006). A single base word–form by means of inflections and compounding may have a huge number of derivative words. This greatly complicates the problem of building a speech recognition system with comparable word error rate (WER) performance to English systems. A common approach is to employ some type of subword systems, the goodness of which can be compared to each other and/or a word–based system (Hirsimäki et al., 2005). This paper is devoted to building of such word–based system and reports on results we obtained.

The first comprehensive description of work done on Estonian speech recognition appeared only recently (Alumäe, 2006). A huge number of experiments is conducted on two databases: Estonian part of Babel multi–language database (Eek and Meister,

1998) and Estonian SpeechDat–like database (Meister et al., 2003). The language modeling is performed both on a word and subword level. Our set of experiments is much more modest as compared to that work. However, we do not replicate the work already done but provide a completely independent set of results on Estonian part of Babel database.

The rest of the paper is organized as follows: in Section 2 language modeling is described. Section 3 is devoted to acoustic modeling. Section 4 describes experiments we performed and Section 5 makes conclusions drawn from this study.

2 Language Modeling

Experimental work with language modeling is performed on the Mixed Corpus of Estonian (MCE) – a set of written texts collected and maintained by University of Tartu[1] The total size of MCE is approximately 77M words excluding such special tags like sentence beginning (`<s>`), sentence ending (`</s>`) and number (`<NUMBER>`) symbols.[2]

A number of competitive bigram and trigram language models (LMs) is created using the HTK toolkit[3] The vocabulary of LMs is fixed to 65,000 most frequent words. All the diversity of LMs is obtained by application of different cut–off values to the number of bigrams and trigrams left in the model. The *cut–off value* specifies the least number of times any n–gram should have been seen in the

---

[1] http://www.cl.ut.ee/

[2] All numbers in this study are mapped to a common tag `<NUMBER>` since there is no known to us application capable of expanding them into verbal representations.

[3] http://htk.eng.cam.ac.uk/

Joakim Nivre, Heiki-Jaan Kaalep, Kadri Muischnek and Mare Koit (Eds.)
NODALIDA 2007 Conference Proceedings, pp. 249–252

corpus to be included in the model. Standard Good–Turing discounting is applied to refine parameters of LMs. The discounting factor k is kept greater from the cut–off value by seven for both bigrams and trigrams. Table 1 provides information about cut–off values for bigrams and trigrams, number of n–grams and size (for ARPA–compatible textual representation) of corresponding trigram LM. The size of tri-

Cut-off	Bigrams	Trigrams	Size (MB)
0	11,676,757	34,166,450	–
1	3,855,881	5,760,565	111.7
10	635,555	507,714	14.3
100	66,440	38,885	2.4

Table 1: Characteristics of trigram LMs

gram LM with cut–off values of 0 significantly exceeds the amount of available computer memory so it is not used in further experiments.

3 Acoustic Modeling

3.1 Babel Multi–Language Speech Database

Experimental work with acoustic modeling is performed on Estonian part of Babel multi–language speech database (Eek and Meister, 1998). The database consists of three subsets: *very few*, *few* and *many* talker sets. The recordings are made in a clean recording environment from the set of 40 text passages, 2 sets of numbers and 4 sets of sentences with multiple occurrence of acoustically confusable words (e.g., *Lina* and *liina*, *türi* and *tüüri*). The recorded speech is sampled at 20,000 Hz and digitized using 16-bit integers.

The training part in this study is composed from the very few and many talker sets. The few talker set is used for development and testing. Basic statistics for training, development and testing parts is summarized in Table 2.

	Train	Dev	Test
Passages	163	40	40
Sentence groups	67	0	8
Number groups	64	0	8
Hours	7.4	0.3	0.9

Table 2: Statistics for training, development and testing parts of Babel Speech Database

All audio data in this study is preprocessed using Mel–Frequency Cepstral Coefficients (MFCC) feature extraction scheme with default values of configurable parameters (Young et al., 2006).

3.2 Unit Selection

The first step in acoustic modeling is to decide upon basic modeling units. There are many options to choose from: words, syllables, phonemes. The large vocabulary speech recognition is best done with phoneme units. There are two possible phoneme sets: orthographic and phonetic set. Experiments conducted on two different Estonian speech corpora revealed no preference in WER figures between these two representations (Alumäe, 2006). The orthographic representation used in this study is based upon the letters of Estonian alphabet with some minor modifications to the loaned letters such as *c, q, x,* etc. These letters are substituted with a sequence of common letters following the generic rules of Estonian pronunciation.

There are 32 letters in Estonian alphabet and 27 of them are considered to be common letters. The remaining 5 letters are substituted with one or more letters from the first set. In addition, two models are created for representing *short pause* (usually between two words) and *silence* (usually between two phrases or sentences) events. Thus the monophone set consists of 29 models:

```
a, b, d, e, f, g, h, i, j, k,
l, m, n, o, p, r, s, sh, z, zh,
t, u, v, io, ae, oe, ue, sp, sil
```

where `sh` corresponds to *š* letter, `zh` to *ž*, `io` to *õ*, `ae` to *ä*, `oe` to *ö* and `ue` to *ü*.

3.3 Acoustic Models

Acoustic model (AM) training follows the generic training procedure described in (Young et al., 2006): a single 3–state left–to–right hidden Markov model (HMM) is constructed for each monophone except for short–pause (`sp`) model which is a single state HMM tied to the central state of silence (`sil`) model; once the monophone models are trained, the next stage of training procedure is to create a set of cross–word triphone models the parameters of which are tied using a phonetic decision–tree state tying procedure implemented in HTK; the number of mixtures is gradually increased until each model in the final set is represented at each state by the weighted sum of eight Gaussian probability density functions (pdfs).

4   Experiments

A large vocabulary speech recognizer implemented in the HTK toolkit (HDecode) is used to transcribe test sentences. There are many configurable parameters to alter the decoding process in some direction (speed, depth, accuracy, etc). For some of them the default values are used, for others, values giving the lowest WER are estimated on the development set.

Fig. 1 gives an example of influence imposed by the value of *word insertion penalty* on resulting WER figures. The word insertion penalty is a fixed

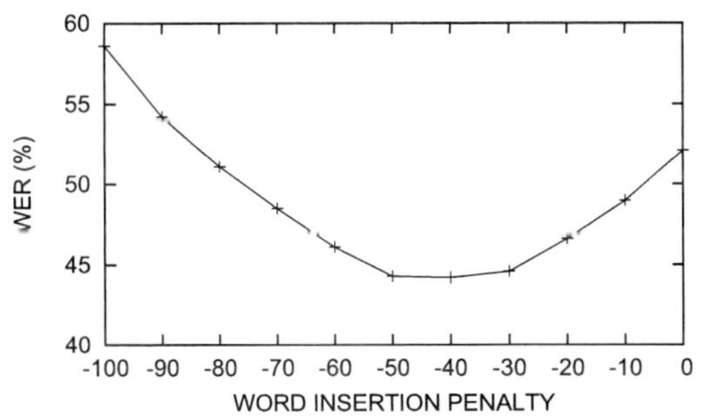

Figure 1: WER at different values of word insertion penalty

value added to each token when it transits from the end of one word to the beginning of another. By penalizing inter–word tokens we can force the appearance of new words only when their probability becomes sufficiently high.

Fig. 2 shows the performance of recognizer at different widths of decoding beam. The *main beam width* restricts the growth of recognition network and token propagation only to those HMM models the likelihoods of which fall no more than a beam width from the most likely model. Narrow beam width results in a smaller number of tokens considered at any given time, thus increasing the decoding speed. The time spent for recognition of test utterance is usually given as a portion of utterance real length called real–time ratio (RT). In Fig. 2 the decoding time varies between 0.2xRT and 7xRT. (Es-

timation of parameters and evaluation of test data is performed at the main beam width value of 200 with 2xRT speed of decoding unless otherwise stated.)

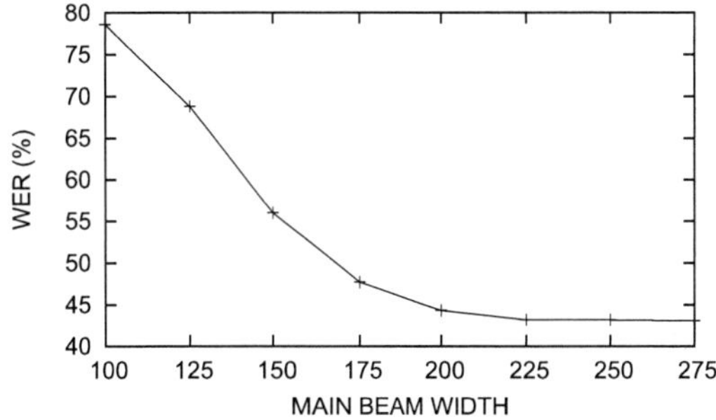

Figure 2: WER at different values of main beam width

Fig. 3 shows WER figures on the development set when LM and AM likelihoods are scaled. Giving a

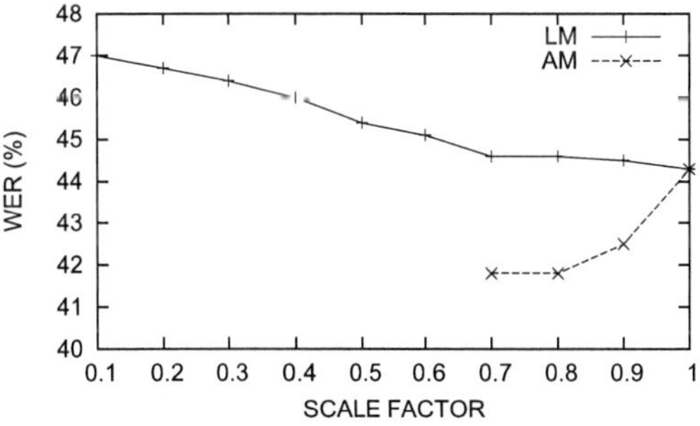

Figure 3: Effect of scaling down AM and LM likelihoods (results for up to 10xRT performance are shown)

preference to AM likelihoods by scaling down LM likelihoods leads to increased error rates; decreasing AM likelihoods, on contrary, enhances the accuracy of recognition with degradation in RT–performance.

Fig. 4 shows the improvement in recognition accuracy obtained by incrementing number of pdfs in the HMM state output distribution. The major drop in WER occurs when the number of pdfs is increased from three to five (13.4% absolute or 25.0% relative). Additional pdfs, however, lead to negligible reduction in WERs (1.8% absolute or 4.5% relative).

Final results of evaluation are given in Table 3. The first column describes the LM used in recog-

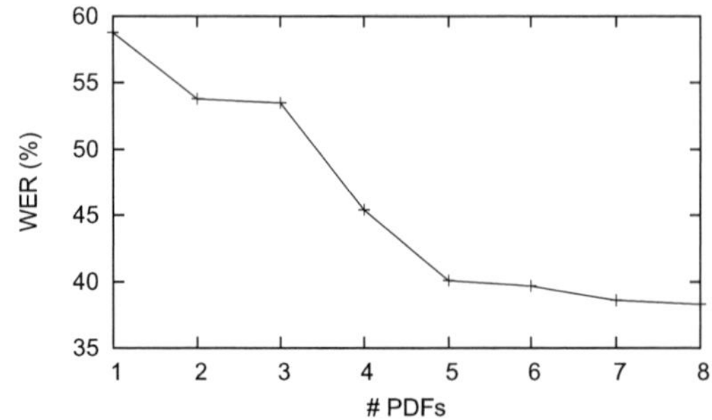

Figure 4: WER at different number of pdfs in HMM state distribution

LM	Del.	Subs.	Ins.	WER
bg100	420	1494	89	38.9
bg10	417	1472	86	38.3
bg1	417	1447	84	37.8
bg0	416	1438	81	37.5

LM	Del.	Subs.	Ins.	WER
tg100	420	1494	89	38.9
tg10	417	1471	86	38.3
tg1	417	1446	84	37.8

Table 3: Number of errors and corresponding WER figures for bigram and trigram LMs

nition: bg stands for bigram, tg for trigram and appended with the cut–off value for any order of n–grams. Next three columns specify the amount of different errors made by recognizer. As can be noted, 75% of all errors are substitution errors which can be originated from the lack of proper n-grams or weakly representative AMs, or both. LM's hit–ratios on the testing set confirm at least the first assumption: average hit–ratios for bigrams and trigrams are 50% and 11%. Since the number of trigram hits is very low, in major cases bigram instances are used instead. This also explains a comparable WER figures of bigram and trigram LMs. The lowest WER of 37.5% is obtained by the most comprehensive LM – bigram LM with more than 11M of distinct bigrams (113MB).

5 Conclusions

In this paper we described briefly the initial set of experiments with Estonian speech recognition using Estonian part of Babel speech database. The lowest WER reported in this paper (37.5%) can be compared to recently reported value of 36.2% (Alumäe, 2006) if we account for reduced amount of training data available to us. The recognition of test data is performed using a single–pass best hypothesis strategy which generally loses considerably to multi–pass N–best list strategies with a lattice stage rescored using more comprehensive LMs. However, this is an example of things needed to be done in the future using baseline systems built and described in this paper.

References

T. Alumäe. 2006. *Methods for Estonian Large Vocabulary Speech Recognition*. PhD thesis, Tallinn University of Technology.

A. Eek and E. Meister. 1998. Estonian speech in the babel multi–language database: Phonetic–phonological problems revealed in the text corpus. In *LP*, volume II, pages 529–546.

T. Hirsimäki, M. Creutz, V. Siivola, and M. Kurimo. 2005. Morphologically motivated language models in speech recognition. In *AKRR*, pages 121–126, Espoo, Finland.

M. Kurimo, A. Puurula, E. Arisoy, V. Siivola, T. Hirsimäki, J. Pylkkönen, T. Alumäe, and M. Saraclar. 2006. Unlimited vocabulary speech recognition for agglutinative languages. In *HLT-NAACL*, New York, USA.

M. Maučec, T. Rotovnik, and M. Zemljak. 2003. Modelling highly inflected slovenian language. *Int. J. of Speech Tech.*, 6:245–257.

E. Meister, J. Lasn, and L. Meister. 2003. Development of the Estonian SpeechDat–like database. In *Proceedings of Eurospeech*, pages 1601–1604, Geneva, Switzerland.

S. Young, G. Evermann, M. Gales, T. Hain, D. Kershaw, X. Liu, G. Moore, J. Odell, D. Ollason, D. Povey, V. Valtchev, and P. Woodland. 2006. *The HTK Book*. Cambridge University Press.

Grammar Sharing Techniques for Rule-based Multilingual NLP Systems

Marianne Santaholma

University of Geneva, ETI/TIM/ISSCO

40, bd du Pont-d'Arve, CH-1211 Geneva

`Marianne.Santaholma@eti.unige.ch`

Abstract

Rule-based multilingual natural language processing (NLP) applications such as machine translation systems require the development of grammars for multiple languages. Grammar writing, however, is often a slow and laborious process. In this paper we describe a methodology for multilingual and multipurpose grammar development based on grammar sharing. This paper presents the first step towards a language independent core grammar used for recognition, analysis and generation of English, Japanese and Finnish used in a domain specific spoken language translation system. The paper focuses on the grammar architecture and rule writing principles. Evaluation on analysis and generation has shown that two thirds of the rules are shared between these three typologically different languages.

1 Background

Grammar is a central component of many natural language processing (NLP) applications including grammar checkers, rule-based machine translation, and speech recognition systems. It formally describes the structure of a language and the way in which linguistic units such as words are combined to produce sentences in the language (Abeillé, 2000). Hence they are essential for tasks like the analysis and generation of languages. NLP grammars differ from each other, among other things, in their coverage, in the grammar formalisms used and the linguistic theories on which they are based. NLP grammars can further be categorized on whether they are used for processing spoken or written language.

A grammar writer is often confronted by both linguistic and purely practical issues. Firstly, language is a complex system and the development of a grammar requires a solid theoretical base in order to capture all the phenomena of a language relevant to a particular type of application. From the point of view of implementation a grammar without a firm theoretical basis remains difficult to maintain and expand systematically. Additionally one bad design decision can have unforeseen consequences later in other parts of the grammar.

Due to the complex nature of languages grammar writing, and consequently grammar-based system development, is time consuming and expensive. This is naturally even more so the case when developing multilingual applications. A multilingual spoken language translation system might be regarded as one of the "worst" cases since it implies not only the development of grammars for multiple languages but also for multiple purposes: speech recognition, analysis and generation. For these practical reasons grammar-based methods are often complemented or even replaced by statistical methods. During the last decade the increased availability of data, including spoken data, in multiple languages has indeed favoured the development and use of such alternative methods. However, when necessary data is not available, as it is often the case with "minor" languages at the beginning of a project, grammar writing remains as the only realistic option. Additionally when reliable and more predictable results are prioritized over robustness,

Joakim Nivre, Heiki-Jaan Kaalep, Kadri Muischnek and Mare Koit (Eds.)
NODALIDA 2007 Conference Proceedings, pp. 253–260

linguistic rule based processing is usually preferred (for example in speech recognition Rayner et al, 2005).

Different approaches to lessen the development burden of grammars have been implemented. For the case of multilingual grammars these approaches include *domain specific grammar development, grammar adaptation* (also called '*grammar porting*') and *grammar sharing*. The first concerns grammars that cover a certain domain specific language, a sublanguage (Kittredge, 2003). Compared to the standard, general language, sublanguages make use of limited vocabulary, syntax and semantics. Given this narrower extent, it is possible to produce a relatively complete linguistic description of the sublanguage structures. Consequently these grammars are less ambiguous and they perform generally better compared to general grammars. Sublanguage grammars for several languages are quicker to develop; however, since the coverage of grammar remains significantly restricted, porting them to new domains can be labourious (Kittredge, 2003).

Instead of limiting the coverage, the second approach, grammar adaptation, reuses the information from an already existing grammar of a language in building a grammar for a new language. The existing grammar rules for the use in same application and preferably of a closely related language are adapted for this new language. This approach has been applied in different types of grammar formalisms and applications (among others by Alshawi et al. 1992; Kim et al. 2003; Santaholma, 2005) and it appears to represent a reduction of effort regardless of the languages used and the linguistic framework adopted. However, the approach still requires a separate grammar for each new language, and thus a fair amount of development work.

Grammar adaptation can be seen as an approach that exploits the common features of languages in NLP grammar development. This is taken further in the third approach, grammar sharing. Instead of just reusing the information of an existing grammar, the grammar rules are actually shared between different languages. This is motivated by the fact that languages are structured by similar underlying principles and hence languages share structure and properties at least to some extent (for an overview see Comrie, 1981; Croft, 1990). There is a vast amount of research done in the field of linguis-

tic universals and language typologies comparing the properties of different languages, and the results of this research are exploited in NLP grammar development different ways by different grammar development projects, including ParGram (Butt et al., 2002) and Grammar Matrix (Bender et al., 2002).

To the best of our knowledge, the actual grammar sharing approach, where rules are directly shared between several languages, has only been implemented for closely related languages, such as Romance languages (Bouillon *et al.* 2006). Grammar sharing has both linguistic and practical advantages. Linguistically more coherent analyses are obtained when rules are written to be used for several different languages. On the practical, system development level the approach contributes to reuse of code and hence to the reduction in the number of rules linguists have to write. Furthermore modifications and debugging are carried out just on one grammar instead of several.

This paper presents a grammar architecture and rule writing principles for development of parameterized core grammar rules for languages that represent different types of languages: English, Finnish and Japanese. These rules are developed for a domain specific spoken language translation system and used for recognition, analysis and generation of these languages.

The rest of this paper is organised as follows. Section 2 briefly presents the Regulus toolkit used for grammar development, and the MedSLT system for which the language independent core grammar is implemented. Section 3 describes the grammar development principles with examples and section 4 summarizes the preliminary evaluation results. Section 5 presents our conclusions.

2 Tools and application

2.1 Regulus grammar development toolkit

The parameterized core grammar rules for English, Finnish and Japanese are implemented using the Regulus grammar development platform. Regulus is an Open Source toolkit for the development of unification grammars for spoken language (Rayner et al, 2006; Regulus, 2007). The main components include an environment for writing and debugging typed unification grammars, tools to support corpus-based specialization of general grammars, and a compiler which is used to turn unification grammars into Context-free Grammar (CFG) language models that are often used in speech recognition.

This compilation into CFG models imposes certain restrictions on the possible grammar formalism that can be employed. Firstly only finite feature-value pairs are allowed in the grammar rules and secondly the features cannot take any complex values. Hence the theoretically stable grammar formalisms that provide detailed syntactic and semantic analysis like Head Phrase Structure Grammar (Pollard & Sag, 1994) and Lexical functional grammar (Kaplan & Bresnan, 1982) are difficult to implement in the context of current speech recognition systems. For more details of Regulus grammars see Rayner et al, 2006.

2.2 The application: Spoken language translation system – MedSLT

The core rules implemented on Regulus are used in the medical domain spoken language translation system, MedSLT (MedSLT, 2007; Bouillon et al, 2005), which is developed to translate doctor-patient examination dialogues. Typical dialogues consist of medical examination questions about the intensity, location, duration or quality of pain, factors that increase/decrease the pain, medical/therapeutic processes and family history of the patient. The syntactic coverage mainly consists of yes-no questions where the patient's response can either be affirmative or negative. Content wise coverage is divided in subdomains based on specific symptoms (for example, headaches or chest pain).

The desired features of this type of medical domain translator include reliability of translation, flexibility in use and rapid portability to new languages and medical domains. These requirements have significantly influenced the MedSLT architecture. To obtain the reliability of translations and flexibility in use, the basic architecture adopted in MedSLT is a compromise between fixed-phrase translation and rule-based linguistic methods complemented by statistical language modelling as backup (Bouillon et al, 2005). Despite its hybrid architecture the heart of the MedSLT is the linguistic Regulus grammars.

To overcome the common difficulties of multilingual grammar development discussed in the introduction, a number of solutions have been implemented in MedSLT. First of all, one

single grammar of a language is automatically compiled by Regulus into the different formalisms needed in all the major components of the translator: speech recogniser, parser and generator. Another significant feature is that a general grammar of a language can be automatically specialized using Regulus for different domains (Rayner et al, 2006). In this way the system combines the advantages of general grammars (applicable in a wide range of domains) and domain specific grammars (less ambiguous).

The most significant drawback of the MedSLT approach, in terms of grammar development, remains, however, the laborious and time-consuming development of the general grammars. One solution to this problem is to share grammars between languages. This approach has been investigated by Bouillon et al. (2006) by developing parameterized rules for Romance languages French, Spanish and Catalan. Bouillon et al. (ibid) concluded that only few language specific rules were needed and that the recognition and generation results were equally good for all these three languages. We are extending this approach to non related languages. In the next section we describe the principles defined to develop these common rules.

3 MedSLT Regulus core grammar architecture and rule writing principles

3.1 Structure of grammar

The MedSLT Regulus core grammar consists of modules that form a three level inheritance structure. This is illustrated in Figure 1. "Language independent rules", the most generic level contains the parameterized language-independent rules that are stored in the "*Common core*" module. This module is shared with all the languages, and its information is inherited by all the lower levels (see section 3.2 for details).

The second level contains separate modules for different language families. According to language typology research one of the evident reasons for similarities between languages is that they are related (Comrie, 1981). In the core grammar we use this fact to reduce redundancy in rule writing. Hence, for example, the properties which are not common for all languages but typical for all Germanic languages, like English and Swedish, would be stored in the *"Germanic languages"* module. Finally the language specific information is stored in language specific modules, i.e. in separate English, Finnish, and Japanese modules.

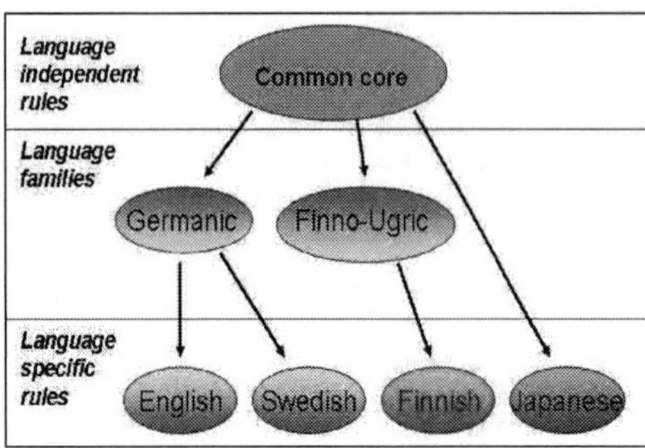

Figure 1: Structure of grammar

3.2 Rule writing principles

The methodology assumes two levels of syntactic representations: constituents and lists of feature-value pairs. In order to divide the constituents and feature-value pairs into the common and language specific modules, the linguistic phenomena necessary to express the concepts of MedSLT diagnosis questions (see Section 2.2) were first defined by analysing the MedSLT corpora of different languages. In a second step the structures used to express the extracted phenomena were compared between languages and the common properties for each structure were extracted. Some general rule writing principles were defined both for the constituents and the features. These principles are presented in the following.

3.2.1 Constituent level

Order of constituents. The basic order of constituents differs remarkably between languages. English and Finnish belong to SVO languages while Japanese is a verb final language, SOV. The first rule writing principle applied (at the constituent level) is that the order of constituents is expressed in a neutral way in the common rule set, "Common core". Instead of hard coding some specific constituent order, only the possible constituents are given, and the order itself is specified by language specific rules. The common rules are parameterized by macros as illustrated in the following.

Example 1 shows a simplified **vbar**[1] rule for phrases containing an auxiliary verb (**aux**) and a main verb (**verb**), for example *"The pain **has been** in the front of the head"*. In Finnish and English the auxiliary precedes the main verb, while in Japanese the auxiliary (marker) is at the end of the sentence after the main verb. These constituents are given in the common rule: vbar → aux verb. Furthermore the macro @vbar_aux_vbar in the common rule points to language specific rules that define the order of these constituents in each language. (The macros follow the Regulus macro writing definition (Rayner et al., 2006)). In Finnish and English the macro points to the identical language specific rule macro(vbar_aux_vbar(AuxV, V),(*AuxV, V*)) that defines that **auxiliary verb** (with semantic value **AuxV**) should precede the **Verb** (with the semantic value **V**) *(AuxV, V)*. The Japanese rule expresses the reverse constituent order by *(V, AuxV)*.

```
COMMON RULE
vbar:[sem=concat(AuxV, V),
vform=finite] -->
@vbar_aux_vbar(
        aux:[sem=AuxV, vform=finite,
participle_vform=Participle_form],
        verb:[sem=V,
vform=Participle_form]
        ).
*ENG + FIN* (aux+verb)
macro(vbar_aux_vbar(AuxV, V), (AuxV,
V)

*JAP* (verb+aux)
macro(vbar_aux_vbar(AuxV, V), (V,
AuxV)
```

Example 1. Constituent order

Variety of constituents. Besides the order of constituents also the variety of constituents varies between languages. Similarly to the constituent order, also the range of constituents is parameterized in the common rules by using macros. This is illustrated by Japanese and English/Finnish noun phrases (Example 2).

Particles (including case particles, topic particles, and postpositions) are very frequent in Japanese and they have various functions in Japanese syntax. In a noun phrase case parti-

---

[1] See Rayner et al., 2006 for detailed description of Regulus grammars.

cles are used to mark subcategorized verbal arguments for which English and Finnish apply other linguistic means (word order, inflectional case). Consequently Japanese requires a `case_particle` constituent that the other two languages do not. Hence the common noun phrase (**np**) rule in Example 2 is formed of a **nbar** and a macro `@case_particle`. As in the case of constituent order, a macro specifies the rule in different languages: in English and Finnish the macro `@case_particle` takes the value "empty" (`_`) and in Japanese the language specific rule introduces the particle constituent:

```
particle:[sem=Particle,
@noun_head_features(Head)].
```

```
COMMON RULE

np:[sem=@np_nbar(Nbar, Particle),
@noun_head_features(Head)] -->

nbar:[sem=Nbar, @noun_head_features(Head)],
@case_particle(particle:[sem=Particle,
@noun_head_features(Head)], _).

*ENG + FIN* (empty)
Macro(case_particle(Yes, No), No)

*JAP* (constituent case_particle)
Macro(case_particle(Yes, No), Yes).
```

Example 2. Variety of constituents

3.2.2 Feature-value pairs

In Regulus grammars, as in other constraint-based grammars, the feature-value pairs encode the fine-grained information, e.g. about the number, person, subcategorization, and semantic categories. As both the required feature-value pairs and the values that the features can take differ between languages, they are parameterized in the language independent rules. The basic principal applied is that the features that differ between languages, like agreement, are generalised under the head feature macros. The head features are the features that are provided by the heads (like noun or verb) of the compositional grammatical constituents such as noun phrases and verb phrases. These are referred as head feature macro rules such as `@noun_head_features(Head)`. Furthermore these macros point to the language specific rules where the needed language specific features are defined. This can be illustrated by noun and verb head features that include, e.g. agreement features.

Agreement is a highly language specific system. In English subjects and predicates agree in person and number. Finnish has number, person, and case agreement between subject and predicate, and Japanese doesn't apply any of these agreement features. The rule in Example 3 shows a simplified declarative sentence rule. The sentence (**s**) consists of a noun phrase (**np**) and of a verbal phrase (**vp**) (`s -> np vp`). The agreement features are parameterized in the **np** by the macro `@noun_head_features(Head)` and in the **vp** by `@verb_head_features(Head)` that point to language specific information.

```
COMMON RULE

s:[sem=concat(Np, Vp),
@verb_type(Type)] -->
        np:[sem=Np,
sem_np_type=SemType,
@noun_head_features(Head)],
        vp:[sem=Vp,
subj_sem_np_type=SemType,
@verb_head_features(Head),
vform=finite, inversion=false,
@verb_type(Type)].
```

Example 3. Phrasal head features

In the case of Finnish, the **noun_head_features** macro evokes the language specific rule:
```
macro(noun_head_features
([Number,Person,Case]),
[number=Number, person=Person,
case=Case]).
```

This specifies that **noun_head_features** include the features called `number` (singular/plural), `person` (1/2/3) and `case` (inflectional case). The **verb_head_features** macro evokes a similar language specific rule:
```
macro(verb_head_features(
[Number,Person,Case]),
[number=Number, person=Person,
subj_n_case=Case]).
```

In English the `case` and `subj_n_case` features are ignored by language specific declarations. The language specific macros corresponding to the Finnish ones are

```
macro(noun_head_features
([Number,Person]),
[nuber=Number,person=Person])
and
macro(verb_head_features
([Number,Person]),
[number=Number,person=Person]).
```

In Japanese all three features are ignored. The examples 4, 5 and 6 show the Finnish, English and Japanese declarative sentence rules after these language specific features have been applied.

```
s:[sem=concat(Np, Vp),
@verb_type(Type)] -->
np:[sem=Np, sem_np_type=SemType, per-
son=Person, number=Number, case=Case],
vp:[sem=Vp, subj_sem_np_type=
SemType, inversion=false, per-
son=Person, number=Number,
subj_n_case=Case, vform=finite,
@verb_type(Type)].
```

Example 4. Agreement in Finnish

```
s:[sem=concat(Np, Vp),
@verb_type(Type)] -->
        np:[sem=Np,
sem_np_type=SemType, person=Person,
number=Number],
        vp:[sem=Vp,
subj_sem_np_type=SemType, inver-
sion=false, person=Person, num-
ber=Number, vform=finite,
@verb_type(Type)].
```

Example 5. Agreement in English

```
s:[sem=concat(Np, Vp),
@verb_type(Type)] -->
        np:[sem=Np,
sem_np_type=SemType],
        vp:[sem=Vp,
subj_sem_np_type=SemType, inver-
sion=false, vform=finite,
@verb_type(Type)].
```

Example 6. Agreement in Japanese

4 Evaluation

To evaluate the common parameterised rules the MedSLT core grammar was tested on analysis and generation of MedSLT English, Finnish and Japanese examination questions. Instead of a large lexical coverage, the focus was on the covered linguistic phenomena. The test corpora contained MedSLT sentences including the variety of phenomena presented in Table 1. The aim of the evaluation was to find out how many rules were shared with all three languages and how many language specific rules were necessary in order to analyse and generate the corpora for each language.

To cover these phenomena in English, Finnish and Japanese total of 65 rules were written[2]. The number of rules used per language varies: English uses 54 out of 65 rules, including 3 language specific rules, Finnish uses 56 of 65 and has no language specific rules. Japanese makes use of 51 common rules and has 5 language specific rules.

Covered phenomena	
Sentence types	declarative, yn-question, wh-question, subordinate "when" clause
Tenses	present, past(imperfect), present perfect, past perfect
Aspects	Continuous
Verb subcategorisation	transitive, intransitive, predicative (be+adj), existential (there+be+np),
Determiners	article, number, quantifier
Adpositional modifiers	prepositional, postpositional
Adverbial modifiers	verb modifying and sentence modifying adverbs, comparison
Pronouns	personal, possessive, dummy pronouns
Adjective modifiers	predicative, attributive, comparison

Table 1. Covered phenomena

As Table 2 summarizes, two thirds (43/65) of parameterized rules are used by all three languages. Additionally in total 22 % of rules

---

[2] This number includes the language independent parameterized rules and languages specific rules.

are used for two languages. Only 12% of rules are strictly language specific.

Languages	No of rules	%
ENG + FIN + JAP	43	66
FIN + JAP	7	22
ENG + FIN	6	
ENG + JAP	1	
ENG	3	12
FIN	0	
JAP	5	
TOTAL	**65**	**100**

Table 2. Rules summarized

Furthermore, the grammar has altogether 57 declared features, 30 of them are common for all three languages. English ignores 13 features, Finnish 15 and Japanese doesn't make use of 19 of total 57 features. The used features vary significantly between languages depending on the typological character of language. Important features, like different case-features in Finnish, are ignored in English, while Japanese omits features including the agreement features like number and person that are significant in English and Finnish.

Based on the above presented figures we can conclude that the defined grammar architecture and rule writing principles captures the cross linguistic similarities and variations efficiently both on constituent and feature-value level.

5   Conclusion

This paper has presented a methodology for more efficient multipurpose and multilingual grammar development for typologically different languages based on rule sharing. The common parameterized rules were developed and tested on English, Finnish and Japanese on medical sublanguage. Evaluation showed that two thirds of rules were shared by all languages when parsing and generating the MedSLT medical examination questions.

We have shown that the defined grammar architecture that a) has a modular structure (a language independent module and language specific modules) and that b) assumes two levels of syntactic representations (constituents and feature-value pairs) that are both parameterized and generalized in the common rule level, captures efficiently the similarities and differences of typologically different languages.

Acknowledgements

I would like to thank Pierrette Bouillon and Manny Rayner for their advice. The MedSLT system is developed at TIM/ISSCO, University of Geneva, and funded by Swiss National Science Foundation.

References

Abeillé A. 1993. Les nouvelles syntaxes: grammaires d'unification et analyse du français. A. Colin, Paris.

Alshavi H (ed). 1992. *The core language engine.* Cambridge, Massachusetts: the MIT press.

Bender E, Flickinger D, Oepen S. 2002. The Grammar Matrix. An Open Source Starter-Kit fort he Rapid Development of Cross-Linguistically Consistent Broad-Coverage Precision Grammars. In *Proceedings of the 19th International Conference on Computational Linguistics*, Taipei, Taiwan, p. 8-14.2002.

Bouillon B, Rayner M, Chatzichrisafis N, Hockey B A, Santaholma M, Starlander M, Isahara H, Kanzaki K, Nakao Y. 2005. A Generic Multi-Lingual Open Source Platform for Limited-Domain Medical Speech Translation. In *Proceedings of EAMT 2005*, Budapest, Hungary, pp. 50-58.

Bouillon P, Rayner M, Novellas Vall ., Nakao Y, Santaholma M, Starlander M, Chatzichrisafis N (2006). Une grammaire multilingue partagée pour la traduction automatique de la parole. In *Proceedings of Traitement Automatique des Langues Naturelles*, 10 - 13 avril 2006, Leuven, Belgique.

Butt M, Dyvik H, King T H, Masuichi H, and Rohrer C. 2002. The Parallel Grammar Project. In *Proceedings of COLING-2002 Workshop on Grammar Engineering and Evaluation.* pp. 1-7.

Comrie B. 1981. *Language Universals and Linguistic Typology.* University of Chicago Press, USA.

Croft W. 1990. *Typology and universals.* Cambridge University Press.

Kaplan R & Bresnan J. 1982. Lexical-Functional Grammar: A formal system for grammatical representation. In Joan Bresnan (editor), *The Mental Representation of Grammatical Relations*, pp. 173-281. Cambridge, MA: The MIT Press.

Kim R, Dalrymple M, Kaplan R, King T H, Masuichi H, Ohkuma T. 2003. Multilingual Grammar development via Grammar Porting. In *Proceedings of the ESSLLI 2003 Workshop on Ideas and Strategies for Multilingual Grammar Development.* Vienna, Austria, pp.49-56.

Kittredge R. 2003. Sublanguages and controlled languages. In *Mitkov, Ruslan (ed.), The Oxford Handbook of Computational Linguistics*, pp. 430-447. Oxford University Press, Oxford.

MEDSLT 2007. https://sourceforge.net/projects/medslt/. As of 15 Mars 2007.

Pollard C & Sag I. 1994. *Head-Driven Phrase Structure Grammar*. University of Chicago Press, Chicago.

Rayner M, Bouillon B, Chatzichrisafis N, Hockey B A, Santaholma M, Starlander M, Isahara H, Kanzaki K, Nakao Y. 2005. A Methodology for Comparing Grammar-Based and Robust Approaches to Speech Understanding. In *Proceedings of Eurospeech-Interspeech*, 4-8, September, 2005, Lisboa, Portugal.

Rayner M, Hockey B A. and Bouillon P. 2006. *Regulus. Putting Linguistics into Speech recognition*. Stanford University Center for the Study of language and information, Stanford, California.

REGULUS.2007.https://sourceforge.net/projects/regulus/. As of 15 Mars 2007.

Santaholma M. 2005. Linguistic representation of Finnish in a limited domain speech-to-speech translation system. In *Proceedings of the 10th Conference on European Association of Machine Translation, 2005,* Budapest, Hungary, pp. 226-234.

Using a Wizard of Oz as a baseline to determine which system architecture is the best for a spoken language translation system

Marianne Starlander

ETI-TIM-ISSCO, University of Geneva

40, bd du Pont d'Arve, 1211 Genève 4

`Marianne.Starlander@eti.unige.ch`

Abstract

This paper is part of an extended study on system architectures, the long term aim being to determine if a unidirectional, a bidirectional or a fixed-phrase architecture is more suitable in the context of the spoken language translator in the medical domain (MedSLT). Our aim here is to compare data collected during a Wizard of Oz (WOz) experiment with data collected using a beta bidirectional version of our system.

1   Introduction

The most common architectures for a spoken language translation (SLT) system are unidirectional, bidirectional or fixed-phrase systems. Unlike most commercial SLT systems for medical diagnosis, MedSLT is grammar-based. The aim is to provide reliable translations of the doctor/patient interview (Bouillon et al., 2005) in a context of controlled dialogue. In this domain precision is more important than robustness for out-of-coverage sentences since the medical user will be trained with the coverage before using the system. At first we implemented a unidirectional version because most doctor-patient interviews are doctor-initiated. However, the demand for a bidirectional system has grown and we decided to start to build such a system, but the question of which system is really best suited for such a task remained open. The aim of this study is to collect evidence to justify the choice of building a bidirectional system.

We will describe the experiments (section 2) we carried out and the resulting evaluation (section 3), before concluding in section 4.

2   Experiment

In the first phase, we constructed a WOz experiment where the participants used three different architectures (bidirectional, unidirectional and fixed-phrase) inspired from the actual MedSLT system. The users were then asked to answer a usability questionnaire where they conclude by citing their preferred architecture. In a second phase, once the actual bidirectional system was built, our aim was to conduct an experiment that would confirm the WOz user's preferences for a bidirectional system. We thus asked the same subjects to use both the beta-version of the bidirectional system and the unidirectional system and to rank the systems again according to their preference. The purpose was to check whether the constrained bidirectional system as opposed to the WOz system was still the preferred architecture. This second experiment also allowed us to study how the users adapted to a system restricted by limited coverage. In this sense, the WOz plays the role of a baseline.

2.1   WOz

Our source of inspiration was the use of a WOz experiment to collect natural data as a working basis to develop the Spoken Language Translator in the ATIS domain (Bretan et al., 2000). This type of experiment is often used for the purpose of developing a spoken dialogue system because it enables (1) the collection of representative speech data and (2) the observation of human-computer interaction in order to improve or create the interface design (Life et al., 1996). In our case, the aim is to enable users to experiment with different architectures of a system in a WOz setting. This experiment also gave us the opportunity to observe the natural interaction of doctor-patient users if they were not

Joakim Nivre, Heiki-Jaan Kaalep, Kadri Muischnek and Mare Koit (Eds.)
NODALIDA 2007 Conference Proceedings, pp. 261–264

restricted to limited coverage. Our experimental environment was simple: the computer running the simulated MedSLT system by the doctor and patient was connected through a VNC connection to two computers in a separate room where two wizards were in reality recognizing and translating instead of MedSLT. The users were not aware that the system was actually run by humans.

2.2 Beta bidirectional MedSLT

MedSLT's bidirectional version works in a manner similar to the unidirectional version: recognition and translation is based on general unification grammars written in the Regulus format (Rayner et al., 2006). The new part is the integration of a second system for the treatment of answers. These are currently limited to elliptical sentences directly related to the question asked, so that the same ellipsis resolution can be applied to them (Bouillon et al., 2007). In order to compensate for the fact that the coverage is quite restricted due to this grammar-based approach, we provide the user with a help module that guides them towards the correct formulation. This module simply uses the result of the secondary statistical recognition to derive a list of in-coverage sentences.

For this second phase of the experiment the major challenge was to find an efficient way of training the users with the real system without interfering too much with their natural interaction with it. This training included four steps for the doctor: (1) learning the interface and the mechanical use (e.g. clicking before talking), (2) learning how to formulate questions through given controlled language rules (derived from the observations made during the WOz experiment), (3) reading through a list of in-coverage sentences during a limited amount of time, and (4) by testing the system with a member of a team to check that the microphone position and the basic usage of the system is adequate. For the patient training the main rule to observe was to answer with elliptical sentences.

2.3 Set-up

In both cases, the task was the following: the doctor or the final year medical student had to make a diagnosis for a patient who only spoke Spanish. The patients were native-Spanish speakers who were asked to pretend not to understand any French or English if they happened to do so, and to simulate sore-throat symptoms described in the task scenario. The doctor had to determine whether they suffered from a strep throat or a viral sore-throat.

In the WOz, we had eight patient-doctor pairs, each using the three different architecture versions (unidirectional, bidirectional and fixed-phrase) varying between the headache and sore-throat domains. For the actual system, three of the same doctors participated and interviewed five out of the eight original patients, and each interviewed two to three patients during a session using first the bidirectional and then the unidirectional system.

At the end of each diagnosis, lasting between ten and fifteen minutes for the real system and fifteen to thirty minutes with the WOz, the doctors filled out a diagnosis form to check on the completion of the task. In the end both doctors and patients filled in a questionnaire. This data plays a key role in the evaluation we will now describe.

3 Evaluation

We follow the classical divide in our evaluation between objective and subjective data. In the first category we decided not to include WER and SER as these measures are not really very efficient to judge the quality of a SLT system (Wang et al., 2003). Instead of WER and SER, we checked the percentage of sentences correctly translated by the system and those that were out of coverage, as this is the most important in order to guarantee an efficient doctor-patient communication. We kept the following usual measures in SLT evaluation campaigns (Stallard, 2000): task completion, and duration. We also decided to carry out a close analysis of the collected speech data regarding the type of answer formulation used by the patients. Finally in the subjective evaluation category we used a utility questionnaire.

3.1 Translation quality and task completion

In this section we will briefly comment on the quality of the translation with the bidirectional system: we divided the collected data into well translated (68.5%), badly translated (0.5%) and out-of-coverage sentences (31%). It is important to note that although the rate of out-of-coverage (OOC) sentences is quite high - it still remains clearly under the WOz OOC percentage of 74.1% - this did not affect efficiency as the average duration of a diagnosis was 12.57 minutes (compared to 20.72

min. for the WOz), and the percentage of successful task completion was around 72%. However it is important to note that this rate would be even higher if our patients really suffered from these symptoms. Patients indeed sometimes gave the doctors incoherent information, not written in their scenario, which explains most of the diagnosis errors.

3.2 Data analysis

As we were beginning to build the bidirectional version of the system, we wanted to have data about the types of answers a patient would give in response to diagnosis questions, in order to gather information on how well the users can adapt to a more limited coverage.

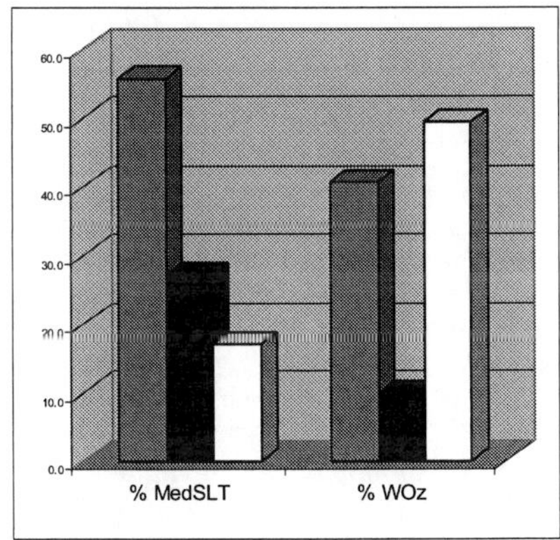

Figure 1. Ellipsis use with System X and WOz

For this reason, we specifically analyzed the proportion of ellipsis, compared to full sentences and yes/no answers. Figure 1 gives a synthesis of this study (grey = ellipsis, black = yes/no and white = full sentences).

From Figure 1 we can draw the following conclusions. First, the patient could adapt to the use of ellipsis, as shown by the fact that they used full sentences only 17.1% of the time while this percentage was far higher in the WOz. It is interesting to note that the gap in ellipsis use between WOz and MedSLT is not as wide as expected (55.7% vs. 40.7%). This would tend to prove that the use of ellipsis is quite natural when answering certain questions (e.g.: temporal questions « *Desde cuándo le duele la garganta* » - *For how long have you had your sore throat*). While questions about the location (*where is your pain?)* and the nature of symptoms (*do you have a rash?)* seem to be answered more naturally with full sentences (*sí, tengo una erupción cutánea* » - *yes, I have a rash*). Finally, patients answer much less frequently with yes/no in the WOz, since the doctor can ask more open questions like « so, what is the problem » than with the actual bidirectional system where the secondary symptoms had to be enumerated, which explains why 27.1% of the answers are of the yes/no type.

3.3 Questionnaire

Based on (Lewis, 1991) we constructed a usability questionnaire, using a 1-5 Likert scale to grade the answers given to the following questions :

Q1	Easy to use the system
Q2	Clear instructions on task
Q3	Good response time
Q4	Could ask enough questions to be sure of diagnosis
Q5	System more efficient than non-verbal communication
Q6	User-friendly interface
Q7	Utility of CL rules
Q8	Help window very useful to learn coverage
Q9	Have often taken sentences directly from help window

Table 2. Abstract of questions

Figure 2 synthesizes the answers to the questionnaire. The real system obtains higher scores than the WOz for all questions apart from Q5, where both obtain almost equally high results. This tells us that both systems are more efficient than non-verbal communication. The less differentiated scores for Q4 are due to simulation of symptoms which sometimes made patients answer in a less clear-cut manner which sometimes puzzled the doctors. This probably explains why the score is no higher than 4 for MedSLT and 3.7 for the WOz. Interestingly MedSLT gets higher scores. This would definitely tend to prove that the constraints due to limited coverage were not impeding the dialogue interview. The most important gap between MedSLT (4.3) and the WOz (2.1) is quite logically found in the question about the speed of the system (Q3). The results for Q1 show that the participants declare that they could easily learn how to use the system thanks to the given instructions. Interestingly, the gap between the WOz and the real system is not wider, as we would have expected since the users have to adapt to the limited coverage.

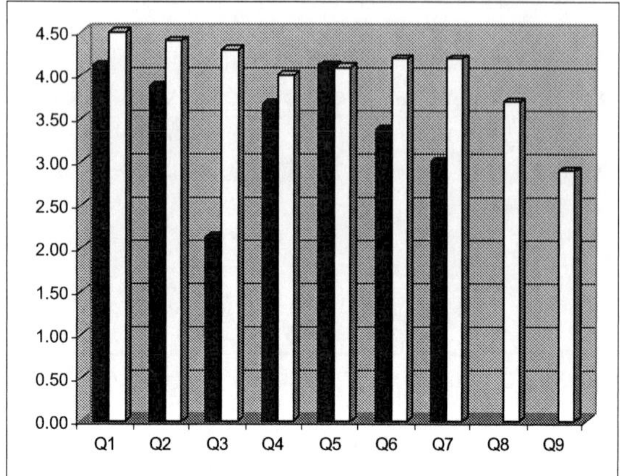

Figure 2. Answers to the questionnaire (white=our system, black=WOz)

This leads us to the results for Q7-Q9 that all concern the learning of the system's coverage. The real system scores high on Q7 about the utility of the controlled language (CL) rules which were given in order to guide the user's formulation. However, the participants gave mitigated answers about the utility of such rules, which can be explained by the unrestricted nature of the WOz. The CL rules were considered to be more useful to learn the coverage than the sentences displayed in the help window (Q 7), whereas these were deemed very useful in previous studies (Starlander et al., 2005).

Finally, the questionnaires tell us that when comparing the different available architectures, the users always prefer a bidirectional architecture, even with the beta version of MedSlt where the coverage is more restricted.

4   Conclusion

After this study using a WOz as a baseline system we can conclude that the bidirectional MedSLT system is performing well; and that the users still prefer this architecture. The users, especially the patients, can adapt to its limited coverage, by using ellipsis and thus achieving a very acceptable task completion. The overall translation quality is acceptable.

This work is only part of a more extended study comparing different architecture with regard to usability and user satisfaction. The next step, be-

fore an extended evaluation, involves a further development phase, after which we would like to compare the actual restricted version of the bidirectional system with a wider version allowing full sentences in some extent.

References

Bouillon, P., M. Rayner, et al. (2005). A generic Multlingual Open Source Platform for Limited-Domain Medical Speech Translation, *10th Conference of the European Association of Machine Translation*, Budapest, Hungary: 50-58.

Bouillon, P., M. Rayner, et al. (2007). Les ellipses dans un système de Traduction Automatique de la Parole, to appear in *TALN 2007*, Toulouse.

Bretan, I., R. Eklund, et al. (2000). Corpora and Data Collection. *The Spoken Language Translator*. M. Rayner, D. Carter, P. Bouillon, V. Digalakis et M. Wirén. Cambridge, Cambridge University Press: 131-144.

Brooke, J. (1996). SUS-A quick and dirty usability scale. *Usability Evaluation in Industry*: 189-194.

Life, A., I. Salter, et al. (1996). Data collection for the MASK kiosk: WOz vs prototype system. *ICSLP '96*, Philadelphia, USA: 1672-1675.

Lewis, J. R. (1991). "Psychometric evaluation of an after-scenario questionnaire for computer usability studies: the ASQ " *SIGCHI Bulletin* 23(1): 78-81.

Rayner, M., B. A. Hockey, et al. (2006). *Putting Linguistics into Speech Recognition*. Stanford, California, Stanford University Center for the Study of Language and Information.

Stallard, D. (2000). Evaluation Results for the Talk'n'travel System. *Applied Natural Language Processing Conference, Seattle*, Washington.

Starlander, M., P. Bouillon, et al. (2005). Practising Controlled Language through a Help System integrated into the Medical Speech Translation System (MedSLT). MT Summit X, Phuket, Thailand: 188-194.

Wang, Y.-Y., A. Acero, et al. (2003). Is Word Error Rate a Good Indicator for Spoken Language Understanding Accuracy. *Workshop on Automatic Speech Recognition and Understanding*, St Thomas, US Virgin Islands.

A Method for Recognizing Temporal Expressions in Estonian Natural Language Dialogue Systems

Margus Treumuth
Institute of Computer Science
University of Tartu, Tartu, Estonia
`treumuth@ut.ee`

Abstract

Extraction of temporal expressions from an input text is an important step in natural language processing tasks. Automated extraction of temporal expressions can be used in dialogue systems where temporal constraints need to be enforced. The paper proposes an algorithm for processing temporal information in natural language. The algorithm was implemented as a standalone rule-based temporal expression recognizer and was made available as a web-service. Finally the implemented module was partially integrated into a spoken language dialogue system that is an interface to a theater information database.

There is no evaluation as this work is still in progress.

1 Introduction

Temporal information can often be a significant part of meaning communicated in dialogues. There are various kinds of dialogues where people negotiate dates and times. Therefore, the automatic extraction of temporal expressions in natural language is required in building dialogue systems where temporal constraints need to be enforced.

Temporal expressions in text vary from explicit references, e.g. *June 1, 1995*, to implicit references, e.g. *last summer*, to durations, e.g. *four years*, to sets, e.g. *every month*, and to event-anchored expressions, e.g. *a year after the earthquake*. (Hacioglu, et al., 2005)

The paper proposes an algorithm for processing temporal information in natural language. The algorithm was implemented to work on Estonian texts and partially integrated to an Estonian spoken language dialogue system that is an interface to a theater information database (Treumuth, et al., 2006).

The extraction tool of time expressions was implemented as a standalone non domain specific module, and was made available as a web-service, that can be plugged into dialogue systems with some minor adjustments.

The time expression recognizer could be a useful software tool in the following list of currently available Estonian language technology software tools:

- Text-to-speech synthesizer (Meister, et al, 2003) (Mihkla, et al, 1999)

- Speech recognizer (speech-to-text): experimental version (Alumäe, 2004)

- Morphological analyzer + generator => spelling checker, hyphenator (Kaalep, 1997)

- Shallow syntactic analyzer => experimental versions: noun phrase extractor, text summarizer, grammar checker (Müürisep, et al, 2006)

- Word sense disambiguator: experimental version (Kaljurand, 2004)

- Dialogue act recognizer: experimental version (Fišel, 2005)

Joakim Nivre, Heiki-Jaan Kaalep, Kadri Muischnek and Mare Koit (Eds.)
NODALIDA 2007 Conference Proceedings, pp. 265–268

2 Algorithm

The rule-based algorithm involves a grammar and a parser. A top down approach is used in matching the regular expressions to input text. The more specific patterns precede the less specific ones in the matching cycle.

The input to the algorithm is text in Estonian, e.g. an utterance from the user of a dialogue system.

The output of the system is:
1. recognized time expression as text
2. recognized time expression as a logical expression (query constraint in meta SQL)

For example:

> **INPUT**: *veebruari teises pooles* (second half on February)
>
> **OUTPUT:**
> RECOGNIZED: *veebruari lõpus* (in the end of February)
>
> CONSTRAINT = DATE between 15.02.$YEAR and last_day(01.02.$YEAR)

Notice that the input term and the output term differ slightly, yet their meaning is the same. The output term is used in generating the answer and is a predefined term for each rule. This will be explained in more detail in the following sections.

The output can contain many sets of recognized expressions and constraints. The more specific ones are listed prior to less specific ones.

The Estonian Morphological Analyzer (Kaalep, 1997) was not used in generating the grammar and was also not used in parsing the grammar. The inflections and agglutinations of Estonian date expressions are easily predictable and can be handled manually. The morphological analyzer will be used as this work is continued. At this time the morphological analyzer is being used in the dialogue system, that employs the temporal recognition module. The input to the temporal recognition module coming from a dialogue system is morphologically analyzed, providing lemmas or base forms, if no other forms yielded a recognition result.

When integrating the parser with a dialogue system, it would be useful to get some additional input from the dialogue system in addition to the current utterance. For instance, knowing the dates that were recognized earlier in the current conversation would provide a way to accept corrections from a user, in case the user would like to clarify prior temporal expressions.

2.1 Grammar

The analysis for the grammar generation process involved studying some real-life dialogues that were held with a dialogue system. It turned out that the users of the dialogue system often like to query the database for intervals of time, rather than for a specific date. That is, instead of requesting information for a specific date as *"January 11th"*, the users often tend to say *"something in January"*.

In addition, students of computational linguistics were used in checking corpora for various representations of Estonian time expressions, finding out all the different ways to refer to a same single date expression.

The grammar consists of 1405 rules where regular expressions are mapped to corresponding SQL constraints as follows:

> regular expression ==> SQL constraint

For example:

> / (oktoober|oktoobri)\S* laupäev\S* /U
> ==>
> weekday(DATE) = 'laupäev' and DATE between 01.10.$YEAR and last_day(01.10.$YEAR)

This rule would recognize expressions like *"oktoobris laupäeviti"*, *"oktoobri laupäevadel"* (in October on Saturdays) and the corresponding SQL constraint can be enforced on a relational database.

The grammar can handle various constructions of time expressions where names of months and weekdays are used to represent an interval of time. Following are a few examples of some date expressions that are recognized by the temporal recognition agent:

> *pühapäeviti ja esmaspäeviti jaanuaris* - on Sundays and Mondays in January
> *jaanuaris ja veebruaris* - in January and in February
> *esmaspäeviti ja laupäeviti* - on Mondays and on Saturdays
> *aprilli lõpus* - at the end of April
> *juuni keskel* - in the middle of June
> *oktoobri alguses* - in the beginning of October
> *mais neljapäeviti* - on Thursdays in May

If the regular expressions in grammar are matched to a natural language input, the corresponding SQL constraints are integrated into a SQL query's template *WHERE clause* as follows:

```
<SELECT clause>
<FROM clause>
<WHERE clause
  [temporal constraints]
  [all other constraints]>
```

For example:

```
SELECT title
FROM performances
WHERE
weekday(DATE) = 'Saturday' and DATE
between 01.10.2007 and
last_day(01.10.2007)
[all other constraints]
```

Upon execution of this query the dialogue system would return the performances that match the time constraint and other constraints. These SQL constraints can easily be altered to suit the needs of a specific database. Also the functions *weekday* and *last_day* are available in most database engines or can easily be implemented.

It was more efficient and extendable to create an explicit grammar, rather than trying to implement an rule based program to cope with these expressions. The grammar is residing in a text file (outside of program code) and can easily be altered and extended. This approach is similar to the one described by Berglund (2004).

2.2 Deictic Expressions

Deictic expressions are expressions that refer to temporal aspect of an utterance and depends on the context in which they are used (Wiebe, et al., 1998). For example "*tomorrow*" depends on current date and is recognized as "*current date + 1 day*" (with respect to the conversation date).

The grammar currently contains a non-terminal *$YEAR*, that is used to enforce dependencies to current date by avoiding looking in past dates. No other deictic expressions are represented in grammar. The algorithm copes with deictic expressions in a separate parser. It can recognize patters like "*on weekends*", "*day after tomorrow*", "*today*", "*next Monday*" and so on.

3 Extensions to Grammar

3.1 Answer Phrases

While the grammar is used to recognize time expressions and execute queries based on returned constraints, there is also need to provide input for the answer generation, as the answer should also contain the recognized time expression in correct form.

For that reason, the grammar that was described above, was extended by adding the recognized term into the rule as follows:

```
oktoobris laupäeviti
        ==>
/ (oktoober|oktoobri)\S* laupäev\S* /U
        ==>
weekday(DATE) = 'laupäev' and DATE between
01.10.$YEAR and last_day(01.10.$YEAR)
```

The recognized term, in correct form, can be used in generating an answer to the user by plugging it in a sentence. Assume a conversation:

<User>: Are there any performances in **October on Saturdays**?
<System>: Here are the plays that I found in **October on Saturdays** …

The pattern can match multiple formats, yet the answer phrase can be fixed to one format, as the rules are built to support this approach.

3.2 Constraint Relaxation

Partial constraint relaxation is implemented in a dialogue system that uses the temporal constraint grammar, yet the rules for constraint relaxation are not defined in the grammar.

For example, the user might mention a date, that would result in *"not found"* response. Then it would be appropriate to relax this constraint, as in the following dialogue.

<User>: Are there any performances on **Saturdays**?
<System>: No, yet I found one on this **Sunday** …

Here we saw an example of a constraint relaxation where the original date constraint was relaxed by adding one day. This way the users of the system can receive some alternative choices, instead of plain *"not found"* responses.

The constraint relaxation properties can be held in the grammar as long as they stay separate from the dialogue domain.

3.3 Correction Questions

There are a some problems with deictic expressions that can be solved by correction questions.

For example, if user mentions the word "*week-end*" on Sunday evening, does the user mean next weekend or the current weekend.

The correction questions are not implemented in the grammar, as they tend to be domain specific. The grammar could be extended by adding correction questions and choices for corresponding answers, also as long as they stay separate from the dialogue domain.

4   Conclusion

The paper has described an algorithm that was implemented as a standalone automated extraction tool for processing temporal information in Estonian natural language. This rule-based approach can be used for other languages (English). The main idea and benefit of current approach is the output of logical expressions that can be used in SQL queries.

The rule-based approach was chosen, as it turned out to save a lot of time to implement an explicit grammar by automatically generating hundreds of rules and a parser (regular expression pattern matching), rather than trying to implement a clever, yet implicit black-box algorithm to cope with all these rules. Also a grammar generator was built, which is able to re-generate the grammar of 1405 rules, making it easy to manage and extend the grammar.

The grammar can be improved in using constraint relaxation options and predefined question-answer sets for correction sub-dialogues.

It would also be useful to get some additional input from the dialogue system in addition to the current utterance. For instance, knowing the dates that were recognized earlier in the current conversation would provide a way to accept corrections from a user, in case the user would like to clarify prior temporal expressions.

The time expression recognizer (e.g. as tagger) could be a useful software tool among the other currently available Estonian language technology software tools.

References

Tanel Alumäe. 2004. Large Vocabulary Continuous Speech Recognition for Estonian Using Morphemes and Classes. *TSD 2004*: 245-252.

Anders Berglund. 2004. Extracting Temporal Information and Ordering Events for Swedish. *Master's thesis report.*

Mark Fišel. 2005. Dialogue Act Recognition in Estonian Dialoguesusing Artificial Neural Networks, *Proceedings of the International Conferenc The Second Baltic Conference on Human Language Technologies,* 231-235;

Kadri Hacioglu, Ying Chen, and Ben Douglas. 2005. Automatic Time Expression Labeling for English and Chinese Text. *In Proceedings of CICLing-2005,* pages 348-359; Springer-Verlag, Lecture Notes in Computer Science, Vol. 3406.

Heiki-Jaan Kaalep. 1997. An Estonian Morphological Analyser and the Impact of a Corpus on Its Development. *Computers and the Humanities* 31: 115-133.

Kaarel Kaljurand. 2004. Word Sense Disambiguation of Estonian with syntactic dependency relations and WordNet. *In Proc. ESSLLI-2004*, Nancy, France, 128-137.

Einar Meister, Jürgen Lasn, Lya Meister. 2003. SpeechDat-like Estonian database. - In: *Text, Speech and Dialogue* : 6th International Conference, TSD 2003, Czech Republic, September 8-12, 2003 / Eds. Matoušek [et al.]. Berlin [etc.] : Springer, Lecture Notes in Artificial Intelligence, Vol. 2807. 412-417.

Meelis Mihkla, Arvo Eek, Einar Meister. 1999. Text-to-Speech Synthesis of Estonian. – *Proceedings of the 6th European Conference on Speech Communication and Technology*, Budapest, Vol. 5 2095-2098.

Kaili Müürisep, Heli Uibo. 2006. Shallow Parsing of Spoken Estonian Using Constraint Grammar. In: *Treebanking for Discourse and Speech. Proceedings of NODALIDA-2005 special session on treebanking*: NODALIDA-2005 special session on treebanking, Joensuu, 2005. (Ed.) Peter Juel Henrichsen, Peter Rossen Skadhauge. Frederiksberg, Denmark: Samfundslitteratur, 105 - 118.

Margus Treumuth, Tanel Alumäe, Einar Meister. 2006. A Natural Language Interface to a Theater Information Database. *Proceedings of the 5th Slovenian and 1st International Language Technologies Conference 2006 (IS-LTC 2006)*, 27-30.

J. M. Wiebe, T. P. O'Hara, T. Ohrstrom-Sandgren and K. J. McKeever. 1998. An Empirical Approach to Temporal Reference Resolution. *Journal of Artificial Intelligence Research*, 9, 247-293.

IV Posters

LinES: An English-Swedish Parallel Treebank

Lars Ahrenberg
NLPLab, Human-Centered Systems
Department of Computer and Information Science
Linköpings universitet
lah@ida.liu.se

Abstract

This paper presents an English-Swedish Parallel Treebank, LinES, that is currently under development. LinES is intended as a resource for the study of variation in translation of common syntactic constructions from English to Swedish. For this reason, annotation in LinES is syntactically oriented, multi-level, complete and manually reviewed according to guidelines. Another aim of LinES is to support queries made in terms of types of translation shifts.

1 Introduction

The empirical turn in computational linguistics has spurred the development of ever new types of basic linguistic resources. Treebanks are now regarded as a necessary basic resource (Nivre et al, 2005) and many of the parallel corpora that were created in the nineties are being developed into parallel treebanks. A parallel treebank extends the usability of a parallel corpus in several ways:

- The application of syntactic annotation schemes can be tested on several languages and enables multi-lingual evaluation and/or training of parsers.

- With access to syntactic relations and alignments we can provide much more fine-grained characterizations of structural correspondences and automatically identify and count such correspondences in the corpus.

- We can investigate the distribution of different kinds of shifts in different sub-corpora and characterize the translation strategy used in terms of these distributions.

In this paper the focus is mainly on the second aspect, i.e., on identifying translation correspondences of various kinds and presenting them to the user. When two segments correspond under translation but differ in structure or meaning, we talk of a translation shift (Catford, 1965). Translation shifts are common in translation even for languages that are closely related and may occur for various reasons. This paper has its focus on structural shifts, i.e., on changes in syntactic properties and relations.

Translation shifts have been studied mainly by translation scholars but is also of relevance to machine translation, as the occurrence of translation shifts is what makes translation difficult. While not all types of translation shifts need to be handled by a machine translation system at least the ones that are due to differences in grammar must be, and, generally speaking, the more of the others that can be handled, whether motivated by style or translator preferences, the better the system.

2 LinES

LinES, Linköping English-Swedish Parallel Treebank, is created on the basis of LTC, The Linköping Translation Corpus (Merkel, 1999). The selection of sentences from the sources are somewhat arbitrary. It has been assumed that whatever selection is made, as long as it is random, will provide typical examples of the usage of function words and grammatical

Joakim Nivre, Heiki-Jaan Kaalep, Kadri Muischnek and Mare Koit (Eds.)
NODALIDA 2007 Conference Proceedings, pp. 270–273

Eng. *Did you see the elephants ?*
Swe. *Såg ni elefanterna ?*
Links: (0,0,-1,-1,5)#(1,1,1,1,5)#(2,2,0,0,5)
#(3,4,2,2,5)#(5,5,3,3,5)

Figure 1: Encoding of word alignments in short format.

constructions and their translation.

2.1 Sub-corpora

The current version of LinES has two sub-corpora, Access, that includes sentences from MS Access online Help texts, and Bellow, with sentences taken from the novel *Jerusalem and Back* written by Saul Bellow. Each sub-corpus contains 600 sentence pairs that have been parsed and aligned at the word level. The goal is to include 1-2 more genres with different texts from each genre and about 1000 sentence pairs from each text.

A sub-corpus of LinES consists of three files: a source file, a target file, and a link file. Source and target files of LinES are XML-formatted monolingual files. These files are structured in terms of segments and words. Segments are demarcated by <s>-tags and words by <w>-tags.

A word normally corresponds to an orthographic word of the source text. However, punctuation marks and clitics are treated as separate words, and a restricted set of multi-word units, such as *of course, each other* are treated as single words.

Each segment has a unique identifier, its s-id. Corresponding source and target segments are assigned identical s-ids. Similarly, each word has a unique identifier, its word-id. In addition, each word has an identifier that states its relative position in the segment.

There are two formats for link files: an XML-format and a short format, where a correspondence is identified by five numbers. The first two numbers identify a word sequence from the source segment, and the next two numbers a word sequence from the target segment. (0,0) is the index for the first word. The pair (-1,-1) is used to represent a null alignment. The fifth number classifies the link as independent or as part of a discontinous alignment. An example of this encoding is shown in Figure 1.

2.2 Linguistic annotation

Words carry a number of attributes for linguistic annotation. The most important of these attributes are `base` for the word stem, `pos` for the part-of-speech, `msd` for morpho-syntactic properties, `func` for dependency relation with respect to a head word, and `fa` for the position of the head word.

Base forms are identical to one of the actually occurring forms of a word. Thus, the base form generally is not a proper lemma, as words of different parts of speech, and words of the same parts of speech with different inflections, may have the same base form.

A common set of parts of speech and morphological properties are used for both languages. While all part-of-speech categories apply to both languages, some morphological properties are used only for one of them. For instance, participial forms are sub-categorized differently in English and Swedish, and only Swedish nouns are sub-categorized for definiteness.

The syntactic annotation in LinES is based on dependency relations. Each segment is assumed to have a single head token and all other tokens, except punctuation marks, are direct or indirect dependents of the head. The analysis is projective, i.e., no discontinuous phrases are allowed. This makes conversion to flat phrase structure representations simple. Dependency analysis has an advantage for parallel treebanks in that phrase alignment to a large extent is given for free from the word alignment.

For parsing, the Machinese Syntax parsers for English and Swedish from Connexor Oy, have been used[1]. These parsers supply initial values for base form, part-of-speech and morphological categorization. However, the annotation in LinES differ in several respects from the parser output. First, postprocessors that convert annotations and add morpho-syntactic information not provided by the parsers are applied. Some function words have also been given different parts-of-speech in LinES.

The dependency functions used in LinES also differ from those of the parsers. The main difference is that they are structure-oriented. In particular, many functions with a primarily semantic flavour that the parses use are encoded as adverbials or modifiers,

---

[1]See http://www.connexor.com/

while others have been added. For instance, LinES distinguishes both prepositional objects and particles from adverbials and employs some additional functions not used by the parsers, such as vocative.

2.3 Alignment

Sentence alignment in LinES is taken over from LTC, while the guidelines for word alignment are slightly different. All of the alignments are manually reviewed, using the interactive word alignment system I*Link (Merkel et al, 2003).

The basic rule for alignment in LinES is the same as the one used in many other projects, namely "Align as short segments as possible, and as long segments as necessary". This guideline means that if we cannot find a good link for a word that we are looking at, we try to find a segment that includes that word that has a better correspondent. However, if the argument can go either way, we prefer many small links to few large ones. For example, a correspondence such as *the house ~ huset* is aligned $(0,0,-1,-1)\#(1,1,0,0)$ rather than $(0,1,0,0)$. Thus, so called level shifts (Catford, 1965) are normally encoded with the aid of null links in LinES.

3 Querying LinES

A word-aligned parallel corpus can easily be queried for word correspondences, using whatever linguistic information is associated with the words. A parallel treebank can in addition be queried for functional information and, in principle, arbitrary subtrees and their correspondences.

The query interface for LinES is in development. The current web-based interface supports link-based search, while tree-based search is still in the pipeline.

3.1 Link-based queries

A link-based query can specify constraints on segments that have been aligned as a pair. In the simplest case the query specifies constraints on a single node of the dependency tree. In this case LinES supports any combination of constraints on base forms, parts-of-speech, morphological information, and dependency relation. Constraints can also be placed on the number of nodes. Moreover, constraints can be specified only for one of the languages, or for both of them. An example is shown in Figure 2.

obj ~ subj: (Count = 9)

[bellow-290]	The Americans wanted the new **regime** to make the populace literate , to create ' a large and stable middle class a sufficient identification of local ideals and values , so that truly indigenous democratic institutions could grow up . '	Amerikanerna ville att den nya **regimen** skulle göra befolkningens breda lager läskunniga och skapa ' en stor och stabil medelklass och en tillräcklig identifiering med landets egna ideal och värderingar , så att verkligt inhemska demokratiska institutioner kunde växa fram ' .
[bellow-325]	I had been telling Shahar when we were walking in the Gai-Hinnom that I had n't liked **it** when David Ben-Gurion on his visits to the United-States would call upon American Jews to give up their illusions about goyish democracy and emigrate full speed to Israel .	När Shahar och jag promenerade i Gai-Hinnom hade jag sagt att **det** stötte mig att David Ben-Gurion på sina besök i USA brukade uppmana de amerikanska judarna att ge upp sina illusioner om gojernas demokrati och emigrera till Israel i flygande fläng .
[bellow-348]	This is a thought that sometimes crosses Jewish **minds** .	Detta är en tanke som judars **medvetande** snuddar vid ibland .
[bellow-394]	I trust that they will give us better **love** than they are getting from us , for ours is a very low-quality upward-seeping vegetable-sap sort of love , as short-lived as it is spontaneous .	Jag hoppas att den **kärlek** de skänker oss är av bättre kvalitet än den de får av oss , för vår egen är av en mycket lågklassig uppåtsipprande växtsaftsliknande sort som är lika kortlivad som spontan .

Figure 2: Output from LinES. The query concerns nodes with an object function in the source text corresponding to subjects in the target text.

3.2 Subtree search

In principle any subtree of a full dependency tree could be the object of an alignment relation. Moreover, if we wish to explain the occurrence of a certain structural shift, the relevant information may be located anywhere in the tree and even outside the tree. While it would be desirable to have a rich language for specifying tree queries, such as that used with Tgrep2 (Rhode, 2004), we do not initially aim for handling arbitrary combinations of constraints, but want to handle queries that classify a correspondence in terms of types of shifts such as deletion, addition, convergence, head switch, and so on.

We restrict consideration to subtrees that form a connected part of a full tree with a single node as its head and zero or more dependent nodes. If the head node has no dependents, the subtree and the node are identical.

A subtree is *inclusive* if it contains all (direct and indirect) dependent nodes of its head node. It is *unilevel* if its longest branch has length one, and is complete wrt to this depth if it contains all direct dependents. In addition to these two types of subtrees, queries for single branches and their correspondents need to be supported.

A subtree and its image are *isomorphic* if (i) they have the same number of nodes, (ii) the same number of branches, and (iii) the n:th branch of the image is an isomorphic image of the n:th branch of the given subtree, where n identifies left-to-right order. For a branch to be an isomorphic image of another branch we require that its m:th subtree of depth 1 is the image of the m:th branch of the other one.

Even if a subtree and its image are isomorphic, they are not necessarily free of shifts. This is so, because the notion of isomorphism so far defined does not take associated linguistic information into account. We believe that a simple formal solution is hard to find in spite of the fact that our categories are uniform. Thus, we need to treat correspondence in annotations notionally. Starting from a simple formal notion of regular correspondence for subtrees and their images, we may consider extending it by adding explicit equivalence relations that express normal relations when translating from English to Swedish.

4   Related work

Several projects for the creation of parallel treebanks have recently been launched. The FuSe project (Cyrus, 2006) annotates parts of the English and German sections of the Europarl corpus with regard to predicates and their arguments. LinES is different from FuSE in that it aims for complete alignments of segment pairs and (semi-)automatic derivation of shifts.

The CroCo-project (Hansen-Schirra et al, 2006) also works with German and English but has a larger scope. Complex queries based on the annotation for many types of shifts can be formulated, though so far only with detailed knowledge of the XML-format and the details of the annotation.

The SMULTRON corpus (Volk et al, 2006; Samuelsson and Volk, 2006) includes data from three languages (English, German, and Swedish). The annotation is based on phrase structure analyses. This project is primarily oriented towards machine translation and the recognition of translation equivalents that can "serve as translations outside the current sentence context" (Samuelsson and Volk, 2006). For this reason, phrase alignment of a sen-

tence pair need not be complete and, contrary to LinES, the alignment of non-equivalent phrases are avoided rather than sought for.

References

J. C. Catford 1965. *A Linguistic Theory of Translation: An Essay in Applied Linguistics*, London, Oxford University Press

Lea Cyrus 2006. Building a resource for studying translation shifts. Proceedings of LREC 2006, Genoa, May 24–26, 2006 1240-1245.

Silvia Hansen-Schirra, Stella Neumann, and Mihaela Vela. 2006. Multi-dimensional Annotation and Alignment in an English-German Translation Corpus. Proceedings of the EACL Workshop on Multi-dimensional Markup in Natural Language Processing (NLPXML-2006), Trento, Italien, 4. April 2006, 35-42.

Magnus Merkel 1999. Understanding and enhancing translation by parallel text processing. *Linköping Studies in Science and Technology, Dissertation No. 607.* Linköping, 1999.

Magnus Merkel, Michael Petterstedt, and Lars Ahrenberg. Interactive Word Alignment for Corpus Linguistics. Proceedings of Corpus Linguistics 28-31 March, 2003, Lancaster. UK.

Joakim Nivre, Koenraad de Smedt, and Martin Volk 2005. Treebanking in Northern Europe: A White Paper. Holmboe, Henrik (ed.) Nordisk Sprogteknologi 2004: Årbog for Nordisk Sprogteknologisk Forskningsprogram 2000-2004, 97-112. København: Museum Tusculanums Forlag.

Yvonne Samuelsson and Martin Volk. 2006. Phrase Alignment in Parallel Treebanks Jan Hajiĉ and Joakim Nivre (eds.) *Proceedings of the Treebank in Linguistic Theory Workshop*, Prague, Czech Republic, December 2006. 91-102.

Douglas T. L. Rhode 2004. TGrep2 - the next-generation search engine for parse trees. http://tedlab.mit.edu/~dr/Tgrep2/.

Martin Volk, Sofia Gustafson-Capková, Joakim Lundborg, Torsten Marek, Yvonne Samuelsson, and F. Tidström. 2006. XML-Based Phrase Alignment in Parallel Treebanks. *Proceedings of EACL Workshop on Multi-dimensional Markup in Natural Language Processing*, Trento, Italy, April 2006.

Posterior Probability Based Confidence Measures Applied to a Chidren's Speech Reading Tracking System

Daniel Bolanos
HCTLab-EPS. Universidad Autónoma
de Madrid, SPAIN
daniel.bolanos@uam.es

Wayne H. Ward
CSLR, University of Colorado at
Boulder USA
whw@cslr.colorado.edu

Abstract

In this paper, we present improved word-level confidence measures based on posterior probabilities for children's oral reading continuous speech recognition. Initially we compute posterior probability based confidence measures on word graphs using a forward-backward algorithm. We study how an increase of the word graph density affects the quality of these confidence measures. For this purpose we merge word graphs obtained using three different language models and compute the previous confidence measures over the resulting word graph. This produces a relative error reduction of 8% in Confidence Error Rate compared to the baseline confidence measure. Moreover the system operating range is increased significantly.

1 Introduction

When dealing with children's continuous speech recognition, it is difficult to obtain satisfactory acoustic models due to the great variability of children's speech. Oral reading tracking systems use a speech recognizer to determine whether a child has read a known passage correctly. Such systems often cope with lack of adequate acoustic models by taking advantage of very tight language models that reflect what the child is supposed to be reading. A recognizer for a reading tracking system was developed in this context (Hagen, 2006) in which the single best scoring hypothesis from the recognizer is used as the hypothesis for what the child read. Comparing these hypotheses against the hand transcriptions for the speech yields a Word Error Rate around 10% when tested on 3rd, 4th and 5th grade children. However, the use of this kind of restrictive language model can make rejection of errors difficult and leads the system to consider misread words as correct. We apply confidence measures to the recognized words as a basis for detecting words that have been misread or skipped.

Previous work has shown (Wessel, 2001) that confidence measures based on word posterior probabilities estimated over word graphs outperform alternative confidence measures (Kemp, 1997) such as acoustic stability and hypothesis density. In the following discussion we will take advantage of this technique in order to obtain word level confidence estimates in the context of children's speech reading tracking.

2 Posterior Probability Based Confidence Measures

SONIC (Pellom, 2001), the continuous speech recognizer used in this work, is able to output the results of the first-pass decoding process in the form of word lattices. Each of these lattices can be considered as an acyclic, directed, weighted word graph, and used (Hacioglu, 2002) during the decoding process to calculate word posterior probabilities. This calculation is carried out by the forward-backward algorithm considering edges as HMM-like states, where emission probabilities are the acoustic models scores and transition probabilities between links are obtained from the trigram language model used. Taking these posterior probabilities attached to each word on the graph we estimate the following confidence measures, where $[w;s,e]$ is a word hypothesis starting at time s and ending at time e and $p([w;s,e]|x_1^T)$ is the posterior probability for the hypothesis word w for the acoustic observation sequence x_1^T.

$$C([w;s,e]) = p([w;s,e]\,|\,x_1^T)$$

$$(1)$$

Joakim Nivre, Heiki-Jaan Kaalep, Kadri Muischnek and Mare Koit (Eds.)
NODALIDA 2007 Conference Proceedings, pp. 274–277

$$C_{sec}([w; s, e]) = \sum_{\substack{[w; s', e']: \\ \{s,...,e\} \cap \{s',...,e'\} \neq 0}} p([w; s', e'] \mid x_1^T)$$

(2)

$$C_{med}([w; s, e]) = \sum_{[w; s', e']: s' \leq \lceil \frac{s+e}{2} \rceil \leq e'} p([w; s', e'] \mid x_1^T)$$

(3)

$$C_{med'}([w; s, e]) = \sum_{\substack{[w; s', e']: \\ s' \leq \lceil \frac{s+e}{2} \rceil \leq e' \wedge (s=s' \vee e=e')}} p([w; s', e'] \mid x_1^T)$$

(4)

$$C_{max}([w; s, e]) = \max_{e_{max} \in \{s,...,e\}} \sum_{[w; s', e']: s' \leq e_{max} \leq e'} p([w; s', e'] \mid x_1^T)$$

(5)

In (1) posterior probabilities are taken directly as a confidence measure for a word hypothesis. However, previous work (Wessel, 2001) has demonstrated that this measure of confidence does not give satisfactory results. The reason is that the fixed starting and ending time frames of a hypothesis word strongly determine the paths involved in the calculation of the forward-backward probabilities. The following confidence measures calculated (2), (3), (4) and (5) take advantage of the fact that, usually, word hypotheses with similar starting and ending time frames represent the same word and therefore makes sense to consider the summation of the posterior probabilities of these words as a confidence measure. The differences between them consist basically of how word hypotheses are selected to be used in the posterior probability accumulation process. In (2) word hypotheses that overlap in time are considered, this procedure has been shown to perform very well as a confidence measure but suffers from a lack of normalization since the summation of the accumulated posterior probabilities over all different words on a single time frame no longer sums to one. To cope with this drawback (3), (4) and (5) are used. In all of them, the posterior probability accumulation process is carried out over all different hypotheses of a word with at least one time frame in common.

Note that while Csec, Cmed and Cmax were proposed on (Wessel, 2001) Cmed' is a variation of Cmed in which only words with the same first or last frame are taken into account in the posterior probability accumulation process. Cmed' performs slightly better than Cmed in terms of Confidence Error Rate as can be seen in Table 1.

2.1 Score normalization

One of the characteristics of children's oral reading is the propagation of errors due to repetitions of text segments, self-corrections and other kinds of disfluencies. We compensate for these events by doing the following normalization over the confidence measures applied to each word. The parameters μ and λ are estimated on a development set distinct from the testing set to avoid over-adaptation.

$$C_{norm}([w_i, s_i, e_i]) = \mu C_{max}([w_{i-1}, s_{i-1}, e_{i-1}]) + \lambda C_{max}([w_i, s_i, e_i]) + (1 - \mu - \lambda) C_{max}([w_{i+1}, s_{i+1}, e_{i+1}])$$

(6)

2.2 Experimental results

We present experimental results on a corpus composed of the CU Prompted and Read Children's Speech Corpus (Cole, 2006), the OGI Kid's speech corpus (Shobaki, 2000) and the CU Read and Summarized Story Corpus (Cole, 2006). Children's acoustic models are estimated from over 62 hours of audio from the CU Prompted and Read Children's Speech Corpus, the OGI Kids' speech corpus grade K through 5, and data from 1st and 2nd graders found in the CU Read and Summarized Story Corpus. Confidence measures are evaluated on the 106 3rd, 4th and 5th graders from the CU Read and Summarized Story Corpus.

To evaluate the performance of the confidence measures applied we use the confidence error rate (CER), defined as the number of incorrectly assigned tags divided by the total number of recognized words. The CER of the baseline system is calculated by dividing the number of insertions and substitutions by the number of recognized words. Since the CER depends on the tagging threshold selected, as well as the acoustic and language model scaling factors, these parameters are adjusted not on the test corpus but on a different cross-validation corpus.

Confidence Measure	CER	Error reduction
Baseline	9.70%	0.00%
C	9.24%	4.74%
C_{sec}	8.05%	17.01%
C_{med}	8.11%	16.39%
$C_{med'}$	8.08%	16.70%
C_{max}	8.05%	17.01%
C_{norm}	7.93%	18.25%

Table 1. Confidence error rates and error reduction

Table 1 summarizes the CER for the confidence measures applied. It can be seen that while word posterior probabilities used directly as a confidence measure don't perform well, the normalized version of C_{max} performs better than the others.

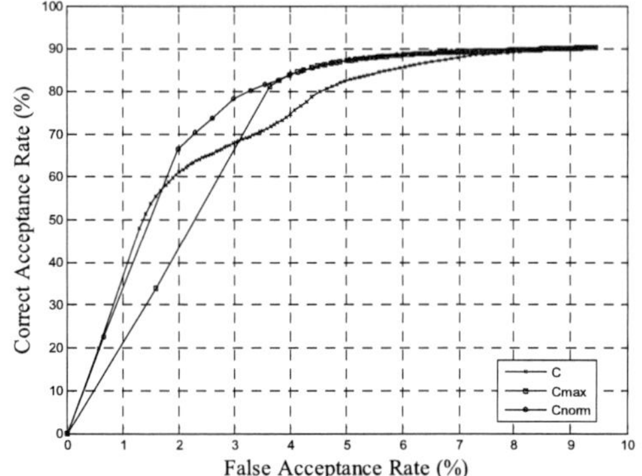

Figure 1. Receiver operating characteristic (ROC) curves.

As can be seen in Figure 1, the C_{norm} measure also has the best performance for the ROC. Note that correct acceptance is tagging a correct word as correct and false acceptance is tagging an incorrect word as correct.

3 Increasing Word Graph Density to Improve the Quality of Confidence Measures

During the decoding process an adaptive language model is used due to the fact that words that are likely to be spoken next can be anticipated based upon the words in the text that are currently being read. For this purpose position-sensitive trigram language models are obtained (Hagen, 2006) partitioning the training text into overlapping regions. After decoding each utterance, the position-sensitive language model that gives a higher probability to the last recognized words is selected for the first pass decoding of the subsequent utterance. This results in a very low perplexity language model.

The main problem when estimating posterior probability based confidence measures over a word graph generated using a very tight language model is the low word graph density, defined as the word hypotheses per spoken word. Previous work (Wessel, 2001; Fabian, 2003) has shown that the word graph density has a clear impact on the quality of confidence measures and therefore it is necessary to adjust the WGD in order to get the best confidence error rates.

To cope with this problem we generate word graphs using the following language models.

1) The original trigram adapted language model that produces the best output in terms of WER.

2) A trigram language model without adaptation.

3) A bigram language model without adaptation.

For each utterance we take the three word graphs generated and merge them into one graph, and then we use it to estimate the confidence measures over the hypothesis generated. During the posterior probability accumulation process, hypotheses coming from different graphs are weighted differently. From now we refer to this confidence measure as C_{merge}.

$$C_{merge}([w,s,e]) = \alpha C_{max(adapted)}([w,s,e]) +$$
$$\beta C_{max(trigram)}([w,s,e]) + (1-\alpha-\beta)C_{max(bigram)}([w,s,e])$$

$$(7)$$

After doing the merging process we also do a score normalization as described in 2.1.

3.1 Experimental results

We conducted experiments with two configurations, in the first one we build a word graph merging word graphs obtained with language models 1 and 2. In the second configuration we build a word graph that merges all three language models in order to increase the graph density further. The results are shown in Table 2. Increasing the word graph density does provide better performance of the confidence estimation measure. The ROC curves shown in Figure 2 also demonstrate that the confidence measures generated from the more dense graphs perform better.

Confidence Measure	WGD	CER	Error Reduction
Baseline	6.45	9.70%	0.00%
C_{norm}	6.45	7.93%	18.25%
C_{merge} (config. 1)	16.64	7.51%	22.58%
C_{merge} (config. 2)	32.79	7.44%	23.30%

Table 2. Word graph densitiy (WGD), confidence error rate (CER) and error reduction respect the baseline for the confidence measures applied using the different configurations.

In the first configuration, the value for α, i.e., the weight applied to the hypotheses coming from the word graph obtained with language model 1, that yields the best performance is in the range of (0.7-0.77), while the weighting value for hypotheses coming from the graph obtained with language model 2 is in the range of (0.23-0.3). In the second configuration, the values for α, β and (1-α-β), that yield the best performance are in the range of (0.65-0.7), (0.15-0.2) and (0.1-0.15). These values show that hypotheses coming from graphs generated with smoother languages models must be weighted less during the posterior probability accumulation process in order to obtain satisfactory results.

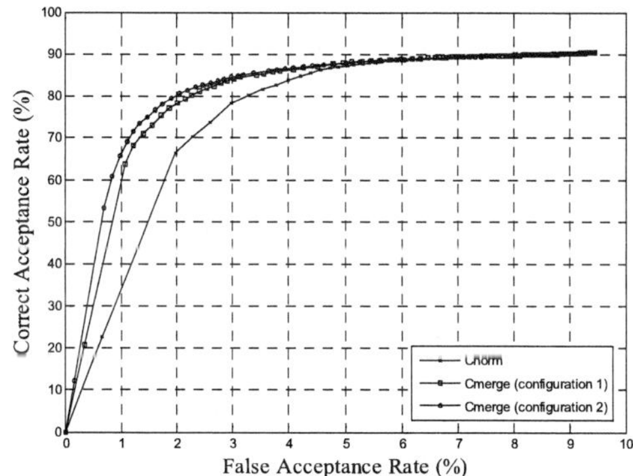

Figure 2. Receiver operating characteristics (ROC) curve.

4   Conclusions

We have evaluated the performance of using confidence measures based on word posterior probabilities to reject misrecognized words in hypotheses generated by a speech recognizer in a reading tracker task. While this technique has been shown to work relatively well for large vocabulary speech recognition, the task of a reading tracker presents a special case. A very tight language model produces the best word error rate, but does not produce a dense enough graph to provide good confidence estimates. We have shown that, adding hypotheses generated from more smoothed language models to increase the word graph density and doing a score normalization based on word context information, the performance of the confidence measures is improved significantly.

5   Future Work

The current work uses posterior probabilities of words to generate confidence scores that are used to make accept/reject decisions on the words in a hypothesis produced by the recognizer. In a reading tracker, the final goal is to estimate whether words in the reference string were read correctly. We will apply the confidence measures estimated for the words in the speech recognition output as features to make a classification as to whether words in the reference string were read correctly.

References

R. Cole, P. Hossom, and B. Pellom. University of Colorado prompted and read children's speech corpus. Technical Report TR-CSLR-2006-02, University of Colorado, 2006.

R. Cole and B. Pellom. University of Colorado read and summarized story corpus. Technical Report TR-CSLR-2006-03, University of Colorado, 2006.

T. Fabian, R. Lieb, G. Ruske and M. Thomae. "Impact of Word Graph Density on the Quality of Posterior Probability Based Confidence Measures," in Proc. 8th Eur. Conf. Speech, Communication, Technology, Geneva, Switzerland September 1-4, 2003, pp. 917–920.

K. Hacioglu and W. Ward, "A Concept Graph Based Confidence Measure", in ICASSP, Orlando-Florida, USA, 2002.

A. Hagen, "Advances in Children's Speech Recognition with Application to Interactive Literacy Tutors", *Ph.D. thesis*, University of Colorado, Dept. of Computer Science, 2006.

T. Kemp and T. Schaaf, "Estimating confidence using word lattices," in Proc. 5th Eur. Conf. Speech, Communication, Technology 1997, Rhodes, Greece, Sept. 1997, pp. 827–830.

B. Pellom, "Sonic: The University of Colorado Continuous Speech Recognizer", Technical Report TR-CSLR-2001-01, CSLR, University of Colorado, March 2001.

K. Shobaki, J.-P. Hosom, and R. Cole. The OGI kids' speech corpus and recognizers. In 6th ICSLP, Beijing, China, 2000.

F. Wessel, R. Schlüter, K. Macherey, and H. Ney, "Confidence Measures for Large Vocabulary Continuous Speech Recognition," IEEE Transactions on Speech and Audio Processing, vol. 9, pp. 288–298, March 2001.

Estonian-English Statistical Machine Translation: the First Results

Mark Fishel
Department of Informatics
University of Tartu
`phishel@gmail.com`

Heiki-Jaan Kaalep
Dept of General Linguistics
University of Tartu
`Heiki-Jaan.Kaalep@ut.ee`

Kadri Muischnek
Dept of General Linguistics
University of Tartu
`Kadri.Muischnek@ut.ee`

Abstract

This paper describes the experiments that apply phrase-based statistical machine translation to Estonian. The work has two main aims: the first one is to define the main problems in the output of Estonian-English statistical machine translation and set a baseline for further experiments with this language pair. The second is to compare the two available corpora of translated legislation texts and test them for compatibility. The experiment results show that statistical machine translation works well with that kind of text. The corpora appear to be compatible, and their combining – beneficial.

1 Introduction

Machine translation and automatic processing of the Estonian language in general is a considerable challenge. The language is highly inflective, which causes a great number of different word-forms. It has a complex system of joining and splitting compound nouns, which is hard to grasp even for a human learner. Finally, the word order is very heterogeneous.

The work described in this paper focuses on statistical machine translation (SMT) from Estonian into English. It has two aims. The first one is to examine, how well SMT works with this language pair, and to determine the main problems in its output. We thus want to set a baseline, which can be used by further experiments in the same area.

The second aim is to compare and evaluate the available resources. There are two sufficiently large parallel Estonian-English corpora, both consisting of translations of legislation texts. It is therefore necessary to compare them from the perspective of suitability for SMT, and to see whether these are similar enough to be combined to enrich the resulting translation and language models.

2 The grammatical system of Estonian

In this section we will briefly discuss some linguistic features of Estonian in order to better understand the challenges that the Estonian-English machine translation has to face.

Estonian has rich inflectional morphology: the nouns inflect for number and 14 cases, the verbs inflect for person, number, mood and tense. This means that we need great amounts of parallel data as, for example, one noun lemma can have 28 different word-forms in text. Compounding is free and productive in Estonian; orthography of a NP depends largely on semantics.

The morphological richness of Estonian is one of the main reasons for using Moses as we hope that in our future experiments we can split the word-forms into lemmas and grammatical categories and ease the data sparseness problem this way.

The syntactic relations (subject, object etc) in Estonian are coded mostly using morphological devices; the word order does not differentiate between the syntactic functions. The word order or, rather, constituent order of Estonian reveals remarkable heterogeneity. For example, a sentence consisting of three words (or constituents) can have nine different word order variants as exemplified in (1) (all the example sentences mean roughly

Joakim Nivre, Heiki-Jaan Kaalep, Kadri Muischnek and Mare Koit (Eds.)
NODALIDA 2007 Conference Proceedings, pp. 278–283

the same, namely 'The child is eating a bun'). The actual word order in text depends on the pragmatics, information structure, clause type etc.

```
(2) Laps       sööb      saia
    child-NOM  eat-3SG  bun-PART

Laps saia sööb.
Saia sööb laps.
Saia laps sööb.
Sööb laps saia.
Sööb saia laps.
```

Contrary to the constituent order of the clause, the order of the components of a noun phrase is fixed. But this fixed word oder can be diametrically opposite to that in English. For example, in a nominalization (3) the head of the NP, namely the word-form 'hospitalization' begins the phrase in English and ends it in Estonian.

```
(3) vältimatut psühhiaatrilist
    emergency-PART psychiatric-PART

    abi       vajava        isiku
    care-PART needing-PART person-PART

    haiglasse     paigutamine
    hospital-ILL  allocation-NOM

    'hospitalization of a person in
    need of  emergency psychiatric
    care'
```

If the predicate of the clause is an analytic or perifrastic verb, the parts of the predicate can be separated from each other by several intervening constituents in certain clause types. In example (4) the predicate is a particle verb vastu võtma 'to adopt'.

```
(4) nõukogu võttis 13. novembril
    council      took    november-ADE

    vastu     resolutsiooni
    PARTICLE  resolution-GEN

    'The Council adopted a resolu-
    tion on 13th of November'
```

3   Corpora Description

As mentioned in the introduction, there exist two partially overlapping Estonian-English parallel corpora, which are sufficiently large for training SMT models. The source of both are translated legislation texts. Firstly, this means that it should be possible to combine the two and therefore to enrich the trained SMT models. Secondly, the contained language is considerably more constrained than spoken language — it should therefore be easier to model it. Thirdly, the law text domain potentially has a higher demand for translating huge amounts of texts, and would therefore benefit from a semi- or fully automatic translation system.

3.1   The UT Corpus

The first of the abovementioned corpora [1] was created at the university of Tartu. The corpus contains 7.8 million words in English and 5.0 million in Estonian.

The corpus is sentence-aligned using the Vanilla aligner (Danielsson and Ridings, 1997), based on the algorithm by Gale and Church (1993). The total number of aligned units is 435 700.

3.2   The JRC-Acquis Corpus

The second used corpus consists of the Estonian and English parts of the JRC-Acquis multilingual parallel corpus (Steinberger et al., 2006). The used corpus contains 7.6 million English and 5 million Estonian words. The corpus is initially aligned on the level of paragraphs, but these are usually short and do usually contain one sentence, or even only part of a sentence. Automatic alignment was also performed using the Vanilla aligner. The total number of aligned units is 295 000. Regardless of the amount of words being almost the same as in the UT corpus, the more general alignment level causes the number of the alignment units to be smaller (and the units themselves, longer on the average).

4   Experiments and Results

4.1   Experiment setup

To ensure statistical significance of the results both corpora were randomly split into the training and

---

[1] http://www.cl.ut.ee/korpused/paralleel

the testing set; the latter initially consisted of 0.1% of the corresponding corpora. We further filtered both testing sets manually, leaving out alignment errors, pairs with one of the sentences empty, sentences witout a single word in the source or target language and paragraph and section numbering sentences. This way the results would show the performance of the SMT system applied to natural language sentences only. Finally, we removed the testing sentences that also appear in the training set. As a result, the size of the test sets was reduced to 749 sentences in the UT, and 649 – in the JRC-Acquis corpus.

Since manual filtering of the training sets wasn't feasible due to the set sizes, only automatic filtering was performed. The excluded sentence pairs were the ones which included sentences longer than 100 words and the ones where the ratio of the word numbers exceeded 9. This left 429 000 and 272 000 parallel units in the UT and JRC-Acquis training sets, respectively. In order for the corpora to suit with the requirements of the used software they were preprocessed in the following way. The UT corpus was converted to UTF-8 encoding and HTML entities in both corpora were replaced with corresponding UTF-characters. All sentences were lower-cased. Finally, the punctuation was separated from the words in order for the translation model training script to recognize them as separate words.

We used n-gram language models, trained with the SRI LM package (Stolcke, 2002). Word alignments were obtained using GIZA++ (Och and Ney 2003). Phrase table composition and decoding was done with Moses[2] and the software included with it.

The automatic evaluation metric, used in the experiments, is BLEU. However, in order not to limit the comparison to that, we performed a limited human evaluation of the output. In addition, the testing results are available online[3].

4.2 Results

We trained three models: on the UT corpus, on the JRC-Acquis corpus and combining both corpora. These models we evaluated against the UT corpus and the JRC-Acquis corpus.

Table 1 presents the quality of the translations measured by BLEU.

Trained on Tested on	UT	JRC	Combined
UT	39.26	29.80	41.60
JRC	38.45	42.38	45.22

Table 1. Translation quality of SMT systems trained /tested on different corpora as measured by BLEU.

Intra-corpus translation

In the first set of experiments we trained and tested the SMT model on the same corpora. This would show the relative corpus performance when used in SMT.

The BLEU scores for UT and JRC-Acquis corpora were 39.26 and 42.38 respectively. The scores are noticeably higher than the ones, published for spoken/written language baseline translation – e.g. (Bojar et al, 2006), (Koehn and Knight, 2003) – which is most probably explained by the highly constrained nature of the legislation language.

Inter-Corpus Translation

We continued by taking a SMT model trained on one corpus and testing it on another. This would show how similar the two corpora are from the SMT perspective.

Training the model using the UT corpus and testing it on the JRC-Acquis test set produced a BLEU score of 38.45, this is only slightly lower than the JRC-Acquis-trained model score. On the other hand, the JRC-Acquis-trained model gave a 29.8 BLEU score when trained on the UT test set. This suggests that the SMT model, trained on the UT corpus is more applicable to the extra-corpus language phenomena. We suggest that the reason is in the more detailed alignment in the UT corpus: this most probably causes less corpus-subjective word alignments and phrase table entries.

Combined corpora experiments

Finally we tested the compatibility of the two corpora from the perspective of combining them for SMT training. Although the corpora have overlapping sources, only 18 000 and 27 000 unique parallel units coincide completely in the Estonian and

---

[2] http://www.statmt.org/moses
[3] http://ats.cs.ut.ee/u/fishel/smt

English corpora parts, respectively. Therefore corpora are combined by simple concatenation.

The BLEU score of the SMT models trained on the combined corpus is 41.6 and 45.22 when tested on the UT and JRC-Acquis test set, respectively. When compared to the intra-corpus translation results, the improvement of the UT test set score (2.34 BLEU) is slightly lower than the improvement of the JRC-Acquis one (2.84 BLEU). This supports the hypothesis made in the inter-corpus experiment section: the models built on the UT training set generalize better on the JRC-Acquis test set than vice versa.

4.3 Manual Output Evaluation

It has been pointed out (Callison-Burch et al, 2006) that while BLEU attempts to capture allowable variation in the translation, it allows random permuting of phrases in the hypothesis compared with the reference translation. In our opinion it also explains the relatively high BLEU score in our experiments.

In order to balance these shortcomings, we carried out a limited human evaluation of the results. The human evaluator gave 6 x 250 output sentences one of the following ratings: 1) good translation, i.e. expresses the same meaning as the source sentence and is grammatically correct; 2) an acceptable translation with minor errors, i.e. expresses the same meaning as the source sentence, but has some grammar errors; 3) does not express the same meaning as the source sentence. The third group covers both the cases if the output is an unintelligible mess of words and if the sentence has a meaning, but that is different from that of a source sentence.

While the UT corpus test set was evaluated as it is, the JRC-Acquis one had the paragraphs split manually into sentences before evaluating; however, approximately every 10th paragraph contained more than one sentence. Results of the human evaluation are presented in table 2.

The shortcomings of the human evaluation are that the sub-clauses of a long sentence have not been evaluated separately. If one sub-clause of a long sentence consisting of several sub-clauses is unintelligible, the sentence gets the overall "wrong" rating.

Trained on	UT	Cmb	JRC	UT	Cmb	JRC
Tested on	UT	UT	UT	JRC	JRC	JRC
Good	16%	15%	8%	13%	15%	11%
Accept able	11%	15%	9%	9%	15%	14%
Wrong	73%	70%	83%	78%	70%	75%

Table 2. Human evaluation of the SMT output. Cmb – combined corpora.

5 Discussion

The results of human evaluation mostly support the conclusion, initially based on BLEU results: combining the corpora results in slight improvement in the SMT output. This conclusion, however, remains so far subjective to the used corpora and requires further testing. In addition, we believe that the sources of the corpora might overlap much more than indicated in the subsection 3.2, which doesn't show due to differences in version/encoding etc. This has to be regarded in the further experiments.

The main problem that distorts the meaning and grammar of the resulting translations is the failure to place the parts of the translation in the right order. The legislative language that the corpora contains is characterized by heavy use of nominalisations, the resulting noun phrases are long and tend to have a complicated structure. So, if the word order (constituent order) in Estonian source sentence is too different from the correct English one, the system fails to make the needed permutations in long sentences. We had hoped that using a phrase-based statistical machine translation system helps us to overcome the word order differences in the source and target languages, but apparently additional techniques are required to do so.

To exemplify the problems with word/constituent order, let's take an Estonian sentence from the JRC-Acquis test corpus and have a closer look at its reference translation and the output of our system. In order to see what has gone wrong in our translation, the phrases (in the meaning used in the phrase-based SMT) that represent the same meaningful units in both Estonian and English have been numbered according to their order in the Estonian sentence.

```
(5) source:
[1 euroopa majandusühenduse ja
Šveitsi konföderatsiooni]
[2 vaheliste kokkulepete]
[3 kohaldamisel]
[4 rakendatakse ühenduses]
[5 ühiskomitee]
[6 otsust nr 5 / 81]

SMT output:
[1 the european economic
community and the swiss
confederation]
[2 of agreements between]
[3 the application]
[5 of the joint committee]
[4 shall apply in the community]
[6 decision no 5 / 81]

reference:
[3 for the purposes of
application]
[2 of the agreements between]
[1 the european economic
community and the swiss
confederation] ,
[6 decision no 5 / 81]
[5 of the joint committee]
[4 shall apply in the community]
```

We can see that the output of the SMT system contains all the correct phrases except for the translation of the word *kohaldamisel* 'applying', translated in the reference translation as 'for the purposes of application' and as 'the application' in the system output. But the order of the phrases in the system output follows too much the phrase order in the source sentence - the system has failed to make the long-distance permutations. The phrase order of the source sentence is 1-2-3-4-5-6; the order of these constituents in the reference sentence is 3-2-1-6-5-4, but our system produces 1-2-3-5-4-6.

At the moment reordering is purely the task of the distortion model of the SMT algorithm, and as indicated by the results, this is not enough. One of the ways to solve the problem is described in (Nießen and Ney, 2001). According to this method the input sentence can be reordered using morphosyntactic information, so that the word order resembles better that of the target language. Another approach to the same problem would be to

re-rank the n-best output list and/or reorder the output sentences.

The incapability of our baseline-model to consider grammatical information creates translations where adverbial NP is translated into subject NP (as the first NP in an English sentence is usually the subject, but in Estonian the order of the syntactic constituents is more varied (cf. also example 2).

```
(6) source:
selles      tunnistuses
this-INE certificate-INE
esitatakse
are-reproduced
kontrollimise     tulemused
verification-GEN result-PL.NOM

output:
this certificate shall be sub-
mitted to the results of verifi-
cation

reference translation:
this certificate shall reproduce
the findings of the examination
```

Another frequently examined disadvantage of the SMT output is the failure to translate several Estonian word-forms into English. The probable cause is the data sparseness, caused by the Estonian morphology and free compounding.

So the systems gives a correct translation of the noun *eeskiri* 'regulation', but fails to give any translation of the compound *finantseeskiri* 'financial regulation'. Needless to say that a case-form of a noun that has appeared several times in the training corpus, but not in this particular form is a new unknown word for the system.

One of the possible solutions is to use the factored translation models of the Moses decoder by translating vectors of base forms and morphological features instead of the words themselves. Also, several preprocessing techniques exist that can reduce the problematic effect, e.g. (Koehn and Knight, 2003), (Perez et al, 2006).

6   Conclusions

This paper described a set of experiments, in which statistical machine tanslation was applied to the Estonian language. The first objective of this work was to test, how well SMT translates from Estonian into English, when trained on the available corpora, and to determine the main output problems. The second one was to compare two existing parallel corpora for this language pair, and to test whether combining the two can bring benefit to the resulting SMT models.

The experiment results show that SMT is applicable to Estonian and the domain, represented in the corpora. The output of the SMT was analyzed, and the main output problems were determined: these being the wrong order of phrases and sparse data. Still, the BLEU scores of the output are higher than the ones reported for spoken language translation, most probably due to the constrained nature of the language of the corpora. Furthermore, combining the two corpora appears to improve the translation output.

Future work includes testing the techniques, used for reducing the data sparsity problem and output quality improvement. In addition, the opposite translation direction has to be inspected.

References

Ondrej Bojar, Evgeny Matusov and Hermann Ney. 2006. Czech-English phrase-based machine translation. In *Proceedings of the 5th International Conference on NLP, FinTal* 2006, pp 214-224. Turku, Finland.

Chris Callison-Burch, Miles Osborne and Philipp Koehn. 2006. Re-evaluating the role of BLEU in machine translation research. In *Proceedings of the 11thh Conference of the European Chapter of the Association for Computational Linguistics, EACL*, pp 249-256. Trento, Italy

Pernilla Danielsson and Daniel Ridings. 1997. Practical presentation of a "Vanilla" aligner. In *TELRI Workshop in alignment and exploitation of texts*, Ljubljana, Slovenia. Available at http://nl.ijs.si/telri/Vanilla/doc/ljubljana/

William A. Gale and Kenneth W. Church. 1993. A program for aligning sentences in bilingual corpora. Computational Linguistics, 19 (1), pp 177-184.

Philipp Koehn and Kevin Knight. 2003. Empirical methods for compound splitting. In *Proceedings of the 10th Conference of the European Chapter of the Association for Computational Linguistics, EACL*, pp 187-193, Budapest, Hungary.

Sonja Nießen and Herman Ney. 2001. Morpho-syntactic analysis for reordering in statistical machine translation. In *Proceedings of MT Summit VIII*, pp 1081-1085, Santiago de Compostela, Galicia, Spain.

Franz J. Och and Hermann Ney. 2003. A systematic comparison of various statistical alignment models. *Computational Linguistics*, 29 (1), pp 19-51.

Alicia Pérez, Inés Torres and Francisco Casacuberta. 2006. Towards the improvement of statistical translation models using linguistic features. In *Proceedings of the 5th International Conference on Natural Language Processing FinTal*, pp 716-725. Turku, Finland.

Ralf Steinberger, Bruno Pouliquen, Anna Widiger, Camelia Ignat, Tomaž Erjavec, Dan Tufis and Dániel Varga. 2006. The JRC-Acquis: A multilingual aligned parallel corpus with 20+ languages. In *Proceedings of the 5th International Conference on Language Resources and Evaluation, LREC*, pp 2142-2147, Genoa, Italy.

Andres Stolcke. 2002. Srilm – an extensible language modeling toolkit. In *Proceedings of the International Conference on Spoken Language Processing*, vol 2, pp 901-904. Denver, Colorado, USA.

A Hybrid Constituency-Dependency Parser for Swedish

Johan Hall
Växjö University
jha@msi.vxu.se

Joakim Nivre
Växjö University and
Uppsala University
nivre@msi.vxu.se

Jens Nilsson
Växjö University
jni@msi.vxu.se

Abstract

We present a data-driven parser that derives both constituent structures and dependency structures, alone or in combination, in one and the same process. When trained and tested on data from the Swedish treebank Talbanken05, the parser achieves a labeled dependency accuracy of 82% and a labeled bracketing F-score of 75%.

1 Introduction

Most natural language parsers use representations that are based on constituency or dependency. While the relative merits of constituency and dependency representations are still a matter of debate, it is quite clear that they provide partly independent, complementary views of syntactic structure. It is therefore increasingly common that syntactic representations combine elements of both, in particular in annotation schemes for treebanks, such as the TIGER Treebank for German (Brants et al., 2002), the Alpino Treebank for Dutch (Van der Beek et al., 2002), and Talbanken05 for Swedish (Nivre et al., 2006c).

However, there are not many parsers available that can produce hybrid constituency-dependency representations. Widely used statistical parsers, like those of Collins (1997; 1999) and Charniak (2000) output a pure constituency representation (despite making heavy use of lexical dependencies for internal processing) and have to rely on post-processing to add information about grammatical functions (Blaheta and Charniak, 2000). More recently, Gabbard et al. (2006) have shown how a version of the Collins parser can be used to derive the full Penn Treebank annotation including both constituent structure and grammatical function tags. It is also worth mentioning that many grammar-driven parsers, based on frameworks such as LFG (Riezler et al., 2002) and HPSG (Toutanova et al., 2002), produce representations that combine elements of constituency and dependency.

In this paper, we show how hybrid representations can be parsed in a dependency-based encoding inspired by Collins (1999). We evaluate the technique using an existing data-driven dependency parser (MaltParser), trained and tested on Swedish treebank data (Talbanken05). The results show that it is possible to derive hybrid constituency-dependency representations with only a marginal loss in accuracy compared to pure representations of either kind.

The rest of the paper is structured in the following way. Section 2 introduces hybrid constituency-dependency representations, and section 3 describes the dependency-based encoding and parsing strategy adopted in this paper. Section 4 presents the results of the experimental evaluation, and section 5 contains our conclusions.

2 Hybrid Representations

A constituent structure representation for a sentence $w_1, \ldots, w_n$ typically consists of a rooted tree where leaf nodes are labeled with the words $w_1, \ldots, w_n$ and internal nodes are labeled with constituent categories, as illustrated in figure 1.

A dependency structure representation instead consists of a rooted tree where *all* nodes are labeled with the words $w_1, \ldots, w_n$ and edges are labeled

Joakim Nivre, Heiki-Jaan Kaalep, Kadri Muischnek and Mare Koit (Eds.)
NODALIDA 2007 Conference Proceedings, pp. 284–287

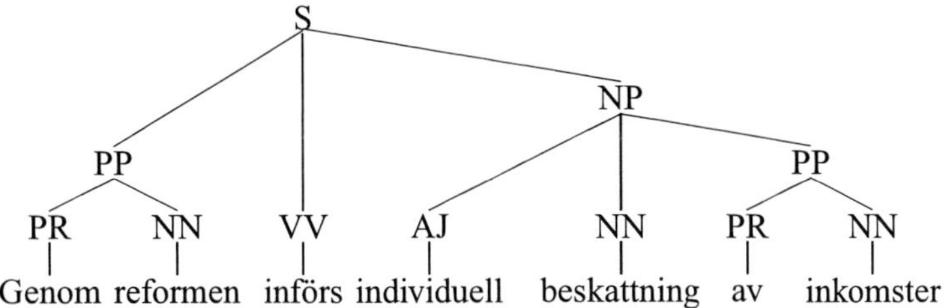

Figure 1: Constituent structure for Swedish sentence

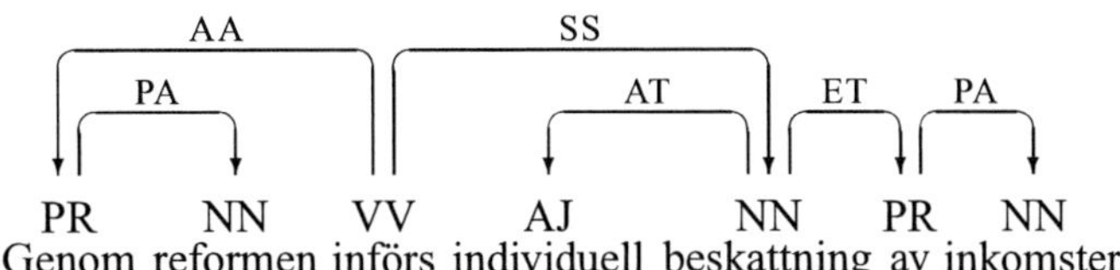

Figure 2: Dependency structure for Swedish sentence

with dependency types, as seen in figure 2.

In the general case, there is no simple mapping from constituent structures to dependency structures or vice versa, especially not if non-projective dependencies are permitted (which correspond to discontinuous constituents). But under certain conditions it is possible to merge the two types of representations into one. Let w_j^* be the substring $w_i, \ldots, w_k$ of the sentence such that all the words in $w_i, \ldots, w_k$ are dominated by w_j in the dependency representation (where dominance is the reflexive and transitive closure of the edge relation). Then, the two representations can be merged if, for every word w_j, w_j^* is the yield of some nonterminal N_j in the constituency representation. In the merged representation, the dependency label of the incoming edge of w_j is added to the incoming edge of the corresponding nonterminal N_j, while other nonterminals get their incoming edge labeled HD (for *head*). Figure 3 shows the hybrid representation obtained by merging the representations in figures 1 and 2.

3 Dependency-Based Hybrid Parsing

Hybrid representations can be parsed in a variety of ways. In this paper, we investigate a dependency-driven approach, where hybrid representations are encoded as dependency structures, by extending the dependency label l_j on the incoming edge to w_j into

$l_j|N_j$, if the corresponding nonterminal N_j is not a preterminal, and into $l_j|*$ otherwise. This dependency encoding of the hybrid representation is illustrated in figure 4.

Given such an encoding, any dependency parser can be used to derive hybrid representations. However, in order for the dependency structure output by the parser to be mappable to the desired hybrid representation, we must impose an additional constraint on the relation between the constituent structure and the dependency structure, namely that only preterminal nodes in the constituent structure may have a yield that does not coincide with the complete projection of a lexical head w_j^*. (Note that we can also derive a pure dependency representation or a pure constituency representation by omitting the second half or the first half of the labels, respectively.) In the experiments below, we use the freely available Malt-Parser (Nivre et al., 2006a) to evaluate this parsing scheme.

4 Experimental Evaluation

The data for the experiments are taken from the professional prose section of the Swedish treebank Talbanken05 (Nivre et al., 2006c), derived from the older Talbanken76 (Einarsson, 1976), developed at Lund University in the 1970s. More precisely, we use the Deepened Phrase Structure version of the

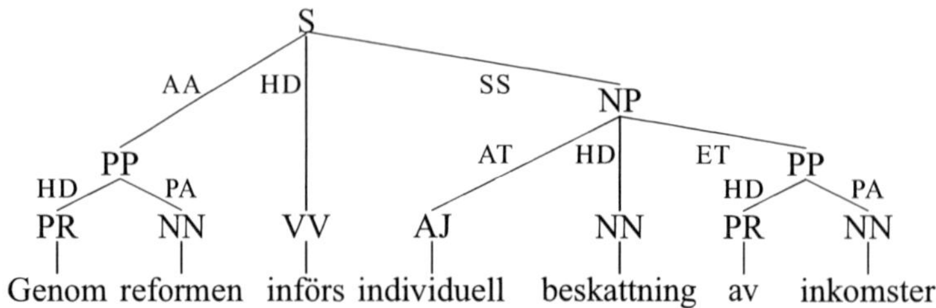

Figure 3: Hybrid representation

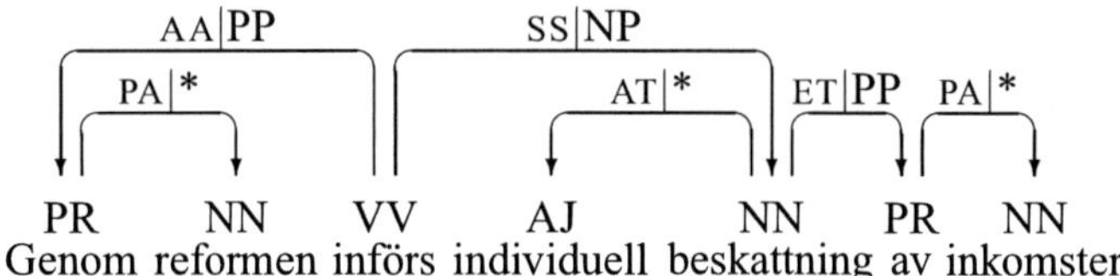

Figure 4: Dependency encoding of hybrid representation

treebank, which combines constituency and dependency annotation in a way that satisfies the constraints discussed in sections 2 and 3.

The data from the professional prose section (roughly 100,000 tokens) were first converted to a dependency-based encoding, as defined in section 2, with three different sets of labels:

1. Constituency only (C)
2. Dependency only (D)
3. Constituency + Dependency (C+D)

While it is only the composite encoding (C+D) that allows the target representation to be derived, the pure constituency (C) and dependency (D) versions are useful for comparison.[1]

The data were then split into 80% for training, 10% for development, and 10% for final testing, and MaltParser was trained on the three versions of the training set (C, D, and C+D). Parsing accuracy was evaluated using two sets of evaluation metrics:

1. The labeled (LR, LP, LF) and unlabeled (UR, UP, UF) recall, precision, and F-measure, as implemented in the evalb software (Sekine and Collins, 1997), measure the percentage

of correct constituents in relation to true constituents (recall) and output constituents (precision), with the F-measure being the harmonic mean of recall and precision. As is customary, these measures are reported both for sentences up to 40 words and sentences up to 100 words.

2. The labeled (LAS) and unlabeled (UAS) attachment score, as implemented in the official scoring software of the CoNLL-X shared task (Buchholz and Marsi, 2006), measure the percentage of tokens that have the correct head and (if labeled) the correct dependency relation.

Note that the constituency-based evaluation metrics (LR, LP, LF, UR, UP, UF) can only be meaningfully applied to representations C and C+D, while the dependency-based metrics (LAS, UAS) are only applicable to representations D and C+D.

The results of the evaluation on the final test set are found in table 1. We see that the best dependency accuracy (LAS = 82.43%, UAS = 88.93%) is obtained with the pure dependency representation (D), but we also see that the drop in accuracy when requiring the parser to derive constituent structure as well is less than one percentage point for LAS (81.48%) and only 0.4 percentage points for UAS (88.53%). For constituency, the difference is a little greater, with a drop of about 1.5 percentage points

---

[1]Note that it is not possible, in the general case, to derive C and D in parallel and simply merge them, since the two output representations may fail to satisfy the constraints required for merging.

	LAS	UAS	LR	LP	LF	UR	UP	UF	
C			75.94	76.54	76.24	80.51	81.15	80.83	≤ 40
			74.56	75.20	74.88	79.15	79.83	79.49	≤ 100
D	82.43	88.93							
C+D	81.48	88.53	74.62	74.76	74.69	79.26	79.41	79.33	≤ 40
			73.39	73.54	73.47	78.12	78.27	78.19	≤ 100

Table 1: Results of the experimental evaluation

in both labeled and unlabeled F-measure (both for sentences up to 40 words and sentences up to 100 words), and the best result is again obtained with the pure representation (C) (LF = 74.88%, UF = 79.49% for sentences up to 100 words).

The results for dependency accuracy are comparable to the best reported results for Talbanken05. It is a little lower than the top score in the CoNLL-X shared task, but that result was based on a training set twice as large (Buchholz and Marsi, 2006; Nivre et al., 2006b). For constituency parsing there is no previous work on Talbanken05, but the results look promising and can probably be improved with better tuning of the parser.

5   Conclusion

We have presented a novel technique for syntactic parsing with hybrid constituency-dependency representations through dependency-based encodings. The method has been evaluated on Swedish, using an existing data-driven dependency parser. The evaluation shows that hybrid representations can be produced with only a marginal loss in accuracy for dependency and constituency considered separately. With better tuning we believe it will be possible to eliminate this loss and perhaps even achieve better accuracy than for separate constituency and dependency parsing.

References

D. Blaheta and E. Charniak. 2000. Assigning function tags to parsed text. In *Proceedings of NAACL*, 234–240.

S. Brants, S. Dipper, S. Hansen, W. Lezius, and G. Smith. 2002. TIGER treebank. In *Proceedings of TLT*, 24–42.

S. Buchholz and E. Marsi. 2006. CoNLL-X shared task on multilingual dependency parsing. In *Proceedings of CoNLL*, 149–164.

E. Charniak. 2000. A maximum-entropy-inspired parser. In *Proceedings of NAACL*, 132–139.

M. Collins. 1997. Three generative, lexicalised models for statistical parsing. In *Proceedings of ACL*, 16–23.

M. Collins. 1999. *Head-Driven Statistical Models for Natural Language Parsing*. Ph.D. thesis, University of Pennsylvania.

J. Einarsson. 1976. Talbankens skriftspråkskonkordans. Lund University, Department of Scandinavian Languages.

R. Gabbard, S. Kulick, and M. Marcus. 2006. Fully parsing the Penn treebank. In *Proceedings of HLT-NAACL*, 184–191.

J. Nivre, J. Hall, and J. Nilsson. 2006a. MaltParser: A data-driven parser-generator for dependency parsing. In *Proceedings of LREC*, 2216–2219.

J. Nivre, J. Hall, J. Nilsson, G. Eryiğit, and S. Marinov. 2006b. Labeled pseudo-projective dependency parsing with support vector machines. In *Proceedings of CoNLL*, 221–225.

J. Nivre, J. Nilsson, and J. Hall. 2006c. Talbanken05: A Swedish treebank with phrase structure and dependency annotation. In *Proceedings of LREC*, 1392–1395.

S. Riezler, M. King, R. Kaplan, R. Crouch, J. Maxwell, and M. Johnson. 2002. Parsing the Wall Street Journal using a Lexical-Functional Grammar and discriminative estimation techniques. In *Proceedings of ACL*, 271–278.

S. Sekine and M. J. Collins. 1997. The evalb software. http://cs.nyu.edu/cs/projects/proteus/evalb.

K. Toutanova, C. D. Manning, S. M. Shieber, D. Flickinger, and Stephan Oepen. 2002. Parse disambiguation for a rich HPSG grammar. In *Proceedings of TLT*, pages 253–263.

L. Van der Beek, G. Bouma, R. Malouf, and G. Van Noord. 2002. The Alpino dependency treebank. In *Language and Computers, Computational Linguistics in the Netherlands 2001. Selected Papers from the Twelfth CLIN Meeting*, 8–22. Rodopi.

Íslenskur Orðasjóður - Building a Large Icelandic Corpus

Erla Hallsteinsdóttir

erlahall@yahoo.dk

**Thomas Eckart, Chris Biemann,
Uwe Quasthoff, Matthias Richter**
Natural Language Processing Group
University of Leipzig
Johannisgasse 26, 04103 Leipzig, Germany
{teckart,biem,quasthoff,mrichter}
@informatik.uni-leipzig.de

Abstract

We introduce an Icelandic corpus of more than 250 million running words and describe the methodology to build it. The resource is available for use free of charge. We provide automatically generated monolingual lexicon entries, comprising frequency statistics, samples of usage, co-occurring words and a graphical representation of the word's semantic neighbourhood.

1   Introduction

Corpora are important language resources for a variety of Natural Language Processing tasks, especially in semi-supervised settings, where corpora are used to build e.g. language models. In (Biemann et al., 2004) and (Quasthoff et al., 2006) design and implementation of an architecture capable of building numerous of large corpora for different languages with little manual effort have been introduced. This infrastructure has been used to produce an Icelandic corpus based on web pages. In this paper we present the steps undertaken to digest unstructured clutter of HTML pages into a ready for use linguistic resource that provides rapid access through search indices on different language units.

2   Motivation

Icelandic is considered a small language with around 300,000 native speakers. Most linguistic research on Icelandic has been highly dominated by ideological premises of a linguistic purism driven by the mission of the preservation of the ancient Icelandic language (cf. Kristmannsson, 2004). But, despite a politically initiated language technology campaign in order to strengthen an effective language purity policy, there still has been only little empirical research on the Icelandic language, partially due to the lack of a large corpus. Recent endeavours, as e.g. used by (Helgadóttir, 2004) or the search interface of Iceland's Lexicological Institute[1] operate on small-scale corpora. Here, our data basis is the entirety of all Icelandic websites officially collected by the National and University Library of Iceland.

The corpus "Íslenskur Orðasjóður" is first of all a comprehensive corpus-based lexicon of modern Icelandic. Its data on current language use is also an important and long needed basis for empirical linguistic research (e.g. lexical research on neologisms, the use of word-formation rules, foreign lexical units), computational linguistics and applications in language technology. Furthermore the corpus provides a basis for diachronic comparison as it documents are a to-date snapshot of Icelandic.

3   Data Cleaning

Automated collection of text cannot avoid unwanted junk in the raw data. We apply a heuristic means of separating well-formed from inappropriate sentences. The overall procedure is the same for each language.

3.1 Text Extraction

The National and University Library of Iceland has kindly provided its internet archive of web pages from all `.is` domains as text basis. Our starting point was approximately 120 GB of zipped

---

[1] http://www.lexis.hi.is/corpus/leit.pl

Joakim Nivre, Heiki-Jaan Kaalep, Kadri Muischnek and Mare Koit (Eds.)
NODALIDA 2007 Conference Proceedings, pp. 288–291

Rule	Description	Examples	Hits
too many periods	unseparated sentences gluing words together or incomplete sentences ending with "…"	Upp í flugvél, burt úr kuldanum......	1,300,000
link artifacts or |	navigation boilerplates	Example: Forsíða > Túlkanir og þýðingar > Þýðingar Heim | Hafa samband | Veftré Leitarvél: Alþjóðahús Gagnlegar upplýsingar Algengar	220,000
begins with number dot blank	enumeration items	1. innkaup hlutu: Gláma/Kím arkitektar ehf., Laugavegi 164.	200,000
too many capital letters or digits in a row	headlines glued together with sentences or enumerations	LEIÐBEININGAR UM NOTKUN Gríptu um borðana og togaðu niður og í sundur. 7.3.2005 Tilkynning frá Högum hf. 7.3.2005 Verslunarrekstur Skeljungs komin til 10-11 25.10.2004 Tilkynning frá Högum hf. 22.6.2004 Tilkynning (...)	198,000
contains too many ":"s	Lists, e.g. of sports results	steini :: Comment :: 10 hugmyndir af bloggi.	166,000
too many {/&:}s	itemizations	Ferðaönd - Svara - Vitna í - Stelpið 31/10/05 - 0:25 Soffía frænka - Svara - Vitna í - aulinn 31/10/05 - 8:39 Kona í bleikum slopp með rúllur í hárinu.	153,000
expression too short	incomplete sentences	10. Valur ? _\ǎv,c ?	100,000
too many "_"s in a row	clozes	a) _____________, b) _____________ og c) _____________ Hvað myndast í kynhirslunum að lokum?	58,000

Table 1: Text cleaning rules used for dropping undesired sentences, their rationale and impact.

HTML pages downloaded by the library in November 2005. From these pages the document text has been extracted and segmented into sentences leaving 29,718,528 unique sentences after duplicate sentence removal.

3.2 Language Identification

To reliably detect different languages, high text coverage can be achieved with the 10,000 most frequent words per language. We use these words extracted from previously built corpora for sentence-based language identification, see e.g. (Dunning, 1994) for an overview.

From the 29,718,528 unique sentences, merely 19,112,187 of them were identified as Icelandic. The remainder was predominantly identified as English (about 4 million sentences).

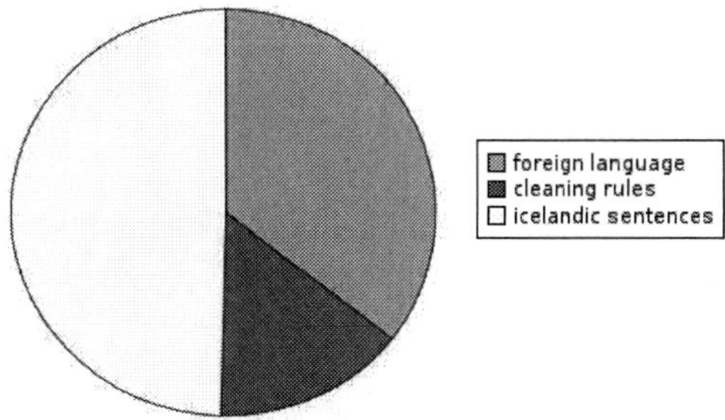

Figure 1: Fractions of the raw material as determined by the cleaning procedures

3.3 Text Cleaning

A set of 65 rules (SQL-statements) was used to get rid of unwanted, ill-formed sentences. Table 1 contains a description of the rules with highest coverage in natural language, their rationale and the number of sentences affected here. Eventually 14.742.802 sentences make up the remaining corpus, approximately half the amount of the raw material. Figure 1 shows the fractions of the raw material removed in the cleaning procedures.

4   Corpus Building

From the remaining sentences, a full form dictionary is computed. Currently, we support two language units in our corpora: word forms and sentences. For sentences, we provide information from which source (e.g. webpage) the respective sentence was obtained, yet we do not store full documents but only well-formed sentences extracted from these (see Section 3). Sentences are indexed by words, so it is possible to quickly access all sentences a word form occurs in. For each word form, we automatically extract the following information: frequency (which indicates common vs. uncommon words) and significant co-occurrences based on neighbouring words (mostly containing typical properties of the corresponding concept or idioms the word is a part of) and based on sentences (mostly containing semantically related word forms). As significance measure, the log-likelihood ratio (cf. Dunning, 1993) is used. Our storing scheme is open for additional, manually provided information, such as grammatical data, lemmatization, thesaurus entries and subject area assignments. *Íslenskur Orðasjóður* contains mappings from word forms to lemmas (source: Bjarnadóttir (2004)), see Appendix.

5   Example Data

Frequency statistics can be used for measuring visibility of a concept and commonness of a word. In lexicography this can be an important criterion to explain judgments. For the language researcher this data can tell whether and to what extent a word was in use in the time interval covered by the corpus. Following are the 100 most frequent words in our Icelandic corpus in descending order by frequency: *og, að, í, á, sem, er, til, við, um, var, en, með, fyrir, ekki, því, það, af, hann, eru, hefur, frá, verið, þar, hafa, ég, eftir, þess, sér, Það, þegar, þá, segir, kl, svo, hún, upp, voru, hafi, eða, sé, úr, fram, verður, Í, þeim, hjá, þeirra, eins, Ég, nú, hans, Hann, þeir, sagði, þetta, sig, út, vera, þau, vel, væri, Við, yfir, okkur, vegna, mjög, okkar, mér, f, allt, ára, Á, einnig, koma, þessu, þó, verði, hér, kom, hefði, ár, hafði, saman, hennar, Þetta, þú, sínum, verða, undir, tíma, Íslands, þessum, En, alltaf, Hún, mun, gera, mikið, dag, má.*

Co-occurrence data is meant to be used extensively as a building block for further applications such as word sense disambiguation, extraction of semantic relations and building of ontologies. For the dictionary user and further uses we provide also networks of co-occurrences like depicted in the Appendix. They can be used for example as a navigation aid or for building topic maps.

The Appendix contains the information as displayed on the corpus website. All words occurring in the corpus are linked to their respective entry, so it is possible to navigate through the resource by clicking on the words. Alternatively, a search mask can be used (not shown).

6   Future Work

With the basic language resource available we aim at including all available types of additional information such as dictionary data, part of speech etc. to the Icelandic language resource. This work is also part of a long term plan to provide language resources in comparable format in the Leipzig Corpora Collection at `http://corpora.uni-leipzig.de`, counting 17 languages at the time writing.

References

Chris Biemann, Stefan Bordag, Gerhard Heyer, Uwe Quasthoff, and Christian Wolff. 2004. *Language independent Methods for Compiling Monolingual Lexical Data*. In Proceedings of CIcLING, Springer LNCS 2945.

Bjarnadóttir, Kristín. 2004. *Beygingarlýsing íslensks nútímamáls*. Version 2.0, 30. November 2004.

Ted Dunning. 1993. *Accurate methods for the statistics of surprise and coincidence*. Computational Linguistics, Volume 19, number 1 .

Ted Dunning. 1994. *Statistical identification of language*. In: Technical report CRL MCCS-94-273, New Mexico State University. Computing Research Lab.

Sigrún Helgadóttir. 2004. *Testing Data-Driven Learning Algorithms for PoS Tagging of Icelandic*. Nordisk Sprogteknologi. Årbog 2004. Kopenhagen

Gauti Kristmannsson 2004. *Iceland's "Egg of Life" and the Modern Media*. In: Meta, XLIX, 1, 2004, 59-66.

Uwe Quasthoff, Matthias Richter, and Chris Biemann. 2006. *Corpus Portal for Search in Monolingual Corpora*. In: Proceedings of the LREC 2006.

Appendix: Sample Entry from `http://wortschatz.uni-leipzig.de/ws_ice/`

orðmynd: orðabók (English: dictionary)
tíðni: 120
tíðniflokkur: 13 (þ.e. *og* kemur 2^{13} oftar fyrir en þessi orðmynd)

beygingarmyndir: orðabók, orðabókar, orðabókin, orðabókina, orðabókinni, orðabókarinnar, orðabækur, orðabókum, orðabóka, orðabækurnar, orðabókunum, orðabókanna

dæmi:
Ég nefni fyrst Íslenska **orðabók**. (heimild: *Newspaper*)
Einnig fylgir lítil **orðabók** þýðanda með skýringum. (heimild: *Newspaper*)
Að gefast upp eða tapa, - það var ekki til í hans **orðabók** eða fasi. (heimild: *Newspaper*)
fleiri dæmi

orð með háa tíðni sem nágrannar orðabók:
Menningarsjóðs (85), Íslenskri (64), Íslensk (42), Orðabók (23), Mörður (21), ritstjórn (20), Marðar (20), Í (17), Orðastað (17), lýsingarorðið (15), heiðinn (15), orðabækur (14), orð (14), Háskólans (14), þreyja (13), Árnasonar (13), stórfiskaleikur (13), prentútgáfna (13), lýðveldistímans (13), klyfberi (13), Bókaútgáfu (13), ÍSLENSK (12), uppgjöf (12), delicious (12), útgáfudegi (11), merking (11), lsquo (11), gefast (11), eða (11), Freysteins (11), orðsins (10), orðið (10), orðinu (10), merkir (10), hugum (10), færeyskt (10), fletta (10), ekki (10), dægrastytting (10), Grunnavík (10), Örlygs (9), Íslenska (9), syndrome (9), glöggva (9), forsölu (9), bók (9), Árna (8), viðhorfa (8), slangur (8), samkvæmt (8), samanlögðu (8), ríkjandi (8), nýrri (8), metsölubók (8), heimspekideild (8), forrit (8), endurbætt (8), Blöndals (8), nefni (7), merkingar (7), keyptum (7), er (7), alist (7), Starfaði (7), Orðið (7), Böðvarssonar (7), íslenskri (6), Ö (6), skýringum (6), selst (6), samantekt (6), lektor (6), hinni (6), hin (6), gefin (6), cintök (6), dósent (6), Færeyingar (6), íslensku (5), íslenska (5)

orð með háa tíðni sem vinstri nágrannar orðabók:
Íslenskri (64), Íslensk (34), ÍSLENSK (12), íslenskri (4), Úr (4), Íslenska (4), íslenska (3), samkvæmt (3)

orð með háa tíðni sem hægri nágrannar orðabók:
Menningarsjóðs (50), Freysteins (11), Blöndals (8), ríkjandi (5), Háskólans (5)

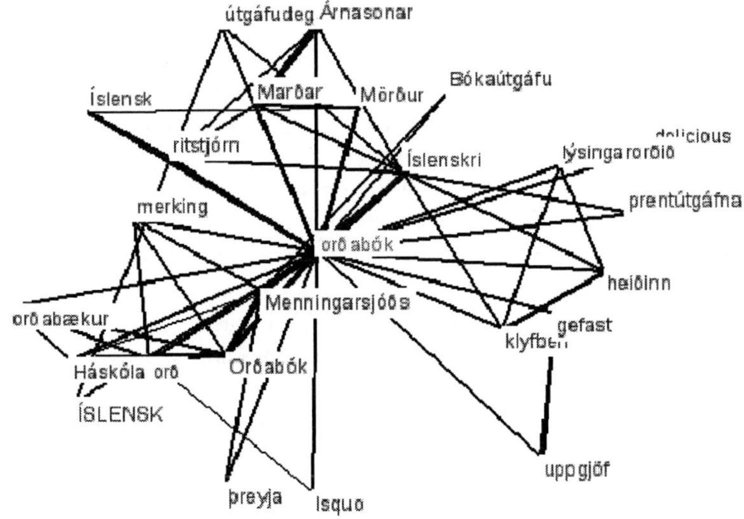

A Survey and Classification of Methods for (Mostly) Unsupervised Learning of Morphology

Harald Hammarström
Dept. of Computing Science
Chalmers University of Technology
412 96, Gothenburg Sweden
`harald2@cs.chalmers.se`

Abstract

This paper surveys work on unsupervised learning of morphology. A fairly broad demarcation of the area is given, and a hierarchy of subgoals is established in order to properly characterize each line of work. All the minor and major lines of work are mentioned with a reference and a brief characterization. Different approaches that have been prevalent in the field as a whole are highlighted and critically discussed. The general picture resulting from the survey is that much work has been repeated over and over, with little exchange and evolution of techniques. All in all, the contribution of this paper is a very brief but comprehensive umbrellic synopsis to the research area.

1 Introduction

The problem of (mostly) unsupervised learning of morphology (ULM) may be broadly delineated as follows:

Input: Raw (unannotated) natural language text data

Output: A description of the morphological structure (there are various levels to be distinguished; see below) of the language of the input text

With: As little supervision, i.e. parameters, annotated bootstrapping data, model selection during development etc., as possible

Some approaches have explicit or implicit biases towards certain kinds of languages; they are nevertheless considered to be ULM for this survey.

Morphology may be narrowly taken as to include only derivational and grammatical affixation, where the number of affixations a root may take is finite and the order of affixation may not be permuted. This survey also subsumes attempts that take a broader view including clitics and compounding (and there seems to be no reasons in principle to exclude incorporation and lexical affixes). A lot of, but not all, approaches focus on concatenative morphology/compounding only.

All works in this survey operate on orthographic words – excluding word-segmentation for languages that do not mark word-boundaries orthographically.

One of the matters that varies the most between different authors is the desired outcome. It is useful to set up the implicational hierarchy shown in Table 1 (which need of course not correspond to steps taken in an actual algorithm). The division is implicational in the sense that if one can do the morphological analysis of a lower level in the table, one can also easily produce the analysis of any of the above levels. For example, if one can perform analysis into stem and affixes, one can decide if two word are of the same stem. The converse need not hold, it is perfectly possible to answer the question of whether two words are of the same stem with high accuracy, without having to commit what the actual stem is.

A lot of recent articles do not deal properly with previous and related work, some reinvent heuristics that have been sighted earlier, and there is little modularization taking place. Thus the time is ripe, even

Joakim Nivre, Heiki-Jaan Kaalep, Kadri Muischnek and Mare Koit (Eds.)
NODALIDA 2007 Conference Proceedings, pp. 292–296

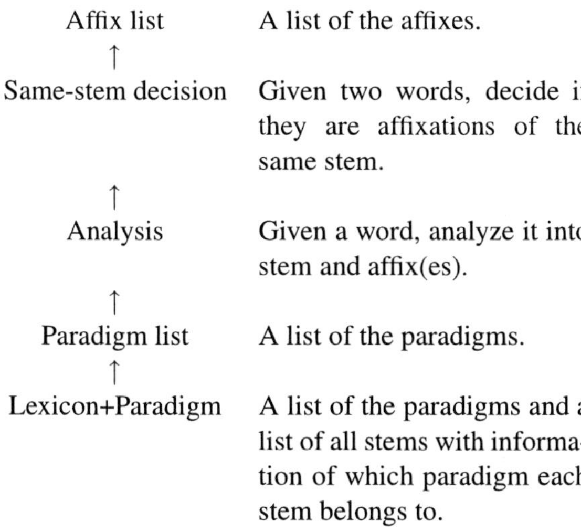

Affix list	A list of the affixes.
↑	
Same-stem decision	Given two words, decide if they are affixations of the same stem.
↑	
Analysis	Given a word, analyze it into stem and affix(es).
↑	
Paradigm list	A list of the paradigms.
↑	
Lexicon+Paradigm	A list of the paradigms and a list of all stems with information of which paradigm each stem belongs to.

Table 1: Levels of power of morphological analysis. We do not make a distinction between probabilistic and non-probabilistic versions.

overdue, for a survey and classification of ideas in this area.

Our full bibliography of ULM-work comprises at least 100 articles/books (more if the level of unsupervised-ness is relaxed out of control) spanning from 1955 to 2006. Clearly, each article cannot be cited or discussed in detail, but we will cover each distinct line of work.

2 Roadmap and Synopsis of Earlier Studies

For reasons of space, very short characterizations of selected representatives of each line of work is given in Table 2. In addition, there is relevant work (Manning, 1998; Borin, 1991; Neuvel and Fulop, 2002) on formalizing morphological regularities but which do not suggest an algorithm that performs on raw text data input.

It was impossible to characterize methods and ideas in brief for each line of work because of the amount of detail necessary to give a relevant comparative picture. However, all work uses some kind of frequency count of n-character grams, and almost all trace their inspiration back to (Harris, 1955). In addition, some recent approches use a Minimum Description Length (MDL)-inspired formula as an optimization criterion of a given model. All the ap-

proaches to non-concatenative morphology involve an alignment-step. A few lines of work have tried to exploit other kinds of clues than character sequences, such as similarities in semantics or syntax between words (also acquired in a semi-supervised manner). A fair comparison of previous work in terms of accuracy figures is entirely impossible, not only because of the great variation in goals but also because most descriptions do not specify their algorithm(s) in enough detail. This aspect is better handled in controlled competitions, such as the Unsupervised Morpheme Analysis – Morpho Challenge 2007[1] which a task of segmentation of Finnish, English, German and Turkish.

3 Discussion

Although the heuristic of Harris has had some success it was shown (in various interpretations) as early as (Hafer and Weiss, 1974) that it is not really sound – even for English. In the 2000s, probably independently, a slightly better extension of the same idea emerged, namely, to compile a set of words into a *trie* and predict boundaries at nodes with high activity, but this is not sound either as non-morphemic short common character sequences also show significant branching.

So far, all the approaches with mixed MDL-optimization are unsatisfactory on two main accounts; on the theoretical side, they still owe an explanation of why compression or MDL-inspired weighting schemes should give birth to segmentations coinciding with morphemes as linguists conceive of morphemes. On the experimental side, thresholds, supervised/developed parametres and selective input still cloud the success of reported results. What is clear, however, apart from whether it is theoretically motivated, is that MDL approaches are *useful*.

4 Conclusion

What emerges from the last 10 years of intensive research is that, essentially, different people have been doing the same thing with little exchange between each other.

---

[1]Website http://www.cis.hut.fi/ morphochallenge2007/ accessed 10 January 2007.

	Model	Superv.	Experimentation	Learns what?
(Harris, 1955)+	C	T	English	Analysis
(Andreev, 1965)	C	T	E-type (I)	Unclear
(Lehmann, 1973)	C	T	German	Analysis
(Hafer and Weiss, 1974)	C	T	English	Analysis
(Wothke and Schmidt, 1992)	C	T	German	Analysis
(Klenk, 1994)+	NC	T	Arabic + E-type	Analysis
(Langer, 1991)+	C	T	German	Analysis
(Flenner, 1995)+	C	T	Spanish	Analysis
(Brent et al., 1995)	C	T	English	Analysis
(Džeroski and Erjavec, 2000)	C	T	Slovene	Analysis
(Kazakov and Manandhar, 2001)+	C	T	French/English	Transducer
(Gaussier, 1999)	C	T + AP	English (I)	Paradigms
(Goldsmith, 2006)+	C	T	E-type (I)	Paradigms+Lexicon
(Clark, 2001)+	NC	# states	German/Arabic/English	Transducer
(Déjean, 1998)+	C	T	E-type	Analysis
(Schone, 2001)+	C	T	E-type	Related pairs of words
(Baroni, 2003)+	C	T	E-type	Analysis
(Jacquemin, 1997)	C	T	E-type	Related pairs of words
(Sharma et al., 2002)+	C	T	Assamese	Paradigms+lexicon
(Baroni et al., 2002)	NC	T	English/German (I)	Ranked list of related word pairs
(Creutz, 2006)+	C	T	Finnish/Turkish/English	Analysis
(Kontorovich et al., 2003)	C	T	English	Analysis
(Snover and Brent, 2003)+	C	T	English/Polish	Related pairs of words
(Johnson and Martin, 2003)	C	T	Inuktitut	Unclear
(Wicentowski, 2004)+	NC	AP	30-ish E-type	Transducers
(Ćavar et al., 2004)+	C	T	Unclear	Paradigms
(Argamon et al., 2004)	C	T	English	Analysis
(Goldsmith et al., 2005)+	NC	T	Unclear	Unclear
(Oliver, 2004, Ch. 4-5)	C	T	Catalan	Paradigms
(Kurimo et al., 2005)	C	T	Finnish/Turkish/English	Analysis
(Hammarström, 2006)+	C	-	Maori to Warlpiri	Same-stem

Table 2: Very brief roadmap of earlier studies. Abbrevations in the Table: C = Concatenative, NC = Also non-concatenative, T = Thresholds and Parameters to be set by a human, AP = Aligned pairs of words, E-type = European Indo-European type languages, I = Impressionistic evaluation. + = entry also covers earlier work by the same author(s).

References

Nikolai Dmitrievich Andreev, editor. 1965. *Statistiko-kombinatornoe modelirovanie iazykov*. Akademia Nauk SSSR, Moskva.

Shlomo Argamon, Navot Akiva, Amihood Amit, and Oren Kapah. 2004. Efficient unsupervised recursive word segmentation using minimum description length. In *COLING-04, 22-29 August 2004, Geneva, Switzerland*.

Marco Baroni, Johannes Matiasek, and Harald Trost. 2002. Unsupervised discovery of morphologically related words based on orthographic and semantic similarity. In *Proceedings of the Workshop on Morphological and Phonological Learning of ACL/SIGPHON-2002*, pages 48–57.

Marco Baroni. 2003. Distribution-driven morpheme discovery: A computational/experimental study. *Yearbook of Morphology*, pages 213–248.

Lars Borin. 1991. *The Automatic Induction of Morphological Regularities*. Ph.D. thesis, University of Uppsala.

Michael R. Brent, S. Murthy, and A. Lundberg. 1995. Discovering morphemic suffixes: A case study in minimum description length induction. In *Fifth International Workshop on Artificial Intelligence and Statistics, Ft. Lauderdale, Florida*.

Damir Ćavar, Joshua Herring, Toshikazu Ikuta, Paul Rodrigues, and Giancarlo Schrementi. 2004. On induction of morphology grammars and its role in bootstrapping. In Gerhard Jäger, Paola Monachesi, Gerald Penn, and Shuly Wintner, editors, *Proceedings of Formal Grammar 2004*, pages 47–62.

Alexander Clark. 2001. Partially supervised learning of morphology with stochastic transducers. In *Proc. of Natural Language Processing Pacific Rim Symposium, NLPRS 2001*, pages 341–348, Tokyo, Japan, November.

Mathias Creutz. 2006. *Induction of the Morphology of Natural Language: Unsupervised Morpheme Segmentation with Application to Automatic Speech Recognition*. Ph.D. thesis, Helsinki University of Technology, Espoo, Finland.

Hervé Déjean. 1998. *Concepts et algorithmes pour la découverte des structures formelles des langues*. Ph.D. thesis, Université de Caen Basse Normandie.

Sašo Džeroski and Tomaž Erjavec. 2000. Learning to lemmatise slovene words. In James Cussens and Saso Dzeroski, editors, *Learning Language in Logic*, volume 1925 of *Lecture Notes in Computer Science*, pages 69–88. Springer-Verlag, Berlin.

Gudrun Flenner. 1995. Quantitative morphsegmentierung im spanischen auf phonologischer basis. *Sprache und Datenverarbeitung*, 19(2):63–78.

Éric Gaussier. 1999. Unsupervised learning of derivational morphology from inflectional lexicons. In *Proceedings of the 37th Annual Meeting of the Association for Computational Linguistics (ACL-1999)*. Association for Computational Linguistics, Philadephia.

John Goldsmith, Yu Hu, Irina Matveeva, and Colin Sprague. 2005. A heuristic for morpheme discovery based on string edit distance. Techincal Report of Computer Science Department, University of Chicago.

John A. Goldsmith. 2006. An algorithm for the unsupervised learning of morphology. *Computational Linguistics*, 12(4):353–371.

Margaret A. Hafer and Stephen F. Weiss. 1974. Word segmentation by letter successor varieties. *Information and Storge Retrieval*, 10:371–385.

Harald Hammarström. 2006. Poor man's stemming: Unsupervised recognition of same-stem words. In Hwee Tou Ng, Mun-Kew Leong, Min-Yen Kan, and Donghong Ji, editors, *Information Retrieval Technology: Proceedings of the Third Asia Information retrieval Symposium, AIRS 2006, Singapore, October 2006*, volume 4182 of *Lecture Notes in Computer Science*, pages 323–337. Springer-Verlag, Berlin.

Zellig S. Harris. 1955. From phoneme to morpheme. *Language*, 31(2):190–222.

Christian Jacquemin. 1997. Guessing morphology from terms and corpora. In *Proceedings, 20th Annual International ACM SIGIR Conference on Research and Development in Information Retrieval (SIGIR '97), Philadelphia, PA*.

Howard Johnson and Joel Martin. 2003. Unsupervised learning of morphology for English and Inuktitut. In *HLT-NAACL 2003, Human Language Technology Conference of the North American Chapter of the Association for Computational Linguistics, May 27 - June 1, Edmonton, Canada*, volume Companion Volume - Short papers.

Dimitar Kazakov and Suresh Manandhar. 2001. Unsupervised learning of word segmentation rules with genetic algorithms and inductive logic programming. *Machine Learning*, 43:121–162.

Ursula Klenk. 1994. Automatische morphologische analyse arabischer wortformen. In Ursula Klenk, editor, *Computatio Linguae II: Aufsätze zur algorithmischen und Quantitativen Analyse der Sprache*, volume 83 of *Zeitschrift für Dialektologie und Linguistik: Beihefte*, pages 84–101. Franz Steiner, Stuttgart.

L. Kontorovich, D. Don, and Y. Singer. 2003. A markov model for the acquisition of morphological structure. Technical report, CMU-CS-03-147, School of Computer Science, Carnegie Mellon University, June.

Mikko Kurimo, Mathias Creutz, Matti Varjokallio, Ebru Arisoy, and Murat Saraclar. 2005. An introduction and evaluation report. In Mikko Kurimo, Mathias Creutz, and Krista Lagus, editors, *Unsupervised segmentation of words into morphemes – Challenge 2005*.

Hagen Langer. 1991. *Ein automatisches Morphsegmentierungsverfahren für deutsche Wortformen*. Ph.D. thesis, Georg-August-Universität zu Göttingen.

Hubert Lehmann. 1973. *Linguistische Modellbildung und Methodologie*. Max Niemeyer Verlag, Tübingen. Pp. 71-76 and 88-93.

Christopher D. Manning. 1998. The segmentation problem in morphology learning. In Jill Burstein and Claudia Leacock, editors, *Proceedings of the Joint Conference on New Methods in Language Processing and Computational Language Learning*, pages 299–305. Association for Computational Linguistics, Somerset, New Jersey.

Sylvain Neuvel and Sean A. Fulop. 2002. Unsupervised learning of morphology without morphemes. In *Workshop on Morphological and Phonological Learning at Association for Computational Linguistics 40th Anniversary Meeting (ACL-02), July 6-12*, pages 9–15. ACL Publications.

A. Oliver. 2004. *Adquisició d'informació lèxica i morfosintàctica a partir de corpus sense anotar: aplicació al rus i al croat*. Ph.D. thesis, Universitat de Barcelona.

Patrick Schone. 2001. *Toward Knowledge-Free Induction of Machine-Readable Dictionaries*. Ph.D. thesis, University of Colorado.

Utpal Sharma, Jugal Kalita, and Rajib Das. 2002. Unsupervised learning of morphology for building lexicon for a highly inflectional language. In *Proceedings of the 6th Workshop of the ACL Special Interest Group in Computational Phonology (SIGPHON), Philadelphia, July 2002*, pages 1–10. Association for Computational Linguistics.

Matthew G. Snover and Michael R. Brent. 2003. A probabilistic model for learning concatenative morphology. In S. Becker, S. Thrun, and K. Obermayer, editors, *Advances in Neural Information Processing Systems 15*, pages 1513–1520. MIT Press, Cambridge, MA.

Richard Wicentowski. 2004. Multilingual noise-robust supervised morphological analysis using the word-frame model. In *Proceedings of the ACL Special Interest Group on Computational Phonology (SIGPHON)*, pages 70–77.

Klaus Wothke and Rudolf Schmidt. 1992. A morphological segmentation procedure for german. *Sprache und Datenverarbeitung*, 16(1):15–28.

Marvina – A Norwegian Speech-Centric, Multimodal Visitors' Guide

Ole Hartvigsen[1], Erik Harborg[2], Tore Amble[1] and Magne Hallstein Johnsen[1]

[1] Norwegian University of Science and Technology (NTNU), N-7491 Trondheim, Norway

[2] SINTEF ICT, N-7465 Trondheim, Norway

hartvigs@stud.ntnu.no, Erik.Harborg@sintef.no, toreamb@idi.ntnu.no, mhj@iet.ntnu.no

Abstract

This paper describes the development and testing of a multimodal visitors' guide service for guests to the city and university in Trondheim. The system is under continuous development. At the present state it serves as a help for visitors to Trondheim aiming at meeting people at the university. Using a natural speech interface with a mobile phone it provides help in finding the right bus connection, how to find your way on the campus, and finally how to find the office inside the building where you are going to meet. Information is provided to the user in the form of speech and graphics (maps, illustrations). It is also illustrated how a robot-guide can be used in helping the visitor in finding his way inside a building. Presently, the user end of the demonstrator is implemented on a standard PC, using IP-based telephony (Skype Out). However, in order to utilize all aspects of the system, a practical implementation would require a type of PDA-based phone.

1 Introduction

Spoken dialogue information systems over the telephone line have enjoyed growing commercial interest over recent years, and a large number of such systems have been developed and tested, e.g. (Gupta et al., 2006). The systems vary a lot in complexity, not only due to the variation in tasks and design techniques, but also because of the difference in targeted user friendliness.

The introduction of new PDA-based mobile phones has increased the interest in developing phone-based services utilizing additional modalities to speech, e.g. graphics through the enhanced screen on those units, e.g. (Bühler and Minker, 2005). Our work has been performed as a part of the collaborative, multidisciplinary BRAGE-project[1]. One of the main tasks within this project has been the development of spoken dialogue systems. The work presented here, is our first attempt of a multimodal add-on to a speech-only based system. It represents a merge and enhancement of previous work in various areas.

2 Human-machine dialogue systems

2.1 Human-human versus human-machine dialogues

It is a long way to go before human-machine dialogue systems can emulate real human-human spoken dialogues. When humans talk with each other the spoken dialogues are characterized by spontaneous speech with an "infinite" vocabulary, unfulfilled sentences with incorrect syntax, interrupts, corrections, filled pauses, false starts, repetitions, topic changes, change of dialogue initiative, complex reasoning, and use of "world" knowledge. In addition, a face-to-face dialogue between humans also applies meta-information such as gestures, mimics and voice mode to communicate the meaning of the spoken utterances.

In contrast, current human-machine dialogue systems are limited to a specific task, a finite vocabulary, moderate reasoning, and usually have no knowledge of the "world" outside the task. Further, the systems have only a limited ability to handle

---

[1] BRAGE homepage: *http://www.iet.ntnu.no/projects/brage/*.

Joakim Nivre, Heiki-Jaan Kaalep, Kadri Muischnek and Mare Koit (Eds.)

NODALIDA 2007 Conference Proceedings, pp. 297–304

"

spontaneous speech, interrupts, topic changes, and discourse.

2.2 Human-machine dialogue structures

A query system is a degenerate dialogue structure as the input must be a grammatically correct, complete request to which the system can respond in a single turn.

On the other end we find the so-called system driven dialogue. This dialogue is characterized by a predetermined sequence of system-initiated turns; i.e. questions which the user must respond to accordingly. Usually only a single semantic entity is asked for in each turn.

A more human-human like (and thus user-friendly) dialogue structure is used in so called mixed-initiative systems, where both the user and the system can take control of the dialogue flow.

Some tasks are complex to solve even for human-human dialogues. These cases are often termed problem-based dialogues. Developing automatic systems which can handle problem-based dialogues is a huge challenge and a current research topic within the field dialogue theory and formalisms.

2.3 Text-based versus speech centric systems

The Internet offers a variety of text-based information systems. Many of these are query based. Further, text-based system driven services (booking, bank etc.) are more or less used by everyone.

Only a few text-based mixed-initiative dialogue systems are public available and rarely any systems deal with tasks which need a problem-based strategy.

In many everyday situations, people need instant information without having access to a PC (keyboard). By enabling access to the information by a phone (or a PDA with GSM, GPRS or UMTS), this problem can be solved. This, however, implies that the users must be allowed to carry out the dialogue by using their voice and also receive the information by speech. A speech only dialogue system is shown in Figure 1, and typically consists of several modules; automatic speech recognition (ASR) including a semantic extractor, text-to-speech synthesis (TTS), a dialogue manager including a reasoning module, a database and a re-

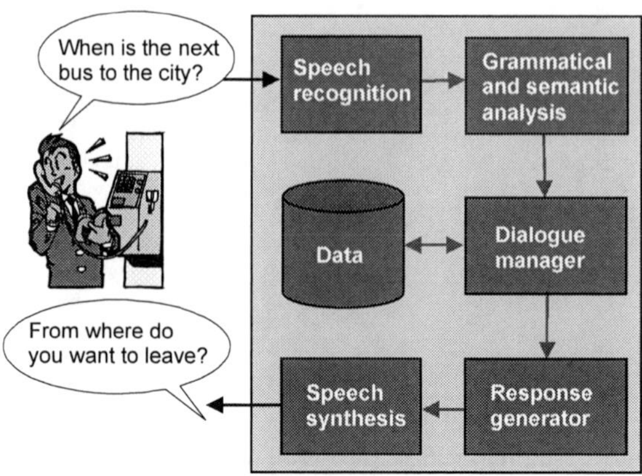

Figure 1. A speech only based dialogue system.

sponse generator. The last three are needed also for a corresponding text-based system.

Note, however, that the ASR performance in a dialogue context means semantic instead of word accuracy; i.e. the goal is to extract the user's meaning or intention correctly. Further, the success of any automated service is strongly correlated to user friendliness. For dialogue systems this calls for a mixed-initiative control between a user and the system. This implies that the system should accept partial information, corrections, change of (sub)task, etc. Finally, it is mandatory that the user should not be restricted to speak in a "read-text" mode; i.e. natural, spontaneous speech must be accepted.

2.4 Speech centric multimodal dialogue systems

The convergence between mobile phones and PDAs is accelerating. Thus the display as a second input-output channel has now become an option. For these terminals we believe that multimodal inputs in the form of "tap and talk" will be useful. (Kvale et al., 2005; Almeida et al., 2002) The tap-option can replace or enhance the speech-option and thus reduce the ASR-complexity. Further, the corresponding outputs will have a richer and more compact form; i.e. a combination of graphics, text and speech. Thus, this type of multimodality will result in a simple and user-friendly interface and thus also opens for solving more complex tasks for the users in a convenient manner.

3   The modules of the Marvina system

Marvina is the result of a continuous activity and collaboration between the project partners going on for several years. This has led to the development of several subsystems, which for some parts have been previously reported. In this section we present a walkthrough of the various pieces which now has merged into the Marvina system.

3.1   Speech I/O

For speech input, an Automatic Speech Recognition (ASR) system is needed. Typically, a speech detector and a feature extractor forms the front-end of the recogniser. The feature extractor performs a sequence of short time-frequency conversions (typically every 10 msec.) and processes the frequency information in a perceptual way (mimics parts of the ear and brain). The output in the form of a sequence of feature vectors is used by the decoder in order to obtain a recognized text string. In this process, acoustic models, a pronunciation lexicon and a language model is used.

The acoustic models are a moderately sized set of phoneme based HMMs[2], and are thus responsible for the core conversion between the acoustic signal and the linguistic representation. The pronunciations lexicon gives the mapping between a phoneme/HMM sequence and a corresponding word. The language model is tailored to the dialogue task, and defines the allowable utterance (word sequence) structures. Thus the decoder maps the incoming feature sequence to the most likely sequence of phoneme HMMs corresponding to a legal word sequence. In some cases, several (ranked) utterance hypotheses can be produced. Further, the likelihood scores are often used to calculate a confidence score for the (best) proposal. The system uses this confidence score and dialogue knowledge to accept or reject the sentence hypothesis (or parts of it). If so, the system can ask the user to repeat the corresponding rejected utterance.

In our particular design a flexible speech recogniser was implemented based on an improved version of the procedure developed in COST Action 249, Continuous Speech Recognition over the Telephone (Johansen et al., 2000). The recognition

engine was the HAPI recogniser (Odell et al., 1999). The Norwegian SpeechDat database (Höge et al., 1999) was used for training. For Norwegian, this database was restricted to 1000 speakers, which was recorded over ISDN-based fixed lines, i.e. the resulting acoustic models are not specifically adapted for mobile phone callers. The acoustic models consist of a context dependent phone set (triphones) with a relatively strong degree of state tying. In addition models for the SpeechDat defined noise labels (man-made and background) were trained. Finally, to cope with Out-Of-Vocabulary (OOV) words, a lexical based filler model was designed from a set of monophones, according to a simplified version of the procedure presented in (Méliani and O'Shaughnessy, 1996). Thus the user is allowed to speak in a natural language.

System prompts are transformed into speech by a text-to-speech system (TTS-synthesis). TTS for Norwegian is an ongoing research topic for one of our partners in another project[3]. For the time being we are using a commercially available TTS engine; RealSpeak from Nuance[4].

3.2   The BusTUC system

BusTUC (Amble, 2000) is a text-based question answering system about bus transportation. The NLP module is based on a complex set of rules, and is implemented in Prolog. It is versatile with respect to understanding and answering a variety of alternative formulations requesting the same kind of information. This question-answering system consists of three modules. The bottom module, BusLOG, includes the bus route database, the bus-stop list of names (including mappings from area descriptions to bus stops), and a route analyzer/planner, which finds the shortest/best route between two given bus stops. Bus transfer is handled if there is no direct route. The second module is a general text understanding module (Text Understanding Computer - TUC) which performs a rule based grammatical and semantic parsing. The third and main module integrates TUC and Bus-LOG, and tailors the system to process a complete inquiry in a single sentence. In fact this is the part

---

[2] HMMs - Hidden Markov Models are well suited for representing statistical sequences.

[3] The FONEMA project homepage:
http://www.iet.ntnu.no/projects/fonema/
[4] Information about the Nuance RealSpeak TTS can be found at: *http://www.nuance.com/realspeak/telecom/*

which is called BusTUC, as it is the part specifically made for the question-answering mode. Thus one could call this module for a degenerate dialogue manager, i.e. with only one turn. BusTUC will thus perform a full sentence analysis. However there is no memory as there is no dialogue; i.e. every question is concerning a new, independent inquiry and must contain all the semantic entities necessary to provide an answer from the bus route database. This can be regarded as an extreme variant of a so-called 'User-initiative' system. Thus, BusTUC will typically understand and respond to sentences like:

- *I would like to travel from Ila to Saupstad in about one hour from now.*
- *When is the next bus from the City Centre to Dragvoll?*

The BusTUC system has now been commercialized, and is publicly available as a service from the bus company in the city of Trondheim. A web-service[5] has been operational since 1998 and a SMS-service since 2002. In 2006 about 678.000 inquiries was made on the web, and about 100.000 on SMS. This is a considerable amount for a city of about 160.000 inhabitants. Inquires are logged and used to continuously improve the performance of the system.

3.3 The BUSTER system

BUSTER (Johnsen et al., 2003) was originally developed as a text based and mixed initiative version of the inquiry system BusTUC, based on an existing system driven approach (Johnsen et al., 2000). It was designed as a first step towards a mixed initiative spoken dialogue system. Thus the system is made robust with respect to inputs which reflect recognition errors in a corresponding speech based system. To accomplish this, BUSTER gracefully degrades the dialogue towards a system driven approach.

As BUSTER includes BusTUC and thus allows inputs with more than one semantic entity, both BusLOG and TUC were needed. In order to allow mixed-initiative turn-taking, a complex dialogue structure was implemented, based on a dialogue grammar using a slot-filling formalism.

We have added a speech interface to BUSTER, as described in Section 3.1. The size of the vocabu-

lary is about 800 words in this case, where around 700 contain names of bus stops and area description in the city of Trondheim. Based on logs from real use of the text-based system, Wizard-of-Oz (WoZ) experiments and online use of the speech based system, we have enhanced the system to its present state. Also, evaluation reports from the WoZ-callers have been used for this purpose. The system has now been publicly available for about one year.

3.4 The DAter system

The text-based Directory Assistance system, DAter is based on the same technology as BUSTER, and illustrates the portability of that design to another domain. It covers all employees at the Norwegian University and other cooperating institutions connected to the same telephone central, summing up to about 5000 names. You may ask questions about the following information:

- Telephone numbers
- Employee names
- Job position
- Street address
- Office location (room number)
- Associated institution
- Email-address

Also for this system a speech interface has been added in order to facilitate usage over the phone. However, the present version is restricted to a subset of the employees for demonstration purposes and due to limitations in the speech recognition system. For this application the vocabulary includes about 350 words, covering all the 250 employees at the dept. of Computer and Information Science at NTNU.

The DAter system was originally developed as a question answering system based on the TUC framework. However, as for BUSTER, it has been extended to deal with dialogue handling.

3.5 The dialogue handling system

The BUSTER system is built upon BusTUC using a generic dialogue handling system. The dialogue system described here is common to BUSTER and DAter.

In general terms, the following functions are new when added to a working question answering system:

- *Decomposition:* Dialogue systems make it easier to convey complex information between the participants, because the information can be broken down into smaller components, and conveyed separately.
- *Anaphoric references:* Decomposition makes it natural to refer to earlier elements by anaphoric references of various kinds.
- *Elliptic references:* Incomplete parts of a sentence that is supposed to be supplemented by the use of earlier text.
- *Augmentation*: The user can on his own initiative add more constraints to a previous query, using ellipsis or otherwise.
- *Modification:* The user can modify the last query, using ellipsis or otherwise.
- *Additional information:* The user may need extra information about something that has come up in the dialogue.
- *Confirmation:* The user may need confirmation of something the system has uttered. Either because the output is ambiguous or unclear, or (in a speech environment) because he is uncertain if he has misheard.

The input from the user is broadly classified into 4 groups of "User Speech Acts":

- *Question:* A question. E.g. "when does the bus leave?"
- *New:* A complete non-question sentence. E.g. "I want to go to Lade".
- *Item:* A single item, not a complete sentence. E.g. "NTH", "Lade allé 80".
- *Modifier:* An elliptic utterance, e.g. "to NTH", "from Lade to NTH".

User dialogue terminals

The terminals for user speech acts are based on these classes. We defined separate terminals based on where in the dialogue the speech acts occurred, because the speech acts should be treated differently based on this.

Dialogue grammar

With these terminals as building elements, the whole dialogue can be modelled by a dialogue grammar. A dialogue grammar is analogous to a sentence grammar, but the nodes in the dialogue grammar are phrases, annotated with their corresponding dialogue terminal types.

```
Dialog    → UserQs, [dialogerror], SystemDialog
UserQs    → UserQ, UserQs | [ ]
UserQ     → [uin], UiqRepl | [uiq], UiqRepl
UiqRepl   → [sant] | Askrefs, Askfors, UiqRepl2
Askrefs   → Askref, Askrefs | [ ]
Askref    → [sqd], SqdRepl
Askfors   → Askfor, Askfors | [ ]
Askfor    → [sqt], UserQs, SqtRepl
UiqRepl2  → [sat], Modify | [sal], Modify |
              [relax], sat, Modify | [saf]
Modify    → [uim], UiqRepl | [ ]
SqdRepl   → [uadi] | [uadm] | [uadn] | [uadq]
SqtRepl   → [uati] | [uatc] | [uatm] |
              [uatn] | [uatg] | [uatf]
```

Figure 2. Generic Dialogue Grammar.

Figure 2 presents a flavour of this grammar, which is further explained in (Fledsberg and Bjerkevoll 1999).

Grammar execution

The BUSTER grammar is interpreted by a grammar engine. The grammar engine stores the state of the analysis in a stack of frame nodes containing the following information:

- The name of the current non-terminal.
- A focus-structure defining the focus of the dialogue at this point in the dialogue.
- A frame node containing the values of the required slots.
- A list of last mentioned referents.

3.6 The Telebuster system

Telebuster is a unified system for BUSTER and DAter. It uses the same generic dialogue handling system that was used for BUSTER and DAter.

The first step was to make the one and same system to handle two different kinds of dialogues, one for buses and one for directory assistance. The next step was to handle both domains integrated in the same dialogue. As the examples will show (see Section 4.1), this is well on its way to be successful.

The Telebuster dialog system resides upon a complete question understanding system. One of the additional functions of the dialog handler is to maintain a context frame which is updated during the dialogue. This context will then contain all possible referents to anaphoric references that are extracted from the users' queries and from essential information of the answers.

Another function is to ask for missing information from the user in order to be able to formulate a meaningful query to its databases.

Implicit in the multi-domain dialogue handling is the decision, what type of question or dialogue-act it is confronted with. For example, for the question:

"How do I get to Erik Harborg",

the system may decide to find and give information about Erik Harborg, and thereby make salient the information of his location. Thereafter, the location is extracted from the answer, and stored in the context frame.

The system may not automatically go on to find a bus route, but on a later question:

"How do I get there",

the location is already available, and the query can be processed as a yet incomplete bus route query. This demands an origin of departure and time constraints, and will be prompted unless given earlier or decided by defaults.

Similarly, a later question :

"What is his phone"

is easily resolved because Erik Harborg is the last mentioned person in the dialogue.

The approach shows its generality in a common handling of the language analysis (both English and Norwegian), the same semantic based translation for two languages and two domains and a unified treatise of dialogues.

3.7   The Marvin system

Marvin (Hartvigsen, 2006) was the first attempt to create an "Intelligent Helper" system built on top of the previously Telebuster system. The original task was to create a text based natural language user interface for a virtual robot. The robot is a "guide" or "helper" for people visiting a certain floor in a building with an office environment. Marvin used the Telebuster system for semantic and syntactic analyses of input sentences, and for getting information about people and offices, however the bus route part of the system was not used in Marvin. Telebuster also returned a logical representation (TQL[6]) of the sentences, which Marvin used to interpret some ad-hoc requests that Telebuster would normally not understand. The movements of the virtual robot were simulated in real

time in a Java program called WSU Khepera Robot Simulator[7]. The Marvin system would also show maps of the floor or surrounding buildings to supplement the textual answers.

4   Connecting the pieces – Marvina

4.1   A typical scenario

Marvina is a modular demonstrator, making it easy to change/substitute parts of the system and utilize parts of previous demonstrators. It utilizes both the BUSTER and DAter system in order to provide information about bus transportation in the city of Trondheim, and information about employees at the university and cooperating organizations. It uses the Marvin system in order to provide localization information within a building for employees at the university area. A speech interface has been added to this originally text-based system.

A typical scenario for the demonstrator will be a visitor to the city of Trondheim, who is going to meet an employee of the university at his office. The visitor stays at a hotel downtown and has no idea about how to get to the university and to the office of the person he is going to meet. He calls in to the University Visitors' Guide service from his PDA-based phone to get help. The dialogue might proceed as follows:

- *S:* Welcome to the Marvina Visitors' Guide. How may I help you?
- *U:* I am going to visit Tore Amble.
- *S:* Tore Amble's office is in the IT-building, room no. 312. The street address is Sem Sæland Street 9.
- *U:* How do I get there?
- *S:* You will go to Gløshaugen Syd. Where are you travelling from?
- *U:* I am staying at Hotel Augustin and have a meeting at 3 o'clock.
- *<A map of the city pops up on the PDA-screen showing the hotel and bus stop in question>*
  S: The bus stop closest to Hotel Augustin is Torget. You will go from Torget to Gløshaugen Syd before 15:00. Bus no. 5 passes Torget at 14:51 and Gløshaugen Syd at 14:56.
- *U:* What is his phone number?
- *S:* Tore Amble has phone no. 73594451.

---

[6] TQL – TUC Query Language (Amble, 2000).

[7] Khepera info page:
http://carl.cs.wright.edu/reg//ksim/ksim.html

- *<The user takes the bus to the Gløshaugen Syd bus stop, and calls in again>*
- *U:* How do I get from Gløshaugen Syd to Tore Amble's office?
- *<A map pops up on the PDA screen with a marked walking route>*
  S: Please follow the marked route on the map to the IT-building, and take the stairs to the 3rd floor.
- *<The user finds his way to the 3rd floor of the IT-building, and finds a visitors' guide robot in the hall. He addresses the robot and says:>*
  U: Where is Tore Amble's office?
- *S:* Tore Amble's office is in room no. 312. Do you want me to follow you there?
- *U:* Yes, please!
- *<The robot moves down the corridor and stops outside Tore Amble's office>*

Presently, the system is not implemented on a PDA, however a PC-based demonstrator is implemented. Also, the robot is not yet physically implemented, but simulated as a moving avatar on a floor map presented on the PC screen. This simulation is similar to the one used in the Marvin system (see Section 3.7).

4.2 Marvina architecture

Marvina runs across three different computers. A Linux server runs the speech recognition and a Windows server runs the text-to-speech synthesizer. Finally, the main Marvina application and

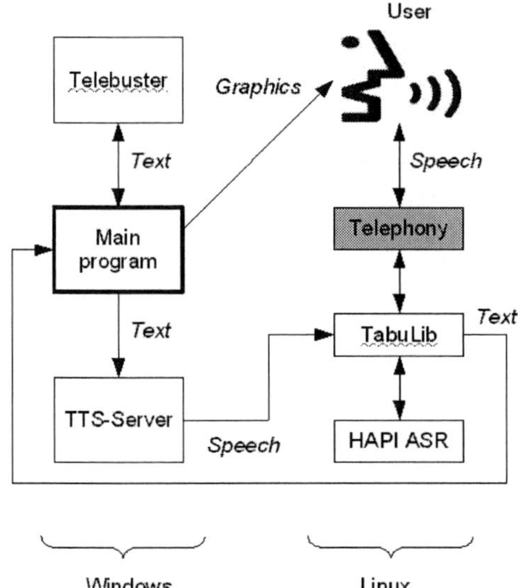

Figure 3. Marvina architecture.

Telebuster is running on another Windows system. Telebuster may also look up information about employees from an LDAP[8] database located elsewhere. The structure of the system is shown in Figure 3.

The TabuLib program library (Knudsen et al., 2005) controls the ISDN telephony interface and the HAPI speech recognizer. Using this library we avoid low level programming of the I/O system.

The user calls up the speech recognizer via telephone (using Skype). The recognized sentence is sent to the main program as a text string, and the main program decides what to answer in cooperation with Telebuster. An output string is sent to the text-to-speech server, which synthesizes an audible speech output sent back to the user via telephony. The main program also outputs graphics to the user.

4.3 Merging the ASR language models

To make use of the complete Telebuster system, the language models for the BUSTER and DAter system had to be merged. The language model has also been extended to cope with special case sentences for the Marvina system. Such sentences include queries like "Where is the toilet?" and "I'm on the third floor of the IT-building". To keep the dictionary size at a reasonable level, names are limited to people working at the Department of Computer and Information Science at NTNU.

4.4 Dynamic answers

An important feature in Marvina is the ability to answer dynamically, based on the location of the user and the desired destination. A question about the location of a person's office will be answered in different ways by Marvina depending on the "closeness" of the user. For instance, a user located in a different suburb of the city than the destination will be advised to take certain buses that will bring him closer to the destination. Maps and spoken answers can, for instance, guide the user from his current location to the bus stop, from the bus stop to the desired building, from the building to the correct floor and from the entrance of a floor to the correct office.

---

[8] LDAP – Lightweight Directory Access protocol.

5 Present experience and future work

At present, Marvina works as a fully functional demonstrator. The user may call in from any phone, however, in order to use the graphics capabilities, he must use a PC. The system seems to work quite well within the domain, though extensive user tests have not yet been performed.

Also, the speech interface seems to work quite nicely, however, we are close to a limit for the lexicon size and complexity of the language model in order to maintain acceptable speech recognition rates for the limited training speech data we have available, in particular when mobile phones are used (speech for ASR training is solely based on fixed network recordings). The robust grammar and semantic analysis are helpful in obtaining a graceful degradation when error occurs.

Obvious tasks for the future include performing extensive user tests/evaluation in order to verify/improve the usability of the system. Standard methods for evaluation of spoken dialogue systems have been suggested (Walker et al., 2000). Also, an implementation on a PDA-based phone is foreseen. At the Department of Computer and Information Science (NTNU), there are plans to implement the robot visitors' guide, which would serve as a natural extension of the present demonstrator.

Acknowledgement

This work has mainly been financed by the Norwegian Research Council as a part of the BRAGE project.

We would like to thank our colleagues at NTNU, SINTEF and Telenor R&D for valuable and fruitful discussions and cooperation with the work within BRAGE.

References

Luís Almeida et al.: "The MUST guide to Paris - Implementation and expert evaluation of a multimodal tourist guide to Paris," in Proc. ISCA Tutorial and Research Workshop on Multi-Modal Dialogue in Mobile Environments, Kloster Irsee, Germany, 2002.

Tore Amble: "BusTUC – A Natural Language Bus Oracle," in Applied Natural Language Processing Conference, Seattle, USA, April 2000.

Dirk Bühler and Wolfgang Minker: "Mobile Multimodality – Design and Development of the SmartKom Companion," International Journal of Speech Technology, vol, 8, pp. 193-202, 2005.

Øystein Fledsberg and Kim Bjerkevoll: *Buster - Robust dialogue management*, MSc thesis, Norwegian University of Science and Technology (NTNU), December 1999.

Narendra Gupta et al.: "The AT&T Spoken Language Understanding System," IEEE trans. on Audio, Speech, and Language Processing, vol. 14, no. 1, pp. 213-222, January 2006.

Ole Hartvigsen: *Marvin - Intelligent Corridor Guide*, MSc Thesis, dept. of Computer and Information Science, Norwegian University of Science and Technology (NTNU), June 2006.

Harald Höge et al.: "SpeechDat multilingual speech databases for teleservices: Across the finish line," in Proc. EUROSPEECH, Budapest, Hungary, pp. 2699–2702, September 1999.

Finn Tore Johansen et al.: "The COST 249 SpeechDat multilingual reference recogniser," in Proc. LREC, Athens, Greece, pp. 1351–1354, May 2000.

Magne Hallstein Johnsen et al.: "TABOR - A Norwegian Spoken Dialogue System for Bus Travel Information," in Proc. International Conference on Spoken Language Processing (ICSLP), Beijing, China, October 2000.

Magne Hallstein Johnsen et al.: "A Norwegian Spoken Dialogue System for Bus Travel Information", Telektronikk (2), 2003.

Jan Eikeset Knudsen et al.: *Tabulib Reference Manual*. Version 1.5.0, Telenor R&D, February 23, 2005.

Knut Kvale et al.: "Evaluation of a mobile multimodal service for disabled users," in Proc. MMUI, Gothenburg, Sweden, April 2005.

Rachida El Méliani and Douglas O'Shaughnessy: "New efficient fillers for unlimited word recognition and keyword spotting," in Proc. International Conference on Spoken Language Processing (ICSLP), Philadelphia, USA, pp. 590–593, October 1996.

Julian Odell et al.: *The HAPI Book*, Version 1.4, Entropic Ltd., January 1999.

Marilyn Walker et al.: "Developing and Testing General Models of Spoken Dialogue System Performance," in Proc. International Conference on Language Resources and Evaluation (LREC), Athens, Greece, pp. 189–192, May 2000.

A Norwegian letter-to-sound engine
with Danish as a catalyst

Peter Juel Henrichsen
Center for Computational Modelling of Language (CMOL)
Copenhagen Business School
Dalgas Have 15, DK-2000 Copenhagen F, Denmark
`pjuel@id.cbs.dk`

Abstract

Danish phonetics and Norwegian phone-tics are not all that different. This fact is exploited in an ongoing project establishing a phonetic transcription algorithm for (East-) Norwegian. Using methods known from machine learning we exploit a publicly available phonetic database for Danish (based on the Danish PAROLE corpus) arriving at a cost-competitive phonetic database for Norwegian. While the ultimate goal of this enterprise is a low-budget complete phonetic transcription of the NoTa corpus of Norwegian spontaneous speech, this paper presents the subparts related to Danish phonetics.

1 Introduction

Politically, Norwegian and Danish[1] are treated as distinct languages as a matter of course. From a linguistic point of view the distinctness is more dubious: it is not difficult to suggest a pair of Norwegian dialects differing more from each other (at least phonetically) than do the vernaculars of Copenhagen and Oslo[2]. Similarly, in a recent study based on statistical methods, Danish and Swedish spoken

languages were shown to be in many respects better described as mutual dialects than distinct tongues (Henrichsen et al 2005). Recycling of linguistic resources across Scandianvian boundaries thus seems to be a natural idea.

In this short paper we present our Danish-to-Norwegian phonetic mapping algorithm based largely on publicly available resources. A dedicated homepage is found via a link in the author's homepage,
`www.id.cbs.dk/~pjuel`

The paper is sectioned as follows. In section 2 we introduce the Danish resources that have played a role in the present project. In section 3, the algorithm is presented, while section 4 presents some results. Finally section 5 puts the letter-to-sound enterprise in a wider perspective.

2 The Danish PAROLE project

The Danish PAROLE corpus was established in the early nineties as a part of the pan-European PAROLE project representing all the official EU languages. In each participating country, a local project group was appointed and commissioned to establishing a (by that time's standards) large text corpus. A substantial subpart of this corpus (at least 250k words) was then manually annotated for part-of-speech using a common annotation format allowing for easy transfer of PoS information across language boundaries.

Annotation work on the Danish PAROLE corpus has been continued at CMOL. Today PAROLE is a poly-dimensional corpus structure comprising these annotation dimensions (in various stages of completion):

- Tree structure (dependency based)
- Rhetorical structure

---

[1] In this paper, 'Norwegian' and 'Danish' refer to the East-Norwegian dialect spoken in and around Oslo, and the lect termed "advanced standard Copenhagen", respectively – unless otherwise stated.

[2] In Denmark, the former dialectal diversity is now largely lost, probably due to the denser and more evenly distributed Danish population.

Joakim Nivre, Heiki-Jaan Kaalep, Kadri Muischnek and Mare Koit (Eds.)
NODALIDA 2007 Conference Proceedings, pp. 305–309

- English translation
- Russian translation
- Tamil translation
- Phonetic annotation (*)
- Prosodic annotation (*)
- Sound track (by one male speaker), including:
    - *Fundamental frequency measurements* (*)
    - *Intensity measurements* (*)

Of these, the dimensions marked with * have played a role in the project reported. Contact the author for information on access to the Danish PAROLE corpus including the various annotation dimensions.

3 The transfer component

The transfer component includes several strategies. Those involving Danish are shown in fig. 1.

Figure 1. Norwegian letter-to-sound mapper

The topmost box represents the Norwegian orthographic input. One of two paths may be tried, in this order: (i) via NO2DO, DO2DP and DP2NP to the end state (the phonetic form), or (ii)via NO2NP. The modules are introduced below. As will be explained, DO2DP as well as DP2NP are informed by the phonetic forms inventory called *DanPO,* the Danish phonetic dictionary developed at CMOL as a part of the long-term PAROLE annotation project.

3.1 Orthographic preliminaries

It is conventional knowledge that many Norwegian orthographic forms have identical Danish equivalents; examples are "notat", "notere", "ignorerer", and "ignorant", just to mention a few. Other forms have near-equivalents, such as "infisere" (Danish *inficere*), "notasjon" (*notation*), "ignorerte" (*ignorerede*) and "ignorantene" (*ignoranterne*) differing only superficially. Only a very small fraction of Norwegian stems are completely absent in Danish, as can be verified in any ordinary word frequency list.

Inspired by these facts, a Norwegian-Danish orthography-to-orthography mapping (NO2DO) was established in a preparatory stage. In the text box below some of the most productive NO2DO rules are presented as (Perl-style) regular expressions.

NO2DO (Nor. orthograpy to Dan. ortography)

Orthographic surface rules

General equivalents
  s/kj/k/, s/kt/gt/, s/øy/øj/, s/au[dt]/ød/, ...

Morphological equivalents
  s/sak/sag/, s/skap/skab/, s/sjon/tion/, ...

Rules informed by PoS

Verbs:	s/a$/e/, s/ert$/eret/, ...
Nouns:	s/ene$/erne/, s/a$/en/, ...
Adjectives:	s/aktig$/agtig$/, s/ert$/eret/,

...

Legend
s/x/y/ = substitute x by y
...$/ = matches string-final position only
[xy] = matches one instance of either x or y

Table 1

Using NO2DO conversion, the recognition rate of Norwegian-Danish equivalent word forms (based on a reference list of 1000 hand-picked equivalences) rose from an initial 75% precision and even lower recall, to more than 95% for both precision and recall[3].

3.2 Danish phones to Norwegian phones

In order to exploit our Danish source as far as possible, we based the mapping algorithm on a phonetic alphabet relating as closely as possible to the Danish PAROLE phonetics annotation (cf. author's homepage). This means that we had to deviate slightly from the de facto standard of SAMPA[4], the most substantial difference being that the retroflexes are not fully instantiated in the adopted version. Discussions with several Norwegian phoneticians have made us aware that the

---

[3]The actual figures should be taken with a grain of salt: the procedures of hand-picking and manual rule-adjustment may sometimes lead to artificially boosted results; still a considerably improved recognition rate is beyond doubt.

[4]Cf. www.phon.ucl.ac.uk/home/sampa

patterns of retroflexation are not completely consistent among East-Norwegian speakers (or even among Oslovians). The full definition of the Norwegian sound alphabet can be consulted at the Dphon2Nphon homepage (via link above).

In the following we demonstrate our treatments of a few of the most important systematic differences between Danish and Norwegian phonetic realisation of common underlying phonological forms.

In Norwegian, the stops /p/ /t/ /k/ are always realised as [p] [t] [k]; Danish /p/ /t/ /k/, in constrast, are only maintained in syllable-initial positions before full wowels; in other positions they reduce to [b] [d] [g], as marked in **bold** in fig. 2.

	Norwegian	*Danish*
"titte"	[t"it0]	[t`id0]
"statsmakter"	[st'A:tsmAkt0r]	-
"statsmagter"	-	
		[sd`{:?dsmAgdC]
"straffbart"	[str"AfbA:rt]	-
"strafbart"	-	[sdr`AfbA:?d]

For Norwegian: ['] – accent I, ["] – accent II.

Figure 2. Danish-Norwegian equivalent forms

The Danish *stød* (sometimes described as a quick glottal contraction or even a glottal stop, but actually better described as instance of 'creaky voice') has no articulatory equivalent in Norwegian. By and large, Danish stød corresponds to Norwegian accent I (as exemplified in fig. 2). The general correlation pattern is however overruled by two facts: (i) in Norwegian, the distinction between accent I and II is only relevant in polysyllabic words; Danish has no similar restriction for stød (e.g. "mand"/"man" [m`an?]/[m`an], "Hans"/"hans" [h`an?s]/[h`ans]; (ii) Danish stød only occurs in syllables with either a long vowel or a short vowel followed by a sonorant consonant ("tænger" [t`EN?C], "koen" [k2o:?0n], but not in e.g. "takker" and "hoppen"). No similar restriction applies for the Norwegian accents.

These and numerous other productive subsitutions rules (165 in all) have been identified by automatic and semi-automatic methods and incorporated in the DP2NP mapping algorithm.

<table>
<tr><td>DP2NP(Dan. phonetics to Nor. phonetics)</td></tr>
</table>

s/`D?/'NVow/   (select accent I)
s/d/t/   for "t" in Danish orthography
s/D/d/   for "d" or "t" in Dan. orthography
s/b/p/   for "p" in Dan. orthography
s/g/k/   for "k" in Dan. orthography
s/v/N/   for "gn"

Legend
`DVow?* = matches any stressed vowel with stød
[D] = Danish /d/ without stop

Table 2

By way of example, Norwegian "adoptant" transcribes to [AdOpt'Ant] in these steps:

```
"adoptant"
                              via NO2DO
"adoptant"
                          via DO2DP
[adCbt`an?d]
  ||  ||  |                via DP2NP
[AdOpt'An t]
```

Observe that (in this case) the proper accent I is selected as signalled by the Danish stød.

3.3 Norwegian orthography-to-phonetics

Even if most Norwegian word forms by far have Danish equivalents, not all of them are within reach of automatically derived (i.e. machine learned) rules. A rule discovering the equivalence of, say, Norwegian "tvil" and Danish "tvivl" (*doubt*) might also – and erroneously – postulate the equivalence of "sal" (*hall*) and "savl" (*saliver*). Foreign words tend to maintain their original spelling in Danish ("bassin", "orange"), but not in Norwegian ("basseng", "oransje"). Finally, some Norwegian lexemes do not have equivalents in contemporary Danish, such as "kanskje" and "slik".

In all such cases, the Danish-to-Norwegian transliteration regime clearly does not suffice. Thus a third mapper had do be designed for the cases where no Danish equivalents can be identified, the Norwegian letter-to-sound module (NO2NP). This module cannot boast innovation, neither in function nor implementation, so we shall not care to present the details here. It follows principles and details from the literature (e.g. Sahajpal (05), Andersen (96), Black (91)). Our results are probably comparable to those reported in the literature, as far as can be judged from the sparse information given; but we wish to stress the fact that we only included the NO2NP for our transformation algorithm to be complete. Details and references will be presented in Henrichsen (2007).

3.4 Compounding

Of course, rules for analysing lexically unrecognized words using rules of compounding have also been implemented. However, as such rules are not special to the current project, we do not present the details here. Suffice it to say that the Danish glue elements (fuger) "e" and "s" are matched by virtually similar Norwegian equivalents "e" and "s". The Norwegian s-fuge usually does not alter the accent of the first component while the e-fuge usually produces accent II. Likewise, fuge-e induces loss of stød in Danish. Otherwise, the implications of compounding are very similar to the Danish rules (e.g. main stress retained by the first compound element only).

4 Some results

We selected 50,000 word forms randomly from the Oslo corpus of mixed text genres (cf. www.tekstlab.uio.no/norsk/bokmaal). Of these, 23,939 were processable by the NO2DO-DO2DP-DP2NP strategy (i.e. recognized in DanPO after NO2DO treatment). We then scored the results using three success definitions: *(i)* exact match with the phonetic form found in a standard Norwegian phonetic dictionary; *(ii)* a single phonetic conflict permitted (e.g. [e] mistaken for [0], or long-instance for short-instance of the same vowel), *(iii)* exact match when ignoring type-of-accent. Table 3 presents our results.

Word length	*(i)- correct*	*(ii)- correct*	*(iii)- correct*
2-5	78%	89%	84%
6-10	68%	79%	75%
11-15	59%	68%	66%

*Table*3

As seen, we get a good estimate of the Norwegian phonetic form of short words (up to ninety percent accuracy, relaxing the

success criterion a little). Also, most errors made are not very disturbing (many are recurrent errors in transcriptions made by humans too), e.g. the confusion of [e]/[0], [o]/[u], accent I/II. As the large majority of words given the NO2DO-DO2DP-DP2NP treatment are shorter than 10 letters after compound decomposition, our preliminary conclusion is optimistic. The low-budget Norwegian phonetic annotation engine may be within reach.

5 Discussion

Phonetic translating between Scandinavian (or other cognate) languages is interesting in its own right, providing a constructive and directly testable way of pursuing 'micro-typology' and language history. To this comes the practical usefulness. The sub-project reported here together with its results constitute the first steps in an ongoing larger scale annotation project which as its primary goal has the phonetic annotation of the newly published NoTa corpus of about 900,000 words (cf. http://www.tekstlab.uio.no/nota/). The annotation task must be carried out on a very tight (almost non-existing) budget, so the recycling of readily avaliable resources for Danish including phonetics and even prosodic markup is – for several reasons – an attractive strategy.

The new NoTa data-tier is of course of lesser value to the linguist than real descriptive phonetics would be. However, for certain purposes, lexical phonetics may well suffice. Say you want to investigate the cross-speaker realisation of a particular phoneme or phoneme-combination that cannot be reliably traced by its orthographic image – then a lexical-phonetic search dimension may be just what you need.

Acknowledgements

Thanks to Janne Bondi Johannessen, Torbjørn Nordgård, and many others for loads of information and good sparring. Without them being Norwegian this project would have been impossible.

References

Andersen, Ove; Roland Kuhn; Ariane Lazaridès; Paul Dalsgaard; Jürgen Haas; Elmar Nöth (1996) *Comparison of Two*

Tree-Structured Approaches for Grapheme-to-Phoneme Conversion; ICSLP 1996 (cd-rom), 4pp

Black, A; Joke van de Plassche, Briony Williams (1991) *Analysis of Unknown Words through Morphological Decomposition*; proceed. of 5th EACL, 101-106

Grønnum, Nina (1998) *Fonetik og Fonologi - Almen og Dansk*; Copenh.: Akademisk Forlag

Henrichsen, Peter Juel; Jens Allwood (2005) *Swedish and Danish, Spoken and Written Language - a statistical comparison*; J. of Corpus Ling. 17/3:2005

Henrichsen, Peter Juel (2007) *NoTa – nu med lydskrift;* in book on NoTa (Oslo Univ., ed. by Janne Bondi Johannessen), *in prep.*

Nordgård, Torbjørn (2000) *NorKompLeks. A Norwegian Computational Lexicon*; COMLEX-2000, Patras, Hellas

Sahajpal, Anurag; Terje Kristensen (2005) *Transcription of Text by Incremental Support Vector Machine*; proceed. of Norsk Informatikkonferanse 2005, 79-87

Skadhauge, Peter Rossen; Peter Juel Henrichsen (2005) *DanPO - a transcription-based dictionary for Danish speech technology*; *NODALIDA-2005,* Joensuu, Finland

Dialogue Simulation and Context Dynamics for Dialogue Management

Simon Keizer and **Roser Morante**
Department of Communication and Information Sciences
Faculty of Humanities
Tilburg University, The Netherlands
{s.keizer,r.morante}@uvt.nl

Abstract

In this paper we describe DISCUS, a research tool for developing a context model and update algorithm for dialogue management. The model builds on Dynamic Interpretation Theory (DIT), in which dialogue is modelled in terms of dialogue acts operating on the information state of the dialogue participants. On the basis of dialogue act specifications of both system and user utterances, DISCUS performs the update of the system's context model. The context model is structured into several components and contains complex elements involving the beliefs and goals of both system and user. We will present simulations of two dialogues, one for demonstrating the context update model, and another in which the system utterances are generated automatically.

1 Introduction

DISCUS (Dialogue Simulation and Context Update System) is a research tool for simulating dialogues between a user and a dialogue system. On the basis of dialogue act specifications of both system and user utterances, DISCUS executes an algorithm for updating the system's context model and displays the results on the screen. The tool is used to test, experiment with, and further develop the context model and update algorithm, by abstracting away from the processes of dialogue act recognition and generation in the dialogue system and focusing on the context dynamics. The model is integrated in the dialogue manager of an interactive question answering system.

The context update algorithm is built on Dynamic Interpretation Theory (DIT), (Bunt, 2000), in which dialogue utterances are interpreted as having intended context–changing effects that are determined by the dialogue act(s) being performed with the utterance. So, generally speaking, we follow an approach that fits in the Information State Update paradigm of dialogue modelling (Traum and Larsson, 2003), but with a strong emphasis on dialogue acts and an information state representation that goes beyond a dialogue history and task-specific information.

Dialogue acts in DIT are organised in a multidimensional dialogue act taxonomy, which means that an utterance gets at most one dialogue act from each dimension. The dimensions reflect different aspects of communication that can be addressed simultaneously, such as the underlying task itself, but also the aspect of how the participants were able to process each other's utterances (auto- and allo-feedback), or aspects of interaction-management like turn-taking and topic-management, or social aspects like greetings and apologies. Following this multidimensional organisation of the taxonomy, DISCUS allows to select several dialogue acts from different dimensions to represent a single, multifunctional, utterance.

The starting point for the model for context update are the preconditions of the dialogue acts, which represent the motivation and ability for an agent to perform a dialogue act. These preconditions are represented in terms of beliefs and goals in the information state of the speaker; in that sense we fol-

Joakim Nivre, Heiki-Jaan Kaalep, Kadri Muischnek and Mare Koit (Eds.)
NODALIDA 2007 Conference Proceedings, pp. 310–317

low an approach that is similar to the BDI (Beliefs, Desires, Intentions) paradigm (Allen and Perrault, 1980). The information state of a dialogue system is represented in its context model, which is structured into different components, representing different kinds of information, such as an extended dialogue history and future (the 'linguistic context'), information about the underlying task (the 'semantic context'), the participants' states of processing each other's utterances (the 'cognitive context'), and information about communicative pressures (the 'social context').

The structure of the context model can be employed in the process of dialogue act generation: for the generation of dialogue acts in specific dimensions, only specific components in the context are relevant.

After discussing the theoretical background of DIT (Section 2) and the concrete specification of the context model used and how it is updated (Section 3), we will discuss the simulation in DISCUS of an example dialogue (Section 4). In Section 5, we discuss a second simulation, but now one in which the system acts are no longer simulated, but generated automatically.

2   DIT

In Dynamic Interpretation Theory (DIT) (Bunt, 2000), a dialogue is modelled as a sequence of utterances expressing sets of *dialogue acts*. These are semantic units, operating on the information states of the participants. Formally, a dialogue act in DIT consists of a *semantic content* and a *communicative function*, the latter specifying how the information state of the addressee is to be updated with the former upon understanding the corresponding utterance. Communicative functions are organised in a taxonomy[1] consisting of 10 *dimensions* (Bunt, 2006) that reflect different aspects of communication speakers may address in their dialogue behaviour. In each utterance, several dialogue acts can be performed, each dialogue act from a different dimension. The overview below shows a layered structure in which the dimensions are given in boldface italic. So, besides the *task/domain* dimension,

---

[1]See web page http://let.uvt.nl/general/people/bunt/docs/dit-schema2.html.

the taxonomy provides for several *dialogue control* dimensions, organised into the layers of *feedback*, *interaction management (IM)* and *social obligations management (SOM)*.

- *Task/domain*: acts that concern the specific underlying task and/or domain.

- **Dialogue Control**
  - **Feedback**
    * *Auto-Feedback*: acts dealing with the speaker's processing of the addressee's utterances; contains positive and negative feedback acts on different levels of understanding;
    * *Allo-Feedback*: acts dealing with the addressee's processing of the speaker's previous utterances (as viewed by the speaker); contains positive and negative feedback-giving acts and feedback elicitation acts on different levels of understanding;
  - **Interaction management**
    * *Turn Management*: turn accepting, giving, grabbing, keeping;
    * *Time Management*: stalling, pausing;
    * *Partner Processing Management*: completion, correct-misspeaking;
    * *Own Processing Management*: error signalling, retraction, self-correction;
    * *Contact Management*: contact check, contact indication;
    * *Topic Management*: topic introduction, closing, shift, shift announcement;
  - *Social Obligations Management*: salutation, self-introduction, gratitude, apology, valediction;

A participant's information state in DIT is called his *context model*, and contains all information considered relevant for his interpretation and generation of dialogue acts. A context model is structured into several components:

1. *Linguistic Context*: linguistic information about the utterances produced in the dialogue so far (a kind of 'extended dialogue history'); information about planned system dialogue acts (a 'dialogue future');

2. *Semantic Context*: contains current information about the task/domain, including assumptions about the dialogue partner's information;

3. *Cognitive Context*: the current processing states of both participants, expressed in terms of a level of understanding reached (see below);

4. *Physical and Perceptual Context*: the perceptible aspects of the communication process and the task/domain;

5. *Social Context*: current communicative pressures.

In keeping track of the participants' processing states in the cognitive context, four levels of understanding are distinguished: 1) *perception*: the system was able to hear the utterance (successful speech recognition), 2) *interpretation*: the system understood what was meant by the utterance (successful dialogue act recognition), 3) *evaluation*: the information presented in the utterance did not conflict with the system's context (successful consistency checking), and 4) *execution*: the system could act upon, do something with, the utterance (for example, answering a question, adopting the information given, carrying out a request, etcetera).

These levels of understanding are also used in distinguishing different types of auto- and allo-feedback dialogue acts, each for signalling processing problems on a specific level.

3   Context specification and update model

The context model we propose follows the general structure according to DIT as described in the previous section. In Figure 1, a feature structure representation is given of our context model. Currently, information about the physical and perceptual context is not relevant for the type of dialogues and the underlying task we consider, and therefore is left out.

The Linguistic Context contains features for storing dialogue acts performed in the dialogue so far: *user_utts* and *system_utts*. In addition, *topic_struct* and *conv_state* contain information about the topical and conversational structure. The other two features in the linguistic context are related to the generation of dialogue acts (see Section 5). The feature *candidate_dial_acts* stores the dialogue acts that are gen-

erated by separate agents responsible for dialogue acts from a specific dimension in the taxonomy. The feature *dial_acts_pres* stores the current combination of dialogue acts available for direct presentation as a multifunctional system utterance.

The Semantic Context contains information related to the underlying task, in our case interactive question answering. The feature *task_progress* allows to distinguish between different stages of performing the task. In the case of an interactive question answering system containing separate QA modules that take self-contained questions as input, we distinguish the states of composing a self-contained question for the QA modules (*comp_quest*), waiting for QA results after submitting a question (*quest_qa*), evaluating the QA results (*answ_eval*), and discussing the results with the user (*user_sat*). Besides this task-specific feature, there is a feature *user_model* containing information about the user's beliefs and goals concerning the task-domain. For question answering, this information can be interpreted as a specification of the user's information needs (as built up through the questions asked by the user), and of the user's current knowledge about the domain (as built up through the answers and other information given by the system).

The Cognitive Context contains two features, representing the processing states of the system (*own_proc_state*) and the user (*partner_proc_state*) as viewed by the system. Both contain two features: one indicating whether or not a processing problem was encountered, and if so, on which level of processing this happened, and one containing information about the user's beliefs and goals related to the processing state. The Cognitive Context also has a feature *common_ground*, containing beliefs the system believes to be mutually believed. Finally, a feature *belief_model* is used, containing all (non-mutual) beliefs in the context model. This feature is used to have a reference to all beliefs in one place, making part of the update mechanism more convenient. These beliefs have cross-links to other parts of the context model, wherever appropriate (e.g., to the user model of the Semantic Context).

The Social Context is specified in terms of communicative pressures; currently, we only use one feature indicating whether or not a reactive pressure exists for performing a social obligations

$$
\begin{bmatrix}
LingContext : \begin{bmatrix}
user\_utts : \langle last\_user\_dial\_act = uda_0, uda_{-1}, uda_{-2}, \ldots \rangle \\
system\_utts : \langle last\_system\_dial\_act = sda_0, sda_{-1}, sda_{-2}, \ldots \rangle \\
topic\_struct : \langle referents \rangle \\
conv\_state : opening|body|pre-closing|closing \\
candidate\_dial\_acts : \ldots \\
dial\_acts\_pres : \ldots
\end{bmatrix} \\[6pt]
SemContext : \begin{bmatrix}
task\_progress : comp\_quest|quest\_qa|answ\_eval|user\_sat \\
user\_model : \langle beliefs \rangle
\end{bmatrix} \\[6pt]
CogContext : \begin{bmatrix}
own\_proc\_state : \begin{bmatrix} proc\_problem : perc|int|eval|exec|none \\ user\_model : \langle beliefs \rangle \end{bmatrix} \\
partner\_proc\_state : \begin{bmatrix} proc\_problem : perc|int|eval|exec|none \\ user\_model : \langle beliefs \rangle \end{bmatrix} \\
belief\_model : \langle beliefs \rangle \\
common\_ground : \langle mutual\_beliefs \rangle
\end{bmatrix} \\[6pt]
SocContext : \begin{bmatrix} comm\_pressure : none|grt|apo|thk|valed \end{bmatrix}
\end{bmatrix}
$$

Figure 1: Feature structure representation of the context model used.

management act, and if so, for which one (e.g., *comm_pressure: grt* indicates a pressure for the system to respond to a greeting).

3.1 Context update model

The model for updating the context makes explicit how every dialogue act contributes to changing the information state, it defines the types of effects that an utterance provokes in dialogue participants, and it establishes the operations that cause the change of state in the context.

The aspect of the context model related to information transfer and grounding is represented in terms of beliefs. Basically, the types of beliefs we distinguish are represented by means of several operators (weak belief, strong belief, mutual belief, knows value of, wants), that allow to represent the meaning of dialogue acts. As a dialogue evolves, new beliefs are created and existing beliefs may change or be cancelled. Those changes are modelled by means of the operations of *creation, strengthening, cancellation* and *adoption*. Dialogue acts have different types of effects on dialogue participants: effects of understanding and adopting information in the addressee, and effects of expectations of understanding and adoption, and strengthening in speaker and addressee. For more details about this aspect of the context update model, see (Morante et al., 2007).

4   Simulating a QA dialogue

In this section we will discuss the simulation of a dialogue in which the user (U) asks a question that gets answered by the system (S):

U0: *what causes the flu?*

S1: *excuse me?*

U2: *what causes the flu?*

S3: *the flu is caused by the influenza virus*

U4: *thank you*

S5: *you're welcome*

With DISCUS, we can simulate dialogues from the perspective of one of the participants. In this case, we simulate the above dialogue from the system's perspective. In Figure 2, a screenshot of the interface is given. The components in the bottom part of the GUI can be used to specify who is the speaker of the utterance simulated, the system's understanding level reached (in case of a user utterance), a literal text representation of the utterance, and the communicative function (CF) and semantic content (SC) of the dialogue act performed in the utterance. A dialogue act is specified in terms of its *Communicative Function* and its *Semantic Content*, the last of which could be very complex. Here it is specified in terms of at most three arguments. It is also possible to simulate processing problems encountered by the system by identifying a specific level of understanding reached.

Simon Keizer and Roser Morante

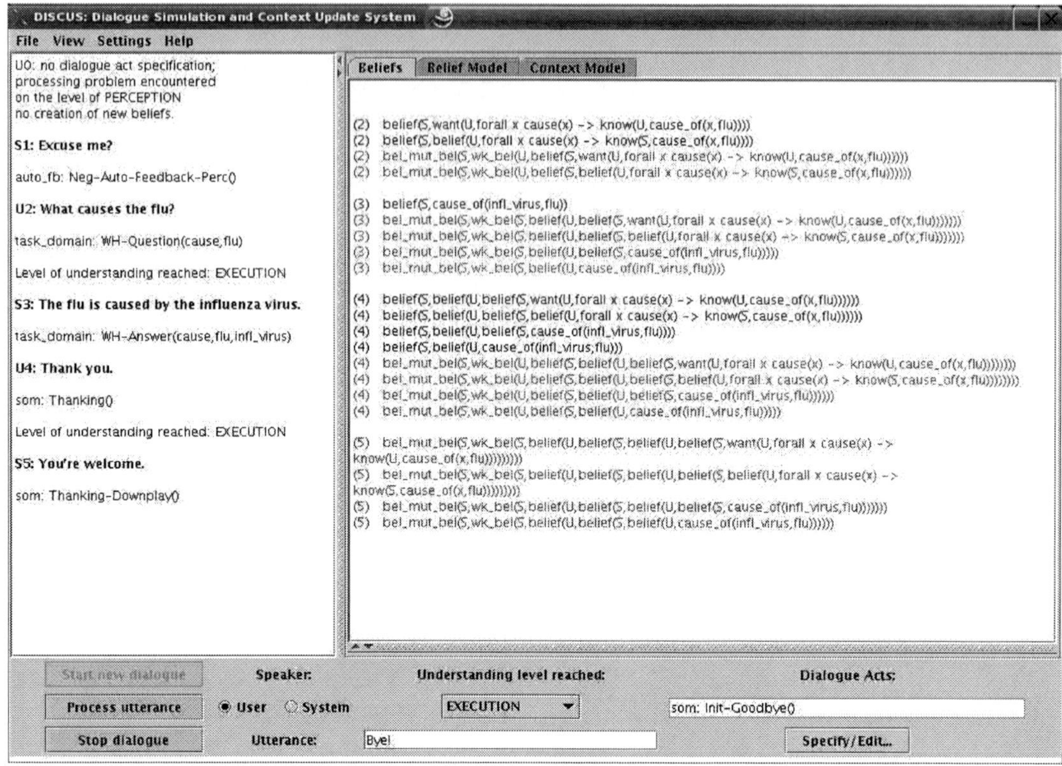

Figure 2: Screenshot of the DISCUS interface.

The text panel in the top left part of the GUI displays the simulated dialogue (Dialogue History). For each utterance in the dialogue, the literal utterance, the speaker (S or U), the dialogue act information along the dimensions of the taxonomy, and in case of user utterances, the processing level reached by the system, can be indicated.

The text panel in the top right part of the GUI displays the beliefs and goals in the context model (Information State). The various kinds of beliefs are displayed in different colours; cancelled beliefs get a 'strike-through' font. Not visible in the screenshot is a separate tab for displaying the full context model.

In processing the first utterance, the system encounters speech recognition problems. This is simulated by specifying a processing level of value 'none' in the interface. Hence, there will be no dialogue acts to specify for this utterance. Updating the context with U1 will create a processing problem on the level of perception being recorded in the own processing state of the cognitive context.

Next, the system signals this processing problem to the user in S1 by means of a negative auto-feedback dialogue act on the level of perception.

In U2, the user repeats his question, and now the system is able to perceive the user's utterance and interpret it as a question about the domain. So, we simulate that the system has reached interpretation level understanding. The interpretation result consists of a dialogue act in the task-domain dimension with a communicative function WH-QUESTION. The semantic content of WH-Questions is specified by means of two arguments, indicating the domain and specific property of the elements from that domain that are asked for by the speaker. In the case of U2, these arguments are *cause* and *flu* respectively.

Updating the system's context model with a dialogue act results in a number of beliefs, based on the preconditions of the dialogue act. As indicated in Section 3.1, these beliefs are the result of different types of effects.

The beliefs in 1 and 2 form the effects of understanding the WH-QUESTION in U2.

$$belief(S, want(U, \forall x \; cause(x) \rightarrow$$
$$know(U, cause\_of(x, flu)))) \quad (1)$$
$$belief(S, belief(U, \forall x \; cause(x) \rightarrow$$
$$know(S, cause\_of(x, flu)))) \quad (2)$$

Belief 1 is about a new user goal, i.e., the user wants to know something; belief 2 is about the user believing that the system has the information the user wants.

The user goal is recorded in the *Semantic Context*, because it is related to the underlying task/domain. This is based on the fact that the belief stems from one of the two preconditions associated with the user's WH-QUESTION, a dialogue act in the task-domain dimension.

The beliefs in 3 and 4 form the effects of expected understanding.

$$mut\_bel(S, wk\_bel(U,$$
$$belief(S, want(U, \forall x \; cause(x) \rightarrow$$
$$know(U, cause\_of(x, flu)))))) \quad (3)$$
$$mut\_bel(S, wk\_bel(U,$$
$$belief(S, belief(U, \forall x \; cause(x) \rightarrow$$
$$know(S, cause\_of(x, flu)))))) \quad (4)$$

These are mutual beliefs that are recorded in the cognitive context as part of the common ground.

Next, we can simulate the system's response, assuming it is cooperative and has been able to find the information requested. This information is represented in the semantic context as the following belief:

$$belief(S, cause\_of(infl\_virus, flu)) \quad (5)$$

This belief, together with 1 and 2 form the preconditions for S3, which is specified as a WH-ANSWER with a semantic content represented by three arguments, two of which correspond to the user's information need created by the WH-QUESTION. The third argument represents the information the system thinks the user asked for, here, *infl(uenza)_virus*.

$$wk\_bel(S, belief(U,$$
$$belief(S, want(U, \forall x \; cause(x) \rightarrow$$

$$know(U, cause\_of(x, flu))))) \quad (6)$$
$$wk\_bel(S, belief(U,$$
$$belief(S, belief(U, \forall x \; cause(x) \rightarrow$$
$$know(S, cause\_of(x, flu)))))) \quad (7)$$

$$wk\_bel(S, belief(U, belief(S,$$
$$cause\_of(infl\_virus, flu)))) \quad (8)$$
$$wk\_bel(S, belief(U,$$
$$cause\_of(infl\_virus, flu))) \quad (9)$$

Updating the context model with this system dialogue act results in beliefs about expecting that the user understands the system's reply (6, 7, and 8) and that the user adopts the information given by the system (9). These beliefs are also considered by the system to be mutually believed. Such beliefs about mutual beliefs are placed in the common ground of the cognitive context.

Utterance U4 is represented by a dialogue act in the Social Obligations Management dimension, with the communicative function THANKING. Updating the context with this dialogue act creates a so-called reactive pressure, set in the *Social Context*. The system releases this pressure in utterance S5 by means of a THANKING-DOWNPLAY.

5 Dialogue act generation

A more recent feature of DISCUS is that a dialogue act generator (Keizer and Bunt, 2006) can be connected to the simulator and can take care of generating the system's actions. In this case, system utterances no longer need to be simulated through the GUI. The dialogue act generator also follows the multidimensional organisation of the taxonomy in that it consists of several agents, each dedicated to the generation of dialogue acts from a particular dimension. As illustrated in Figure 3, the dialogue act agents monitor and write to different parts of the context model. Dialogue act candidates produced by these agents are recorded in the so-called 'dialogue future' as part of the *Linguistic Context*. The additional Evaluation agent selects a combination of dialogue acts from the dialogue future to form the next system utterance.

Below is a dialogue in which the user utterances are simulated and the system utterances are

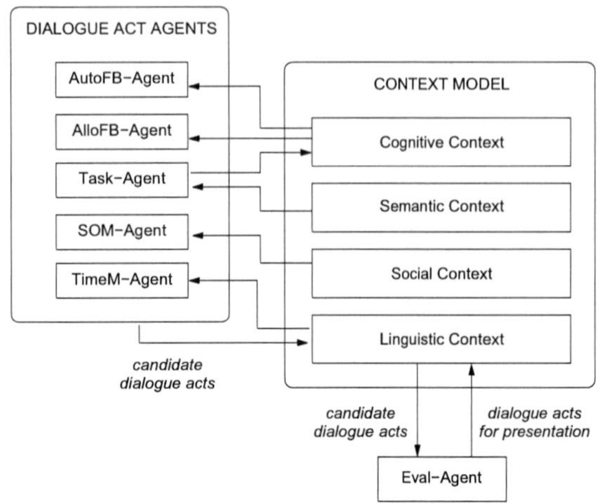

Figure 3: Dialogue act generation architecture.

automatically generated. For this simulation, the task/domain information is contained in a structured database the Task Agent has at its disposal (instead of using separate QA modules, requiring selfcontained, natural language questions as input).

U0: *what are the causes of RSI?*
    WHQ(cause,rsi)

S1: *repetitive movements.*
    WHA(cause,rsi,rep_movs)

U2: *and what are the causes?*
    WHQ(cause,rsi)

S3: *but I just told you!*
    NEG-AUTO-FB-EVAL

U4: *oh sorry, I meant symptoms*
    APO; allo-fb:INF

S5: *so you want to know the symptoms of RSI*
    auto-fb:CHECK

U6: *yes*
    auto-fb:CONF

S7: *just a moment please*
    PAUSE

U8: *ok*
    POS-AUTO-FB-EXE

S9: *unfortunately, I could not find any information*
    APO; NEG-AUTO-FB-EXE

U10: *okay, thanks anyway*
    POS-AUTO-FB-EXE; APO-DP; THK

S11: *you're welcome*
    THK-DP

In U0, the user asks a question about the domain, i.e., the system interprets the user utterance as a WH-QUESTION in the task-domain dimension. Updating the context with this dialogue act results in a number of beliefs (see Section 4), one of which involves a new user goal, i.e., the user wants to know something. This new user goal, that is recorded in the *Semantic Context*, triggers the Task Agent that will try to satisfy it by finding the information requested by the user in the database with domain information.

In this case, the information is found and the Task Agent can construct a WH-ANSWER with that information as the semantic content. This dialogue act is recorded in the dialogue future of the *Linguistic Context*, which results in generating S1.

Next, the user asks another question about the domain, but mistakenly says "causes" instead of the intended "symptoms". The system interprets U2 again as a WH-QUESTION with the same semantic content as in U0. After updating his context with this dialogue act, the system detects an inconsistency: the user cannot have the goal of wanting to know the causes of RSI and at the same time believe that the causes of RSI are 'repetitive movements', as was established in the previous utterances. Therefore, an evaluation level processing problem is recorded in the *Cognitive Context*, causing the Auto-feedback Agent to be triggered and generate a negative auto-feedback act on the level of evaluation. For S3, only this negative feedback act is selected for generation by the Evaluation Agent; any answer to the user's question that might have been generated by the Task Agent is ignored.

In U4, the user realises he made a mistake, apologises and makes a correction to his earlier question. The system interprets this as a dialogue act in the allo-feedback dimension with a communicative function INFORM. In updating his context, the system corrects the effects from his earlier interpretation, including the replacement of the user goal regarding the causes of RSI with a new user goal regarding the symptoms of RSI. Now, the Auto-feedback Agent is triggered to make sure that the system understood the user's question correctly and constructs a CHECK, leading to S5. At the same time, the Task Agent may have been triggered to find the answer to the (corrected) question and already have generated that answer as a candidate.

After the user's confirmation in U6, the system can proceed to produce an answer. In this case however, the Task Agent was not able to return any results within reasonable time. This 'time-out event' is recored in the *Linguistic Context* and triggers the Time-management Agent to generate a PAUSE dialogue act, leading to S7. While the user responds with an overall positive feedback in U8, the Task Agent has finished his attempt to retrieve the required information, but was not successful, and therefore recorded an execution level processing problem in the *Cognitive Context*. The Auto-feedback Agent gets triggered by this new information and generates a negative auto-feedback act on the level of execution. The occurrence of processing problems also triggers the SOM Agent to generate an apology. These two dialogue acts are combined to generate system utterance S9.

Finally, in U10, the user gives overall positive feedback, downplays the apology and thanks the system, thereby pre-closing the dialogue. In updating the context, the THANKING dialogue act causes a reactive pressure of type 'thanking' to be recorded in the *Social Context*. This pressure triggers the SOM Agent, which then constructs a THANKING-DOWNPLAY dialogue act, leading to system utterance S11.

6 Conclusions and Future work

We have presented the DISCUS system as a convenient simulation environment for developing a theory of dialogue management. Building on the DIT framework, we have developed a context model and update algorithm that has been integrated in an interactive question answering system. The rich context model and system of dialogue acts allows for the generation of dialogue behaviour involving different kinds of feedback, interaction management, and social obligations. The multi-agent design of the dialogue manager allows for the generation of multifunctional system utterances.

In general, future work will consist of further improving the tool and extending the implementation of the theory. Particular focus will be on the process of selecting and combining candidate dialogue acts from different dimensions. We will also experiment with different task models via different application agents that the Task Agent can turn to, for example, a database agent or a QA engine.

Acknowledgements

This research is partly funded through the PARADIME project, which falls under the IMIX research programme, funded by the Dutch national research foundation NWO. Roser Morante's research is funded by the EX2005–1145 grant awarded by the Spanish *Ministerio de Educación y Ciencia*. We thank the anonymous reviewers for their useful comments.

References

J. F. Allen and C. R. Perrault. 1980. Analyzing intention in dialogues. *Artificial Intelligence*, 15(3):143–178.

H. Bunt. 2000. Dialogue pragmatics and context specification. In H. Bunt and W. Black, editors, *Abduction, Belief and Context in Dialogue*, Studies in Computational Pragmatics, pages 81–150. John Benjamins.

H. Bunt. 2006. Dimensions in dialogue act annotation. In *Proceedings 5th International Conference on Language Resources and Evaluation (LREC 2006)*, pages 1444–1449, Genova, Italy.

S. Keizer and H. Bunt. 2006. Multidimensional dialogue management. In *Proceedings of the SIGdial Workshop on Discourse and Dialogue*, pages 37–45, Sydney, Australia.

R. Morante, S. Keizer, and H. Bunt. 2007. A dialogue act based model for context updating. In *Proceedings of the 2007 Workshop on the Semantics and Pragmatics of Dialogue (DECALOG)*, Rovereto (Italy), May. To appear.

D. R. Traum and S. Larsson. 2003. The information state approach to dialogue management. In Jan van Kuppevelt and Ronnie Smith, editors, *Current and New Directions in Discourse and Dialogue*, pages 325–354. Kluwer, Dordrecht.

Managing Keyword Variation with Frequency Based Generation of Word Forms in IR

Kimmo Kettunen
Department of Information
Studies
University of Tampere
kimmo.kettunen@uta.fi

Abstract

This paper presents a new management method for morphological variation of keywords. The method is called FCG, Frequent Case Generation. It is based on the skewed distributions of word forms in natural languages and is suitable for languages that have either fair amount of morphological variation or are morphologically very rich. The proposed method has been evaluated so far with four languages, Finnish, Swedish, German and Russian, which show varying degrees of morphological complexity.

1 Introduction

Word form normalization through lemmatization or stemming is a standard procedure in information retrieval because morphological variation needs to be accounted for and several languages are morphologically non-trivial. Lemmatization is effective but often requires expensive resources. Stemming is also effective, generally almost as good as lemmatization and typically much less expensive; besides it also has a query expansion effect. However, in both approaches the idea is to turn many inflectional word forms to a single lemma or stem both in the database index and in queries. This means extra effort in creation of database indexes.

In this paper we take an opposite approach: we leave the database index un-normalized and enrich the queries to cover for surface form variation of keywords. A potential penalty of the approach would be long queries and slow processing. However, we show that it only matters to cover a negligible number of possible surface forms even in morphologically complex languages to arrive at a performance that is almost as good as that delivered by stemming or lemmatization. Moreover, we show that, at least for typical test collections, it only matters to cover nouns and adjectives in queries. Furthermore, we show that our findings are particularly good for short queries that resemble normal searches of web users.

Our approach is called FCG (for Frequent Case (form) Generation). It can be relatively easily implemented for Latin/Greek/Cyrillic alphabet languages by examining their (typically very skewed) nominal form statistics in a small text sample and by creating surface form generators for the 3–9 most frequent forms. We demonstrate the potential of our FCG approach for four languages of varying morphological complexity: Swedish, German, Russian, and Finnish in well-known test collections (CLEF 2003 and 2004). Applications include in particular Web IR in languages poor in morphological resources.

2 Word Form Distributions

It is well known that the distributions of words and word forms are not even in texts. Some word forms occur often, some are rare. Even the distributions of different morphological categories have rates of their own, and both semantic and morphological factors play a role in distribution of word form frequencies (Baayen, 1993, 2001). Karlsson (1986, 2000) shows with some semantically distinctive word types, how the case distributions of the words differ in Finnish. A word denoting a place, like

Joakim Nivre, Heiki-Jaan Kaalep, Kadri Muischnek and Mare Koit (Eds.)

NODALIDA 2007 Conference Proceedings, pp. 318–323

Helsinki, has besides the dominating nominative and genitive singular forms mainly occurrences of locative cases. A person's name like *Martti* occurs mostly in nominative singular. Same kind of analysis is given by Kostić et al. (2003) for Serbian, although they seem to be hesitant about the semantic origins of the phenomenon. We shall not explore the semantic factors of case distribution any deeper, but analyze the distribution of cases on morphological level only.

In Kettunen and Airio (2006) we first sought for corpus statistics of Finnish nominal word forms. Then we verified these statistics with two independent automatic analyses of larger corpora. Our analysis and earlier corpus statistics showed, that six cases (out of 14) constituted about 84 – 88 % of the token level occurrences of case forms for nouns – thus covering 84 – 88 % of the possible variation of about 2000 distinct inflectional forms of nouns. Our analysis also showed that the huge number of grammatical forms is mainly due to clitics and possessive endings that are almost non-existent even in a reasonably large textual corpus (10.3 M nouns). This analysis demonstrated that, while a language may in principle be morphologically complex, in practice it is much less so.

2.1 Distribution Based Management of Keyword Variation for IR

Our FCG method and its language specific IR evaluation are simply as follows:

1) For a morphologically complex enough language the distribution of different nominal case/other word forms is first studied through corpus analysis (if such results are not available for the language). The used corpus can be quite small, because variation at this level of language can be detected even from smaller corpora. Variation in textual styles may affect slightly the results, so a style neutral corpus is the best. If style specific results are sought for, then an appropriate corpus needs to be used in word form occurrence analysis.

2) After the most frequent (case) forms for the language have been found with corpus statistics, the IR results of using only these forms for noun and adjective keyword forms are evaluated in a standard IR collection. As a comparison best available normalization method (lemmatization or stemming) is used. The number of tested FCG processes depends on the morphological complex-

ity of the language: more processes can be tested for a complex language, only a few for a simpler one.

3) After evaluation, the best FCG process with respect to normalization is usually distinguished. The evaluation process will probably also show that more than one FCG process is giving quite good results, and thus a varying number of keyword forms can be used for different retrieval purposes, if necessary.

We have been simulating the process of keyword generation in our tests, but as word form generation programs are available for many languages, their output could be modified accordingly for real use, i.e., only the most frequent forms of generated forms would be used in search.

Based on this method, we evaluated four different FCGs in two different full-text collections of Finnish, TUTK (with multi-valued relevance) and CLEF 2003 (with binary relevance) with long title and description queries. The results of Kettunen and Airio (2006) showed that frequent case form generation works in full-text retrieval of inflected indexes in a best-match query system and competes at best well with the gold standard, lemmatization, for Finnish. Our best FCG procedures, FCG_9 and FCG_12 - with 9 and 12 variant keyword forms - achieved about 86 % of the best average precisions of FINTWOL lemmatizer in TUTK and about 90 % in CLEF 2003. We thus performed successful information retrieval of Finnish with nine and twelve variant keyword forms, which is 0.48 % and 0.64 % of the possible grammatical forms of Finnish nouns ($\sum$ = 1872) and about 34.6 % and 46.2 % of the productive forms ($\sum$ = 26).

We now evaluated performance of Finnish short title queries in the CLEF 2003 collection. Results of the Finnish short queries (mean length 2,55 words when stop words were omitted) are shown in Table 1.

Method	Mean average precision
FINTWOL, compounds split	42.8 %
Stemmed	41.3 % (-1.5)
FINTWOL, compounds not split	40.5 % (-2.3)
FCG_12	38.1 % (-4.7)
FCG_9	37.9 % (-4.9)
Inflected	22.6 % (-20.2)

Table 1. Finnish CLEF 2003 results, 45 title queries

As can be seen from Table 1, difference between the best FCG method and the best achieved results, FINTWOL with index where compounds are split, is about 5 absolute per cent with short queries. Thus the method works also well with short and realistic queries, and about 88–89 % of the maximal retrieval result is achieved with both nine and twelve most frequent nominal forms of the keywords.

Figure 1 shows P/R-curves of the best Finnish FCG procedure (FCG_12), FINTWOL with split compound index and plain query words for short queries.

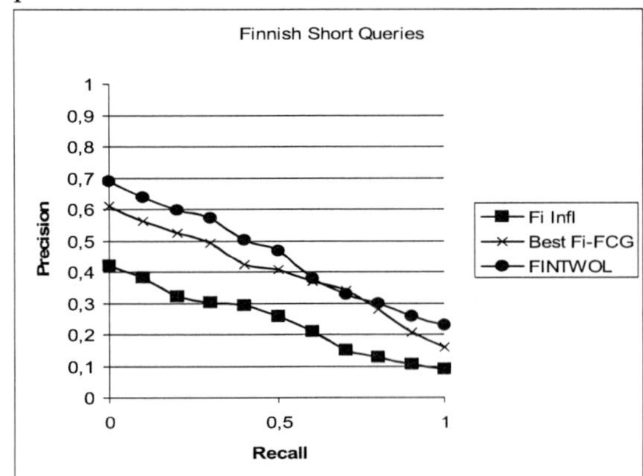

Figure 1. P/R-curves for Finnish short queries: precision by eleven recall levels 0.0–1.0

3 FCGs for Three More Languages

In this study we evaluated further our word form frequency based method with three European languages, Swedish, German, and Russian. They are all morphologically moderately complex, i.e. clearly much more complex than English, but also clearly much simpler than Finnish (or Hungarian) measured in the number of possible word forms

per lexeme. The chosen languages represent two major language groups of the Indo-European language family, Germanic (German and Swedish) and Slavonic (Russian), and are thus also characteristic samples for other languages in the same language groups. The languages were chosen on the basis of available IR collections and complex enough nominal morphology from the CLEF materials. From the morphological complexity point of view there would have been other and perhaps more interesting languages among the official EU languages (e.g., Estonian, Lithuanian, Latvian, Slovak, Czech and Hungarian), but either lack of available IR collections or detailed enough linguistic knowledge in the languages made inclusion of these languages impossible in this study.

3.1 Materials and Methods

CLEF collections for all the three languages were utilized in this study. For Swedish and German we used materials of CLEF 2003. The retrieval system was InQuery. For Russian we used Russian collection of CLEF 2004 and the Lemur retrieval system. Character encoding for Russian was UTF-8. In Table 2, the number of documents and topics in each collection is shown (Airio, 2006; Tomlinson, 2004).

Language	Collection	Collection size (docs)	Topics
Sv	CLEF 2003	142 819	54
De	CLEF 2003	294 809	56
Ru	CLEF 2004	16 716	34

Table 2. Swedish, German and Russian collections used in the study

For Swedish we analyzed the most frequent word forms to be used as keywords in FCG queries on the basis of a SWETWOL analysis of newspaper material from Helsingborgs Dagblad 1994 and Göteborgs posten 1994 texts, altogether 161 336 articles (Ahlgren, 2004, 61). For German word form frequency analysis we used an existing morphologically annotated Tiger corpus. For Russian we obtained the case distribution information from the Russian national corpus. Statistics of the distribution analysis are published in Kettunen et al. (2007).

On the basis of these corpus analyses we formed FCG procedures for each language with different number of keywords. Swedish got two procedures, Sv-FCG_2 and Sv-FCG_4, as did also German with procedures De-FCG_2 and De-FCG_4. As Russian was morphologically the most complex language of these, it got three FGC procedures, Ru-FCG_3, Ru-FCG_6 and Ru-FCG_8. The figure in the name of the procedure gives the approximate number of morphological keyword variants for each procedure.

Queries for the FCG procedures of each language were formed manually from the topics by using different language tools in the web (electronic dictionaries, word form generators or both). After we had formed the queries, we evaluated the retrieval results for each language. As a comparison we used lemmatization with TWOL programs for Swedish and German and also Snowball stemmers for both of the languages. For Russian we only had access to Snowball stemmer. Also plain topic words were used in the queries of all languages to get a baseline result.

Our queries were structured with InQuery's #SYN operator. With the operator morphological variant forms of the keyword are treated as synonyms of the key, and InQuery treats them all as instances of one key.

As a FCG query example we can take one query from the CLEF 2003 collection. A short version of query #142 for the Sv-FCG_4 process is as follows:

```
#q142 = #sum(#syn( christo )
#syn( paketerar ) #syn( det )
#syn( tyska tyskt ) #syn(
riksdagshuset riksdagshus
riksdagshusen));
```

As can be seen from the query example, only nouns and adjectives of the query are expanded with variant forms, all words of other categories are left in the form they were in the original topic. Nouns are self-evidently most important for queries, but adding variant forms of adjectives seems

also to increase mean average precision of queries with 1–3 % in each language.

4 Results

4.1 Swedish results

We ran both long and short queries for all the languages. Here we show and discuss only results of short title queries. Full results are presented in Kettunen et al. (2007).

Results of the Swedish very short queries (average length 3.17 words with stop words) are shown in Table 3.

Method	Mean average precision
SWETWOL, compounds split	32.6 %
Sv-FCG_4	30.6 % (-2.0)
Sv-FCG_2	29.1 % (-3.5)
Stemmed	28.5 % (-4.1)
SWETWOL, compounds not split	26.3 % (-6.3)
Inflected	24.0 % (-8.6)

Table 3. Results of the 54 Swedish title queries

SWETWOL with split compounds in the database index gets the best results, but the best Sv-FCG procedure is not far behind. The margin between non-processed keywords and best normalization result is 8.6 %. Both Sv-FCGs outperform stemming and SWETWOL without compound splitting.

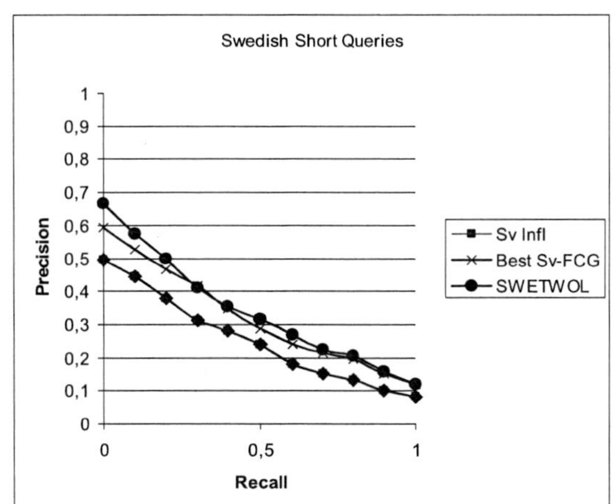

Figure 2. P/R-curves for Swedish short queries: precision by eleven recall levels 0.0–1.0

Figure 2 shows P/R-curves of the best Swedish FCG procedure (Sv-FCG_4), SWETWOL with split compounds and plain query words for short queries.

4.2 German results

Results of the German very short queries (average length 3.15 words with stop words) are shown in Table 4.

Method	Mean average
GerTWOL, compounds split	29.6 %
Stemmed	30.9 % (+1.3)
De-FCG_4	29.9 % (+0.3)
De-FCG_2	29.0 % (-0.6)
GerTWOL, compounds not split	28.1 % (-1.5)
Inflected	25.4 % (-4.2)

Table 4. Results of the 56 German title queries

The Snowball stemmer performs the best with a 1.3 % margin to GERTWOL using split compound index. De-FCG_4 is also slightly better than GERTWOL, and De-FCG_2 outperforms also GERTWOL without compound splitting. Non-processed queries perform worst, and the margin of non-processing to the best performing system, Snowball, is 5.5 %. The margin of non-processing to the worst performing normalization is 2.7 %.

Figure 3 shows P/R-curves of the best German FCG procedure (De-FCG_4), German Snowball and plain query words for short queries.

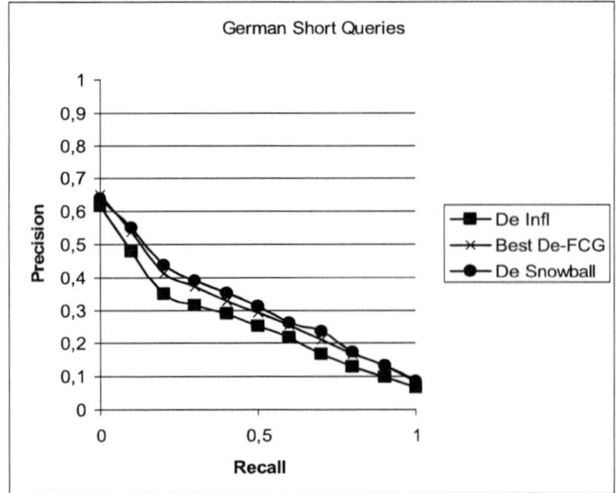

Figure 3. P/R-curves for German short queries: precision by eleven recall levels 0.0–1.0

4.3 Russian results

Results for Russian short queries are shown in Table 5. Mean length of the queries was 3.18 words (with stopwords).

Method	Mean average precision
Ru-FCG_6	32.0 %
Ru-FCG_8	31.7 % (-0.3)
Ru-FCG_3	31.2 % (-0.8)
Snowball Ru	27.2 % (-4.8)
Inflected	25.1 % (-6.9)

Table 5. Results of 34 Russian title queries

Our Russian results are not as clear as those of Swedish and German, because results of long and short queries in Russian were quite different. Overall it seems that short Russian queries show some advantage for FCGs, but as the collection is small and has very few relevant documents, the interpretation of the Russian results remains inconclusive.

Figure 4 shows P-R-curves of the best Russian FCG procedure (Ru-FCG_6), Russian Snowball and plain query words for short queries.

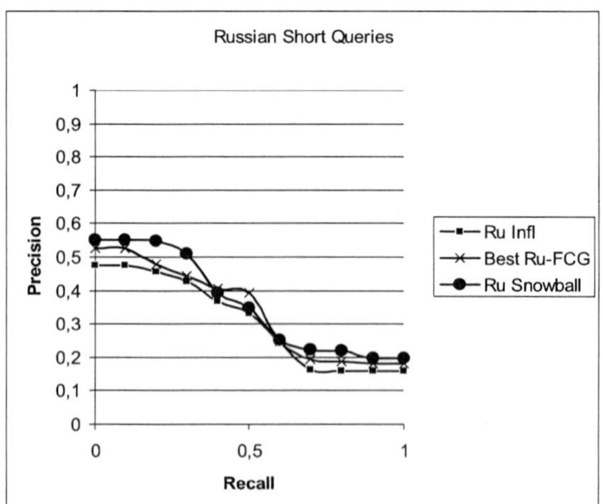

Figure 4. P/R-curves for Russian short queries: precision by eleven recall levels 0.0–1.0.

5 Discussion

The main reason for using stemming, lemmatization or any kind of morphological processing with IR is improvement in precision and recall of searches. Although the gains of morphological processing are varying, they are real. The usual way to estimate the performance gains is relative percentage improvement of mean average precisions between different methods. For comparison purposes of methods a slightly different point of view could also be used: the difference between doing nothing for the query words and the best mean average precision shows the need of morphological processing for the language in question. The bigger the discrepancy between these figures, the bigger the need to do something for the keywords.

In Figures 1–4 P/R-curves of Finnish, Swedish, German and Russian short queries for the best normalization method, best FCG method and no processing at all were shown. As can be seen from the figures and Tables 1, 3, 4 and 5, the largest difference between non-processing and best normalization method is in Finnish (20.4 %) and smallest in Swedish (4.1 %). German and Russian have slightly greater differences than Swedish, 5.7 % and 6.9 % respectively. Figures show that the FCG method gives clear gains for Finnish and smaller gains for German, Swedish and Russian. For three languages FCG works well in comparison to lemmatization; for Finnish 88 % of the performance of lemmatization is achieved and 95 % for Swedish and German. The P/R graphs also show that the FCG method pushes close to normalization even when the gap between normalization and non-processing is narrow. Gains over no morphological processing at all are greater than losses against normalization.

For the three new languages evaluated two, Swedish and German, showed quite clearly that the FCG method works well for both languages. In short queries the differences between all the methods were smallest, but also the margin between plain keywords and the best method increased. In German runs overlap of inflectional noun forms slightly disturbed results.

Our Russian results remained partly counterintuitive. Although recall rose steadily when more case forms were put into the query, the mean average precision of short queries did not get much better, when forms were added. Overall it seemed that short Russian queries showed some advantage for FCGs. As the collection was small and had very few relevant documents, the interpretation of the Russian results remained inconclusive. Thus the method should be re-evaluated in a better Russian collection.

References

Per Ahlgren. 2004. *The effects of indexing strategy-query term combination on retrieval effectiveness in a Swedish full text database.* Department of Library and Information Science/Swedish School of Library and Information Science. University college of Borås/Göteborg University.

Eija Airio. 2006. Word Normalization and decompounding in mono- and bilingual IR. *Information Retrieval 9*: 249–271.

R. Harald Baayen. 1993. Statistical Models for Word Frequency Distribution. *Computers and the Humanities 26*: 347–363.

R. Harald Baayen. 2001. *Word Frequency Distributions.* Kluwer Academic Publishers, Dordrecht Boston London.

Fred Karlsson. 1986. Frequency Considerations in Morphology. *Zeitsschrift für Phonetik, Sprachwissenschaft und Kommunikationsforschung 39*: 19–28.

Fred Karlsson. 2000. Defectivity. In: Booij G. et al. (eds.): *Morphology. An International Handbook on Inflection and Word-Formation.* Volume 1. Walter de Gruyter, Berlin, 647–654.

Kimmo Kettunen and Eija Airio. 2006. Is a morphologically complex language really that complex in full-text retrieval? In T. Salakoski et al. (Eds.): *Advances in Natural Language Processing,* LNAI 4139. Springer-Verlag Berlin Heidelberg, 411–422.

Kimmo Kettunen, Eija Airio and Kalervo Järvelin. 2007. Restricted Inflectional Form Generation in Management of Morphological Keyword Variation. *Information Retrieval* (to appear).

Alexandar Kostić, Tanja Marković and Alexandar Baucal. 2003. A. Inflectional Morphology and Word Meaning: Orthogonal or Co-implicative Cognitive Domains. In: Baayen, R.H. and Schreuder R. (eds.): *Morphological Structure in Language Processing.* Trends in Linguistics, Studies and Monographs 151. Mouton de Gruyter, Berlin, 1–43.

Tiger corpus. http://www.ims.uni-stuttgart.de/projekte/-TIGER/TIGERCorpus/ (visited June 7th, 2006).

Stephen Tomlinson. 2004. Finnish, Portuguese and Russian Retrieval with Hummingbird SearchServerTM at CLEF 2004. Working Notes for the CLEF 2004 Workshop, 15-17 September, Bath, UK. <http://clef.isti.cnr.it/2004/working_notes/WorkingNotes2004/21.pdf>. Accessed October 10th, 2006.

Developing and Evaluating a Searchable Swedish-Thai Lexicon

Wanwisa Khanaraksombat and Jonas Sjöbergh
KTH CSC
{wanwisa, jsh}@kth.se

Abstract

We present an automatically created Swedish-Thai lexicon. The lexicon was created by matching the English translations in a Thai-English and a Swedish-English lexicon. The search interface to the lexicon includes several NLP tools to help the target group: second language learners of Swedish. These include automatic generation of inflectional forms of words, automatic spelling correction, lemmatization and compound analysis of queries. A user study was performed and showed that while erroneous translations sometimes fool the users, they still find the lexicon good enough to be useful. They also like the NLP tools, though some grammatical information is presented in a hard to understand way. The lexicon and the interface tools were built using commonly available NLP tools.

1   Introduction

Since the world is rapidly becoming more and more interconnected, reading, writing and speaking foreign languages play important roles and have received much attention. Language technology can be an important tool to aid people when learning a new language and can improve efficiency of human activities and communication. One often used tool for understanding foreign languages is a bilingual lexicon.

This paper presents an automatically created large Swedish-Thai lexicon, a search interface for the lexicon with language tools and a user study evaluating the lexicon and the user interface. Everything was created from readily available tools, to see what results can be achieved with currently available NLP using very little manual work. A total of a few days of work was spent on creating the lexicon and the interface.

There are many ways to create bilingual lexicons. Traditionally it has been done by hand, which is time consuming and thus expensive if the desired lexicon is large, but it generally yields very high quality lexicons. Since manual work is expensive, automatic methods for creating lexicons have been devised. While they have drawbacks, such as including noise in the form of erroneous translations, they are still popular because of the enormous time saving potential. Automatic methods can be used to generate a first noisy lexicon which is then cleaned up and extended by manual work.

2   Related Research

There are many methods for generating bilingual lexicons from a parallel corpus, i.e. a corpus where the same text is available in different languages. Koehn and Knight (2001) discuss different methods using bilingual corpora, monolingual corpora and lexicon resources to extract bilingual dictionaries.

Other approaches use existing bilingual lexicons from the source and target language to some common intermediate language. Usually, English is used as the "interlingua", since there exist large bilingual lexicons between English and many other languages. This is the approach we used, since there were lexicons available but no parallel corpora.

The fact that many English words are ambiguous is a problem that can lead to erroneous translations in the new lexicon. A similar problem is English translations with a wider meaning than the original word. Paraphrasing is another problem. The same meaning is often described in very different ways by different lexicographers, so even though two translations are both in English it can be hard to automatically match them. Is a small difference in translation indicative of a difference in nuance or is it just different lexicographers describing the same thing? This can lead to many "missing" translations in the new lexicon. Another problem with the same effect is

Joakim Nivre, Heiki-Jaan Kaalep, Kadri Muischnek and Mare Koit (Eds.)
NODALIDA 2007 Conference Proceedings, pp. 324–328

that many words in the source language do not have directly corresponding words in the target language. The same meaning would instead be described using several words.

Work on automatic bilingual lexicon creation using existing bilingual lexicons and an intermediate language has been done before (Tanaka and Umemura, 1994; Shirai et al., 2001; Shirai and Yamamoto, 2001). The problem of ambiguity can be mitigated by using several intermediate languages (Paik et al., 2001) and using part of speech and semantic categories (Bond et al., 2001). Hopefully different intermediate languages will not be ambiguous in the same way. The impact of using lexicons in different directions, i.e. a source language-English or an English-source language lexicon, has also been examined (Paik et al., 2004).

The two biggest problems in our lexicon is that common words are often not translated and that there are erroneous translations in the resulting lexicon. Common words are often ambiguous, and thus hard to automatically translate with our method. Hopefully, learners of a new language will learn the common words quickly through some other means, and thus not need them in the lexicon.

Filtering out erroneous translations can as mentioned above be done using several intermediate languages. In our case, we only found lexicons with translations to English. It is also possible to use information from parallel corpora, but as mentioned before, we had no such corpora.

There are other methods that can be used too, for instance the monolingual frequencies of different translation candidates, or the "burstiness" of the words in monolingual news data (Schafer and Yarowsky, 2002). Words common in one language are often common in other languages, and words with the same meaning are often used in describing the same events.

While we could likely have found enough resources to use such methods, we did not. One problem that occurs is that Thai is non-trivial to segment into words, and we had very little experience in processing Thai.

3 Creating the Lexicon

The method used to create the lexicon was a fairly standard method. We used a program that was previously used in generating a Japanese-Swedish lexicon (Sjöbergh, 2005) with only slight modifications. All English descriptions of Thai words were matched to all English descriptions of Swedish words. Matches are basically word overlap, and the best matches are selected as translation candidates.

Quality	Words
All OK	66
Most OK	4
Some OK	3
Similar	11
Wrong	16

Table 1: Translation quality of a random sample of 100 Swedish words and their translation.

The English words were weighted with a measure similar to idf (Inverse Document Frequency), which is useful when ranking several poor translation candidates. Words marked as being a certain word class were not allowed to match words in the other language marked with another word class. Many words in the lexicons used have no word class markings at all, though.

The created lexicon consists of over 20,000 words, which is the largest Swedish-Thai lexicon known to us. The next largest machine searchable lexicon known contains about 2,000 words, though in book form there are lexicons of about 7,000 words available. The main drawback of the automatically created lexicon is of course that it contains erroneous translations.

For creating the Swedish-Thai lexicon, the Thai-English lexicon Lexitron (Palingoon et al., 2002) was used. It is a freely available dictionary from NECTEC (downloadable from http://www.nectec.or.th/) which includes not only translations but also word class information, example sentences and pronunciation. It contains over 40,000 words.

The Swedish-English lexicon used contains about 160,000 Swedish words or expressions with their corresponding translations in English. Many of these Swedish words are old words that are somewhat rare in modern Swedish though.

A Swedish-Thai lexicon was created by for each Swedish word in the Swedish-English lexicon taking the top scored suggestions in Thai. If the top suggestion for a word had a score lower than 0.75, the word was not translated. A Thai-Swedish lexicon was also created, by taking the top scoring Swedish suggestions for each Thai word in the same way. When searching the lexicon in Swedish, the Swedish-Thai lexicon can be used, and then when searching in Thai the Thai-Swedish lexicon. Of course, for very many words the closest matching Swedish word for a Thai word will have the same Thai word as its closest match.

A small evaluation of the translation quality was done by having a native speaker of Thai who is quite fluent in Swedish manually check translations. For 100 Swedish words, how well the translations matched the actual meaning was checked. The results are shown in Table 1.

Since there are often many translation suggestions for each word, the quality was classified into the following classes: *All OK*, meaning all suggested translations are correct translations of the Swedish word. *Most OK*, if there are more correct translations suggested than incorrect translations. *Some OK*, if there is at least one correct suggestion. If the word occurs in a context, the correct meaning would likely still be understood using these suggestions. *Similar* is the case that the translations at least give enough information so that the general idea will come across in most contexts. An example would be "vehicle" instead of "car", or "radio broadcast" instead of "TV broadcast". Finally, the class *Wrong* is used when the translation is simply wrong.

4 NLP Tools for Searching the Lexicon

A simple web interface for looking up words in the Thai-Swedish lexicon from the previous section was created. To help users of the lexicon interface, especially the main target group which was second language learners of Swedish, some readily available language technology tools were added. These include spelling checking (Domeij et al., 1994), lemmatization (Domeij et al., 2000), and compound analysis (Sjöbergh and Kann, 2006). These tools were only implemented for searches in Swedish. In the spirit of believing that the user is probably right if the system understands the query, these tools are only used if the search fails to return any matches.

The first tool is spelling correction. Experiences from other popular lexicon services on the Internet indicate that a substantial part of all queries are misspelled, even by native speakers. Thus, if a query returns no results, the word is put through a spelling checker. If there are suggested corrections from the spelling checker, all such suggestions are automatically used as search queries and the resulting translations are shown.

The second tool is a lemmatizer. When there are no results, the lemma form of the word is used instead, since some word classes have quite rich inflection in Swedish but only the lemma forms are listed in the lexicon. A possible improvement that was discovered during the evaluations is that verbs were generally not listed in their lemma form but

in their present tense in the Swedish-English lexicon used, so for verbs the present tense form would likely be a better choice than the lemma.

Since Swedish has very productive compounding where the compound components are concatenated into one word, the third tool is compound splitting. Search queries that return no results can be automatically split into their compound components. The translations of each component are presented to give an indication of the meaning of the whole compound.

It is also possible to search the lexicon using words in Thai (or even English), though the language tools only work for Swedish. The interface also allows for choosing which of the lexicons, the Thai-Swedish or the Swedish-Thai, to search in.

Since there is a possibility of erroneous translations, mainly caused by ambiguous English words, it is also possible to view the original English translations, color coded to show which parts have a matching word in the corresponding translation.

The lexicon also presents other helpful information, such as example sentences, pronunciation information and inflectional forms for some words. Inflections are automatically generated by the same NLP tool that performed the lemmatization of queries (Domeij et al., 2000), example sentences and pronunciations are taken from another lexicon[1] when available there.

5 User Study

To evaluate if the resulting lexicon is useful for learners of Swedish a small user study was done. For a detailed account of this study written in Swedish, see (Khanaraksombat, 2007). Five native speakers of Thai with eight to twelve months of studies of Swedish were observed while doing two exercises using the lexicon and then interviewed. The first task was to create a story, in Swedish, from a series of eight pictures. The second task was to translate a short Swedish text into Thai. Thus, one task was intended to make the users search the lexicon using Thai words to find the wanted Swedish word and the other to make them look up Swedish words they did not know. These tasks were done in two groups, one with two persons and one with three.

5.1 Results from Observing the Users

During the exercises, there were quite a few examples of problems related to the somewhat poor quality of the translations in the lexicon:

Sometimes the word that was sought after was not found by the users despite it being present in

---

[1]Swedish-English Lexin, http://lexin.nada.kth.se/

the lexicon, because there were too many suggested translations of a word. This was mainly a problem of English ambiguous word giving many too many mappings between Thai and Swedish words.

Sometimes a word was mistranslated, confusing the users. This was usually caused by translations such as *"kort"* (Swedish word corresponding to the English word "card"), translated as "card, for example playing card, post card etc". This type of translations made the Swedish word for post card match the translation for the Thai word for playing card. There were also examples where the users understood that a translation was wrong, though this of course did not help them in understanding the correct translation.

Sometimes the sought after word was not available in the lexicon. Especially troublesome is that many common words are highly ambiguous, and thus very hard to translate automatically. Sometimes the word itself was not translated, but a short phrase containing the word was. This also confused the users, for instance when searching for the Swedish word *"finns"* (is/are/exists) which only matched a phrase meaning "there are some friends", which matched the translation of the Thai word for "friend". So if one does not look too carefully at the results, it appears that "exists" should be translated as "friend".

There were also problems with understanding the grammatical information displayed by the search interface. For instance for verbs, the uninflected form, the past tense and the present perfect is shown. This determines what inflectional pattern a verb belongs to, but the users generally wanted the present tense, which was not available, and were not familiar enough with inflectional rules to have much use of the presented information. The same was true for nouns, where the inflectional pattern was shown but the much sought after gender information was not explicitly stated, because it is implicitly available in the inflectional information and normally not presented to native speakers (the target group of the resource this information was taken from).

5.2 Results from the Interviews

On the whole, the users believed that lexicons are very important to them. They found the automatically created lexicon to be fairly useful, despite the erroneous translations. They did however think that there were too many results, fewer translations would be better as long as the important ones are present, i.e. less commonly used meanings of a word should preferably be removed from the lexicon. When it comes to the NLP tools the users were satisfied, and thought that the option to turn them off should be

removed from the interface to make it cleaner. As explained in the previous section, the presented grammatical information was not what the users wanted. Similar but slightly different information would be much appreciated though. The users also found the layout of the interface to be a bit messy, making it hard to find the most important information.

6 Discussion

The problems related to the presentation of the grammatical information can be easily improved. The information the users wanted can easily be generated automatically from the resources available in the same way that the currently displayed information is.

Some of the other problems can be mitigated by using smaller Thai-English and Swedish-English lexicons, or by filtering out only important words from some list of what is considered important. Automatically determining which words are important is likely quite hard, though a rough estimate could be gained by concentrating on highly frequent words, for instance determined from some topically relevant corpus.

The translation quality was evidently good enough for the users to find the resource useful, but since there were quite a few problems for the users related to erroneous translations, it should preferable be improved. Having smaller lexicons to start with removes some erroneous matches, but probably not enough. Using more than one intermediate language is easy and generally also removes many faulty translations, but no other large lexicons are available for either Swedish or Thai, as far as we know. Monolingual corpora could be used to filter out translation suggestions were the monolingual frequencies are very different, and it would also likely be a good idea to remove longer phrases from the Swedish-English lexicon.

7 Conclusions

We automatically created a large Thai-Swedish lexicon and built a search interface for the lexicon including NLP tools. In a user study it was found that the users were generally satisfied with the NLP tools. Though some of the automatically generated grammatical information presented was not what the users wanted, the wanted information could easily be generated and the interface changed to display the more relevant information.

Regarding translations, the users ran into some problems caused by the translation quality of the lexicon being poor, though the they still found the lexicon useful. The users would prefer a lexicon containing only important words to a lexicon with a large coverage, so as not to be confused by rare translations.

In conclusion, it seems that it is possible to create a quite useful tool for second language learners with minimal amounts of manual work.

Acknowledgements

We would like to thank Viggo Kann, Ola Knutsson and our anonymous reviewers for valuable comments.

References

Francis Bond, Ruhaida Binti Sulong, Takefumi Yamazaki, and Kentaro Ogura. 2001. Design and construction of a machine-tractable Japanese-Malay dictionary. In *Proceedings of MT Summit VIII*, pages 53–58, Santiago de Compostela, Spain.

Rickard Domeij, Joachim Hollman, and Viggo Kann. 1994. Detection of spelling errors in Swedish not using a word list en clair. *Journal of Quantitative Linguistics*, 1:195–201.

Richard Domeij, Ola Knutsson, Johan Carlberger, and Viggo Kann. 2000. Granska – an efficient hybrid system for Swedish grammar checking. In *Proceedings of Nodalida '99*, pages 49–56, Trondheim, Norway.

Wanwisa Khanaraksombat. 2007. Utvärdering av ett svensk-thailändskt elektroniskt lexikon. Master's thesis, KTH CSC, Stockholm, Sweden.

Philipp Koehn and Kevin Knight. 2001. Knowledge sources for word-level translation models. In *Proceedings of EMNLP 2001*, Pittsburgh, USA.

Kyonghee Paik, Francis Bond, and Shirai Satoshi. 2001. Using multiple pivots to align Korean and Japanese lexical resources. In *Proceedings of NLPRS-2001*, pages 63–70, Tokyo, Japan.

Kyonghee Paik, Satoshi Shirai, and Hiromi Nakaiwa. 2004. Automatic construction of a transfer dictionary considering directionality. In *Proceedings of MLR2004: PostCOLING Workshop on Multilingual Linguistic Resources*, pages 31–38, Geneva, Switzerland.

Pornpimon Palingoon, Pornchan Chantanapraiwan, Supranee Theerawattanasuk, Thatsanee Charoenporn, and Virach Sornlertlamvanich. 2002. Qualitative and quantitative approaches in bilingual corpus-based dictionary. In *Proceedings of SNLP-O-COCOSDA 2002*, pages 152–158, Hua Hin, Thailand.

Charles Schafer and David Yarowsky. 2002. Inducing translation lexicons via diverse similarity measures and a bridge lexicon. In *Proceedings of the 6th Conference on Natural Language Learning (CoNLL-2002)*, pages 146–152, Taipei.

Satoshi Shirai and Kazuhide Yamamoto. 2001. Linking English words in two bilingual dictionaries to generate another language pair dictionary. In *Proceedings of ICCPOL-2001*, pages 174–179, Seoul, Korea.

Satoshi Shirai, Kazuhide Yamamoto, and Kyonghee Paik. 2001. Overlapping constraints of two step selection to generate a transfer dictionary. In *Proceedings of ICSP-2001*, pages 731–736, Taejon, Korea.

Jonas Sjöbergh and Viggo Kann. 2006. Vad kan statistik avslöja om svenska sammansättningar? *Språk och Stil*, 16:199–214.

Jonas Sjöbergh. 2005. Creating a free digital Japanese-Swedish lexicon. In *Proceedings of PACLING 2005*, pages 296–300, Tokyo, Japan.

Kumiko Tanaka and Kyoji Umemura. 1994. Construction of a bilingual dictionary intermediated by a third language. In *Proceedings of COLING-94*, pages 297–303, Kyoto, Japan.

Identification of Entity References in Hospital Discharge Letters

Dimitrios Kokkinakis
Göteborg University
Department of Swedish Language,
Språkdata
Sweden

svedk@svenska.gu.se

Anders Thurin
Clinical Physiology
Sahlgrenska University Hospital/Östra
Sweden

anders.thurin@vgregion.se

Abstract

In the era of the Electronic Health Record the release of medical narrative textual data for research, for health care statistics, for monitoring of new diagnostic tests and for tracking disease outbreak alerts imposes tough restrictions by various public authority bodies for the protection of (patient) privacy. In this paper we present a system for automatic identification of named entities in Swedish clinical free text, in the form of discharge letters, by applying generic named entity recognition technology with minor adaptations.

1 Introduction

There is a constantly growing demand for exchanging clinical and health-related information electronically. On a daily basis, hospitals store vast amounts of patient data as free text, but due to confidentiality requirements these texts remain inaccessible for research and knowledge mining. Therefore, an anonymisation or de-identification system can provide a broad spectrum of services related to the growing demands for better forms of dissemination of confidential information about individuals (Personal Health Information – PHI) found in electronic health records (EHR) and other clinical free text (e.g. discharge letters).

In this paper we present an anonymisation system for Swedish, which re-uses components of a generic named entity recognition system (NER) (Kokkinakis, 2004). Generic NER is the process of identifying and marking all single or multi-word named persons, location and organizations, including time and measure expressions, or other entities of interest in free text. NER is considered a mature technology that has numerous applications in a number of human language technologies, including information retrieval and extraction, topic categorization and machine translation. NER serves also as an important supporting technology for providing annotations for the Semantic Web.

We start by defining the notions of anonymisation and de-identification (Section 2) and give an overview of related work in Section 3. The method we use is described in Section 4. The system is based on two major components, a rule-based mechanism which makes use of classificatory criteria provided by the local context (e.g. trigger words, morphological prefixes/suffixes), and extended lists of various types of named entities. Section 5 provides a description of the medical data, while experimental results and evaluation are described in Section 6. Finally, Section 7 presents our conclusions.

2 Anonymisation *vs.* De-Identification

We define as *permanent anonymisation*, or simply *anonymisation* the process of recognizing and deliberately removing named entities and other identifying information about entities, including time expressions. Information about individuals, e.g. patients, may also include numerical, e.g. demographic or nominative information, such as age, sex, nationality and social security number, hence making the re-identification of those entities (particularly individuals) extremely difficult.

We further define as *de-identification* or *de-personalization* the process of recognizing and deliberately changing, masking, replacing or concealing the names and/or other identifying information of relevance about entities. Identified information

Joakim Nivre, Heiki-Jaan Kaalep, Kadri Muischnek and Mare Koit (Eds.)
NODALIDA 2007 Conference Proceedings, pp. 329–332

may be stored separately in an identification database. The linking between text and the identification database can be made by a unique identifier. Hence, making the re-identification or linking of individuals extremely difficult without the use of an appropriate "key".

3 Related Work

Sweeney (1996) describes the "Scrub" system, a set of detection algorithms utilizing word lists and templates that each detected a small number of name types in 275 pediatric records. Sweeney reports high rates on identified PHIs, 99-100%. Ruch et al. (2000) present comparable results with a similar system. However, it is unclear in both studies what the recall figures were. Taira et al. (2002) present a de-identification system using a variety of NLP tools. Each sentence found in a medical report was fed into a lexical analyzer (a database of 64,000 names) which assigned to each token syntactic and semantic information. Rule-based pre-filters were then applied to eliminate non-name candidates (e.g. by using drug name lists). 99,2% precision and 93,9% recall figures are reported. Thomas et al. (2002) used a method based on lists of proper names and medical terms for finding and replacing those in pathology reports. Their approach was based on identifying trigger words such as "Dr" and on the heuristic that "proper names occur in pairs". 98,7% correct identification on the narrative section and 92,7% on the entire report were reported. Sweeney (2002) describes a method, *k-anonymisation*, which de-associates sensitive attributes from the corresponding identifiers. Each value of an attribute, such as date of birth, is suppressed (i.e. replacing entries with a "*") or generalized (i.e. replacing all occurrences of for instance "070208", "070209" etc. with "0702*"). Gupta et al. (2004) discusses the interplay between anonymisation and evaluation within the framework of the *De-Id system* for surgical pathology reports. Three evaluations were conducted in turn, and each time specific changes were suggested, improving the system's performance. As the authors claim, "by the end of the evaluation the system was reliably and specifically removing safe-harbor identifiers and producing highly readable de-identified text". For a description of a number of methods for making data anonymous, see Hsinchun et al. 2005.

Finally, in the "Challenges in NLP for Clinical Data" workshop (Uzuner et al., 2006) one can find details of the systems that participated in a shared task dealing with the automatic de-identification (age, phone, date, hospital, location, doctor and patient) of medical summaries.

4 Method

Parts of the NER system we use for the annonymisation originate from the work conducted between 2001-03 in the Nomen-Nescio (*cf.* Bondi Johannessen et al., 2005). Five are the major components of the Swedish system:

- lists of multiword entities

- a rule-based component that uses finite-state grammars, one grammar for each type of entity recognized

- a module[1] that uses the annotations produced by the previous two components in order to make decisions regarding entities not covered by the previous two modules[2]

- lists of single names (approx. 80 000)

- a revision/refinement module which makes a final control on an annotated document with entities in order to detect and resolve possible errors and assign new annotations based on existing ones, e.g. by combining annotation fragments.

In the current work, seven types of NEs are recognized[3]: *persons*, *locations*, *organizations*, names of *drugs* and *diseases*, *time expressions* and a set of different types of *measure expressions* such as "age" and "temperature" (Table 1). The annotation uses the XML identifiers ENAMEX, TIMEX and NUMEX; for details see Kokkinakis (2004).

The lack of annotated data in the domain prohibits us from using, and thus training, a statistically

---

[1] The module is inspired by the *document centred approach* by Mikheev et al. (1999). This is a form of on-line learning from documents under processing which looks at unambiguous usages for assigning annotations in ambiguous words. A similar method has been also used by Aramaki et al., 2006, called *labelled consistency* for de-identification of PHIs.
[2] This module has not used in the current work, since we applied bulk annotation on a very large sample, while this module has best performance in single, coherent articles.
[3] These name categories are a subset of the original system which also covers three more entities, namely *artifacts*, *work&art* and *events* (e.g. names of conferences).

based system. Since high recall is a requirement, and due to the fragmented, partly ungrammatical nature of the data, the rule-based component of the system seemed an appropriate mechanism for the anonymisation task. Only minor parts of the generic system have been modified. These modifications dealt with: i) multiword place entities with the designators "VC", "VåC", "Vårdc" and "Vård-central" in attributive or predicative position, which all translate to *Health Care Center*, e.g. "Tuve VC" or "VåC Tuve" – designators frequent in the domain, which were inserted into the rule-based component of the system; ii) the designators "MAVA" *acute medical ward*, "SS", "SS/SU" and "SS/Ö", where "SS" stands as an acronym for the organization "Sahlgrenska Sjukhuset" *Sahlgrenska Hospital* and iii) the development and use of medical terminology, particularly names of pharmaceutical names (www.fass.se) and diseases, particularly eponyms (mesh.kib.ki.se), in order to cover for a variety of names that conflict with regular person names. E.g., the drug name "Lanzo" *lansoprazol* is also in the person's name list, while "Sjögrens" in the context "Sjögrens syndrom" *Sjogren's syndrome* and "Waldenström" in the context *Mb Waldenström* could also be confused with frequent Swedish last names. Therefore, the drug's and disease's modules (which were also evaluated, see Section 6) are applied before the person/location in order to prohibit erroneous readings of PHIs.

An example of annotated data, before [a] and after [b] anonymisation, is given below. The content of anonymised NEs (b) is translated as: uppercase *X* for capital letters, lowcase *x* for lower case characters, and *N* for numbers, while punctuation remains unchanged. The number of the dummy characters in each anonymised NE corresponds to the length of the original NE. However other translation schemes are under consideration. Examples of various NE types are given in table 1.

a. Pat från <ENAMEX TYPE="LOC">Somalia </ENAMEX> op <TIMEX TYPE= "TME">-91</TIMEX> med [...] får <ENAMEX TYPE= "MDC">Waran</ENAMEX> [...] <ENAMEX TYPE="PRS">dr Steffan A. Janson </ENAMEX> rekommenderar biopsi [...]

b. Pat från <COUNTRY>Xxxxxxx </COUNTRY> op <TIME>-NN</TIME> med [...] får Waran [...] <PERSON>dr Xxxxxxx X. Xxxxxx</PERSON> rekommenderar biopsi [...]

Entity	Examples
Person	HUM[human]: Dr Janson CLC[group]: 10 HIV-patienter
Location	LOC[country]: Somalia FNC[functional]: Åre VåC
Organization	ORG[organization]: VOLVO
Measure	PSS[pressure]: 120/80 mmHg DSG[dosage]: 10 mg 1x1
Time	TME[time]: aug. 2006
Disease	MDD[disease]: Tourettes
Drugs	MDC[drug]: Waran

Table 1.Entity examples

5 A Corpus of Clinical Data

In this study we used a large corpus (~1GB) of discharged letters extracted from the EHR system MELIOR© used by the Sahlgrenska Univ. Hospital. The corpus consists of database posts taken from tables of special interest for further research (text and data mining) such as "clinical history" and "final diagnoses". The subcorpus we used for the evaluation consists of 200 randomly extracted passages, which we believe gives a good indication of the performance of the NER system. A passage may consist of one or more sentences. The size of the evaluation material was 14,000 tokens. The only pre-processing of the texts has been the tokenization, while the anonymisation and evaluation work was conducted on a locally installed version of the system at the department of Clinical Physiology, at the Sahlgrenska/Östra Univ. Hospital in Gothenburg, behind a firewall, which, at this stage, guarantees maximum security[4].

6 Results and Evaluation

For the evaluation we manually examined the selected sample. We calculated precision, recall and f-score using the formulas: *P = (Total Corr. + Partially Corr.) / All Produced* and *R = (Total Corr. + Partially Corr.) / All Possible*. Partially correct means that an annotation is not completely correct but partial credit should be given, e.g., if the system produces an annotation for "Alzheimers sjukdom" (Alzheimer's disease) as *<ENAMEX TYPE="MDD">Alzheimers</ENAMEX>sjukdom*, instead of *<ENAMEX TYPE="MDD">Alzheimers*

---

[4] We are currently investigating ways to get the appropriate clearance by the hospital's ethical committee in order to make some of the material available for research, although this might be difficult if results don't reach almost perfect scores.

sjukdom</ENAMEX>, then such annotations are given a half point, instead of a perfect score. F-score is calculated as: $F=2*P*R/P+R$.

Entity	P	R	F-score
Person	95,65%	95,65%	95,65%
Location	94,11%	59,25%	72,71%
Organization*	60%	85,71%	70,59%
Time	98,99%	76,03%	86%
Measure	99,19%	93,75%	96,39%
Disease	97,94%	86,81%	92,03%
Pharma/names	95,16%	92,63%	93,82%
Total	96,97%	89,35%	93%

Table 2. Evaluation Results (* only 7 occurr.)

The error analysis we conducted indicates that the performance of the generic NER system is influenced by the features of the domain. We emphasize the word "generic", since simple means can increase the P&R figures dramatically. E.g., the majority of unmarked time expressions were of the form "Number/Number –Number" (1/7 -00), characteristic of the data and not part of the Swedish standard for designating time. The analysis of the results, particularly for the cases that the system failed to produce an annotation (insufficient coverage) or when the annotation was erroneous, revealed that many errors where due to 3 types: i) spelling errors & ungrammatical constructions (e.g. 'ischaemi' – instead of 'ischemi'), ii) insufficient context/short sentences (e.g. 'ACB-op -94' – 'by-pass operation 1994') and iii) abbreviations (e.g. 'på Ger' – at the Geriatric unit – instead of 'på Geriatriken' and 'skivepitel-ca' – squamous cell cancer – instead of 'skivepitel-cancer').

7   Conclusions

We have described a system for anonymising hospital discharge letters using a generic NER system slightly modified in order to cope with some frequent characteristic features of the domain. The coverage of our approach provides a ground for accessing the content of clinical free text in a manner that enables one to draw inferences without violating the privacy of individuals, although some work still remains to be done. For the near future, we intend to: i) evaluate a larger sample and propose adjustments for increased performance; ii) integrate more NE types and iii) get the appropriate approval from the appropriate ethical committees, for releasing some of the data for further research.

Acknowledgements

This work has been partially supported by the "Semantic Interoperability and Data Mining in Biomedicine" – NoE, under EU's Framework 6.

References

Aramaki E., Imai T., Miyo K. and Ohe K. 2006. *Automatic Deidentification by using Sentence Features and Label Consistency*. Challenges in NLP for Clinical Data Workshop. Washington DC.

Bondi Johannessen J. et al. 2005. *Named Entity Recognition for the Mainland Scandinavian Languages*. Literary and Linguistic Computing, Volume 20:1.

Gupta D., Saul M. and Gilbertson J. 2004. *Evaluation of a Deidentification (De-Id) Software Engine to Share Pathology Reports and Clinical Documents for Research*. Am. J. of Clin. Pathology. 121(6): 176-186.

Hsinchun C., Fuller S.S., Friedman C. and Hersh W. 2005. *Medical Informatics – Knowledge Management and Data Mining in Biomedicine*. Pp. 109-121. Springer Series in Information Systems.

Kokkinakis D. 2004. *Reducing the Effect of Name Explosion*. LREC-Workshop: Beyond Named Entity Recognition - Semantic Labeling for NLP. Portugal.

Mikheev A., Moens M. and Grover C. 1999. *Named Entity Recognition without Gazeteers*. Proc. of the 9th European Chapter of the Assoc. of Computational Linguistics (EACL). Pp. 1-8, Bergen, Norway.

Ruch P. et al. 2000. *Medical Document Anonymisation with a Semantic Lexicon*. AMIA: Session S81 - Clinical Information Confidentiality and Security.

Sweeney L. 1996. *Replacing Personally-Identifying Information in Medical Records, the Scrub System*. J. of the American Medical Informatics Association. Washington, DC: Hanley & Belfus, Inc. Pp. 333-337.

Sweeney L. 2002. *k-anonymity: a Model for Protecting Privacy*. Int. J. Uncertain. Fuzziness Knowl.-Based Syst. 10(5): 557-570.

Taira R.K, Bui A.A. and Kangarloo H. 2002. *Identification of Patient Name References within Medical Documents Using Semantic Selectional Restrictions*. AMIA. Pp. 757-61.

Thomas S.M., Mamlin B., Schadow G. and McDonald C. 2002. *A Successful Technique for Removing Names in Pathology Reports Using an Augmented Search and Replace Method*. AMIA. Pp. 777-81.

Uzuner O., Kohane I. and Szolovits P. 2006. *Challenges in NLP for Clinical Data*. (www.i2b2.org/NLP/)

Lexical Parameters, Based on Corpus Analysis of English and Swedish Cancer Data, of Relevance for NLG

Dimitrios Kokkinakis
Maria Toporowska Gronostaj
Göteborg University
Department of Swedish Language,
Språkdata
Sweden

{svedk,svemt}@svenska.gu.se

Catalina Hallett
David Hardcastle
Centre for Research in Computing
The Open University
Walton Hall
Milton Keynes MK7 6AA

{c.hallett,d.w.hardcastle}@open.ac.uk

Abstract

This paper reports on a corpus-based, contrastive study of the Swedish and English medical language in the cancer sub-domain. It is focused on the examination of a number of linguistic parameters differentiating two types of cancer-related textual material, one intended for medical experts and one for laymen. Language-dependent and language independent characteristics of the textual data between the two languages and the two registers are examined and compared. The aim of the work is to gain insights into the differences between lay and expert texts in order to support natural language generation (NLG) systems.

1 Introduction

Health care consumers are constantly exposed to the rapidly growing overload of medical information, e.g. general information on health and medication issues, electronic health records written by and for health care providers, individual advisory information given by net doctors for laypersons. The language of these texts manifests a variety of levels of difficulty, with e-health records and research-oriented texts at one end and ask-the-doctor texts and web portals driven by health care consumers at the other. To make information accessible to the health care consumers, it has to be tailored to their individual needs. However, making the issue of empowerment of health care consumers (e.g. patients) is a challenging task

because health care consumers make up a heterogeneous group of individuals with widely differing medical needs, educational background, medical literacy and age. In line with these challenges, the issue of patient empowerment, as well as the development and evaluation of methods and tools for assisting patients to better understand their health and health care, has been one of the many goals of the EU-funded *Semantic Mining* network. A strand of this research is developing means for generating patient-friendly, readable texts that paraphrase the content of the electronic health records and other types of health-related information.

There are several ways to approach the task and our study focuses on examining on an empirical basis, linguistic factors that involve contrastive characteristics of the medical sub-corpora. In our study it is assumed that effective lexical guidance is a prerequisite for consumers' access to medical information in these texts. Our study[1] is restricted to the subfield of *cancer* while our intended readership is the group of patients. The aim of our study is to gain insights into the differences between languages and registers for supporting systems that generate patient-friendly language.

Points of related work are given in (Section 2). In Section 3 we present a concise view of the findings in the corpora and in Section 4 we discuss the results. Finally, Section 5 summarizes the paper and provides some topics for future research.

---

[1] Our work belongs to the area of *consumer health informatics* which is the branch of medical informatics that analyses consumers' needs for information; it studies and implements methods of making information accessible to consumers, and also models and integrates consumers' preferences into medical information systems (Eysenbach, 2000).

Joakim Nivre, Heiki-Jaan Kaalep, Kadri Muischnek and Mare Koit (Eds.)
NODALIDA 2007 Conference Proceedings, pp. 333–336

2   Background

The assessment of reading comprehension, on one hand, and the discrepancy between reading abilities of patients and written patient information, on the other, have been in the focus of a number of studies in the past. Campbell & Johnson (2001) investigated the syntactic differences between medical and non-medical corpora. Various experiments showed significant differences in syntactic content and complexity, for instance in the distribution of both simple part-of-speech and part-of-speech bigrams between discharge summaries and the Brown corpus. Cantalejo & Lorda (2003) analyzed the readability of health education materials and proposed improvements, emphasizing the issue of cooperation: "Invite target readers to help write and design the material". Soergel et al. (2004) propose an interpretive layer framework for helping consumers "find, understand and use medical information when and where it is needed". The authors claim that this is something that can be accomplished by bridging mismatches in knowledge representation between the professional's perspective and the lay perspective and by filling in gaps in consumer knowledge. Soergel et al. (2004) also propose that such a system needs a knowledge base for a consumer health ontology and relevant context-based usage information. Hsieh et al. (2004) explore the level of the appropriateness of MetaMap (part of the UMLS - nlm.nih.gov/pubs/factsheets/umls.html) in capturing linguistic meaning of the terms used by patients in free text. In 53% of the cases MetaMap captured the linguistic meaning of the parsed terms used by the patients participating in the study, which is regarded by the authors as a very encouraging figure that demonstrates the possibility of using natural language processing (NLP) tools to automatically extract and capture the linguistic meaning of the terms patients used in their e-mail messages. Finally, Ownby (2005) investigated the influence of several aspects of the readability (e.g. use of passive voice) of health care information from websites intended for the elderly. His results show that easier-to-read sites could be differentiated most consistently from more difficult ones by vocabulary complexity.

3   Comparing Corpora

We have collected and analysed two different corpora in two registers (Section 3.1) along different, particular lexical, dimensions. These included loan/native words, lexical choice, periphrastic constructions, the use of pronouns and the use of a number of meta-markers as indicators for epexegesis.

3.1   Swedish and English Cancer Corpora

Two types of registers for each of the two languages are examined, namely expert-lay [lay] corpora and expert-expert [expert] corpora (Table 1). The English expert corpus consists of case studies and manual for medics, while the English lay corpus includes manuals for patients, patient information leaflets and patient testimonials. The Swedish expert corpus consists of internet-based material for experts while the lay part of the corpus is acquired from various news sites as well as patient-oriented sites (e.g. the Swedish Netdoktor).

	English	Swedish
Expert (size #words)	140 000	190 000
Lay (size #words)	155 000	170 000
Expert (words/sentence)	17.67	17.03
Lay (words/sentence)	18.95	15.18
Expert (complex words)	30.38%*	11.45%**
Lay (complex words)	14.61%*	8.94%**

Table 1. Qualitative profile of the corpora (*>3 syllables; **solid compounds)

3.2   Loan/Native words

We considered 30 suffixes, prefixes and infixes that are indicative of medical words of Greek or Latin origin. We specifically selected those affixes that are, at the same time, representative for the cancer domain and are less likely to appear in general purpose vocabularies. We associated with each affix one or more English/Swedish words that correspond to the loan suffix, e.g.

- #mammo#/breast-/bröst-
- #nephr/nefr#-/kidney/njur-
- #angio#/artery-/artär-/-åder

- #hepat#/liver-/lever-
- #oesophag/esofag#/throat-/matstrup-

Whilst the English expert corpus exhibited an almost equal distribution of loan and English equivalents, the lay corpus contained predominantly English equivalents, with a much smaller number of loan terms. The Swedish data exhibits similar results, although the Swedish expert texts show rather less uniformity in the distribution of loan/native words (Table 2).

	English		Swedish	
	Lay	Expert	Lay	Expert
Loan	0.76%	3.65%	0,67%	1,04%
Native	3.99%	3.42%	3,27%	2,95%

Table 2. Distribution of loan/native words

3.3 Lexical Choice

For English and Swedish, there is a pretty clear tendency of using lay terms in lay corpora, instead of more specific terms, as compared to the expert corpus. We examined constructions containing a number of cancer-related terms in the subdomain. The sample of examples listed in Table 3 is indicative of the preferable vocabulary choice for the two types of corpora.

	English		Swedish	
	Lay	Expert	Lay	Expert
tumour/tumor	697	1532	578	710
cancer*	2690	548	1172	997
carcinoma	177	773	18	83
malignancy	1	98	5	56
neoplasm	-	165	-	7
metastasis	14	114	78	524

Table 3. Lexical choice (*including "cancersjukdom" – cancer disease)

3.4 Periphrastic Constructions

Many medical terms have a lot of justifiable alternate forms with several orthographic and lexical variants. The analysis of the English corpora showed a clear preference of compounds constructions in both lay and expert texts (Table 4). The analysis of the Swedish showed a similar tendency, with a few exceptions, e.g. 'tjocktarmscancer' (cancer of the colon) occurred 69 times in the expert and 38 in the laytexts, while its periphrastic "cancer i tjocktarmen" occurred 44 times in the expert and 18 times in the lay texts.

We could not draw any clear conclusions from this exercise, apart from the fact that the compound forms (e.g. "breast cancer", "bröstcancer") are the preferred expressions in both corpora.

	English		Swedish	
	Lay	Expert	Lay	Expert
breast cancer	221	37	471*	460*
cancer of/in the breast	2	0	9	2
lung cancer	75	44	108*	64*
cancer of/in the lung	4	0	8	1

Table 4. Periphrastic writing (*solid compounds, "bröstcancer", "lungcancer")

3.5 Pronouns

There is a clear preference of using the pronouns "you/your/yours/yourself/yourselves" in the lay texts in both languages (Table 5). Also, in the Swedish data the use of the pronoun "man" (one) is also very common, with 1707 occurrences in the lay and 671 in the expert texts.

	English	Swedish
Lay	757	511
Expert	9	15

Table 5. Distribution of 2nd person pronoun

3.6 Epexegesis

We investigated the use of connective phrases, denoted by a handful words and punctuation marks, which signal the presence of synonyms, paraphrases, or substitution (*cf.* Pearson, 1998). We considered for instance the following words and expressions that may indicate explanations: *call(ed), known as, aka, layman's terms, mean(s), in other words, what is.* We found 378 occurrences in the English lay corpus (0.24%) and 76 occurrences in the English expert corpus (0.05%). Corresponding expressions in Swedish, such as "så kallade" (so called) were four times more frequent in the lay texts.

4 Discussion

Target text analysis is the very first step in the design and development of Natural Language Generation systems. Moreover, several researchers have emphasised the fact that corpus analysis is instrumental in reducing the effort involved in constructing the complex knowledge bases generally required by NLG systems (Knight & Hatzivassiloglou 1995, Langkilde & Knight 1998, Pan & Shaw 2004).

Since our intended target texts emulate the style and lexical content of the analysed corpora (Hallett & Scott, 2005), we are able to offer several recommendations and scoring mechanisms for bilingual English-Swedish NLG systems. More specifically, we are able to:

- informing an NLG system with regard to the appropriate lexical choices and syntactic constructions

- assess whether an automatically generated text is appropriate as patient information material, by analysing its readability level, lexical composition and syntactic complexity and comparing with the reference lay corpus. Similarly, for NLG systems that generate multiple variants, our analysis can help score the alternatives in order to make the best choice

5 Conclusions

In this study, we have compared the language in two types of register, i.e. expert and non-expert English and Swedish texts in the domain of cancer. A series of corpus-based experiments were conducted in order to assess the lexical variety of the corpora. The main question that arises from this work is: *what are the practical benefits, if any, brought about by this study particularly for the field of natural language generation.*

We hope that our work provides some insights and relevant pragmatic implications on how to support the generation of patient-friendly documents (particularly electronic health records and discharge letters) at the lexical and terminological level (use of explanations and definitions, use of paraphrased terms, use of "patient" terms etc.).

In the near future, we are planning to extend the analysis to discover discourse-related features, such as rhetorical relations, and actually look into more detail into semantic features. Moreover, we are currently in the process of adapting an existing NLG-system (Hallett et al., 2007) to both Swedish as well as to the cancer subdomain for English.

Acknowledgements

This work has been supported by the "Semantic Interoperability and Data Mining in Biomedicine", a Network of Excellence (NoE) funded by the European Commission under Framework 6.

References

Campbell DA and Johnson SB. 2001. *Comparing Syntactic Complexity in Medical and Non-Medical Corpora.* Proc AMIA Symp. 2001;90-4

Cantalejo B. IM. and Lorda S. P. 2003. *Can Patients Read What We Want Them to Read? Analysis of The Readability of Printed Materials for Health Education.* Aten Primaria. 30;31(7):409-14.

Eysenbach G. 2000. Consumer Health Informatics. *British Med. J.* 320:1713-1716

Hallett C. and Scott D. 2005. *Structural Variation In Generated Health Reports.* Proc. of the 3rd International Workshop on Paraphrasing (IWP2005). Korea.

Hallett C., Scott D. and Power R. 2007. *Composing Questions through Conceptual Authoring.* J. of Computational Linguistics. (to appear).

Hsieh Y., Hardardottir G. A. and Brennan P. F. 2004. *Linguistic Analysis: Terms and Phrases Used by Patients in E-mail Messages to Nurses.* MEDINFO. Amsterdam: IOS Press.

Knight K. and Hatzivassiloglou V. (1995). *Two-Level, Many-Paths Generation.* Proc. of the 33rd Annual Meeting of the Association for Computational Linguistics (ACL-95), Cambridge, MA.

Langkilde I. and Knight, K. (1998). *Generation that Exploits Corpus-Based Statistical Kn*owledge. Proc. of Coling-ACL'98. Quebec, Canada.

Ownby R.L. 2005. *Influence of Vocabulary and Sentence Complexity and Passive Voice on the Readability of Consumer-Oriented Mental Health Information on the Internet.* Proc. AMIA, USA.

Pearson J. 1998. *Terms in Context.* Amsterdam: John Benjamins Publishing Company

Shimei Pan and James Shaw. 2004. *SEGUE: A Hybrid Case-Based Surface Natural Language Generator.* Proc. of ICNLG, Brockenhurst, U.K.

Soergel D., Tse T. and Slaughter L. 2004. *Helping Healthcare Consumers Understand: an "Interpretive Layer" for Finding and Making Sense of Medical Information.* MEDINFO. IOS Press.

Anatomy of an XML-based Text Corpus Server

Mikko Lounela
Research Institute for the Languages of Finland
Sörnäisten rantatie 25
00500 Helsinki
Finland
`mikko.lounela@kotus.fi`

Abstract

This document describes an XML-based data model for annotated, modular text corpora along with a WWW-interface for browsing such corpora, reading the texts, searching for examples, and extracting information of word usages. The interface is based solely on programs and techniques belonging to the XML-family. The corpus model is designed in such a way that new parts (texts, sub-corpora) can be easily plugged in the system as far as they fit into the model. Furthermore, the model includes slots for such parts that are not conventionally included in text corpora. These may include (digitized) originals of the texts and links to other relevant documents. The searching interface for the model is based on XML query language that enables the developers to add queries to the system for extracting detailed linguistic information from the texts, depending on their annotation level. The corpus model and its interface can be seen as a step towards a general quantitative tool for text linguistic research, including the data model and programs for browsing, querying, and analyzing the texts.

1 Credits

I am indebted to Outi Lehtinen, who has worked on developing the database environment for the searching interface, and helped in numerous other ways. I am also indebted to Mikko Virtanen, who has carried out a lot of important work in encoding the corpus and developing the style sheets for the corpus interface. He has also designed modifications for the metadata model.

2 Introduction

The Research Institute for the Languages of Finland (RILF) has developed a text corpus data model in recent years. The model is based on de facto standards belonging to the XML family, which offers a well-defined, consistent set of languages for defining and processing structured documents. Further, the processes modelled by XML-related definitions can often be executed using free, high quality applications. The main goal of this work has been to develop a consistent, easy-to-use model for text collections, text documents, and their metadata. The corpus model is easy for the developers in the sense that new texts and sub-corpora can be added to the collections with little effort. Browsing and searching applications are also relatively easy to build and maintain. As a matter of fact, the browsing interface is implemented by adding style sheets to the metadata and text files. The searching interface can be implemented in many ways. The current searching interface is built on top of an XML database. The ease for developers should naturally lead to ease of use for linguist researchers and other corpus end users.

The model has been implemented as part of a web-based text corpus service, belonging to the RILF data service Kaino (RILF, visited 27.2.2007). The service was opened to public in December

Joakim Nivre, Heiki-Jaan Kaalep, Kadri Muischnek and Mare Koit (Eds.)
NODALIDA 2007 Conference Proceedings, pp. 337–344

2006[1]. The text corpus interface of Kaino service is divided into two parts: a browsing interface, which is built on top of the file system of the corpus server, and a searching interface, which uses a free XML database as the search engine. The interfaces are cross-linked. The definitions used in the system are well-known and XML-based, being very close to de facto standards. The tools used in the system are free and have an open source code.

In this article, I will present the data models and techniques included in the corpus model, as well as the implementation of the model. First, I will present the XML structure of the corpus texts, and the metadata model of the corpus. Then I will go through the technicalities of the current browsing interface and searching interface. After that I will introduce briefly the corpora included in the RILF text corpus collection, and their annotation and special features. Finally, I will consider the expandability of the interface and some future prospects for the model.

The documents referred to in this paper include web pages of institutions, in which case the authors are anonymous, and the publishing dates unrevealed. I refer to these documents using the institutions' names instead of authors' names, and visiting dates instead of publishing years. Some of the references concern research carried out in Finnish language, in which case the publications are in Finnish.

3   Corpus Data Structure

Figure 1 presents an overview of the modular corpus model. Metadata files include descriptions of the corpus, its sub-corpora, and individual texts belonging to the sub-corpora, as well as links that connect the parts to each other. New parts can be added to the corpus simply by inserting links pointing to them into the description file at suitable level of the corpus structure. At the moment, the RILF text corpus collection includes generally four levels. There can be more levels of collections in the corpus. In principle the corpus tree can be of any depth.

The links connect the corpora to their parts, each being represented by their metadata files. In the top of the tree, the metadata descriptions of the text files

are linked to the corpus text files. In some text collections, the descriptions are also linked to the digitized originals of the texts. Links to any other versions of the texts can be added to the descriptions, as well as links to any other relevant documents.

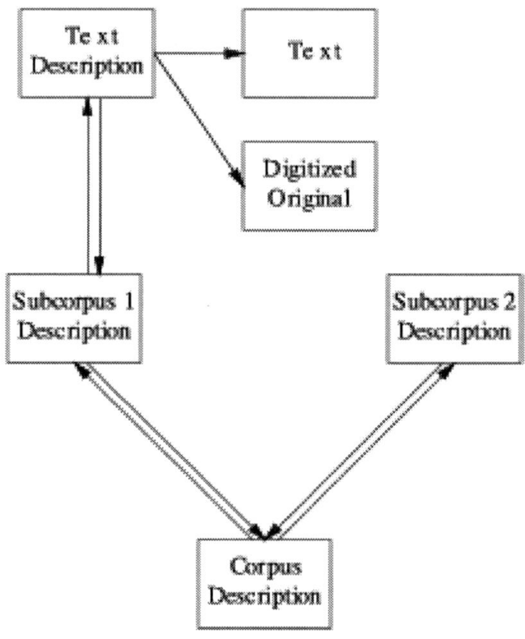

Figure 1: Overall corpus structure

3.1   Text Structure

The text structure of the corpus model is based on Text Encoding Initiative TEI P4 XML data model (TEI, visited 27.2.2007 a). Depending on the sub-corpus, the texts may be encoded to the paragraph level, sentence level or word level. The word level analysis includes morpho-syntactic tagging, and possibly semantic elements. The semantic elements may denote persons, names, dates, addresses etc. In our experience, almost any element may need further classification, when texts are used for text linguistic research. The needs above require some alternations to the original TEI structure (eg. an attribute for the word element to carry the morpho-syntactic description, and a global type attribute for sub-classifying any element). On modifications to

---

the TEI P4 structure for research corpora, see Lehtinen and Lounela (2004).

Some sub-corpora include texts with alternative structures, such as dictionary, drama and poetry. For these, customized structure definitions (DTDs) have been created using the automatic DTD generator TEI Pizza Chef (TEI, visited 27.2.2007 b). These DTDs have not been modified.

3.2 Metadata Structure

The metadata model of the RILF text corpus collection uses the Dublin Core metadata Initiative (DCMI, visited 27.2.2007) element set, expressed in the Resource Description Framework (W3C, visited 27.2.2007 a) data model. About the DCMI metadata structure, expressed in the RDF/XML format, see Beckett et al., (2002) and Kokkelink and Schwänzl, (2002). A model for using these techniques to form a metadata backbone for a structured corpus has been outlined in Lounela (2002).

We have made some additions to the information content of the DCMI element set. The motivation for them is to make it more convenient to browse the corpus. The additions consist of including one extra element and some attributes into the definition. The element included in the descriptions is kotus:label, and it is used to label a (sub)corpus, a text, or a link in the browsing interface. Links are presented as dc:Relation-elements. In the browsing system, a relation-element contains two elements: a selected DCMI-element that expresses the URL and classifies the relation, and a kotus:label-element for labeling the link. The DCMI elements classifying the relations used in the RILF text corpus collection are the following.

- dcterms:isPartOf for linking a collection to its super-collection.

- dcterms:hasPart for linking a collection to its sub-collection.

- dcterms:isReferencedBy for linking a collection or a text either to a search engine or an external document of some relevance.

- dcterms:isFormatOf for linking a text document to its digitized original.

The attributes added to the DCMI/RDF/XML for use in the RILF corpus model add some information to the existing elements. This information typically helps in grouping some links or adds linking information to the browsing system. The added attributes are the following.

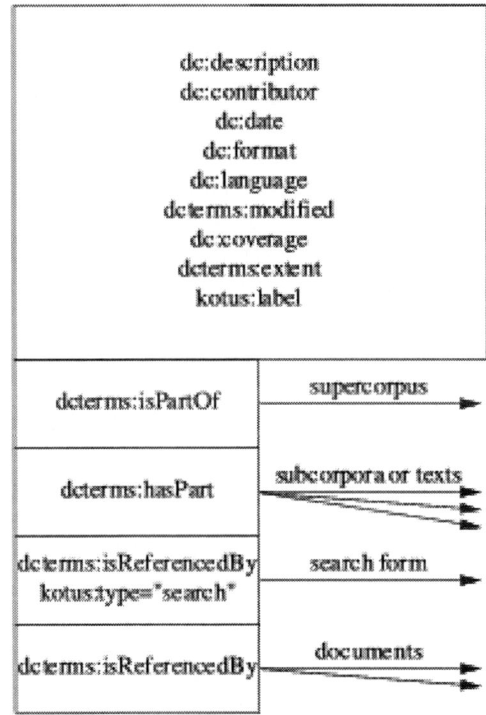

Figure 2: Meta-information of a sub-corpus

- kotus:unit-attribute to qualify the dcterms:extent-element. In corpora, the unit is normally a word.

- kotus:type-attribute is added to the DCMI elements classifying the relations. At the moment, type-attribute is used for separating links to the searching interface from links to other documents, as all of these are expressed by dcterms:isReferencedBy-element.

- kotus:metalink-attribute for adding an URL of a metadata description of a resource to the relation-classifying elements.

- kotus:class-attribute to group the sub-corpora of a corpus and label the groups. The sub-corpora are referenced using dcterms:hasPart-elements.

Figure 2 illustrates the meta-information structure of a sub-corpus in the RILF corpus system. The large box in the figure includes the elements used to describe the current collection. The small boxes and arrows below the large box represent linking that implements the hierarchical corpus structure. Links to other relevant documents (expressed by dcterms:isReferencedBy-element) are optional. Description of a text document has no links to sub-corpora, but it may have dcterms:isFormatOf-links to digitized originals. A text document has a dc:title-element that expresses the original title of the text.

The following code extract represents a meta description of a text document. After the XML formalities, it contains an rdf:RDF-element that includes all the DCMI elements describing the current document, and the links forming the browsing system. The links are expressed as dc:Relation-elements. The first of them links the text to the search form (teko-haku.xql), the second one links the text to the collection in which it belongs to (Speeches of President Halonen), and the third one links it to its original HTML version on the web.

The text content of the elements and links in the example are edited for presentation purposes. The original meta description can be found in the Kaino data service.

```
<?xml version="1.0"
 encoding="iso-8859-1" standalone="yes"?>
<?xml-stylesheet
 type="text/xsl" href="/tyyli/dc_teksti.xsl"?>

<rdf:RDF
 xmlns:rdf="http://www.w3.org/1999/02/22-rdf-syntax-ns#"
 xmlns:dc="http://purl.org/dc/elements/1.1/"
 xmlns:kotus="http://www.kotus.fi/"
 xmlns:dcterms="http://purl.org/dc/terms/">

<rdf:Description
 rdf:about="../halonen/halonen_2003.xml">

<dc:title>New Year's Speech 2003</dc:title>
<dc:creator>Halonen, Tarja</dc:creator>
<dc:date xml:lang="FI">2006</dc:date>
<dc:format>TEXT/XML</dc:format>
<dc:language>FI</dc:language>
<dc:coverage>1.1.2003</dc:coverage>
<dcterms:extent
 kotus:unit="words">985</dcterms:extent>
<dcterms:modified>20.12.2006</dcterms:modified>
<kotus:label>New Year's Speech 2003</kotus:label>

<dc:Relation>
```

```
<rdf:Description>
<dcterms:isReferencedBy
 kotus:type="search"
 rdf:resource="/korpushaku/teko-haku.xql"/>
<kotus:label>Search Form</kotus:label>
</rdf:Description>
</dc:Relation>

<dc:Relation>
<rdf:Description>
<dcterms:isPartOf
 rdf:resource="../teksti/presidentti/halonen/"
 kotus:metalink="../halonen_coll_rdf.xml"/>
<kotus:label>Speeches of President Halonen</kotus:label>
</rdf:Description>
</dc:Relation>

<dc:Relation>
<rdf:Description>
<dcterms:isFormatOf kotus:type="external_link"
 rdf:resource="http://www.tpk.fi/"/>
<kotus:label>HTML text</kotus:label>
</rdf:Description>
</dc:Relation>

</rdf:Description>
</rdf:RDF>
```

4 Browsing Interface

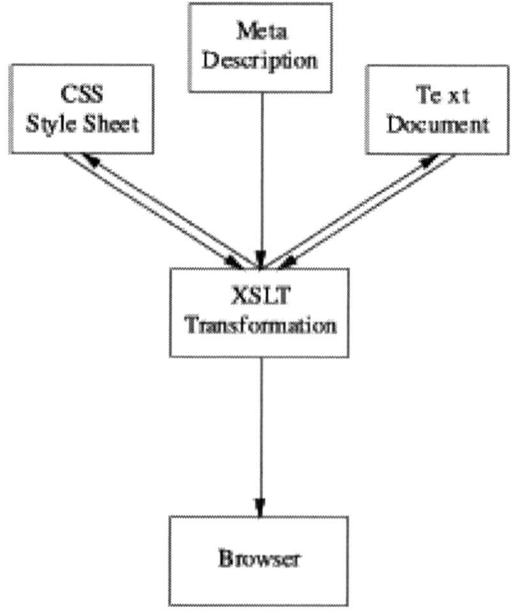

Figure 3: Browsing interface

The browsing interface for the corpus model described above is implemented in XSLT transformation language (W3C, visited 27.2.2007 b) and

Cascading Style Sheet language CSS (W3C, visited 27.2.2007 c). Figure 3 illustrates the browsing system, in which the meta descriptions are attached to XSLT transformation definitions that rearrange them and transform them to HTML documents. These documents get their appearance from CSS style sheets. In the case of text documents, XSLT transformations rearrange meta descriptions and fetch corresponding text documents to be displayed along with them.

This arrangement is modular in the sense that new material can be easily plugged in at any level of the system. Because the transformations are performed dynamically by the web browser, the corpus can be browsed on the spot, as it is, with all its meta information and text content

5 Searching Interface

The searching interface of the current RILF text corpus collection is built on top of eXist XML database (Meier, 2007). The queries are implemented in Xquery language, using some database-specific extensions. When a query is carried out, the text documents of the sub-corpus to be queried are identified and located using the meta descriptions of the documents. After that, the documents are queried one by one.

Figure 4 illustrates the basic functions of the searching interface. Search form sends a query to the database, where the search is performed. The resulting elements are formatted with an XSLT transformation and embedded in the reloaded query form. The XSLT transformation links search results to the corresponding passages of text in the browsing system.

Using Xquery makes it straightforward to use meta information included in the DCMI/RDF descriptions for filtering text documents to be queried. This makes it possible to use publishing date or language of a text as a key for fetching documents. At present, in the RILF text corpora, the publishing dates of the old texts are not consistently accurate, and all the texts are in Finnish, so this feature is not implemented in the current version of the system.

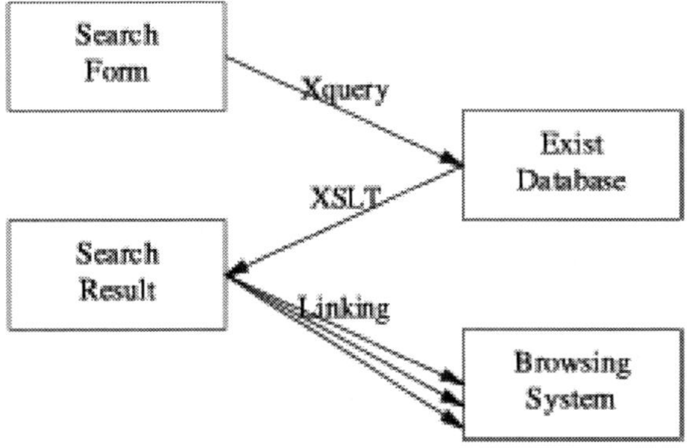

Figure 4: Searching interface

Xquery, being close to a full programming language, offers good options to process the query results further. At the moment the searching interface offers a possibility for producing a frequency list of occurrences of the queried word in a sub-corpus, but there are many more ways of producing summaries of linguistic features of the sub-corpora (or sets of selected text, if that feature will be implemented).

6 RILF Text Corpus Collection

The system, including separate but interlinked browsing and searching interfaces, is currently implemented at RILF. Publicly available parts of the text corpora possessed by RILF are served through it. The major part of the RILF collections form a diachronic corpus collection of Finnish literary texts. The oldest collected texts date back to the birth of the Old Finnish Literary Language in the sixteenth century. The collection goes diachronically through the Early Modern Finnish Literary Language from the nineteenth century to the present day Literary Finnish. Because of copyright issues, the public texts of the modern language available in the Kaino data service are very few. In addition to the diachronic, literary texts, the corpus includes a collection of Finnish proverbs, collected in the 1930s.

The current structure of the public RILF text corpus collection is presented in the list below (the names of the corpora on the list are not official). The corpus collection consists of different levels as explained above. The corpus collection root contains the diachronic corpora and the proverb collection. These corpora are further divided into sub-collections. The nature of the division depends on the corpus. In the historical corpora of old texts (corpora of Old Literary Finnish and Early Modern Finnish and the collection of Literary Classics), the division into sub-collections is mainly based on authorship. In the proverb collection, the division is regional. In the collection of texts in Modern Finnish, the division is based on text types, and the sub-corpora may be divided further according to author, source or some other property.

- The RILF Text Corpus Collection

    - The Corpus of Old Literary Finnish
        * 12 sub-collections
        * 132 texts
        * 3.5 million words
    - The Corpus of Early Modern Finnish
        * 94 sub-collections
        * 761 texts
        * 6.5 million words
    - Early Classics of Modern Finnish Literature
        * 13 sub-collections
        * 89 texts
        * 1.35 million words
    - Texts of Modern Finnish
        * 1 sub-collection
        * 76 texts
        * 62 105 words
    - Finnish Proverbs
        * 20 parishes
        * 72 580 proverbs

The corpora of Old Literary Finnish and Early Modern Finnish are results of many years of persistent work. The texts included in these collections are carefully selected and then digitized, either by hand or even by scanning at a later stage. The texts are marked up to the sentence level, and references to corresponding passages in the original publications are added to each sentence. Some of the texts in the corpus of Early Modern Finnish are word lists, and follow the TEI P4 dictionary structure.

The collection of the Early Classics of Modern Finnish Literature includes short stories, poems, plays and novels from the period of the beginning of modern Finnish literature. The markup goes down to the smallest structural (non-linguistic) level of the text. This may mean paragraphs in the prose texts, lines or stage descriptions in a play, or lines in a poem. For drama and poetry, new DTDs were created using the TEI Pizza Chef.

The collection of Modern Finnish is special in the sense, that the texts currently belonging to it are marked up to the word level and annotated morphologically. On the annotation scheme, see Lehtinen and Lounela (2004). Also, the text type division adds one level to the corpus structure, as the texts in the collection (at present) are divided further based on the author. At the moment the modern Finnish collection is very limited, consisting only of a collection of New Year's speeches of the presidents of the republic. In the near future certain legislative texts will be added, and we are planning to identify and encode other current texts that are not bound by the copyright laws. RILF has at its possession more texts from the twentieth century than the Kaino data service contains. These texts are arranged according to the corpus model described in this paper, and structured to the paragraph level. This material, however, is bound by copyright law, and cannot be re-published freely by RILF.

The collection of Finnish proverbs is a part of larger collection, which is digitized only partly. The collection is arranged regionally according to parishes where the proverbs were originally collected in the 1930s. The subcollections are structured according to the same DTD as the word lists and dictionaries in other collections.

7 Expandability

The corpus model of the RILF text corpus collection allows many possibilities of expanding it: by size, by function, and by information. Increasing the size of the corpus is straightforward. A compatible corpus tree (or document) can be plugged in by adding a link to it to the meta description in a suitable place in the existing tree. The new part will be readily integrated into the structure.

Expanding the corpus system by function is possible by enhancing the query interface. Exploring the XML-encoded documents with Xquery language is limited practically only by the richness of the annotation expressed with the XML code. A way of exploring morphologically annotated texts is presented in Lounela (2006). This type of a summarizing analysis can be a natural part of a corpus user interface, such as the one described in this article. Linguistic summaries can be added statically, by producing them off-line and linking the reports to the existing collections in the browsing system, or dynamically, by adding queries to the searching interface.

Expanding the corpus system by information can be done by using the linking capabilities of the metadata system of the browsing interface. Above, I mentioned the possibility to link linguistic summaries or reports describing the textual properties of the collections. It is also possible to enhance the metadata system by linking the collection descriptions to external documents. The external documents may concern research that describes or uses the corpus, or is relevant to the potential corpus users in some other way.

8 Discussion

Above, I have described a corpus structure and interface that is modular, and is based on (slightly modified) de facto standard definitions belonging to the XML family. The implementation of the described interface uses open source tools. I am now going to sum up and discuss some advantages and uses of this type of a system for using corpora in linguistic work, and outline some possible future developments for such a system.

- The de facto standard -boundedness of the system makes it relatively easy to understand, implement and alter according to local needs. The existing implementation shows that a versatile user interface for the corpora can be implemented with a reasonable effort using free software.

- The modularity of the system makes it easy to add or remove corpora, sub-collections or documents, or to rearrange the corpora. Normally, parts of the system are only attached to one well-defined location in the metadata structure, which makes altering the linking straightforward.

- The integrated metadata system makes it easy to express, add, and use meta information at all levels of the corpus. The metadata can be used for browsing and searching.

- The linking system of the meta descriptions, and the use of Xquery language for the searching interface lead to expandability in many directions. New collections and documents can be plugged in, new, intelligent queries can be programmed and included, and new links, internal or external, can be added to the system in a well-defined, controlled manner.

- The searching interface can use the meta descriptions for forming new collections of already existing texts. Also, new sub-collections can be dynamically formed, regrouping the existing text documents, using existing meta information about the texts. With consistent instructions, humanistically oriented researchers can collect and annotate text materials of their own interest to be plugged in the system, and to be used in connection with previously collected materials.

- Summarizing linguistic properties with Xquery, in connection with controlled use of TEI XML structure for morphologically annotated text sets makes it possible to use text collections for text linguistic research. In Kankaanpää (2006) and Tiililä (2007) quantitative properties of text sets are examined and compared automatically in this manner as a part of text linguistic research. The techniques used in these research projects are very similar to the techniques used in the RILF corpus system.

- The corpus system could be expanded to a direction where it could be used as a tool for analyzing and recognizing text types according to frequencies of linguistic categories. On this type of research, see Biber (1988) and Saukkonen (2001).

- The mechanism of linking external documents to the metadata system of a corpus makes it possible to offer the corpus users information about research carried out using the corpus. If this possibility was used in its full potential, the corpus could include a structured research reference database concerning the corpus and its use.

The points listed above lead to two possible (not mutually exclusive) directions of development for the corpus system. First, the system can be directed towards a research reference database where, in addition of the text materials, knowledge of relevant research is accumulated to be easily used by the researchers. Second, the system can be directed towards a general quantitative tool for text linguists. The latter would be done by expanding the searching interface to a full-blown analysis tool that offers a possibility for creating varied quantitative reports for text sets that are morphologically annotated in the standard way.

References

Douglas Biber. 1988. *Variation Across Speech and Writing*. Cambridge University Press, Cambridge.

Dave Beckett, Eric Miller, and Dan Brickley. 2002 *Expressing Simple Dublin Core in RDF/XML*. http://dublincore.org/documents/dcmes-rdf-xml/. The Dublin Core Metadata Initiative.

Salli Kankaanpää. 2006. *Hallinnon lehdistötiedotteiden kieli*. [Language of Administrative Press Releases.] Finnish Literature Society (SKS), Helsinki.

Stefan Kokkelink and Roland Schwänzl. 2002 *Expressing Qualified Dublin Core in RDF / XML*. http://dublincore.org/documents/dcq-rdf-xml/. The Dublin Core Metadata Initiative.

Outi Lehtinen and Mikko Lounela. 2004. A model for composing and (re-)using text materials for linguistic research. *Papers from the 30th Finnish Conference of Linguistics*. University of Joensuu, Joensuu.

Mikko Lounela. 2002. Aiming Towards Best Practices in XML Techniques for Text Corpora Annotation: City of Helsinki Public Works Department - A Case Study. *Towards the Semantic Web and Web Services. Proceedings of the XML Finland 2002 Conference*. Institute for Information Technology, Helsinki.

Mikko Lounela. 2006. Exploring morphologically analyzed text material. *Inquiries into words, constraints and contexts. Festschrift in the honour of Kimmo Koskenniemi on his 60th birthday*. Gummerus, Helsinki

Wolfgang Meier et al. 2007. *Open Source Native XML Database*. http://exist.sourceforge.net/. Open Source Technology Group, Fremont, California.

Pauli Saukkonen. 2001. *Maailman hahmottaminen tekstein*. [Perceiving the world by texts.] Helsinki University Press, Helsinki.

Ulla Tiililä. 2007. *Tekstit viraston työssä*. [Texts in the work of a city department.] Finnish Literature Society (SKS), Helsinki.

DCMI visited 27.2.2007. *Dublin Core Metadata Initiative*. http://dublincore.org/. The Dublin Core Metadata Initiative.

RILF visited 27.2.2007. *Kaino - Kotuksen aineistopalvelu*. [Kaino - RILF Data Service.] http://kaino.kotus.fi/. Research Institute for the Languages of Finland, Helsinki.

TEI visited 27.2.2007 a. *TEI: Yesterday's information tomorrow*. http://www.tei-c.org/. The Text Encoding Initiative, Charlottesville, Virginia.

TEI visited 27.2.2007 b. *TEI Pizza Chef*. http://www.tei-c.org/pizza.html. The Text Encoding Initiative, Charlottesville, Virginia.

W3C visited 27.2.2007 a. *Resource Description Framework (RDF)*. http://www.w3.org/RDF/. The World Wide Web Consortium, Cambridge.

W3C visited 27.2.2007 b. *XSL Transformations (XSLT)*. http://www.w3.org/TR/sxlt. The World Wide Web Consortium, Cambridge.

W3C visited 27.2.2007 c. *Cascading Style Sheets*. http://www.w3.org/Style/CSS/. The World Wide Web Consortium, Cambridge.

Perceptual Assessment of the Degree of Russian Accent

Lya Meister
Laboratory of Phonetics and Speech Technology
Institute of Cybernetics
Tallinn University of Technology
Akadeemia tee 21, Tallinn 12618, Estonia
lya@phon.ioc.ee

Abstract

This paper deals with the perceptual assessment of Russian-accented Estonian. Speech samples were recorded from 20 speakers with a Russian background; clips of about 20 seconds from each speaker were selected for this perceptual study. The accentedness was rated in two tests: first, 20 native Estonian speakers judged the samples and rated the degree of foreign accent on a six-point interval scale; secondly, two experienced phoneticians carried out a perceptual study of the same samples and compiled the list of pronunciations errors. The results of both listening tests were highly correlated – the higher the degree of accentedness given to a L2-speaker by naïve listeners, the more pronunciation errors were found by trained experts. The classification of most frequent pronunciation errors based on acoustic-phonetic features is given, as well.

1   Introduction

Native speakers/listeners can easily identify non-native speech and are able to rate the degree of foreign accent (FA). Naïve listeners' judgments of FA degree are based on their general perceptual impression rather than on conscious use of acoustic-phonetic knowledge about their own first language (L1). Accentedness ratings result in the degree of global foreign accent which is an impressionistic measure to which the speech of a second language (L2) speaker deviates from that of L1-speakers (Southwood & Flege, 1999). On the contrary, a trained phonetician should be able to identify and classify different accent phenomena as well as describe them in terms of deviations of acoustic-phonetic features.

Following the findings and methodology presented in a recent paper (Meister, 2006; for methods employed in different studies see Jesney, 2004) on the accentedness rating of foreign-accented Estonian, two further listening experiments have been designed. The aim of these experiments is to compare the accentedness ratings given by naïve listeners, and the results of perceptual analysis of pronunciation errors carried out by experienced phoneticians. It is expected that the results of these two groups of raters harmonize quite well, i.e., the higher the accentedness ratings by naïve listeners of L2 speakers are, the more pronunciation errors are listed by experts. The study serves also a long-term goal – the development of criteria for speaking proficiency assessment, including the degree of FA.

2   Method

2.1   Speech samples and speakers

The speech material used in the study was recorded from 20 L2-speakers (14 female, 6 male) during the high-level language test at the National Examination and Qualification Centre. One of the sub-tasks the examinees have to perform is the conversation in pairs on a given topic which should demonstrate different speaking skills: expression of opinion, argumentation, turn-taking and carry-

Joakim Nivre, Heiki-Jaan Kaalep, Kadri Muischnek and Mare Koit (Eds.)
NODALIDA 2007 Conference Proceedings, pp. 345–348

Lya Meister

ing on the conversation, etc. (Pajupuu et al., 2002). It is expected that a person with high-level language skills is able to communicate in written and spoken Estonian with near-native proficiency.

The recordings of the conversations were carried out using a digital recorder (sampling frequency 44.1 kHz, 16 bit, mono) and a high-quality microphone placed at a ca. 1 m distance from the speakers. With each pair of subjects, six to eight minutes of spontaneous conversation was recorded. A continuous clip of speech with the duration of ca. 20 seconds from each subject's speech was chosen for perceptual assessment. The clips were stored into an audio file in random order with an inter-stimuli interval of five seconds.

In addition to the speech recordings, each subject filled out a questionnaire concerning their linguistic background, age of L2 acquisition, use of L1, L2, etc. The summary of the speakers' information is presented in Table 1.

2.2 Listeners

Two groups of listeners were employed in the study. First, a group of naïve (non-linguist) listeners was composed of 20 native Estonians (10 female, 10 male) in the age range of 17 to 62. All of them had some knowledge of Russian and diverse exposure to foreign-accented Estonian spoken by Russians; none of them reported any hearing problems.

A second group of judges consisted of two trained phoneticians (native Estonians, one female, one male, both 49 years of age) with good knowledge of Russian and experience in experimental studies of Estonian as L2.

2.3 Experimental setup

Before the test a foreign accent scaling technique was introduced and several examples of L2 speech with different degrees of accentedness were played to the listeners. The participants were instructed to focus only on deviations in pronunciation, while grammatical and lexical errors should be ignored.

In the first part of the experiment the stimuli were played to subjects from a notebook computer via headphones in a quiet environment. The task of the judges was to rate the degree of foreign accent of each stimulus on an interval scale from 1 – "no foreign accent" to 6 – "very heavy foreign accent". The group of naïve listeners heard each stimulus only once; during the inter-stimulus intervals they had to write down their ratings on an answer sheet. The duration of the listening session was about nine minutes.

In the second part of the experiment, two experts carried out an exhaustive perceptual analysis of each stimulus and compiled the list of perceived pronunciation errors classified into five major groups typical to Russian-accented Estonian: (1) deviation of temporal structure, (2) location of word stress, (3) quality of vowels and diphthongs, (4) palatalization, and (5) voicing of voiceless consonants (Meister and Meister, 2005).

In the first stage the experts carried out error analysis independently from each other using repeated listening: this resulted in two different lists of pronunciation errors. Later, the disagreements in errors were discussed and analyzed together until the experts reached a common agreement.

Table 1. Summary of the background information of L2-speakers (EST = Estonia(n), RUS = Russia(n), UKR = Ukraine (Ukrainian)).

	L2-speakers' data																			
Speaker's ID	Sp1	Sp2	Sp3	Sp4	Sp5	Sp6	Sp7	Sp8	Sp9	Sp10	Sp11	Sp12	Sp13	Sp14	Sp15	Sp16	Sp17	Sp18	Sp19	Sp20
Age	52	23	19	19	16	25	26	32	19	18	20	51	19	43	20	33	18	46	45	32
Gender	F	M	F	F	F	M	F	F	F	F	M	F	M	F	M	F	F	M	F	F
Country of birth	Est	Ukr	Est	Est	Est	Est	Est	Est	Est	Est	Rus	Est	Est	Est	Est	Est	Est	Rus	Rus	Est
Age of L2 acquisition	5	9	5	7	7	1	12	12	9	5	9	5	9	8	9	20	5	30	23	9
Language(s) used at home	Rus	Rus	Rus	Rus	Rus	Est Rus	Rus	Rus	Ukr	Rus	Rus	Rus	Rus	Est	Rus	Rus	Rus	Rus	Est	Rus
Language(s) used at work	Rus Est	Est Rus	Rus	Est	Rus	Est Rus	Est Rus	Est Rus	Rus	Rus	Est	Est	Rus	Est Rus	Est	Rus Est	Rus Est	Rus	Est Rus	Rus Est
Friends include Estonians	No	Yes	No	Yes	Yes	Yes	Yes	Yes	Yes	Yes	No	Yes	Yes	Yes	No	No	Yes	No	No	No

Table 2. The results of the perceptual assessment in ascending order by the mean of the perceived degree of global foreign accent (L2 speakers marked as Sp1…Sp20, raters marked as R1…R20).

	Perceptual ratings given by 20 raters (R1 - R20)																			
	Sp14	Sp12	Sp4	Sp6	Sp5	Sp13	Sp1	Sp7	Sp10	Sp16	Sp2	Sp9	Sp8	Sp19	Sp20	Sp15	Sp3	Sp11	Sp17	Sp18
R1	2	1	1	1	2	3	3	2	3	4	4	3	3	5	6	5	5	5	5	6
R2	1	2	1	1	2	3	2	3	4	4	4	3	4	4	3	5	4	5	5	6
R3	1	1	1	3	2	2	2	3	3	4	4	3	4	4	5	5	5	5	5	6
R4	1	2	1	1	1	2	2	2	2	3	3	[2]	4	3	4	3	4	[3]	4	4
R5	1	1	1	1	2	2	2	3	3	4	5	5	5	4	5	5	5	5	6	6
R6	1	1	2	3	2	3	4	4	4	5	4	4	[6]	5	6	6	5	6	6	6
R7	1	1	1	1	1	2	2	2	2	2	5	3	5	3	4	4	6	6	5	6
R8	1	1	2	1	2	2	3	2	[6]	5	5	5	3	4	3	6	6	6	6	6
R9	2	2	1	1	2	2	3	3	2	4	3	5	5	5	5	6	5	6	6	6
R10	1	1	1	2	2	3	3	4	5	5	3	5	5	5	5	4	5	6	6	6
R11	1	1	2	1	3	2	2	3	3	4	3	4	4	5	5	4	4	5	5	6
R12	1	2	2	3	3	3	2	4	3	4	4	3	5	3	4	5	5	6	6	6
R13	1	1	2	1	1	2	4	2	3	3	3	4	4	4	6	4	5	5	5	6
R14	1	1	2	1	2	2	3	3	4	3	4	4	5	5	5	5	5	6	6	6
R15	1	1	2	1	2	3	4	4	3	2	4	3	5	4	4	5	[3]	5	5	5
R16	2	2	3	3	3	3	4	4	4	3	4	4	4	4	4	4	4	5	5	6
R17	1	1	1	2	2	2	3	3	5	4	4	5	5	5	5	5	5	6	6	6
R18	1	1	1	2	2	2	2	2	3	2	3	3	3	3	3	3	4	4	[3]	4
R19	1	1	1	1	1	2	2	2	4	2	3	4	3	5	5	4	5	6	6	6
R20	1	1	1	1	2	2	2	3	5	5	3	4	3	4	3	6	5	6	6	6
Mean	1,2	1,3	1,5	1,6	2,0	2,4	2,7	2,9	3,4	3,6	3,8	3,9	4,2	4,2	4,5	4,7	4,8	5,5	5,5	5,8
Stdev	0,37	0,44	0,60	0,83	0,60	0,49	0,80	0,79	0,96	1,05	0,72	0,81	0,83	0,77	1,00	0,92	0,60	0,61	0,61	0,64
CI 95%	0,16	0,19	0,27	0,36	0,27	0,21	0,35	0,35	0,42	0,46	0,31	0,35	0,37	0,34	0,44	0,40	0,26	0,27	0,27	0,28

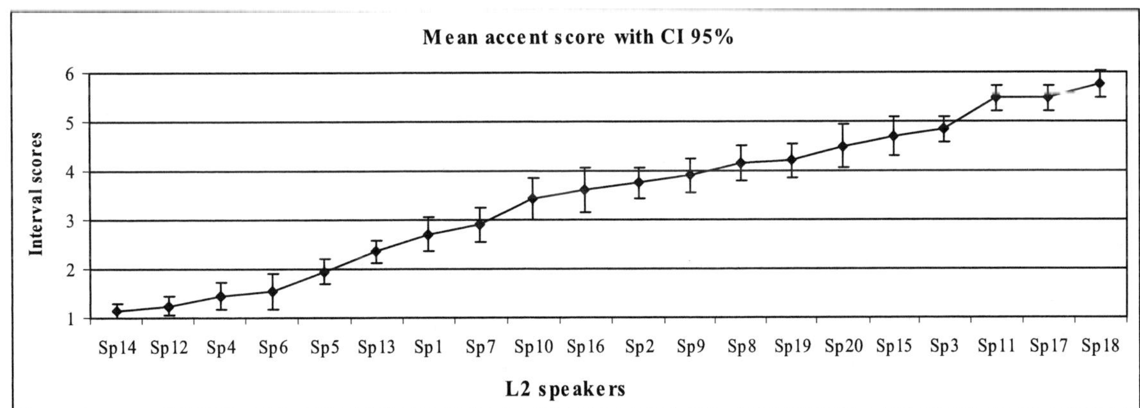

Figure 1. The mean scores of global foreign accent with a confidence interval of 95 %. L2 speakers (Sp1 … Sp20) ordered by the mean accent score in ascending order.

3   Results

The rating results of the first group of judges (Table 2 and Figure 1) show high inter-rater consistency. Correlation for all possible pairwise combinations of two raters was computed while a few outliers were excluded from the statistics (see Table 2 numbers in square brackets). The average correlation is r = 0.85 (min r = 0.7, max r = 0.96); a correlation of 0.75 is considered acceptable (Shrout and Fleiss, 1979). Good inter-rater correlation shows that the duration of stimuli of 20 seconds is sufficient for reliable results (cf. (Meister, 2006), where five- and 60-seconds clips were used). Also, the narrower six-point interval scale (compared to the nine-point scale used in (Meister, 2006)) may result in less dispersed ratings.

Variability of judgments among different listeners and the occurrence of few deviating ratings suggest that listeners' internal standards of accentedness are different. Also, it can not be excluded that grammatical and lexical errors made by L2 speakers influenced the individual accent scores.

Table 3. Classification of pronunciation errors of L2 speakers in ascending order by error rate.

Speaker ID	Number of words	Type and amount of errors					Total number of errors	Error rate
		Temporal structure	Word stress	Vowel quality	Palatalization	Voicing of consonants		
Sp14	34						0	0
Sp12	40						0	0
Sp4	40						0	0
Sp6	45	2				1	3	0,07
Sp5	33	3					3	0,09
Sp1	40	2		1		1	4	0,10
Sp13	36	3				3	6	0,17
Sp10	23	2	1	2	2		7	0,30
Sp7	41	4		2	1	6	13	0,32
Sp2	34	4	1	1	2	3	11	0,32
Sp8	56	8		7	4		19	0,34
Sp9	23	5		1	2	3	11	0,48
Sp16	33	10	2	1		4	17	0,52
Sp3	23	5		4	5	1	15	0,65
Sp15	27	9		1		8	18	0,67
Sp11	31	9		3	3	6	21	0,68
Sp20	29	9		6		5	20	0,69
Sp17	27	10		2	3	4	19	0,70
Sp19	23	8	1	2	4	3	18	0,78

The findings of two experts (Table 3) show that the most frequent errors are related to temporal structure, voicing of voiceless consonants, and quality of some vowels and diphthongs; other errors are less frequent. These results confirm earlier findings (Meister and Meister, 2005).

In order to compare different L2-speakers, a simple measure of error rate has been formed by dividing the total number of errors by the number of words produced by the speaker during a 20 second clip (see Table 3).

4   Summary

The results of the two groups of listeners are highly correlated – the correlation between the mean accent score (Table 2) and the error rate (Table 3) is 0.94. It has been shown that for L1 speakers of a non-quantity language it is difficult to acquire a contrastive temporal category of L2 as a quantity language (McAllister et al., 2000). The same seems to hold true for the case of Russian as L1 and Estonian as L2 – the errors in the temporal domain contribute most to the error rate and probably to the perceived degree of FA, as well.

Further work will focus on the analysis of relationships between the degree of global FA and the types of pronunciation errors, as well as the role of deviations of acoustic features in the perception of accentedness.

References

Jesney, K. 2004. *The Use of Global Foreign Accent Rating in Studies of L2 Acquisition.* Calgary, AB: University of Calgary Language Research Centre Reports.

McAllister, R., Flege, J. and Piske, T. 2000. Aspects of the Acquisition of Swedish Quantity by Native Speakers of English, Spanish and Estonian. *In: Proceedings of FONETIK 2000.* Skövde, Sweden.

Meister, L. and Meister, E.. 2005. Acoustic correlates of Russian accent in Estonian. *In: Proceedings of SPECOM 2005,* University of Patras, 437 - 440.

Meister, L. 2006. Assessment of the degree of foreign accent: a pilot study. *In: Fonetiikan Päivät 2006 = The Phonetics Symposium 2006,* University of Helsinki, 53:113 - 119.

Pajupuu, H., Reins, P. and Kerge, K. 2002. *Eesti keele kõrgtaseme test. Käsiraamat.* Tallinn: Riiklik Eksami- ja Kvalifikatsioonikeskus.

Shrout, P.E. and Fleiss, J.L. 1979. Intraclass correlations: uses in assessing rater reliability. *Psychological Bulletin*, 86, 420-428.

Southwood, H. and Flege, J. 1999. Scaling foreign accent: direct magnitude estimation versus interval scaling. *Clinical Linguistics & Phonetics*, Vol. 13, No. 5, 335-349.

Terminology Extraction and Term Ranking for Standardizing Term Banks

Magnus Merkel
Department of Computer and Information Science
Linköping University
Linköping, Sweden
magme@ida.liu.se

Jody Foo
Department of Computer and Information Science
Linköping University
Linköping, Sweden
jodfo@ida.liu.se

Abstract

This paper presents how word alignment techniques could be used for building standardized term banks. It is shown that time and effort could be saved by a relatively simple evaluation metric based on frequency data from term pairs, and source and target distributions inside the alignment results. The proposed Q-value metric is shown to outperform other tested metrics such as Dice's coefficient, and simple pair frequency.

1 Introduction

Quality assurance (QA) of products and services is standard procedure in most industrial areas today. In the area of document production and localization, quality assurance has been deemed to be both time-consuming and costly as most of the linguistic quality assurance has to be made manually. Of course, if used, spell and grammar checkers, and controlled language checkers for assuring that manuals are created using a special variety of Simplified English, will identify some errors, and sometimes also help to correct them. The major problem for technical writing and localization quality is to be found in inconsistent use of terminology. Or as Sue Ellen Wright puts it: "The primary source of rework is inconsistent terminology" (Wright 2006). Inconsistent terminology is perhaps most crucial in source language documentation (originals) as mistakes there will multiply by every translation. Lombard (2006) illustrates this phenomenon by an example where an American software development company may use a great

variety of terms to refer to a closing or stopped application by inconsistently using terms such as *cancel, quit, close, end* and *stop* in the user interface and in the accompanying documentation. This is, as Lombard puts it, not a problem for the development team as they know what all these terms mean. The translators/localizers, however, will be tempted to translate every distinct source term choice to distinct target terms, thereby multiplying the inconsistency.

Poor quality in documentation could result not only in dissatisfied clients and users, but also in substantially increased costs for revisions, retranslations and delays. In addition, legal damages could make things worse, for example through lawsuits for serious factual mistakes in the source documentation or in translations. Capturing mistakes in documentation before they reach the users/readers is the only way to avoid the extra costs and inconvenience that poor quality will yield.

The obvious solution to the inconsistency dilemma can be found in a *standardized term bank*. Creating a term bank is very time consuming if it is done in the old way, i.e. by hand. During the last decade word alignment techniques have been used to create practically usable resources for translation activities, much faster than the manual way. However, as word alignment can never produce 100 per cent accurate term pairs, methods of how to filter out erroneous entries and efficiently revise the output from alignment systems need to be developed. Even if an alignment system is close to perfect, the data itself (the source and target texts) will contain errors, omissions and additions that will result in terminological entries that are unwanted in a standardized term bank. Perhaps most interesting, high quality alignments will produce a map of the

Joakim Nivre, Heiki-Jaan Kaalep, Kadri Muischnek and Mare Koit (Eds.)
NODALIDA 2007 Conference Proceedings, pp. 349–354

source and target texts that reveals how consistent, or inconsistent, term usage is in reality.

In this paper we will address the issue of how to create standardized term banks by using word alignment techniques. The focus lies on the ranking of the term entries produced by the alignment system and on the evaluation of a proposed metric.

2 Motivation

The focus of this paper is to explore how term candidate validation can be improved by using a good ranking metric. A good ranking metric correlates to the precision of a term candidate. This means that using a good term ranking metric makes it possible to select a set of term candidates which when processed will result in a higher number approved terms compared to selecting the set of term candidates to be processed by random or using a bad ranking metric.

3 Approach

The ranking metrics used here are based on data from a set of word aligned term candidates. This means that the presented method can be used on all term candidate sets, without regard to how the term candidates have been extracted or produced. A corpus-based approach relies on the existence of a corpus from which statistics can be calculated.

The set of term candidates used in this paper were extracted using an align-filter method. The extracted term candidates are then ranked using term pair frequency, Q-value and Dice's coefficient (see Metrics below). The ranking order produced by these metrics is then compared using accumulated precision.

The word alignment system used is the ITools suite, developed at Fodina Language Technology and Linköping University (Ahrenberg et al. 2003; Deléger et al. 2006; Nyström et al. 2006; Foo & Merkel 2007). The source and target texts used in the alignment case study consisted of around 35,000 sentence pairs (English-Swedish) from patent texts from the subject area *Animal care*.

3.1 The ITools suite

The ITools software suite three major applications interactive word alignment (ILink), automatic word alignment (ITrix), viewer for editing and browsing alignment data (IView).

The ITools suite also includes functions for sampling test and training data sets, automatic evaluation, statistical processing and conversion from XML to SQL database format.

The basic approach used for alignment in the ITools suite combines evidence from a variety of different sources by assigning each piece of evidence a score and then calculating a joint score for all of them (cf. Tiedemann 2003).

The ITools suite is supported by Connexor's Machinese Syntax parsers (Tapanainen & Järvinen 1997) which provide the grammatical information for English, Swedish and several other western European languages.

A typical word alignment process using the ITools suite consists of the following steps:

1. Morphological, syntactic and dependency analysis of source and target files
2. Statistical processing of source and target files
3. Sampling test and training data sets
4. Training, i.e. creating dynamic resources interactively (ILink)
5. Running automatic alignment (ITrix)
6. Conversion to SQL database
7. Verification, filtering and categorization of extracted term candidates (IView)

In step 1 the sentence aligned source and target text are parsed independently using the Machinese Syntax parsers for the source and target languages.

In step 2 statistical resources are created both for the word form level (inflected words) and lemma level (base forms). We use t-score and dice associations on co-occurrences between items in the bitext and thereby create a bilingual dictionary which is used as a static resource in the automatic alignment. Other statistical approaches can also be used, such as the Giza++ kit (Och & Ney 2005). In the third stage, a test set and a training set of aligned sentence pairs are randomly sampled. The size of these sets varies depending on the project and time available.

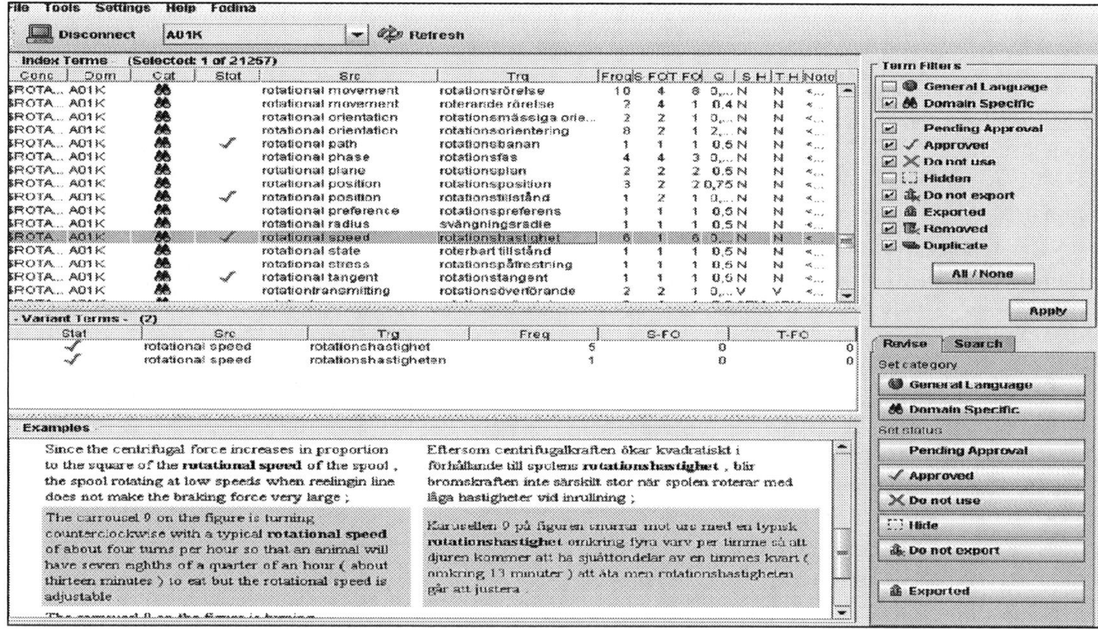

Figure 1. IView application. Used for filtering, categorization and revision.

In step 4, a training environment is set up in the interactive ILink tool where the training results in dynamic resources on four levels: 1) the word form level, 2) the base (lemma) level, 3) the parts-of-speech level, and 4) the syntactic function level.

In step 5 the automatic alignment is performed using ITrix, which results in thousands of pointers between the source and target texts containing the actual token links. These token links are then used to create an SQL database, keeping all grammatical information from the XML files as well as creating a structured term data base containing a concept level, index term level, term variant level and examples (see Figure 1).

However, to arrive at a usable term collection, the output from the word alignment needs to be verified. The IView application can be used during this last step (see Figure 1), which consists of verifying extracted term pairs with access to sample contexts as well as statistical data. In IView all token alignments made by ITrix are compiled into a table of translation pair types in a graphical environment where the annotator can confirm translation pairs as domain specific terms or as belonging to "general language", i.e., they are correct align-ments but cannot be considered as terms in a specific domain.

3.2 Metrics

As hinted in the introduction, it is desirable to optimize the quality of the aligned data by stripping away poor quality alignments and keeping the high quality ones as this will leave less manual work in the actual standardization process. To achieve this, one needs to order the proposed term pairs in, for example, descending quality order. Ordering term candidates can be done using different metrics.

One such metric that has been used in term extraction research is the Dice's coefficient of association (Dice 1945). A common approach in applying Dice's coefficient as a ranking metric is to collect corpus statistics (Pazienza et al. 2005). The second metric used in this study is the Q-value, a metric specifically design to operate on aligned data (Deléger et al. 2006). These two metrics are compared to a third baseline, which is a straightforward pair frequency.

The input data used for these metrics are all available in the SQL database, which contains information such as

- **T**ype **P**air **F**requencies (TPF), i.e. the number of times where the source and target types are aligned
- **T**arget types **p**er **S**ource type (TpS), i.e. the number of target types a specific source type has been aligned to. E.g. if the source type A is aligned to the target types B and C, two type pairs exist – A-B and A-C. For both these type pairs, the TpS value is 2.
- **S**ource types **p**er **T**arget type (SpT), i.e. the number of source types a specific target type has been aligned to. Given the example provided to explain the TpS, the SpT values for the two type pairs would be 1 for A-B, and 1 for A-C. This means that low SpT and TpS values correspond to consistent usage of target and source types if the aligned data is fairly correct.
- **S**ource **T**ype **F**requency (STF), i.e. the accumulated frequency of a source type in the set of aligned type pairs.
- **T**arget **T**ype **F**requency (STF), i.e. the accumulated frequency of a target type in the set of aligned type pairs.

Using this information, we can calculate the following metrics:

$$Q\text{-}value = \frac{TPF}{TpS + SpT}$$

$$Dice = \frac{2 \times TPF}{STF + TTF}$$

#	Src	Trg	TPF	TpS	SpT	STF	TTF
1	fatty acid	Fett syra	2	2	1	7	2
2	fatty acid	fettsyra	5	2	1	7	5

Table 1. Two type pairs and their frequencies.

Given the complete set of type pairs in Table 1, the Q-value of pair 1 is 0.67 and the Dice coefficient is 0.45. The Q-value of pair 2 is 0.71 and the Dice coefficient is 0.83.

The main conceptual difference between the Dice coefficient and the Q-value is that the Dice coefficient focuses on positive association between source and target type, whereas the Q-value focuses on the association between the current source and target type, but also between the current source and target types with other source and target types.

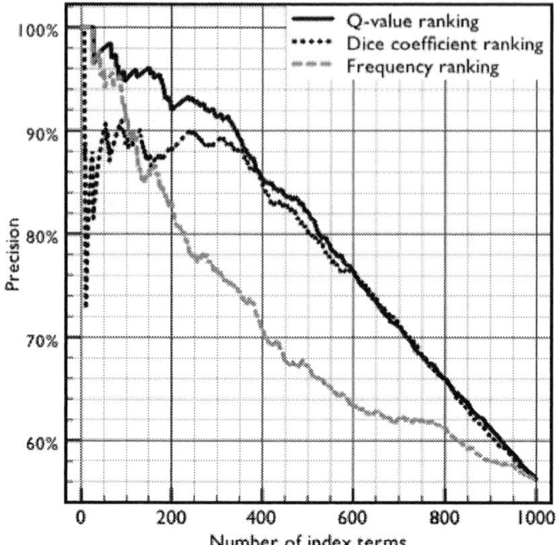

Figure 2. Precision fall-off using different metrics to rank 1000 randomly sampled term candidates

In other words, a high Q-value indicates a term candidate pair with few similar candidates whereas a high Dice coefficient indicates a common term.

4 Evaluation and results

Processing the patent texts in the ITools suite resulted in over 60,000 term candidate pairs in the term bank. One thousand entries were sampled randomly from these term pairs and evaluated manually for correctness. The manually corrected test set of term candidates was then ordered by using the three different metrics: term pair frequency, Dice coefficient, and Q-value. The results are presented in Figure 2.

As can be seen in Figure 2, ranking the term candidates using the Q-value results in the best accumulated precision curve. Both Q-value and Dice coefficient metrics rank the term candidates in a fairly linear correlation with term candidate precision, whereas the term pair frequency curve has a bad precision fit. The Dice coefficient does not perform well at its highest scores, which could be explained by the fact that the term pairs contain a considerable amount of term pairs where frequency is equal to one (1) (over 50 per cent of the term pairs).

5 Discussion

As stated earlier, the motivation of finding a good term ranking metric is to increase the efficiency of the validation process – the process of going from term candidates to standardized terms. If we assume that the random sample is representative of the total 60,000 term candidates generated by ITools, we can choose a combination of precision and coverage by setting a threshold at the appropriate Q value.

Precision	Q-value	Number of term candidates to process	Estimated number of approved terms
95.8%	0.53	10,400	9963
91.0%	0.50	20,040	18236
~80.0%	0.20	~30,000	~24,000

Table 2. Estimated term volumes and precision for different Q-values.

In table 2, three different Q-values have been chosen resulting in three sets of term candidates to process. Set 2 is double the size of set 1, and set 3 is three times the size of set 1. The increases in size can roughly be translated into the same increase in time needed to process the term candidates. The precision of the sets gives us an estimate of how many approved terms we can expect from processing a given number of term candidates. Furthermore, given a scenario where there are no resource restrictions enforced on the validation process, processing the full set of term candidates will of course result in the highest number of approved terms.

However, resources available for the validation process are often limited. In this case the precision of the set of term candidates becomes interesting as this can roughly be translated into processing efficiency. If we assume that all term candidates require the same amount of processing time, we can use the data in Table 1 to derive the earnings and costs connected to the different sizes of term candidate sets. An example of such calculations is presented in Table 3.

Increase in term candidate volume	Additional effort required	Additional approved terms gained	Difference between effort and gain
10400-20040	92.7%	83%	-9.7
20040-30000	49,7%	31.6%	-18.1

Table 3. Earnings and costs when increasing the volume of term candidates to process.

Using the three sets of term candidates presented in Table 2, the relative increases in effort (spent time) and number of approved terms, as well as the difference between these gains and efforts have been calculated in Table 3. As we can see, an additional increase in candidate terms from 20 000 to 30 000 results in half the effective gain of the resources spent, compared to an increase in term candidates to process from 10 000 to 20 000. In effect, having a good term ranking metric with a predictable precision fall rate can provide the information necessary to come to the decision on how term processing resources can be spent in the most effective way, depending on the present requirements on the size of the final set of approved terms.

6 Conclusion and future work

In this paper we have shown that time and effort could be saved by a relatively simple evaluation metric based on frequency data from term pairs, source and target distributions inside the alignment results. The proposed metric Q-value is shown to outperform other tested metrics such as the Dice coefficient, and simple pair frequency. The Q-value is better at handling low frequency data. The results point to that one could realistically decide on what goals a term standardization endeavor should aim for in terms of volume, and time spent.

The next step to develop the methodology for revising term candidates further is to test it on several alignment projects. We are currently investigating techniques to cluster term pairs conceptually by using semantic mirroring using a Q-value filter. The initial results look promising in that they make it possible to group synonym variants within a conceptual cluster and thereby making it possible to automatically filter out undesired term synonyms.

References

Ahrenberg L, Merkel M, Petterstedt M. 2003. Interactive Word Alignment for Language Engineering. In *Proceedings of the 10th Conference of the EACL*, Budapest.

Deléger L, Merkel M, Zweigenbaum P. 2006. Enriching Medical Terminologies: an Approach Based on Aligned Corpora. In the *Proceedings 20th International Congress of the European Federation for Medical Informatics (MIE 2006)*.

Dice, L R. 1945. Measures of the Amount of Ecologic Association Between Species. *Ecology*, Vol 26, pp 297-302.

Foo J, Merkel M. 2007. Building standardized term banks through automated term extraction and advanced editing tools. To be published in the *Proceedings from the International Conference on Terminology* 2006, November 16-17 Antwerp.

Och F, Ney H. 2003. A Systematic Comparison of Various Statistical Alignment Models, *Computational Linguistics,* vol 29, number 1, pp. 19-51.

Lombard R. 2006. Managing source-language terminology. In K. J. Dunne (ed.), *Perspectives on Localization.* John Benjamins Publishing Company. Amsterdam.

Nyström M, Merkel M, Ahrenberg L, Zweigenbaum P, Petersson H, and Åhlfeldt H. 2006. Creating a medical English-Swedish dictionary using interactive word alignment. In *BMC Medical Informatics and Decision Making 2006,* 6:35.

Pazienza M. T, Pennacchiotti M, Zanzotto F M. 2005. Terminology extraction: an analysis of linguistic and statistical approaches. In: S. Sirmakessis (ed.) *Knowledge Mining.* Series: Studies in Fuzziness and Soft Computing, Vol.185, Springer Verlag.

Tapanainen P and Järvinen T. 1997. A non-projective dependency parser. In *Proceedings of the 5th Conference on Applied Natural Language Processing: 31 March-3 April 1997; Washington D.C* , pp. 64-71.

Tiedemann J. 2003. Combining clues for word alignment. In *Proceedings of the 10th Conference of the EACL*, Budapest

Wright, S. E. 2006. *The role of terminology management in Localization.* Teminology seminar given on Internet (webinar), SDL, May 20, 2006.

Representing Calendar Expressions with Finite-State Transducers that Bracket Periods of Time on a Hierarchical Timeline

Jyrki Niemi and **Kimmo Koskenniemi**
University of Helsinki,
Department of General Linguistics,
PO Box 9, FI–00014 University of Helsinki, Finland
`{jyrki.niemi, kimmo.koskenniemi}@helsinki.fi`

Abstract

This paper proposes representing the semantics of natural-language calendar expressions as a sequence of compositions of finite-state transducers (FSTs) that bracket the denoted periods of time on a finite timeline of nested calendar periods. In addition to simple dates and times of the day, the approach covers more complex calendar expressions. The paper illustrates the model by walking through the representation of the calendar expression *January to March and May 2007*. The representation of the expressions considered is compositional with reference to their subexpressions. The paper also outlines possible applications of the model, based on finding the common periods of time denoted by two calendar expressions.

1 Introduction

Temporal information is essential in various applications, for example, in event calendars and appointment scheduling. A common class of temporal information are calendar expressions, which range from simple dates and times of the day to more complex ones, such as *the second Tuesday following Easter*. In applications, calendar expressions and other temporal information should often be both processed by software and presented for a human to read.

Numerous approaches and models have been developed to represent and process temporal information in various fields, from temporal databases to natural-language processing. Temporal information often contains cycles and repetition, such as the cycle of hours within a day. A natural means to process cyclical structures could be provided by finite-state methods. These methods have a sound theoretical basis, and they are easier to control than ad hoc methods. Finite-state transition networks may also provide a usable representation for sparse sets of sets. Despite these advantages, explicitly finite-state methods and representations seem to have been relatively little used in temporal representation and reasoning. (However, see Sect. 4 for previous work.) Although these methods indeed have their limitations, in particular their restricted numerical calculation ability, we believe that they would suit well to representing and processing various kinds of temporal information.

In this paper, we use finite-state transducers (FSTs) in representing the semantics of calendar expressions and in finding the common periods of time denoted by two or more calendar expressions. We start from the (intensional) meaning of a natural-language calendar expression; we do not treat the extraction of the meaning from the original expression. We use FSTs to mark the denotations of calendar expressions with brackets on a timeline string. Thus we call the representation presented here the bracketing FST model. We also use the composition operation of FSTs both to construct more complex expressions from simple ones in a compositional way, and to find the common periods of time denoted by several expressions.

Some aspects of the present bracketing FST model are based our earlier model presented in

Joakim Nivre, Heiki-Jaan Kaalep, Kadri Muischnek and Mare Koit (Eds.)
NODALIDA 2007 Conference Proceedings, pp. 355–362

Niemi et al. (2006). That temporal model and representation of calendar expressions was based on a string of hierarchical calendar periods, expanded to finer ones by FSTs as needed. Although the approach seemed to promise to make reasoning tractable, it was non-compositional and rather procedural. In that respect, we regard the present model as a marked improvement.

The rest of the paper is organized as follows. Section 2 presents the basic principles of the bracketing FST model and illustrates them with examples. Section 3 describes some possibilities of simple temporal reasoning using the model in such applications as event calendars and appointment scheduling. Section 4 presents some related work in temporal representation and reasoning research. Section 5 concludes the paper with discussion and some directions for further research.

2 Calendar Expressions in Bracketing FST Model

In this section, we present the basic principles of the bracketing FST model. We illustrate the principles primarily with the representation of a fairly simple calendar expression, *January to March and May 2007*. The expression contains four basic calendar expressions corresponding to specific calendar periods of the Gregorian calendar, combined with an interval, a list and a refinement. Before the example, we briefly discuss the levels of representation of calendar expressions.

2.1 Calendar Expressions and their Levels of Representation

A calendar expression generally denotes a period of time that does not depend on the time of use of the expression, such as *25 May 2007*. However, the denotation may be vague or underspecified without context, as in *September* or *in the morning*. The denotation may also be ambiguous; for example, *a week* may denote either a calendar period or a duration. In this paper, we model the disambiguated meanings of natural-language calendar expressions, while trying to retain underspecification wherever possible.

A calendar expression can denote disconnected periods (non-convex intervals) of time, as well as connected ones. For example, *two Sundays* denotes a period consisting of two Sundays without the intervening days.

Calendar expressions can be represented at several different levels. We distinguish between the following levels of representation: (1) a natural-language calendar expression: *January to March 2007*; (2) a semi-formalized term representation of its semantics: intersect(interval(mon(jan), mon(mar)), year(y2007)); (3) the representation of this as a regular (relation) expression or a sequence of compositions of them; (4) the FST constructed from the regular expression; and (5) the string or set of strings specified by the FST composed with a string representing a timeline. In this paper, we present natural-language expressions, regular expressions at the level of macros and composed timeline strings. The parametrized regular relation macros can be regarded as the basic building blocks of calendar expression FSTs.

Our work does not cover the conversion of a natural-language calendar expression to the term representation. Instead, we assume the semantic term representation as a starting point. The semantic representation is then converted into a regular expression, which is further compiled into an FST.

The term representation is similar to the calendar XREs (extended regular expressions) of Niemi and Carlson (2006) in that they are structurally fairly close to natural language calendar expressions. Thus it should be relatively simple to generate a natural-language calendar expression from the term representation. It should also be possible to parse a natural-language calendar expression to a term representation.

2.2 FST Expressions and Macros

We represent the denotation of the example expression *January to March and May 2007* as the complex term intersect(union(interval(mon(jan), mon(mar)), mon(may)), year(y2007)). This in turn translates to the following sequence of compositions of FSTs. (The parameters i*n* refer to marker bracket indices, explained below.)

$$mon(\text{Jan}, \text{i1}) \circ mon(\text{Mar}, \text{i2})$$
$$\circ\, interval(\text{i1}, \text{i2}, \text{i3})$$
$$\circ\, mon(\text{May}, \text{i4}) \circ union(\text{i3}, \text{i4}, \text{i5})$$
$$\circ\, year(\text{y2007}, \text{i6}) \circ intersect(\text{i5}, \text{i6}, \text{i7})$$

Remarkably, this composition sequence corresponds directly to a postfix representation of the term expression.

The denotation of a calendar expression is represented by indexed marker brackets that delimit the denoted periods on a timeline. Marker brackets are added by FSTs corresponding to either basic calendar expressions or operations combining simpler expressions to more complex ones. Basic expression FSTs add new marker brackets to each calendar period denoted by the expression, whereas operation FSTs add brackets based on their operands that are denoted by previously added brackets. A composite expression is represented as a sequence of compositions of such FSTs.

We present FSTs at the level of simple parametrized macros, as above. For example, the FST constructed from *mon*(Jan, i1) marks each January with the marker brackets i1, whereas *intersect*(i5, i6, i7) marks with the marker brackets i7 the periods of time that are inside both marker brackets i5 and i6. More generally, each operation FST macro takes as its arguments marker bracket indices corresponding to the subexpressions of a calendar expression.[1] The last argument of each macro indicates the marker bracket index with which the FST marks the result of the operation.

The representation of a calendar expression is compositional as each operation operates on the indicated periods marked on the timeline and marks its own denotation on the timeline.

2.3 The Representation of a Timeline

To illustrate the representation of a calendar expression, we need a timeline on which to mark the denotation of the expression. We use a simplified timeline consisting solely of the year 2007 at the level of months. We begin with the following timeline without marker brackets. (We separate the symbols of a string with spaces.)

> [y y2007 [m Jan m] [m Feb m] [m Mar m]
> [m Apr m] [m May m] [m Jun m] ... [m Dec
> m] y]

Largely following Niemi et al. (2006), we represent a finite timeline as a string consisting of hierarchical (nested) markings for different calendar periods. Each calendar period is delimited by granularity-specific begin and end markers: for example, [y marks the beginning of a year and m] marks the end of a month. A begin marker is followed by a symbol indicating a specific period, such as y2007 for the year 2007 and Jan for a January. A day is marked for both the day of the month and the day of the week. The period indicator may be followed by a sequence of markers for a finer granularity.

A timeline string can be constructed by a sequence of compositions of FSTs that expand the timeline a granularity at a time to finer granularities, for example, a year to contain months.[2] Granularities need not be strictly nested, which allows the representation of weeks. The level of detail in a timeline can vary: for example, if hours are not referred to in the expression, they are not needed in the timeline.

A calendar expression is represented on a timeline by enclosing the denoted periods of time in marker brackets which have an index corresponding to the expression: {in ... }in. The indices distinguish between the denotations of different subexpressions in a composite expression.

2.4 Basic Calendar Expressions

Basic calendar expressions correspond to the basic periods of the Gregorian calendar. Basic calendar periods include both generic periods, such as hour, day, month and year, and specific ones, such as each hour, day of the week, day of the month, month and year. We also assume expressions for seasons and holidays, such as Easter and Christmas Day.

A basic calendar expression such as *January* is represented as an FST that adds marker brackets on the timeline around each period denoted by the expression.[3] In the present example (see Sect. 2.2), the first FST *mon*(Jan, i1) adds marker brackets i1 around each month identified by the symbol Jan,

---

[1] Macros may also have integer arguments.

[2] To be able to expand the months of a year and the days of a month independently of the neighbouring periods, each year contains symbols indicating its leap-year status and the day of the week of its first day, and each month, the number of its days and the day of the week of its first day. However, for clarity, we omit this information in the examples of this paper.

[3] Although unqualified natural-language calendar expressions, such *January*, typically refer to the nearest past or future period relevant in the context, in this work we interpret them as underspecified, for example, referring to any January.

that is, each January: {i1 [m Jan ... m] }i1. Similarly, *mon*(Mar, i2) adds i2 around each March. The timeline is now as follows. (Boldface indicates brackets added at this stage.)

> [y y2007 **{i1** [m Jan m] **}i1** [m Feb m] **{i2** [m Mar m] **}i2** [m Apr m] [m May m] ... [m Dec m] y]

Basic calendar expressions form the basis for more complex expressions. The complex example expression *January to March and May 2007* contains three basic constructs used to combine calendar expressions: an interval, a list and a refinement. We treat each of them in the following subsections.

2.5 Interval

In the example, the subexpression *January to March* denotes an interval which begins from the beginning of a January and ends at the end of the closest following March. The January and March marked above are combined to the interval by the FST *interval*(i1, i2, i3), which marks with i3 the intervals beginning from i1 and ending to i2:

> [y y2007 **{i3** {i1 [m Jan m] }i1 [m Feb m] {i2 [m Mar m] }i2 **}i3** [m Apr m] [m May m] ... [m Dec m] y]

In general, an interval FST adds a begin marker bracket for the result at the beginning of each begin period of the interval and an end marker bracket at the end of the closest following end period.

2.6 List

The next step is to combine the interval *January to March* with *May* to a list representing *January to March and May*. We treat all list expressions as disjunctive; for example, *January and May* is interpreted as "any January or May".

In the example, the FST *mon*(May, i4) marks May with i4, and *union*(i3, i4, i5) adds i5 around the periods marked with i3 or i4 or both:

> [y y2007 **{i5** {i3 {i1 [m Jan m] }i1 [m Feb m] {i2 [m Mar m] }i2 }i3 **}i5** [m Apr m] **{i5** {i4 [m May m] }i4 **}i5** ... [m Dec m] y]

More generally, we represent a list as the union (disjunction) of its elements. A (binary) union FST adds result marker brackets around the periods covered by at least one of the operands.

2.7 Refinement

Finally, we combine the previous subexpression with the year 2007 to the final expression *January to March and May 2007*. We call this construct a refinement, following Niemi et al. (2006), as each of the subexpressions refines or restricts the denoted period of time. We implement refinement as an intersection (conjunction). In the example, the FST *year*(y2007, i6) marks the year 2007 with i6, and *intersect*(i5, i6, i7) marks the denotation of the final expression with i7:

> **{i6** [y y2007 **{i7** {i5 {i3 {i1 [m Jan m] }i1 [m Feb m] {i2 [m Mar m] }i2 }i3 }i5 **}i7** [m Apr m] **{i7** {i5 {i4 [m May m] }i4 }i5 **}i7** ... [m Dec m] y] **}i6**

An intersection FST adds result marker brackets around periods covered by both the operands.

From this final timeline, we can then remove all other marker brackets except the i7s that mark the denotation of the whole expression:

> [y y2007 {i7 [m Jan m] [m Feb m] [m Mar m] }i7 [m Apr m] {i7 [m May m] }i7 ... [m Dec m] y]

We now take a brief look inside an FST expression, followed by an outline of the representation of a few other calendar expression constructs and discussion about the interpretation of calendar expressions.

2.8 The Implementation of an FST Expression

The FST expressions used above in representing calendar expressions are rather abstract in that they use macros which correspond to parametrized regular relation expressions. For example, the following macro implements the union operation:

$$union(i, j, r) =$$
$$noijrs$$
$$. (\varepsilon{:}\{r . (\{i \cup \{j)$$
$$. (noijrs \cup ((\{i \cup \{j) . noijrs . (\}i \cup \}j)))^*$$
$$. (\}i \cup \}j) . \varepsilon{:}\}r . noijrs)^*$$

Here *noijrs* is an abbreviation of the expression $(\sim(\{i \cup \}i \cup \{j \cup \}j \cup \{r \cup \}r))^*$, ε denotes the empty string, $A{:}B$ the transduction from symbol A to B, $A . B$ the concatenation of A and B, and $\sim\!A$ the symbols of the alphabet excluding those in A.

In effect, the expression inserts the marker brackets {r...}r around each brackets {i...}i or {j...}j, which may contain or overlap with one or more instances of the other pair of marker brackets. The definition assumes that marker brackets with a certain index appear neither nested nor overlapping with themselves. Moreover, this slightly simplified version does not consider the special cases that may occur at the beginning or the end of the timeline, such as an end marker bracket not preceded by a corresponding begin marker bracket.

2.9 Other Calendar Expression Constructs

In addition to intervals, lists and refinement expressions, it is relatively straightforward to represent in the bracketing FST model also various more complex types of calendar expressions. They include constructs presented in Niemi et al. (2006): exception expressions (*8 am, except Mondays 9 am*), various kinds of anchored expressions (*the second Tuesday following Easter*) and consecutiveness expressions (*two consecutive Sundays*). Furthermore, the model can represent a number of deictic and anaphoric temporal expressions. In this subsection, we outline the representation of these types of expressions. In several examples below, we present the corresponding term representation instead of or in addition to the FST macro representation.

The expression *8 am, except Mondays 9 am* (except(h08, mon, h09)) is an exception expression. Such an expression consists of two or three parts: a default time, an exception scope and an optional exception time. In the above expression, *8 am* is the default time (*dt* below), *Mondays* the exception scope (*es*) and *9 am* the exception time (*et*). Following Carlson (2003), we express the denotation of an exception expression with union, difference and intersection as $(dt \setminus es) \cup (es \cap et)$. The union and intersection operations are described above, and the difference $dt \setminus es$ corresponds to $dt \cap \neg es$. The complement $\neg es$ is in turn implemented by the macro *complement*(i, r), which precedes each $\{i$ with a $\}r$ and follows each $\}i$ with a $\{r$. For example, the timeline with marker brackets $\ldots \{i \ldots \}i \ldots \{i \ldots \}i \ldots$ becomes $\{r \ldots \}r \{i \ldots \}i \{r \ldots \}r \{i \ldots \}i \{r \ldots \}r$.

An anchored expression denotes a time relative to an anchor time. For example, *the second Tuesday following Easter* (nth_following(2, tue, easter)) refers to a time relative to Easter. To obtain the denotation of the expression, FSTs first

mark each Tuesday and Easter with the respective marker brackets (*wday*(Tue, i1) ∘ *easter*(i2)). The FST *nth_following*(2, i1, i2, i3) then inserts result marker brackets i3 around each Tuesday that is preceded by Easter, with exactly one Tuesday in between. This condition is fairly simple to express in regular relation expressions.[4]

The consecutiveness expression *two consecutive Sundays* (consecutive_n(2, sun)) differs from the other constructs above in that it represents a set of disconnected periods of time, and thus it should be interpreted disjunctively (see Sect. 2.10 below). However, it is simple to implement as an FST that marks any two Sundays with no Sundays in between them and leaves the rest of the timeline intact.

Among other calendar expression constructs that we have represented in the model are parity expressions (*even Tuesdays of the month*), ordinal expressions (*every second Monday of the year*) and containment expressions (*the months with a Friday 13th*). These expressions can be represented in a manner fairly similar to anchored expressions.

The present model can also be extended fairly straightforwardly to simple deictic and anaphoric temporal expressions, such as *today* and *the following month*. Similarly to Carlson (2003), we define FSTs that mark speech time and the reference time of an anaphoric expression: *now*(i) and *then*(i), respectively. With their help, we can represent *today* as containing(day, now) (the day containing the speech time) and *the following month* as following_nth(1, month, then) (the first calendar month following the reference time).

2.10 Conjunctive and Disjunctive Interpretations

Many calendar expressions can be interpreted either conjunctively or disjunctively. For example, *Monday and Thursday* might denote either "a (certain) Monday and a (certain) Thursday" or "any Monday or Thursday", depending on the point of view. The conjunctive interpretation would be feasible for someone who provides a service on the days in question, and the disjunctive one for a client.

---

[4]The first argument of the macro *nth_following* is an integer *n*. In the macro definition it translates to the concatenation power R^{n-1}, where R is the part of the regular expression to be repeated $n - 1$ times.

In the present work, we generally represent the denotation of a calendar expression conjunctively, on a single timeline string, whenever possible. Effectively, the denotation of *Monday and Thursday* is a single disconnected period of time that comprises all Mondays and Thursdays.

However, a purely conjunctive representation would provide an incorrect representation for some types of expressions. In particular, we need to represent disjunctively expressions denoting multiple separate disconnected periods of time and expressions with several possible overlapping denotations. Both of these properties are true of the expression *(any) two Sundays*, for example: if all the possible combinations of two Sundays were represented on a single timeline, it would in effect denote all Sundays. Instead, each possible combination of two Sundays is represented on its own timeline. This set of timelines is represented as an FST with many possible paths, each corresponding to a single timeline.

3   Temporal Reasoning Applications

The bracketing FST model could be used in temporal reasoning. We have mainly considered a form of reasoning that finds the common periods of time denoted by two calendar expressions. Such reasoning could be used, for instance, in querying an event database or in appointment scheduling.

A query to an event database could find out, for example, at what time certain museums are open on Fridays in May, or which museums are open on Fridays in May. For both queries, we should compute the common periods of time denoted by both the query and the target expression. The answer to the first query would be a representation of the common periods, and to the second one, the existence or non-existence of common periods. In our model, we would mark the denotations of both expressions on the same timeline and compute their intersection using the same operation as for a refinement within a single expression.

Although this kind of reasoning might not be efficient enough for large-scale on-line processing, it might be of use in an application in which some information is generated periodically from a database, such as a Web page showing events of the week. Such an application would also need a generation component that would generate from the term representation the corresponding natural-language calendar expressions, possibly in multiple languages, along the lines of Niemi and Carlson (2006).

In appointment scheduling we should find the common free periods of time in the calendars of two or more people or institutions. In addition, the appointment may have further constraints, such as *at least six hours without interruptions*. Finding common periods of time with intersection could be applied to appointment scheduling as well.

4   Related Work

Temporal expressions have been widely researched, including modelling and reasoning with calendar expressions. However, finite-state methods have seldom been used explicitly. In the following, we very briefly relate our work to a few other pieces of work in this area.

Our original inspiration was Carlson's (2003) event calculus, which includes modelling calendar expressions as extended regular expressions (XREs). In Niemi and Carlson (2006) we represented a number of calendar expression constructs as XREs; however, the approach generally appeared computationally intractable.

The Verbmobil project (Wahlster, 2000) had its own formalism to represent and reason with temporal expressions in appointment negotiation dialogues (Endriss, 1998). Its coverage of calendar expressions was similar to our present approach.

The calendar logic of Ohlbach and Gabbay (1998) and its time term specification language can represent calendar expressions of various kinds. However, compared to our term representation, the structure of calendar logic expressions differs significantly more from that of natural-language calendar expressions.

Han and Lavie (2004) and Han et al. (2006) use their own formalism in conjunction with reasoning using temporal constraint propagation. They cover more types of expressions than we do, including durations and underspecified and quantified expressions, such as *every week in May*.

TimeML (Boguraev et al., 2005) is a markup language for marking events and temporal expressions and their relationships in a text. Compared to our present approach, TimeML covers many more kinds of temporal expressions, such as temporal relations, durations and underspecification. However, as Han et al. (2006) point out, in many cases TimeML expresses only the denotation of the expression, such as a certain date, whereas our bracketing FST expressions, as well as and the TCNL representation of Han et al. (2006), represent the intensional meaning of a calendar expression. Moreover, it is unclear how TimeML would suit to the kind of reasoning that we have considered.

Finite-state methods have been explicitly used by a few people to represent or reason with temporal information, but the scope of their work is otherwise mostly rather different from that of ours. Karttunen et al. (1996) express the syntax of fairly simple dates as regular expressions to check their validity. Fernando (2004) uses regular expressions to represent events with optional temporal information, such as *(for) an hour*. Focusing on events, his examples contain only rather simple temporal expressions. Finally, Dal Lago and Montanari (2001) and Bresolin et al. (2004) present automata models that are suitable in particular for representing infinite granularities. Their models are based on Büchi automata.

5 Discussion and Further Work

In the following, we discuss some advantages and disadvantages of the bracketing FST model of calendar expressions presented in this paper. We also mention some directions for further research.

Compared our earlier FST-based temporal model (Niemi et al., 2006), the bracketing FST model is clearly more compositional and less procedural but less efficient in at least some aspects. For instance, it is an open question if it is possible to compute the denotation of an expression a granularity level at a time, or to expand on the timeline only the periods of time relevant to the expression, as in the earlier model. We thus use a pre-expanded timeline, which may be rather long in practical applications.

The FST compositions for calendar expressions can quickly result in very large automata unless we begin the composition sequence from the timeline. In some applications it might nevertheless be useful to combine the expression FSTs before composing them with a timeline, so we also intend to investi-

gate other options for keeping the size of the FSTs manageable even for complex expressions.

Since we use a different marker bracket index for each subexpression, the number of different marker bracket symbols is proportional to the number of nodes in the expression tree of a term expression. This number may be fairly large for complex calendar expressions. An alternative could be to reduce the number of indices by reusing them; for example, an operation could use the brackets of one of its operands to mark the result. However, we probably should preserve the indices of reoccurring subexpressions to avoid having to recompute them.

We found it relatively easy to build FST expressions for the various calendar expression constructs, even though it might be partly explained by the fact that only few special cases were treated. To widen the coverage, we intend to try to represent in the bracketing FST model all the calendar expression constructs mentioned in Niemi and Carlson (2006), and relevant ones probably also from Endriss (1998) and Han and Lavie (2004). We should also test the scalability of the representation to longer and more complex calendar expressions.

Duration expressions are an area still to be investigated in the bracketing FST model, although they can be represented with finite-state methods, as seen in Niemi and Carlson (2006). The representation of durations in general may be intractable, since a disconnected duration, such as in *40 hours a week*, might be composed of an arbitrary number of arbitrarily short periods of time. However, a tractable subset should suffice in a practical application.

Even though finite-state methods can be used to represent many different types of calendar expression constructs, they are unable naturally to represent fuzzy or inexact expressions, such as *about 8 o'clock*, internally anaphoric expressions, such as *9.00 to 17.00, an hour later in winter*, fractional expressions, such as *the second quarter of the year*, or arbitrary repetition expressions, such as *two equally long periods of time*. However, it might be possible to compile at least some expressions of some of these types to a finite-state representation.

Furthermore, there are types of temporal expressions that we have not yet considered but that probably can be represented with finite-state methods. For example, one might want to find in an event database the days on which one could take a boat cruise followed by one to two hours before a theatre play.

We have used the Xerox Finite-State Tool (XFST) (Karttunen et al., 1997) as the main tool for experimenting with regular relation (FST) expressions. However, it would be essential to develop an accompanying compiler to compile term representations of calendar expressions into compositions of FST expressions, instead of translating them by hand.

In summary, although several issues should be investigated and solved before the bracketing FST model could be useful in a practical application. we find it more promising in many respects than that of Niemi et al. (2006). In general, we consider finite-state approaches fairly well suited to modelling the semantics of calendar expressions.

Acknowledgements

This paper represents independent work by the junior author based on the suggestions of the senior author. We are grateful to the anonymous reviewers for their valuable comments. We are also grateful to Nathan Vaillette (personal communication) for his original suggestion to use finite-state transducers in representing calendar expressions.

References

Branimir Boguraev, Jose Castaño, Rob Gaizauskas, Bob Ingria, Graham Katz, Bob Knippen, Jessica Littman, Inderjeet Mani, James Pustejovsky, Antonio Sanfilippo, Andrew See, Andrea Setzer, Roser Saurí, Amber Stubbs, Beth Sundheim, Svetlana Symonenko, and Marc Verhagen. 2005. TimeML: A formal specification language for events and temporal expressions. http://timeml.org/site/publications/timeMLdocs/timeml_1.2.1.html, October.

Davide Bresolin, Angelo Montanari, and Gabriele Puppis. 2004. Time granularities and ultimately periodic automata. In José Júlio Alferes and João Leite, editors, *Logics in Artificial Intelligence: 9th European Conference, JELIA 2004, Lisbon, Portugal, September 27–30, 2004, Proceedings*, number 3229 in Lecture Notes in Computer Science, pages 513–525, Heidelberg, September. Springer-Verlag.

Lauri Carlson. 2003. Tense, mood, aspect, diathesis: Their logic and typology. Unpublished manuscript, February.

Ugo Dal Lago and Angelo Montanari. 2001. Calendars, time granularities, and automata. In Christian S. Jensen, Markus Schneider, Bernhard Seeger, and Vassilis J. Tsotras, editors, *Advances in Spatial and Temporal Databases: 7th International Symposium, SSTD 2001, Redondo Beach, CA, USA, July 12–15, 2001, Proceedings*, number 2121 in Lecture Notes in Computer Science, pages 279–298, Heidelberg, July. Springer-Verlag.

Ulrich Endriss. 1998. Semantik zeitlicher Ausdrücke in Terminvereinbarungsdialogen. Verbmobil Report 227, Technische Universität Berlin, Fachbereich Informatik, Berlin, August.

Tim Fernando. 2004. A finite-state approach to events in natural language semantics. *Journal of Logic and Computation*, 14(1):79–92.

Benjamin Han and Alon Lavie. 2004. A framework for resolution of time in natural language. *ACM Transactions on Asian Language Information Processing (TALIP)*, 3(1):11–32, March.

Benjamin Han, Donna Gates, and Lori Levin. 2006. From language to time: A temporal expression anchorer. In James Pustejovsky and Peter Revesz, editors, *Proceedings of the Thirteenth International Symposium on Temporal Representation and Reasoning (TIME'06)*, pages 196–203. IEEE Computer Society.

L[auri] Karttunen, J[ean]-P[ierre] Chanod, G[regory] Grefenstette, and A[nne] Schiller. 1996. Regular expressions for language engineering. *Natural Language Engineering*, 2(4):305–328, December.

Lauri Karttunen, Tamás Gaál, and André Kempe. 1997. Xerox finite-state tool. Technical report, Xerox Research Centre Europe, Grenoble, France, June. http://www.xrce.xerox.com/ competencies/content-analysis/fssoft/docs/fst-97/xfst97.html.

Jyrki Niemi and Lauri Carlson. 2006. Modelling the semantics of calendar expressions as extended regular expressions. In Anssi Yli-Jyrä, Lauri Karttunen, and Juhani Karhumäki, editors, *Proceedings of the FSMNLP 2005*, number 4002 in Lecture Notes in Artificial Intelligence, pages 179–190. Springer.

Jyrki Niemi, Kimmo Koskenniemi, and Lauri Carlson. 2006. Finite-state transducers and a variable-granularity timeline in modelling the semantics of calendar expressions. In Hans W. Guesgen, Gérard Ligozat, Jochen Renz, and Rita V. Rodriguez, editors, *ECAI 2006 Workshop. Spatial and Temporal Reasoning*, pages 56–62, August.

Hans Jürgen Ohlbach and Dov Gabbay. 1998. Calendar logic. *Journal of Applied Non-classical Logics*, 8(4):291–324.

Wolfgang Wahlster, editor. 2000. *Verbmobil: Foundations of Speech-to-Speech Translation*. Artificial Intelligence. Springer, Berlin.

Parsing Manually Detected and Normalized Disfluencies

in Spoken Estonian

Helen Nigol
University of Tartu
`helen.nigol@ut.ee`

Abstract

An experiment with an Estonian Constraint Grammar based syntactic analyzer is conducted, analyzing transcribed speech. In this paper the problems encountered during parsing disfluencies are analyzed. In addition, the amount by which the manual normalization of disfluencies improved the results of recall and precision was compared to non-normalized utterances.

1 Introduction

Müürisep and Uibo (2006) have made the first attempt at analyzing spoken Estonian via adapting the existing Constraint Grammar based syntactic analyzer for written Estonian. Based on a 2543-word corpus of spoken Estonian, the achieved recall rate was 97.3% and precision 89.2%. Results were surprisingly good, but there is room for some improvement. They were focusing on the problems of parsing incomplete and elliptical sentences as well as problems in finding clause boundaries. In this experiment we investigate how the parser copes with analyzing disfluencies, which adds further difficulty to the task of parsing spoken language. In this paper we will concentrate on certain types of disfluencies: repairs and false starts. Under repairs, we distinguish word fragments and substitutions, wherein the speaker corrects or alters the utterance. A false start is where speaker abandons the utterance entirely and starts over. All the instances were manually annotated and some

words normalized, i.e. ungrammatical utterances were made grammatical.

Disfluencies have been annotated in several corpora of spoken English; the most well-known is the Switchboard Corpus (Meteer et al, 1995). There are also several studies where the detection and correction of disfluencies have been made automatically. E.g. meta-rules (Hindle, 1983; McKelvie, 1998), a statistical approach (Stolcke and Shriberg, 1996), triggers as indicators of repair (Spilker et al, 2000) and prosodic-acoustic cues (Nakatani and Hirschberg, 1993) are used for the detection of disfluencies; for normalization, pattern-matching (Bear et al, 1992; Heeman and Allen, 1994; Kurdi, 2002) is applied; it may also be handled as a machine translation task (Spilker et al, 2000). As the disfluencies are such a heterogenous class of linguistic events, maximum results may only be achieved through combining different methods. So far the best results have been attained when some amount of manual annotation prior to automatic analysis is conducted.

This paper is structured as follows: firstly, the compiled subcorpus is introduced, and the annotation of disfluencies is defined. In section 3, an overview of the parser and the prework for the analysis is given. In section 4, the results of a test run with the Estonian constraint-based parser are presented.

2 Corpus and annotation

Detecting and normalizing disfluencies is a complex task. Classically, the disfluent unit is divided into four: reparandum, interruption point, editing phase, and repair. There are very obvious cases

Joakim Nivre, Heiki-Jaan Kaalep, Kadri Muischnek and Mare Koit (Eds.)
NODALIDA 2007 Conference Proceedings, pp. 363–366

where it is very easy to decide what has been replaced, deleted or added, but there are also very vague cases. During the annotation the annotator detects the extent of the disfluency and annotates the reparandum and repair, as well as the editing phase. The *Disfluency annotation stylebook for the Switchboard corpus* has been used as the model for the annotation of disfluency in spoken Estonian. The tags used in the annotation of spoken Estonian are presented in Table 1. The abbreviations *RP*, *D*, *F*, and *X* specify the content of the brackets, i.e. whether the subject is a repair, particle, filled pause, or non-analyzable unit. A false start is marked with '+/'. As a result of annotation, after the removal of the reparandum and the editing phase (consisting of particle or filled pause), the result should be a syntactically well-formed utterance.

DF class	Tag
Repair	[RP...+...]
Particle	{D...}
Filled pause	{F...}
False start	+/
Non-analyzable unit	{X...}

Table 1. The tags used in annotation of spoken Estonian.

The annotation scheme was applied on an information dialogue subcorpus of Estonian, part of the Estonian Dialogue Corpus[1]. 35 randomly selected information dialogues (13 168 words, 1991 utterances) were analyzed. The shortest dialogue consisted of 31 words and the longest of 1962 words. In Table 2, the occurrence of the types of disfluencies is presented.

Disfluencies	Total
Word fragments	53
Substitutions	50
False starts	33
Total	**136**

Table 2. Occurrence of types of disfluencies in corpus.

---

3   Experiment

The experiment was conducted with Estonian constraint-based parser, which was originally designed to analyze written language. The parser gives a shallow surface oriented analysis to a sentence, in which every word is annotated with the tag corresponding to its syntactic function. For analyzing spoken language, two additional tags were adapted: @B – particle; @T – unknown syntactic function. In the adapting process, clause boundary detection rules as well as some syntactic constraints were changed. The process of syntactic analysis consists of three stages: morphological disambiguation, identification of clause boundaries, and identification of the syntactic functions of words. The syntax used in CG is word based, i.e. no hierarchical phrase structure is constructed. (Müürisep and Uibo, 2006)

All utterances containing word fragments, substitutions and/or false starts were analyzed twice. The first run parsed the corpus in its original form; the second run parsed the same corpus after its normalization. The original utterance was retained in the corpus, but the input to the parser did not include the disfluencies. As the analysis of disfluencies is in the preliminary stage and the syntactic analyzer does not count the tags used in annotation, the reparandum and editing phase were manually removed to get the normalized utterances. The corpus of original utterances contained 4701 words and the corpus of normalized utterances 3864 words; thus, 837 words were removed by normalization.

When analyzing the original utterances, it was assumed that mistakes occurring during analysis would be related to the disfluencies, as all utterances contained one of the disfluencies. For normalized utterances the assumption was that as the obvious reasons of mistakes had been removed, the occurred mistakes would be caused by other things, e.g. an incorrect clause boundary detection causing the wrong analysis of a whole utterance. Thus, the encountered mistakes in the original and normalized utterances are not analyzed in further detail. However, the achieved recall (the ratio of number of correct assigned syntactic tags to the number of all correct tags) and precision (the ratio of number of correct assigned syntactic tags to the number of all assigned syntactic tags) of repairs and false starts is compared and the main problems encountered in parsing word fragments, substitutions and false starts are discussed.

4 Results and analysis

In this section, the problems encountered during parsing the three types of disfluencies are analyzed, as well as the amount by which the manual normalization of disfluencies improved the results. The results of the experiment are given in Table 3. As the morphological disambiguation was made manually, the statistics show only the problems of syntax.

	Repairs		False starts	
	Original	Norma-lized	Original	Norma-lized
Recall	94.4%	96.2%	97.4%	98.9%
Preci-sion	84.6%	87.3%	90.0%	93.8%

Table 3. Results of the experiment.

The results showed significant improvement. For repairs, the recall rate rose 1.8% and precision 2.7%. For false starts, recall rate rose 1.5% and precision 3.8%.

4.1 Word fragments

In the majority of the cases the analysis of word fragments did not present a problem, as long as the word in question was changed into another.

Original utterance

sööke	# food
söök+e //_S_// @SUBJ	
nende	# these / pl gen
see+de //_P_// @NN>	
hin-	# pri-
hin+0 //_T_// @T	
selle	# this / sg gen
see+0 //_P_// @NN>	
hinna	# price
hind+0 //_S_// @P>	
sees	# in
sees+0 //_K_// @ADVL	
ei	# is not
ei+0 //_V_// @NEG	
ole	# included
ole+0 //_V_// @+FMV	

Example 1. sööke **[RP** nende hin- + selle hinna**]** sees ei ole ('food is not included in price').

The problems were in analyzing phrases that contained a disfluent element. In this case the word fragment is automatically assigned with the tag @T, but the other element of the phrase is analyzed as if it still were part of the utterance, although it is not, e.g. Example 1.

The reparandum in Example 1 is 'nende hin-' and the speaker has corrected it to 'selle hinna'. But from this analysis it is possible to determine that the word 'hinna' has two attributes, 'nende' and 'selle'. The analysis will be adequate assuming the whole phrase is assigned with the tag @T or is somehow otherwise marked. But as was mentioned earlier, the Constraint Grammar syntactic analyzer is word-based; no phrase structure is constructed.

4.2 Substitutions

Substitutions are more complex to detect and normalize than the word fragments. The syntactic analyzer examines the utterance from left to right, i.e. from the beginning of utterance, but in a disfluent utterance the repair is always situated at the end of the utterance. This proves the need for normalization as a preprocessing task as long as the constraint-based syntactic analyzer is being used. Example 2 shows what happens when the reparandum is part of the utterance.

Original utterance

erinevatel	
erinev+tel //_A_// @AN>	# different / pl ade
päevadel	
päev+del //_S_// @ADVL	# day / pl ade
on	
ole+0 //_V_// @+FMV	# is
võimalik	
võimalik+0 //_A_// @AN>	# possible
sis	
sis+0 //_D_// @ADVL	# then
mägi	
mägi+0 //_S_// @SUBJ	# mountain / sg nom
mäge	
mägi+0 //_S_// @OBJ	# mountain / sg part
valida	
vali+da //_V_// @-FMV @<INF_N @ADVL	# to choose

Example 2. erinevatel päevadel on võimalik sis [RP mägi + mäge] valida ('every day you may choose a new mountain').

The word 'mägi' evoked that the adjective 'võimalik' is analyzed as an attribute and the verb 'valida' had three different tags: non-finite main verb, infinitive as a modifier and adverbial. The correct parse would have been that 'võimalik' is predicative and 'valida' a subject.

4.3 False starts

Müürisep and Uibo (2006) found that false starts are detectable with rules by marking them with clause boundary tags, but this is possible only if there is a verb in the false start phrase. In Example 3 is presented an utterance where the false start does not have a verb. The utterance with the false start has dictated the analysis of the entire utterance, though the real subject is the word 'seda'.

Original utterance

```
kui
    kui+0 //_J_//  @J              # if
ta
    tema+0 //_P_//  @SUBJ          # he/she
seda
    see+da //_P_//  @ADVL @NN>     # this / sg  part
seda
    see+da //_P_//  @PRD @ADVL     # this / sg  part
tükina
    tükk+na //_S_//  @ADVL         # as a single piece
siin
    siin+0 //_D_//  @ADVL          # here
ei
    ei+0 //_V_//  @NEG             # not
ole
    ole+0 //_V_//  @+FMV           # is
```

Example 3. kui ta seda +/ seda tükina siin ei ole ('we don't have it here as a single piece').

5   Conclusion

In this paper we presented how the Constraint Grammar based syntactic analyzer handles the problems of parsing disfluent spoken Estonian and how much the manual normalization of disfluencies improved the results of recall and precision compared to non-normalized utterances. An experiment was conducted. The utterances containing word fragments, substitutions and/or false starts were analyzed twice. The first run parsed the corpus in its original form; the second run parsed the same corpus after its normalization. For repairs the recall rate rose from 94.4% to 96.2% and precision from 84.6% to 87.3%. For false starts recall rose from 97.4% to 98.9% and precision from 90.0% to 93.8%.

The main objective is to identify regularities in different kinds of disfluencies, focusing on repairs and false starts. The future plan is to increase the annotated corpus and to use it as a training corpus to train the parser to automatically detect disfluencies in order to save time in manual annotation.

References

Bear, John, John Dowding, and Elizabeth Shriberg. 1992. Automatic Detection and Correction of Repairs in Human-Computer Dialog. Proceedings of the DARPA Speech and Natural Language Workshop.

Heeman, Peter, and James Allen. 1994. Tagging Speech Repairs. ARPA Workshop on Human Language Technology, pp. 187–192.

Hindle, Donald. 1983. Deterministic Parsing of Syntactic Nonfluencies. Proceedings of the 21st Meeting of the Association of Computational Linguistics.

Kurdi, Mohamed-Zakaria. 2002. Combining pattern matching and shallow parsing techniques for detecting and correcting spoken language extragrammaticalities. 2nd Workshop on Robust Methods in Analysis of Natural Language Data, Italy, pp. 1–9.

McKelvie, David. 1998. The syntax of disfluency in spontaneous spoken language. Technical Report HCRC/RP-95, Edinburgh University, Edinburgh, Scotland.

Meteer, M., A. Taylor, R. MacIntyre, R. Iver. 1995. Dysfluency annotation stylebook for the Switchboard corpus. Distributed by LDC.

Müürisep, Kaili, and Heli Uibo. 2006. Shallow Parsing of Spoken Estonian Using Constraint Grammar. In Proceedings of NODALIDA special session on treebanking (ed. Peter Juel Henrichsen and Peter Rossen Skadhauge). Copenhagen Studies in Language #33/2006.

Nakatani, Christine, Julia Hirschberg. 1993. A Speech-First Model for Repair Detection and Correction. Proceedings of the 31st Annual Meeting on Association for Computational Linguistics, pp. 46–53.

Spilker, Jörg, Martin Klarner, and Günther Görz. 2000. Processing Self-Corrections in a Speech-to-Speech System. W. Wahlster (ed.) *Verbmobil: Foundations of Speech-to-Speech Translation*. Springer, pp. 131–140.

Stolcke, Andreas, and Elizabeth Shriberg. 1996. Statistical Language Modeling for Speech Disfluencies. Proceedings of the International Conference on Audio, Speech and Signal Processing.

Designing a Speech Corpus for Estonian Unit Selection Synthesis

Liisi Piits
Institute of the Estonian Language
Roosikrantsi 6, Tallinn 10119, Estonia
liisi@eki.ee

Meelis Mihkla
Institute of the Estonian Language
Roosikrantsi 6, Tallinn 10119, Estonia
meelis@eki.ee

Tõnis Nurk
Institute of the Estonian Language
Roosikrantsi 6, Tallinn 10119, Estonia
tonis@eki.ee

Indrek Kiissel
Institute of the Estonian Language
Roosikrantsi 6, Tallinn 10119, Estonia
indrek@eki.ee

Abstract

The article reports the development of a speech corpus for Estonian text-to-speech synthesis based on unit selection. Introduced are the principles of the corpus as well as the procedure of its creation, from text compilation to corpus analysis and text recording. Also described are the choices made in the process of producing a text of 400 sentences, the relevant lexical and morphological preferences, and the way to the most natural sentence context for the words used.

1 Introduction

Text-to-speech synthesis means that synthetic speech is automatically generated from a written text. The understandability and naturalness of output speech depends on linguistic preprocessing of the input text, the prosody generator, signal processing and the quality of the speech database used. It has been argued - and proved in practice - that the large number of concatenation points make the synthetic speech sound unnatural, even if the spectral discontinuities have been minimized by carefully smoothing the concatenation points, considering phonetic criteria (Donovan and Woodland 1999). The idea of corpus-based, or unit-selection synthesis is that the corpus is searched for maximally long phonetic strings to match the sounds to be synthesized. As compared to diphone or triphone synthesis, corpus-based speech tends to elicit considerably higher ratings of naturalness in auditory tests (Nagy et al., 2003). As the corpus in

its entirety provides the acoustic basis for such synthesis, the development of an optimal corpus represents an essential task of corpus-based synthesis. A system with a good selection module and a high-quality speech corpus may yield output speech of extremely high quality, even if the signal processing module is rather simple (Bozkurt et al., 2002).

Considering an optimal database for Estonian text-to-speech synthesis it should obviously contain phonetically rich sentences and different phonological structures of Estonian. The corpus words should also include all Estonian diphones. The first database for Estonian speech synthesis consisted of ca 1700 diphones (Mihkla et al., 1998). The experience accumulated during the creation of that database came in handy while developing our corpus. Aim was a speech corpus that would not be too big (up to 60 minutes), yet representative enough from phonetic and phonological aspects, containing many numbers and years, alongside with frequent Estonian words and expressions. Even though a necessity for repeat recordings to complement the corpus cannot be ruled out entirely, material should serve for synthesis of an arbitrary text as well as for limited domain applications.

2 Text corpus development

The first decision to be made concerned the size of the corpus. This meant a compromise between the minimum and maximum sizes. A maximum size would mean a greater probability of the corpus containing the biggest possible units to match the text to be synthesized- from sound strings to words or even phrases. Unfortunately, big databases have

Joakim Nivre, Heiki-Jaan Kaalep, Kadri Muischnek and Mare Koit (Eds.)
NODALIDA 2007 Conference Proceedings, pp. 367–371

been found complicated to maintain and even more complicated to annotate (Breen and Jackson, 1998). Moreover, segmentation and tagging of corpus units is a cumbersome and time-consuming process - it has been found that a one-minute corpus takes 1000 minutes to mark up (Mihkla et al., 1998). This is why we decided to make the corpus as small as possible, yet containing as much relevant material as possible.

2.1 Stage 1: diphones

It was decided that the smallest searchable unit of the corpus would be a diphone. Therefore it was important to ensure that the corpus contains all diphones possible in Estonian. We already had a word list, compiled for an earlier synthesizer based on diphone selection, featuring all diphones occurring in Estonian (Mihkla et al., 1998). Most of those words were taken as the basis for the new corpus. However, as the words had not been included in the list in their natural sentence context, our first task was to provide a sentence context for them.

So, Stage 1 of the corpus development started with combining the list words to make meaningful sentences. During that process one had to keep a watchful eye on the pronounceability of words and sentences, considering sentence length as well as word structure. Both too long and too short sentences were to be avoided. For English sentences it has been argued that too short sentences (less than 5 words) have a deviant prosody, while too long ones (more than 15 words) tend to elicit more mistakes when read out (Kominek and Black, 2003). As Estonian is a more synthetic language than English we did not stick to the five-word limit, ending up at seven words in an average sentence.

Among the sound combinations and syllable types of a natural language there are some that are easy to pronounce and some others that are not. The latter, being more demanding on speech organs, are used less frequently. Such sound sequences and syllable types are called marked ones (Hint, 1998). As the word list was meant to include all diphones possible in Estonian it contained not only frequent words but also the rare words with marked structure. There were even some diphones not allowed by Estonian phonotactics, but they had to be included because of their occurrence in foreign words. In addition, the list contained some nonsense words with sound combinations theoreti-

cally allowed by the rules of Estonian word structure, yet not realized. For example, the diphone *üf* can be found in the 2nd quantity degree, as in the loanword *küfoos* 'kyphosis', but for the 3rd-quantity diphone *üf:* a nonsense word **süf:fi* had to be made up, as the theoretically possible diphone cannot be derived from its 2nd-quantity equivalent. The number of such nonsense strings included in the corpus was 18.

In sentences we generally tried to disperse the words with a marked structure among the unmarked ones. Most of the nonsense strings, however, were given a concentrated presentation in special sentences: e.g. **Puls:s *kõõ:l'is seda *võõ:ba ehk* mõõ:du.*

At the end of Stage 1 the corpus contained 178 sentences, with 1244 words all told.

2.2 Stage 2: words and phrases

While diphone is a minimal unit of the corpus, a word or even a phrase is seen as a unit of maximal length. The aim of stage 2 was to supply sentences containing the most frequent Estonian words and phrases. As the synthesizer is meant for texts without domain limitations the corpus vocabulary was to cover a wide selection of spheres. The words were selected from *Frequency Dictionary of Standard Estonian* (Kaalep and Muischnek, 2002), which is based on texts from media and fiction.

The aim was to make an addition of 1000 most frequent words. Frequency measurement is complicated due to Estonian morphology. The numerous cases of stem alternation and agglutination are the reason why a word may have many forms. A noun, for example, may yield 28 word forms, each of a different grammatical meaning. As generally most of the forms are made up of a word stem and various grammatical morphemes it was found sufficient to include just the stem of a high-frequency word, which could take certain grammatical morphemes also present in the corpus. The word forms contained in the corpus were to cover all paradigms of declinable as well as conjugable words. Also, the formative variants containing different allomorphs were to be represented.

Besides agglutinative formation there was inflection to be reckoned with. In Estonian, meaning can also be conveyed by stem alternation. Gradational words have at least two stem variants, both taking different grammatical markers and endings. Therefore, different stem variants also needed to be included, if at all possible, e.g. **haka**-*ta* 'to begin' and **hakka**-*b* 'begins', **mees** 'man Nom. Sg.' and **mehe** 'man Gen. Sg.', **krooni** 'crown Gen. Sg.' and **kroo:ni** 'crown. Part. Sg'.

Besides grammatical markers and endings the corpus was provided with words containing the most productive derivational suffixes like in: *moodusta**mine*** 'formation', *must**lanna*** 'gypsy woman', *võist**kond*** 'team', *rahandus* 'finance' etc.

The nominative and genitive forms of cardinal and ordinal numerals were also included, and the most frequent place names - not only Estonian ones, but also some foreign toponyms salient in the Estonian cultural context, such as *Soome* 'Finland', *Rootsi* 'Sweden', *Venemaa* 'Russia', *Läti* 'Latvia', *Ameerika* 'America', *Saksamaa* 'Germany' etc.

While constructing sentences we always aimed at finding the most natural context for the words to be included. To find the normal sentence context of the words we used a corpus portal developed at the University of Leipzig[1] to compute the most frequent left and right collocations from a large database. This provided the background for sentence compilation.

The final corpus consisted of 400 sentences with 2811 words.

3   Corpus analysis

In parallel with corpus compilation a constant process of analysis was going on to diagnose its possible weak points. First we had to find out if all Estonian diphones, existing as well as theoretical, are present in the corpus and with what frequency.

	m	n	n'	o	p	r	s
#	141	79	✕	105	205	71	171
a	3	55	13	9	86	52	140
e	35	52	14	4	15	48	19
f		1	✕	11		3	2
h	2	3	✕	12		1	
i	34	80	15	4	18	17	174
j	✕	✕	✕	10	✕	✕	✕
k	4	3	✕	85	2	20	71
l	14	8	✕	19	6	1	4
l'	2		✕	lo	2		2
m	31	8	✕	11	10	1	6

...

Table 1. Frequency of diphone occurrence at an intermediate stage of corpus compilation

The gray cells stand for diphones missing from the corpus, however possible theoretically. As Estonian is fond of active compounding we had also to consider such sound combinations as might emerge at compound boundary. So some additional words (mostly compounds) were found to fill in the gray cells. The crossed cells stand for diphones theoretically impossible in Estonian, or at least impossible to find by the means available.

As our corpus was meant to be as rich as possible phonetically and phonologically we had to include many sound combinations that were less frequent, yet vital for TTS. As can be seen in Figure 1 the synthesis corpus has considerably more of rare phonemes than the mixed corpus of Estonian[2], although in general there is no significant difference between the phoneme frequencies across the two corpora.

4   Recording

The main criterion in voice donor selection was their ability to read out the whole text at relatively constant prosodic parameters. As a result, a professional radio announcer (female) was chosen. The recording (sampling frequency: 44.1 KHz, resolution: 16 bits) was made at a studio of the Estonian Radio. The recording session lasted about an hour, yielding 51 minutes of recorded speech. The text was read out relatively monotonously, as the pitch amplitude was to be kept relatively low. The reason is that although the pitch of the synthetic signal is later subjected to modification by some signal processing methods, a large-scale interference is bound to have an undesirable effect on the quality of synthesis.

The recording pursued canonical Estonian pronunciation. It was based on the pronunciation received by *Estonian orthological dictionary* (ÕS 2006) as the would-be source of diacritics to aid text synthesis. Problems ensued from the word-final *s, n, t,* and *l*, as the orthological dictionary requires their palatalization in some positions (*roos'* 'rose', *geen'* 'gene'), although their palatalization has ceased to be consistent in modern Estonian. Even though no studies have been conducted to prove it, it seems that there is a tendency to use the non-palatalized variants in those positions.

---

[1] http://corpora.informatik.uni_leipzig-de/

[2] http://www.cl.ut.ee/korpused/segakorpus

Therefore those cases were recorded relying on the speaker's pronunciation.

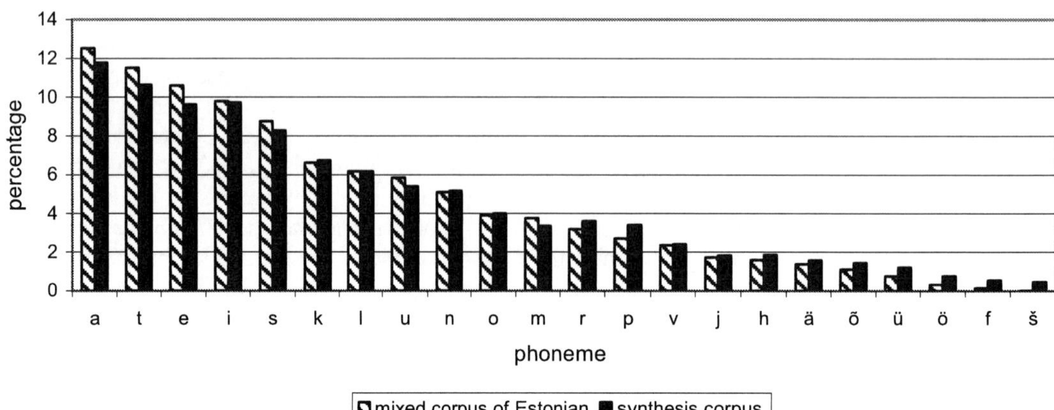

Figure 1. Frequency of phoneme occurrence in a mixed corpus of Estonian vs. the synthesis corpus.

Problems were also caused by some occasional fluctuations of the speech rate. Some of the corpus sentences included rare diphones, which may occur only in words extremely rare in Estonian, or in artificial compounds. This caused the speech rate to drop as compared to the sentences with frequent words in their normal contexts of occurrence. Whether and to what extent such fluctuations in speech rate may affect the quality of the synthesis will be revealed in the practical use of the synthesizer, which is also the proof of a necessity for additions to the corpus and for repeat recordings.

5   Conclusion

The aim of the speech corpus described was to develop an acoustic basis for a relatively naturally sounding synthetic speech. To reduce the number of concatenation points in the synthetic utterance it was necessary to create a speech corpus enabling searching for units larger than diphones. The article provides specifics on the material included in the 400-sentence corpus. Corpus development being the first step towards natural-like synthetic speech, we are now busy tagging and segmenting the speech material and laying a phonological structure on the speech corpus.

Acknowledgement

The support from the program Language Technology Support of the Estonian has made the present work possible.

References

Baris Bozkurt, Thierry Dutoit, Romain C. Prudon, Christophe D'Alessandro and Vincent Pagel. 2004. Reducing discontinuities at synthesis time for corpus-based speech synthesis, in *Text To Speech Synthesis: New Paradigms and Advances,* (S. Narayanan, A. Alwan, ed.), Prentice Hall PTR.

Andy P. Breen and Peter Jackson. 1998. Non-Uniform Unit Selection and the Similarity Metric within BT's Laureate TTS System. *Proceedings of the Third ESCA Workshop on Speech Synthesis.*

Robert E. Donovan and Phil C. Woodland. 1999. A hidden Markov-model-based trainable speech synthesizer. *Computer Speech and language,* 13:223-241.

Mati Hint. 1998. *Häälikutest sõnadeni. Eesti keele häälikusüsteem üldkeeleteaduslikul taustal.* Tallinn.

Heiki-Jaan Kaalep and Kadri Muischnek. 2002. *Eesti kirjakeele sagedussõnastik*, Tartu.

John Kominek and Alan W. Black. 2003. *CMU ARCTIC databases for speech synthesis.* Carnegie Mellon University.

Meelis Mihkla, Arvo Eek and Einar Meister. 1998. Creation of the Estonian Diphone Database for Text-to-Speech Synthesis. *Linguistica Uralica,* 34(3):334-340.

András Nagy, Péter Pesti, Géza Németh and Tamás Bőhm. 2005. Design Issues of a Corpus-Based Speech Synthesizer, *Hungarian Journal on Communications,* 6:18-24.

ÕS 2006 – *Eesti õigekeelsussõnaraamat 2006.* Eesti Keele Sihtasutus, Tallinn.

Evaluating Evaluation Measures

Ines Rehbein
NCLT
School of Computing, DCU,
Dublin, Ireland
irehbein@computing.dcu.ie

Josef van Genabith
NCLT,
School of Computing, DCU,
Dublin, Ireland
josef@computing.dcu.ie

Abstract

This paper presents a thorough examination of the validity of three evaluation measures on parser output. We assess parser performance of an unlexicalised probabilistic parser trained on two German treebanks with different annotation schemes and evaluate parsing results using the PARSEVAL metric, the Leaf-Ancestor metric and a dependency-based evaluation. We reject the claim that the TüBa-D/Z annotation scheme is more adequate then the TIGER scheme for PCFG parsing and show that PARSEVAL should not be used to compare parser performance for parsers trained on treebanks with different annotation schemes. An analysis of specific error types indicates that the dependency-based evaluation is most appropriate to reflect parse quality.

1 Introduction

The evaluation of parsing results is a crucial topic in NLP. Despite severe criticism for PCFG parsing the PARSEVAL metric is still the standard evaluation measure. PARSEVAL has been criticised for not representing 'real' parser quality (Carroll et al., 1998; Brisco et al., 2002; Sampson et al., 2003).

Recent studies investigating the impact of different treebank annotation schemes on unlexicalised probabilistic parsing of German (Kübler, 2005; Kübler et al., 2006; Maier, 2006) have been using the PARSEVAL metric for evaluation. Results (labelled bracketing f-score) are about 16% higher for a parser trained on the TüBa-D/Z treebank (Telljohann et al., 2004) than for a parser trained on the NEGRA treebank (Skut et al., 1997). Maier (2006) takes that as evidence that the NEGRA annotation scheme is less adequate for PCFG parsing, while a parser trained on the TüBa-D/Z yields PARSEVAL results in the same range as a parser trained on the English Penn-II treebank (Kübler et al., 2006). These results are based on the assumption that PARSEVAL is an appropriate measure for comparing parser performance of a PCFG parser trained on treebanks with different annotation schemes.

This paper presents parsing experiments with the PCFG parser BitPar (Schmid, 2004) trained on two German treebanks. The treebanks contain text from the same domain, namely two German daily newspapers, but differ considerably with regard to their annotation schemes. We score parsing results using three different evaluation measures and show that the PARSEVAL results do not correlate with the results of the other metrics. An analysis of specific error types shows the differences between the three measures. Our results indicate that dependency-based evaluation is most appropriate to compare parser output for parsers trained on different treebank annotation schemes.

Section 2 describes the main features of the two German treebanks, and Section 3 gives an overview over the metrics used for evaluation. Section 4 presents the parsing experiments. In Section 5 we describe the behaviour of the different evaluation metrics for specific error types. Section 6 concludes.

Joakim Nivre, Heiki-Jaan Kaalep, Kadri Muischnek and Mare Koit (Eds.)
NODALIDA 2007 Conference Proceedings, pp. 372–379

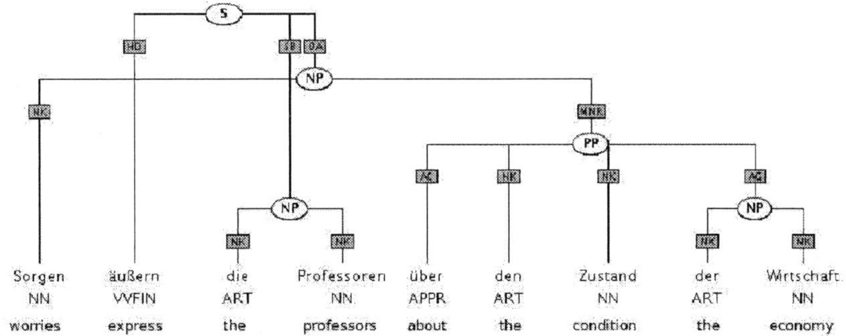

"The professors express their concerns about the state of the economy."

Figure 1: TIGER Treebank tree

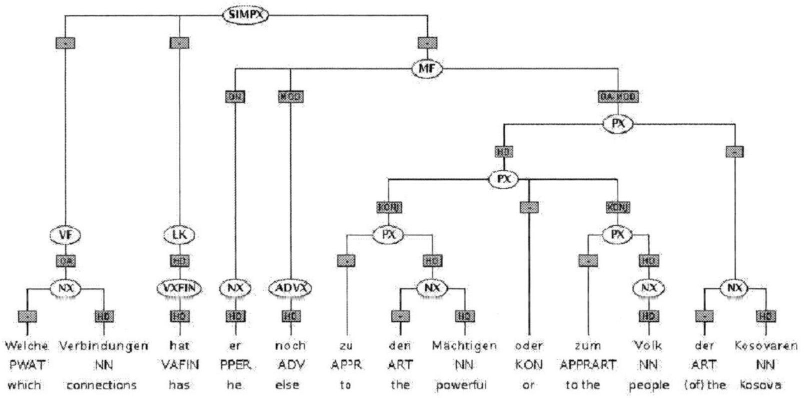

"What connections does he still have with those in power or with the people of Kosovo."

Figure 2: TüBa-D/Z Treebank tree

2   TIGER and TüBa-D/Z

The two German treebanks used in our experiments are the TIGER Treebank (Release 2) and the Tüba-D/Z (Release 2). The TüBa-D/Z consists of approximately 22 000 sentences, while the TIGER Treebank is much larger with more than 50 000 sentences. TIGER is based on and extends the NEGRA data and annotation scheme. Both treebanks contain German newspaper text (Frankfurter Rundschau for TIGER and 'die tageszeitung' (taz) for TüBa-D/Z) and are annotated with phrase structure and dependency (functional) information. Both treebanks use the Stuttgart Tübingen POS Tag Set (Schiller et al., 1995). TIGER uses 49 different grammatical function labels, while the TüBa-D/Z utilises only 36 function labels. For the encoding of phrasal node categories the TüBa-D/Z uses 30 different cat-

egories, the TIGER Treebank uses a set of 27 category labels.

Other major differences between the two treebanks are: in the TIGER Treebank long distance dependencies are expressed through crossing branches (Figure 1), while in the TüBa-D/Z the same phenomenon is expressed with the help of grammatical function labels (Figure 2). The annotation in the TIGER Treebank is rather flat and allows no unary branching, whereas the nodes in the TüBa-D/Z do contain unary branches and a more hierarchical structure, resulting in a much deeper tree structure than the trees in the TIGER Treebank. This results in an average higher number of nodes per sentence for the TüBa-D/Z. Table 1 shows the differences in the ratio of nodes for the TIGER Treebank and the TüBa-D/Z.

	phrasal nodes/sent	phrasal nodes/word	words /sent
TIGER	8.29	0.47	17.60
TüBa-D/Z	20.69	1.20	17.27

Table 1: Average number of phrasal nodes/words in TIGER and TüBa-D/Z

Figures 1 and 2 also illustrate the different annotation of PPs in both annotation schemes. In the TIGER Treebank the internal structure of the PP is flat and the adjective and noun inside the PP are directly attached to the PP, while the TüBa-D/Z is more hierarchical and inserts an additional NP node. Crossing branches show the long distance dependency between the PP and the noun *Sorgen* (worries) in the TIGER tree, while in the TüBa-D/Z the node label OA-MOD encodes the information that the PP modifies the accusative object *Verbindungen* (connections).

Another major difference is the annotation of topological fields in the style of Drach (1937) in the TüBa-D/Z. The model captures German word order, which accepts three possible sentence configurations (verb first, verb second and verb last), by providing fields like the initial field (VF), the middle field (MF) and the final field (NF). The fields are positioned relative to the verb, which can fill in the left (LK) or the right sentence bracket (VC). The ordering of topological fields is determined by syntactic constraints.

2.1 Differences between TIGER and NEGRA

To date, most PCFG parsing for German has been done using the NEGRA corpus as a training resource. The annotation scheme of the TIGER Treebank is based on the NEGRA annotation scheme, but it also employs some important extensions, which include the annotation of verb-subcategorisation, appositions and parentheses, coordinations and the encoding of proper nouns (Brants and Hansen, 2002).

3 The Evaluation Measures

The three evaluation metrics used in our experiments are:

- the PARSEVAL metric (**PV**)
- the Leaf-Ancestor metric (**LA**)
- a dependency-based evaluation (**DB**)

Below we demonstrate the differences between the three evaluation measures, using Sentence 4 from the TIGER test set as an example:

(1) Die Regierung rief   zum weltweiten Kampf
     the government called to the worldwide fight
     gegen   Terror auf.
     against terror up

  "The government called for a worldwide war against terror."

3.1 PARSEVAL

PARSEVAL checks label and wordspan identity in parser output compared to the original treebank trees, but neither weights results, differentiating between linguistically more or less severe errors, nor does it give credit to constituents where the syntactic categories have been recognised correctly but the phrase boundary is slightly wrong.

Figure 3 shows the gold tree for our example sentence (1). In the parser output the second PP was incorrectly attached to the sentence level (Figure 4) instead of being attached to the noun inside the PP.

```
(TOP
    (S
        (NP
            (ART Die [the] )
            (NN Regierung [government] )
        )
        (VVFIN rief)
        (PP
            (APPR zum [to the] )
            (ADJA weltweiten [worldwide] )
            (NN Kampf [fight] )
            (PP
                (APPR gegen [against] )
                (NN Terror [terror] )
            )
        )
        (PTKVZ auf)
    )
    ($. .)
)
```

Die Regierung rief zum weltweiten Kampf gegen terror auf.
"The government called for a worldwide war against terror."

Figure 3: Gold tree for example (1)

PARSEVAL counts 4 (out of 5) matching brackets, which results in a precision and recall of 80.00% respectively.

(TOP
  (S
    (NP
        (ART Die [the])
        (NN Regierung [government])
)
    (VVFIN rief)
    (PP
        (APPR zum [to the])
        (ADJA weltweiten [worldwide])
        (NN Kampf [fight])
)
    (PP
        (APPR gegen [against])
        (NN Terror [terror])
)
    (PTKVZ auf)
)
  ($. .)
)

Die Regierung rief zum weltweiten Kampf gegen terror auf.
"The government called for a worldwide war against terror."

Figure 4: Parser output tree for example (1)

3.2 Leaf-Ancestor

LA (Sampson et al., 2003) measures the similarity between the path from each terminal node in the parser output tree to the root node and the corresponding path in the gold tree. The path consists of the sequence of node labels between the terminal node and the root node, and the similarity of two paths is calculated by using the Levenshtein distance (Levenshtein, 1966).

For each terminal node in the parser output the sequence of node labels between the terminal node and the root node is compared to the same path in the gold tree. This results in an evaluation result for string similarity for each terminal node. The score for the whole tree is the average of the values for all terminals in the tree. Figure 5 shows LA evaluation results for example (1). The numbers in the left column give the LA scores for each terminal node, which results in an average score of 0.963 for the whole sentence.

Phrase boundaries are taken into consideration, in order to distinguish between paths like the one for *zum* (`[PP S TOP`) and the one for *weltweiten* (`PP S TOP`) in Figure 5. The LA metric does this as follows: for each terminal at the beginning of a phrase LA looks for the highest non-terminal node governing the phrase which also starts with the terminal, and inserts a left boundary marker before the categorial label of the non-terminal node, if the phrase starts with the terminal node. For *Die* [the] the high-

1.000	Die			NP	S	[		TOP	: NP		S	[	TOP
1.000	Regierung			NP	]	S		TOP	: NP		]	S	TOP
1.000	rief					S		TOP	: S				TOP
1.000	zum			[		PP	S	TOP	: [			PP S	TOP
1.000	weltweiten					PP	S	TOP	: PP			S	TOP
0.857	Kampf					PP	S	TOP	: PP		]		S	TOP
0.889	gegen	[	PP			PP	S	TOP	: [			PP S	TOP
0.889	Terror	PP	PP		]		S	TOP	: PP		]	S	TOP
1.000	auf				S	]		TOP	: S		]		TOP
1.000	.							TOP]	: TOP]				

Sentence 1: avg. 0.963

Figure 5: LA result for example (1)

est non-terminal governing node is TOP. As the sentence starts with *Die*, a left boundary marker is inserted before the TOP node. For *zum* the highest governing non-terminal node which starts with the word *zum* is the PP, therefore the left boundary marker is inserted before the PP node.

Additionally, LA looks at each terminal node at the end of a phrase and inserts a right boundary marker after the label of the highest non-terminal node of the phrase ending with the terminal node. In the gold tree of our example the terminal node *Kampf* [fight] is not the final node of the PP. Due to the PP attachment error in the parser output tree, on the other hand, *Kampf* [fight] is in a phrase-final position, with the PP as the highest non-terminal node governing the terminal. Therefore a right boundary marker is inserted after the PP node in the path of the parser output, which results in a score of 0.889 for path similarity between gold tree and parser output.

The average result for the whole sentence is 0.963, while a perfect sentence would get a score of 1. If LA encounters a mismatch between the words in the gold tree and the parser output, it simply stops without returning a result for the whole sentence.

3.3 Dependency-Based Evaluation

The dependency-based evaluation used in the experiments follows the method of Lin (1998) and Kübler et al. (2002), converting the original treebank trees and the parser output into dependency relationships of the form WORD POS HEAD. Functional labels have been omitted for parsing, therefore the dependencies do not comprise functional information.

Figure 6 shows the dependency relations for example (1), indicated by arrows. Converted into a

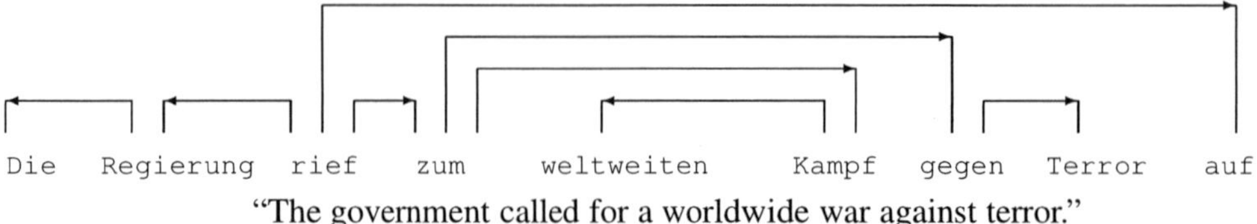

"The government called for a worldwide war against terror."

Figure 6: Dependency relations for example (1)

WORD POS HEAD triple format the dependency tree looks as follows (Table 2).

WORD		POS	HEAD
Die	[the]	ART	Regierung
Regierung	[government]	NN	rief
rief	[called]	VVFIN	-
zum	[to the]	APPRART	rief
weltweiten	[worldwide]	ADJA	Kampf
Kampf	[fight]	NN	zum
gegen	[against]	APPR	zum
Terror	[terror]	NN	gegen
auf	[up]	PTKVZ	rief

Table 2: Gold dependency triples for example (1)

The PP attachment error in the parser output leads to an error in the dependency triples, incorrectly assigning *rief* [called] as the head of *gegen* [against] (Table 3), while in the gold triples the PP *gegen Terror* [against terror] is a dependent of the preposition *zum* [to the].

WORD		POS	HEAD
gegen	[against]	APPR	rief

Table 3: Error in parser output dependency triples

For our example we get a precision and recall of 88.89 respectively. Following Lin (1998), our algorithm computes precision and recall:

- **Precision**: the percentage of dependency relationships in the parser output that are also found in the gold triples

- **Recall**: the percentage of dependency relationships in the gold triples that are also found in the parser output triples.

We assessed the quality of the automatic dependency conversion methodology by converting the 1024 original trees from each of our test sets into dependency relations, using the functional labels in the original trees to determine the dependencies. We then removed all functional information from the trees and converted the stripped trees into dependencies, using heuristics to find the head. We evaluated the dependencies for the stripped gold trees against the dependencies for the original gold trees including functional labels and obtained an f-score of 99.65% for TIGER and 99.13% for the TüBa-D/Z dependencies. This shows that the conversion is reliable and not unduly biased to either the TIGER or TüBa-D/Z annotation schemes.

4 Experimental Setup

For the experiments we trained the PCFG parser BitPar (Schmid, 2004) on the TIGER treebank and the TüBa-D/Z. The training sets for each treebank contain 21067 sentences, while the test sets include 1024 sentences each. To allow a meaningful comparison of parsing results we selected sentences comparable with regard to sentence length, syntactic structure and complexity from both treebanks for our test sets. This resulted in an average sentence length of 14.5 for the TIGER test set and of 14.7 for the TüBa-D/Z. Before extracting the grammars we inserted a virtual root node and resolved the crossing branches in the TIGER treebank by attaching the non-head child nodes higher up in the tree. After this preprocessing step we extracted an unlexicalised PCFG from each of our training sets. We parsed our test sets with the extracted grammars, using raw text as parser input.

5 Results

Table 4 shows the evaluation results for the different metrics.[1] PARSEVAL shows higher results for

---

[1]PARSEVAL results report *labelled* precision and recall.

precision and recall for the TüBa-D/Z. For DB evaluation the parser trained on the TIGER training set achieves about 7% higher results for precision and recall than the parser trained on the TüBa-D/Z. The LA results are much closer to each other, but also show better results for the TIGER parse trees.

	PARSEVAL		Dependencies		LA
	Prec	Rec	Prec	Rec	Avg.
TIGER	81.21	81.04	85.78	85.79	0.9388
TüBa	87.24	83.77	78.63	78.61	0.9258

Table 4: Parsing results for three evaluation metrics

Comparing the f-score learning curves in the three metrics shows that for PARSEVAL the gap between TIGER and TüBa-D/Z is consistent throughout the whole training process. But while during the first stages of training the difference in results adds up to around 12%, the gap becomes smaller with more training data. When trained on 90-100% of the training data, the difference in f-scores decreases to around 5% (Figure 7).

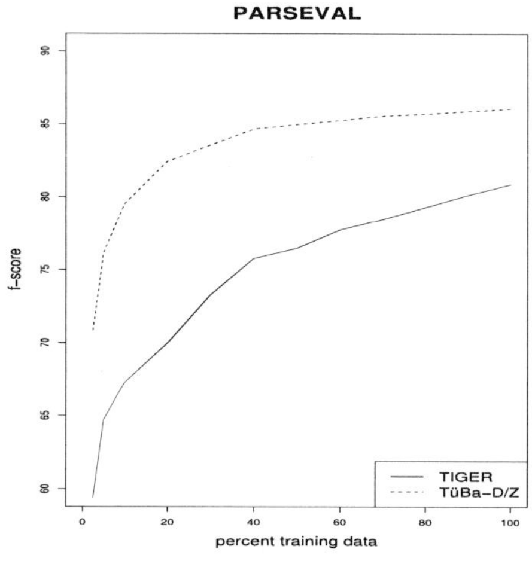

Figure 7: F-score learning curves for TIGER and TüBa-D/Z (PARSEVAL)

The LA learning curve shows an advantage for TüBa-D/Z during the first stages of training. When training the parser on less than 20% of the training data, the TüBa-D/Z-trained grammar yields better results. Training the parser on more than 50% of the sentences in the training set reverses the picture:

while the f-score for TüBa-D-Z does not seem to improve further, the TIGER results clearly show an ongoing learning effect (Figure 8).

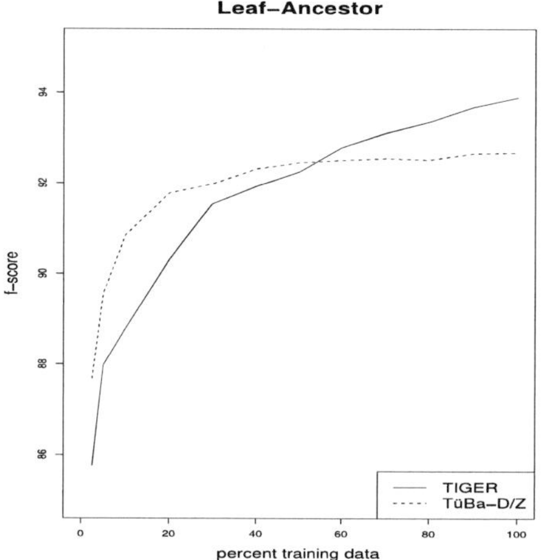

Figure 8: F-score learning curves for TIGER and TuBa-D/Z (Leaf-Ancestor)

The learning curve for the dependency based evaluation (Figure 9) shows a similar tendency. While the TüBa-D/Z yields better results when trained on a small amount of training data only, and from more than 20% of the training set onwards only shows a moderate increase, the f-score for TIGER improves faster and shows an advantage of more than 6% over the TüBa-D/Z f-score when trained on the whole training set.

The wide difference between the results raises the question, which of the metrics is the most adequate for judging parser quality. The next section approaches this question by looking at the behaviour of the different metrics with regard to specific error types.

5.1 Part-of-Speech Errors

Parse trees yielding 100% precision and recall for PARSEVAL and 100% for LA, but failing to get 100% precision and recall for the DB evaluation, often contain POS errors. In most cases the parser assigned a noun tag instead of a proper name, an adjective tag instead of a cardinal number, or mixed up attributive adjectives with predicative adjectives. These error types are attested in 32 sentences in the TIGER and in 23 sentences in the TüBa-D/Z test set.

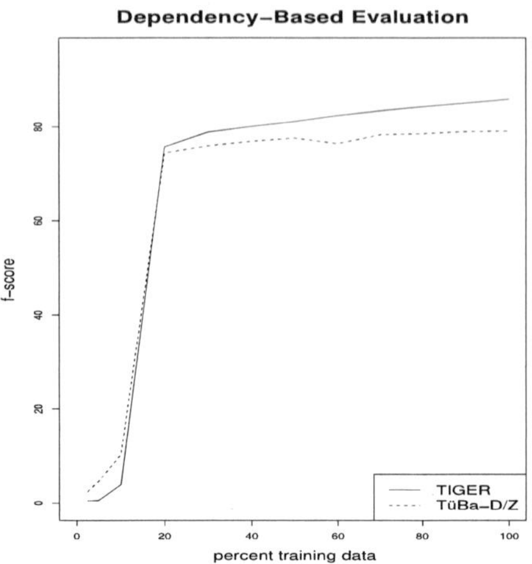

Figure 9: F-score learning curves for TIGER and TüBa-D/Z (Dependencies)

5.2 Missing Nodes / Additional Nodes

Parse trees achieving 100% precision and recall for DB evaluation, but not for the PARSEVAL and LA metric mostly lack a non-terminal node such as a proper name node enclosing an NP, a multi-token number for the TIGER treebank or the *Nachfeld* (final field) for the TüBa-D/Z. This applies to 23 sentences in the TIGER test set and to 29 sentences in the TüBa-D/Z test set. In the parser output of the parser trained on the TIGER treebank there are also sentences which show additional categorial nodes not present in the gold trees, such as prepositional phrases enclosing a pronominal adverb, adverbial phrases or adjectival phrases. Both the missing and the additional nodes do not translate into dependency errors as the dependencies for the trees can be extracted correctly. Nonetheless they lead to a significant decrease in precision and recall for the PARSEVAL scores and, to a lesser extent, also for the LA scores.

5.3 PP Attachment Errors

Parse trees with attachment errors often get reasonable results for the PARSEVAL metric but only show mediocre scores for DB evaluation. We demonstrate this for two sentences with PP attachment errors from the TIGER test set (Figure 1) and the TüBa-D/Z (Figure 2).

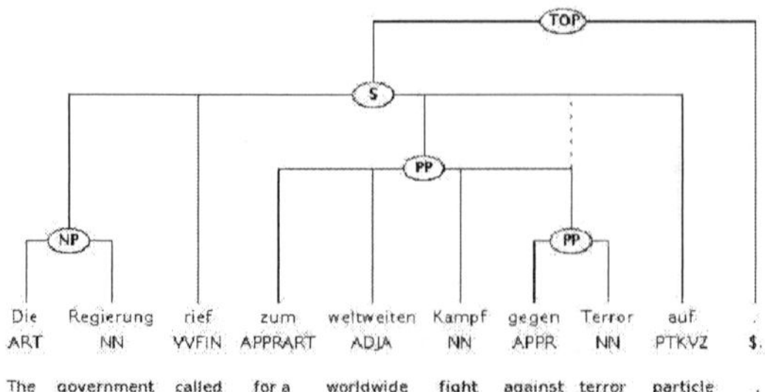

Figure 10: TIGER (dotted line: parser output)

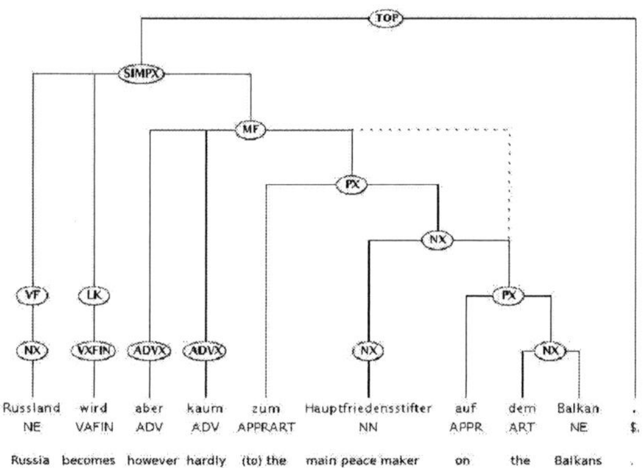

Figure 11: TüBa-D/Z (dotted line: parser output)

In the gold trees one of the PPs is a child respectively grandchild of the other PP, while in the parser outputs both PPs are mis-attached to the same mother node (dotted lines). Table 5 shows the evaluation results for the two sentences.

	PARSEVAL		Dependencies		LA
	Prec	Rec	Prec	Rec	Avg.
TIGER	80.00	80.00	88.89	88.89	0.963
TüBa	92.31	85.71	88.89	88.89	0.935

Table 5: Parsing results for PP attachment error

Despite the similarity of the two trees concerning sentence length and syntactic complexity PARSEVAL yields strongly different results for the TIGER and the TüBa-D/Z parser output. The LA scores are much closer, giving better results for the TIGER parse tree, while the PARSEVAL results are clearly in favour of the TüBa-D/Z tree. The difference between the PARSEVAL results for two comparable trees is caused by the higher ratio of nodes per words in the TüBa-D/Z annotation scheme. For the TIGER tree the parser is able to match 4 out of 5 brackets which yields a recall of 4/5 = 80%. For the TüBa-D/Z the parser correctly identifies 12 out of 14 brackets in the gold tree and therefore achieves a recall value of 12/14 = 92.31%. The dependency-based evaluation gives identical results for the two sentences, which is what linguistic intuition would ask for.

6 Conclusions

In this paper we rejected the claim that the German TüBa-D/Z is more appropriate for PCFG parsing than the TIGER treebank. We showed that the PARSEVAL metric cannot be used to compare parser output from parsers trained on different treebanks, because it favours annotation schemes with a high ratio of nodes per word. We have also shown that PARSEVAL results do not correlate with other evaluation measures like the Leaf-Ancestor metric or a dependency-based evaluation, and that the results of a dependency-based evaluation best reflect the linguistic notion of a good parse.

References

Dipper, S., T. Brants, W. Lezius, O. Plaehn, and G. Smith. 2001. The TIGER Treebank. *In Third Workshop on Linguistically Interpreted Corpora LINC-2001*, Leuven, Belgium.

Brants, Sabine, and Silvia Hansen 2002. Developments in the TIGER Annotation Scheme and their Realization in the Corpus. *In Proceedings of the Third Conference on Language Resources and Evaluation (LREC 2002)*, pp. 1643-1649. Las Palmas, Canary Islands.

Briscoe, E. J., J. A. Carroll, and A. Copestake. 2002. Relational evaluation schemes. *In Proceedings Workshop 'Beyond Parseval - towards improved evaluation measures for parsing systems', 3rd International Conference on Language Resources and Evaluation*, pp. 4-38. Las Palmas, Canary Islands.

Carroll, J., E. Briscoe and A. Sanfilippo. 1998. Parser evaluation: a survey and a new proposal. *In Proceedings of the 1st International Conference on Language Resources and Evaluation*, Granada, Spain. 447-454.

Dipper, S., T. Brants, W. Lezius, O. Plaehn, and G. Smith. 2001. The TIGER Treebank. *In Third Workshop on Linguistically Interpreted Corpora LINC-2001*, Leuven, Belgium.

Drach, Erich. 1937. *Grundgedanken der Deutschen Satzlehre*. Frankfurt/M.

Kübler, Sandra, and Heike Telljohann. 2002. Towards a Dependency-Oriented Evaluation for Partial Parsing. *In Proceedings of Beyond PARSEVAL – Towards Improved Evaluation Measures for Parsing Systems (LREC 2002 Workshop)*, Las Palmas, Gran Canaria.

Kübler, Sandra. 2005. How Do Treebank Annotation Schemes Influence Parsing Results? Or How Not to Compare Apples And Oranges. *In Proceedings of RANLP 2005*, Borovets, Bulgaria.

Kübler, Sandra, Erhard Hinrichs, and Wolfgang Maier. 2006. Is it Really that Difficult to Parse German? *In Proceedings of the 2006 Conference on Empirical Methods in Natural Language Processing, EMNLP*, Sydney, Australia.

Levenshtein, V. I. 1966. Binary codes capable of correcting deletions, insertions, and reversals. *Soviet Physics - Doklady*, 10.707-10 (translation of Russian original published in 1965).

Lin, Dekang. 1998. Dependency-based Evaluation of MINIPAR. *Workshop on the Evaluation of Parsing Systems*, Granada, Spain.

Maier, Wolfgang. 2006. Annotation Schemes and their Influence on Parsing Results. *In Proceedings of the COLING/ACL 2006 Student Research Workshop)*, Sydney, Australia.

Sampson, Geoffrey, and Anna Babarczy. 2003. A test of the leaf-ancestor metric for parse accuracy. *Natural Language Engineering*, 9 (4):365-380.

Schmid, Helmut. 2004. Efficient Parsing of Highly Ambiguous Context-Free Grammars with Bit Vectors. *In Proceedings of the 20th International Conference on Computational Linguistics (COLING 2004)*, Geneva, Switzerland.

Skut, Wojciech, Brigitte Krann, Thorsten Brants, and Hans Uszkoreit. 1997. An annotation scheme for free word order languages. *In Proceedings of ANLP 1997*, Washington, D.C.

Telljohann, Heike, Erhard W. Hinrichs, Sandra Kübler, and Heike Zinsmeister. 2005. *Stylebook for the Tübingen Treebank of Written German (TüBa-D/Z)*. Seminar für Sprachwissenschaft, Universität Tübingen, Germany.

Schiller, Anne, Simone Teufel, and Christine Thielen. 1995. *Guidelines fr das Tagging deutscher Textcorpora mit STTS*. Technical Report, IMS-CL, University Stuttgart.

Development of a Modern Greek Broadcast-News Corpus and Speech Recognition System

Jürgen Riedler
SAIL Labs Vienna, Austria
juergen@sail-labs.at

Sergios Katsikas
Department of German Linguistics
University of Pécs, Hungary
Katsikas@btk.pte.hu

Abstract

We report on the creation of a Modern Greek broadcast-news corpus as a pre-requisite to build a large-vocabulary continuous-speech recognition system. We discuss lexical modelling with respect to pronuciation generation and examine the effects of the lexicon size on word accuracies. Peculiarities of Modern Greek as a highly inflectional language and their challenges for speech recognition are discussed.

1 Introduction

Modern Greek *Koine* or Standard Modern Greek, the official language of Greece and Cyprus, is the latest variety of Europe's oldest literary language following Mycenian, Ancient, Hellenistic, and Byzantine Greek. Research objectives within the REVEAL THIS[1] project comprise also the development of a Modern Greek (MG) automatic speech recognition (ASR) system. In constrast to recent efforts on MG ASR focussing on dictation (Digalakis et al., 2003), our interests are in the broadcast news domain.

After providing a short linguistic overview of MG we specify the prerequisites for ASR, which would be: audio recordings with corresponding transcriptions to train acoustic models, text corpora for language modelling, and recognition lexicon inclusive pronunciation generation. Finally we disclose word error rates of experiments employing various recognition dictionaries and discuss major problems of lexical and language modelling for a highly inflectional language.

---

[1]Retrieval of **V**ideo **A**nd **L**anguage for **T**he **H**ome user in an **I**nformation **S**ociety – funded by the IST Frame Programm 6/2003/IST/2.*Scientific and technological objectives:* 1) Augmentation of the content of multimedia documents with entity, topic, speaker, and fact information; 2) Development of cross-media and cross-language representations; 3) High-level functionalities, like search, retrieval, categorization, and summarization, from 1) and 2).

2 Notes on Modern Greek structure

In the following we briefly present a linguistic introduction into MG - see (Katsikas, 1997), (Mackridge, 1985) and references therein - and comment on its implications to ASR.

2.1 Phonological system

The phonological system of MG consists of five vowel phonemes: /a/, /ɛ/, /i/, /o/, /u/ and 20 consonant phonemes: the plosives /p/, /b/, /t/, /d/, /k/, /g/, the fricatives /f/, /v/, /θ/, /ð/, /s/, /z/, /x/, /ɣ/, the affricates /t͡s/, /d͡z/, the nasals /m/, /n/, the lateral /l/ and the apical trill /r/. The most important allophone-generating phonological processes are:

- palatalisation of /k/, /g/, /x/, /ɣ/ to [c], [ɟ], [ç], [j] before /i/ or /ɛ/

- /k/, /g/, /x/, /ɣ/, /n/, /l/ merge with following glide [j] (non-syllabic allophone of /i/) to palatals: [c], [ɟ], [ç], [j], [ɲ], [ʎ], *e.g.* εννιά /ɛni'a/ → *[ɛ'nja] → [ɛ'ɲa]

- sonorisation of /p/, /t/, /k/, /t͡s/ to [b], [d], [g], [d͡z] after /n/, often with denasalisation in informal speech, *e.g.* τον πατέρα /ton pa'tɛra/ → [tomba'tɛra] or [toba'tɛra]

- regressive assimilation of place of articulation of /n/ to the following consonant
    - /n/ → [m] before /p/, /b/, see former example
    - /n/ → [ŋ] before /k/, /g/, /x/, /ɣ/, *e.g.* τον Κώστα /ton 'kosta/ → [toŋ'gosta] or [to'gosta]

- sonorisation of /s/ to [z] before voiced consonants, *e.g.* της λέω /tis 'lɛo/ → [tiz'lɛo]

Within syntactic phrases (*e.g.* article - noun - possesive pronoun) certain phonological processes usually extend even across word boundaries (see examples above), but only if there is no pause between the words.

This can cause homophony of phrases, *e.g.* [tim'bira] or [ti'bira] could mean both την μπίρα "the beer {acc.}" or την πήρα "I picked her up/I called her *etc.*", and represents an almost inevitable source of word errors for ASR (*cf.* Section 4).

Joakim Nivre, Heiki-Jaan Kaalep, Kadri Muischnek and Mare Koit (Eds.)
NODALIDA 2007 Conference Proceedings, pp. 380–383

2.2 Prosody

The functional load of prosodic features in MG is extremely high, since word stress and intonation are highly distinctive. There are hundreds of prime-stress minimal pairs (*e.g.* πότε "when" *vs.* ποτέ "never"), stress fulfills various morphological functions and moreover, intonation patterns provide in most cases the only distinction between declarative clauses and yes-no questions (*e.g.* [o ˈjanis ˈin(ε) εˈðoˎ] "John is here" *vs.* [o ˈjanis ˈin(ε) εˈðoˏ] "Is John here?").

This is the reason why we introduced word stress as a part of suprasegmental structure into our phone sets, see Section 3.

2.3 Morphology

MG is a prototypical inflectional language, *i.e.* a potentially huge number of different word forms may be derived from one basic stem (lemma). In particular verb inflection is very rich: by combining two stems, three sets of endings, a few modal particles, an auxiliary verb and the participle, every active verb can produce about 200 forms, if we take all syntactically defined categories (three aspects, six moods, eight tenses, *etc.*) into account, despite of (partial) homonymies. This number is twice as big for verbs that exhibit a medio-passive voice, which is formed synthetically. Different verb forms can differ from each other in the ending, in accentuation as well as in the stem (there are also irregular verbs with suppletive roots, *e.g.* βλέπω [ˈvlεpo] "I see" *vs.* είδα [ˈiða] "I saw"), and finally, active verbs consisting of two syllables have in past tense a sort of prefix (augment) carrying the stress on the antepenultimate syllable. Nouns show, depending on their inflectional class, between 4 and 7 different forms, adjectives about 40 (including comparative and elative). Due to ambiguities of various morphological rules and the bistructurality of MG (parallel use of old and new forms), inflectional forms are often hardly predictable.

MG word formation processes are very complex though not very productive. Various mutations of morphemes and bistructurality prevent the predictability of derivatives and compounds. For example, the stems within the verb forms κλέβω "I steel", έκλεψα "I stole" do not evidently imply those in derivatives like κλέφτης "thief", κλοπή "theft" or in a compound like κλεπτομανής "cleptomaniac".

Since syntactic relations between constituents of a sentence are mostly expressed by inflection, MG constituent order is fairly free Word order has rather a pragmatic than syntactic function (e.g. topicalisation).

It is obvious from the above that inflection as well as syntactical freedom present outstanding demands on lexical and language modelling.

3 Phonetic transcription and lexicon

MG grapho-phonemic correspondences are mostly unambiguous from grapheme to phoneme, *i.e.* the pronunciation of written text is predictable to a high degree. However, as a result of historical spelling some phonemes comply with more than one grapheme (*e.g.* /i/ may be represented by six different graphemes: ⟨ι⟩, ⟨η⟩, ⟨υ⟩, ⟨ει⟩, ⟨οι⟩, ⟨υι⟩), hence the text-to-speech task or pronuciation generation, respectively is less problematic than ASR.

Recognition dictionaries map lexical words to their corresponding phonetical transcriptions. This was accomplished by an automatic grapheme-to-phoneme (g2p) conversion applying about 70 rules in consideration of:

- structure words like τον, την (male and female definite article in accusative) and very frequent monosyllabic words were transcribed manually because of their manifold phonetical realisations

- the ⟨γγ⟩-digraph resulting from 'learned' formations of the prefixes {εν-, συν-} and stems with initial /γ/, *e.g.* έγγραφο "document", is phonetically transcribed as [ŋɣ] (in contrast to [ŋg] as usual)

- company or product names and acronyms written in latin characters (*e.g.* BBC, Unesco, Löwenbräu) also had to be transcribed manually

g2p makes use of the following phone inventory: 26 consonants (except for affricates like /t͡s/, /d͡z/, which were separated as /t/+/s/, /d/+/z/, respectively), 5 vowels, the non-syllabic /i/ plus one additional phone for every stressed vowel and 4 artificial phones (SILence, BReaTh, LIPsmack, GaRBage).

Aside from the phonological processes described above (*cf.* Section 2.1) the following phenomena were found to be relevant for phonetic transcription:

- pronunciations of the consonantal digraphs ⟨μπ⟩, ⟨ντ⟩, ⟨γκ/γγ⟩ within words vary between [b], [d], [g] and [mb], [nd], [ŋg] (not at word beginnings) due to regional, stylistic, and individual differences

- digraphs $\langle \alpha \upsilon \rangle$, $\langle \epsilon \upsilon \rangle$, $\langle \eta \upsilon \rangle$ are pronounced as [af], [ef], [if] before voiceless consonants and as [av], [ev], [iv] before voiced consonants or vowels

- within pronunciations of the digraphs $\langle \alpha \acute{\upsilon} \rangle$, $\langle \epsilon \acute{\upsilon} \rangle$, $\langle \eta \acute{\upsilon} \rangle$, the vowel has to be stressed, although for reasons of orthography the written accent is put on the consonantal component

Obeying the specified phonological rules lead to 1.9 pronunciations per lexeme on average.

4 Experimental setup

4.1 Corpora

Experiments were carried out using audio recordings (mono, 16kHz sampling rate, 16 bit resolution) of various news shows broadcasted via the Greek satellite-TV channel EPT . Transcription into text as well as XML-annotation (timing, speaker turns and names, topics, non-speech utterances, *etc.*) of the collected audio data was done at ILSP[2]. The recorded data comprise

- ~ 27000 pure speech segments (utterances)

- ~ 1200 individual speakers of which ~ 300 could be identified by name

- ~ 1500 segments (stories) annotated according to a topic hierarchy derived from Reuters

and were randomly divided into a training set of $36^h 05^{min}$ and a disjoint test set of $1^h 35^{min}$.

Two corpora made up of newspaper texts of approximately 25 million words altogether were provided by ILSP and had to undergo several pre-processing steps in order to obtain clean and convenient text for language modelling. This gave an exhaustive word list of about 350k different lexical terms of which 200k occur more than once, see *e.g.* (Oikonomidis and Digalakis, 2003) for a comparison with other European languages.

4.2 Recognizer

Acoustic models are context-dependent triphone (1984 codebooks) and quinphone models (76432 codebooks) derived from mel-frequency cepstra (cepstral coefficients up to 14th order as well as their first and second derivatives) extracted from the audio. Several normalisation and adaptation techniques like cepstral mean subtraction are applied on a per-utterance base. The phone models are continuous-density Hidden Markov Models with state-tied Gaussian mixtures employed in two subsequent decoder passes.

---

[2]Institute for Language and Speech Processing $\langle$http://www.ilsp.gr$\rangle$

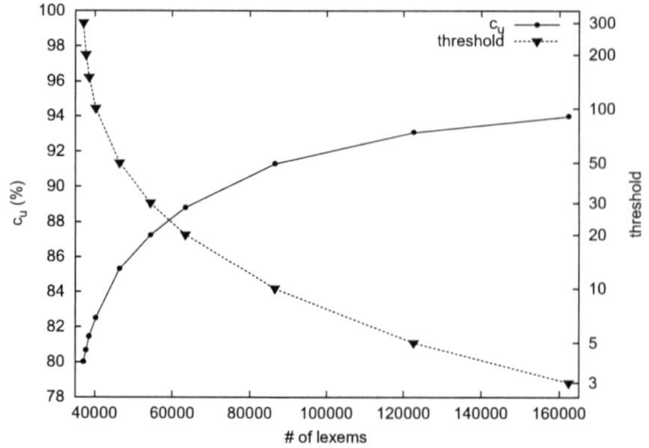

Figure 1: *Lexical coverages c_u obtained by using all words from the audio transcripts supplemented by those words with occurences of more than a minimum-threshold in the text corpus.*

We adopted back-off trigram language models with modified Witten-Bell smoothing. Language models were trained on the audio transcripts as well as the newspaper corpora, in which the audio data were given a higher weight (because audio vocabulary and n-gram inventory is supposed to be more similar to the ASR's actual operational area).

The decoder is part of the next-generation SAIL Labs Media Mining System. It is designed to run in real-time on state-of-the-art PC hardware (details will be published elsewhere).

4.3 Experiments

The recognition lexicon was assembled by taking all words from the audio transcripts as a basis, and extending it by those words of the text corpora with frequencies higher than a given threshold. Figure 1 depicts lexical coverages on the test set as a function of the number of lexical terms. In addition one can read off that coverages due to a cut-off of no more than 3 yields a dictionary of about 160k lexems, *i.e.* only the inclusion of words with rather small unigram probability, lead to coverages generally reported for recognition dictionaries of comparable utility, *cf.* (Oikonomidis and Digalakis, 2003).

We tested several ASR systems with respect to lexicon size and got almost constant word error rates of about **38%** for recognition lexicons with **90k-160k** entries, corresponding to lexical coverages of greater than **90%**, see Figure 2. Additional words of low frequency don't reduce word error

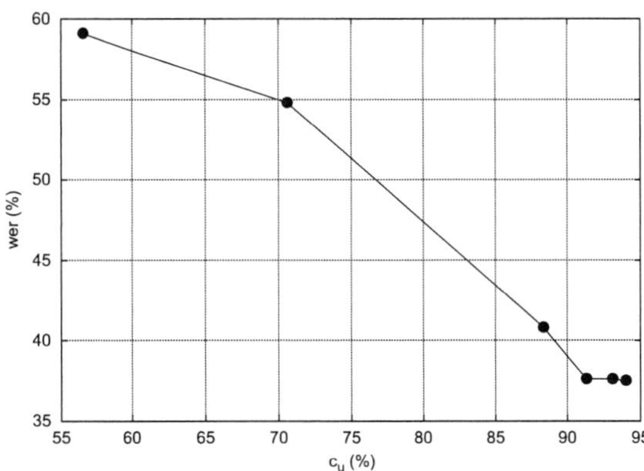

Figure 2: *Word error rates versus lexical coverage of the recognition dictionary on the test set.*

rates further as support by the language model collapses due to missing trigrams. This is also reflected in trigram perplexity figures ranging within **320-330**.

Apart of problems due to out-of-vocabulary words, the most frequent types of errors are insertions and deletions of common, poorly articulated, short words like negative and modal particles, articles, prepositions, and conjunctions. Another source of error is provoked by homophonies of word transitions within different word sequences, which cause wrong word boundary settings, *e.g.* note the displacement of initial [s] in the REFerence (Σ, σ) to final [s] in the HYPothesis (ς):

REF: ...στη Λεωφόρο Σπάτων στη ...
HYP: ...στη Λεωφόρος πάντως τη ...

A well endowed language model seems to be the only way out in this case.

5   Conclusions and Perspectives

Governed by the Modern Greek (MG) phonolocical and prosodical system we presented a grapheme-to-phoneme conversion for pronunciation generation necessary for ASR dictionaries. Several experiments were carried out employing language models and lexica of different extent. The resulting word error rate of around 38% may seem rather high, but is indeed within the ballpark for systems of comparable resources of training data. On the other hand, high perplexity values (compared to other European languages) is another indication of a rather difficult test set.

Concurrent ASR systems for inflectional languages, *e.g.*   for Czech (Byrne et al., 2001),

try to solve the problem of enormous vocabulary growth by performing automatic stemming and sophisticated morpheme-based language modelling. These techniques require grammatically tagged corpora and a morphological lexicon. However, as argued in Section 2, morphological decomposition is extremely non-systematic for Modern Greek and thus difficult to implement by means of rule-based stemming.

In (Oikonomidis and Digalakis, 2003) a maximum entropy language model incorporating n-gram (with Kneser-Ney smoothing) as well as stem constraints (word classification according to about 30k stems!) has been examined and a small but statistically significant improvement was achieved. Similar results were obtained from a factored language-modeling approach (Vergyri et al., 2004) with data-driven parameter optimization by genetic algorithms. Again small reductions of perplexity and word error rates are reported.

In view of the minor gain in performance using morphologically motivated language models, we expect considerable improvements by reducing the n-gram sparseness problem via incorporating much more language model data (keeping full form word lexica at the moment).

References

W. Byrne, J. Hajič, P. Ircing, F. Jelinek, S. Khudanpur, P. Krbec and J. Psutka. 2001. *On Large Vocabulary Continuous Speech Recognition of Highly Inflectional Language - Czech.* Proc. of Eurospeech 2001, Vol. 1: 487–490.

V. Digalakis, D. Oikonomidis, D. Pratsolis, N. Tsourakis, C. Vosnidis, N. Chatzichrisafis, V. Diakoloukas. 2003. *Large Vocabulary Continuous Speech Recognition in Greek: Corpus and an Automatic Dictation System.* Proc. of Eurospeech 2003: 1565–1568.

S. Katsikas. 1997. *Probleme der neugriechischen Graphematik aus der Perspektive des Fremdsprachenlernens* in H. Eichner et al. (eds): *Sprachnormung und Sprachplanung*: 419–474.

P. Mackridge. 1985. *Modern Greek Language - A Descritpive Analysis.* Oxford University Press, 1985.

D. Oikonomidis and V. Digalakis. 2003. *Stem-based Maximum Entropy Language Models for Inflectional Languages.* Proc. of Eurospeech 2003: 2285–2288.

D. Vergyri, K. Kirchhoff, K. Duh, A. Stolke. 2004. *Morphology-Based Language Modeling for Arabic Speech Recognition* Proc. of ICSLP 2004: 2245–2248

Role of Different Spectral Attributes in Vowel Categorization:

the Case of Udmurt

Janne Savela
Department of Information Technology
University of Turku
janne.savela@utu.fi

Stina Ojala
Department of Information Technology
University of Turku
stina.ojala@utu.fi

Olli Aaltonen
Department of Phonetics
University of Turku
olli.aaltonen@utu.fi

Tapio Salakoski
Department of Information Technology
University of Turku
tapio.salakoski@utu.fi

Abstract

The present study examines the difference between categorization and goodness ratings in Udmurt (Finno-Ugric language) using different sets of spectral attributes. The tendency to have two areas of /u/ vowels was observed in languages with unrounded non-front closed vowels during the TUR-VOTES project. Our study explores whether this can be due to the different acoustic attributes used in the identification and goodness ratings of these vowels. The identification and goodness-rating of Udmurt close vowels confirmed the observation. The model using only formants was not significant for identification data, but did explain the goodness rating data. The spectral moments explained both identification and goodness ratings.

1 Introduction

The vowel perception is a process in which the auditory pattern induced by the perceived stimulus is categorized with the stored auditory patterns of similar stimuli. The basic question in speech perception studies is to understand the role of the dif-

ferent spectral attributes within these processes and the actual similarity of two sounds within a chosen scale. This is crucial in the interpretation of the patterns observed in human performance based on these similarities (e.g. identification and discrimination and linguistic use of the same physical stimuli). The crucial question is: what type of similarity the listener use, if asked to identify the stimuli or to estimate its goodness. The knowledge on these features makes possible to predict, how people would perceive the stimuli they have not heard before, and consequently categorization in accordance with their linguistic knowledge about the speech sounds.

The long time problem of the vowel identification studies has been the discrepancy between the whole spectral attributes and formants that give different information about the physical similarity of the stimulus. According to Rosner (1994) the discrepancy may be related to the difference between general acoustic distance and the phonetic distance between the same vowel pair (also Granstrom & Klatt, 1979). The general assumption has been that the formant hypothesis, formant peak picking, is enough to explain the attentive vowel identification responses. Savela et al. (2003) showed that the formant peak picking and the general acoustic distance can be related to the different types of perceptual processes: automatic and post-perceptual. The automatic process buffers the fea-

Joakim Nivre, Heiki-Jaan Kaalep, Kadri Muischnek and Mare Koit (Eds.)
NODALIDA 2007 Conference Proceedings, pp. 384–388

tures of the stimuli, using intuitive knowledge on the important information within the stimulus. It was shown (ibidem) that the formant information can be considered as an intuitive indexical knowledge on the category and the whole spectral information was shown to be post-perceptual language independent general information about the similarity of two stimuli. In extreme cases the general auditory knowledge and the formant based linear knowledge can result non-continuous areas within the vowel space.

The aim of the present study is to use comparison of the identification and goodness rating data in order to show the role of formant based intuitive (indexical) similarity and the whole spectral based auditory similarity between the synthetic stimuli, using familiarity based indexical (goodness ratings) and analytical symbolic strategies. The idea is to identify the attributes sufficient to explain the identification and goodness ratings adequately.

First two models are tested, in the first model the efficiency of two formant model is tested and in the second model with the spectral moments added is tested. The aim of the present study is to show that vowel identification and goodness rating are based on different spectral attributes in terms of vowel space. The chosen vowels are Udmurt /ɨ/ (unrounded close central vowel) and /u/ (rounded close back vowel) which both cover the same areas of the F1-F2 vowel space. This area of the perceptual vowel space is critical, because it has been revealed as the most challenging area of the vowel space in using of the formant based models. In this particular area of the vowel space the F1, F2 and F3 are distinct and no trivial fusion of the formants can be observed.

2 The TURVOTES data for Udmurt

2.1 Methods

Stimuli

The test consisted of synthetic vowels which covered the entire vowel space except for diphthongs and nasal vowels. The stimuli were synthesized with Klatt parallel synthesizer (Klatt 1980). The vowel space was created by varying F1 from

250 to 800 Hz with steps of 30 mel and F2 from 600 to 2800 Hz with steps of 50 mel. F3 is 2500 Hz as long as F2 is 2000 Hz or below and higher by 200 mel when F2 is above 2000 Hz. The duration of the vowel stimuli was 350 ms and their pitch rose first from 100 Hz to 120 Hz (until 120 ms) and fell then to 80 Hz during the rest of the stimulus. The amplitude of the formants were not damped which can lead to the higher amplitudes of higher formants.

Procedure

There were six subjects (mean age 28,5). They were asked to name the vowel they heard (using Udmurt orthography) and to evaluate the goodness of the vowel (grades 1 – 7). The test for whole database took about 45 minutes. The stimuli were delivered through headphones in a sound hampered room at the Turku University Language centre.

2.2 Results

The identification data for the Udmurt data is drawn in Figure 1.

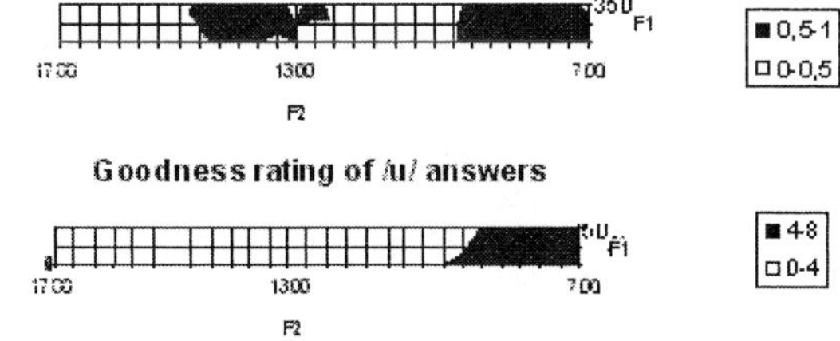

Figure 1. The identification of the non front back vowels in Udmurt. The goodness is described using 1 – 7 goodness scale (two steps) and the identification is described on percent of answers (over 50 % categorization is presented with black color).

The results were clear. In categorization data the area of /u/ was divided into the two different areas whereas the goodness rating data showed only one area of high goodness. Our finding is against the assumption of existence of linear prototype-based categorization of the vowel stimuli. This is because identification of the category can not be explained by two lowest formants of prototypical exemplars.

3   Statistical evaluation of the Udmurt data

3.1   Methods

In order to study the similarity between proto-typical areas and vowel boundaries, two binominal regression models were made. The stimuli that the subjects had perceived as /u/ or /ɨ/ were chosen to analysis. Four models were tested in binominal logistic regression mode. In two of them the stimulus category was the dependent parameter and in two of the models the stimulus goodness served as the dependent parameter respectively. The independent parameters were the formants or the formants with spectral moments respectively.

The spectral moments in the signals were analyzed using the PRAAT speech analysis program. First the Fourier analysis of the vowels was made for all stimuli, using sampling frequency 11024 Hz. The measuring of the spectral moments was based on the power spectrum in which the magnitudes of the spectral components are squared. It has been used by Forrest (1988) in measuring of the fricatives. The centre of gravity describes the average frequency of the spectral components in signal (Figure 2).

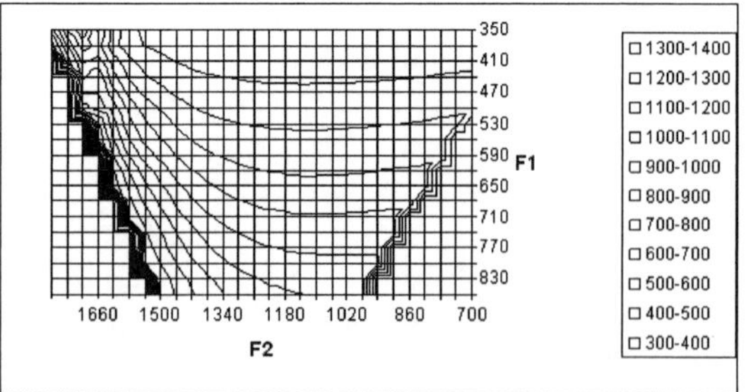

Figure 2. Center of gravity in power spectrum of the synthetic vowel in mel scale plotted against the formant values. The analyzed area is marked with boundaries.

The standard deviation describes the mean difference between the spectral components and the centre of gravity. It is a square root of the second central moment of the spectrum. It describes how much the spectral components differ from the centre of the gravity (Figure 3).

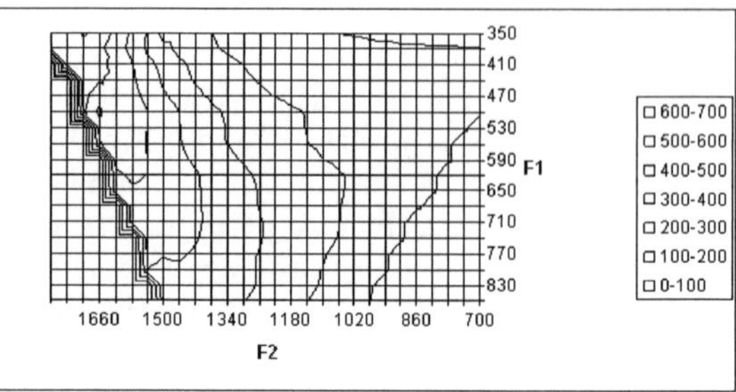

Figure 3. Standard deviation in the power spectrum of the synthetic vowel in mel scale plotted against the formant values. The analyzed area is marked with boundaries.

The (normalized) skewness tells the asymmetry in the shape of the spectrum between the lower and higher areas in the vowel spectrum. It is measured by dividing the third spectral moment (non-normalized skewness) with the 1.5 power of the second spectral moment Figure 4.

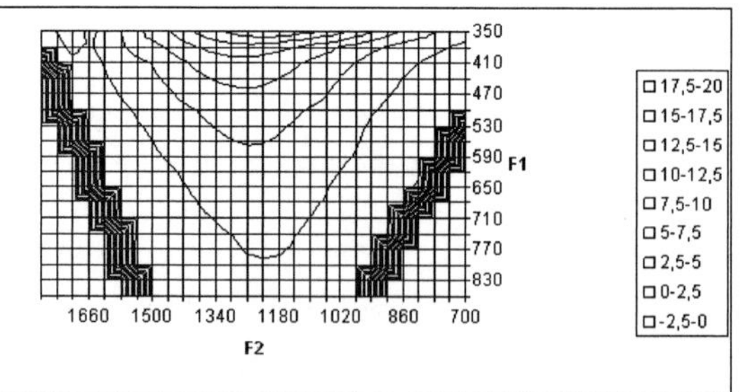

Figure 4. Skewness in the power spectrum of the synthetic vowels plotted against the formant values. The analyzed area is marked with boundaries.

The (normalized) kurtosis describes how much the spectrum differs from the Gaussian distribution (Figure 5).

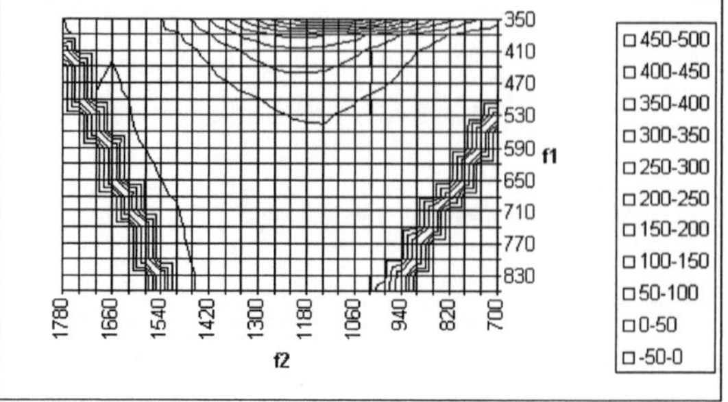

Figure 5. Kurtosis in the power spectrum of the synthetic vowels plotted against the formant values. The analyzed area is marked with boundaries.

3.2 Results

The results of the study are shown in Table 1.

	Chi square	DF	VOWEL NAME /ɨ - u/			VOWEL GOODNESS/ɨ - u/		
			sig.	-2 log	Chi square	DF	sig.	-2 log
F1F2	4,444	2	0,108	424,287	115,488	2	,000	346,146
F1F2 + SPEC	113,799	6	0,00	314,932	143,548	6	0,00	318,086

Table 1. The strength of models in the Udmurt /ɨ-u/ identification.

The first column shows the chi-square value of the model that tells the general fit of the variables in the model (omnibus test on the variables within the model). The next column (DF) tells the degrees of freedom in model and the third column (sig.) tells omnibus significance of the model. In fourth column (-2log likelihood) presents a value that gives the deviation of the likelihood function of the logistic model and makes possible to compare the fits of the models.

The results show that the identification of vowels was not predicted by formants (insignificant) only whereas the goodness ratings could be evaluated using formant values. The effect of the difference between goodness rating models was smaller, although significant. However looking at the individual formants gives a clearer picture (Table 2).

	VOWEL NAME /ɨ - u/			VOWEL GOODNESS/ɨ - u/		
	Chi-square	DF	P	Wald	DF	p
F1	,803	1	,370	10,019	1	0,002
F2	13,194	1	,000	17,829	1	0,000
COG	3,148	1	,076	5,366	1	0,21
STD	7,897	1	,005	5,089	1	0,24
SKEWNESS	18,618	1	0,00	6,540	1	0,011
KURTOSIS	16,748	1	0,00	17,693	1	0,00

Table 2. The statistical significance of different spectral attributes in identification and goodness rating of Udmurt vowels in models with spectral moments.

In goodness ratings F1 was more important than in categorization that was more the importance of skewness and kurtosis was more significant. The results showed that the identification and goodness ratings were based on different acoustic criteria although many features had similar significance.

4   Discussion and Conclusion

The present study was designed to show that the goodness ratings and identification of the vowels use different spectral attributes in the vowel space. The results argued against the use of the similar model of predictive acoustic parameters for goodness rating data and identification data, providing that the formant based similarity does not fit the identification functions of the Udmurt identification data. It was shown that the identification can be based on post-perceptual process different to goodness rating. The plasticity to the general acoustic features can lead to the areas of similarity that are not similar to the proto-typical exemplars of the category, but still categorized as the same.

The general acoustic features can lead to the areas of similarity that are not similar to the prototype. Recently, the understanding of the phonetic experience has exploded. The present study showed that the many questions concerning the area of prototypical vowels and their relationship to the rest of the category can be elaborated using auditory model in which spectral moments are added to the model. In comparison to the Rosner and Pickering's theory in which the vowel categories are always linear in terms of formant space model (1994) which do not explain the identification data. Additionally, a present study provides information about the perception of open back vowels and their relationship to closed back vowels. It can be speculated, that the perceptual similarity between /u/ and /y/ in some languages may be related to the listeners' habits to use spectral moment information, if synthetic stimuli covering large areas of the vowel space is used. In conclusion, to obtain a more comprehensive description of vowel category, the person-independent formant tracking model has to be extended with spectral moment information dependent on person and culture.

References

Aaltonen, O., Eerola, O., Hellstrom, A., Uusipaikka, E. and Lang, A. H. (1997). Perceptual magnet effect in the light of behavioral and psychophysiological data, *Journal of the Acoustical Society of America* 101(2): 1090-105.

Carlson, R., Granström, B. and Klatt, D. (1979). Vowel perception: the relative perceptual salience of selected acoustic manipulations, *TMH-QPSR* 3-4.

Ito, M., Tsuchida, J. and Yano, M. (2001). On the effectiveness of whole spectral shape for vowel perception, *Journal of the Acoustical Society of America* 110(2): 1141-1149.

Rosner, B. S. and Pickering, J. B. (1994). *Vowel perception and production.* Oxford, Oxford Univ. Press.

Savela, J., Kleimola, T., Mäkelä, L., Tuomainen, J. and Aaltonen, O. (2003). The effects of distinctive features on the perception of vowel categories. *The 15th International Congress of Phonetic Sciences*, Barcelona, Spain, Universitat Autònoma de Barcelona.

Thyer, N., Hickson, L. and Dodd, B. (2000). The perceptual magnet effect in Australian English vowels, *Perception and Psychophysics* 62(1): 1-20.

Recreating Humorous Split Compound Errors in Swedish by Using Grammaticality

Jonas Sjöbergh and Kenji Araki
Graduate School of Information Science and Technology
Hokkaido University
{js, araki}@media.eng.hokudai.ac.jp

Abstract

We present a program that recreates split compound errors with amusing effects in written Swedish. Two useful criteria for funniness is that the result should be grammatical and that the compound words should not be split into many short components.

1 Introduction

While humor is often used by humans, computational humor is an area of language processing that has seen relatively little attention. Most attempts have focused on language related humor, such as word play jokes. Languages with compounding where compound components are concatenated, i.e. combining several words into a single long word, have the possibility for compounding jokes, which seem fairly simplistic and thus achievable by computer.

Swedish is a language where compound components are concatenated and where compounding is very productive. Creating new quite long words from several shorter words is very common. If a word that should be written as one compound word is split up into several words, the meaning might be changed. Recently, many people have been annoyed by a perceived increase in this type of error in newspapers, signs and society. There was even a movement called *"skrivihop.nu"* (compound now!) which gathered over 25,000 members.

When a word is erroneously split so that the meaning is changed, the effect is sometimes amusing. Collections with examples of amusing mistakes from newspapers, restaurant menus, signs etc. are available on many humor sites on the Internet and seem to be an appreciated form of language humor.

We present a program that can recreate most examples from such humor collections given the intended (non-mistaken) text. It uses an automatic compound analyzer and an automatic grammar checking program. It turns out that grammati-

cality is a helpful criteria to tell if an erroneously split compound is amusing or not. To our knowledge, this is the first system for automatically generating this type of jokes, though other types of humor has been automatically generated (Binsted, 1996; Binsted et al., 2003; Stark et al., 2005; Yokogawa, 2001; Binsted and Takizawa, 1998; Sjöbergh and Araki, 2007). The system works on written Swedish, but a similar system for other languages with compounding, such as German or Norwegian, should be straightforward to create given a compound analyzer and a grammar checking program.

2 Description of the Program

Our program is quite simple. It uses a freely available program for analyzing compound words in Swedish (Sjöbergh and Kann, 2006) and an automatic grammar checking program for Swedish freely usable online (Domeij et al., 2000).

Given a sentence the program generates all possible compound analyses (according to the compound analysis program) of all the words. Each compound analysis of a word is then used to replace the word with the components of the compound separated into separate words. Compounds with several components or components that are in turn compounds need not be split fully, but can be. So given the word *"barnunderkläder"* (children's underwear), which can be analyzed as *"barn-under-kläder"* (children-below-clothes), the suggestions *"barn underkläder"* (children underwear), *"barnunder kläder"* (miracle-child clothes), *"barn under kläder"* (children under clothes) are generated.

Words with the character "-" are also processed in the same way, replacing the "-" with whitespace. The "-" has several uses, including some forms of conjunctions of compounds, e.g. *"hund- och katthår"* (dog [hair] and cat hair), and line breaks inside words.

From the complete sentence, new sentences are

Joakim Nivre, Heiki-Jaan Kaalep, Kadri Muischnek and Mare Koit (Eds.)

NODALIDA 2007 Conference Proceedings, pp. 389–393

generated by replacing one, two or three compounds with the suggested split variations. All combinations are generated. This of course generates very many variations for sentences with many compounds or compounds with many possible analyses or many components. Most of these are not amusing.

To remove unamusing sentences, two methods are used. The first is a powerful heuristic for removing over generation from the compound analyzer. If an analysis of a compound word results in more components than the analysis with the fewest components, the one with many components is ignored. Analyses with many short components are rarely amusing. There can of course be several different analyses with the same number of components.

The second method is to send the generated sentences to the automatic grammar checker. If the generated sentence is considered ungrammatical it is disregarded. The exception is the error type "split compound", which is ignored since the program is trying to add split compounds on purpose. The error type "no active verb" is also ignored, since many examples do not contain a verb, such as signs outside shops, e.g. *"Dansk fårost"* (Danish sheep cheese).

A small variation of this method is to remove suggested sentences for any grammar checking error, including the two exceptions above, if another suggestion for the same original sentence exists that has no errors at all. This was also tried.

For some sentences there is no suggested humorous variation from the program. This can be caused by either the compound analyzer failing to find any compounds to split in the sentence, or all suggestions being removed because they are considered ungrammatical.

3   Evaluation: Recreating Humor

A test corpus was created by searching the web for collections of amusing split compounds. Many examples are very similar, such as *"fryst kyckling lever"* (deep freezed chicken is still alive) with the intended sentence being *"fryst kycklinglever"* (deep freezed chicken liver) and *"djupfryst kyckling lever"* (same as previous example). In such cases, only one example from the set of variations of basically the same mistake was used in the corpus. This gave 230 examples of amusing split compounds from the real world. A few example sentences are given in Appendix A.

All examples were also fixed by hand, to recreate the intended meaning. Examples with only a word with no context are common in the split compound collections. These are often taken from signs with few words or leave out the original context because it was not very amusing. To get more information from

the grammar checker, such examples were also given a simple context, so the grammar checker had something to base the analysis on. For example *"pris för slag"* (prices for being beaten), fixed to *"prisförslag"* (price suggestions), were at the same time put in the context *"Vi erbjuder: pris för slag."* (We are offering prices for being beaten.).

The program was run on the fixed sentences, with the goal of recreating the amusing split compounds. Not all split compounds can be recreated, since some of the corpus sentences contain words that are not covered by the compound analyzer. Several examples are words that are not strictly compound words, but were split into more than one word anyway by the original writer.

Generated sentences were classified as "Correct" if perfectly fitting the amusing original, "Almost" if almost fitting the original or "Wrong". "Almost" was used for sentences that found some but not all of the funny parts of a sentence, meaning that any compound which was split in the suggested sentence must be split in the same way as in the original, but if some compounds are correctly split it is an almost match if some compound is left untouched despite being split in the original. The sentence is thus a little bit funny, but has not achieved its full humorous potential. Sentences that are "wrong" are those that contain compounds that were split by the program that were either not split in the funny sentence or split in some other way than the one chosen by the program.

An example is *"datorn visar: fel meddelande, felkod 47"* (the computer is showing: the wrong message, error code 47) which is an almost match for *"datorn visar: fel meddelande, fel kod 47"* (the computer is showing: the wrong message, wrong code 47), both related to the error free sentence *"datorn visar: felmeddelande, felkod 47"* (the computer is showing: an error message, error code 47). Outputting *"datorn visar: fel med delande, fel kod 47"* (the computer is showing an error with dividing, wrong code 27) would be considered wrong, since the first compound is split in a different way than it should be.

The results are shown in Table 1. Both the few components heuristic and the grammar checking reduces the number of generated unamusing sentences considerably, while removing only one amusing sentence each. They can also be used together with even better effect, since the overlap in removed sentences is not very large. If suspicious suggestions are removed when a grammatical suggestion exists, many of the correct suggestions are removed. Thus the recall is decreased considerably, though precision is

	All	Gr.	Full Gr.	Few	Few, Gr.	Few, Full Gr.
Not found	16	17	31	17	18	26
Correct	214	213	199	213	212	204
Almost	43	40	37	40	40	37
Wrong	450	322	216	271	183	112
Recall (%)	93	93	87	93	92	89
Precision (%)	30	37	44	44	49	58
Precision (%, no A)	32	40	48	48	54	65

Table 1: "All", all suggestions from the compound analyzer. "Gr.", removing most ungrammatical suggestions. "Full Gr.", removing all ungrammatical suggestions. "Few", removing compound analyses with many components. "Precision, no A", the precision if sentences of type "Almost" are ignored.

increased.

It is also possible to increase the precision further by only using the suggestion with the most splits for each sentence. This reduces the number of generated suggestions drastically, since there is only one suggestion for each sentence, but while the precision rises to well over 70% the recall drops to about 70%, of course varying a bit depending on other settings.

Sentences for which the correct suggestion is not found generally contain split words that the compound analyzer does not consider to be compounds at all, often correctly. One example is *"Dagens prognos är öm som snö, slask och regn."* (Today's forecast is hurting like snow, slush and rain.), created from *"Dagens prognos är ömsom snö, slask och regn."* (Today's forecast is a mix of snow, slush and rain.). *"Ömsom"* is not a compound word, though it happens to become two words if a space is inserted in the right place. The fact that this word is not actually a compound word but was still split into two words by the original author and made sense is probably a large part of what makes this sentence funny (and thus made it appear in the joke collections the corpus is based on). This lack of recall could be mitigated by having a more aggressive compound analyzer, looking for any way to split a word that results in new words. This will however generate very many new suggestions. Most real life examples are split at the compound component borders, so the loss of recall from generating only such sentences is low.

Grammaticality is a useful filter. Only three of the real world sentences in the corpus are considered ungrammatical by the grammar checker. Requiring the amusing sentences to be grammatical is thus a good way to filter out bad suggestions with low risk of loosing actually amusing suggestions. It does however not remove as many bad suggestions as the heuristic for removing over generation from the compound analyzer. This heuristic is also very powerful, only

removing one correct suggestion in the corpus while removing many faulty suggestions.

As a side note, the actual results are slightly funnier than what is suggested by Table 1. Several of the suggestions classified as "Wrong" are still funny, though in a different way than the real world example. Two examples are *"matt trea"* (fatigued letter three) instead of *"matt rea"* (fatigued sale) for *"mattrea"* (carpet sale) and *"brun stens batterier"* (the batteries belonging to a brown stone) instead of *"brunstens batterier"* (the batteries for when in heat) for *"brunstensbatterier"* (zinc-carbon batteries).

4 Evaluation: Creating New Humor

In the previous section, all sentences in the corpus had the potential to become funny. Taking a Swedish sentence in general, this is much less likely to be true. A (very) small test to get an indication of the potential on more general text was also performed. The front page of the Internet version of the Swedish newspaper Metro[1] was downloaded and the program run on the text. Removal of ungrammatical suggestions and suggestions with many short components was done.

The Metro text contains 335 sentences or phrases. From these, the program outputs 26 suggestions. Evaluating whether these are funny or not is of course subjective, though many cases where the program fails are easy to spot.

The following 10 suggestions were deemed (by the author, native speaker of Swedish) to be in the vein of the funny examples in the previous corpus, and somewhat funny (some are funny, some are very faintly funny):

- *En ja mes, men ingen Bond* (A yes saying wimp, but no Bond) *En James, men ingen Bond* (A James, but no Bond)

---

[1] http://www.metro.se/se/nyheter/

- *fort sätt* (quick way) *fortsätt* (continue)

- *Flykting mot tagande ska utredas* (Refugee against taking will be investigated) *Flyktingmottagande ska utredas* (Refugee welcoming procedures will be investigated)

- *Flyktingmott agande ska utredas* ("Butterfly refugee"-like beatings will be investigated) Original same as above.

- *Se fler bilder på Bil bo.* (See more pictures of Car nests.) *Se fler bilder på Bilbo.* (See more pictures of Bilbo (a lemur at the zoo).)

- *Tal man utmanar Bush i Syrien* (Speakable man challenges Bush in Syria) *Talman utmanar Bush i Syrien* (Speaker of the parliament challenges Bush in Syria)

- *Fri lans* (Free lance) *Frilans* (Freelance)

- *Quelle pastell le!* (Smile in the way of Quelle Pastell!) *Quelle pastelle!* (Quelle Pastelle!)

- *Play station 3 vapen i kampen mot Alzheimers* (The Playstation is 3 weapons against Alzheimer's) *Playstation 3 vapen i kampen mot Alzheimers* (The Playstation 3 as a weapon against Alzheimer's)

- *Pandaporren miss lyckades* (Miss Success, the panda porn) *Pandaporren misslyckades* (The panda porn failed)

Another six suggestions were deemed to also be in the vein of the funny corpus examples, though even less funny.

This means that a surprisingly high 10 or 16 of the 26 sentences were in some way joke like (though, as said before, the judgements are very subjective and were done by only one person). This means that about one suggestion in two was joke like, and about one sentence in 30 from the newspaper could be made into a joke. Of course, the attention seeking nature of a front page of a newspaper is still a fairly good source of funny formulations. Less successful results can probably be expected from other genres.

5   Conclusions

Amusing split compounds can successfully be recreated by a program, with very high recall. The program also generates sentences that contain split compounds that are not amusing. Grammaticality of the sentence is a good criteria for removing unamusing

suggestions, filtering out many unamusing suggestions and only one of the amusing sentences. Another useful criteria is that the compounds should not be split into many short components. This also removes only one amusing suggestions while removing many unamusing ones. These two methods also complement each other, each removing many suggestions that the other method lets through. So, to be funny, be grammatical and don't overdo it!

With a recall of recreating 92% of the original amusing sentences, more than one suggestion in two is funny. At a quite high cost in recall, lowering it to 70%, it is possible to increase precision to over 75%.

While grammaticality seems to be almost a requirement for amusing split compounds, it is far from enough. Many texts can be split and still grammatical without amusing results. A small evaluation on the front page of a newspaper showed promising results on more general text, though. About half the generated suggestions were deemed amusing, and about one sentence in 30 from the newspaper could be turned into a joke.

Acknowledgments

This work has been funded by The Japanese Society for the Promotion of Science, (JSPS).

References

Kim Binsted and Osamu Takizawa. 1998. BOKE: A Japanese punning riddle generator. *Journal of the Japanese Society for Artificial Intelligence*, 13(6):920–927.

Kim Binsted, Benjamin Bergen, and Justin McKay. 2003. Pun and non-pun humour in second-language learning. In *Workshop Proceedings of CHI 2003*, Fort Lauderdale, Florida.

Kim Binsted. 1996. *Machine Humour: An Implemented Model of Puns*. Ph.D. thesis, University of Edinburgh, Edinburgh, United Kingdom.

Richard Domeij, Ola Knutsson, Johan Carlberger, and Viggo Kann. 2000. Granska – an efficient hybrid system for Swedish grammar checking. In *Proceedings of Nodalida '99*, pages 49–56, Trondheim, Norway.

Jonas Sjöbergh and Kenji Araki. 2007. Automatically creating word-play jokes in japanese. In *Proceedings of NL-178*, pages 91–95, Nagoya, Japan.

Jonas Sjöbergh and Viggo Kann. 2006. Vad kan statistik avslöja om svenska sammansättningar? *Språk och Stil*, 16:199–214.

Jeff Stark, Kim Binsted, and Benjamin Bergen. 2005. Disjunctor selection for one-line jokes. In *Proceedings of INTETAIN 2005*, pages 174–182, Madonna di Campiglio, Italy.

Toshihiko Yokogawa. 2001. Generation of Japanese puns based on similarity of articulation. In *Proceedings of IFSA/NAFIPS 2001*, Vancouver, Canada.

A Example Sentences

Here are some example sentences from the evaluation corpus, both the mistaken/funny versions and the intended versions are given.

- *Vi behöver tio öringar.* (We need ten salmon trouts.) *Vi behöver tiooringar.* (We need 10 "cent" coins.)

- *Vi skulle gärna vilja ha en flaggstång och några barn och vuxen cyklar också när vi ändå är på gång.* (Now that we are at it anyway, we would like a flagpole and some kids, and an adult is riding a bicycle.) *Vi skulle gärna vilja ha en flaggstång och några barn- och vuxencyklar också när vi ändå är på gång.* (Now that we are at it anyway, we would like a flagpole, bicycles for kids, and bicycles for adults.)

- *Vila under armarna mot skrivbordet.* (Rest below your arms on the desk.) *Vila underarmarna mot skrivbordet.* (Rest your wrists on the desk.)

- *Äldre dam eller herrcykel köpes billigt.* (Will buy cheaply: older lady or a bicycle for men.) *Äldre dam- eller herrcykel köpes billigt.* (Will buy cheaply: older bicycle, either men's or women's model.)

- *Behöver du extra knäck på lovet?* (Do you need more caramel during the vacations?) *Behöver du extraknäck på lovet?* (Do you need a part time job during the vacations?)

- *Brun hårig sjuk sköterska strök Herr skjorta.* (Brown, hairy and sick nurse ironed Mr. Shirt.) *Brunhårig sjuksköterska strök Herrskjorta.* (Brown haired nurse ironed a shirt [men's model].)

- *Dagens rubrik är svensk general agent för Kinaföretag.* (Today's headline is: Swedish general a spy for Chinese company.) *Dagens rubrik är svensk generalagent för Kinaföretag.* (Today's headline is: Swedish general representative for Chinese company.)

- *Dagens rätt är halvgrillad kyckling med kul potatis.* (Today's lunch is half grilled chicken with amusing potatoes.) *Dagens rätt är halvgrillad kyckling med kulpotatis.* (Today's lunch is half grilled chicken with round potatoes.)

- *Det finns en telefonservice som under normal arbetstid ger hjälp med svensk talande personal.* (We have a phone service that during normal working hours gives assistance with Swedish staff that can speak.) *Det finns en telefonservice som under normal arbetstid ger hjälp med svensktalande personal.* (We have a phone service that during normal working hours gives assistance with staff that can speak Swedish.)

- *Företaget bjuder samtliga anställda på Jullunch, för utom stående 50 kr* (The company treats all employees to a Christmas lunch, except people who are standing up who pay 50 kronor.) *Företaget bjuder samtliga anställda på Jullunch, för utomstående 50 kr* (The company treats all employees to a Christmas lunch, non-company people pay 50 kronor.)

A Re-examination of Question Classification

Håkan Sundblad
Linköpings universitet
581 83 Linköping
Sweden
`hakjo@ida.liu.se`

Abstract

This paper presents a re-examiniation of previous work on machine learning techniques for questions classification, as well as results from new experiments. The results suggest that some of the work done in the field have yielded biased results. The results also suggest that Naïve Bayes, Decision Trees and Support Vector Machines perform on par with each other when faced with actual users' questions.

1 Introduction

One of the most important factors for a question answering system to succeed is the ability to correctly identify the expected answer's semantic type (Moldovan et al., 2002).

This paper presents results from an evaluation of five different machine learning approaches to question classification (Naïve Bayes, k Nearest Neighbours, Decision Tree Learning, Sparse Network of Winnows, and Support Vector Machines). The paper also presents a review of earlier work on question classification as well as results from experiments using slightly different data than used in previous work. The reason for re-examining the results from previous work is that only performance in terms of accuracy has been reported in the literature. No significance testing has been made to see if there really is a difference in results between learners. Furthermore, the data used in many of the experiments have been submitted to manual selection, and also the test data is slightly different from the training data.

2 The Question Classification Task

Question classification can loosely be defined as the task of given a question (represented by a set of features), assign the question to a single or a set of categories (answer types). Adopting the formal definition of text categorization (Sebastiani, 2002) to the problem of question classification, the task can be defined as follows: Question classification is the task of assigning a boolean value to each pair $\langle q_j, c_i \rangle \in \mathcal{Q} \times \mathcal{C}$, where $\mathcal{Q}$ is the domain of questions and $\mathcal{C} = \{c_1, c_2, \ldots, c_{|\mathcal{C}|}\}$ is a set of predefined categories. The task therefore requires a taxonomy of answer types according to which questions should be categorized on the on hand, and a means for actually making this classification on the other.

3 Previous Work

Radev et al. (2002) experiment with machine learning for question classification using decision rule learning with set-valued features. This is a standard decision tree/rule approach that has been augmented in that instead of being restricted to features with single values, the values can also be a set of values. The answer type taxonomy consists of 17 types, and the training data is TREC-8 and TREC-9 data. Testing data is TREC-10. In the experiment, questions are represented by 13 features, 9 of which are semantic features based on WordNet.

Li and Roth (2002) use a Sparse Network of Winnows (SNoW) to classify questions with respect to their expected answer type. The taxonomy consists of 6 coarse and 50 fine semantic classes. The training corpus used consists of 5,500 questions. Some

Joakim Nivre, Heiki-Jaan Kaalep, Kadri Muischnek and Mare Koit (Eds.)
NODALIDA 2007 Conference Proceedings, pp. 394–397

of these are manually constructed, while other stems from the TREC-8 and TREC-9 conferences. The test corpus comprise 500 questions from the TREC-10 conference. The input to the classifiers is a list of features. The features used were words, part-of-speech tags, chunks, named entities, head chunks (e.g. the first noun chunk in a sentence), and semantically related words (words that often occur with a specific question class). Apart from these primitive features, a set of operators were used to compose more complex features.

Zhang and Lee (2003) used the same taxonomy as Li and Roth (2002), as well as the same training and testing data. In an initial experiment they compared different machine learning approaches with regards to the question classification problem: Nearest Neighbors (NN), Naïve Bayes (NB), Decision Trees (DT), SNoW, and Support Vector Machines. The feature extracted and used as input to the machine learning algorithms in the initial experiment was bag-of-words and bag-of-$n$grams (all continuous word sequences in the question). Questions were represented as binary feature vectors. In a second experiment the linear kernel of the SVM was replaced with a tree kernel developed by the authors.

Suzuki et al. (2003b) used a SVM with a hierarchical directed acyclic graph kernel (Suzuki et al., 2003a) for the question classification problem. The answer type taxonomy used consists of 150 different types. The corpus used was in Japanese and consisted of 1011 questions from NTCIR-QAC, 2000 questions of CRL-QA data, and 2000 other questions reported to be of TREC-style (Suzuki et al., 2002). After removing answer types with too few (less than 10) examples, a total of 68 answer types were actually used.

Hacioglu and Ward (2003) used a SVM with error correcting codes to convert the multi-class classification problem into a number of binary ones. In essence each class is assigned a codeword of 1's and -1's of length m, where m equals or is greater than the number of classes. This splits the multi-class data into m binary class data. Therefore, m SVM classifiers can be designed and their output combined. The SVM:s also used linear kernels. The same taxonomy, training and testing data was used as in Li and Roth (2002)

4 Method

In order to compare the five algorithms (Naïve Bayes (NB), k Nearest Neighbours (kNN), Decision Tree Learning (DT), Sparse Network of Winnows (SNoW), and Support Vector Machines (SVM)) significance testing have been used. Significance scores can not be found in any previous work on question classification and hence it is difficult to draw any real conclusions from this work. For present purposes the micro and macro sign tests established by Yang and Liu (1999) have been used. Thses were originally developed for the text categorization task, but as question classification bears many resemblances and can be seen as a special case of text categorization.

The taxonomy used is the taxonomy proposed by Li and Roth (2002). This taxonomy has been chosen since it is the most frequently used one in earlier work in the field (Li and Roth, 2002; Zhang and Lee, 2003; Hacioglu and Ward, 2003). The corpora used is both the corpus constructed and tagged by Li and Roth (2002), as well as a newly tagged corpus extracted from the AnswerBus logs. AnswerBus is a question answering system that has been online and logged real users questions. The AnswerBus corpus consists of 25,000 questions. For present purposes 2,000 questions have been selected and tagged according to the aforementioned taxonomy. Questions are in all experiments treated as a bag-of-words and represented as binary feature vectors.

The results will be reported in terms of micro- and macro-averaged precision, recall and F-score. Micro-averaged precision and recall are dominated by the large categories, whereas macro-averaged precision and recall illustrate how well a classifier performs across all categories. Micro-averaged precision is denoted as π^μ, macro-averaged precision as π^M, micro-averaged recall as ρ^μ, and macro-averaged recall as ρ^M. Combined measures for micro-averaged results is denoted as F_1^μ while the corresponding macro-averaged measure is denoted as F_1^M.

Performance is for the purpose of this paper seen as solely related to accuracy in terms of precision and recall. The learning and classification speed of the algorithms are ignored.

5   Experiment 1

The first experiment is intended to be a straight-forward re-examination of previous work to establish what differences in performance there really are between machine learners. This experiment has been done under two different settings. First, we have used the corpus originally developed by (Li and Roth, 2002), but since the test corpus used consists of questions solely from TREC-10 and the TREC conferences have a specific agenda the test corpus might be slightly different from the training data. Therefore, a second setting was used where the questions from the training and test corpora were pooled together and a randomized test corpus was extracted. This will be refered to as the repartitioned corpus. The performance of the different learners on setting 1 can be found in table 1, setting 2 in table 2 while significance testing between the learners is shown in table 3

Classifier	π^μ	ρ^μ	F_1^μ	π^M	ρ^M	F_1^M
kNN	.6720	.6720	.6720	.6002	.5028	.5472
NB	.7162	.7120	.7141	.5979	.5775	.5875
SNoW	.7642	.7535	.7588	.7080	.6413	.6730
DT	.7780	.7780	.7780	.7460	.6819	.7125
SVM	.8149	.8100	.8124	.7574	.6655	.7085

Table 1: Performance of classifiers on original TREC data.

Classifier	π^μ	ρ^μ	F_1^μ	π^M	ρ^M	F_1^M
kNN	.6285	.6260	.6273	.6196	.5557	.5859
NB	.6713	.6700	.6707	.5970	.6498	.6223
SNoW	.6633	.6593	.6613	.6511	.4999	.5656
DT	.7194	.7180	.7187	.6381	.6202	.6290
SVM	.7820	.7820	.7820	.8122	.7112	.7584

Table 2: Performance of classifers on repartitioned TREC data.

As can be seen in table 1 and 2 the performance of the different learning algorithms with regards to micro-averaged precision and recall is at best equal to and in most cases worse on the repartitioned data than on the original data. When it comes to macro-averaged precision and recall the results are more varied.

In table 3 we can find differences when comparing the algorithms with regards to significant differences in performance. In the table, "$<$" means a

		Original		Repartitioned	
sysA	sysB	s-test	S-test	s-test	S-test
kNN	NB	$<$	-	$<$	$\ll$
kNN	SNoW	$\ll$	$<$	-	-
kNN	DT	$\ll$	$\ll$	$\ll$	$\ll$
kNN	SVM	$\ll$	$\ll$	$\ll$	$\ll$
NB	SNoW	$<$	-	-	-
NB	DT	$\ll$	$\ll$	$\ll$	-
NB	SVM	$\ll$	$\ll$	$\ll$	$\ll$
SNoW	DT	$<$	-	$\ll$	-
SNoW	SVM	$\ll$	-	$\ll$	$\ll$
DT	SVM	$\ll$	-	$\ll$	$\ll$

Table 3: Sigificance testing of classifiers on both original and repartitioned TREC data.

significantly on the .05 level, "$\ll$" and "$\gg$" means a difference on the .01 level. NB $<$ SNoW should be read as NB performs significantly worse than SNoW on the .05 level. The column "s-test" means micro sign test, and "S-test" means macro sign test. It is interesting to note that where there were no significant differences in performance on the original corpus there now are to some extent differences on the repartitioned corpus and also the other way around to a smaller extent. This might be an indication that the training and test corpora in fact are not balanced in the original setting, and some of the results reported in previous work is somewhat biased.

6   Experiment 2

To further investigate the performance of different machine learners in the face of a corpus consisting of actual users' questions a second experiment was conducted. As mentioned earlier, in this setting 2,000 questions from the AnswerBus logs are used, but everything else remains the same as in experiment 1. Results in terms of performance is found in table 4 and significance testing is found in table 5.

Classifier	π^μ	ρ^μ	F_1^μ	π^M	ρ^M	F_1^M
kNN	.7159	.7076	.7117	.6088	.5252	.5639
NB	.8000	.7953	.7976	.6959	.6605	.6778
SNoW	.6913	.6588	.6746	.6138	.7702	.6831
DT	.8143	.7953	.8047	.6871	.6583	.6724
SVM	.8176	.8128	.8152	.7319	.6499	.6885

Table 4: Performance of classifiers on AnswerBus data.

As can be seen in table 4 the performance in terms of micro-averaged precision and recall is higher on the AnswerBus corpus than on any of the TREC corpora. When it comes to macro-averaged perfor-manve the results are more varied and it is hard to draw any clear conclusions.

		Original	
sysA	sysB	s-test	S-test
kNN	NB	≪	<
kNN	SNoW	-	-
kNN	DT	≪	≪
kNN	SVM	≪	≪
NB	SNoW	≫	-
NB	DT	-	-
NB	SVM	-	-
SNoW	DT	≪	-
SNoW	SVM	≪	-
DT	SVM	-	-

Table 5: Sigificance testing of classifiers on Answer-Bus data.

In terms of significant differences between classi-fiers, the results from the AnswerBus corpus devi-ates from what could have been expected given the results on the TREC corpora. It seems than Naïve Bayes, Decision Trees and Support Vector Machines are on par with each other, while k Nearest Neigh-bours and Sparse Network of Winnows are sigifi-cantly worse in terms of performance.

7   Conclusions

The results in this paper indicate that some of the results found in previous work (Li and Roth, 2002; Zhang and Lee, 2003; Hacioglu and Ward, 2003) on question classification might be incorrect due to an unbiased training and test corpus. This bias stems from the fact that the training corpus is derived ex-clusively from TREC-10 data, while the training data stems from other sources. Since the TREC conferences have an explicit agenda that shifts from year to year this is perhaps no surprise. In relation to this, TREC material is maybe not the best source of information if one is interested in how different machine learners might perform on actual user data.

8   Future Work

The results from experiment 2 in this paper stems from a corpus of 2,000 questions. We will go on to categorize 3,000 more questions from the Answer-Bus logs and run the learners on this data in order to get even more accurate results. This work is well on the way.

We will also go on to make a deeper analysis of exactly which questions that pose problems for learning algorithms. Such work has not been re-ported in the literature thus far.

References

K. Hacioglu and W. Ward. 2003. Question classifica-tion with support vector machines and error correcting codes. In *Proceedings of HLT-NACCL 2003*.

X. Li and D. Roth. 2002. Learning question classifiers. In *Proceedings of the 19th International Conference on Computational Linguistics (COLING 2002)*, pages 556–562.

D. Moldovan, M. Paşca, S. Harabagiu, and M. Surdeanu. 2002. Performance issues and error analysis in an open-domain question answering system. In *Proceed-ings of the 40th Annual Meeting of the Association for Computational Linguistics*, pages 33–40, Philadel-phia.

D. Radev, W. Fan, H. Qi, H. Wu, and A. Grewal. 2002. Probabilistic question answering on the web. In *Pro-ceedings of the eleventh international conference on World Wide Web (WWW2002)*, Hawaii.

F. Sebastiani. 2002. Machine learning in automated text categorization. *ACM Computing Surveys*, 34(1):1–47, March.

J. Suzuki, Y. Sasaki, and E. Maeda. 2002. SVM an-swer selection for open-domain question answering. In *Proceedings of the 19th International Conference on Computational Linguistics (COLING 2002)*.

J. Suzuki, T. Hirao, Y. Sasaki, and E. Maeda. 2003a. Hierarchical directed acyclic graph kernel: Methods for natural language data. In *Proceedings of the 41st Annual Meeting of the Association for Computational Linguistics (ACL2003)*, pages 32–29.

J. Suzuki, H. Taira, Y. Sasaki, and E. Maeda. 2003b. Question classification using HDAG kernel. In *The ACL 2003 Workshop on Multilingual Summarization and Question Answering*.

Y. Yang and X. Liu. 1999. A re-examination of text categorization methods. In *Proceedings of the 22nd Annual International ACM SIGIR Conference on Research and Development in Information Retrieval*, pages 42–49, Berkeley, CA.

D. Zhang and W. S. Lee. 2003. Question classification using support vector machines. In *Proceedings of the 26th Annual International ACM SIGIR Conference on Research and Development in Informaion Retrieval*, pages 26–32.

Interpretation of Yes/No Questions as Metaphor Recognition

Tarmo Truu   **Haldur Õim**   **Mare Koit**

University of Tartu
Liivi 2, Tartu 50409
Estonia
{tarmo.truu, haldur.oim, mare.koit}@ut.ee

Abstract

Estonian institutional phone calls are analyzed with the further aim to develop a human-computer dialogue system. The analysis is based on the Estonian Dialogue Corpus. Linguistic cues of yes/no questions are found out that can be used for their automatic recognition.

1   Introduction

Automatic recognition of user questions is one of the main tasks of a dialogue system (DS) which interacts with a user in a natural language. An analysis of human-human conversations is needed in order to find out how do speakers formulate their requests and how hearers understand them.

When a speaker wants the hearer to perform an action, he can express his request directly, using an imperative form (*pass me the salt*); however, it is more polite to use an indirect request (such as *would you pass me the salt?*), which doesn't presuppose any hearer's attitude towards the requested action (in fact, she is questioned about that). Various methods for modulating the strength of utterances are chosen according to the degree of familiarity, respect, relative social roles of the participants of communication, and the impact that the contents of the acts might have on them (Brown and Levinson, 1987). Indirect speech acts may also be considered as allowing more than one characterization. On the standard view, an indirect speech act occurs when a speaker uses an utterance to perform an additional speech act to the one that is 'directly' associated with the utterance in view of its appearance, as illustrated by *Do you know what time it is?* (as a request to tell what time it is) or *What time do you think it is?* as a reproach for being late (Bunt and Girard, 2005).

The idea that constructing new meanings from explicitly given ones forms an inherent part of text understanding process is well known in (cognitive) linguistics. The situation where in order to understand a text one should, proceeding from what is explicitly said in the text, carry out certain operations to reach the 'real' (intended) meaning of the text is in fact much more common in natural communication. Processing indirect speech acts (such as a request in the form of a question) constitutes just one – but very common – case/example of quite analogous processes. Would it be possible to establish some more general mechanisms in human communication which underlie and unite different meaning construction processes? This is the problem we will approach from the point of view of modeling the process of recognizing (understanding) indirect speech acts.

Let's take two examples, one of which is a typical example in the cognitive theory of metaphor and the other – a typical example in the treatment of indirect speech acts. The sentence *My dentist is a real robber* represents a typical use of metaphor. On the other hand, such sentences express indirect speech acts, in the given case e.g. an accusation. The indirect meaning is recognized through interpreting the sentence as metaphorical. Such cases apparently will be outside the abilities of a DS in the near future. On the other hand, in the treatment of indirect speech acts one popular type is request in the form of a question concerning some aspect – as a rule, a pre-requirement of the requested action, e.g. *Can you tell me the arrival time of the bus?* From the point of view of cognitive semantics we can treat such uses as the above question as cases

Joakim Nivre, Heiki-Jaan Kaalep, Kadri Muischnek and Mare Koit (Eds.)
NODALIDA 2007 Conference Proceedings, pp. 398–401

of metonymy: being able to do some D is just one part (prerequisite) of doing D. For the computational analysis of dialogue and recognition of indirect acts this offers a much more clear possibility, especially in the context of institutional information-seeking phone calls. One of the (hypothetical) rules here could be: if the customer is asking whether a prerequisite for an action expected from the information operator does hold then he in fact intends to get the action performed (can you tell me => tell me). The types of actions performed by information agencies can be delimited and their structures where their prerequisites are explicitly formulated can be realized in the corresponding DS (e.g. in the form of frames of actions they are expected to carry out).

In this paper, we will analyze yes/no questions. There are two subtypes of such questions which could be called as direct and indirect ones: (1) (direct) yes/no questions which expect a simple answer *yes* or *no* (e.g. asking *Can you tell phone numbers of private persons?* a speaker intends to get the answer *yes* or *no*), (2) (indirect) yes/no questions which expect giving information (e.g. by asking *Can you tell me the arrival time of the bus?* a speaker intends to receive the arrival time of the bus, the answer *yes* would be insufficient). Let us call these two subtypes as closed (CYN) and open (OYN) yes/no questions, respectively (Gerassimenko et al., 2004). Our aim is to find out (1) how to recognize yes/no questions, (2) how to differentiate these two subtypes, (3) how to model it in a DS.

The rest of the paper is organized as follows: the second section describes the corpus and tools used for the analysis; the third gives an overview of the results of analysis – some linguistic cues which have been found out for recognition of yes/no questions; the fourth section represents some ideas how to model the interpretation of speech acts in a DS. Finally, some brief conclusions are presented.

2 Corpus and Tools Used

Our current study is based on the Estonian Dialogue Corpus (EDiC). The corpus contains over 900 authentic human-human spoken dialogues, including over 800 phone calls. Dialogue acts are annotated in the corpus using a DAMSL-like typology of dialogue acts (Gerassimenko et al., 2004).

Dialogue acts used for requesting information form a certain act group which is differently classified in different typologies. In the typology used by us, questions are determined as the utterances which have a specific form in Estonian: interrogatives, a specific word order and/or intonation. Questions are differentiated from directives. For example, *Can you tell me the arrival time of the bus?* is considered as a question (indirect request, OYN) but *Tell me the arrival time of the bus* is a directive (request). OYN and CYN have similar form in Estonian but they expect different reactions from the partner. A CYN is a direct dialogue act and expects the answer *yes* or *no* (e.g. *Are you open in winter? – Yes.*) while an OYN expects giving information (e.g. by asking the question *Is there a bus that arrives after 8 p.m.?* the customer intends to learn the departure times of buses). An OYN is an indirect dialogue act – the speaker forms his actual request as a question (an act of another type, Hennoste et al., 2005).

For the analysis, a sub-corpus of EDiC was chosen consisting of 312 directory inquiries. Customers ask phone numbers, addresses, opening hours of institutions, etc. The Workbench of EDiC was used for calculations and analyses.[1]

3 Corpus Analysis

Our first aim is to find out some linguistic cues which can be used for recognition of yes/no questions. Let us consider two examples from EDiC, the first one is annotated as a closed and the second one as an open yes/no question[2]:

```
'kas te mulle 'saate firma 'nime
vaadata 'numbri järgi,=
```
can you give me the name of a firm on the basis of a
phone number?   CYN
```
.hh kas teie käest saaks informat-
siooni kui palju võiks maksta sõit
'Inglismaale.
```
could you give information about how much does a
trip to England cost?   OYN

The linguistic form of both utterances is the same but the expected responses are different.

Customers asked 76 and operators 67 CYNs. The number of OYNs is 163 and 19, respectively. The reason of the significant difference in numbers

---

[1] http://math.ut.ee/~treumuth/
EDiC is accessible via the Workbench, but it is password-protected.
[2] Transcription of conversation analysis is used in examples (Schegloff, 1986).

of OYN is that the goal of a customer is to get information, and it is reasonable for him to expect a longer answer to a yes/no question than simply *yes*. An indirect question includes both direct and indirect meanings (Clark, 1991). In our case, an OYN includes two meanings – a direct and an indirect wish of the speaker.

We analyzed only customers' yes/no questions having an aim to find out how the computer performing the role of an operator could recognize users' dialogue acts. The analysis was carried out in two parts. The first part examined most important cue words, and the second one considered the same cue words together with the interrogative *kas* (whether) which is a significant key of yes/no questions in Estonian. The Table represents the results of our analysis: the numbers of cues found in OYNs, CYNs and in the remaining part of the sub-corpus, and possible recognition percents which one can expect to achieve using these cues.

The most interesting cue includes the word *saama* (to be able). Using only this word alone as a cue one can achieve the recognition percents 3.9 and 12.3 for CYN and OYN, respectively. But using this word together with the interrogative *kas* (whether) the percents increase to 22.5 and 52.5, respectively. It is not surprising because the question *kas sa saad teha D (are you able to do D)* includes a prerequisite of doing D.

The amount of the analyzed sub-corpus is too small to make some general conclusions. Still, it is clear that there exist linguistic cues which can be used for automatic recognition of yes/no questions.

4 Computational Model of Interpretation of Yes/No Questions

Communication is the intentional exchange of information. The speaker S wants to inform the hearer H about proposition p. H infers that S intended to convey q (where q=p in ideal case). S is not intentionally ambiguous but most utterances have several interpretations. H infers the most probable interpretation of p (speaker's interpretation or metaphorical interpretation). Such framework can be implemented both for dialogue analysis and recognition of metaphors (or metonymes) where the task of a hearer (reader) is to understand the actual intention of the speaker (author).

Table. Cues, their numbers and percents in open and closed yes/no questions

Cue	# OYN	# CYN	# other acts	% OYN	% CYN
kas (whether)	92	53	75	41.8	24.0
mingi (some, a certain, a kind of)	38	1	52	41.7	1.1
vä (or)	3	6	0	33.3	66.6
mõni (some, any, a few)	5	0	2	71.4	0.0
midagi (something, anything)	21	0	24	46.6	0.0
ütlema (to tell)	27	1	43	38.0	1.4
võimalik (possible)	9	4	24	24.3	10.8
näiteks (for example)	10	3	48	16.3	4.9
saama (to be able)	31	10	210	12.3	3.9
ega (nor)	8	1	9	44.4	5.5
kas + another interrogative	7	0	0	100.0	0.0
kas + mingi	17	0	6	73.9	0.0
kas + mõni	3	0	0	100.0	0.0
kas + midagi	9	0	1	90.0	0.0
kas + võimalik	5	2	0	71.4	28.5
kas + ütlema (to tell)	13	0	11	54.1	0.0
kas + näiteks	4	3	1	50.0	37.5
kas + saama	21	9	10	52.5	22.5
tahtsin + küsida (I wanted to ask)	6	0	1	85.7	0.0

Similar methods have been used for solving of both tasks. The computational models of both dialogue act interpretation and metaphor recognition can be divided into two classes. The first class has been called cue-based or probabilistic. The idea is that the hearer (or reader) uses different linguistic cues of the utterance to build its non-literal meaning. Sometimes, an utterance can be considered as an idiom. The second class of models implements the inferential approach. Such models are based on belief logics and use logical inference to reason about the speaker's intentions (Jurafsky and Martin, 2000).

We are working on a computer model of information seeking dialogues in Estonian and experimenting with different approaches to recognizing communicative intentions, including indirect ones, and expressing these intentions (by the computer) in a human manner. Recognizing and using metaphorical and metonymic expressions is one of the methods investigated, the general and uniting key-concepts being 'meaning construction' and 'communication through reasoning'. Our work is based on the EDiC and our general framework is one kind of BDI model worked out in Artificial Intelligence (Koit and Õim, 2004).

How to differentiate the OYNs and CYNs? We propose the following analysis cycle: first, linguistic cues are used to recognize the type of a dialogue act (a yes/no question), and secondly, frame representations of dialogue acts are used to interpret the act. We have built frames of questions, and a frame of an OYN is a combination of the frames of the CYN and wh-question. On the ground of the hypothetical rule formulated in Section 1 a frame of request can be inferred and constructed. Therefore, we try to combine the two kinds of computational models to interpret questions as dialogue acts – cue-based and inferential-based.

Solving of metaphors, metonymes and indirect speech acts can be considered as meaning disambiguation: the task is to choose one of several possible meanings which suits with a context. The hearer has to find out the most probable intention of the speaker.

5   Conclusion and Future Work

Estonian directory inquiries were analysed with the further aim to develop a DS. Yes/no questions were considered in order to find out some cues which can be used for their automatic recognition. It turned out that the most important linguistic cues of yes/no questions are (1) the interrogative *kas* (whether), (2) the pronouns *mingi* (some, a certain, a kind of), *mõni* (some, any, a few), *midagi* (something, anything), 3) the verb *saama* (to be able). By combining of these cues, the recognition accuracy can be increased. For example, *kas + saama* is a significant cue.

The first task of the computer is to recognize a yes/no question. After that, a closed and an open yes/no question can be differentiated as direct and indirect dialogue acts. An indirect dialogue act includes at least two meanings while the partner has to react to the most important one.

A simple DS is implemented which gives information about flights leaving from the Tallinn Airport. Our future work concerns implementation of the described method of recognition of yes/no questions in the DS.

Acknowledgement

This work is supported by Estonian Science Foundation (grant No 5685).

References

Penelope Brown and Stephen C. Levinson. 1987. Politeness: some universals on language usage. *Studies in Interactional Sociolinguistics* 4. Cambridge University Press.

Harry Bunt and Yann Girard. 2005. Designing an Open, Multidimensional Dialogue Act Taxonomy. Claire Gardent and Bertrand Gaiffe (eds). *Dialor'05. Proc. of the ninth workshop on the semantics and pragmatics of dialogue (SEMDIAL)*. Loria, 37-44.

Herbert II. Clark. 1991. Responding to Indirect Speech Acts. *Pragmatics.* Ed S. Davis. Oxford: Oxford University Press.

Olga Gerassimenko, Tiit Hennoste, Mare Koit, Andriela Rääbis, Krista Strandson, Maret Valdisoo and Evely Vutt. 2004. Annotated dialogue corpus as a language resource: an experience of building the Estonian dialogue corpus. *The first Baltic conference "Human language technologies. The Baltic perspective"*. Riga, 150–155.

Tiit Hennoste, Olga Gerassimenko, Riina Kasterpalu, Mare Koit, Andriela Rääbis, Krista Strandson and Maret Valdisoo. 2005. Questions in Estonian Information Dialogues: Form and Functions. *Text, Speech and Dialogue. 6th International Conference TSD 2005.* Ed. V. Matousek, P. Mautner. Springer, 420-427.

Daniel Jurafsky and James H. Martin. 2000. *An introduction to natural language processing, computational linguistics, and speech recognition.* Prentice Hall.

Mare Koit and Haldur Õim. 2004. Argumentation in the Agreement Negotiation Process: A Model that Involves Natural Reasoning. *Proc. of the Workshop W12 on Computational Models of Natural Argument. 16th European Conference on Artificial Intelligence.* Valencia, Spain, 53-56.

Emanuel Schegloff. 1986. The routine as achievement. - *Human Studies,* 9, 111-152.

Rule-based Logical Forms Extraction

Cenny Wenner

Department of Computer Science, Faculty of Science
Lund University, Sweden
`cwenner@gmail.com`
`http://cennywenner.com`

Abstract

In this paper, we present concise but robust rules for dependency-based logical form identification with high accuracy. We describe our approach from an intuitive and formalized perspective, which we believe overcomes much of the complexity. In comparison to previous work, we believe ours is more compact and involves less rules and exceptions. We also provide the reader with a comparison of the respective impacts of the most essential rules on the logical form identification task of the 2004 Senseval 3 test set.

1 Introduction

The logical form of a text segment is a first-order logic (FOL) well-formed formula (wff) representing the meaning of the segment. Such a representation is used for a number of problems involving semantics and inference, for instance question answering (QA) (Moldovan et al., 2003) and textual entailment (TE) (Bar-Haim et al., 2006; Tatu et al., 2006). Moldovan and Rus (2001) introduced a simplified representation where the wff is restricted to a conjunction of predicates and where functions/functors are not allowed as arguments. The arguments are partitioned into two sets: events and objects. Conventionally, objects are called entities and we extend that term to refer to both events and objects. With this representation, more complicated constructions of natural language are ignored but these are not crucial to the previously mentioned problems.

As an example, the representation of *John and the dog ran to his car* is

$$\text{John:}\_n(x_1), \text{and}(x_2, x_1, x_3), \text{dog:}\_n(x_3),$$
$$\text{run:}\_v(e_1, x_2; x_4), \text{to}(e_1, x_4), \text{his}(x_4), \text{car:}\_n(x_4),$$
$$(1)$$

where the arguments of the form x_i and e_i denotes objects and events respectively. In this particular example, x_1 is John, x_3 the dog, x_2 John and the dog as a group, x_4 his car, and e_1 the event that they are running. The *to* predicate expresses a relation between the event *run* and the car, while the predicate *his* expresses a quality of the car alone. Note that John is not present in the *his* predicate, this is a task for a coreference solver. The suffixes *:_n* and *:_v* denote nouns and verbs respectively. For verbs, complements are listed after a semicolon.

A task for identifying these logical forms was introduced at the 2004 Senseval 3 conference. 27 teams were registered, although only five submitted sensible results, whereof one involved manual parsing (Rus, 2004). Our work builds on the results of these systems and we use the conference's annotated and unannotated data sets to evaluate and verify our approach.

The goal of this article is to present the reader with a robust rule-based scheme which only relies on a few exceptions to the simple default search rules. The transformation takes as input a dependency graph, a sequence of tokens, the tokens' parts of speech (POS), and morphological base forms (lemmatised word form). We briefly describe how to produce the input from raw English text in Sect. 3. The transformation is done in two steps. The first step constructs predicates with argument placeholders, called slots, and we cover this in Sect. 4. Sect. 5 deals with the second step where we substitute the placeholders with real arguments. The later step is more complicated and we devote several subsections to it. We evaluate the system on the Senseval 3 test set in Sect. 6 and concludes the paper with a discussion of these results and potential further work.

Joakim Nivre, Heiki-Jaan Kaalep, Kadri Muischnek and Mare Koit (Eds.)
NODALIDA 2007 Conference Proceedings, pp. 402–409

2   Previous Work

All contemporary systems for logical form identification rely on a syntactical parser. Constituent trees appear to be the most frequent approach today, introduced by Rus (2001). Two rivals to this approach are depedency graphs (Anthony and Patrick, 2004) and link grammar (Bayer et al., 2004). However, these systems seems to employ a large number of rules for only a slight improvement in accuracy. Some systems seems to use over a hundred rules (Bayer et al., 2004; Ahn et al., 2004). Unfortunately, descriptions of these systems only mention a few of the rules and do little evaluation of their respective impacts. We aim to give a concise but robust overview that will allow the readers to replicate the system and compare the different rules.

Other work on logical form identification includes Mohammed et al. (2004), Moldovan and Rus (2001), and van Eijck and Alshawi (1992).

3   Preprocessing

As mentioned in the introduction, the system's transformation from a sentence to a simplified logical form relies on a dependency graph, an associated sequence of tokens, the tokens' parts of speech, and morphological base forms. Five modules are used to extract this information: a sentence splitter, a tokenizer, a POS tagger, a dependency-graph parser, and a morphological parser. For the first two modules we use simple regular expressions. We also check each subsequence of tokens and substitute collocations with a single token. For this, we use a list containing collocations extracted from WORDNET, that was supplied for the Senseval 3 task.

We represent the sequence, or list, of lexical tokens with $W = (w_1, \ldots, w_n), w_i = (i, t_i)$ where i is the position of the token in the sequence and t_i is the string representation. We also define a total order $w_i \prec w_j \equiv i < j$.

3.1   Part-of-speech tagging

We denote the particular part of speech of a token with $\text{POS}(w_i)$. As POS tagger we have tried the STANFORD LOG-LINEAR POS TAGGER (Toutanova and Manning, 2000; Toutanova et al., 2003), MXPOST (Ratnaparkhi, 1996), and TREETAGGER (Schmid, 1994). The results we list in Sect. 5 are for MXPOST.

3.2   Dependency-graph parsing

We consider dependency graphs to be directed acyclic graphs (DAGs) $D = (W, A)$ where A is the ordered set of labeled arcs $(w_i, r, w_j), r \in R$, r the dependency function,[1] and where R in particular contains the functions subject (SUB), object (OBJ), and verb chain (VC). We also use the notation $w_i \xrightarrow{r} w_j$ to denote $(w_i, r, w_j) \in A$ and $rel(w_i, w_j) = r \Leftrightarrow (w_i, r, w_j) \in A$. We have tried MSTPARSER (McDonald et al., 2006) and Nivre's MALTPARSER 0.4 ENGSVM (Nivre et al., 2006). The results in Sect. 5 are for MALT-PARSER.

3.3   Morphological parsing

For the simplified logical forms, the head of the predicates should consist of the token's base form and a part-of-speech suffix. We use WORDNET to identify the base forms, performing a call for each token independent of its neighbours. See for instance Fellbaum (1998).

4   Predicate Introduction

Tokens are divided into two simple groups based on the class of supported and ignored parts of speech. The forms used at Senseval 3 ignores for instance determiners because they complicate matters and do not have a great impact for many inference and semantics tasks. For each token of a supported part of speech, we create a predicate with its base form as head and a number of slots equal to its arity[2]. Table 1 lists the arities of different part-of-speech classes. For the tokens of parts of speech in the ignored set, we do nothing. The exceptions to this are noun groups and noun compounds for which an additional predicate is introduced to refer to the group/compound rather than to the components.

After these steps, our first example (Eqn. 1) would be equivalent to

$$\text{John:\_n}(s_{1,1}), \text{and}(s_{2,1}, s_{2,2}, s_{2,3}),$$
$$\text{dog:\_n}(s_{3,1}), \text{meet:\_v}(s_{4,1}, s_{4,2}, s_{4,3}),$$
$$\text{at}(s_{5,1}, s_{5,2}), \text{his}(s_{6,1}), \text{car:\_n}(s_{7,1}), \quad (2)$$

where $s_{i,j}$ are argument placeholders. We repeat that we call the placeholders slots.

---

[1] Also called the dependency relation and dependency label.

[2] The arity of a predicate is the number of parameters it has.

Table 1: Suffixes and arities of our part-of-speech classes, and the classes equivalences in the PTB.

POS	Suf.	Arity	PTB
Nouns, regular	:_n	1	NN, NNS, NP, NPS
Nouns groups /compounds		3	(We call this _NN)
Verbs	:_v	2-3	V[B]?[DGNPZ]?
Adjectives	:_a	1	JJ, JJR, JJS
Adverbs	:_r	1	RB, RBR, RBS, WRB
Conjunctions		3	CC, UH
Unary mods.		1	POS, PP\$, WP\$
Binary mods.		2	IN, TO

The dependency graph models relations between nodes. This is interpreted here as relations between entities. The entity that is involved in this kind of relation is the first argument of each predicate. For example, the arguments of the *to* predicate in our first example (Eqn. 1) are e_1 and x_4. These two entities are also the first arguments of other predicates, x_4 is the first argument of the *dog* predicate and e_1 is the first argument of the event *run*. Furthermore, every entity in Eqn. 1 is the first argument of a verb, noun, or conjunction.

The primary POS tags that we use are listed in Table 1 along with the equivalent tags in the Penn-Treebank (Santorini, 1991).

We believe our system can relatively easily be extended to different arities and with support for any part of speech. At least as long as inference is not required in the transformation step. For instance, the meaning of the sentence *Do not not breathe* is that one should breathe, with a slightly different emphasis. This sentence is represented as

$$\text{do:\_v}(e_1, x_1, e_2) \wedge \text{not:\_r}(e_2, e_3)$$
$$\wedge \text{not:\_r}(e_3, e_4) \wedge \text{breathe:\_v}(e_4, x_1), \quad (3)$$

which could be reduced to

$$\text{do:\_v}(e_1, x_1, e_4) \wedge \text{breathe:\_v}(e_4, x_1) \quad (4)$$

(*Do breathe*). If reductions such as the above are required, it might not be straightforward to extend the system.

Let $\{p_i = pred_i(s_{i,1}, \ldots, s_{i,\text{arity}(p_i)})\}$ denote the set of created predicates where $w(p_i)$ is the associated token, $\text{POS}(p_i)$, its part of speech[3], $\text{arity}(p_i)$, the predicate's arity, and $s_{i,j}$, the jth slot of the ith predicate.

5 Argument identification

So far, the steps have only involved simple rules directly given by the representation or relying on existing systems. The last step is less trivial and consists of identifying the real arguments for the slots.

5.1 Formalization

We introduce some notation that we use in the latter sections. We let $\text{arg}(s_{i,j})$ be the function that maps the jth slot of the ith predicate to an entity. With $\text{arg}(s_{i,j}) \in E$ and $\text{arg}(s_{i,j}) \in O$ we denote that the argument is an event and object, respectively.

The meaning of Eqn. 1 would be the same if we replaced all the occurrences of x_1 with x_5, since x_5 does not appear elsewhere in the formula, i.e. we merely create an unique entity for it. At this point, we therefore concentrate on finding out what slots are mapped to the same arguments and not so much which specific entity it is. In fact, once we know which arguments should be same and which ones should not, it is an easy task to find a satisfying substitution since there are no restrictions on the number of entities we may create.

Aside from identifying which arguments are the same, we must determine if they are events or objects. We will handle these two tasks in different sections even though the problems overlap.

5.2 Simplifications

Each predicate has an associated token and this token has a node in the dependency graph. We also said that the first slot of each predicate should be the entity that participates in the relation that the dependencies model. We therefore do not always distinguish between tokens, predicates, nodes, and entities when talking about argument identification.

We define the argument search space of a slot to be a list of nodes in the DG that will we search through for a suitable argument. The slot is contained in a predicate and the predicate has an associated node in the dependency graph. The space we use is defined as a region in relation this node.

---

[3] Also defined for the noun groups/compounds even though there are no associated tokens.

Note that the space is over nodes in the graph and not entities.

For a dependency graph, the arguments of a predicate are usually found in the near vicinity of its node in the dependency graph. Particularly often among its children or siblings, and occasionally its parent or grandchildren. It is also not certain that a suitable argument exists in the sentence. We therefore restrict our argument search space to consist of the node's parent, children, and siblings. If no suitable argument is found among these, we assume that the slot should contain an entity that does not appear elsewhere in the formula. To model preferences between nodes, we order the search space in different ways depending on the parts of speech. This is covered in Sect. 5.3.

Different parts of speech also put different requirements on their arguments. For instance, adjectives generally only modify objects, not events. We collect these constraints under a function that depends on the parts of speech, among other things. We handle these functions, which we call argument constraint functions, in Sect. 5.4.

5.3 Argument search spaces

If p is a node in the dependency graph, then let $P(p), C(p), S(p), S_L(p), S_R(p)$ be the lists of, respectively; the parents of the node[4], the children of the node, the siblings of the node, the left siblings of the node, and the right siblings of the node. The lists should be sorted according to the order of appearance of the nodes' respective tokens in the token sequence.

We use the set notation for operations on ordered lists and with this, we implicitly mean that the elements of the resulting list follow the same order as the source list. One could see it as picking elements from left to right from the input list, process it, and place the result in the output list from left to right.

Take these equations as an example:

$$Y = (x \in X | x \in Nouns),$$
$$X = (saw, cat, yard, in). \qquad (5)$$

We first pick *saw* and discard it. Next we pick *cat* and place it in Y, and *yard* which we place to the right of *cat*. We finally discard *in* to get the resulting list: $(cat, yard)$.

---

[4]N.B. there is only one parent per node in dependency graphs.

With the described notation, we may formally define the left- and right-siblings:

$$S_L(p) = (p' \in S(p) | t(p') \prec t(p)) \qquad (6)$$
$$S_R(p) = (p' \in S(p) | t(p') \succ t(p)) \qquad (7)$$

For our simplified logical forms, we search for suitable arguments for up to two slots for each predicate. The slots for which we do not perform search we call stable, and the remaining slots unstable. The stable slots are the first slots of all noun, verb, and conjunction predicates. Since the only classes with an arity of three are noun groups/compounds, verbs, and conjunctions, no predicate contains more than two unstable slots.

We have noticed that the arguments for the first and second unstable slots are found in a bit different locations. We therefore separate the argument search space for the first and second unstable slot. Note that the spaces contains the same nodes, we only permute them differently. We call these $\mathcal{A}_1(p)$ and $\mathcal{A}_2(p, q)$, where the latter term is the argument search space for the second unstable slot of a node p, given that we have identified the first argument as q (which is another node in the graph, recall that the argument spaces consists of nodes). We first introduce some of our common spaces that we then use to define the above mentioned terms with respect to the nodes' part of speech. The selection of the proper order is part linguistics and part understanding or making observations about the structure of dependency graphs. The permutations we describe are those that we through iterative experiments and analysis have found work well.

Let X^R denote the list X in reverse order, and let multiplication implicitly denote concatenation of tuples, we describe the most common permutations of the search space with

$$\mathcal{A}_{Lcrp}(p) = S_L(p)^R \cdot C(p) \cdot S_R(p) \cdot P(p) \qquad (8)$$
$$\mathcal{A}_{pLcr}(p) = P(p) \cdot S_L(p)^R \cdot C(p) \cdot S_R(p) \qquad (9)$$
$$\mathcal{A}_{rpLc}(p) = S_R(p) \cdot P(p) \cdot S_L(p)^R \cdot C(p) \qquad (10)$$
$$\mathcal{A}_{crpL}(p) = C(p) \cdot S_R(p) \cdot P(p) \cdot S_L(p)^R \qquad (11)$$

Notice how $\mathcal{A}_{Lcrp}(p)$ is equivalent to a preorder traversal of the nodes in the argument search space, except with the left siblings reversed. The other spaces are also given by shifting terms.

We now define the default search methods for the first and second arguments. With $\mathcal{A}_{\text{Def},1}(p)$ we denote the default argument search space for the first unstable slot of node p, and with $\mathcal{A}_{\mathrm{Def},2}(p,q)$, the argument space function for the second unstable argument of node p, given that its first identified argument is q. We define a *shifted* order, $\mathcal{A}_{\mathrm{Shi},1}(p)$, because it is very similar to the default and we refer to it later.

$$\mathcal{A}_{\mathrm{Def},1}(p) = \begin{cases} \mathcal{A}_{Lcrp}(p) & p, P(p) \in Nouns \\ \mathcal{A}_{pLcr}(p) & \text{else} \end{cases} \tag{12}$$

$$\mathcal{A}_{\mathrm{Shi}}(p) = \begin{cases} \mathcal{A}_{rpLc}(p) & p, P(p) \in Nouns \\ \mathcal{A}_{crpL}(p) & \text{else} \end{cases} \tag{13}$$

$$\mathcal{A}_{\mathrm{Def},2}(p,q) = \begin{cases} \mathcal{A}_{\mathrm{Def},1}(p) & q \notin S_L(p) \\ \mathcal{A}_{\mathrm{Shi}}(p) & q \in S_L(p) \end{cases} \tag{14}$$

The default argument search spaces are used for nouns (N), conjunctions (C), adjectives (A) and adverbs (R). If $k = 1, 2$, then

$$\mathcal{A}_{N,k} = \mathcal{A}_{C,k} = \mathcal{A}_{A,k} = \mathcal{A}_{R,k} = \mathcal{A}_{\mathrm{Def},k} \tag{15}$$

The three exceptions to the default rule are: verbs (V), for which we prefer subject, object or verb chain functions, and unary (U) and binary (B) modifiers, for which we always use the shifted order.

$$\mathcal{A}_{\mathrm{V},1}(p) = (p_i | w(p) \xrightarrow{SUB} w(p_i)) \cdot \mathcal{A}_{\mathrm{Def},1}(p) \tag{16}$$

$$\mathcal{A}_{\mathrm{V},2}(p,q) = (p_i | w(p) \xrightarrow{r} w(p_i)) \cdot \mathcal{A}_{\mathrm{Def},2}(p,q), \\ r \in \{OBJ, VC\} \tag{17}$$

$$\mathcal{A}_{U,1}(p) = \mathcal{A}_{B,1}(p) = \mathcal{A}_{B,2}(p,q) = \mathcal{A}_{\mathrm{Shi}}(p) \tag{18}$$

We may now define the search space for the first and secon arguments with respect to their part of speech as

$$\mathcal{A}_k(p) \equiv \mathcal{A}_{\mathrm{POS}(p),k}(p) \tag{19}$$

5.4 Argument constraint functions

The default constraint function, which we call c_{Def}, merely ensures that the first and second arguments are different, the arity of both is at least zero and if both belong to the preceding siblings, then the first argument must not precede the second. q and r are here the first and second identified arguments of the node p.

$$c_{\mathrm{Def}}(p,q,r) \Leftrightarrow \mathrm{arity}(q), \mathrm{arity}(r) > 0 \\ \wedge q \neq r \wedge (q, r \in S_L(p) \Rightarrow q \succeq r) \tag{20}$$

As with the argument search space, we define the constraint function c with respect to its part of speech,

$$c(p,q,r) \equiv c_{\mathrm{POS}(p)}(p,q,r) \tag{21}$$

There are five classes with more specific requirements than the default but at least unary and binary modifiers are defined as the default constraint function and the rest rely on it. Furthermore, during evaluation, we found that the special constraint functions for conjunctions and adverbs virtually contribute with nothing over the default.

- **Noun groups/compounds (N):** All arguments are restricted to nouns.

- **Verbs (V):** Except for SUB/OBJ/VC functions, arguments must be nouns, conjunctions or verbs. These three classes are called stable and are described in the next section.

- **Conjunctions (C):** Generally both arguments, and subsequently its first argument, are either all events or all objects.

- **Adjectives (A):** Restrict to objects.

- **Adverbs (R):** We restrict adverbs to only modify events.

Recall that E is the set of events, O the set of objects, and with $rel(w_i, w_j)$, we denote the dependency relation between nodes w_i and w_j. The above explanations are formally defined as

$$c_N(p,q,r) \Leftrightarrow \mathrm{POS}(q), \mathrm{POS}(r) \in Nouns \\ \wedge c_{\mathrm{Def}}(p,q,r) \tag{22}$$

$$c_V(p,q,r) \Leftrightarrow (\mathrm{POS}(q) \in Stable \vee rel(p,q) \in (*)) \\ \wedge (\mathrm{POS}(r) \in Stable \vee rel(p,r) \in (*)) \\ \wedge c_{\mathrm{Def}}(p,q,r) \tag{23}$$

$$c_C(p,q,r) \Leftrightarrow (q \in E \Leftrightarrow r \in E) \\ \wedge c_{\mathrm{Def}}(p,q,r) \tag{24}$$

$$c_A(p,q,r) \Leftrightarrow q, r \in O \\ \wedge c_{\mathrm{Def}}(p,q,r) \tag{25}$$

$$c_R(p,q,r) \Leftrightarrow q, r \in E \\ \wedge c_{\mathrm{Def}}(p,q,r) \tag{26}$$

$$(*) = \{SUB, OBJ, VC\}$$

5.5 Argument introduction

The next step is merely to test each predicate or pair of predicates in the argument search spaces for each predicate. The first predicate or pair of predicates that fulfills the constraint function is the best candidate as argument(s).

As mentioned earlier, the first slot of each node represents it in the relations. With potential arguments identified, we may therefore simply introduce equalities to represent these in terms of the predicates' slots. If we find that p_k is the first predicate in the search space for slot $s_{i,j}$ that satisfies the constraints, then $\arg(s_{i,j}) = \arg(s_{k,1})$.

Whenever we during search encounter nouns in the argument search space, we first check any associated noun groups/compounds and any children that are conjunctions. This could be formalized as a function of a node which by default only lists the node itself and where nouns are the only exceptions.

The constraint functions are defined with respect to both arguments, but in our system we use a simplified version; we begin by selecting a first argument that could fulfill the constraints for some second argument, we then search for the second argument. If no satisfying second argument can be found, we still keep the first:

$$\hat{c}(p, q) \equiv \exists_r c(p, q, r) \tag{27}$$

It would be preferable to balance the position of the first and second argument in the ordered argument space.

We conclude this step by merely going through slots and assigning entities. If an equality to another slot with an assigned entity exists, we assign the same entity to this slot; if none exists, we create a new entity.

5.6 Entity partitioning

By default, all entities are considered objects. If it appears in the first slot of a verb, or in a conjunction where all the children are events, it is however considered an event. Because some constraint functions require knowledge of whether an entity is an event or not, the argument identification and entity partitioning decisions cannot be made independently. To handle this, our system identifies equalities like the ones above in two steps: the first step containing predicates which do not rely on whether slots refer to events or not, and the second containing those that do.

Table 2: Argument and predicate F-score for the systems of Senseval 3. The values are ± 0.001.

Team	Argument	Predicate
University of Amsterdam	0.709	0.801
LCC	0.776	0.892
MITRE	0.694	0.809
University of Sydney	0.705	0.844
Our system	0.649	0.845

5.7 Verb complements

As mentioned in Table 1 and as seen in Eqn. 1, verbs may have additional arguments besides their standard one or two. We have taken a simple approach for identifying these modifier arguments: We check every path from the parent that does not contain another verb node. If a modifier *at, by, for, from, in, of, on* or *to* is encountered, introduce an equality to its second argument. Preferably one would want to require the first argument to refer to be the verb in question but this lowers the accuracy of our system. This list needs to be extended but we have not explored this further.

6 Results

For the logical forms identification task at Senseval 3, evaluation was done on a test set of 300 sentences. Participating teams submitted their outputs, which were compared to a gold standard. To evaluate our system, we have use the annotated test set of the Senseval 3 conference and a released evaluation script. The evaluation is done in two parts: F-score on predicates and F-score on arguments. The systems at Senseval 3 achieved an argument F-score between 0.694 and 0.776 and a predicate F-score between 0.801 and 0.892. We report here an argument F-score of 0.649 and a predicate F-score of 0.845 on this test set[5]. Table 2 lists the respective systems and their F-scores. The values have been calculated from Rus (2004).

We therefore do worse than the systems at Senseval 3 on the argument level but good on the predicate level, placing just below second place. The evaluation script does not seem to take into consideration all the equalities or inequalities between arguments or whether they are events or entities though.

---

[5]We have only run the system on the test set for three configurations with minor changes besides the purpose of testing modifications such as those listed in Table 3. The reported results are for a scheme selected prior to these tests. Development was done on a separate supplied set.

Table 3: Impact on the argument precision, recall and F-score for different modifications. The changes are absolute, not relative.

Modification	Prec. %	Rec. %	F-sc. %
No collocations	+1.5	−0.1	−0.7
Noun in cases	−4.7	−4.8	−5.4
Not noun in cases	−1.0	−0.5	−1.3
Parent first	−2.0	−2.3	−2.0
Only parent	−7.4	−9.8	−8.5
$\mathcal{A}_k \leftarrow \mathcal{A}_{\mathrm{Def},1}$	−4.0	−3.7	−4.7
$\mathcal{A}_k \leftarrow \mathcal{A}_{\mathrm{Shi}}$	−9.5	−9.1	−10.7
$\mathcal{A}_{\mathrm{Def},2} \leftarrow \mathcal{A}_{\mathrm{Def},1}$	−0.2	−0.4	−0.5
$\mathcal{A}_{V,k} \leftarrow \mathcal{A}_{\mathrm{Def},k}$	−1.2	−1.0	−1.4
$\mathcal{A}_{U/B,k} \leftarrow \mathcal{A}_{\mathrm{Def},k}$	−0.4	−0.3	−0.4
Grandchildren	−0.3	+0.4	+0.1
Ignore $p \succeq q$	−0.8	−0.7	−0.8
$c_N \leftarrow c_{\mathrm{Def}}$	−0.4	−0.3	−0.4
$c_V \leftarrow c_{\mathrm{Def}}$	−1.3	−1.6	−0.5
$c_C \leftarrow c_{\mathrm{Def}}$	±0.0	±0.0	±0.0
$c_A \leftarrow c_{\mathrm{Def}}$	−0.2	−0.3	−0.4
$c_R \leftarrow c_{\mathrm{Def}}$	−0.1	−0.3	−0.1
No noun checks	+0.7	−3.2	−1.1

The impact on the argument F-score for different rules are given in Table 3.

7 Discussion

Observing the mean F-score, our system, the University of Amsterdam, and MITRE are very close to each other. There is then a large difference with University of Sydney and even greater with LCC. We still believe our results are good in comparison to the other systems if they have larger rule sets. Our approach is simple, robust, general and uncluttered and there is a lot of work that can be done to improve it further without being constrained by a complicated or brittle design.

Auxiliary verbs are ignored by the simplified logical forms but it is not trivial as to what should be considered auxiliary verbs in specific contexts. We have difficulties in consistently separating the cases without introducing rules which are too specific. Since this appears even in the development set, we expect it to have a large impact on the test set.

All argument search spaces we described have been permutations of the nodes in the subgraph rooted at a node's parent, excluding the node itself. It seems like the argument search space should frequently contain grandchildren or nodes past the parent, such as the grandparent or uncles. However, carelessly including these classes in all the argument search spaces reduces the accuracy. This is because the search then discovers too many false equalities.

We notice that a fairly large portion of the errors originate from the preprocessing step. A mistake by the POS tagger propagates to the dependency graph, morphological parser, and the application of transformation rules. On the development set, we at one point noticed a difference of 4% in the logical form identification accuracy caused only be a 1% improvement in POS tagging (absolute units). It seems the accuracy would benefit a fair amount from further improvement of the part-of-speech and dependency-graph modules in particular.

Our system assumes that all noun groups/compounds should consist of components of exactly two objects each. In one example however, a noun group/compound of three objects was used with an arity of four. A related difficulty is the nesting of conjunctions in which its not immediately clear how the dependency-graph parser deals with them from case to case.

8 Conclusions

It appears as though we can conclude that transforming dependency graphs to the simplified logical forms with high accuracy is possible through a few simple rules. Formalizing them as search rules has reduced the complexity particularly and we believe this scheme should make further improvement easy. Previous work in the area (Ahn et al., 2004) confirms the conclusion that it is relatively straightforward to implement a fair transformation scheme. We would like to add that implementing such a system is anything but complex or time-consuming, given the modules mentioned above.

9 Future Work

Systems for inference and semantics tasks involving logical forms frequently use different certainty factors for making the right choices. Taking a more probabilistic approach to logical forms identification, which does not necessarily need to be statistical, should both improve the accuracy of the logical forms identification as be of use for the reasoning tasks. This is also partly our way to approach the last paragraph of the discussion.

We have experimented with statistical logical form identification and believe that the scheme we have presented here provides a useful basis. There are however still a variable number of parameters for the decisions and they might not be as independent as preferable. A downside today is the lack of training data.

We have described three simplifications in our system: 1) we restrict the search space to nodes at distance one and two, 2) we greedily select the first argument before the second even though this is not warranted, and 3) we process slots which depend on whether other slots are events or not without any particular order after those that do not share this dependency. It would exciting to explore how to relieve or better handle these simplifications, in particular without causing an explosion of the argument search space.

10 Acknowledgment

The work presented here has received much support and guidance from Pierre Nugues at Lund university, both on the construction of the system and in particular on the authoring of this paper. He would likely have wanted to make many more suggestions on both.

References

David Ahn, Sisay Fissaha, Valentin Jijkoun, and Maarten De Rijke. 2004. The University of Amsterdam at Senseval-3: Semantic roles and Logic forms. In *Senseval-3*, pages 49–53. Association for Computational Linguistics.

Stephen Anthony and Jon Patrick. 2004. Dependency based logical form transformations. In *Senseval-3*, pages 54–57. Association for Computational Linguistics.

Roy Bar-Haim, Ido Dagan, Bill Dolan, Lisa Ferro, Danilo Giampiccolo, Bernardo Magnini, and Idan Szpektor. 2006. *Proceedings of the Second PASCAL Challenges Workshop on Recognising Textual Entailment.*

Samuel Bayer, John Burger, John Greiff, and Ben Wellner. 2004. The mitre logical form generation system. In *Senseval-3*, pages 69–72. Association for Computational Linguistics.

Fellbaum. 1998. *WordNet: An Electronic Lexical Database*. The MIT Press.

R. McDonald, K. Lerman, and F. Pereira. 2006. Multilingual dependency analysis with a two-stage discriminative parser.

Altaf Mohammed, Dan Moldovan, and Paul Parker. 2004. Senseval-3 logic forms: A system and possible improvements. In *Senseval-3*, pages 163–166. Association for Computational Linguistics.

Dan I. Moldovan and Vasile Rus. 2001. Logic form transformation of wordnet and its applicability to question answering. In *ACL '01*, pages 402–409. Association for Computational Linguistics.

Dan Moldovan, Christine Clark, Sanda Harabagiu, and Steve Maiorano. 2003. Cogex: a logic prover for question answering. In *NAACL '03*, pages 87–93. Association for Computational Linguistics.

Joakim Nivre, Johan Hall, and Jens Nilsson. 2006. Maltparser: A data-driven parser-generator for dependency parsing. pages 2216–2219.

Adwait Ratnaparkhi. 1996. A maximum entropy model for part-of-speech tagging. In *Proceedings of the Conference on Empirical Methods in Natural Language Processing*.

Vasile Rus. 2001. High precision logic form transformation. In *ICTAI*, pages 288–.

Vasile Rus. 2004. A first evaluation of logic form identification systems. In *Senseval-3*, pages 37–40. Association for Computational Linguistics.

Beatrice Santorini. 1991. Part-of-speech tagging guidelines for the penn treebank project.

Helmut Schmid. 1994. Probabilistic part-of-speech tagging using decision trees. In *International Conference on New Methods in Language Processing*. unknown.

Marta Tatu, Brandon Iles, John Slavick, Adrian Novischi, and Dan Moldovan. 2006. Cogex at the second recognizing textual entailment challenge. In *Proceedings of the Second PASCAL Challenges Workshop on Recognising Textual Entailment.*

Kristina Toutanova and Christopher D. Manning. 2000. Enriching the knowledge sources used in a maximum entropy part-of-speech tagger. In *EMNLP/VLC-2000*.

Kristina Toutanova, Dan Klein, and Christopher D. Manning. 2003. Feature-rich part-of-speech tagging with a cyclic dependency network. In *Proceedings of HLT-NAACL 03*.

J. van Eijck and H. Alshawi. 1992. Logical forms. In *The Core Language Engine*, pages 11–40. MIT Press.

Author Index